The European Discovery of America

THE NORTHERN VOYAGES
A.D. 500–1600

OTHER BOOKS BY SAMUEL ELIOT MORISON

The Life and Letters of Harrison Gray Otis, 2 vols., 1913
The Maritime History of Massachusetts, 1921, 1941
The Oxford History of the United States, 2 vols., 1927
Builders of the Bay Colony, 1930, 1964
The Tercentennial History of Harvard University, 4 vols., 1929–36
Three Centuries of Harvard, 1936, 1963
Portuguese Voyages to America, 1940
Admiral of the Ocean Sea: A Life of Christopher Columbus, 1942
History of U. S. Naval Operations in World War II, 15 vols., 1947–62
By Land and By Sea, 1953
The Intellectual Life of Colonial New England, 1956
Freedom in Contemporary Society, 1956
The Story of the "Old Colony" of New Plymouth, 1956
John Paul Jones: A Sailor's Biography, 1959
The Story of Mount Desert Island, 1960
One Boy's Boston, 1962
The Two-Ocean War, 1963
Vistas of History, 1964
Spring Tides, 1965
The Oxford History of the American People, 1965
Old Bruin: Commodore Matthew C. Perry, 1794–1858, 1967
Harrison Gray Otis, The Urbane Federalist, 1969

WITH HENRY STEELE COMMAGER AND WILLIAM E. LEUCHTENBURG

The Growth of the American Republic, 2 vols., 1930, 1969

WITH MAURICIO OBREGÓN

The Caribbean as Columbus Saw It, 1964

The European Discovery of America

of America

THE NORTHERN VOYAGES
A.D. 500–1600

SAMUEL ELIOT MORISON

OXFORD UNIVERSITY PRESS
New York   Oxford

Oxford University Press

Oxford   New York   Toronto
Delhi   Bombay   Calcutta   Madras   Karachi
Kuala Lumpur   Singapore   Hong Kong   Tokyo
Nairobi   Dar es Salaam   Cape Town
Melbourne   Auckland   Madrid

and associated companies in
Berlin   Ibadan

Copyright © 1971 by Samuel Eliot Morison

First published in 1971 by Oxford University Press, Inc.,
200 Madison Avenue, New York, New York 10016

First issued as an Oxford University Press paperback, 1993

Oxford is a registered trademark of Oxford University Press

Library of Congress Cataloging-in-Publication Data
Morison, Samuel Eliot, 1887–1976.
The European discovery of America / Samuel Eliot Morison.
p.   cm.
Includes bibliographical references and index.
Contents: [1] The northern voyages, A.D. 500–1600 — [2] The
southern voyages, 1492–1616.
ISBN 0-19-508271-0 (pbk. : v. 1). — ISBN 0-19-508272-9 (pbk. : v. 2)
1. America—Discovery and exploration.   I. Title.
E101.M85   1993   970.01—dc20   93-20183

2   4   6   8   10   9   7   5   3   1

Printed in the United States of America

To my Dearest Wife

Priscilla Barton Morison

Who has followed all these Voyages with me
in spirit, and some of them in person

Preface

The book here presented to the public is devoted to European voyages to North America prior to 1600. Together with a similar volume on the Southern Voyages to follow (God willing), it should replace John Fiske's classic *Discovery of America* (2 vols., 1893) and supplement an irreplaceable work, the first four volumes of Justin Winsor's *Narrative and Critical History of America* (1884–89). Nobody in the present century has followed Winsor in attempting to cover the entire field of New World discovery. I have used Winsor's method of following each narrative chapter by a section of bibliography and notes, including a *précis* of the major controversies and of alleged voyages that never took place.

All honest efforts to throw light on historical darkness, such as this era, have my enthusiastic support. But it has fallen to my lot, working on this subject, to have read some of the most tiresome historical literature in existence. Young men seeking academic promotion, old men seeking publicity, neither one nor the other knowing the subject in depth, only a particular voyage or a particular map, write worthless articles; and the so-called learned journals are altogether too hospitable to these effusions. Some of these stem from mere personal conceit; others from racial emotion. Canada and the United States seem to be full of racial groups who wish to capture the "real" discovery for their medieval compatriots. They argue that Colombus and Cabot had so many predecessors as to deserve no more credit than a person who buys a ticket for a cruise at a tourist agency. In my bibliographies I have mentioned a few of these articles for the unconscious humor they provide, but for the most part only those which contribute something to the subject are recorded here.

The cartographical aspect deserves special notice. Literary evidence of these early Northern Voyages must be supplemented by that of early maps showing bits and pieces of the New World. Most of these are in European libraries or museums. I have attentively examined almost every one, as even the excellent Edward Luther Stevenson full-scale black-and-white photographs do not bring out every detail of a colored original. Several learned and excellent studies of these maps, especially of the projections they used, have been published by R. A. Skelton, G. R. Crone, Heinrich Winter, and others. But nobody has yet penetrated the secret of how the maps were made. Did the cartographer call on individual discoverers and explorers, record what they said, and borrow their own charts? Did he simply depict his own notion of the relation of early North American discoveries to Asia, and dub in the names of bays and promontories told to him by the sailors, or even make them up? Peculiar features of early maps, which may have been nothing but a draftsman's whimsy, have inspired pages of vain conjecture. Dozens of islands, rocks, and shoals that do not, and never did, exist are depicted on charts of the Atlantic, even down to the nineteenth century; and some have been avidly seized upon as evidence of pre-Columbian voyages. Williamson well observed, "All this map interpretation is hopelessly uncertain, and from it one may argue almost anything that comes into one's mind. The historian wants written statements."

Alas, he does not often find them, for the earliest period. He has to apply his background knowledge, his common sense, and (rarest of all qualifications) his personal knowledge of sailing to make sense out of the sources. Accordingly, I have handled cartographical evidence with respect, but somewhat gingerly, ever conscious that I am writing a history of voyages, not of maps.

The reproduction of old maps in a book presents typographical problems. Nobody likes a big pull-out; but if the size is too much reduced, one cannot read the names of places. I have tried whenever possible to obtain a photo directly from the map, and to keep the scale as big as possible by using only the immediately relevant portion. Most of the libraries and museums in Europe and America which possess these treasures have been very generous, helpful, and reasonable in their charges about reproduction.

The pursuit of suitable illustrations of places discovered by the early explorers has been interesting and time-absorbing. Not one government in the New World, to my knowledge, has made a complete photographic coverage of its shores. Hence I have been compelled to cover them by air, and do my best to photograph them from the fast-flying Beechcraft of my friend James F. Nields. The results, as the reader will observe, are very spotty, but the best I can offer.

Finally, there is oral evidence. We have precious little of that for so early a period, a notable exception being the Eskimo tradition about Frobisher; but as oral evidence I would include what professional sailors have taught me about coastal and blue-water sailing, and what fishermen have told me about their art. Just as old Horace wrote that his rustic poems came not only from personal experience but from his farmer Ofellus, *rusticus abnormis sapiens;* so much of what I know comes from a succession of Maine sailors who initiated me into the mysteries of the sea. Among these, I am especially indebted to Enos Verge, *nauta abnormis sapiens,* who sailed with me for years, mostly from Nova Scotia to Cuba. My knowledge of seafaring, acquired from such oral sources and from books over a period of seventy years, enables me to stretch back across the centuries and understand not only the triumphs of the navigators but their day-by-day problems. And, of late, Alan Villiers has been very generous to me from his vast fund of sea experience.

There is something very special about these northern voyages. In contrast to the fair winds that Columbus experienced and which made an outward Atlantic crossing easy from the navigator's point of view, anything might happen to you in the North Atlantic, even in summer; and in the sixteenth century everyone but French fishermen avoided sailing in winter. Westerly gales hurled crested seas against your little bark and forced it to lay-to for days; easterly gales drenched the sailors with chilling rain; fierce northerlies ripped their sails and cracked their masts. Between weather fronts even the whisper of a wind would often die and a white calm descend, so calm that one might think that the winds were worn out; then the fog closed in and the sea became a shimmering mirror reflecting the filtered rays of the sun. In high latitudes in summer one could forget whether it was day or night, while the sails slatted monotonously and the yards and rigging dripped rime. Plenty of men died on these northern voyages, but never of thirst. In a big fishing fleet, two centuries later, days of white calm might pass with jollity and humor from ship to ship, but for little knots of men confined to a small vessel, and no other human being within a thousand miles, the experience might be maddening. In the era of discovery, sailors would break out their sweeps and try to row their heavy vessels out of the calm, just to have something to do. It was a life for strong men and boys, not for women; the Greenlanders did indeed take women on their short voyages to Vinland, but there is no record of French or English taking them to America before Cartier's second voyage; and they were *forçats*, convicts.

People ask me to compare the hazards of the early navigators and those of the modern single-handed breed. The Atlantic was crossed many years ago by a Gloucester fisherman rowing a dory; and since Captain Slocum sailed around the world in his little *Spray*, with not one modern gadget, there have been countless one-man ocean crossings and a number of non-stop circumnavigations with self-inflicted hardships perhaps equal to those of the crews of Cabot and Frobisher. But these modern "loners" know where they are going; they have accurate charts, many instruments, and an auxiliary engine; they are in communication with the world by radio; naval vessels, airplanes, and coast guards shepherd them, drop food and water, and even, on occasion, take them on board for a rest; and, perhaps most important, they have no unruly, timid, and suspicious crew to govern and cajole into doing their duty.

Consider also the hazards of a sixteenth-century navigator exploring an unknown coast in a square-rigged vessel, incapable of quick maneuvering like a modern sailing yacht. With an onshore wind, the discoverers had to sail close to shore if they wanted to learn anything; yet it was always risky, especially on a fog-bound coast like Newfoundland. Submerged just below the surface, rocks capable of ripping the guts out of a ship were difficult to see in northern waters—dark green, opaque waters, not transparent like those of the Caribbean and the Coral Sea. Every harbor you entered added a new risk, even if a boat were sent ahead to sound. Would your anchor hold, or was the bottom hard rock, eel grass, or kelp, along which your hook would skid like a sled, requiring quick and efficient action to prevent your ship's crashing? If the wind is offshore when you sight land, you might be blown seaward again and have to beat back, which could take weeks—we shall see many instances of this. As Alan Villiers wrote, "The plain everyday difficulties of handling these ships . . . are already so forgotten as to seem incredible. Their means of movement was the wind properly directed to their sails. . . . They had to *fight* for their way, fight for their lives at times." * And so many lost their lives: John Cabot, both Corte Reals, Sir Humfry Gilbert, for instance. North America became a graveyard for European ships and sailors.

I wish that everyone who imagines that the "perils and dangers of the sea" have vanished before modern science would read Captain K. Adlard Coles's *Heavy Weather Sailing* (1967), with its hair-raising stories of sailing yachts no smaller than those of the era of discoveries, but laden with gadgets. There you have first-hand accounts of some of the hazards that the early navigators encountered as a matter of course—enormous freak waves, pitch-poling, capsizing; and although hurricanes were rarely encountered on these northern voyages of discovery, very strong gales and immense seas were common. Please remember, too, that these seamen had no storm warnings, no "law of storms" enabling them to evade the eye; and that even sailing in a fleet gave little protection. Under certain conditions a ship that foundered, like Gilbert's, or crashed on a lee shore, could expect no help even from another ship within sight. There is no basis of comparison between the astronauts who first landed on the moon on 20 July 1969, and discoverers like Columbus, Cabot, Verrazzano, and Cartier. Those four were men with an idea, grudgingly and meanly supported by their sovereigns. The three young heroes of the moon landing did not supply the idea; they bravely and intelligently executed a vast enterprise employing some 400,000 men and costing billions of dollars; whilst Columbus's first voyage cost his sovereigns less than a court ball; and Cabot's, which gave half the New World to England, cost Henry VII just fifty pounds. The astronauts' epochal voyage into

* Alan Villiers, *Captain James Cook* (1967), pp. 146–47.

space, a triumph of the human spirit, was long prepared, rehearsed, and conducted with precision to an accurately plotted heavenly body. Their feat might be slightly comparable to Cabot's if the moon were always dark and they knew not exactly where to find it—and if they had hit the wrong planet.

Abbé Anthiaume, a pioneer historian of French navigation, wrote many years ago of the early explorers by sea, "What superhuman energy a captain needed to triumph over these terrors of the ocean, to free his mind of ancient prejudices . . . and to carry his crew through these obscurities! . . . He knew very well that he risked his life and that of his shipmates for a hypothesis." The Abbé asks us to remember the common sailor who, "lost in an immensity of ocean that he suspected to be endless," imagined an island behind each cloud on the horizon, and anxiously followed with his eyes the birds which, as evening fell, flew in the same direction, hoping to be able, like them, to sleep ashore again.

Finally, I am highly conscious of writing amid "the tumult of the times disconsolate"—as Longfellow wrote of the 1860's. And to those now whimpering about the state of the world, and especially Americans predicting the collapse of society, I will say, "Have faith! Hang on! Do something yourself to improve things!" What if England and France had given up trying to establish colonies after the failures we are about to relate, and had become ingrown like certain other European countries, or Japan? What if they had written off North America as worthless, for want of precious metals? Where, then, would you be?

Just before the discovery of America, thinking men in western Europe believed that their world, already crumbling, would shortly crash; the stately Nuremberg Chronicle dwelt on "the calamity of our time . . . in which iniquity and evil have increased to the highest pitch," and gave its readers six blank pages to record events from 1493 to the end of the world. Nevertheless, a new era of hope and glory and enlargement of the human spirit, some aspects of which we shall now relate, was about to begin.

In human affairs there is no snug harbor, no rest short of the grave. We are forever setting forth afresh across new and stormy seas, or into outer space.

Morison, Nields, and Obregón setting forth to check on Leif Ericsson and John Cabot, 1968. Photo by Señora Obregón.

Rather than weary the reader with a long list of the persons and institutions that have helped me in my tortuous way, I shall mention them in the notes to each chapter. But I must here make a special tribute to those who have been with me all the way: my beloved wife Priscilla, who has not only accompanied me around the world in my quest for material, but has heard, read, and corrected my prose and created perfect conditions for work, whether in Boston, Northeast Harbor, or overseas. Second, my secretary Antha Eunice Card, who not only with exemplary cheerfulness has typed and retyped my drafts, but on occasion pointed out *le mot juste*, and executed many pieces of research. Third, my daughter Catharine Morison Cooper who has acted as my London agent and has been assiduous in looking up the scattered facts on early shipping in the British Museum and the National Maritime Museum at Greenwich (two institutions to which I am greatly indebted), and obtaining photographs of persons, places, and ships. Finally, James F. Nields of Ware, Massachusetts, and Mauricio Obregón of Bogotá, Columbia, both eminent in the new world of aviation, who have flown me, in Nields's plane, along the coasts discovered by Cabot, Cartier, and Verrazzano.

By the time this volume is published, I shall already be working on its companion, the Southern Voyages of Discovery, beginning with Columbus and concluding with Cavendish. Then, if time and strength permit, I shall return to the northern voyages of the early seventeenth century—those of Hudson, Champlain, Captain John Smith, Gosnold, Pring, and Captain Thomas James.

So, dear reader, this is au revoir, not (I hope) adieu!

"Good Hope"   S. E. Morison
Northeast Harbor, Maine
January 1971

Contents

I The Mysterious Ocean   3
Bibliography and Notes, 9

II St. Brendan and the Irish A.D. 400–600   13
Sea-going Monks, 13   Voyages of St. Brendan, 18
Irish Refugees in America? 26   Bibliography and Notes, 28

III The Norsemen and Vinland *c.* A.D. 800–1400   32
Norse Ships, Sailors, and Navigation, 32   Leif's First
Settlement, 39   Grapes, Wild Wheat, and Mosür Wood, 51
Expeditions of Thorvald and Karlsevni, 53   Expedition
of Thorvard and the Two Brothers, 57   The Later
History of Greenland and Vinland, 58   Bibliography and
Notes, 62

IV Flyaway Islands and False Voyages 1100–1492   81
The Background and the Problem, 81   Prince Madoc and
the Welsh Indians, 84   The Zeno Brothers and
"Zichmni," 87   Pining, Pothorst, and Scolvus, 89   The
Discovery of the Azores, 94   The Fabulous Antilia
Group, 97   Hy-Brasil, 102   Bibliography and Notes, 105

v   English Ships and Seamen 1490–1600   112
    Design, Build, and Rigging, 112   Getting Under Way, 128
    Food, Cooking, and Clothing, 130   The Sailor, His Wages
    and Division of Labor, 132   Ballast and Bilgewater, 134
    Navigation, 136   Shipboard Religion, 142   Weapons,
    Sweeps, and Anchors, 143   Bibliography and Notes, 148

vi John Cabot's Voyages 1497–1498   157
    Who Was John Cabot? 157   Bristol and the Transatlantic
    Passage, 161   The Landfall, 24 June 1497, 170   The
    Coastal Voyage, 177   His Homeward Passage, 185
    Cabot's Second Voyage, 189   Bibliography and Notes, 192

vii Voyages to the Labrador and Newfoundland
    1500–1536   210
    João Fernandes, Lavrador, 210   Gaspar and Miguel Corte
    Real, 213   The Anglo-Azorean Syndicate and Sebastian
    Cabot, 218   Fishermen and Newfoundland Cartography,
    1502–1524, 225   João Alvares Fagundes, 228   Robert
    Thorne's Letter and John Rut's Voyage, 233   Master Hore's
    Tourist Cruise, 237   Bibliography and Notes, 238

viii The French Maritime Background 1453–1590   252
    Emerging Normandy, 252   Brittany, 263   La Rochelle, 264
    Bordeaux and the Gironde, 267   Shipbuilding, 268
    Inauguration of the Grand Bank Fishery, 270
    Bibliography and Notes, 274

ix The Voyages of Verrazzano 1524–1528   277
    François-premier and the Search for a Northern Strait, 277
    Giovanni da Verrazzano, Gentleman Explorer, 282   From
    Deserta to the "Isthmus," 287   Et in Arcadia Ego, 295
    Angoulême and Refugio, 301   Maine—"Land of Bad
    People," 308   End of the Voyage, and of Giovanni, 313
    Bibliography and Notes, 317

x   Gomez and Ayllón 1524–1530   326
    Estévan Gomez, 326   Luís Vasquez de Ayllón, 332   The
    Ribero Maps of 1529, 334   Bibliography and Notes, 336

XI   Cartier's First Voyage 1534   339

Le Maître-Pilote Jacques Cartier, 339   Cartier's First Voyage
Gets Under Way, 345   South Shore of The Labrador, 348
West Coast of Newfoundland, 355   Brion, Magdalen, and
Prince Edward Islands, 361   Gaspé, 368   Anticosti and
Home, 375   Bibliography and Notes, 381

XII   Cartier's Second Voyage 1535–1536   388

To Sea with Royal and Episcopal Blessing, 388   Retracing
First Voyage, 392   *Le Chemyn de Canada*, 395
Stadaconé—Quebec, 405   Hochelaga, 410   First Winter
in Canada, 417   Bibliography and Notes, 424

XIII   The Search for Saguenay 1538–1543   430

Preparations for Cartier's Third Voyage, 430   Roberval
and Diplomatic Snooping, 434   Cartier's Third Voyage, 437
Cartier Meets Roberval and Goes Home, 442   The Valiant
Demoiselle, 445   France-Roy and Search for Saguenay, 448
Bibliography and Notes, 455

XIV   England, France, and the Northwest 1553–1600   464

The Glorious Kingdom of Norumbega, 464   The
Newfoundland Cod Fishery, 470   The Gulf Whale and
Walrus Fisheries, 478   A French Colony on Sable Island, 480
English Voyages "Around the Clock," 482
Bibliography and Notes, 488

XV   Queen Elizabeth and Her Master Mariners   494

Gloriana, 494   Enter Gilbert and Frobisher, 497   Martin
Frobisher's First Voyage, 1576, 500   Bibliography and
Notes, 510

XVI   Frobisher's Second and Third Voyages 1577–1578   516

Second Voyage Begins, 516   Frobisher Bay Again, 519
Conclusion of Second Voyage, 528   Third Voyage, 531
The "Mistaken Straits," 535   A Summer's Ore-Gathering, 537
Homeward Bound, 543   Conclusion, 545
Bibliography and Notes, 550

XVII   Hakluyt and Gilbert 1578–1585   555

Richard Hakluyt, 555   Sir Humfry Gilbert and His First

Voyage, 561   Gilbert's Second and Last Voyage, 569
Bibliography and Notes, 578

XVIII The Northern Voyages of John Davis 1585–1587   583
John Davis, Master Mariner, 583   First Voyage, 1585, 587
Second Voyage, 1586, 592   Third Voyage, 1587, 598
Bibliography and Notes, 605

XIX The First Virginia Colony 1585–1586   617
Walter Raleigh and the Amadas-Barlowe Voyage of 1584, 617
Windgandcon Becomes Virginia, 626   Grenville's 1585
Voyage, to Puerto Rico and Hispaniola, 631   Lane's
Colony at Roanoke Island, 1585–86, 640   Drake and
Grenville Relief Expeditions of 1586, 649
Bibliography and Notes, 651

XX The Second Virginia Colony 1587–?   656
John White's Colony and Settlement, 656   Thomas
Hariot's Account, 666   Relief Expeditions of 1588–1590, 669
The Lost Colony, 677   Bibliography and Notes, 679

List of Illustrations, 685
Index, 693

The European Discovery of America

THE NORTHERN VOYAGES
A.D. 500–1600

✳ I ✳

The Mysterious Ocean

The European discovery of America flows from two impulses. One, lasting over two thousand years and never attained, is the quest for some "land of pure delight where saints immortal reign"; where (in the words of Isaac Watts's hymn) "everlasting spring abides, and never fading flowers." The other impulse, springing into life in the thirteenth century, was the search for a sea route to "The Indies," as China, Japan, Indonesia, and India were then collectively called. This search attained success with the voyages of Columbus and Cabot—who (by the greatest serendipity of history) discovered America instead of reaching the Indies—and with the voyage of Magellan which finally did reach the Indies and returned around the world.

The story of how this happened—so far as we can piece it out from the imperfect records of the past—is the subject of this book. It is convenient to cover the Northern Voyages first, because they had a certain unity of purpose as well as of geography. But we must briefly consider the heritage of classical antiquity which is basic to all European westward ventures.

When primitive man first reached the shores of the Mediterranean and the Atlantic, his first impulse, no doubt, was to cast a line into this new and apparently limitless fish pond; and his second, to wonder what

3

lay "over there," beyond the Ocean's rim. He built himself rafts, dug-out canoes, and finally boats for fishing and coastwise trading, he discovered that manipulating a sail saved him a lot of manual labor, and in the course of experimenting with winds and currents, some men ventured, or were blown, out of sight of land. No matter how far they sailed beyond the Pillars of Hercules (the Strait of Gibraltar) or off the western coast from Scotland to Spain, the same watery horizon greeted them. So, naturally, poets and priests adopted the theory of a never-never land where the souls of the meritorious faithful live happily without work before proceeding to one of God's many mansions. It must have been a consoling thought for the families of sailors who never returned, that God had provided for them in these Happy Isles.

Hesiod, Greek poet of the eighth century B.C., was the first man (so far as we know) to give these Islands of the Blest literary expression. Speaking of a "godlike race of hero-men" who preceded us on earth, he said that some were killed in battles such as the siege of Troy, but to the others, "Father Zeus, at the ends of the earth, presented a dwelling place, apart from man and far from the deathless gods. In the Islands of the Blest, bounded by deep-swirling Ocean, they live untouched by toil or sorrow. For them the grain-giving earth thrice yearly bears fruit sweet as honey." These *Insulae Fortunatae*, or Happy Isles, which are also called the Hesperides, the Elysian Fields, and other names in every European vernacular, were believed in throughout the period of classical antiquity and well into the Middle Ages. Even the sophisticated Horace, despairing of the Republic in time of civil war, urged his noble Roman friends to "cease their effeminate complaints and go," leaving the vile, indocile plebeians to fight it out among themselves. "Happy fields surrounded by Ocean await us and invite us to their shores. Go, then, to these fortunate islands, where the land without tillage produces grain abundantly, the vine bears grapes without pruning, ripe figs may be plucked the year round, the olive ever bears fruit, honey drips from the live-oak, the streams make a pleasant murmur as they flow from the mountains and tumble over rocky ledges; she-goats with full udders beg one to milk them; neither bears nor vipers are there. . . . The Argonauts never rowed along these coasts; Medea, the shameless woman of Colchis, never set foot there; neither sailors of Sidon nor shipmates of Ulysses have ranged this coast under sail. There is no pestilence to hurt the cattle. Eurus, the tempestuous

east wind, here brings a gentle, fertile rain, and never is there drought.
. . . Jupiter has reserved for the just these happy countries, whenever
the golden age turns to brass, and an iron era succeeds the brass. Only
by following my advice may the just escape the horrors of this age of
iron."

Carthage, founded by Phoenicians from Tyre and Sidon, became the
greatest sea power in antiquity. Carthaginians certainly discovered and
partially colonized the Canary Islands, whose salubrious climate caused
them to be confounded with the *Insulae Fortunatae*. Unnamed Phoenicians, manning "a number of ships" in the navy of the Egyptian
Pharaoh Necho, who reigned from 609 to 595 B.C., performed one of
the most remarkable voyages of history, the circumnavigation of
Africa from east to west. These big row galleys took their departure
from Egypt by way of the Erythraean Sea, weathered the Cape of
Good Hope, entered the Mediterranean, and reported to Pharaoh at the
mouth of the Nile. Since sea-going row galleys, with little storage
space, had to keep a crew of at least fifty officers and oarsmen live and
healthy, this Egyptian fleet had to stop ashore "when autumn came"
to plant, grow, and reap a crop of grain; that was their only means of
solving the logistic problem. Thus the voyage consumed three years.
Herodotus, our sole source, disbelieved the story because, as it came to
him, "in sailing round Libya" they had the sun upon their right hand;
and for over a thousand years almost everyone followed the Greek
historian in writing off this voyage as fabulous. Alexander von Humboldt first noted that, on the contrary, this observation was good evidence that the voyage did take place. Except when they crossed the
Gulf of Guinea, these galley sailors must have seen the sun rise on their
starboard hand.

"No evidence from the classic writers justifies the assumption that
the ancients communicated with America," wrote Justin Winsor in
1889; nor has anyone since discovered any such evidence.

The Greeks were never "light-hearted masters of the waves," as
Matthew Arnold described them; they, like Ulysses, regarded the sea
as an element "laden with suffering," necessary as a means of fishing and
transportation, but to be used cautiously and avoided whenever possible. Nevertheless, one of the boldest voyages of history was made by
Pytheas of the Greek colony in Marseilles, at a time when Alexander
the Great reigned. In a sailing ship with auxiliary oar power he sailed

beyond the Pillars of Hercules into the broad Atlantic, north along the coasts of Portugal, France, and Britain, reaching a place that he named *Thule*, where he observed the midnight sun and was told that darkness lasted all winter. This voyage, which we know only through the works of Pliny and other ancient historians, gave Thule an almost fabulous importance as the uttermost land that man had reached—*Ultima Thule*. Columbus's son, for instance, boasted that his father had fulfilled the prophecy in Seneca's *Medea*, that some future Argonaut would discover a vast new world, when Thule would no longer be the ultimate.

But where and what was Thule? The Faroes, Iceland, or the northern coast of Norway? Not that it matters; nobody sailed north to check on Pytheas. The importance of his voyage lay in the fact that he made a startling discovery which led other men of enterprise to believe that they could do even better.

A contribution of antiquity far more important to the cause of discovery was scientific geography—especially determination of the shape and size of the earth, and the distribution of land, water, and climates. The Pythagoreans of the sixth century B.C. taught that the world was spherical; Aristotle proved it from the circular shadow of the earth on the moon during an eclipse. Plato rendered the concept popular, as did Virgil and Ovid, and although there were many "flat-earth" dissenters (and still are), Aristotle's authority, supported by the common observations of sailors, caused the spherical earth to be taught not only in ancient schools of learning but in medieval universities. The story that Columbus was trying "to prove the world was round" and that he was held up by flat-earth monks, is one of those vulgar errors that no amount of denial can dispel. Scientific demonstration of the earth's rotundity was enforced by religion; God made the earth a sphere because that was the most perfect form. In the Old Testament there is a reference to this in Isaiah xl.22: "It is he that sitteth upon the circle of the earth"—"circle" being the translation of the Hebrew *khug*, sphere. The ancients also drew logical conclusions from the earth's sphericity; they postulated a south temperate zone corresponding to the one with which they were familiar, and a land therein, the Antipodes, to balance Europe.

Three men especially moved people in the Middle Ages and Renaissance. A Greek whose name we do not know invented the degree, one three-hundred-sixtieth of a circle or sphere, as a unit of measurement.

When Alexander the Great's armies marched to India and back, it became necessary, for logistic purposes, to have accurate measurements, and the school of geography founded by the Ptolemies in Alexandria studied the problem. Eratosthenes, librarian at Alexandria around 200 B.C., made a laudable attempt at measuring the degree by making meridian observations of the sun from the bottoms of wells at two distant points (Cyene and Alexandria), supposedly on the same meridian of longitude. Although he made sundry errors in his calculations, they canceled each other out so that his answer was very nearly correct; translated into modern nautical miles, Eratosthenes' degree was 59.5 instead of the correct 60.

The most influential geographer of antiquity, though not the most accurate, was Claudius Ptolemy (c. A.D. 73–151). His geography spotted the position—so far as he could ascertain it—of some 8000 places in the known world, and he drew both general and detailed maps which were not superseded for fourteen centuries. Ptolemy's Geography, known in a Latin translation from about 1406 and printed in edition after edition after 1475, exercised a tremendous authority over the human mind. It is no exaggeration to say that the learned world was more interested in the discovery of Ptolemy than in the discovery of America. A geography book with any pretense to authority was long called a "Ptolemy," just as manuals of geometry are still called "Euclids" and the official compendium of navigation a "Bowditch." The Bologna Ptolemy of 1477 has latitude and longitude grids on the margins, and the Ulm edition of 1482, edited by Nicholaus Germanus, includes a very early world map. Anyone like the Scandinavians, who objected to his attenuated depiction of the northern kingdoms, had to prove their case; for dixit Ptolemaeus—Ptolemy said it—was generally held to be conclusive. Ptolemy was grossly inaccurate in spots: his Mediterranean was far too long, his Italy sloped too easterly, his Scotland leaned over backwards, his Ceylon was bigger than India. But Ptolemy was the best, indeed the only, world geographer that Europe had in the fifteenth century. And Ptolemy's biggest mistake, making the length of Eurasia from Cape St. Vincent to the coast of China 177 degrees (the correct figure being 131), was a happy mistake. For it encouraged navigators like Columbus and Cabot to believe that the Atlantic could be crossed in a reasonable time.

Columbus liked Ptolemy because he marked down Eratosthenes'

length of the degree to 56.5 nautical miles; but he loved Marinus of Tyre (of the second Christian century) even better. For Marinus, by totting up what the silk caravan camel drivers told him about the length of their journeys to China and back, and assuming that a camel walked an average of twenty miles per day for seven months, figured out that Eurasia measured 225 degrees from Cape St. Vincent to the coast of China—48 degrees more than Ptolemy's already overblown reckoning.

Another and older Greek geographer who became known to Europe in the fifteenth century was the Greek Strabo (born c. 63 B.C.), extracts of whose *Geographika* and *Diorthosis* were copied by the Byzantine scholar Pletho and printed as early as 1469. Columbus made much of Strabo's statements that it would be possible to sail from Spain to the Indies, and that certain sailors had tried to do it but gave up their quest for want of provisions.

Eratosthenes, as reported by Strabo, stated that it was theoretically possible to sail from Spain to the Orient along the same parallel of latitude. Seneca the philosopher gave Columbus considerable comfort by writing that the ocean from Spain to the Indies could be traversed *paucis diebus;* but Seneca meant "few" in a sense relative to eternity and the higher interests of the soul. Ancient sea craft were not adequate for an Atlantic crossing both ways. In the late twentieth century the ocean has been crossed successfully by men in open dories or tiny sailboats; but it is one thing to do that when you know exactly your destination and can rely on coastguards and aviators to feed or to rescue you; and another to thrust forth into the unknown on a voyage of undetermined length and dubious destination.

In the ancient world, moreover, there was no international competition for trade routes. The Roman empire, which succeeded to and absorbed the commercial supremacy of the Phoenicians, had no competitors. Thus the motives for financing the voyages of Columbus, Cabot, Cartier, and the rest did not then exist. And whilst the scientific findings of the Greeks were of great help to navigators of the Renaissance, their offhand remarks about the Atlantic were anything but encouraging. Aristotle taught that the sea was shallow and becalmed a few miles out from the Pillars of Hercules. Plato declared that the mythical Island of Atlantis—created by his imagination—had submerged into a vast mudbank. Tacitus believed that there was a built-in resistance to sailing ships in northern waters; a sort of jellied or coagulated sea. Not far wrong, when we think of the pack-ice.

In conclusion, the philosophers and other writers of ancient Greece and Rome laid a scientific basis for the discoveries of the fifteenth and sixteenth centuries. To what extent these theories reached the common people is unknown. Doubtless fishermen and sailors were familiar with the Islands of the Blest hypothesis, especially through the familiar story of Hercules searching for the golden apples of the Hesperides. These happy or fortunate isles shone as an enticing mirage through the Middle Ages and almost to our own times. Many, many attempts were made to locate them, notably the Voyage of St. Brendan. But there is no evidence from classic writers to justify any assumption that the ancients communicated with America.

Bibliography and Notes

GENERAL BIBLIOGRAPHY

Justin Winsor, *Narrative and Critical History of America*, I–IV (1884–89), in my opinion, will always stand first. Other giants of early American historiography, are Henry Harrisse, *Discovery of North America* (1892) and his many other works; Henry Vignaud with his many works on Columbus; Cesare De Lollis, who edited the great *Raccolta di Documenti e Studi* on Columbus, which also contains data on Northern Voyages; Charles de La Roncière, who wrote the monumental *Histoire de la marine française*; Francis Parkman, whose *Pioneers of France in the New World* (1865) has become a classic, and Edward G. Bourne, whose one-volume *Spain in America* (1904) is an example to all historians of condensation without becoming dull. They are long since dead, and peace to their souls! In a class with them, among twentieth-century writers, are the late J. A. Williamson, the greatest authority on the Cabots; D. B. Quinn, on Gilbert and Raleigh; and the Canadians H. P. Biggar and Marcel Trudel. France, too, has produced worthy successors to La Roncière in Mollat, Chaunu, Julien, and Bernard; their works are not only scholarly but comprehensive, relating the economic context in which voyages took place, and preventing us from (too easily) imagining that the Discovery of America consumed all the maritime energy of Europe. We shall mention their works in due course in our chapter bibliographies and notes.

Scholarship in the United States has ebbed during the last fifty years, so far as this subject is concerned; but the foundation at the Smithsonian Institution of a Society for the History of Discoveries, with a learned journal, *Terrae Incognitae* (Vol. I, No. 1, of 1969 on hand as I write), is a hopeful sign that the tide is turning. Our young aspirants to the mantle of

Justin Winsor suffer from two handicaps. Having been deprived of a classical education, they find the learning of a foreign language very difficult, and they dislike getting their feet wet. One cannot do much about their want of basic Latin; but if only they would take a cruise in a sailing vessel they might learn something about the facts of life at sea and not write the nonsense they do about voyages. The late Eva G. R. Taylor, professor of geography in the University of London, once laughingly admitted, "I am absolutely terrified of the water and would not go on it for anything!" * Yet for years she pontificated about the great navigators of history in a highly disparaging fashion.

Unfortunately, there is no corpus of sources for the Northern Voyages corresponding to De Lollis's for Columbus. Three recent compilations are notable: Armando Cortesão and Avelino Teixera da Moto, *Portugalae Monumenta Cartographica* (5 vols., Lisbon, 1960–62, Vol. I, to 1564); and Duque de Alba *et al.*, *Mapas Españoles de America Siglos XV–XVII* (Madrid, 1951). Both are beautifully printed with many maps in color, toponymy, and analysis. There is no such corpus for Italian, English, or French maps, which are fewer in number, and, all but the French, inferior in execution. A particularly useful series is Carlos Sanz's *Mapas Antiguas del Mundo (Siglos XV–XVI)*, privately printed in Madrid, c. 1965. The black-and-white reproductions are on separate sheets.

In the nineteenth century there were produced several big folio albums of map reproductions, of which the best are Friedrich Kunstmann, *Die Entdeckung Amerikas* (1859); E. M. Jomard, *Les Monuments de la géographie* (Paris, 1862); A. J. Nordenskiöld, *Facsimile Atlas* (Stockholm, 1880), and *Periplus* (Stockholm, 1891; see facsimile of title page in Notes to Chapter V below); Konrad Kretschmer, *Die Entdeckung Amerikas . . . mit einem Atlas* (1892). A very careful photographic compilation is Edward L. Stevenson, *Maps Illustrating Early Discovery and Exploration in America 1502–1530* (1905). Although none of these, except Stevenson, are photographic reproductions, they are nonetheless useful; an artist making a line drawing sometimes sees things that the camera misses. A moderate-sized (and priced) book with a large number of clear illustrations and sound comment is R. A. Skelton, *Explorers' Maps* (1958).

Two excellent guides to important maps on early America are M. Foncin, Marcel Destombes, and Monique de La Roncière, *Catalogue des cartes nautiques sur vélin conservées au département des cartes et plans* (Paris, 1963) and [Theodore E. Layng] *Sixteenth-Century Maps Relating to Canada, A Checklist and Bibliography* (Ottawa, 1956). I wish here to express my gratitude to Mlle de La Roncière (daughter of my eminent friend of other days, Charles de La Roncière) for her help in studying the amazing resources of the Bibliothèque Nationale; as also to Dr. Layng, head of the Map Room of the Canadian Public Archives, to Mr. Frank E.

* *Geographical Journal*, CXXVII (1961), 156.

Trout, curator of the Justin Winsor Map Room of the Harvard College Library, to Mr. George Naish of the National Maritime Museum, to Miss Oloronshaw, exec. of the Manuscript Room, and Mr. E. J. Huddy, both of the British Museum, for their frequent, untiring help in running down early maps in their collections.

BIBLIOGRAPHY FOR CHAPTER I

William H. Tillinghast, "The Geographical Knowledge of the Ancients" ꞏ in Justin Winsor, *Narrative and Critical History*, I (1889), is still the best scholarly account of this subject. Richard Hennig, *Terrae Incognitae* (4 vols., Leiden, 1936–39), is a useful compilation of sources on all voyages and extensive journeys down to 1490, with notes; but he translates all sources ꞏ into German, and is unduly credulous. Vincent H. Cassidy, *The Sea Around Them* (Baton Rouge, 1968), summarizes all geographical knowledge and theory to A.D. 1250. Milton V. Anastos, *Pletho, Strabo and Columbus* (Brussels, 1953), is an important contribution. G. R. Crone, *Maps and Their Makers* (1953), chapters i and v, is a good starting point for Ptolemy and his influence. Crone believes that Ptolemy's maps are no older than the early fourteenth century, and were drafted in Constantinople.

My classical quotations are from Hesiod, *Works and Days*, 160–73, Horace, *Epodes*, xvi, and Rawlinson's translation of Herodotus, *History*, III, 28–29.

THE "PHOENICIAN DISCOVERY OF AMERICA"

There are still advocates for this happening before 146 B.C., when Rome destroyed Carthage; and Phoenician script is so simple that, as with the later Norse runes, it is easy for an overimaginative searcher to read Punic, like Runic, in natural grooves and scratches on rocks. A Brazilian gentleman named Bernardo da Silva Ramos claimed to have collected 2800 Phoenician inscriptions in a voyage up the Amazon! C. M. Boland assigns "Mystery Village" at North Salem, New Hampshire (see notes to Chapter II below) to the sea-going Carthaginians, and has another favorite site in Pennsylvania, complete with "Punic inscriptions" and flat "sacrificial stones" where obscene rites were supposedly performed. See C. M. Boland, *They All Discovered America* (1961), chap. 2. The most "solid" evidence, one of those fakes which never dies, is the reported discovery in 1872 by a slave belonging to Joaquim Alves da Costa in Brazil, of an inscribed stone tablet. Costa's son allegedly copied the inscription and sent it to Ladislau Netto, then director of the National Museum at Rio de Janeiro, who rendered it into Portuguese:

> We are sons of Canaan from Sidon, the city of the king. Commerce has cast us on this distant shore, a land of mountains. We set [sacrificed] a youth for the exalted gods and goddesses in the eighteenth year of Hiram, our mighty king. We embarked from Ezion-Geber into the Red Sea and voyaged

with ten ships. We were at sea together for two years around the land belonging to Ham [Africa] but were separated by a storm [literal translation: "from the hand of Baal"] and we were no longer with our companions. So we have come here, twelve men and three women, on a new shore which I, the Admiral, control. But auspiciously may the exalted gods and goddesses favor us!

Obviously, this is an attempt to hook up the tablet with the circumnavigation of Africa ordered by Necho.

Investigation failed to locate either the stone or Senhor da Costa, and the whole thing was dropped as a hoax. But Professor Cyrus H. Gordon of Brandeis University revived it in 1968, made the English translation quoted above, and argued for its authenticity. Professor Frank M. Cross of Harvard promptly demonstrated its falsity on linguistic grounds. It is a mixture of letters from different periods, with many anachronisms. (New York *Times*, Washington *Post*, and other newspapers of 16–19 May; *Time* magazine, 24 May 1968; *Saturday Review*, 18 July 1970).

Armando Cortesão is also partial to the Phoenician discovery of America. In his *Nautical Chart of 1424* (Coimbra, 1954), chap. ii, he assumes that the Phoenician galleys spread square sails when ranging the west coast of Africa, and that some "must" have been "blown across" to the New World. The obvious question is, if Necho's fleet that made the periplus of Africa had been a sailing fleet, why was it necessary to stop over twice to grow food for the crew? And, if one of these row galleys, which might well have used auxiliary sail in a fair wind, got "blown across" the Atlantic, how did her skipper find food enough to keep his galley slaves alive and rowing? I confess I am rather tired of "blown across the Atlantic" hypotheses. Naturally, a vessel in the easterly trade wind belt could, if partially disabled and using some sort of jury rig, have been "blown across"; but how would she have got back?

✻ II ✻
St. Brendan and the Irish
A.D. 400-600

Sea-going Monks

"What wonderful happiness there was, then," wrote Thomas Morton of the early Middle Ages. "There were still men on this miserable, noisy, cruel earth, who tasted the marvelous joy of silence and solitude, who dwelt in forgotten mountain cells, in secluded monasteries, where the news and desires and appetites and conflicts of the world no longer reached them." And also at sea.

Ireland, already a land of high culture in comparison with most parts of Europe, was converted to Christianity by St. Patrick and others in the fourth and fifth centuries. Christianity in Ireland assumed peculiar forms. Monasticism flourished in a hundred or more convents, as the best means of leading the New Testament life with a minimum of temptation. Yet even in a monastery the sight of a pretty barefoot colleen delivering the milk, or of a noble lady riding by on her palfrey, might afflict the brethren with wicked thoughts. So, really to "get away from it all," your typical Irish monk indulged in long voyages in small frail boats. Thereby he served both piety and pleasure; piety because no woman could be there to tempt him; pleasure because since time immemorial the Irish had loved salt water. "What joy to sail the

St. Brendan's Bay, County Kerry. Courtesy Bord Fáilte Photo, Dublin.

crested sea!" is one of the recorded sayings of St. Columba. Yet every voyage must end; so, in order to prolong isolation from the world and the other sex, Irish clerics built themselves tiny monasteries or single cells on almost inaccessible rocks surrounded by the ocean. There were scores of them off the west coast, such as the famous cluster of cells atop Skellig Michael. Anchorites who lived on these spurs of rock had to be ascetic; they caught fish and snared sea fowl, and let down baskets which pious fishermen, eager to win grace through a holy man, filled with bread and fruits of the soil. They believed that they were obeying the divine command (Genesis xii.1): "Now the Lord had said unto Abram, Get thee out of thy country, and from thy kindred, and from thy father's house, unto a land that I will shew thee." Iona was begun as just such an island monastery by St. Columba in A.D. 563.

These rock-anchored monastic cells were dead ends, in a double sense; but the voyages led to discoveries—Iceland and the Faroes certainly, possibly further. Early Irish literature, both pagan and Christian, abounds in *imrama*, as these Irish voyages are called. The *imram* tells

The Skelligs, from Skellig Michael. Courtesy Bord Fáilte Photo, Dublin.

the tale of an ocean voyage, embellished by marvels and miracles; and of all *imrama*, that of St. Brendan is the best. It enjoyed a popularity in the Middle Ages equal to that of the Song of Roland and the legends of King Arthur. No fewer than one hundred and twenty manuscripts of the *Navigatio Sancti Brendani Abbatis*, the principal text, exist, and three are from the early eleventh century. In addition, there is a contemporary *Vita S. Brendani* which has few details on the voyage but more on the saint's life and career.

St. Brendan the Navigator was born in the last quarter of the fifth century—perhaps in 484 if you must have a date—near Tralee, County Kerry. He became a famous churchman and great organizer, founding four monasteries in western Ireland and making several voyages to England, Scotland, and Wales, and to Brittany, with MacLaw (St. Malo), one of his disciples. At the time when he shoved off into the unknown, Brendan was over seventy years old and abbot of the monastery of Clonfert in Galway, on the verge of the sea. One suspects that his eyes often strayed westward, and that he wondered over the meaning of

15

the green flash when the sun set behind a clear horizon. But he was too involved with monastic business to go on a cruise without a pious objective. That was furnished by his aged friend Abbot Barinth, who came to tell him how his son Mernoc, sailing westward, had discovered not only a "delicious island" full of monks, but the *Terra Repromissionis Sanctorum*, the Promised Land of the Saints, and had sailed his father there and back. As proof that he had been in this terrestrial paradise, Barinth invited Brendan's monks to sniff his garments, which still, after a forty-day sea voyage, retained the floral perfumes of the blessed isle.

Brendan, deeply impressed by these divine manifestations, selected fourteen monks and asked how they felt about seeking the promised land. They replied with one accord, "Abbot, thy will is ours; have we not rejected our inheritance and placed our bodies in thine hands? We are prepared to follow thee to death, God willing."

Brendan and the chosen fourteen fasted forty days; not a very good preparation, one would think, for the next job, shipbuilding. They constructed (says the *Navigatio S. Brendani*) "a very light little vessel, ribbed and sided with wood, but . . . covered with oak-tanned ox-hides and caulked with ox-tallow." This is a good description of the *curragh*, the skin-covered boat which the Celts invented—Julius Caesar described them in Britain. The type has lasted to this day, in the wicker-framed boats of the west coast of Ireland, now covered with tarred cotton cloth instead of greased hides. The Irish built not only small curraghs for fishing and inshore work, but big, sea-going ones with mast, square sail of woolen cloth, cordage of ox-hide strips,* and lashings of deer sinews or vine roots in lieu of metal fastenings. This type could not sail to windward like the Portuguese caravels, but it had many merits. In a country where timber was scarce but cattle plentiful, the Irish built with what they had, and the resulting curragh had excellent qualities. Being little more than a big wicker basket covered with skins, she rode the waves like a cork and stayed dry in heavy seas which broke over any heavy wooden ship. Modern rowing curraghs

---

* My friend Mauricio Obregón tells me that Indians in the cattle country of Colombia still make their cordage by cutting an oxhide spirally into one long strip and drying it in the sun, and the resulting line is as strong as a hemp or manila rope.

Drying nets and carrying a curragh at Brandon Harbour, County Kerry.
Courtesy Bord Fáilte Photo, Dublin.

are carried upside-down by their crews, as college oarsmen do a racing shell.

Brendan's curragh, to accommodate eighteen men (three more having joined him at the last minute), probably had a half-deck for extra protection, and a tiny altar where the Abbot could celebrate mass; it was equipped with mast, sail and cordage, provision for forty days, and plenty of spare tallow to keep the skin tight. There seem to have been no cooking facilities; the crew lived on cold victuals except when they had a chance to kindle a fire ashore—or on a whale's back. They carried water, and wine for mass, in goatskins, hair side in, just as Orientals do today; with practice one gets to like the high flavor and bouquet that the goat imparts to the wine. The curragh used a stone killick for anchoring; but whenever possible they beached her ashore, unstepped the mast, turned her bottom up, and serviced the ox-hide sheathing with tallow or pine resin. Smaller and less seaworthy vessels than this have crossed the Western Ocean in our own day. The Saint and his crew were too wise to count on holiness to offset clumsiness at sea. Familiar with curraghs from childhood, they knew both how to build them and how to handle them in all kinds of weather; and with beds of grass or heather, to sleep well. Being ascetics, they did not expect comfort.

Voyages of St. Brendan

When ready for sea, the Abbot ordered his crew on board and set sail with a fair breeze, shaping a course "against the summer solstice," northward. A fortnight later the wind dropped dead, and the crew made way with their long oars. After forty days at sea, with ship's stores spent, they sighted a high, rocky island over whose cliffs waterfalls fell into the sea, but they could find no harbor. The hungry monks were in despair, but Brendan assured them that Our Lord would show them a port within three days. Of course He did. After beaching and securing their curragh, the brethren decided to explore the island. Suddenly a dog appeared and, instead of snarling and barking, fawned on Brendan as if he had been his long-lost master. "What a good messenger God has given us!" said the Abbot to his men. "Let's follow him." The dog, frisking and gamboling, led them to a town where the principal building was an immense castle. They entered, to find themselves in a vast hall hung with necklaces and other articles of pure silver. A table had already been set for them, laden with bread and fish. They fell to greedily, and after making a hearty supper retired to guest cells; but one of the three Johnny-come-latelys sneaked out, stole a silver necklace from the wall, and hid it in his cowl. Brendan caught him in the act, absolved him after confession, and then saw the devil in the form of a black dwarf hop out of the monk's cowl and curse the Abbot for robbing him of a victim! The errant brother died that night.

Next morning, when the seventeen remaining monks walked down to their ship, a human being, the first to be seen on this island, approached. He was a young man, bringing great baskets of bread and an amphora of water for their voyage. The procurator (business manager) of this monastery, as he proved to be, kept turning up during the seven years' voyage to see that Brendan's men had meat and drink, being transported by magic from island to island.

A day or two later, Brendan's crew landed on an island where they celebrated Good Friday and Easter. Here they found flocks of white sheep bigger than oxen, and a lamb which they slaughtered for the paschal feast. A man in shining garments appeared, offered them provision for eight days, and gave them the course for an island called the Paradise of Birds. En route, they landed on a bare, treeless, black island and kindled a fire to prepare a hot meal. The island then slipped away from under them! It turned out to be a whale named Jasconius (as they later learned) who did not appreciate back-burning saints but forgivingly invited them to return, provided they ate their victuals cold.

Now the brethren sail away to the Paradise of Birds. Here they find a river flowing into the sea and haul their vessel ashore. The island is so thick with birds that one can scarcely see the trees for them. A big one perches on the ship's prow and explains, in good Latin, that he and his fellows are fallen angels of Lucifer's host who, as the less guilty, have been placed here by a merciful God. "We are not punished. Here we can see the presence of God. . . . We fly to all parts of air, earth and heaven . . . but on Sundays and holy days we assume bodies such as you now see, and here we abide and glorify our creator. Thou and thy brethren have been a year on thy journey; six more remain. Where this day thou celebratest Easter, there shalt thou keep it every year, and again after thou hast found the land of thy heart's desire, the Promised Land of the Saints." Thus saying, the bird spread his wings and joined his fellows on the trees.

These were obviously no common birds—they both spoke and sang Latin! When the hour of vespers approached, "All birds in the tree sang in unison, 'Thou, O God, art praised in Sion, and unto thee shall the vow be performed in Jerusalem.' " They sang the responses correctly and so continued for an hour, accompanying themselves by a rhythmic flapping of wings. That night Brendan awoke his brethren to sing lauds, opening with the verse "O Lord, open thou my lips," to which the drowsy birds responded, "Praise the Lord all ye angels of his, praise him, all his host." At prime, terce, sext, and none they sang the appropriate psalms, ending, "Behold how good and joyful a thing it is for brethren to dwell together in unity." And when the monks departed on the octave of Pentecost, all the birds sang with one accord, "Hear us, O God our saviour, our hope to the ends of the earth and in the deep sea."

"Now the holy father with his people sailed to and fro over the ocean for three months," says the *Navigatio*. "They could see neither sky nor sea," evidently being enveloped by the thickest sort of fog. The provisions donated by the procurator ran low, and they ate only every two or three days. Finally an island appeared, around it they sailed and sailed, looking for a harbor; then there opened up a narrow slit, just big enough for their curragh. Feeling very dry and famished, they followed an uphill path. A venerable man with white hair approached and prostrated himself thrice before Brendan. After exchanging a kiss of peace, this ancient led Brendan and the crew to the monastery, which turned out to have been founded by Ailbe, a noted Irish saint, eight years before. Presently eleven monks came forward bearing crosses and images and singing a hymn of welcome. The seafarers had their feet washed in scriptural fashion by their hosts, dined on white bread—a great luxury in the early Middle Ages—and roots of exquisite flavor. The ancient, St. Ailbe himself, informed Brendan that he never knew who baked the bread or whence it came. "We are twenty-four brethren," he said. "Daily we have twelve loaves of bread for our refreshment, double on holy days, and in anticipation of your arrival we received the same extra rations today." After dinner they went to vespers. The church was lighted by seven lamps of crystal. After the

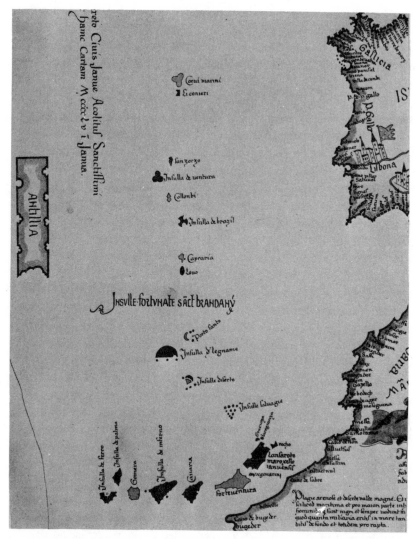

The medieval conception of St. Brendan's Isles. Bartolomeo Pareto's Map of 1455, now in the Biblioteca Vittorio Emanuele, Rome. Photographed from Kretschmer's *Atlas* Plate V. From north to south: *Corui marini* (sea crows), *Li conieri* (rabbits), *San Zorzo* (St. George), Ventura, *Collonbi* (doves), Brazil, *Capraria* (goats), and *Louo* (wolf). South of these are two groups of real islands:—(1) Porto Santo, *legname* (Madeira), Deserta and Salvagio; and (2) the Canaries: Ferro, Palma, Gomera, *Inferno* (Santa Cruz), The Grand Canary, Forteventura, and Lanzarote. For Antilia, the big square island to the westward and Isle of Brasil, see Chapter IV below.

brethren had proceeded to their cells, Brendan and Ailbe remained in the church. As they were conversing, a burning arrow flew in at one window of the church, lighted every lamp, and flew out again. "Where did *that* come from?" asked Brendan. "Haven't you ever heard of the burning bush on Mount Sinai?" replied Ailbe.

The octave of Epiphany having passed, Brendan and his men set sail and visited various places until Ash Wednesday. On that day they sighted another island, where they found a glistening spring of sweet water surrounded by herbs with edible roots; various species of fish sported in the clear water below. Again they made sail and steered north into the ocean. The wind dropped dead and the sea became coagulated. Brendan ordered the sail to be furled and the oars shipped, and drifted, trusting in God. They remained in this coagulated sea—probably pack-ice—for twenty days. Then the wind rose, and they steered westward. Three days later there appeared an island surrounded by clouds. Brendan recognized it as the same island where the procurator lived, and at that the happy but famished brethren bent so hard to their oars that the man of God said, "Boys, don't wear yourselves out. Is not Almighty God pilot of our little craft? Lay off, since He directs our voyage whither He wilt." Sure enough, the procurator stood on the shore to greet them. He provided them with baths and new clothes—their first for over a year, so that they would be clean and decent for Holy Week. Here they passed Good Friday. Their host replenished the ship's stores, and they set off on what proved to be a six-year cruise, as the talking bird had predicted.

During these six years the same islands were revisited, but the brethren encountered many more marvels, and saw new places. An enormous sea monster came roaring up, to make one mouthful of them; Brendan reminded God of how He had saved David and Jonah, and lo! a second monster attacked and killed the leviathan. A portion of his body, found by the brethren stranded at their next island of call, afforded them food during three foggy months; Brendan, who had had his fill of fog sailing, stayed ashore until the weather cleared. A great bird dropped on the ship a branch with fruit resembling apples, as a sign that they were near land. It turned out to be an island covered with trees and grapevines, which gave forth a spicy odor. Here they tarried forty days and reprovisioned their curragh with fruits of the earth. Sailing away from this Isle of Grapes, a huge bird, a griffon, flew

over them as if to attack, but a mysterious power killed him on the
way, and his carcass fell plunk! into the sea. One day the skipper and
his men sighted an object rising from the sea, so high that three days'
rowing was required to get near enough for a good look. It had the
color of a silver veil but seemed to be harder than marble, and there
was a hole in it big enough for their vessel to sail through. Luckily,
they did not try, for the mysterious object must have been a melting
iceberg. The top fell off while they were gaping at it, and the sea
around was smooth as glass and white as milk. Brendan figured that the
berg was 1400 cubits high. Its towers and pinnacles reminded him of
the New Jerusalem in the Apocalypse.

At a rocky, fire-scarred island with neither trees nor grass, a horrid,
subhuman, hairy creature rushed down to the shore and hurled at the
ship a red-hot mass of lava or slag, which fell hissing into the sea. "Let's
get out of here!" said Brendan. They made sail and plied their oars
just in time to escape a crowd of similar monsters who threw more hot
stuff at them, but fortunately they were out of range. Next day they
saw a volcano with smoking summit, evidently the source of this
ammunition; it discharged flames as they sailed away. Seven days' sail
southward, they sighted a rock with a man sitting thereupon. He
identified himself as Judas Iscariot, doing penance for his great sin.
He alternated sitting on this rock where demons from the volcanic
isle came nightly to bite him, with sessions in hell in company with
Herod, Pontius Pilate, Annas, and Caiaphas. Brendan interceded with
God to give Judas a night off, which He did. The demons turned up
just the same and were furious with Brendan for doing them out of
their nocturnal sport of biting Judas.

Nearing the end of her seventh year's wanderings, the curragh
reached a little, high, circular island inhabited only by Paul the Hermit.
Brought up in St. Patrick's own monastery, Paul had lived on this rock
for sixty years. During the first thirty he had been fed by a kindly
beast, but for the last thirty he had had nothing to eat, though plenty
of spring water to drink. The hermit was clothed only in long white
hair. Brendan invited him to have his hair cut, accept a spare cowl, and
join the party; but Paul felt himself to be unworthy and preferred his
own style of living.

Forty days they were at sea again, sailing hither and yon and living
largely on water obtained from Paul's spring. En route they enjoyed a

cold picnic on board Jasconius the whale, who considerately returned the iron pot in which they had started to cook a meal years before. Finally they reached *Terra Repromissionis Sanctorum*, the Promised Land. It was full of trees bearing ripe apples, on which they lived for forty days while exploring; and all this time there was no night. Upon reaching a wide river that they hesitated to cross, a youth came forth, called each monk by name, kissed him, and sang the 84th Psalm—"How amiable are thy dwellings, thou Lord of hosts." He informed them that this island was indeed the place God left to them and their successors to have and to hold until the persecution of Christians shall have ceased. The Brendan party are not to explore further, but to return home laden with fruits and precious stones of the island. This they did, first passing Mernoc's "Island of Delights," a sort of antechamber to the island Paradise.

The *Navigatio* ends as abruptly as does the mass, with a simple statement that everyone got home safely, and that Brendan died among his disciples, "whence he departed to God, *cui est honor et gloria in secula seculorum*." From the *Vita* we learn that he was ninety-three years of age; scholars believe that the date lies between A.D. 577 and 583. He was shortly after canonized, and in the hierarchy of Irish saints Brendan ranks only after Patrick, Brigit, and Columba.

Such, in shortest outline, is the story of the celebrated Voyage of St. Brendan. What are we to make of it, in terms of discovery?

Most readers in this skeptical generation will dismiss the story as mere fantasy, like Edward Lear's Voyage of the Owl and the Pussy Cat. But people believed in it for centuries, just as they believed the legends of King Arthur and the Round Table. Miracles did not trouble them, for they had been taught to believe the miracles in the Bible. In 1580, when John Dee entered on his map a brief defense of the English title to North America, he mentioned St. Brendan's voyage along with those of the Cabots as evidence. *Insulae Sancti Brendani*, sometimes with individual names corresponding to those of the *Navigatio*, but more frequently with strange names, appear on European maps from the thirteenth century on. Columbus in 1484, and eight years later when he called at the Canaries on his first voyage, heard of reported sightings of *Isla de San Borondon*, as the Spaniards called the Saint's Promised Land; and it even appears on post-Columbian maps due west of the Canaries. Efforts to locate it extended into the eighteenth century.

Brendan was a real person, and in my opinion his *Navigatio* is based on a real voyage or voyages, enhanced by Celtic imagination. The whole atmosphere of the story is northern. We can accept the Faroes and Soay as the Islands of Birds and of Sheep, although the millions of birds now scream rather than sing psalms, and the wild sheep later found there by the Norsemen were runts, not monsters. The volcano might well have been Hecla in Iceland or Beerenberg on Jan Mayen or even Tenerife. Waterfalls drop directly into the sea from St. George in the Azores and from Iceland; icebergs occasionally drift as far south as the Azores, and east to within a few hundred miles of the coast of Europe. Three centuries after Brendan's death, the raiding Vikings found Irish monks in Iceland, the Faroes, the Shetlands, and the Orkneys, and picked up Irish bells and croziers in Iceland. We are not straining the evidence to conclude that Brendan sailed for several trips, if not for seven years, on the circuit Hebrides-Shetlands-Faroes-Iceland, possibly as far as the Azores. Presumably some bard or writer who heard the story of the real voyage was clever enough to see that it would make, in modern terms, "good copy," especially if embellished by marvels. The whaleback island and the talking birds had been stock stories of earlier Irish *imrama*, and one can also detect borrowings from Lucian, Virgil, Homer, and other ancient writers.

But, discovery of America—no! The imagination of certain modern Irish writers, no whit less than that of the early storytellers, has brought Brendan to Newfoundland, the West Indies, Mexico, and even the Ohio River! They do not even boggle at peppering the Antilles with Irish monasteries which have disappeared, or ascribing to Brendan's curragh the speed and endurance of a clipper ship. If one pieces together end-to-end all Brendan's forty-day voyages, you can certainly get his curragh to the American strand; but it seems obvious that the author of the *Navigatio* used "forty" because that was the duration of Lent—he even sailed for forty days *around* one of the islands looking for a harbor! No, here is not a discovery of a New World, but a captivating tale which led men of later centuries to sail into the unknown, hoping to find Brendan's islands, confident that God would watch over them. In that sense the *Navigatio* may be said to have stimulated oceanic exploration for nigh one thousand years, and to have been a precursor of Columbus.

As literature, the *Navigatio* is imperishable. It reflects all seafarers' experiences in northern waters—the translucent sea swarming with fish, the sporting of whales, icebergs melting in the summer sunlight, dungeon fogs, rocky isles crowned with trees and grass, pinnacle rocks. And the story beautifully expresses the Celtic ideal. All is fair, pure, and innocent; no brutality, no lechery, no weakness or illness that the saintly skipper cannot cure, no suffering but from hunger and thirst, always miraculously relieved. Never has so gentle and benevolent a skipper as this Irish saint sailed the Western Ocean—he even begs relief for Judas. Evil appears only in the form of sea monsters or malicious gnomes against whom God protects the voyagers; and in the end they reach a Promised Land where the faithful may delightfully sojourn before their souls ascend to Heaven.

Irish Refugees in America?

Very different from these gentle, monkish mariners were the next people with whom we have to deal, the Vikings or Norsemen. A sinister confrontation took place in Iceland around 870, some three centuries after St. Brendan's death.

In the late seventh and early eighth centuries, several hundred Irish ecclesiastics, mostly Culdees, were outraged by the Synod of Whitby's efforts to bring the Irish church into line with Rome. These clerics built curraghs and sailed to Iceland. There they were joined, from the close of the eighth century on, by Irish refugees from Viking raids on the Faroes. Since Iceland had no indigenous population, the Irish made themselves at home, spreading out and forming monastic cells wherever it seemed possible to get a living. Dicuil, a learned Celt at the court of Charlemagne, told in a book that he wrote in 825, *De Mensura Orbis Terrae*, of hearing from a priest who had been to Iceland, a vivid description of the endless day in the Arctic summer, and used a homely example: one could even *pediculos de camisia extrahere*—pick lice out of one's shirt—as easily at midnight as at noon!

For a century and more, these Irish colonists in Iceland were safe from the tyranny of Rome, the rage of the Vikings, and the temptations of the flesh. By the second half of the ninth century, reinforced by subsequent waves of Celtic come-outers, they numbered at least several hundred, possibly more than a thousand. Alas, no part of the world could then ensure one a quiet life, any more than in our time. One fine day in the summer of 870, an alarming sight met Irish eyes on

the Icelandic shore—a fleet of long Viking ships with attendant merchant vessels. One can imagine the consternation. What, in the name
of Heaven, is this? asks one. Viking ships, m'lad; this is it! They are
about to land! Mother of God, they are bringing cattle with them—
and women—they mean to stay! Are those blue-eyed people with long
yellow hair *women*, father? They are that, m'lad, and we shall have to
leave this island to preserve our Christian purity!

The Norsemen kept coming, and the Irish *papae* or *papar*, as they
called the monks, did not all leave at once. But within a few years
they had all gone, and the Norsemen had Iceland to themselves.

Where did the Irish Icelanders go? Some, doubtless, went home to
Mother Machree. Many must have perished at sea in their frail cur-
raghs. But there is some reason to believe that a few sailed west, missed
Greenland, and fetched up somewhere on the east coast of North
America.

The evidence is all in the Norse sagas. The *Landnamabok* tells of an
Icelander named Ari who "drifted over the ocean to *Hvitramanna
Land*, which some call Ireland the Great, and lies away west in the
ocean nigh to Vinland the Good." Unable to escape, Ari was baptized
there (obviously by the Irish) and held in great esteem by the natives.
The *Eyrbyggia Saga* adds more detail. One Bjorn, a man with "a grand
bearing," had an affair in Iceland with a lady named Thurid, and she
bore him a boy. After her brother had attempted to kill him, Bjorn
took ship and disappeared to the westward. Some years later, around
1025–30, a certain Gudleif Gunnlangson, sailing from Dublin for Iceland, was driven off his course and anchored in an unknown harbor.
Natives who flocked to the shore, and spoke a language that Gudleif
thought to be Irish, seized him and his crew, and were debating
whether to kill or to enslave them when a tall, old, white-haired man
approached on horseback and was saluted as the natives' leader. He
spoke to Gudleif in Norse, asked about the people in his district of
Iceland, and warned him that the natives would kill the intruders if
they stayed, so they had better get out quick. The old man would not
tell his name but Gudleif recognized him as Bjorn. He gave Gudleif a
gold ring for his former mistress, and a sword for their son.

Finally, we have a passage in the Saga of Eric the Red about the
captives who described men clad in white, who carried poles with
pieces of cloth attached, and yelled loudly; and the Norse who heard

this said to each other, "Sounds like an Irish ecclesiastical procession!" The trouble with these stories is that they are supposed to have happened in the early eleventh century, and the *papae* left Iceland in the ninth. These pioneers, if Irish, must have reached the vast age of Old Testament patriarchs, or else abandoned chastity, mated with native girls, and kept an Irish Catholic community going for a couple of centuries. Gudleif, however, may have been wrong in his belief that the natives who seized him spoke Irish; they may simply have been Indians who had adopted an Icelander as their leader. And where did he get his horse?

All this was long, long ago, when one feels that anything might have happened.

As yet, not one early Irish artifact has been found in North America.

Bibliography and Notes

GENERAL

The quotation from St. Columba is from Adamnan's Life of the saint, Reeves ed., appendix, pp. 255–87.

The sheer weight of literature on St. Brendan is enormous, and most of it is worthless. A guide to what appeared before 1929 is James F. Kenney (ed.), *Sources for the Early History of Ireland*, Vol. I: *Ecclesiastical* (Columbia University Press, 1929). Carl Selmer (ed.), *Navigatio Sancti Brendani Abbatis*, in the Medieval Studies series of the University of Notre Dame (1959), is the best critical edition of the vital text. *Vita S. Brendani* and a metrical version in Latin are in Patrick Cardinal Moran, *Acta Sancti Brendani* (Dublin, 1872). Most translations are souped-up and utterly unreliable. The attempts of Denis O'Donoghue, *Brendaniana* (Dublin, 1893), and George Little, *Brendan the Navigator* (Dublin, 1946), to identify the islands and take the saint to Mexico are fantastic. Geoffrey Ashe, *Land to the West* (New York, 1962), is even more imaginative, but he has beautiful photographs of Irish scenery and curraghs. Torsten Dahlberg, *Brendaniana* (Göteborg, 1958), contains a medieval metrical version in German. The invocation to the Virgin Mary at the end of this poem (p. 140) underlines the curious fact that in the *Navigatio* the Holy Spirit and the Virgin are never mentioned, despite the fact that Mary was regarded as Star of the Sea and protectress of sailors.

Lighting a fire on a whale's back has been a favorite story through the ages. The earliest known version is in the ancient Greek *Physiologus*, ed., Emile Legrand (1873, p. 71). Whilst it is improbable that St. Brendan or his biographers ever saw this, they may well have seen a manuscript of the

Latin translation called *Physiologus Latinus;* it is in F. J. Carmody, ed. (1939), p. 44. Lucian's whale story in his *True Story* (Loeb edition, pp. 285–86) is altogether different.

Many are the attempts to link Columbus with Brendan. Since Columbus went very thoroughly into the history of Western Voyages, he must have heard about the *Navigatio,* but his only reference to the seafaring saint is in the Journal of his first voyage. Denis O'Donoghue (333*n*) declares, "It is a well-known fact that Columbus . . . visited Ireland . . . was assisted in his researches by an Irish gentleman named Patrick Maguire, who accompanied him also on his great voyage of discovery. There are other Irish names on the roster of the ship's crew." This statement is completely fictitious. So is Geoffrey Ashe's (p. 297). "It is almost certain that one of the crew on his [Columbus's] first American voyage was a Galway man. It is absolutely certain that he heard of Brendan and chased him westward beyond all charts." For correct list of Columbus's crew, see S. E. Morison, *Admiral of the Ocean Sea,* I, 190–93, and note 18, p. 197, on the phony crew list printed by Navarrete, including an Irishman and an Englishman, under the erroneous impression that this was Columbus's crew list.

T. C. Lethbridge, *Herdmen and Hermits, Celtic Seafarers in the Northern Seas* (Cambridge, 1930), a chatty book by an imaginative archaeologist, describes and maps Irish monastic settlements in northern seas.

THE CURRAGH, NECKLACE, ICEBERG, PSALMS AND SHEEP

Good studies of the curragh are in George Little's *Brendan the Navigator* (see above) and, by way of comparison, in Edwin T. Adney and Howard I. Chapelle, *The Bark Canoes and Skin Boats of North America* (Smithsonian Institution, 1964).

The stolen necklace (frenum) is usually translated "bit" or "bridle," but Carl Selmer (see above) thinks it is a corruption of an old Irish word for necklace, since monks on an island would have no use for horse tack.

The *Iceberg* is the only item in the *Navigatio* pointing to the saint's having reached American waters, but not unmistakably so. On the Pilot Charts of the North Atlantic Ocean issued by the Oceanographic Office of the Navy Department, the line of "mean maximum iceberg limit" extends eastward only to about latitude 45° N, longitude 38° W in August, with a further extension from south of Cape Farewell, Greenland, to the Icelandic peninsula north of Reykjavik. However, the charts show a number of exceptional sightings of icebergs and growlers (small bergs) outside these limits. For instance, in June 1886 an iceberg was sighted some 400 miles west of Ushant and 250 miles southwest of Fastnet. In July 1918 a berg was sighted in latitude 45° N, longitude 33° W; and another in July 1890 at latitude 48° N, longitude 23° W—positions which Brendan might have crossed in sailing from the Azores to Iceland. Another iceberg was sighted on the Azores-Iceland route in September 1906. In September 1883 and again in September 1923, a growler was sighted very near the Azores, a berg about 240 miles south of Fayal, and another only 60 miles north of Flores. Icebergs drifted south of the Azores in October 1934, and two were sighted within 150 miles of Fayal. In April 1926 a growler was sighted in latitude 61° N, longitude 18° W, on the route between the Hebrides and Iceland. Since there is no reason to assume that the habits of icebergs have changed, it seems possible that Brendan could have sighted one or more if his voyage followed the corridor between the Azores and Iceland, for a period of several years.

The Psalms Sung by Birds. Verses quoted in the *Navigatio,* in order, are: lxv. 1; li. 15; cxlviii. 2; xc. 17; xlvii. 6 and 7; iv. 6; cxxxiii. 1; lxv. 5.

The Sheep. Not only the Faroes, but Soay Island in the St. Kilda group have a goat-like breed of sheep which Julian Huxley (*Memories,* p. 248) believes to have been there since neolithic times.

For Dicuil's statement, see Fridtjof Nansen, *In Northern Mists* (1911), I, 164–65, quoting the Letronne 1814 ed. of Dicuil. See also pp. 160–61 for what Solinus and others say about Iceland. My final paragraph on St. Brendan is a paraphrase of Ernest Renan's beautiful summary in *La Poésie des races celtiques* (1854).

IRISH IN AMERICA BEFORE THE NORSE?

The late William B. Goodwin, an insurance executive of Hartford, Connecticut, spent a fortune following various archaeological will o'the wisps, including an alleged pre-Vinland or at least pre-Columbian "Irish stone village" in North Salem, New Hampshire. Hugh Hencken, the Irish archaeologist, investigated the site and reported it to be unlike anything ever seen or heard of in Ireland (*New England Quarterly,* XII, 1939, 429–42). According to local report, it was the work of a half-crazy Yankee farmer named Pattee in the nineteenth century. The so-called Altar Stone (which those who claim this site to be Phoenician call the Sacrificial Stone) has a gutter around the edge, supposedly to let a victim's blood run off; this, Hencken points out, was one of the lye-stones commonly used in New England to wash out lye from wood ashes. Geoffrey Ashe, who made a special transatlantic trip to see this site, describes it, with illustrations, in his *Land to the West* (1962). He reports mournfully that protracted diggings since Hencken's visit have produced not one artifact, Irish or otherwise. The site is now called "Mystery Village" and is open to the public.

The references to Hvitramanna Land in the sagas may be found in T. Ellwood (trans.), *Landnambok* (1898), p. 81; Paul Schach (trans.), *Eyrbyggia Saga,* pp. 31 ff., 136–38. T. G. Oleson, *Early Voyages,* pp. 97–102, has a theory that Hvitramanna, or White Men's Land, also called "Albania Superior," was either the Norse name for the entire Arctic, or else a corruption of Tir na-Fer Finn, a district in Ireland. Carl Rafn, on the other hand, in his *Antiquatates Americanae* (1837, see Chapter III be-

The "Sacrificial Stone" at Mystery Village, Salem, New Hampshire. Photo by Antha E. Card, October 1968.

low) locates Hvitramanna south of Vinland, in the Carolinas. Hencken, in *New England Quarterly*, XII, 437, concludes that these tales are probably attempts to account for sailors who never returned to Iceland, and belong to a class of folklore which goes back to classical times.

* III *

The Norsemen and Vinland

c. A. D. 800-1400

Norse Ships, Sailors, and Navigation

From the ninth to the twelfth century, Scandinavia was the leading sea
power of Europe. In an era when the English, French, and South
Europeans hardly dared sail beyond sight of land, Scandinavians from
Norway, Denmark, and Sweden, improving the maritime technique
of the Irish, sailed boldly to the Faroes before A.D. 800, to Iceland by
870, and to Greenland c. 985; conquered a good part of Ireland before
800, invaded Normandy in the tenth century and Sicily in the eleventh,
establishing royal dynasties in both countries. And in 1066, the date
everyone knows, William the Norman conquered England. Vinland,
as the Norse called their brief colony in North America, was the
furthest outpost of a loosely knit Scandinavian empire which extended
east to Russia and south to Sicily. And although Vikings were tough
and ruthless freebooters, their countrymen were not lacking in the
fine arts or in politics. The eddas and sagas of Iceland are justly famous
as literature, the Norman adaptations of Romanesque architecture are
second only to Gothic, and the institutions they worked out in Normandy were woven into those of the Anglo-Saxon world.*

* I do not use the popular term *Vikings* because the Norsemen who discovered
Greenland and Vinland were not Vikings but comparatively peaceful traders and

32

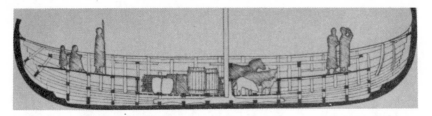

Restored section of the wrecked *knarr* recovered at Roskilde Fjord, 1968.

Bow and triangular forward bulkhead of the smaller cargo ship excavated at Roskilde. From Olsen and Crumlin-Pedersen *Fem vikingeskike fra Roskilde Fjord*, 1969.

Until the age of the Infante D. Henrique (Henry the Navigator) of Portugal, the Norsemen were the most expert navigators of the Western World, comparable only to the Polynesians in the Pacific. Without benefit of compass—invented at Amalfi in the late twelfth century—they crossed the Atlantic and sailed south to the Pillars of Hercules. How did they do it?

Ranging south was not too difficult, as one could keep in touch with the land and seek refuge in a harbor when a tempest threatened. But how could one cross the Atlantic and return, with no compass? The Norsemen managed it by what through the ages has been called "latitude sailing." Once having found the Faroes, Iceland, and Cape Farewell of Greenland, the Norse navigators took the latitude of each place by crudely measuring the angular height of the North Star—and you can do that with a notched stick. So, in preparing for an Atlantic voyage, they sailed along the coast of Norway until they reached the presumed latitude of their destination, then shoved off and sailed with the North Star square on their starboard beam by night and by carefully noting the sun's azimuth by day. In thick weather they had to steer "by guess and by God." When the weather cleared, their crude instrument called the "sun shadow-board" was broken out. This was a wooden disc on which concentric circles were marked, and in the center a gnomon or pin which could be raised or lowered to accord with the sun's declination—and the Norse had declination tables. Floated in a bowl of water to make it level, this shadow-board at high noon would give a rough latitude, indicating how far the ship was off course, and enable her to get on again. These devices were so crude that the Norse occasionally missed Iceland or Greenland, as we shall see; and, returning, they might fetch up in Ireland or Scotland instead of Norway.

Modern sailors are so dependent on the mariner's compass that they find it difficult to imagine how any ship could find her destination across a broad ocean without one. But the Polynesians did so, in a wider ocean than the Atlantic, and simple seafaring folk to this day do it. Fishermen used to sail from Newfoundland to Labrador without

---

farmers. The Vikings were the Norse freebooters and pirates who raided the coasts of Europe in their long ships. The Norsemen we are concerned with did not use the long ship, but the *knarr*, or round ship; and, as for fighting, the plain fact emerges from the sagas that they were run out of Vinland by the natives.

a compass. And as a sojourner on the rocky coast of Maine I have heard a lobsterman say, "I don't need no compass to find my gang o' traps in a fog, or to git home, neither!" Ensel Davis, a mariner and lobster fisherman of Otter Creek, Maine, who died recently at a great age, was asked how he found his way home through fog without a compass. "By the ocean swells," he said; "they always run south to ʳ north." "But supposing there is no swell?" "There always is one, even on the calmest day, if you know how to look for it."

The Norse discoverers of Greenland and Vinland did not use a long Viking ship like the one unearthed at Gokstad and preserved at Oslo. There is ample evidence that they used the *knarr*, a beamy type propelled principally by one big square sail made of a coarse woolen cloth called "wadmal," rigged with an additional sprit to set well close-hauled. Their lines were cut out of walrus hide, or plaited from bast; rings of osier were used to secure the shrouds. The wrecked knarr recently discovered at Roskilde Fjord, Denmark (and on p. 33 depicted as restored) is about 54 feet long, 14 feet 9 inches beam, and stoutly ᵗ clinker-built. Although carbon-dated around the year 1000, this freighter shows a sophisticated manner of shipbuilding. Oak are her keel, knees, and ribs, pine are her planks, and her trunnels (wooden pegs) are of soft linden, but most of her fastenings are iron rivets secured by burrs. Caulking of twisted animal hairs soaked in pine tar is inserted in the overlap. The scarfing of split pine planks is neatly done, and they are beautifully fined off to make the curved stem and stern. There is no big figurehead of a supposedly terrifying sea monster, as she is no warship; but like the long Viking ships she was directed by a steerboard on the right side—hence the word "starboard." She was partly decked forward and aft, and could carry several head of cattle, ᵗ as well as a cargo and thirty or so people. The knarrs used by Leif Ericsson and his successors were probably bigger than the Roskilde example, and had a stout half-deck forward to protect the people from rain and spray. For auxiliary power the crew pulled on long sweeps, for which holes were cut in the upper-most plank. There is no evidence of any means of cooking food on board; the crew must have subsisted on cold victuals and beer, or mead fermented from honey.

These early Scandinavian explorers did not look or dress like Wagnerian heroes. In the restoration depicted on page 33, sailors are correctly dressed in hooded, ankle-length woolen gowns resembling those ᵗ found in Norse graves in Greenland. It was a rough life for the sailors, but life ashore was rough too; and in one respect the Norse seamen were more comfortable than their successors in the great age of discovery. Each mariner had his own big sleeping bag made of sheepskin or cowhide, which kept him warm and dry in the worst weather; and he needed it, since a great disadvantage of the knarr was its receptivity to water. Every leak, every breaking wave, every drop of rain or snowflake which came on board went into the bilges, whence it had to be bailed out with buckets; no evidence of a pump has been found. Two or three centuries elapsed before shipwrights learned to rig permanent pumps, and to deck a vessel over, stem to stern, build bulwarks with drain ports, and camber the deck so that rain, spray, and green water taken on board sloshed overboard automatically. Nothing is said in the literature of the Roskilde ships about ballast, but ballast there must have been to prevent the knarr from capsizing in a sudden squall. Probably the Norse seamen used well-selected flat stones which would nestle between the frames and not shift easily or take up too much space. This type of beamy, single-masted knarr was used for local freighting and fishing along the coast of Norway right down to the twentieth century.

The story that Norsemen early in the eleventh century had discovered a land across the Western Ocean where wild grapes grew, was always known to Scandinavian scholars; and two sagas written from oral sources around A.D. 1250, proud possessions of certain Icelandic families, tell the story in fascinating detail. Thormodus Torfaeus published a Latin translation of the sagas in his *Historia Vinlandiae Antiquae* (Copenhagen, 1705). The data therein, he said, pointed to Newfoundland as Vinland; the scholarly world, after shoving the elusive colony all over the Atlantic seaboard from Baffin Land to Florida, mostly now agrees that the learned Torfaeus was right. But these important records seem to have been ignored, or dismissed as fantasies, like the voyages of St. Brendan, by almost every early historian of America. Henry Wheaton, when United States minister to Denmark, wrote a *History of the Northmen* (London, 1831) which used the sagas and expressed the opinion that Vinland might be found in New England, but he had no effect upon fellow historians such as George Bancroft, who dismissed the sagas as "mythological in form and obscure in meaning." It remained for a later Scandinavian scholar,

Carl C. Rafn, to rock the learned world in 1837 with an impressive quarto printed at Copenhagen called *Antiquitates Americanae sive Scriptores Septentrionales rerum ante-Columbianarum in America.* Rafn introduced the Vinland sagas to the reading public by printing them in three parallel versions—the original Old Norse, Latin and Danish translations—together with his own comments in Latin.

Eager to locate Vinland, Rafn, before publishing his magistral work, sent requests for evidence of Norse antiquities to every historical society in the eastern United States. These sparked off a frenzied hunt for Norse artifacts and inscriptions. Rhode Island and southeastern Massachusetts came off on top, as Rafn indicated in the heading of one of his chapters: "Descriptio Vetustorum quorundam monumentorum in Rhode Island." The excited Yankees produced Dighton Rock, various rocks inscribed with Algonkin petroglyphs, the Newport stone tower, and the remains of an Indian who had been buried with his poor jewelry, little copper discs from the Great Lakes region. This unknown brave became the "Skeleton in Armor" to whom Longfellow, assuming him to be a Viking, wrote a poem describing how, "for my lady's bower," he built the Newport tower.

The story of Vinland fascinated the American public. All the New England poets (and, later, Sidney Lanier) gave tongue, echoing Longfellow's *"Skoal!* to the Northland! *Skoal!"* Local antiquarians found inscriptions carved in the runic letters of Scandinavia on rocky ledges facing the sea, on boulders in their pastures, and almost anywhere. James Russell Lowell's Parson Wilbur even found his private rune stone at "Jalaam" and wrote to the Editors of the *Atlantic Monthly:*

> Touching Runick inscriptions, I find that they may be classed under three general heads: 1°. Those which are understood by the Danish Royal Society of Northern Antiquaries, and Professor Rafn, their Secretary; 2°. Those which are comprehensible only by Mr. Rafn; and 3°. Those which neither the Society, Mr. Rafn, nor anybody else can be said in any definite sense to understand, and which accordingly offer peculiar temptations to enucleating sagacity. . . . To this class the stone now in my possession fortunately belongs.

He translates the runes thus: "Here Bjarna Grímólfsson first drank Cloud-Brother through Child-of-Land-and-Water," which he interprets to mean that the Viking Bjarna inhaled his first tobacco smoke through a reed stem, right in the Wilbur pasture.

This search for the site of Vinland lasted for more than a century; most intensively, however, in New England, although Rafn in his beautifully engraved "General Chart exhibiting the Discoveries of the Northmen," extended Vinland to Chesapeake Bay. There are few local histories of seaport towns between Newfoundland and the Virginia Capes which do not open with a chapter asserting, "Leif Ericsson was here!" And there came a revival in 1893 when Norwegian Americans, resenting the publicity which "that Italian Colombo" was getting, arranged for a Viking ship to sail (or be towed) to Chicago, and even endeavored to project Vinland into Minnesota.

But—nary an artifact to prove any of these claims. The Newport tower was found by incontrovertible evidence to have been erected as a windmill around 1675 by a colonial governor of Rhode Island. Leif Ericsson's signature and date "MI" on a boulder at No Man's Land off Martha's Vineyard proved to have been a practical joke. Alleged runic inscriptions were found to be mere glacial scratches, or had been "lost" before any runic scholar could get a look at them. Attempts to fit the sagas' descriptions of Vinland into the coast of New England and the Middle States were strained and unconvincing.

Finally, in 1960, a Norwegian archaeologist named Helge Ingstad located a spot in northern Newfoundland, L'Anse aux Meadows, which he thought might be "it." Years of summertime diggings by competent archaeologists have (it seems to me beyond reasonable doubt) proved this place to have indeed been Vinland, where Leif Ericsson spent one winter, and where members of his family founded a short-lived colony. So, now that the location of Vinland has been solved, we may proceed with the story as told in the sagas.

First, however, a word as to the sagas. A saga is well defined in the Oxford English Dictionary as a "medieval Icelandic or Norwegian prose narrative, especially one embodying the history of an Icelandic family or Norwegian king." It was not intended to be a coast pilot or to give reliable geographical data, but to amuse, instruct, and leave a family record. The Icelanders, and to a less extent the other Scandinavians, were as family-conscious as a Colonial Dame, and it is fortunate that they were, otherwise these tales of discovery, repeated orally for two centuries before being recorded, would never have been preserved.

Those that describe the voyages to Vinland are two in number—the Saga of Eric the Red (also called the Saga of Thorfinn Karlsevni) in a

manuscript called Hauk's Book (Hauk being a descendant of Karlsevni); and the Tale of the Greenlanders (*Groenlendina thattr*), also
called the Vinland History of the Flatey Book, as it belonged to a
family living on Flatey (Flat Island) off Iceland. This last was thought
by Rafn to be the more authoritative. Gustav Storm, the greatest nineteenth-century authority on Old Norse, denigrated the Tale of the
Greenlanders but authenticated the Saga of Eric the Red. Next, Jón
Jóhannesson, professor of history in the University of Iceland, published in 1956 a reappraisal, again raising the Tale of the Greenlanders
to the top, and his views have been generally accepted. Jóhannesson's
convincing evidence is that the pedigrees inserted in the sagas, and
other data, indicate that the Tale of the Greenlanders is the older of
the two, written before 1263. He believes that the popular account of
Leif's discovering Vinland accidentally when on a mission to introduce
Christianity to Greenland is a pious interpolation in the Saga of Eric
the Red.

Leif's First Settlement

Eric, known as "the Red" from the color of his hair, left Norway for
Iceland to escape punishment for manslaughter. After becoming in-
volved in an Icelandic feud he was outlawed and decided to leave.
Hearing that a friend named Gunnbiorn had seen a land to the west of
Iceland when blown off his course, Eric decided to explore it and, if
practicable, settle there.

Accordingly he set forth, discovered a great peninsula which he
named "Greenland" because, he said, people would be attracted thither
"if the country had a good name." He returned to Iceland, and next
summer (A.D. 985) set out to colonize the country. Twelve or fifteen
shiploads of Icelanders went with him, or followed shortly after. Finding the east coast of Greenland to be sheathed in ice, Eric rounded
Cape Farewell and founded Brattahlid, the Eastern Settlement on
Eriksfjord, near the site of the present Julianehaab; whilst other Icelanders set up the Western Settlement at or near what is now Godthaab.
Both are on the west coast.

In the year 999 or 1000, Leif Ericsson, second son of Eric, sailed
to Norway and at Trondheim met King Olaf Tryggvason, who had
established Christianity as the official religion. Leif was persuaded by

the king to embrace the Christian faith. In the meantime, one Biarni Heriulfson, owner of a ship which traded between Norway and Iceland, had made an important discovery. Accustomed to spend each winter with his father Heriulf in Iceland, Biarni on arriving there in A.D. 986, finding that the old man had gone to Greenland with Eric the Red, persuaded his crew to accompany him to the new colony. Their ship missed Greenland, but made an unknown land "level and covered with woods" which Biarni said could not possibly be Greenland. They sailed north, turned toward shore, and found "a flat and wooded country." Again Biarni said this could not be Greenland, as there were no icy mountains, and he would not allow his people to land. For a second time they put out to sea, with a southwest wind, and not only found Greenland but made land at the very spot where old Heriulf had settled. Biarni never touched foot to earth, but he saw parts of North America—the Labrador and Baffin Island.

Poor Biarni! All we know about him thereafter is that he traded with Greenland for some fourteen years, and returned to Norway. He left no posterity, nobody built a saga around him; and after Gustav Storm had denounced as spurious the Tale of the Greenlanders, in which his inadvertent discovery is related, the name of Biarni ceased to be mentioned. Now, not only has this saga been rehabilitated, but Biarni has received the dubious support of Yale's Vinland Map, which names him not as a predecessor but as a shipmate of *Leiphus-Erissonius*. So, let us give Biarni Heriulfson his due as the earliest, Number One, indubitable European discoverer of America, even if he never landed. But for his voyage, who would ever have heard of Leif?

Ericsson, returning to Greenland in the summer of A.D. 1000 after his brief sojourn at King Olaf's court, heard "much talk about voyages of discovery." His father and other immigrants from Iceland had set up farming and hunting communities in Greenland, but were hampered by want of wood; Greenland had no timber bigger than a willow bush, and for building and fuel they were dependent on turf and driftwood. Might not one of the places that Biarni discovered be the answer? So Leif Ericsson bought Biarni's knarr, collected a crew of thirty-five men including his foster father, a German named Tyrker, and shoved off in the high summer of 1001, avoiding the ice off Baffin Island. Eric the Red would have gone too, had he not been thrown from his horse the day of sailing and regarded the mishap as a warning to stay at home.

Leif Ericsson is described in the saga as "a big, strapping fellow, handsome to look at, thoughtful and temperate in all things." He had all the makings of a folk hero, and has been joyfully accepted as such by Scandinavian-Americans. Nobody knows when or where he was born or died. He came to Greenland with his father as a lad, and was over twenty-one years old when he undertook this voyage.

Setting forth in Biarni's beamy knarr in the summer of 1001, Leif "found first that land which Biarni and his shipmates found last." This was Baffin Island. He landed, observed flat ledges leading to icy mountains, and called it Helluland (Country of Flat Stones)—a very good description of that frore land. Regarding it as valueless—as did all who came later, after finding no gold in the rocks—Leif put to sea again, found a second country, anchored, and went ashore. "This country was level and wooded, with broad white beaches wherever they went and a gently sloping shoreline." Leif said, "I shall give this country a name that fits with its natural character and call it Markland"—Land of Forests.

These furdurstrandir (Wonder Strands), as they are called in both sagas, are our first anchor for the location of Vinland. Without doubt they are the thirty-mile-long stretch of beach on the Labrador coast, between latitudes 53°45′ and 54°09′ N, broken only by Cape Porcupine. Here are magnificent yellow sand beaches with a gentle gradient, longer than any that the Norsemen could ever have seen, and the more wondrous because they occur almost miraculously in the middle of a barren, rocky coast. Behind these Wonder Strands, a level, sandy plain —unique for southern Labrador—nourishes a fine stand of black spruce, and numerous streams wind through the forest and discharge into the ocean across the beach.

Markland, however, did not satisfy Leif. Again he put to sea and sailed from the Wonder Strands for two doegr. This term, which has had all the Vikingologists by the ears, may mean a unit of time, or of distance; both fit the 165 nautical miles which we measured in 1968 from the Wonder Strands to Leif's next anchorage.

The Tale of the Greenlanders says, "After sailing two doegr, they sighted another shore and landed on an island to the north of the mainland." This island must have been Belle Isle. There they found dew on the grass; being very thirsty, they lapped it up and found it sweet. "Then they returned to the ship and sailed through the channel

The Norsemen's "Wonder Strands" and Cape Porcupine, Labrador.

Another view of the Wonder Strands.

Iceberg stranded in cove of southern Labrador. Belle Isle in distance.

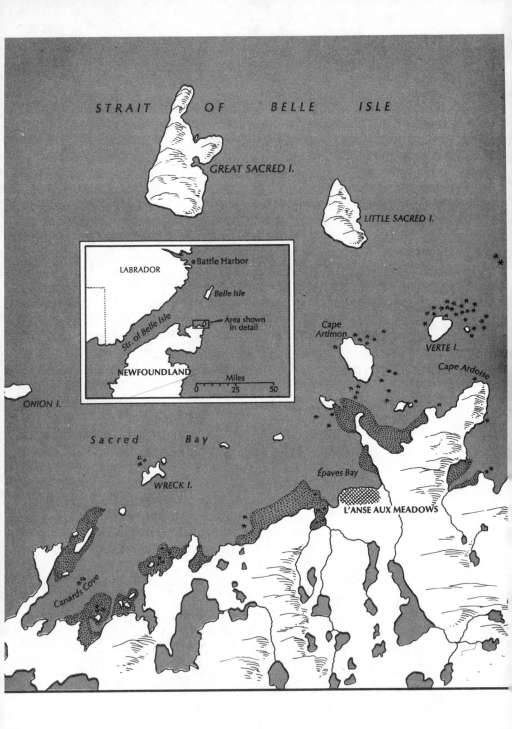

STRAIT OF BELLE ISLE

GREAT SACRED I.

LITTLE SACRED I.

LABRADOR

Battle Harbor

Belle Isle

Str. of Belle Isle

Area shown in detail

Cape Artimon

VERTE I.

Cape Ardoise

NEWFOUNDLAND

Miles

0   25   50

ONION I.

Sacred Bay

Épaves Bay

WRECK I.

L'ANSE AUX MEADOWS

Canards Cove

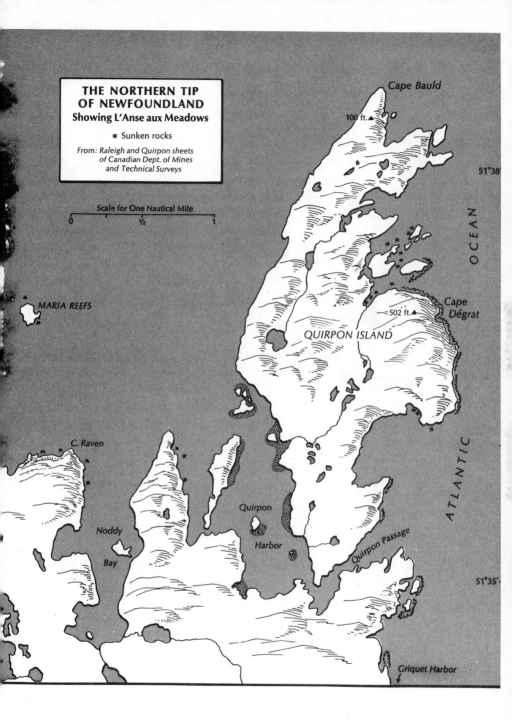

THE NORTHERN TIP
OF NEWFOUNDLAND
Showing L'Anse aux Meadows

* Sunken rocks

From: Raleigh and Quirpon sheets
of Canadian Dept. of Mines
and Technical Surveys

Scale for One Nautical Mile
0   ½   1

Cape Bauld

100 ft.▲

51°38'

OCEAN

MARIA REEFS

Cape
Dégrat

502 ft.▲

QUIRPON ISLAND

ATLANTIC

C. Raven

Quirpon

Quirpon Passage

Noddy

Harbor

51°35'

Bay

Griquet Harbor

45

L'Anse aux Meadows: Air view of Epaves Bay.

between the island and a cape jutting out to the north of the mainland"—Cape Bauld, Newfoundland. "They steered a westerly course past the cape and found great shallows at ebb tide, so that their ship was beached and lay some distance from the sea. But they were so eager to go ashore that they could not wait until the tide rose under their ship. They ran up on the shore to a place where a stream flows out of a lake, where they cast anchor." After towing their ship to shore when the tide rose, "they took their leather sleeping bags ashore and built themselves shelters. Later they decided to stay there during the winter and set up large houses. There was no lack of salmon either in the river or in the lake, and it was bigger salmon than they had ever seen. Nature was so generous here that it seemed to them no cattle would need any winter fodder, but could graze outdoors. There was no frost in winter, and the grass hardly withered. The days and nights were more nearly equal than in Greenland or Iceland. On the shortest day of winter the sun was up between breakfast time and late afternoon."

This description well fits the site at L'Anse aux Meadows that Dr. Ingstad has been excavating: the north-facing and shallow Epaves Bay from which one can see the Sacred Islands, Belle Isle, and the Labrador shore; a stream up which salmon run in the spring to spawn in a lake; an extensive natural meadow, biggest in northern Newfoundland; a spruce forest to the southward. The meadow, which might have been grassy in 1001 (since the climate of these northern regions may then have been much less severe), now consists largely of wild cranberry, partridgeberry, cloudberry, bearberry, bunchberry, potentilla, blue iris, and stunted spruce. Any modern English or American cow would turn up her nose at such browse; but we must remember that the curing of grass to make hay for winter fodder was not practised anywhere until the thirteenth century, and the runty cattle of Greenland were used to very poor winter rations, such as seaweed. So this Vinland meadow would have tasted good to them.

On the verge of this meadow, and a stone's throw from the shallow

L'Anse aux Meadows: Excavation of the Great House. Wooden structures are modern.

L'Anse aux Meadows: Salmon stream and meadow.

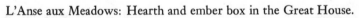

L'Anse aux Meadows: Hearth and ember box in the Great House.

Epaves Bay, Dr. Ingstad has excavated the sites of two great houses, closely corresponding to the Norse dwellings earlier uncovered in Greenland. The bigger is 70 feet long and 55 feet wide. The floors were of hard-pressed clay, the walls of turf, and the roof of timber, covered with sod. There is a central hall with a fire-pit in the center, and a little ember-box of flat stones in which coals were kept alive during the night. Around the fireplace are raised-earth benches which the Norsemen doubtless covered with polar bear and other skins; one can imagine Leif and his particular cronies lounging there at night and exchanging tales about their former adventures. Grouped around the central hall are six to eight small square rooms, some doubtless living rooms as they have center hearths, too; some for storage. Surprisingly, one finds evidence of a primitive ironworks, complete with a forge, for fashioning crude articles such as nails and spikes from the bog iron which abounds in that region. This is not mentioned in the sagas; but there is abundant evidence of similar crude forges in the Norse settlements of Greenland, where there was never enough iron production for the needs of the population. Consequently, the setting up of ironworks at L'Anse aux Meadows is perfectly reasonable.

Besides the two great houses there have been excavated the foundations of several smaller ones, each with a central hearth; a Finnish-type steam bath paved with big pebbles; and a cooking pit paved with large cobblestones. Here the Norsemen could have roasted whole cattle or deer by the same method as the New England clambake—heating up the stones with a hot fire, raking out the coals, and covering the meat with seaweed. Dr. Ingstad figures that seventy-five to ninety people lived here at one time; feeding them must have been a problem, except in the salmon season.

It is not assumed that all this building was done by Leif. The site was used by two later and more populous expeditions from Greenland, which no doubt added to Leif's structures, making a small village.

No runic or other inscriptions have been found, but that is not surprising, as Leif and his crew were busy getting enough to eat, and very probably were illiterate. The only artifacts found of Norse provenance are a soapstone spindle-whorl and a bronze pin, similar to objects found in Greenland, and doubtless brought thence. On the other hand, there is valuable negative evidence: very, very few artifacts

Early Norse ironworks. Wood carving of *c*. A.D. 1100 in Hylestad, Norway.
Note the anvil, the piece of hot iron held by pincers, the sledgehammer, and
the bellows. And a good portrait of eleventh-century Norsemen. Helge
Ingstad, *Westward to Vinland*. Courtesy of Dr. Ingstad.

of Eskimo or Indian provenance have been unearthed on the site.
Charred roof timbers, which by carbon-14 yield dates within a century
of A.D. 1000 each way, prove that the entire complex was burned down
after abandonment by the Norsemen.

Grapes, Wild Wheat, and Mosür Wood

So far, everything meshes with the Greenlanders' saga; but the next episode is an embarrassment to locating Leif's settlement so far north. When they had finished building the houses, says the Tale of the Greenlanders, they missed Tyrker one evening. Before a search party could get going, the German came out of the woods in high spirits, rolling his eyes and babbling, first in a German dialect which none of his shipmates understood, then in Norse. He said, "I have some real news for you. I found grapevines and grapes!" "Is this possible, foster father?" asked Leif. "Certainly," answered Tyrker, "for I was born where there is no lack either of vines or grapes." Leif now set his men to gathering grapes as well as cutting wood. "And it is said that they loaded up the after boat with grapes, and the ship itself with a cargo of timber. When spring came, they made the ship ready and sailed away. Leif gave this country a name to suit its products. He called it Vinland."

Here is the stumbling block. Wild grapes cannot possibly have grown as far north as L'Anse aux Meadows. Their utmost coastal limit in historic times has been southern Nova Scotia, and they are not really abundant until you reach southern New England. Yet the wild grapes were the one outstanding product of this country, besides giving it a name. Adam of Bremen, the first chronicler to write down this discovery, about A.D. 1075, reported after visiting the king of Denmark: "He spoke of an island in that [northern] ocean, discovered by many, which is called *Winland*, for the reason that vines yielding the best of wine grow there wild. Moreover, that grain unsown grows there abundantly is not a fabulous opinion but, from a relation of the Danes we know it to be true."

Grapes and "self-sown wheat," which also appear in the Saga of Eric the Red, were the main reasons for earlier antiquarians locating Vinland between Cape Cod and the Chesapeake Capes. It was assumed that the "wheat" was either Indian corn or wild rice; but even the dumbest Norseman could hardly have mistaken either for wheat. Merritt L. Fernald, professor of botany at Harvard, solved this problem in a paper published in 1910 in the magazine *Rhodora*. He pointed out that *vinber*, the word in the sagas usually translated "grapes," really

meant "wineberry," which might be the wild red currant, the goose-
berry, or the mountain cranberry. If it be objected that Leif Ericsson,
after whooping it up at the court of King Olaf, must have known wine
and would not have been put off by a poor substitute made from
berries; one may reply that, just as father Eric put the "Green" in
"Greenland" to attract settlers, so Leif put the "Vin" in Vinland. And
with such success as to throw off all Vinland-seekers for centuries!

As for the "self-sown wheat" (*hveiti*) which is mentioned as one of
the products of Leif's new-found land in the Saga of Eric the Red,
Fernald, both in his *Rhodora* article and in his revision of Asa Gray's
Manual of Botany, convincingly identified this as Lyme grass (*Elymus
arenarius*, var. *villosus*), a long, wild grass with a wheat-like head which
grows along beaches from Iceland to southern New England. He cites
abundant evidence for the seeds of this plant, in recent times, having
been used to make flour and bread in Iceland, where it was popularly
called *vild hvede* (wild wheat) or *sandhavre* (sand oat). As far back as
1749 Peter Kalm, the Scandinavian botanist and explorer, wrote of the
north shore of the St. Lawrence, west of Murray Bay, "The sand-
wheat was . . . abundant on the strands. . . . The places where these
grew, look from a distance like fields of grain; we may hence be able
to explain what in the old Norse sagas is said of Wineland the Good,
namely, that even there self-sown wheat fields had been found."

A third wild product of Vinland, mentioned in the Eric the Red
saga, is "trees called *mosür*." This, too, has been convincingly identified
by Fernald as the white or canoe birch. Burly birch knobs with tangled
veins were valued in the old country. Linnaeus wrote of the Lapland
birches, "Knobs, tufts, protuberances . . . are often put forth in old
birches from the middle of the trunk. . . . From these they make
their small vessels for foods and drink, generally carved into a roundish
form." And the Saga of Harald Haardraade mentions *mosürbolls* in the
year 1086. There are no birches now in northern Newfoundland big
enough to grow burls; but in the center of the island there are plenty,
and they may have grown further north in 1001.

On the way back to Greenland, Leif rescued fifteen shipwrecked
sailors from a reef and brought them to Ericsfjord and Brattahlid. This
rescue earned him the nickname "Leif the Lucky."

Expeditions of Thorvald and Karlsevni

Eric the Red died in the winter, shortly after Leif's return. A year or two later his son Thorvald, Leif's brother, proposed to explore Vinland. He outfitted a ship, enrolled a crew, Leif lent them his buildings, and at the place that the sagas name *Leifsbudir* (Leif's huts, or temporary houses) they spent the winter of 1004–5, living largely on fish. In the spring, part of the crew explored the coast in their tender, found nothing but woods and white sand, and returned to Leif's place in the fall. During the second summer again they explored; their ship, driven ashore, broke her keel, which at Thorvald's suggestion was set up as a beacon on a cape which they named Keelness. At another cape they saw three kayaks ashore, with three men under each, and wantonly killed all but one, who escaped. This aroused the natives, who attacked in a fleet of kayaks. The Norsemen affixed their shields to the gunwale, standard procedure for repelling arrows or boarders; but one arrow flew between the gunwale and Thorvald's shield and wounded him mortally. His shipmates buried him on the cape Keelness between two crosses, and following his orders renamed it Crossness. This may have been any one of a dozen promontories between Cape Bauld and Cape Porcupine.

Here is the first contact of Europeans with American aborigines, whom they called *Skrellings*. It is a word of contempt meaning "barbarians," "weaklings," or perhaps even "pygmies," and it is still a matter of dispute whether these hardy natives, who eventually succeeded in driving the Norsemen out, were Indian or Eskimo; and, if Eskimo, Dorset or Tunnit.

The survivors returned to Leif's deserted village, spent a second winter, gathered *vinber* and "wine wood," steered their ship to Ericsfjord (Brattahlid, Greenland), "and had plenty of news to tell Leif." Plenty indeed!

The next recorded voyage to Vinland, a serious attempt to colonize the country, was undertaken by Thorfinn Karlsevni. This Icelander, trading between Norway and Greenland, had become intimate with the children of Eric the Red and spent a merry Christmas with them at Brattahlid in 1008. In the new year Karlsevni married Gudrid, the handsome and intelligent widow of Thorstein Ericsson, Leif's brother.

Their expedition started shortly. With them sailed a bastard daughter of old Éric's named Freydis, her husband Thorvard, and Thorvald Ericsson, Leif's brother. We have already buried him; but no matter, let us hear what this saga tells. They had three ships, with 250 men and women. After passing the Wonder Strands, Karlsevni sent ashore for exploration two Scots slaves whom King Olaf had given to Leif Ericsson and Leif had lent to him. The "Gaelic runners," as this pair were called because of their fleetness of foot, brought back a bunch of wild grapes and an ear of the "self-sown wheat." Encouraged, the three ships continued and stood into a fjord past an island about which there were strong currents, and which they named "Straumey"; it was covered with sea birds. This must have been Belle Isle or Great Sacred Island off L'Anse aux Meadows, and the fjord, the Strait of Belle Isle. They landed, and set up housekeeping in Leif's houses, which Leif had given Karlsevni permission to use. That autumn Gudrid gave birth to Snorri, first white child born in America, 575 years before Virginia Dare.

This expedition brought "all kinds of live stock" which did not do well the following winter, a severe one; nor was the fishing much good; by springtime the people were so desperate as to seek fodder and birds' eggs on Straumey, the big island. A dead whale drifted ashore and they tried eating the flesh, but it made them sick. A character named Thorhall the Hunter who had joined the expedition became so disgusted that he sailed away, singing an improvised ditty justifying his desertion. After having been promised wine and good meat in Vinland, he was given only spring water to drink and putrid whale to eat; so he was through and going home. Thorhall missed Greenland and his ship was cast away on the shores of Ireland, where he was killed and his crew enslaved.

Karlsevni, Biarni, and Thorvald now cruised "southward along the coast," looking for a better settlement than Leif's, and found it at a river mouth with sandbars on the east coast, flowing into a small land-locked bay which they named *Hóp*, an old Norse name for that kind of place. This may have been any one of twelve harbors between Quirpon and White Bay. There they found not only grapes and self-sown wheat but caught stranded halibut in beach pools at low water. And there was good pasturage. After two weeks at Hóp, they

had a visit from Skrellings in kayaks, making what the Norsemen interpreted as peace gestures. So they raised a white shield in reply; and the
natives (described as horribly ugly, hairy, and swarthy, with great
black eyes) departed after sampling the milk of the Norsemen's cows
and being given a few strips of red cloth.

After passing a winter in which no snow fell and the cattle grazed
comfortably outdoors, Karlsevni's company had another visitation of
Skrellings in a multitude of kayaks. These natives were looking for
more red cloth and cow's milk; probably they offered in payment furs
and salmon. While the chaffering went on, Karlsevni's bull ran out of
the woods bellowing loudly, and this so alarmed the Skrellings that
they paddled away and were not seen again for three weeks. They returned in a fighting mood. The Norsemen displayed red shields, gave
battle, and were met with a shower of arrows and a primitive weapon
of Skrelling ballistics. The saga describes it as "a pole with a huge knob
on the end, black in color and about the size of a sheep's belly, which
flew . . . over the heads of the men and made a frightening noise
when it fell." Whatever this terrible object may have been—probably
nothing more than a blown-up moose bladder—it panicked the Norsemen. Freydis, Eric's bastard daughter, saved the day. After vainly try- _Freydis_
ing to rally her menfolk with taunts, she bared her breasts, slapped
them with a sword, and screamed like a hellcat. This so alarmed the
Skrellings that they broke off the attack and retreated. It can hardly
escape the reader's notice that Freydis showed more Viking spirit than
Karlsevni and his men.

The leader and his people now decided to give up and go home.
Nature in Vinland was kind, compared with Greenland, but colonists
would be in constant dread of the natives, none of whom as yet had
reached the Greenland settlements. So Karlsevni's people piled into
their ships and sailed north, taking a mean revenge by killing five Skrellings whom they caught asleep on the shore. It was too late in the
season to sail to Greenland, so they passed another winter somewhere
along the shore. In the spring, Karlsevni set forth in his ship, hoping to
find Thorhall the Hunter, passed Keelness, and then bore westerly,
with land to port. Obviously they were sailing along the west coast of
Newfoundland. It was all a wooded wilderness. Finally they reached a
river flowing westerly into the sea. "They concluded that the moun-

tains they found in the country were the same as those they had seen at Hóp." Both places were equidistant from Straumfjord, the Strait of Belle Isle.

Here is an important geographical clue. The long northern peninsula of Newfoundland, with an almost level ridge rising to three thousand feet, is the only place on the Atlantic seaboard where you can see mountains from the sea on each side of a peninsula. The unnamed spot opposite Hóp, where a river flowed from east to west into the sea, could have been St. Geneviève or St. Margaret, about sixty miles from the tip of Cape Bauld. Plenty of choice for an archaeologist who wants to start digging!

One thing the men of science are not likely to find evidence of is the famous Uniped, the ein-foetingr (one-footer) who skipped down to the river bank against which the Norse ship was lying, and mortally wounded Thorvald Ericsson with an arrow. This conflicts with the other saga, which states that he was killed earlier and buried on Keelness. Unipeds were part of the classical tradition. Olaus Magnus has several pages of repulsive monstrosities in his Historia de Gentibus Septentrionalibus (1555), including a Uniped of Ethiopia who is using his foot for a parasol. Travelers to far-off places were supposed to see abnormal and horrible half-beasts, half-humans; and people loved to read about them; that is one reason why the bogus Travels of Sir John Mandeville were so popular. Columbus even apologized in his first Letter to the Spanish Sovereigns for having no monstrosities to report! If not more honorable, it was at least a more notable death for Thorvald to be killed by a Uniped than by a dwarf Skrelling. More than five centuries later, Jacques Cartier reported Unipeds in the mythical Kingdom of Saguenay.

After another winter at Straumfjord, in which the men fought over the women, the Karlsevni colony, with Gudrid and three-year-old Snorri, sailed for home. In Markland (Labrador) they captured two native boys, took them to Greenland, had them baptized, and taught them to speak Norse. They then told the Norsemen many strange things, including a haunting clue to a lost Irish colony: "There was a land on the other side over against their country, where people wore white clothes, and yelled loudly and carried poles with pieces of cloth attached." The Norsemen commented that this must have been an Irish ecclesiastical procession in "Hvitramannaland or Ireland the Great," which they had heard about.

Expedition of Thorvard and the Two Brothers

Now we come to the third and final attempt, of which we have any record, to colonize Vinland. In the summer of 1013, when Karlsevni returned to Greenland, there arrived at Brattahlid a ship from Norway owned by two brothers, Helgi and Finnbogi. Freydis, Thorvard's wife, the tough wench who had routed the Skrellings, made a deal with the brothers. She and they, each in their own ship, would take thirty men and a few women to Vinland, and equally share the profits. Leif lent his half-sister his big house at L'Anse aux Meadows. But Freydis doublecrossed her partners. Upon arriving at the old site in the summer of 1014 she insisted that Leif's house belonged to her, made the brothers build another, and soon the two parties were not on speaking terms. Freydis, having her eye on the brothers' ship as the bigger of the two, stirred up her husband with a lie about Helgi and Finnbogi trying to "make" her, and so teased and taunted Thorvard with the "Are you a man or a mouse?" routine that he summoned his crew and surprised and killed all the men of the brothers' party. Freydis herself finished off the women. "After this monstrous deed," says the saga, Freydis and Thorvard loaded the brothers' ship to the gunwales "with all the products of the land," abandoned their own vessel, and sailed to Ericsfirth, Greenland. Freydis had sworn her accomplices to tell that the brothers' party had simply decided to stay behind; but some of Thorvard's crew blabbed, the story reached Leif, and he had three sailors separately tortured to reveal the truth. Their stories agreed so closely that Leif had to accept his half-sister's guilt. Family feeling prevented him from punishing the guilty couple; but he put a curse on their offspring, who in consequence (we are told) never amounted to anything.

With this sordid episode of murder and perjury, the recorded history of Vinland ends; everything that comes after is mere conjecture. The Greenlanders made no further attempt to exploit their western colony. And it is clear enough that they gave up trying because of the hostile attitude of the Skrellings, especially their ability to deliver surprise attacks almost at will. So Skoal! to the Skrellings. They did well

to run the white men out of their territory, for by so doing they enjoyed American isolation for almost five hundred years.

The Later History of Greenland and Vinland

To conclude what we know about Eric the Red's family: Karlsevni
and Gudrid, with their American-born boy Snorri, made a profitable
voyage to Norway with Greenland products and then bought a farm
in Iceland. After Karlsevni's death, Gudrid managed the property until
Snorri married and took it over. She then made a pilgrimage to Rome
and took the veil. Snorri's daughters married substantial Icelanders.
Distinguished people, including three bishops, traced their ancestry to
the little boy born in Vinland.

Vinland now practically disappears from recorded history. The only
known event, and that conjectural, is a mysterious visit by Bishop
Eric Gnupson, a well-known character whom the Norse nicknamed
"Upsi" (the Pollock). Icelandic annals for 1121 relate that Upsi went
"to look for Vinland" that year, and never returned; but the fishy
cleric returns to life in a legend on the Yale Vinland Map: "Eric,
bishop of Greenland and adjacent regions and papal legate, arrived on
this truly spacious and most opulent land, in the last year of our most
blessed Pope Paschal, remained there a long time both summer and
winter and afterwards returned northeasterly toward Greenland and
proceeded thence in humble obedience to superior will."

Unless this is the work of a recent forger—which I suspect it to be—
the inscription suggests that there was supposed to be still living somewhere on the North American seaboard a Christian community to
which the bishop felt he should minister, and hence made a voyage to
Vinland and back. But apart from the question of forgery, the story is
full of holes. Pope Paschal II died in January 1118, not 1126. Eric had
been consecrated a bishop *in partibus* in 1112-13, but a bishop in or of
Greenland he never was; the first bishop of Greenland was consecrated
twelve years later.

So, what? Every Vinlandologist has had a whack at the problem.
Hennig thinks that the bishop was really looking for the legendary
Irish colony of Hvitramanna Land, the Quii and all that! Skelton sensi-
bly concludes that no European colony could possibly have survived in
North America to 1121, and that Eric's object for this long journey was

to convert the Skrellings. The bishop, having survived the voyage, performed the double service of spreading the Word and topography recorded on the Vinland Map. Very neat! On the basis of very slight
evidence, one may conclude that Bishop Eric made one voyage, or two;
that he returned, or was lost; that he was looking for a Norse colony,
an Irish colony, or heathen ripe for conversion; or nothing. But the
only certain thing that he accomplished was the befuddlement of twentieth-century scholars.

More than a century elapsed before another reference to Vinland or
any adjoining country is recorded. The Icelandic annals for 1347 state
that "a ship came from Greenland, smaller than those which ply to
Iceland. . . . It had no anchor. There were 17 men on board who had
been to Markland and been driven here by the sea." Here is concrete
evidence of a steady trade between Greenland and the spruce forests
near the Wonder Strands of Leif's Markland—the Labrador. It was
no great feat for Norse sailors in summer, when the ice was out, to
cross the Labrador Sea from the Western Settlement and to follow the
coast to Hamilton Inlet. There they could moor their vessel in a land-
locked harbor while the crew rowed in their tender to the Wonder
Strands to fell trees. Having cut all the timber they wanted, they could
sail their vessel to the beach, taking advantage of an offshore wind, and
load up for Greenland. Some ships may have continued their voyage
to Vinland in search of grapes, only to find berries and meet hostile
Skrellings. But the tall timber of Markland was a valuable asset for the
Greenlanders, although they could get it only in two summer months
without being blocked by ice.

This incident of 1347 is the latest documentary record of the lands
discovered by Biarni and Leif. The chronology in the manuscript history of Greenland by Björn Jonsön ends with the consecration of another Henricus (Erik) as bishop of Greenland in 1389; but it is doubtful whether he ever found a ship to take him there.

Of the Norse settlements in Greenland we have abundant evidence,
mainly archaeological, up to a point. Since 1920 there have been extensive excavations by the Danish government and private archaeologists.
They have found evidence of flourishing agricultural communities
radiating from the Western Settlement (Godthaab) and the Eastern
Settlement, Eric's Brattahlid, near Julianehaab. Gardar, in the Eastern
Settlement, had a neat little stone cathedral church, and there were at

least a dozen parish churches in the colony, with an estimated population of around three thousand. Great houses, subdivided like Leif's at L'Anse aux Meadows, were numerous. The Greenlanders had their own national assembly, the *Althing*, and did not pay homage to the king of Norway until 1261. They raised horses, sheep, and cattle on the grass meadows bordering the inner and more sheltered fjords. In addition to making use of edible wild plants and berries, they raised a little barley, and of course had plenty of fish. They fashioned iron implements from bog ore, and others from bones of the walrus which they hunted not for his meat and hide but for his tusks; walrus ivory was a valuable export. So were white falcons, highly valued by noble and royal sportsmen such as the Emperor Frederick II. To while away the long winter nights, the Greenlanders carved walrus-ivory chessmen. The women spun and wove wool from their own sheep, and also imported the latest fashions from Europe; skeletons have been found clothed in woolen gowns, and hoods with a long whip-lash peak, which one sees in portraits of Dante and his contemporaries. But an examination of the human remains in Greenland indicates that the people, or at least those of the fifteenth century, were undersized, ill-nourished, and even rachitic.

Greenland gradually faded out of European cognizance. The last bishop of Gardar whom we know to have visited his see died in 1372. A ship from Norway spent a winter at the Western Settlement between 1406 and 1410; no people were there, only cattle running wild. Pope Nicholas V in 1448 wrote to the archbishop of Trondheim that, some thirty years earlier, "a barbarous and pagan fleet from neighboring shores invaded the island, laying waste the land with fire and sword, and destroying the churches, leaving only nine standing." He begged the archbishop to look into the matter and send out priests to minister to the survivors. Nothing was done. Some forty-five years later, the Borgia pope Alexander VI, of not very blessed memory, evinced a laudable compassion for his lost northern flock. In a letter addressed to two bishops in Iceland he observed that no vessel had touched at Greenland for eighty years, and that although Pope Innocent VIII (1484–92) had appointed one Matthias bishop of Greenland, he had heard nothing from him, not even whether he went there; the Icelandic bishops should do something about it. All papal taxes will be waived for Greenland; their people need not fear being presented with a bill for accumulated Peter's pence.

The rest is silence. What can have happened?
There are several explanations, but the most plausible is the disruption of Greenland's connection with Norway. No European colony
in America could long subsist if connections with the homeland were
cut off—the first English colony in Virginia is an example. And why
did this once fruitful connection cease? Partly for lack of profitable
trade. The bottom fell out of the walrus-ivory market, owing to competition from African elephant-ivory brought home by the Portuguese,
and gentlemen no longer preferred blond falcons. Second, Norse economy recoiled from the Black Death epidemic of 1349 which killed one
person out of three, and in Iceland it was even more devastating. Ships
of the Hansa and of England ran the Norse merchant ships out of business, and instead of Vikings' raiding the shores of northern Europe,
English and Scots pirates began raiding Iceland. The ship which had
been sent at least every few years from Norway to Greenland no
longer came. And in the summer temperature there was a distinct drop,
which Greenland agriculture, always marginal, could not take. There
are hints, too, of a plague of locusts. The priests died and no replacements came from Rome. The men, physically degenerate as their skeletons indicate, grew too weak to hunt.

It is a sad picture, the gradual snuffing out of this far-away colony
so gallantly planted by Eric the Red. His last descendants, hardly able
to find enough food to keep alive, staring their eyes out all through the
short, bright summer for the ship from Norway that meant their salvation. By September it becomes certain that she will not come that
year. The long, dark winter closes in, and there is no more oil for
lamps. Cold and hungry, the people live merely to survive until next
summer when surely the ship will come; but it never does. At some
time in the second half of the fifteenth century, the last Norse Greenlander died, "unknell'd, uncoffin'd and unknown."

There remains the teasing question, what relation do these early
Norse colonies bear to the great discovery by Columbus? In my opinion, nothing. Columbus's son is generous in stating whatever hints encouraged his father's great enterprise, but Vinland is not one of them.
Even Greenland was so forgotten by southern Europe in his day that
when a Portuguese from the Azores made Cape Farewell in 1500, it
was mapped as a new discovery and given a new name.

Columbus as a young man voyaged on a Portuguese ship to the north of Iceland, but there is no evidence that he called at Iceland; or that, supposing someone had translated the saga manuscripts for him, he would have found anything in them to interest him. Columbus was looking for a route to the Indies and for gems, spices, and precious metals, not for walrus ivory and wild grapes; the natives whom he wished to contact were Chinese mandarins and gentlemen of Japan, not rough Skrellings; and he started west along a latitude some 1400 miles further south than that of Leif's Vinland. Valiant efforts have been made to hook up Columbus with Ericsson in order to prove the Greenland and Vinland colonies to be the real start of a causal sequence, instead of the dead end that they actually were; but as honest Halldór Hermannsson wrote, "We can find nothing in the history of Columbus which indicates that he knew anything about the Wineland voyages."

Bibliography and Notes

DRAMATIS PERSONAE

Biarni Heriulfson, "a most promising man," owner of a trading ship, missed Greenland c. 986 and discovered Vinland, Markland, and Helluland.

Eric the Red, who died in Greenland c. 1002, had three sons, Thorstein, Leif (known as "the Lucky"), and Thorvald; and an illegitimate daughter Freydis who married Thorvard, a trader.

Gudrid, daughter of Thorbiorn, a friend of Eric's, married (1) Thorstein Ericsson, who died, and (2) Thorfinn Karlsevni. Their son Snorri was born in Vinland.

Helgi and Finnbogi, brothers, accompanied Freydis and Thorvard to Vinland where they were killed at the instigation of Freydis.

Thorfinn Karlsevni, a gentlemanly trader from Iceland, married the widow Gudrid and attempted to colonize Vinland.

Thorhall "the Hunter" accompanied the Karlsevni expedition but when he found no grapes, deserted and was shipwrecked in Ireland.

Thorvald went on the second voyage to Vinland, and c. 1005 was killed either by Skrellings, and buried on Keelness (according to the Greenlanders' tale), or by a Uniped on the Karlsevni expedition (according to the Eric the Red saga).

Thorvard, a Greenland trader, married Freydis and attempted to colonize Vinland.

Tyrker, a German, Leif Ericsson's foster-father, accompanied him to Vinland and identified the grapes.

CHRONOLOGY

Scandinavian scholars differ as to the dates of the several attempts to colonize Vinland. Those I give are possibly too early by one or two years.

NORSE VOYAGES AND SHIPS

The best recent general accounts of Norse voyages by a competent scholar are Gwyn Jones, *The Norse Atlantic Saga* (1964), and *A History of the Vikings* (1968). But, to my mind, nothing has replaced Joseph Fischer, S.J., *The Discoveries of the Norsemen in America*, Soulsby, trans. (London, 1903). Bertil Almgren *et al.*, *The Vikings* (London, 1968), has articles by specialists and is beautifully illustrated.

William Hovgaard, *Voyages of the Norsemen to America* (1914), began the scientific study of early Norse ships and was the first to prove that the Vinland voyagers used the *knarr*, or round ship. There have been many excavations of Norse ships in recent years. Material will be found in A. W. Brøgger and Haakon Shetelig, *The Viking Ships, Their Ancestry and Evolution* (Oslo, 1951). Even later, the discovery *c.* 1959 of five vessels built *c.* 1000, sunk with stones to close a channel at Skuldelev, Roskilde Fjord, Denmark, and their restoration and preservation in a special museum there, have immensely increased our knowledge of the merchant ship of the period. These are described in Ole Olsen and Ole Crumlin-Pedersen, "The Skuldelev Ships," *Acta Archaeologica*, XXXVIII (1967), 73–175, and the same authors' *Fem vikingeskibe fra Roskilde Fjord* (Roskilde, 1969). I am indebted to Captain Harold E. Rice USN, United States Defense attaché at Copenhagen, for looking these up for me; and to the museum director Mr. Ole Crumlin-Pedersen for answering my questions.

G. J. Marcus, "The Navigation of the Norsemen," in *Mariner's Mirror*, XXXIX, No. 2 (May 1953), 112–31, is the best treatise on that subject. Heinrich Winter, in *Mariner's Mirror*, XXIII (1937), 99, argues that the early Norsemen had the compass, but I find his evidence unconvincing. Farley Mowat, *Westviking* (1965), has a detailed appendix on Norse seafaring and navigation that is somewhat overblown. Fantastic as the Polynesian "sacred gourd" is the story of the "Magical Sun Stones" set forth in *Anglers and Hunters Magazine* (Toronto, 1968). An unnamed Danish archaeologist discovered minerals with molecules aligned parallel, as in a Polaroid filter. The Vikings, by squinting through a slab of this, could sight the sun through heavy overcast!

VINLAND SAGAS AND OTHER EARLY SOURCES

The original manuscripts are in the Royal Library, Copenhagen. The best ⟨ edition of them in the original is Einar Munksgaard's in *Corpus Codicum Islandicorum Medii Aevi* (Copenhagen, Vol. 1, 1930, and later volumes). Arthur Middleton Reeves, *The Finding of Wineland the Good* (London, 1890; offset reprint, New York, 1967), reproduces facsimiles of the manuscripts, line by line transliterated, and a translation which is reprinted conveniently in *Northmen, Columbus and Cabot* of the Original Narratives of Early American History series, with introduction and notes by Julius E. Olson, professor of Scandinavian in the University of Wisconsin. Olson includes translations of the relevant passages in Adam of Bremen and of the papal letters about the lost colony of Greenland. Reeves's translation is unnecessarily pedantic—"a storm made up" becomes "the wind waxed amain," etc.—but reliable. Preferable is the informal but accurate translation by Professor Einar Haugen in his *Voyages to Vinland* (New York, 1942). Another good one is G. M. Gathorne-Hardy's in his *Norse Discoverers of America. The Wineland Sagas Translated and Discussed* (Oxford, 1921).

There is a second manuscript of the Saga of Eric the Red, but it differs little from the one usually translated. Jón Jóhannesson's devastating analysis of this saga as a sophisticated tale written to exalt the descendants of Karlsevni, and his rehabilitation of the Tale of the Greenlanders (Flatey Book) as the older and more authentic narrative, came out originally in a Festschrift to Professor Nordal at Reykjavik in 1956. It is available in an English translation by Tryggvi J. Oleson in *Saga Book of the Viking Society*, XVI (1962), 54–60. The conversion story, Jóhannesson points out, is derived from the Saga of Olaf Tryggvason, written by a monk named Gunnlangr *c.* 1200; the Tale of the Greenlanders, which does not mention these missionary activities, must be earlier, and several early authorities on Olaf's reign mention his having converted the rest of the Norse empire, but not Greenland. "The author of the *Saga of Eirikr* [Eric the Red]," writes Jóhannesson (p. 65), "was, no doubt, a learned man. His work shows acquaintance with the bookish geographical lore of southern Europe, such as the concept of the circle of lands and the Land of the Unipeds." However, details in the Saga of Eric the Red may well be true and they were written down only half a century later than the other saga.

Adam of Bremen's allusion to Vinland is in his *Descriptio Insularum Aquilorum*, an appendix to his *Gesta Hammaburgensis Ecclesiae Pontificum*, composed before 1076, first printed in 1595, lib. iv §38 (Hannover, 1876 ed., p. 186). "Wineland" is also mentioned casually in Ari Thorgilsson's *Islandingabok* (H. Hermannsson (ed.), *Islandica*, XX (Ithaca, 1930), pp. 51, 52, 64, 83).

DETAILS

The Wonder Strands. A map of that part of the Labrador will be found in Chapter XVIII below.

The Doegr. Some say a *doegr* means 12 hours, others 24 hours, and still others that it is a unit of distance, an average day's sail of a Norse ship.

Sleeping Bags. The word is *húdfat*, usually wrongly translated "hammocks," which were an invention of the Arawak and discovered by Columbus in 1492. The *húdfat* was a big bag made of sheepskin or cowhide, which

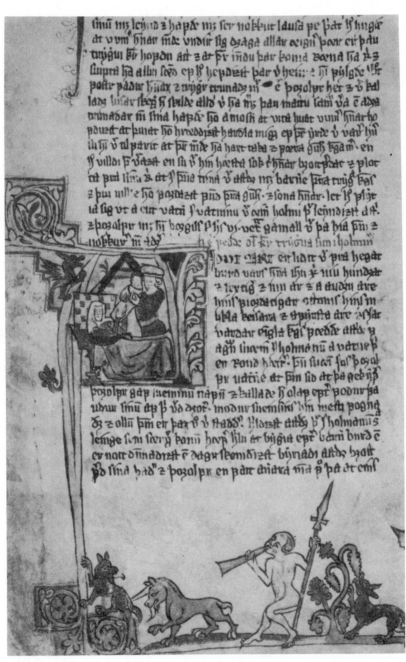

Page from Flatey Book illustrating birth of King Olaf Trygvasson. Courtesy Royal Library, Copenhagen.

Part of page from Flatey Book with reference to "Vÿnlãd," Vinland.
Courtesy Royal Library, Copenhagen.

the Norsemen used both for sleeping and for storing or carrying clothing. Information from Professor Einar Haugen.

Eyktarstad and Dagmalastad. The saga-teller was trying to say that this place was on a lower latitude than Greenland, and enjoyed more winter sun. Everyone works it out as the exact latitude where he thinks Vinland was! Haugen's translation is the simplest and best: "On the shortest day of the year the sun was up from breakfast time to mid-afternoon." This did not occur in Iceland after mid-October (*Voyages to Vinland*, p. 21).

Mosür Wood. This *mosür* became the king-pin of the Horsford theory that Leif's settlement was on the Charles River in Massachusetts. Eben N. Horsford (1818–93), professor of chemistry at Harvard, made a fortune from Rumford Baking Powder and other proprietary products, and spent it on locating Leif and Thorfinn on the banks of the Charles. In his imagination, every colonial ditch or paved cow-yard in that region became Norse. Arguing that *Norumbega*, the name that later explorers found Indians using on the Penobscot, was a corruption of Norway (see Chapter XIV below), he purchased a tract of land on the Charles River which he named Norumbega Park, and erected a stone tower with a bronze tablet setting forth the achievements of the Norse pioneers. He believed that they cut burls and knobs from birch and oak and floated them to a dam at the head of navigation at Watertown, whence a fleet of Viking ships transported them to Iceland and Norway to be fashioned into beer bowls. Horsford gained slight support from the historical profession— Justin Winsor wrote, "The most incautious linguistic inferences, and the most uncritical, cartological perversions, are presented in Horsford's *Discovery of America by Northmen.*" But most of the then simple inhabitants of Boston and vicinity were intrigued by the thought of Vikings shouting *Skoal!* over beer bowls fashioned from New England wood. Hence the odd-looking statue of Leif Ericsson on Commonwealth Avenue, Boston, overlooking the Back Bay where the *mosür* ships were supposed to have plied. Horsford published a score of lavishly illustrated and for the most part privately printed works, of which the most important are *The Defenses of Norumbega* (1891), in which he replies vigorously to his critics, and *The Landfall of Leif Erickson A.D. 1000, and the Site of his Houses in Vineland* (1892).

The Reported Cloth on Poles. The word is *flík*, the same root as English *flitch.* Professor Einar Haugen thinks that here it means a narrow piece of cloth, which must have been a scarce commodity with those people, the best they could do for a banner.

THE GREENLAND COLONY

Accounts of the Danish excavations have been regularly reprinted in the periodical *Meddelelser om Grønland* of Copenhagen. Helge Ingstad includes these, and later excavations of his own, in *Land Under the Pole Star*, translated by Walford (New York, 1966), a fascinating and scholarly book. So is Knud J. Krogh, *Viking Greenland* (Copenhagen, National Museum, 1967), which is lavishly illustrated.

For the controversial voyage of Bishop Eric "Upsi" from Greenland to Vinland, see the books mentioned under the Yale Vinland Map, below, and notes by H. Hermannsson to his edition of the *Islandingabok* in *Islandica*, XX (Ithaca, 1930), 82–83.

The question of what became of the Norse Greenlanders is argued in all the general works, in varying degrees of acrimony; I have discussed it pleasantly and profitably with Dr. Helge Larsen of the National Museum, Copenhagen. T. J. Oleson in his *Early Voyages and Northern Approaches*,

1000–1632 (London, 1964) argues that Greenlanders of the Western Settlement simply wandered off with Dorset-culture Eskimo, becoming the "Quii," and fathering the legendary blond Eskimo. An account of recent excavations on the Ungava Peninsula in Thomas E. Lee, *Fort Chimo and Payne Lake, Ungava, Archaeology 1965* (Centre d'Études Nordiques, Université Laval, 1967), contains few facts but plenty of speculation. Recent archaeologists, whether Canadian or Scandinavian, seem reluctant to admit that the Eskimo could build anything but a snow igloo; so every heap of stones in these northern wastes is joyfully presented as a result of Norse migration. The same writers refuse to admit that their ancestors could have been exterminated by Skrellings. Oleson characterizes the theory that the Skrellings wiped them out as a "hoary" myth and asserts, "There is not a tittle of evidence of this warfare" (p. 9). One "tittle" is Olaus Magnus's picture of it (see illustrations in Chapter IV below), and another is an Eskimo tradition, told to Rockwell Kent in 1929 (his *N By E*, 1930, pp. 210–13). This is a detailed account of their ancestors killing one Olaf, the last surviving Norseman, in the Eastern Settlement. An earlier version of this story is in Gwyn Jones, *Norse Atlantic Saga*, pp. 214–19. Whilst not denying that the Eskimo may have moved in on Brattahlid when its survivors were too weak to resist, Dr. Larsen and I regard any such attack as a mere *coup de grâce* to a dying community; dying from isolation, and undernourishment.

The 1448 letter of Pope Nicholas V, mentioned in my text, known in Scandinavia since 1765, has been attacked by several Scandinavian writers as spurious, ostensibly because addressed to an ecclesiastical swindler named Marcellus, but obviously because the contents do not fit their theories. The letter was published in facsimile by J. C. Heywood in *Documenta Selecta e Tabulario Secreto Vaticano* (Rome 1893), and the Latin text is printed in Joseph Fischer, S.J., *The Discoveries of the Northmen in America* (London, 1903), pp. 51, 52. I have no doubt that it is a genuine papal brief, and the fact that it is addressed to an imposter does not discredit the information which the Pope doubtless received from other sources. For Marcellus the medieval swindler, see S. Hasund, *Det norske folks liv og historie*, III (Oslo, 1934). Note from Professor Haugen.

THE L'ANSE AUX MEADOWS SITE

Helge Ingstad first reported his discoveries in *National Geographic*, CXXVI, No. 5 (November 1964), 708–34. A more complete report will be found in E. J. Friis's translation of Ingstad's Norwegian book, *Westward to Vinland* (New York, 1969), especially pp. 197–203, 210–21. In September 1968, with Mauricio Obregón and James F. Nields, in the latter's Beechcraft, I flew to St. Anthony airfield in Newfoundland and drove to the excavation, which we examined critically and carefully. We believe that Ingstad has it.

Two adverse criticisms of the site at L'Anse aux Meadows that have come to my knowledge are Farley Mowat, *West Viking* (1965), Appendix N, and my Harvard colleague Einar Haugen, orally. Mowat has a rival site; Haugen feels that Ingstad's evidence is inconclusive for want of artifacts and inscriptions of Greenland origin; that *vínber* really are grapes, not berries, and that both they and the *mosür* point to a more southerly site for Vinland. Many Scandinavians feel that it detracts from their ancestors' glory to have Leif and Karlsevni sail no further south than this. To me, it seems enough for a sailor to have found his way to any part of North America and back without benefit of compass or sextant, and to have returned thrice to the same spot. Gwyn Jones, *Norse Alantic Saga* (1964), chap. iii, accepts L'Anse aux Meadows and has an important supporting bibliography in Appendix IV.

Dr. Ingstad wrote to me (26 November 1968) that since his last publication he has had three more carbon-14 datings from the site, making a total of sixteen, all indicating A.D. 1000 ± 100 years.

Some Eskimo soapstone spindle whorls are illustrated in an article by David Sanger in *The Beaver* (Spring 1968). They are very different from those found at L'Anse aux Meadows.

YALE'S VINLAND MAP

With a great fanfare of publicity Yale University brought out, shortly before Columbus Day 1965, *The Vinland Map and the Tartar Relation*, edited by R. A. Skelton, Thomas E. Marston, and George D. Painter. This map, which they date at around A.D. 1440, and the northwestern quarter of which we here reproduce in outline, aroused a storm of controversy altogether incommensurate with its importance. If genuine, it is the only pre-Columbian map to represent Vinland or to make Greenland an island. If genuine, it confirms Biarni Heriulfson's part in the discovery of America, and Bishop Eric's missionary voyage of *c.* 1118–21. It may yet be proved genuine by chemical analysis of the ink, etc.; but I have "serious reservations" about it—the polite scholarly term for saying that you suspect fakery. The ground for my suspicion is this: Whilst the greater part of the map, supposed to illustrate the *Tartar Relation*, is an Andrea Bianco mappemonde type of around 1436, with the usual Ptolemaic errors and mythical islands, the "Isolanda," "Gronelanda" and "Vinlanda" correspond so closely to the outlines and relative positions of Iceland, Greenland below latitude 72° N, and Baffin Island on modern maps, that they must have been dubbed in by some clever forger at a much later date. Note the close resemblance of "Vinlanda Insula" to Baffin Island—Cumberland Sound and Frobisher Bay are there, and Nettining Lake, draining east instead of west to look like the Norsemen's Hóp. Note that Greenland is an island. It was never so depicted on any map prior to 1650, but as a peninsula of Asia. Note the remarkable accuracy of Iceland, and of the east coast of Greenland, which on the Cantino map of 1502 is correctly shown as shrouded with ice. Note the east coast fjord at Angmagssalik (about lat. 65°30′ N, and Scoresby

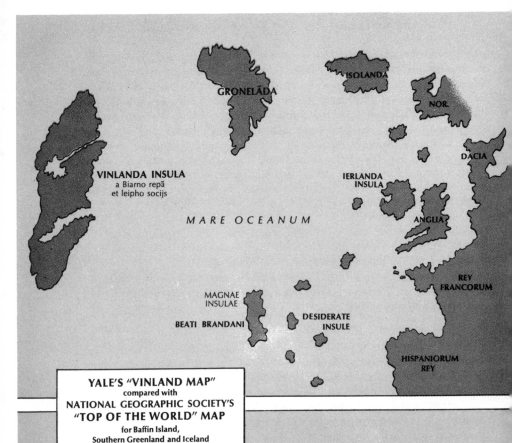

VINLANDA INSULA
a Biarno repã
et leipho socijs

GRONELÃDA

ISOLANDA

NOR.

DACIA

MARE OCEANUM

IERLANDA
INSULA

ANGLIA

REY
FRANCORUM

MAGNAE
INSULAE

BEATI BRANDANI

DESIDERATE
INSULE

HISPANIORUM
REY

YALE'S "VINLAND MAP"
compared with
**NATIONAL GEOGRAPHIC SOCIETY'S
"TOP OF THE WORLD" MAP**
for Baffin Island,
Southern Greenland and Iceland

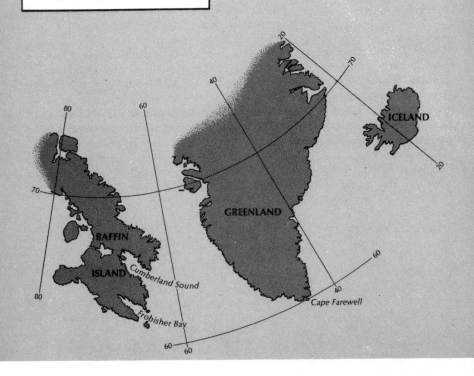

ICELAND

GREENLAND

BAFFIN

ISLAND

Cumberland Sound

Cape Farewell

Frobisher Bay

Sound at lat. 70° N, which could not by any stretch of the imagination have been explored that early; and on the west coast, indentations which correspond closely to the modern Söndre, Strömfjord, Disko Bugt, Karrets Fjord; note the westerly trend of the coast north of Upernavik. No, this map of the northern regions is just too accurate to have been drafted in 1450 or for at least two centuries thereafter. It is a sharp contrast to the grotesquely inaccurate Eurasian part of the map, which is supposed to illustrate the *Tartar Relation.** And what do the three northern islands illustrate, other than some clever forger's appetite for dollars? Not one of the Danish and Icelandic scholars whom I consulted at Copenhagen in May 1969 believes the Vinland Map to be genuine, although they have every national and sentimental reason to accept it as such.

The Latin inscriptions about Bishop Eric and Vinland are suspiciously similar to the chronology at the end of a manuscript in the Royal Library, Copenhagen, dated 1669, *Gronlands Bejkriffvelse* . . . *Antiquitäter* translated by Theodore Thorlacius from Björn Jonsön. Here we have *Biarni*, *Leifus*, *Ericus Rufus*, and *Ericus Gronlandiae Episcopus*, who, however, dies on his journey to Vinland in 1121. The Vinland Map enlarges on this.

In the spate of discussions, the following have something important to say: Einar Haugen's review in *Speculum*, XLI (October 1966), 770–74, "Sources of the Vinland Map" in *Arctic*, XIX (December 1966), 287–95, and Paper presented at Vinland Map Conference at Smithsonian Institution, November 1966. D. B. Quinn, "The Vinland Map" in *Saga Book of the Viking Society*, XVII, Pt. 1 (1966), 63–72. P. G. Foote, "On the Vinland Legends on the Vinland Map," ibid. 73–79, both reprinted in a pamphlet by the Viking Society for Northern Research (London, University College, 1966). J. H. Parry, "The Vinland Story" in *Perspectives in American History*, I (1967), 417–33. Giuseppe Caraci, the eminent Roman geographer, has a scathing assault on the map in *Studi Medievale* of Spoleto, 3d ser., VII, No. 2 (December 1966), pp. 509–615. G. R. Crone, "The Vinland Map Cartographically Considered," *Geographical Journal*, CXXXII (1966), 75–80. V. Slessarev and P. Sablett, "The Vinland Caption Reëxamined," *Terrae Incognitae*, I (1969), 58–67. Wilcomb E. Washburn, "Examen critique des questions cartographiques" in *La Découverte de l'Amérique* (Paris, 1968). The late E. G. R. Taylor's "misgivings" are presented by M. W. Richey in *Journal of the Institute of Navigation*, XIX (1966), 124–25; Skelton's reply, ibid. 171–73. I. R. Kejlbo, "Vinlandskortet og Claudius Clavus," *Saertryk af Kulturgeografi*, No. 106 (1968), pp. 197–220, with summary in English, argues that the author of the Map obtained his data from Claudius

---

* The promoters claim that it was originally intended to illustrate a manuscript of the *Speculum historiale* of Vincent de Beauvais, a copy of which (acquired separately) is alleged to have been formerly married to the Map and the *Relation* by the dubious evidence of corresponding worm holes.

Clavus, the celebrated Norse geographer of the fifteenth century. Michael A. Musmanno's, *Columbus Was First* (1966) is an amusing, emotional assault on what he calls "Scandiknavery." Amintore Fanfani, *The Vinland Map* (New York, Inst. Italiano di Cultura, 1965), tells about the tempest that the Yale publication raised. Bibliography of the discussion in Association de géographes français, *Bibliographie géographique international* (Paris, 1966), p. 38.

THE SKÓLHOLT MAP

This curious map of the northern regions was drafted by Sigardur Stefánsson of Iceland about 1600, when the king of Denmark was contemplating an expedition to repossess Greenland. The original is lost; this illustration is from a copy made by Thorlacius (around 1669) for his translation of Björn Jonsön (see previous page). It expresses a geographical conception which came down from the ancient world, that land surrounded the ocean instead of the ocean surrounding the land. The author was evidently familiar with the Norse sagas as published by Torfæus. Note how closely *Promontorium Winlandiae* resembles the northern cape of Newfoundland. *Frisland*, as the key suggests, comes from the Zeno book (see Chapter VII below). At the end of the manuscript there is a chronology, which, to me at least, suggests that it was read by the author of the Yale Vinland Map, who changed it a little for the Vinland inscription. The Skólholt Map has been frequently reproduced and discussed, notably in Winsor, *Narrative and Critical History*, I (1889), 130, where a translation of the Latin key will be found.

VINLAND'S LOCATION AND "VIKING REMAINS" IN NEW ENGLAND

Halldór Hermannsson, *The Problem of Wineland* (*Islandica*, XXV, Ithaca, 1936), by the curator of the Fiske Icelandic Collections at Cornell, is a triumph of scholarship added to common sense. Merritt L. Fernald in "Notes on the Plants of Wineland the Good," *Rhodora*, XII (1910), 17–38, has collected numerous instances of a fermented drink being made from berries in northern countries. Gwyn Jones, *History of the Vikings* (1968), is the sanest and most scholarly recent discussion.

There are scores of books and articles by assorted oddballs. Edward Reman gets Leif to Grand Manan and Karlsevni to Nelson River, Hudson Bay, in his *Norse Discoveries and Explorations in America* (Berkeley, 1949). Of a different and scholar-in-action category are the works of Vilhjálmur Stefansson, *The Friendly Arctic* (1921), *Ultima Thule, Further Mysteries of the Arctic* (1940), *Three Voyages of Sir Martin Frobisher* (2 vols., London, 1938), etc. Stefansson built up in imagination a vast Greenland-Vinland-European trade in white falcons and walrus ivory, which Columbus learned about on a voyage to Iceland, and which gave him his inspiration. Popes and the Latin monarchs were in a conspiracy to suppress all knowledge of this flourishing empire, according to Stefansson. Evidence

The Skólholt Map of c. 1600. From the copy in the Jónsson Ms. in the Royal Library of Copenhagen, and with their permission and the courtesy of Dr. I. R. Kejlbo.

of undernourishment in the Norse skeletons excavated in Greenland does not bother him; if they were rachitic it was because they overstuffed themselves on dainties imported from Europe!

Thomas C. Webb, secretary of the Rhode Island Historical Society and a correspondent of Carl Rafn when the latter was preparing his *Antiquitates Americanae*, picked on a stone tower at Newport, Rhode Island, to be a surviving Norse structure, and Rafn fell for it as such. Common sense might have told him that anything so conspicuous as a hilltop stone tower, had it

73

existed, would have been noted by the intelligent and well-educated explorers and founders of Rhode Island such as Verrazzano, Roger Williams, William Coddington, and John Clarke. (The English settlers did show great interest in a far less conspicuous monument, the Dighton Rock— see notes to Chapter VII.) Benedict Arnold (1615–77), governor of Rhode Island who owned the land, mentioned it twice in his will of 1677 as "My stone built wind mill" (*R. I. Colonial Records*, I, 511); and John C. Palfrey in his *History of New England*, I (1858), 58, illustrated a very similar stone windmill at Chesterton, England, near Arnold's old home. But, if you imagine that common sense will rule the approach to any of these problems, you are very wrong. As late as 1942, Philip Ainsworth Means, a competent authority on the Inca, published *Newport Tower* to prove that it was Norse; * and other books and articles have come out claiming it to have been erected by the Kensington Rune Stone boys on their way west, a Portuguese chapel erected by Miguel Corte Real around 1511, and a pre-Norse Irish colony.

Thorough excavations of the foundations and surroundings of the tower in 1948–49 by Dr. William S. Godfrey, Jr., have proved beyond any reasonable doubt that the tower was indeed built by Arnold around 1675, possibly to double as fortress against Indian attack. All artifacts turned up, including coins and pieces of mill stone and fragments of a clay tobacco pipe in the foundation, were English colonial; none by any stretch of the imagination could be called anything else. Dr. Godfrey's final report, "The Archaeology of the Old Stone Mill in Newport," is printed in *American Antiquity*, XVII (1951), 120–29, and his Harvard Ph.D. dissertation of the same year, "Digging a Tower and Laying a Ghost," contains additional details.

An alleged runic signature of Leif Ericsson with date MI was observed on a boulder lying on the beach at No Man's Land, an island off Martha's Vineyard, around 1920. It formed the basis of a book by Edward F. Gray, *Leif Eriksson Discoverer of America* (Oxford, 1930), in which it is illustrated. Opinions of runic experts were so disappointing that Mr. Gray finally concluded (p. 159) that it was carved by some later explorer such as Verrazzano or Gosnold as a "monument to Lief" (!) The inscription was thoroughly investigated by Edmund B. Delabarre and Charles W. Brown for *The New England Quarterly*, VIII (1935), 365–78. They concluded that it had been carved in the twentieth century by some joker, probably Walton Ricketson (1839–1923) of New Bedford.

A pamphlet by Olaf Strandwold, *Norse Inscriptions on American Stones* (1948), gives photos and sketches of some thirty alleged North American runic inscriptions, not one of which has been accepted as such by runic scholars. Runes being mostly straight lines, it is easy to imagine them in

---

* Herbert O. Brigham in his valuable booklet *The Old Stone Mill* (Newport Historical Society, 1955) well described (p. 27) Means's *Newport Tower* as "a curious blend of special pleading, wishful thinking and visionary writing."

glacial or other scratches on rocks; and by chalking certain lines and neglecting others you can make the stone say almost anything you like. I have examined the alleged one on Manana Island, Maine, and found no true resemblance to runes. The stone found near Yarmouth, N. S., still being played up as a tourist attraction, is described by Moses H. Nickerson and Harry Piers in Nova Scotia Historical Society *Collections*, XVII (1913), 51–58. After two amateur runologists had made utterly different translations, the inscriptions were submitted to Magnus Olsen the runic scholar and by him pronounced to be *not* runes but "a freak of nature."

A note to John G. Whittier's "The Norsemen, "first published in 1843, explains that "some three or four years since, a fragment of a statue, rudely chiseled" had been found in Bradford, Massachusetts. It was assumed to be Norse. Whittier, who lived near the opposite bank of the Merrimac, accordingly wrote "The Norsemen," imagining them sailing up that river, striking their spears against their shields and

> Keeping a harsh and fitting time
> To Saga's chant, and Runic rhyme.

The "Bradford statue," of course, turned out to be English colonial.

Frederick J. Pohl, *The Lost Discovery* (New York, 1952), centers the drama on Cape Cod and Mount Desert Island, Maine, on the basis of "mooring holes" in the rocks. These were made by the English natives of New England to receive iron eye-bolts through which to reeve a line to a boat mooring or fish trap. I could have shown him some made for me! It is true that Scandinavians then, as now, liked to moor fore and aft, both to an anchor and to a ring-bolt or tree ashore. But in New England there were plenty of stout trees near shore, and no need to drill holes in granite rocks.

Justin Winsor, who reviewed all hoaxes and "finds" up to 1889 in his *Narrative and Critical History*, I, chap. ii, felt impelled to remark of Rasmus B. Anderson, *America Not Discovered by Columbus* (Chicago, 1883), "The author is, we believe, a Scandinavian, and shows the tendency of his race to a facility rather than felicity in accepting evidence on this subject" (p. 97).

Tryggvi J. Oleson, *Early Voyages and Northern Approaches* (1964), is amusingly sarcastic about the Kensington Rune Stone, the Newport Tower, and all that; but he has an odd theory that the Greenlanders in Vinland never encountered an Indian or an Eskimo; their *Skrellings* were four-foot pygmies who were the bearers of the Dorset (pre-Columbian) Eskimo culture, lived in caves and tunnels, and were exterminated. He even identifies these Nibelungs with the slag-hurling gnomes of the *Navigatio S. Brendani!*

KENSINGTON, BEARDMORE, AND HEAVENER

In 1898 a Swedish-born farmer named Olaf Ohman about three miles from Kensington in Douglas County, Minnesota, an area almost exclusively inhabited by Scandinavians, is alleged to have found a stone weighing about 200 pounds enlaced by the roots of an aspen tree that he was grubbing up. Then or later (the matter is disputed) he noticed that the stone bore a runic inscription in a sort of Swedish jargon, and when sketched in a local newspaper it was translated by three local residents as: "8 Goths [Swedes] and 22 Norwegians on a voyage of discovery from Vinland westward. We had our camp by 2 skerries [rocky islets] one day's journey north of this stone. We were out fishing one day. When we came home we found 10 men red with blood and dead. AVM save us from evil. We have 10 men by the sea to look after our ships, 14 days' journey from their island. Year 1362."

Common sense should have dismissed this as a hoax. If you dig up a "Greek vase" resting on a telephone book, it is a waste of time to try to prove the vase genuine. The Kensington story is preposterous. Norsemen were sea discoverers, not land explorers; what possible object could they have had in sailing into Hudson Bay, or through Lake Superior to the Portage, and striking out into the wilderness? Common sense did consider the stone as a joke until 1908 when it was taken up by a Wisconsin cherry farmer named Hjalmar R. Holand, who for over half a century has been attempting to prove the inscription authentic. The controversy shows no sign of abating after creating a bibliography of hundreds of items. Holand took the stone to the Norse Millenary Congress at Rouen in 1911, hoping for support from the assembled Scandinavian scholars, and got none.* Every leading runologist of Scandinavia and Germany who has deigned to examine the inscription has called it a clumsy forgery.** One word alone, *opdagelsefard* (voyage of discovery), which did not occur in any Scandinavian language for several centuries after 1362, gives it away. As Professor Gösta Franzan of Chicago wrote in a review in *The Library Quarterly* for April 1959, almost any one of fifty flaws "would be sufficient to classify the inscription as a fake."

Erik Moltke, "The Ghost of the Kensington Stone," *Scandinavian Studies*, XXV (1953), 1–14, Professor Erik Wahlgren, *The Kensington Stone, a Mystery Solved* (Madison, 1958), and Theodore C. Blegen, *The Kensington Rune Stone: New Light on an Old Riddle* (Minnesota Historical Society, 1968), should put the whole thing to rest. Moltke's article is a devastating analysis of the inscription by an expert runologist; he calls it (p. 9) "a childish fraud . . . made by a farmer who lacked the most elementary knowledge of medieval Scandinavian." "Never has a spurious document

---

* The late Charles H. Haskins, who attended, told me that an even cursory examination of the inscription with a reading glass showed that it had been cut recently, and that the experts from Scandinavia without exception regarded it as an American hoax.

** These include Ludvig F. A. Wimmer, Sophus Bugge, Otto von Friesen, Magnus Olsen, Elias Wessén, Sven B. F. Jansson, Wolfgang Krause, Adolf and Erik Noreen, and Erik Moltke, Director of the National Museum at Copenhagen.

stood on such feeble ground and given such striking proofs of its falsity" (p. 14).* Wahlgren points out that all school children in Norway and Sweden in the period 1870–1900 learned runes as part of their cultural education; the schoolteachers, hundreds of whom emigrated to the American Northwest, taught runes and, just as American and English schoolboys a century ago liked to write their names or messages in Greek letters, so Scandinavian schoolboys found it amusing to write short notes, inscriptions, etc. in runes. Blegen points the finger of suspicion at one Sven Fogelblad (1829–97), brought up in a Swedish area rich in runic inscriptions, a graduate of Upsala, co-minister in Sweden with a noted runologist who wrote a popular book on runes. He emigrated to Minnesota and taught school; he was well known as a joker, and an intimate friend of Ohman's. It is probable that he wrote the inscription (it contains Ohman's name—*Oh* for island and *man* for near, both anachronisms); and that Ohman carved it and buried it as well as dug it up.

Nevertheless, Holand cheerfully went on writing books and articles about it, the latest being *A Pre-Columbian Crusade to America* (New York, 1962). This one is really supernatural; the stone, he says, was carved by an expedition under Paul Knutson which first wintered in Newport and built the stone tower, then explored the coast northerly, entered Hudson Bay, tramped thence to central Minnesota, and after carving this inscription fell in with the Mandan Indians and became rivals to Prince Madoc's Welshmen (see Chapter IV) in converting them. Adopting Pohl's "mooring holes" theory, Holand finds these aids to navigation on the rocky banks of Minnesota rivers. He even takes on board the mysterious Nicholas of Lynn, who stays at Hudson Bay with that section of the party, makes plenty of observations with his astrolabe, and returns home to write that elusive ghost book *Inventio Fortunatae* and present it to Edward III of England.** A "Runestone Memorial Park," with a mammoth reproduction of the Kensington stone, has been established at the nearest county seat, Alexandria, Minnesota.

Supporting the Kensington fake were bogus "Norse halberds" and "Early Scandinavian Battle-Axes" unearthed in various parts of Minnesota. The halberds turned out to be tobacco cutters manufactured by the Rogers Iron Company of Springfield, Ohio, and the battle-axes were premiums given to collectors of labels from Battle-Axe Plug, a popular chewing tobacco around the turn of the century. Even more "convincing" were the "Beardmore Relics." These were a sword, an axe, and another object of undoubted Scandinavian antiquity alleged to have been blown out of the soil at Beardmore near Lake Nipigon, Ontario, in 1931 by a man prospect-

---

* Dr. Moltke, had earlier raked the inscription fore-and-aft in *Antiquity* No. 98 (June 1951), reprinted in the Bulletin of the Mass. Archaeological Society, XIII (1952), 33–37.
** See notes to Day's Letter in appendix to Chapter VI below, and T. J. Oleson, *Early Voyages*, pp. 105–8.

ing for gold. Although no human remains accompanied them, it was assumed that these "relics" belonged to one of the Kensington heroes who died on the long tramp home. They were purchased in 1936 by the Royal Ontario Museum of the University of Toronto, which has issued a booklet by A. D. Tushingham, *The Beardmore Relics, Hoax or History?* (Toronto, 1966). The alleged discoverer was found to have been a friend or neighbor to a collector of Norse antiquities, and his stepson and others deposed that they had seen the "relics" in his cellar before their alleged unearthing.

To the bibliography in Wahlgren (215–22), add a lengthy review of his book by Lawrence D. Steefel in *The Minnesota Archaeologist*, XXVII (1965), No. 3, organ of the Minnesota Archaeological Society. This society, which originally backed Holand, now gives the Stone a place in history with other famous hoaxes such as the Cardiff Giant and the Piltdown Man.

Nevertheless, there will always be people who believe that the Vikings tramped all over North America, shedding implements, battle-axes, and runic inscriptions. The situation now is similar to that in New England around 1837, only the modern "finds" are all thousands of miles inland. Latest addition to this collection of fakes and phonies is the alleged runic inscription at Heavener in the Poteau Mountains of southwestern Oklahoma. This, in so-called Futhauk runes which went out of use before A.D. 800, is rendered in Roman letters as GNOMENDAL, obviously the first initial and surname of an educated Scandinavian pioneer in this region who childishly carved his name in runes. The Heavener inscription, first publicized by Frederick Pohl in *Atlantic Crossings Before Columbus* (1961), has been described in the New England Antiquities Research Association mimeographed *News Letter*, III, No. 3 (September 1968), whose promoter Mr. Robert E. Stone of Derry, New Hampshire, defends all these shadowy footprints on the sands of time. He states that no fewer than fifty runic inscriptions "are claimed to exist in eastern Oklahoma," of which one "unmistakably reads AOIEALW." In 1967 there appeared *Cryptology in Norse Medieval Inscriptions* by Ole G. Landsverk and Alf Monge, who claim to have discovered a secret rune code that enables one to date anything. That for the Heavener inscription is 11 November 1012! Hence this ditty:—

OKLAHOMA!

Newport Tower—fade away!
Kensington—you've had your day;
The Vikings are all over Oklahoma!
Skoal! to Mr. Gnomendal,
Skoal! to Mr. Aoiealw!
Sooner than the Sooners,
Boomier than the Boomers,
They've proved we're real antiques in Oklahoma!

A Uniped and another monster. From Olaus Magnus. Courtesy Harvard
College Library.

Oklahoma (in case you didn't know it)
Means West Viking Land.
Futhauk runes are scattered all over,
All archaeologists are in clover.
Vikings prior to 800 A.D.
Staked their claims for posterity
In the Poteau Mountain Range of Oklahoma!

Local Heavener people, who have been studying the inscriptions for
twenty years, are waging a campaign to have them recognized as genuine,
according to a dispatch in the *Boston Evening Globe* of 5 November 1969.

MONSTERS, MARVELS, AND ACKNOWLEDGMENTS

Fridtjof Nansen, *In Northern Mists*, I: 189, II: 11, 263; Olaus Magnus, *Historia de Gentibus Septentrionalibus* (1555). The same Uniped picture appears in an early edition of *The Voiage and Trauaile of Syr John Maunde-
ville* (1568, and Oxford, 1932, facsimile ed.). For Sir John, the greatest
faker of the fourteenth century, see Zoltán Haraszti in Boston Public Library *Quarterly*, II (October 1950), 306–16. Adolf Rieth, *Archaeological
Fakes* (Imber trans., New York, 1970), tells of European false runic inscriptions and other famous phonies, one of which, the "turkey frieze" in
Schleswig Cathedral, pertains to America.

Many scholars, starting with my Harvard colleague Professor Einar
Haugen, have helped me with this subject. At Copenhagen, thanks to the
arrangements made by Captain Harold E. Rice USN at the American

Embassy, I had the opportunity to consult Drs. Tue Gad, Erik Moltke, Helge Larsen, and Jón Helgason.

As a fitting conclusion to this chapter, the parting words to me in Copenhagen by Dr. Helgason were, "Remember, Morison, that Icelanders are the greatest liars in history—except the Irish!"

✻ IV ✻

Flyaway Islands and False Voyages

1100-1492

The Background and the Problem

From regrettably few facts on the Norsemen we come to fancies, and plenty of them. Between the twelfth-century blackout of America, and the curtain-raising by Columbus in 1492, there are at least ten so-called pre-Columbian voyages of discovery that never took place; and on the maps, dozen of islands that were never seen. Some of the voyages did start, but never reached America; others are purely fictitious. What Henry Harrisse called "l'amour-propre national; la plaie des études historiques," is the origin of many; pure imagination accounts for the rest.

The great Alexander von Humboldt cynically remarked, "There are three stages in the popular attitude toward a great discovery: first, men doubt its existence, next they deny its importance, and finally they give the credit to someone else."

Columbus's discovery ran this gamut very quickly. No sooner was it certain that he had opened to Europe a brave new world, than rival claimants appeared. The French savant Guillaume Postel in mid-sixteenth century declared that the ancient Gauls had been in America before the Christian era but abandoned it because they disliked vast distances, uncultivated land, and the absence of towns! Oviedo, in his *Historia General y Natural de las Indias* which appeared in 1535, staked out a similar claim for the Visigothic kings of Spain—a claim very agreeable to their sixteenth-century successors as it eased royal consciences over the shabby treatment of Columbus. The Portuguese quickly asserted priority, largely on the ground that they, being the best navigators of the fifteenth century, *must* have discovered America first; and England was not far behind, with the mythical voyage of the Welsh prince Madoc. Venice, left by the great discovery a lovely but slightly down-at-heel queen of the Adriatic, invented a voyage of the brothers Zeno, to which a legendary Scots earl became attached. Finally, just in time to get under the wire as pre-Columbian, came Pining and Pothorst, two jolly pirates whose visit to Greenland has been pre-dated and prolonged in order to accommodate, in the same boat, João Vaz Corte Real and Johannes Scolvus, respectively the Portuguese and Polish candidates for Discoverer of America. These do not exhaust the list, but include most who still have a following. Curiously enough, no Scandinavian put in a claim for Biarni or Leif Ericsson until Columbus had been dead two hundred years. The Northmen by A.D. 1200 had lost not only their interest in overseas lands, but the restlessness which took them there.

Closely allied to these phony voyages are the alleged secret ones. It is a favorite theory of recent Portuguese historians that before any recorded voyage of discovery there was a secret Portuguese one that really found the spot. By this ingenious argument the absence of evidence becomes evidence; the kings of Portugal concealed all reports of early discoveries, fearful lest someone else benefit, and hid them so long that Spain, France, and England did benefit. It is assumed that North and South America, the West Indies, the Arctic, the Antarctic, the Moluccas, and the Philippines were discovered by Portugal, or by a Portuguese. And the Moluccas and the Philippines actually were.

Many non-existent Atlantic islands are depicted on medieval and renaissance maps. Several library navigators of this century insist that every mapped island must represent a real one. The contrary is true. "They that go down to the sea in ships, that do business in great waters," know by experience how easy it is to mistake a cloud-bank for an island, especially at sunset when clouds mass on the western horizon. Columbus had one such experience on his outward passage in 1492; the island looked so solid that Captain Pinzón claimed the reward for sighting land, and all hands sang the *Gloria;* but after sailing all night toward the supposed land, they found nothing but water. The same phenomenon frequently occurs nowadays. How often, sailing off shore, has not someone said, "Look! What land is that?" only to be told there is no land there. In the official *Notices to Mariners* one reads how the master of a certain ship reported a shoal spot or a breaking reef at such-and-such latitude and longitude, where the ocean's depth is really several hundred or thousand fathom. The skipper may have seen a spot on the ocean whipped to a white froth by a sudden squall, or by a school of big fish, or there was something wrong with his lead line, or his head; but the Hydrographic Office feels obliged to report the supposed danger to navigators, and even to enter it on charts, just in case it was correct. How much more likely, then, that false islands would be frequently reported in an age when the great ocean was an object of endless wonder and mystery! Sailors had a name for these disappearing bodies of land—"Flyaway Islands."

We must also consider the habits of map-makers. They have always disliked open spaces. In the Middle Ages they peopled unknown interiors with storied cities and Oriental potentates, and peppered the Atlantic with imaginary islands. Once an island became mapped, it took centuries to get it off, since map-makers copied one another—and, after all, the island *might* exist. If some mariner reported a new position for a mythical island, the next map, without apology, would depict two of the same name at different places. After this position had been sailed over again and again and no land appeared, the next map-maker would cheerfully move it to another spot. On a mid-fifteenth-century map in the Library of St. Mark's, Venice, there are no fewer than four Brasil Islands. St. Brendan's group is placed on early maps all the way from Iceland to the Gulf of Guinea, or mixed up with the Azores or the Canaries, or right across to Newfoundland, where there is a St. Brendan's Isle today.

João de Lisboa's *Livro de Marinharia* of the sixteenth century, first printed in 1903, has a chapter devoted to directions from known points to "islands *not* discovered." Even the great Mercator was a glutton for imaginary islands; his World Map of 1569 has at least ten, five appearing there for the first time. Nor did this fakery end with the age of discovery. Frobisher's fleet provided a new one, the "Island of Buss" which stayed on the map for two centuries. Cary's *New Terrestrial Globe* "with Additions to 1840" spots at least five non-existent rocks in the Atlantic "seen between 1773 and 1805"; and in the Pacific, due north of Oahu, a big mythical isle named *Maria Lejara*, "discovered by the ship *Hercules* 1781, well inhabited." *Verde, Maida,* and *Brasil* were not removed from official charts until mid-nineteenth century.

Nevertheless, certain academic geographers will have it that there must be something solid behind these shifting whimsies of the map-makers. William H. Babcock in his *Legendary Islands of the Atlantic* gives a useful list of these elusive bits of real estate, but insists that each one represents some reality—an unrecorded discovery of Bermuda, Bahamas, Newfoundland, or the Greater Antilles. The late Professor E. G. R. Taylor wrote that to her it "seemed out of the question that a cartographical establishment employing skilled craftsmen and carrying on the business of supplying seamen's charts, would insert imaginary islands on these maps." Miss Taylor apparently envisaged the makers of medieval and sixteenth-century maps as having an establishment like Messrs. Bartholomew. Actually, these charts were made by individual cartographers with perhaps a couple of helpers and an errand boy. They had no coast-guard or airplane from which to check, and were eager not to miss anything. If a map-maker compiled a "portolan," a practical chart for mariners, like the Pizzi of 1424, he could not risk a customer's being shipwrecked by leaving any possible obstacle un-charted. If he were preparing an ornamental mappemonde for some great lord, his princely patron would think he was not getting his money's worth if the Atlantic Ocean were left blank. There is a lot of truth in Berry's cartoon of a monk working on a map in the scrip-torum, saying to one of the brothers, "I think I'll throw in a couple of extra islands just for laughs!"

Prince Madoc and the Welsh Indians

The most popular, persistent, and pervasive of these post-Columbian stories of pre-Columbian voyages is that of the Prince of Wales who brought a Cymric colony to America in the twelfth century. By some mysterious process this colony became a Welsh-speaking Indian tribe which moved west from the Atlantic shore until it became the Mandan in the Far West. John Dee added this tale to his map of the 1580's in order to support England's title to North America; numerous travelers for three centuries have sought out the Welsh Indians and compiled impressive (though phony) parallel vocabularies of several different Indian languages with Welsh. By force of mere repetition it even got into American school histories.* The Daughters of the American Revolution embalmed the story in bronze by erecting on Fort Morgan, Mobile Bay, a tablet inscribed "In memory of Prince Madoc, a Welsh explorer, who landed on the shores of Mobile Bay in 1170 and left behind, with the Indians, the Welsh language."

The full story, which first appeared in print in 1583, relates that civil war broke out upon the death of Owen Gwyneth, king of North Wales. Owen's son Madoc, "a man bred to the sea," eager to get away from it all, resolved to lead a colony of his presumably dovish countrymen to a place where they could start life afresh. He sailed west in 1170, found a suitable spot, left there 120 colonists, returned to Wales, fitted out an expedition of ten ships filled with men and women, and passed out of view.

This is the core of a fable that, despite all proofs that it is not and could not be true, would be elaborated and believed wherever there is a Welshman or two. As Bernard De Voto well observed, the insubstantial world of fairies and folklore is as real as the visible world to Celtic peoples; and for this "old and haughty nation, proud in arms," the exploits of Madoc were a partial compensation for her conquest by the Anglo-Saxon. After a Welsh family named Tudor had secured the throne of England, court historians were eager to substantiate Madoc's voyage in order to claim British priority over Spain in the New World. Hakluyt printed the story in his *Voyages* (1589), and anticipated Southey in getting the Welshman to Mexico. Sir Humfry Gilbert even identified Madoc with Quetzalcoatl!

The Welsh-speaking Indian part developed a century later. The Reverend Morgan Jones, traveling through the Carolinas in 1669, fell in with a Tuscaroran tribe called the Doeg, who understood his native Cymric, and among them he happily lived for months, preaching the Gospel in Welsh; so he asserted in a tract written in 1686. There are several eighteenth-century travelers' tales to the same effect, only it is always a different Indian tribe which speaks Welsh, exhibits a relatively

* It was in my first history textbook, about 1895; and I well remember teacher saying with a smile, "Oh yes! the Mandan Indians still speak a kind of Welsh!"

fair complexion, and cherishes Welsh relics such as a printed Bible in that language. The Shawnee, Delaware, Conestoga, and Comanche, and at least nine other actual tribes, in addition to eight imaginary ones, have at one time or another been designated as the pale-complexioned, blue-eyed, Welsh-speaking Indians. Eventually the Mandan became the most favored tribe. They built little hide-covered wicker boats like the Welsh coracles and Irish curraghs; their beautiful and lascivious women babbled when being embraced (as Welsh girls were said to do), and they spoke a language of Welsh origin.

Welsh literati were so deeply stirred by these stories, that a respectable London literary society appointed a twenty-two-year-old Welsh clergyman named John Evans to search for Madoc's descendants and reconvert them to Christianity. Evans, after an adventurous journey, followed the rumor trail to the Rockies, and in 1795 or 1796 reached the country of the Mandan and spent a winter with them in what is now North Dakota. As a result of that experience he honestly reported to one of his London supporters that he had met no Welsh-speaking Indians "and from the intercourse I have had with Indians from latitude 35° to 49° I think you may with safety inform my friends that they have no existence."

Evans's report, and Lewis and Clark's statement that they had found no Welsh traces among the Mandan, should have spiked the venerable myth; but of course they did not—too much racial emotion had been aroused. The legend reached full flower in Robert Southey's epic poem *Madoc*, at which he worked intermittently for seven years, and finally published in 1805. The twenty-seven cantos occupy 148 double columns of fine print in the Paris, 1845 edition of Southey's complete works, together with sixty-nine columns of notes. Probably nobody but patriotic Welshmen has read it for fifty years, but Southey's *Madoc* is the sort of thing that the English-reading public relished in the Romantic era. Madoc in Southey's version does not stop at planting a Welsh colony in North America; he and nephew Llewelyn sail a fleet into the Gulf of Mexico and intervene in Aztec politics, with allies and enemies named Aztlan, Tlalala, and Zezozomoc. In conclusion

Madoc was left sole Lord; and far away
Yuhidthiton led forth the Aztecas,
To spread in other lands Mexitli's name,

And rear a mightier empire, and set up
Again their foul idolatry; till Heaven,
Making blind Zeal and Bloody Avarice
Its ministers of vengeance, sent among them
The heroic Spaniard's unrelenting sword.

In vain did the Welsh historian Thomas Stephens (*Literature of the Kymry*, London, 1849) point out that Welsh annals mention no such person as Madoc. In vain did the Mandan repudiate their supposedly distinguished ancestry; the legend went on and on, gathering trimmings. Madoc preceded Ponce de Leon at Bimini; you can retrace his steps inland from Mobile Bay (scene of the D.A.R. tribute) by prehistoric earthworks; he and his Welshmen were the original Mound Builders of Illinois; they constructed a series of forts around Chattanooga, one on Lookout Mountain; Antilia was Madoc's Atlantic stopover, and the strange names of its Seven Cities are Welsh. To such extravagant fancies there is no end. Madoc even has his phony monument; the press in 1966 or 1967 reported the discovery of a twelfth-century portrait of him carved on a rock near Old Oraibi, Arizona, identified as Madoc's by the three Princes of Wales feathers on his helmet (which date only from 1346) and an inscription in the "ancient Celtic Akadian Coptic alphabet," in which the letters D O K are visible.

We may dismiss the Welsh Indians myth with the authoritative words of the Bureau of American Ethnology: "There is not a provable trace of Welsh, Gaelic or any other European language in any native American language."

The Zeno Brothers and "Zichmni"

In 1558 there was printed in Venice a handsome little book entitled, in translation, *Discovery of the Islands Frislanda, . . . Estotilanda, & Icaria by two Zeni brothers, Nicolò and Antonio.* These Venetian brothers, shipwrecked in 1380 on the island of Frislanda, there met an ancient fisherman, a regular Sinbad. Twenty-six years earlier he had been blown west to an island named Estotiland, where the people read Latin; next he visited a "place called Drogeo," whence he was chased off by cannibals, and finally a third region, replete with towns and temples. At Frislanda the brothers met the local prince, yclept Zichmni, who became so interested that he sailed with them to these odd localities, especially Estotiland, "exploring the whole of the coast with great diligence." The Zeni conveyed this story, with a map, to a third brother in Venice; the manuscript rested in the family muniments until 1558, when a descendant decided to make a printed book of it. Patriotic Venetians received the book with delight; whilst the islands pleased map-makers by providing something new to depict on their maps. Estotiland is usually shown as an island bigger than Newfoundland, blocking the northern passage to the New World.

An ingenious German named Johann R. Forster, in a book published in 1786, identified the mysterious Zichmni as Henry Sinclair, Earl of Orkney and Caithness, who happened to be in the Faroes ("Frislanda" of the narrative) when the Zeni called, and saved the Venetians from being murdered by the natives. Henry Sinclair of the Roslin house of that name was an actual person; but his biography, although dim, is well enough known to prove that he could never have been Zichmni. To many minds, however, this Scots addition to the brew made it more palatable. Zichmni has more probably been identified as the Venetian

The original Zeno Brothers' Map. From their *Scoprimento* (1558). Estland, Frisland, Icaria, Estotiland, and Drogeo are imaginary. Courtesy Harvard College Library.

pronunciation of Wichmann, a Baltic pirate who was killed in 1401 after a lifetime of depredation; and it has been suggested that the Zeno boys might have gone a-pirating with him when they pretended to be exploring. This hint comes from Frederick W. Lucas who, in a volume published in 1898, raked the Zeno-Zichmni craft fore and aft with historical and geographical facts, reducing the story to shreds as far as reputable history is concerned.

Nevertheless, the story has perennial fascination. Professor William H. Hobbs of the University of Michigan and Frederick J. Pohl, the Norse mooring-holes man, have taken it up again. They locate the Zeni's "great mountains which cast forth smoke" in Nova Scotia—not otherwise known as a volcanic region. They have identified Zichmni as Glooscap, legendary hero of the Micmac tribe. William B. Goodwin, paladin of lost causes, even found the likeness of Earl Sinclair on a rock in Westford, Massachusetts, previously called "The Indian Rock." Where others only see a pecked-out outline of an eighteenth-century tomahawk, Goodwin and Pohl find the portrait of a knight in armor, carrying a shield, pronounced to bear the arms of the Sinclairs!

Pining, Pothorst, and Scolvus

The first two members of this trio made their bow to history on a map of Iceland by Hieronymus Gourmont, printed at Paris in 1548, and the story was repeated by Olaus Magnus in his *History of the Northern Peoples* (1555), on the page here reproduced. It tells us that two "notorious pirates" Pining and Pothorst, having been outlawed from all northern kingdoms for their atrocious robberies, located in 1494 on a rocky island called Hvitsark, halfway between Iceland and Greenland, and for some obscurely wicked purpose carved on it a crude mariner's compass. They were finally captured and hanged.

Although these gentry may have come to a bad end, they had been respectable *sceppere* (task force commanders) under Christian I of Denmark. Didrik Pining, sometimes described as a Norwegian nobleman, sometimes as a German in the Danish service, served for a time as governor of part of Iceland. He and Pothorst are mentioned by an early Danish historian, among those pirates who "met with a miserable death by drowning, or on the gallows, or at the hands of friends."

The third member of this alleged partnership, known to contempo-

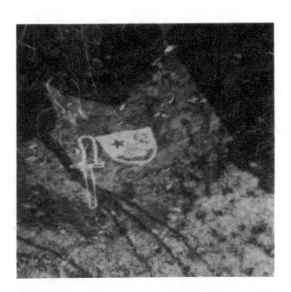

Earl Sinclair—"Zichmni" in Massachusetts. The "Indian Rock" at Westford.
Photo by Antha E. Card, October 1968.

•

raries as Johannes Scolvus or Skolp, and to his recent Polish-American
admirers as Jan of Kolno, was introduced to the general public by the
Dutch geographer Wytfliet in 1597. After describing the voyage of the
Zeno brothers, the Dutchman stated that the honor of a "second discovery" of America "fell to *Johannes Scolvus Polonus*, who in the year
1476 . . . sailed beyond Norway, Greenland, Frisland, penetrated the
Northern Strait under the very Arctic Circle, and arrived at the country of Labrador and Estotiland."

Earlier than Wytfliet, an English document of 1575, apparently
drawn up in preparation for Frobisher's voyage, states, "In the north
side of this passage"—the Northwest Passage—"*John Scolus*, a pilot of
Denmarke, was in anno 1476." Lok's Map of 1582, following Frobisher's
voyage, has a country northwest of Greenland on which is written
Jac. Scolvus Groetland. Even earlier, Francisco López de Gómara in
his *Historia de las Indias y conquesta de Mexico* (Seville, 1553) says of
"la Tierra de Labrador" (i.e. Greenland), "Hither also came men from
Norway with the pilot *Joan Scolvo* and Englishmen with Sebastian
Cabot." And on the Gemma Frisius or Zerbst globe of *c.* 1537, on the
north coast of a northwest passage to Asia, are inscribed two legends:

De Pygmæis Gruntlandiæ, & rupe Huitfark.

CAP. XI.

Huitfark.

Piratę Pining, & Pothorſt.

Vitelliani,de q̃ bus Albertus Crantzius in Vandalia. Kniphoff. Compaſſus.

Pygmæi,ſeu nani.

VPRADICTO capite proximo parumper de excelſa rupe Huitfark medio maris tractu inter Islandiã,& Grunt/ landiam ſita, dictum videtur : nec tædet eam repetere per amplius explanandam. In ea etenim circa annos Domini M. CCCC. XCIIII. duo inſigniores piratæ,Pining, & Pothorſt,ab omni humano conſortio,Aglonarium Re/ gum ſeueriſsimo edicto ob atrociſsima latrocinia , quaſi in deſpectum, & contemptum omnium regnorum , & arma/ torum, cum complicibus ſuis piratis proſcripti habitabãt, multaꝙ crudelia facta in quoſcunꝙ ſiue prope , ſiue à longe nauigantes , commit/ tebant : vti & alio tempore priore Vitelliani plures , & inſigniores piratæ (ſic di/ cti) magna facinora egerunt,& ad vltimum communibus omnium regnorum Aqui/ lonarium armis è viuis ſunt ſublati. Ita & quidam Kniphoff anno M. D. XXV. per Hamburgenſes cũ LXX. cõplicibus è potẽtiſsima naue Galion dicta,extractis, ſupplicio capitis , & rotæ ſuſpenſione ſunt puniti . In huius altiſsimæ rupis ſu/ percilio compaſſus circulis,& lineis plumbeis ſatis ampla rotunditate,opera prædi/ ctorum Pining , & Pothorſt,formatus eſt : quo meta compendioſior latrocinari vo/ lentibus data eſt , vt ſciant,quorſum opulentiores deprædatione extendi poſsint .

Videntur præterea in ſuperiori tabula duo diſparis quantitatis homines bellatores : quorum puſillioris ſtaturæ homunculus intrepi/ dè cum maiori obiiciens , triumphator exultat .
Non enim minori animo in omnem ca/
ſum maioribus ſe obiicit ,
quàm ſi gigantea
poten
tia
gloriari , & præualere poſſet .

Iterum

Page from Olaus Magnus. Head of chapter in Olaus Magnus, *De Gentibus Septentrionalibus* (1555), "Concerning the Pygmies of Greenland and the Rock Hvitsark." The cut shows a Greenlander fighting a Skrelling, a saint in the background giving encouragement, and Hvitsark with its stone compass. Courtesy Harvard College Library.

(1) *Fretum trium fratrum, per quod Lusitani ad Orientem et ad Indos et ad Moluccas navigare conati sunt* (Strait of the Three Brothers, through which Portuguese attempted to sail to the Orient and the Indies and the Moluccas), and (2) *Quij populi ad quos Johannes Scolvus Danus pervenit circa Annum 1476*—"These are the people reached by John Scolvus a Dane about the year 1476." The same *quii populi* legend appears on a bulge of western Greenland on the Rouen (Lecuy) globe of the second half of the sixteenth century. As a sample of the precious nonsense indulged in by recent historians, the words *quii populi*, which are simply bad Latin for "these people," have been exalted to mean a tribe of white Eskimo named Quii. The late Eva Taylor even claimed that it meant "Lequii, Lequio or Lu-Chu," i.e. Okinawa!

Thus we have two distinct stories: Pining and Pothorst having fun off eastern Greenland in 1494, and Scolvus-Skolp sailing to the "Northern Strait" in 1476. The document that made shipmates of the pirate pair and the Pole, along with other distinguished passengers, is a letter of Carsten Grip, burgomaster of Kiel, to King Christian III of Denmark in 1551. Grip, it seems, had been ordered by the king, when on a southern trip, to collect valuable books, maps, and paintings for the royal library. He wrote that there had just been published in Paris a new map of Iceland, on which "it is remarked that Iceland is twice the size of Sicily, and that the two *sceppere, Pyningk* and *Poidthorst* who were sent out by your majesty's royal grandfather King Christian I, at the request of his Majesty of Portugal, with certain [or several] ships to explore new countries and islands in the north, have raised on the rock Hvitsark . . . a great sea-mark on account of the Greenland pirates, who with many small ships without keels fall in large numbers upon other ships."

This is the text which enables certain writers, by heaping inference on inference, to make the two post-Columbian pirates respectable pre-Columbian discoverers, with Scolvus as pilot, and a pair of distinguished Portuguese passengers. The Greenland Eskimo now become the pirates.

The man who arranged this happy union was Dr. Sofus Larsen, a librarian of Copenhagen. His book (published in 1925) has become the Bible of the Pining-Pothorst-Scolvus aficionados. Larsen points out that D. Afonso V of Portugal and Christian I of Denmark (d. 1481) were cousins and correspondents—royal pen pals, as it were. What more natural than that D. Afonso, absorbed in pushing Portuguese ships further south along Africa, should ask Christian to "take over" northern exploration? (Unusually generous for that era, I would say.) Larsen boldly combines what were once considered three separate and unrelated voyages, the Pining-Pothorst location off Greenland in 1494, that of Scolvus to the Northern Strait in 1476, and the discovery of Newfoundland by João Vaz Corte Real in 1472. To put three bogus voyages "all in the same boat" seems to convince many people that they really happened; as if three zeros added made one.

The alleged Corte Real discovery is based on a statement in the *Saudades da Terra* (Souvenirs of the Land) by Gaspar Frutuoso (born 1522), a notoriously unreliable collector of gossip. It was repeated, pushing back the date ten years, in the *História Insulana* (1717) of António Cordeiro, a more respectable Portuguese historian. The story was carefully examined by Ernesto do Canto and by Henry Harrisse in their biographies of the Corte Reals, by the one suspected and by the other overwhelmed with such a weight of evidence that one would suppose it could never have revived.

Nevertheless it was revived by Sofus Larsen and by recent Portuguese historians, who are now bringing up schoolboys to believe that João Vaz Corte Real was the *real* discoverer of America. It is even so stated in mosaic on the Avenida do Liberdade, Lisbon. According to Larsen, João Vaz went on a royal expedition of discovery commanded by Pining and Pothorst, with Scolvus as pilot, and with Diogo Homem (deputy vice-governor of Terceira) as another distinguished guest, courtesy king of Portugal. This happy international expedition took place in 1472.

What can we salvage for sober history from this hodge-podge? First, that Pining and Pothorst varied their piratical activities with a voyage to eastern Greenland at some time prior to 1494, when they carved a mariner's compass on the rock *Hvitsark*, which does not exist, either on an island or on the Greenland coast. Why the king of Portugal should have instigated so trifling an enterprise is left to our imagination. Second, that a Dane or Pole named Skolp or Scolvus made a northern voyage under Danish auspices in 1476, and was reported on certain maps and globes a century later to have found the Northwest Passage long before Frobisher even looked for it. There is absolutely nothing to associate Scolvus-Skolp with the two P's except the circumstance of their names appearing on the same sixteenth-century globe. Whilst there is no reason to believe that the pirate pair discovered anything, it is possible that Scolvus sailed around Cape Farewell, Greenland, and looked into Davis Strait.

Nothing, absolutely nothing, is known about Scolvus-Skolp except what is here repeated. He has never been identified. His name may mean that he came from Kolno or Kovno; but the Danes claim that his being described as *Polonus* on the globe was merely a mistake for *Pilatus* (pilot). Polish-Americans, insisting that his real name was Jan of Kolno, have adopted this man of mystery as a folk hero, a rival to Columbus and Leif Ericsson. Fancy portraits of Jan discovering America are presented to state capitals by Polish groups, and congressmen representing Polish-American districts agitate for a Jan of Kolno day.

Highly unpalatable to these worthy patriots is the thesis of a distinguished Peruvian historian, Luís Ulloa. After "proving" that the name Cristobal Colón was the alias of a Catalan rebel named Joan Baptista Colom, Ulloa transforms him into Scolvus by ellipsis. Both Danes and Catalans place a sibilant "s" before a hard "c," so Joan Colom becomes Johannes Scolom or Scolvus. And as Christopher Columbus is known to have made a northern voyage in 1477, this was it!

The Discovery of the Azores

After these foolish fancies, it is a relief to return to cold facts. Portugal in the early fifteenth century became *the* Atlantic sea power. The Portuguese acquired the cosmic restlessness that the Scandinavians had lost. Their Infante D. Henrique, known in English-speaking lands as Prince Henry the Navigator, established around 1420 a center for exploration and hydrography at Sagres on Cape St. Vincent. There he made fruitful efforts to improve maritime technique, and sent forth captains who extended the bounds of the world known to Europeans. Gil Eanes rounded Cape Bojador in 1434, and Antão Gonçalves brought home the first cargo of gold and slaves from West Africa in 1441. From that time forth the Portuguese mariners, with remarkable skill, enterprise, and courage, continued their progress along the west coast. They developed a fast, seagoing, lateen-rigged vessel called the caravel, which could sail up to five points on the wind, and they learned to find latitude with astrolabe or primitive quadrant, which enabled them to return to an overseas spot once its latitude was ascertained. They discovered the Madeira group as early as 1419; the Canaries had been known since classical days.

Although Prince Henry and his royal successors (Afonso V and João II) were primarily interested in African exploration and the eastern sea route to the Indies, they did not ignore the Western Ocean. On one of the Catalan charts collected by the Infante, he saw depicted the Isles of St. Brendan a few hundred miles off the Strait of Gibraltar, and in 1431 he sent one Gonçalo Velho Cabral to locate them. Velho sailed well to the westward of where the Brendan chain was supposed to be, and discovered the Formigas rocks which break the ocean into a hissing froth some twenty-five miles east of the nearest island of the Azores. The following year he returned and discovered Santa Maria. Thence São Miguel was sighted. Third to be discovered, as its name indicates, was Terceira. São Jorge, Graciosa, the volcanic Pico, and Faial came next; and the group was named Ilhas dos Açores (Isles of the Hawks) by the Infante. King Afonso V in 1439 conferred the privilege of settling and ruling these seven Azorean islands on his uncle, D. Henrique; four years later the Infante and his brother D. Pedro began to people this fertile group, where no natives or trace of former occupants were found. (The story of a hoard of Phoenician coins on one of the Azores is fabulous.) They obtained not only Portuguese settlers but Flemings, owing to royal connections with the dukes of Burgundy.

Two more Azorean islands, Flores and Corvo, remained to be discovered. These were found by a Portuguese resident of Madeira named Diogo de Tieve in 1452. Diogo and a friend named Pedro de Velasco were sent by Prince Henry to try and find the mythical Antilia, or Isle of the Seven Cities (of which more anon). They took their departure from Faial, sailed first southwesterly and then northeasterly to the supposed latitude of Cape Clear, Ireland, without finding land. On their return they discovered Corvo and Flores, westernmost outposts of the Azores, not visible from any other islands, and outside Prince Henry's domain. D. Afonso V in 1453 granted Corvo to his uncle the Duke of Bragança, and Flores to a waiting-lady of the queen.

Apart from its practical value, the discovery of the Azores had an immense psychological influence on discovery. Here for the first time the ocean had loosed her chains as Seneca prophesied, and lands hitherto unpeopled were found where before there was nought but myth and mystery. The crossing to a new world was now more than one-third accomplished; it is 745 nautical miles from the Rock of Sintra, Portugal, to São Miguel in the Azores, and 1054 miles from Corvo to Cape Race, Newfoundland. Furthermore, these newly discovered islands proved to be fertile producers of corn, cattle, and wine, suggesting that more oceanic discovery would be profitable. Since Corvo and Flores were discovered a good twenty years after Santa Maria, the Portuguese had every reason to expect to find more islands in the same direction; and if the Atlantic Plateau, that underwater mountain chain which in mid-ocean extends between latitudes 30° and 50° N, had not subsided some millions of years earlier, they would have discovered plenty. Soundings of thirteen and twenty-eight fathom were reported in 1955–59 on the Chaucer Bank, some two hundred miles north-northeast of Corvo.

Many efforts were made by the Portuguese between 1462 and 1490 to discover other Atlantic islands or to rediscover mythical ones which were presumed to exist. There are on record six *cartas de doação* (letters of donation) of islands not yet found, from the Portuguese sovereigns to their subjects, within thirteen years; and many more voyages were surely made by mariners of this enterprising nation, in the hope of discovering an island which the king would allow them to keep. Such donations might have been highly valuable, since the grantees were accorded the land, civil and criminal jurisdiction, and a monopoly of mills, public ovens, and salt. In 1462 the king granted to one João Vogado the two islands which "according to the sea chart are called respectively Lovo and Capraria." These are two St. Brendan isles that appear on almost every chart of the Atlantic in the fifteenth century. They were not discovered because they did not exist. On 29 October 1462, the king granted to his brother D. Fernando an island which Gonçalo Fernandes had sighted west-northwest of the Canaries and Madeira, on his way home from a fishing expedition. There was no island there. On 21 June 1473, the king granted to Rui Gonçalves da Câmara, for his services in Africa, "an island that shall be found by himself or by his ships." Rui found nothing. On 28 January 1474, he conceded to Fernão Teles "whatever islands he or the one whom he may send to search for them for the first time, shall find, and to choose those which he shall order to be settled," provided they were not in the Guinea region. Teles received an additional grant in 1475 of the Isle of the Seven Cities, if he could find it. He never did.

D. João II, known to his contemporaries as "the perfect prince," suc-' ceeded D. Afonso in 1481 and continued his father's Western Ocean policy. In 1484 he issued a letter of donation to a native of Madeira to be captain of "an island which he is going to find." Two years later he authorized Fernão Dulmo, captain of the northern half of Terceira, to find and rule over the Isle of the Seven Cities. Dulmo took into partnership João Estreito of Madeira, each to provide one caravel. Apparently they sailed in the stormy month of March, and found nothing.

Although Dr. Armando Cortesão and other Portuguese historians insist that some or all of these enterprising sailors "must" have discovered Newfoundland or Hispaniola, there is no evidence that they found anything. With the exception of the Azores, the story of Portuguese westward search before 1500 is a chronicle of failure. The explanation is meteorological. They struck out into the Western Ocean at seasons and in latitudes where strong westerly winds, even today, make navigation for sailing vessels full of danger and uncertainty. Columbus succeeded in reaching land because he sailed west from the Canaries with the northeast trades on his stern. John Cabot took off from Ireland, and in a season when there is a good prospect of fair winds; yet he required thirty-three days to reach Newfoundland, and but for the example of ' Columbus, his men might not have endured that long. Portuguese sailors from the Azores prior to 1492, after a month or so of battering by strong head winds and high seas, "wanted home." Small blame to them!

The Fabulous Antilia Group

Medieval maps covering the Atlantic, as time went on, became fairly crowded with islands big and small. Had they really existed, no ship could have sailed west from Europe without sighting one or more. Nor did the discovery of the Azores make any difference. One would suppose that these would have made map-makers say, "This is it," or "These are them!" The Portuguese crown did give Brendanesque names to Flores and Corvo; but for a long time the nine Azores were simply · spotted in as additions to mythical archipelagoes.

Most interesting of these mythical islands, which Portuguese historians now attempt to identify with a discovery of the New World, is Antilia, or the Isle of the Seven Cities. It appears as a rectangular

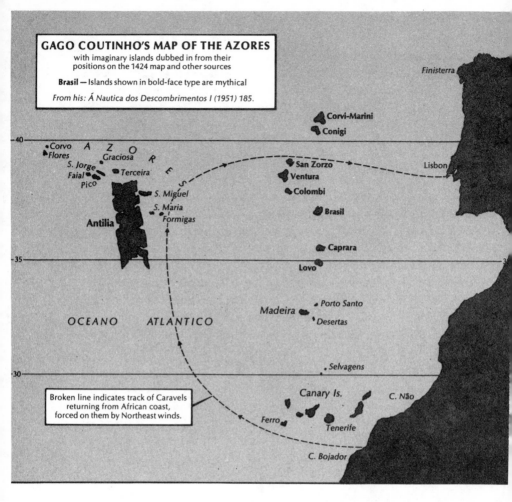

Finisterra

Corvi-Marini
Conigi

—40

•Corvo A Z O
Flores Graciosa *R*
S. Jorge *E* San Zorzo → Lisbon
Faial ●Terceira Ventura
Pico ●Colombi

S. Miguel
S. Maria **Brasil**
Antilia Formigas

Caprara

—35 **Lovo**

• Porto Santo
Madeira **Desertas**

OCEANO ATLANTICO

• Selvagens

—30

Broken line indicates track of Caravels
returning from African coast,
forced on them by Northeast winds.

Canary Is. C. Não
Ferro Tenerife

C. Bojador

island almost as big as Ireland, oriented north-northeast–south-southwest and painted red, on the Pizzi Nautical Chart of 1424, here reproduced in part. The name Antilia means "island opposite" Portugal, or the Pillars of Hercules.

Antilia has always been synonymous with the Isle of the Seven Cities. Nobody as yet has traced this name farther back than 1452, when the Tieve-Velasco expedition, as we have seen, went out to search for the Seven Cities and found Corvo and Flores. Next, Paul Toscanelli's letter of 25 June 1474 to Canon Martins of Lisbon, on which Columbus based his great enterprise, states, "From the island of Antilia, which you call the Seven Cities" to "the most noble island of

Cipangu [Japan] it is 50 degrees of longitude." The same year, D. Afonso V granted to Fernão Teles "The Seven Cities or whatever islands" he may find in the Atlantic north of Guinea.

The story first appears in writing on the 1492 globe of Martin Behaim, who must have picked it up in Portugal or the Azores. Against *Insula antilia septe citade* he states, "In A.D. 734, when the whole of Spain had been won by the African heathen, the above island Antilia, called Seven Cities, was occupied by an archbishop from Oporto, Portugal, with six other bishops, and other Christians, men and women, who had fled thither from Spain by ship, together with their cattle, property and goods. In 1414 a ship from Spain got nearest to it without danger."

Except for the date of this episcopal hegira, which Ferdinand Columbus placed twenty years earlier, this is the full-fledged story, oft repeated. D. Rodrigo, last Visigothic king of Spain (which then included Portugal), was utterly defeated by the Moors at a battle near Salamanca in 713. Sir Walter Scott, Robert Southey, and Washington Irving have made D. Rodrigo the hero of a story or a poem. Seven bishops, unwilling to live under infidel rule, took off, as the Irish *papae* had from Iceland, together with the bolder members of their flocks to seek new homes beyond the horizon's rim. The depicter of Antilia on the 1424 chart obviously regarded it as the seat of the episcopal refugees, for he spotted in seven cities with strange, outlandish names: *Asay, Ary, Vra, Jaysos, Marnlio, Ansuly,* and *Cyodne.* Las Casas, in his *Historia de las Indias* written in mid-sixteenth century, not only records the legend but states that in Columbus's notebooks he found this story: A storm-driven ship landed at the Isle of Seven Cities in the time of the Infante D. Henrique. The crew was welcomed by the natives in good Portuguese and urged to remain, but declined. On the way home they found grains of gold in the sand that they had taken in for their cook-box. When they reported this find to the Infante, he scolded them for not procuring more information, and ordered them to return, which they refused to do. The Portuguese historian António Galvão, in his *Tratado* (1563) adds this incident: In 1447 a Portuguese ship was blown by an easterly gale to an island which had seven cities peopled by Portuguese, who inquired particularly how the home folks were doing against the Moors. Galvão also repeats the story of golden grains in the cook-box sand.

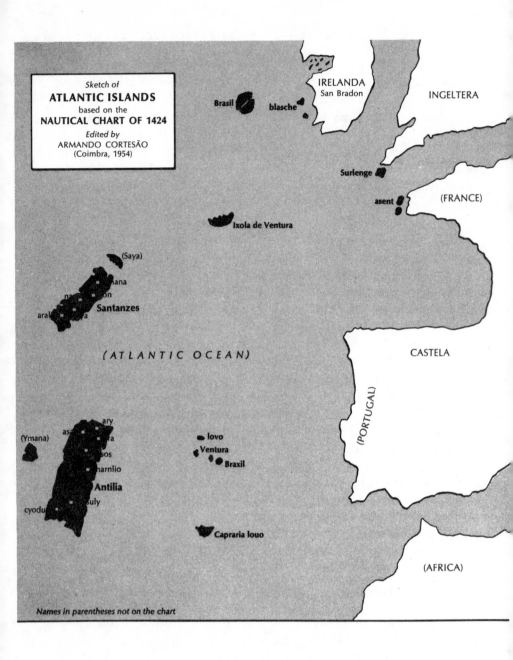

Sketch of
ATLANTIC ISLANDS
based on the
NAUTICAL CHART OF 1424
Edited by
ARMANDO CORTESÃO
(Coimbra, 1954)

IRELANDA
San Bradon

INGELTERA

Brasil
blasche

Surlenge

asent
(FRANCE)

Ixola de Ventura

(Saya)

ana
on
Santanzes
aral
a

(ATLANTIC OCEAN)

CASTELA

(PORTUGAL)

ary
as
a
(Ymana)
os
arnlio
Antilia
cyodu
uly

lovo
Ventura
Braxil

Capraria Iouo

(AFRICA)

Names in parentheses not on the chart

100

North of Antilia on the Nautical Chart of 1424 is a somewhat smaller rectangular island, painted blue, oriented northeast–southwest and named *Satanazes*. It usually appears in the same position relative to Antilia on pre-Columbian maps. This island (also called *Satanaxio*, *Satanagio, Saluaga, Santa Ana, and Salirosa*) has five obviously made-up names of towns. Nobody has yet found a legend to explain Satanazes. Possibly it derives from "hand of Satan," referring to an East Indian legend that off a certain island a giant hand rises from the sea nightly, ꞌ plucks some luckless inhabitant off the shore, and pulls him down to be eaten. Babcock thinks it was Florida, perhaps because one of the towns is named *Con!* Possibly the satanic isle is meant for that island visited by St. Brendan where devils hurled lumps of red-hot slag at his curragh.

The smaller mythical isles of the Antilia group on the 1424 Nautical Chart are *Saya*, the umbrella without a stick lying off Satanazes; this becomes *Tamar* on later maps. West of Antilia is a small, squarish island with one harbor, called *Ymana*. This becomes *Roillo* on later maps. All four names are inexplicable, although Babcock, in one of the wildest guesses of history, asserts that Roillo gave its name to Port Royal, Jamaica.

Columbus believed in the Antilia-Seven Cities legend. Martin Behaim's globe, shows "antilia septe citade" right on latitude 28° N, which Columbus tried to follow from the Canaries to Cipangu. His son states that the Discoverer wished to find "some island" en route, as a convenient staging point for the ocean route to the Indies. And his sea journal for 25 September 1492 proves that he expected to find it about where Behaim placed Antilia.

Babcock and Cortesão argue that each of these islands represents a New World reality, "The Forefront of Eastern America," as the latter calls them. Cortesão insists that the master of an unknown Portuguese caravel, sailing north from the African coast in the late fourteenth or early fifteenth century, was "blown across" to the New World, and discovered Hispaniola and Cuba. He kept his discovery secret at home, ꞌ but reported it to the Venetian cartographer of 1424, on whose Nautical Chart these islands are represented by Antilia and Satanazes.

If you can believe that, you can believe anything! Why would anyone who knew the two biggest islands of the West Indies rotate them almost 90 degrees on the map and place them only a few hundred miles off Portugal? Columbus, when he landed on Cuba, Hispaniola, and Jamaica, did not encounter Portuguese reception committees saying "Welcome to asay, ary, or jaysos," nor did he find similar names attached to an Indian village or region. It is true that many people thought that Columbus had discovered nothing but Antilia and its neighbors; that is why the Portuguese called the West Indies *As Antillas*, and the French, *Les Antilles;* names which carry the memory of the mysterious island to this day. The Seven Cities, too, reappear both as the fabled Seven Cities of Cibola in North America, and the extinct volcano crater now called Septe Citade on São Miguel of the Azores. Antilia, with north-south axis south of Newfoundland, appears on maps right through the sixteenth century.

Also, how can one explain why these supposed Portuguese discoveries appear only on Italian, Spanish, or other maps, never on a Portuguese one; or that the earliest undoubtedly Portuguese map of the Atlantic, the Cantino, has none of them? "Policy of secrecy," the Portuguese historians will doubtless answer; but, how secret is a policy of secrecy when every cartographer outside Portugal gets the word? Finally, João de Lisboa, the official chief pilot of the Portuguese kingdom, writing a book of sailing directions for the entire world dated 1514, devotes a whole chapter to "Courses for the Islands *not yet* discovered," including *Maidas* north-northeast of São Miguel and 7 *Septe citades* 170 leagues south of Cape Race, Newfoundland. There you will find it on several sixteenth-century maps.

Antilia and its appendages by no means exhaust the fictitious islands on the 1424 Nautical Chart. *Man, Mam,* or *Mayda* appears on the Pizzigani Chart of 1367 and several later ones, always in the shape of an inverted open umbrella. Mayda took a long time to disappear from maps. E. M. Blunt's *Chart of the Atlantic,* published at New York in 1841, places it at latitude 46° N, longitude 20° W.

Hy-Brasil

One mythical island never claimed by Portuguese historians is Hy-Brasil. Older, cartographically speaking, than Antilia, it has been left to the Irish, indisputably.

Hy-Brasil appears off Ireland on the Angelino Dulcert Chart of 1325, on numerous charts of the following century, and on many later ones.

It is usually represented as a round island with a strait through the middle, located within a hundred miles of West Ireland; sometimes it is two separate, semi-circular islands like the two halves of a walnut. Hy-Brasil floats off the Irish coast near enough to be sighted from shore. Fishermen of the Aran Islands told Professor Westropp of the Royal Irish Academy that it appeared every seven years; he saw it himself in 1872! "Just as the sun went down, a dark island suddenly appeared far out to sea, but not on the horizon. It had two hills, one wooded; between these, from a low plain, rose towers and curls of smoke."

The name Hy-Brasil (later corrupted to O'Brazil) means simply Isle of the Blest in Gaelic; it has nothing to do with the red dyewood which gave its name to Brazil, or with St. Brendan. It is obviously the product of a legend similar to Brendan's Land of Promise, representing in a rough, hard age the human longing for a land where there is no sorrow or struggle, no old age, no death or dissolution. Nobody, it seems, has traced the origin of Hy-Brasil in Irish literature, but all folk tales respecting it are very similar. The island is a Gaelic Elysian Fields where the souls of the blest sojourn before proceeding to Heaven. It is an enchanted island, never still; now sighted by a shepherd from high Achill, again glimpsed through fog off the Aran Islands, or appearing to the crew of a vessel rounding the Blaskets. For the Irish lived on the fringe of the Old World, and used their vivid imaginations to penetrate the mist and gloom of the unknown ocean. No living man has placed foot on Hy-Brasil, but it is said that if you could get near enough to throw fire ashore, you would be well received.

Gerald Griffin, a nineteenth-century Irish poet, wrote a charming poem about Hy-Brasil, beginning:

> On the ocean that hollows the rocks where ye dwell,
> A shadowy land has appeared, as they tell;
> Men thought it a region of sunshine and rest,
> And they called it O'Brazil, the Isle of the Blest.
>
> From year unto year, on the ocean's blue rim,
> The beautiful spectre showed lovely and dim;
> The golden clouds curtained the deep where it lay,
> And looked like an Eden, away, far away!

Although the Irish nourished this beautiful myth, sober English merchants of Bristol, ignoring the warning that none but a Celt could find it, searched for the elusive island. They financed a series of voyages in search of Hy-Brasil, beginning in 1480; and these, as we shall see, are connected with John Cabot's voyage of 1497, just as Antilia figured in Columbus's plans five years earlier.

Men of Bristol never found Hy-Brasil or any island where it was supposed to be; but the map-makers would not let it go. Successive charts of the sixteenth and seventeenth centuries show it, round as an apple, off the Blaskets, occasionally adding a second "I. de Brazil" off Spain or Africa. As early as 1560 the shadowy isle begins to move west and is found snuggling up to Newfoundland; but it always floats back to Ireland. An account of a fictitious visit to it by Captain John Nisbet was a London best-seller in 1675. Jeffrey's *American Atlas* of 1776 places O'Brazil on latitude 51° N and longitude 17°34' W, but he does call it "imaginary." John Purdy's "New, elegant & highly approved Chart of the Atlantic Ocean, exhibiting every Rock, Shoal and Danger known or supposed to exist" (New York, 1832) lived up to this promise. He even lays down the day-by-day track of the ship *Atlas* from Portsmouth, which *found* "Brasil Rock (high)" on 8 February 1787 at latitude 50°50' N, longitude 15°20' W.

A. G. Findlay's *Memoir, Descriptive and Explanatory, of the North Atlantic Ocean* spots "Brasil Rock" at latitude 51°10' N, longitude 16° W, about 250 miles west of southern Ireland, where the mariners of "Bristowe" were looking for it in the fifteenth century! Findlay admitted that its existence had been doubted, but as it had been "seen" in 1791 by the master of an English merchantman who said it was a high, bold-to islet which he passed within a biscuit-toss, he could not dismiss it as fictitious. Findlay's doubts increased, and he finally eliminated Brasil from his chart in 1865. But it was some years before those old "blue-backs" ceased to be used by mariners; and the British Admiralty, even more conservative, did not take the island off their charts until 1873. The Reverend Edward Everett Hale, visiting the bridge of S.S. *Siberia* in April of that year, was amused to find Brasil in the traditional spot, although the master admitted that steamers had sailed over it hundreds of times. Returning home in July, Hale found a new chart on board with no Isle of Brasil; so he reported to the American Antiquarian Society that he had been "in at the death" of this fabulous island.

Not quite. Map-makers, loath to give up their favorite movable island, attached its name to Brazil Rock, now safely anchored for all time off Cape Sable, Nova Scotia. In the midst of swirling tide rips it constitutes such a hazard in the fogs which infest that coast as to call from mariners sentiments and language highly inappropriate for Hy-Brasil, the Isle of the Blest.

While men of Bristol were still searching for Hy-Brasil and the Portuguese were preparing to follow Bartholomew Diaz to India, there took place the most earth-shaking event in the entire history of discovery—Columbus's first voyage to the Bahamas, Cuba, and Hispaniola. Even though he and many others mistook these islands for outlying parts of the Indies, they proved to be gateways to a whole New World unsuspected by Ptolemy.

Columbus's Letter to the Spanish Sovereigns about his voyage, first printed in April 1493, was promptly translated into Latin and circulated throughout Europe in eleven different editions before the end of that year. Columbus sailed on his second voyage in September 1493, discovered the Lesser Antilles and Puerto Rico, and founded the first Spanish colony in the New World at Isabela, Hispaniola, in January 1494. His flag captain Antonio de Torres returned to Spain in early March, bearing a large quantity of gold, a number of slaves, and samples of alleged Oriental spices.

This news, circulating more by word of mouth than by pen, threw maritime Europe into a whirl of activity. First king to profit by this astounding news, to defy the Pope's division of the New World between Spain and Portugal, and to carve out a share for his own subjects, was Henry VII of England. And his chosen instrument was another Genoese, John Cabot.

Bibliography and Notes

EARLY GAULS

Pierre de Charlevoix, *Histoire et description générale de la Nouvelle France* (Paris, 1744), p. 3, for Postel's yarn. He does not specify in which of Postel's numerous works this statement appeared; probably his *Description des Gaules* or *Des Merveilles des Indes et du nouveau monde* (both Paris, 1553). Fernández de Oviedo y Valdés, *Historia General y Natural de las Indias* (1851 ed.), I,14–18.

MADOC

Sir George Peckham, *A True Report of the late Discoveries of the New-found Landes* (London, 1583), first told this story in print; it was shortly followed by Humphrey Lhoyd, *History of Cambria, now Called Wales* (London, 1584). Hakluyt, too, has it (Everyman ed., V, 79). Morgan Jones's story appeared in *The Gentleman's Magazine* in 1740. John Williams, *An Enquiry into the Truth . . . Concerning the Discovery of America by Prince Madog ab Owen Gwynedd* (London, 1791), adds more travelers' tales. Thomas Stephens, *Literature of the Kymry* (London, 1849), is the classic refutation. *The Magazine of History*, Extra Number No. 78 to Vol. XX (1922), reprints George Burder's curious pamphlet of 1797, *The Welch Indians*. Richard Deacon, *Madoc and the Discovery of America* (London, 1967), pulls all the travelers' tales together. His approach to the subject is uncertain; he feels there must be something in it, but cannot say what. Zella Armstrong, *Who Discovered America? The Amazing Story of Madoc* (Chattanooga, 1950), reproduces some of Catlin's paintings of blue-eyed Mandan, and goes all out for the legend's truth. Bernard DeVoto, *The Course of Empire* (Boston, 1952), amusingly traces the westward course of the Welsh Indians.

David Williams, "John Evans's Strange Journey," *American Historical Review*, LIV (1949), 277–95, 508–29, tells of the legend's growth. All pro-Madoc writers try to refute Evans by attacking his character. In my opinion he was sober, honest, and objective. George Catlin gave the legend a new lease on life in his *Letters and Notes on the Manners, Customs and Condition of the North American Indians* (New York, 1841), I, 206–7; II; 259–61, with phony comparative vocabulary. Justin Winsor lists the older literature in *Narrative and Critical History*, I, 71–73, 109–11, and reviews the subject with common sense; the oft-repeated statement that Winsor believed in the Madoc story is not correct. James Mooney, "Welsh Indians," in F. W. Hodge, *Handbook of American Indians*, II, 931–32, is a good summary.

There is extensive literature on travelers discovering American Indians who were fluent in some European or Asiatic language. Uneducated travelers were apt to regard every Indian language as gibberish, and so compared it with some known language such as Welsh, Basque, Hebrew, or Finnish, that was also gibberish to them. An Irish traveler, Charles Beatty, who entered the Gulf region *c.* 1760 reported that the Indians of Carolina who captured him spoke Irish Gaelic and spared his life when he answered in kind! *Journal of a Two Months' Tour* (1768); quoted by Joseph Dunn in *Catholic Historical Review*, VI (1921), 456. Similar stories are told of Hebrew-speaking Indians, first by Spanish explorers and more particularly by English Puritans, who toyed with the idea that the American aborigines were the Ten Lost Tribes of Israel. This theory, embalmed in the *Book of Mor-*

mon, has become an official dogma of the Latter-Day Saints. The Reverends John Eliot and Jonathan Edwards found analogies between Algonkin and Hebrew (Justin Winsor, I,115–16). Thomas Thorowgood, *Jewes in America* (London, 1650), heard that New England Indians cried "Hallelujah!"

ZENO BROTHERS

The original publication, with the map, is *Dei Commentarii . . . dello scoprimento de dell'Isole Frislanda, Eslanda, Engrouelanda, Estotilanda, & Icarìa da due fratelli Zeni, Nicolò e Antonio* (Venice, 1558). Johann Reinhold Forster, *History of the Voyages and Discoveries Made in the North* (London, 1786), is the book that brought Sinclair and the Zeni together. Frederick W. Lucas, *The Annals of the Voyages of the Brothers . . . Zeno* (London, 1898), includes a facsimile of the 1558 imprint and an expert demolition of the story. His conclusions, in which I concur, are, in brief: "There is no evidence that Antonio Zeno ever visited any part of America, or any of its islands. . . . No such island as Zeno's Frislanda ever existed, his map of it having been compounded from earlier maps of Iceland and the Faroes. . . . Zichmni, if such a man ever existed, was certainly not identical with Henry Sinclair, Earl of Orkney. . . . A sufficient motive for the compilation of Zeno's story and map is to be found in a desire to connect, even indirectly, the voyages of his ancestors with a discovery of America earlier than that by Columbus, in order to gratify the compiler's family pride and his own personal vanity, and to pander to that Venetian jealousy of other maritime nations (especially of the Genoese) which was so strong in the . . . decadence of the great Venetian Republic. . . . Zeno's work has been one of the most ingenious, most successful, and most enduring literary impostures which has ever gulled a confiding public."

Recent attempts at rehabilitation are William H. Hobbs, "The 14th-Century Discovery of America by Antonio Zeno" in *Scientific Monthly*, LXXII (1951), 24–31 (he has Zeno and Zichmni landing in Nova Scotia); Frederick J. Pohl, *Atlantic Crossings Before Columbus* (1951), pp. 226–90; E. G. R. Taylor, "A Fourteenth Century Riddle and Its Solution," *Geographical Review*, LIV (1964), 573–76, and "The Fisherman's Story, 1354," *Geographical Magazine*, XXXVII (1964), 709–12. See also Chapter XIV below, for how the Zeno map befuddled cartographers for over a century.

William B. Goodwin, father of archaeological lost causes, "discovered" at Westford, Mass., an inscribed rock which allegedly showed a portrait of the noble Earl resting on his sword and bearing a shield with the arms of the Sinclairs (*The Ruins of Great Ireland in New England*, Boston, 1946). This is played up by Lawrence F. Willard, "Westford's Mysterious Knight," in *Yankee* magazine of Dublin, New Hampshire, XXII (1958), 60–61, 84–89. William S. Fowler, who examined the rock, reported in the Massachusetts Archaeological Society *Bulletin*, XXI (1960), 21–22, that the only man-made part of the design is the outline of an iron Indian tomahawk of the period 1700–1750, similar to one now in the museum of the Rhode Island Historical Society. That outline had been pecked out with "a case-hardened iron center punch of earlier days, in common use by blacksmiths of those times." Everything else on the rock is nature-made frost pits, so numerous that any design can be made by joining them together with chalk or paint. Thus the tomahawk, despite its awkward design, has been extended into a sword; the knightly head is a pure figment of the imagination; and the shield showing alleged Sinclair arms has been painted on by some enthusiast. This rock is on Depot Street, Westford, about half a mile from the village center, on the right side going north. Antha E. Card, who made the accompanying photo in October 1968, freshly chalked the "sword" and the outline of the "knight's" head and shoulders, but the painted shield was already there.

PINING-POTHORST-SCOLVUS-JOÃO VAZ

Cornelius Wytfliet (*Descriptiones Ptolemaicae augmentum*, Louvain, 1579, p. 188) seems to have been the first to popularize these merry men, and later writers copied him. Charlevoix in his *Histoire . . . de la Nouvelle France* (Paris, 1744), I,4, says: "Quelques Auteurs ont avancé qu'en 1477 Jean SCALVE, Polonois, reconnut *l'Estotiland*, & une partie des Terres de *Labrador*. . . . On ne sçait rien de particulier de l'expedition du Voyageur Polonais, qui n'a eu aucune suite, et qui n'a pas fait beaucoup de bruit dans le monde." The famous illustrated work of the Scandinavian savant Olaus Magnus, *Historia de Gentibus Septentrionalibus* (Rome, 1555), was early translated into French (1561), Italian (1565), and English (1658).

Fridtjof Nansen has a good, common-sense account, with English translation of the Grip letter, *In Northern Mists*, II (1911), 122–33. The Sofus Larsen book, including everything relevant and much more, is *The Discovery of North America Twenty Years Before Columbus* (London and Copenhagen, 1925), on page 86 is a photo of the Quii inscription. I have already dealt with the João Vaz Corte Real part in *Portuguese Voyages to America in the XV Century* (1940), pp. 33–41. Charles Boland, *They All Discovered America* (Garden City, 1961), p. 346, believes that Scolvus was a pseudonym for Pothorst, but one Portuguese historian argues that Scolvus and Corte Real were identical! Eduardo Brazão, *The Corte-Real Family in the New World* (Lisbon, 1965), believes implicitly in the 1472 voyage and scores me in his footnotes. T. J. Oleson in *Early Voyages* (1968), p. 97, writes that Quii means *quit populi*, a translation of the Icelandic *hvitir mann* (white men), and that the *quiteum mare* on Claudius Clavus's Map of 1427, an obvious misspelling of the Latin name for quiet or calm, "is no doubt a mistake for *quitum mare*," White Men's Sea. Eva Taylor's rendering of Quii into Okinawa is in her *Tudor Geography*, p. 81.

Halldór Hermannsson discusses this complex in *The Problem of Wineland* (1936), pp. 80–81, and rejects it as spurious. On page 83n he gives a bibliography of the articles by Ulloa, whose principal writings are: *Christophe Colomb Catalan* (Paris, 1927), *Noves Proves de la Catalanitat de Colom* (Paris, 1927), and *Xristo-Ferens Colom, Fernando el Catolico, y la Cataluña Española* (Paris, 1928).

To preserve my sanity while reading these works of moonstruck historians, I composed this doggerel:—

Pining and Pothorst were two merry men,
They went to sea—we don't know when;
Electing an international cruise,
They invited aboard what made good news:
Two Portugee and a fellow named Skoal
(Who may have been Danish and maybe a Pole).
And maybe, for boy (as you didn't surmise),
The youthful Colón in Catálan disguise.

They sailed away for a year and a day
To the land which the Quii create,
And they danced around with many a bound
On the shores of that Arctic strait.
Pining and Pothorst each married a Quii
And fathered some Quae and some Quod,
While Scolvus-Colón sailed through to Ceylon
And then to the Land of the Cod.

So now you know, unless you're a fool,
That they told you all wrong, when you studied at school!

DISCOVERY OF THE AZORES

Jules Mees, *Histoire de la découverte des Iles Açores* (Ghent, 1901), and Admiral Gago Coutinho, *A Nautica dos Descobrimentos* (Lisbon, 1951), I, 165–95, a salty account by an expert navigator under sail. The Admiral, knowing well the winds of that region, argues that a Portuguese ship discovered the eastern Azores by accident on her way home from West Africa. Portuguese historians, however, thought it "more elegant" to say that they were discovered by order of the Infante! His map illustrating the theory is here reproduced. My late friend Captain A. Fontoura da Costa has a fresh approach to the discovery problem in *Congresso do Mundo Português*, III,i (1940), 240–86, with ample bibliography.

The *Boletim do Instituto Historico da Ilha Terceira* (Angra-do-Heroismo, 1943) contains numerous valuable articles on early Azorean history, many by my esteemed correspondent Tenente Coronel José Agostinho. M. C. Baptista de Lima, *Deux Voyages portugais de découverte dans l'Atlantique Occidental* (Lisbon, 1946), has a fresh interpretation of Diogo de Tieve's voyage. Diogo is the favorite Portuguese candidate for a pre-

Columbian discovery of America, although he distinctly says that he sailed northeast, not northwest, from the Azores. See my *Portuguese Voyages* (1940), pp. 10–16, 21–33, with many references in footnotes.

THE PORTUGUESE "POLICY OF SECRECY"

This theory, first propounded by Jaime Cortesão in 1924, is perhaps the most preposterous in modern history, because it uses absence of evidence as positive evidence that the Portuguese discovered everything. Yet it has converted almost every Portuguese historian and is taught in Portuguese schools. Bailey W. Diffie, "Foreigners in Portugal and the 'Policy of Silence,' " *Terrae Incognitae*, I (1969), 23–34, gives a bibliography and points out that the number of foreigners in Portugal around 1500 precludes the possibility that the government could have kept any discovery secret.

HY-BRASIL AND ANTILIA

Thomas J. Westropp, "Brazil and the Legendary Islands of the North Atlantic," Royal Irish Academy *Proceedings*, 3rd ser., XXX (1912), sec. C, pp. 223–60. Nordenskiöld, *Periplus*, Plate VIII (the Dulcert of 1325), and many that follow, depict it. Denis O'Donoghue, *Brendaniana* (Dublin, 1893), pp. 298–305, has some Irish data. Roger Barlow in his *Briefe Summe of Geographie* (1540–41, Hakluyt Society edition, 1932, p. 52) says, "Weste of Yreland is an ylande called . . . brasyle which standeth in 51 degrees. Hit is almoste rounde. . . . From Yreland to this yle of brasyll is 70 legis." Fridtjof Nansen, *In Northern Mists*, I, 375–79, has a collection of floating-island myths from Norway to China; the Isle of Avalon near Glastonbury was one, and Ireland had others besides Brasil.

Justin Winsor, *Narrative and Critical History*, I, 49–51, and II, 36, tells of Hy-Brasil through the ages. The book on the pretended visit to it in the seventeenth century is *O Brazile, or the Enchanted Island* (London, 1675). Edward E. Hale's report of its disappearance from the charts in 1873 is in American Antiquarian Society *Proceedings* for that year, pp. 6, 84. See also André L'Hoist, "L'origine du nom Brésil" in *Cong. do Mundo Portugues* III, i, 403–26. Brazil Rock, N. S., is in lat. 53°20′ N, long. 65°26′ W. There is also a Brazil Shoal off Grand Manan, N. B.

William H. Babcock, *Legendary Islands of the Atlantic* (American Geographical Society, 1922), catalogues most of them, tracing their history on maps and assigning to each an identity such as Newfoundland, Hispaniola, Cuba, Jamaica, etc. My *Portuguese Voyages to America*, I supposed, had proved to everyone's satisfaction that these islands were really mythical—but how wrong I was! Dr. Armando Cortesão, protagonist of the theory that every island shown on a medieval map was a real one, or a part of North America secretly discovered by some Portuguese, does not even mention poor me in the elaborate bibliography of his sumptuous and scholarly work, *The Nautical Chart of 1424* (Coimbra, 1954), which I reviewed in *Speculum*, XXX (1955), 467–70. E. G. R. Taylor supported Dr.

Cortesão in *Geographical Journal*, CXXX (1964), 105–7. But the Genoese historian Paulo Ravelli, who sees everything as Genoese which Cortesão asserts to be Portuguese, finds Satanazes derived from the Genoese patrician family Salvago or Salvaghi, who discovered it!

Cartographers subsequent to 1492 cheerfully continued to map non-existent islands, often moving them nearer the New World. They even invented new ones. The Globe Verte of *c.* 1515 in the Bibliothèque Nationale, and many later maps, show *I. Verde* south of Newfoundland. Notice the number of them on the maps I have reproduced here to illustrate the voyages of Cartier. The Antilia legend on the Behaim globe is in E. G. Ravenstein, *Martin Behaim* (1908), p. 77 and Plate I, gore B. Las Casas, *Historia de las Indias* (1927 ed.), I, 70, tells the story of the gold grains in the cook-box sand.

João de Lisboa, *Livro da Marinharia*, (Brito Rebêlo, ed., 1903), is from a manuscript finished in 1514; the chapter on "Courses of Islands not [yet] Discovered" is on pp. 121–22. Several others are listed, notably *Ilha dos braçiles* 50 leagues west of Dursey Head, Ireland. Mr. Roger Whidden of Harvard kindly made an exhaustive study of the date of João's *Livro* for me; and the fact that he, the top pilot of Portugal, lists Antilia and Hy-Brasil as *not yet discovered*, is sufficient refutation of the Portuguese and English pre-discovery fables.

✳ V ✳
English Ships and Seamen

1490-1600

Gentyl maryners on a bonne viage
Hoyce up the sayle and let God stere;
In ye bonaventur makyng your passage
It is ful see the wether fayre and clere.

PIERRE GARCIE *Routier* (1520)

Design, Build, and Rigging

Before embarking with Cabot and his successors on their important North Atlantic voyages, my readers will wish to know what sort of a ship they used, how they built and rigged her, and what manner of men sailed her. To cover these topics with any degree of accuracy is a difficult if not impossible task. Records of English shipbuilding, design, rig, and handling for the closing years of the fifteenth century are very scarce. The situation respecting French ships is clearer, owing to the researches of Mollat, Bernard, and others; and we can also learn much from Frederic C. Lane's magistral works on Venetian shipping.

The ships which the English, French, and other northern explorers had at their disposition around 1500 were the result of centuries of trial and error. The English, leaving the basket-like curragh to the Irish, adopted the Scandinavian knarr, which (as we have seen) made an excellent coastwise freighter but took in too much water for off-shore work.

The next development, completed by 1200, was the *cog*, or *cogge* (*coque* in French), invented in Germany or the Netherlands. One of the difficulties in marine research is that the same word means different things at different times. For instance, by 1600 *cog* had become *cock*

Contemporary model of a carvel-built cog, the Spaans Karveel. Courtesy National Maritime Museum, Rotterdam.

or *cock-boat*, a ship's boat propelled by oars and sail; *hulk* became a ship without masts, and *barge* became a flatboat to carry coal, or the admiral's boat on a flagship.

The cog originally was a single-masted ship with one sail and a bank of oars to use to windward or in a calm, but it had four important advantages over the knarr. It was completely decked over, so that water

taken in from sky or sea flowed overboard instead of having to be
pumped or bailed out. It had a rudder, hung to the sternpost by iron
pintles and gudgeons, and a long hardwood tiller mortised to the rudder head, affording the helmsman good leverage, while the sterncastle
protected him from the elements. It had flimsy, openwork "castles"
forward and aft, which were detachable and expendable, together with
what we would call a crow's nest atop the single mast, valuable both
for a lookout station and for defense. It had a bowsprit, first used to
stay the mast. Originally clinker-built like the knarr, the cog, owing
largely to her stern rudder and big mainsail with "bonnet" attached,
was a far better sailer and more efficient cargo carrier. Cogs, built in
great numbers in the Hanseatic League seaports, ran the Scandinavian
merchant fleet out of business, except for local trade in sheltered
waters. A well-built cog was perfectly capable of crossing the Atlantic;
I would choose her every time rather than a modern yacht of her size
with a "self-bailing" cockpit and an open companionway ready to
gobble up a following sea.

The next important development came in the early fifteenth century.
A cog's hull, now carvel-built, lengthened, and provided with two
more masts, became first the *hourque*, or *hulk*, then the *nef*, *nau*, or
full-rigged ship. The first explorers of America used these because they
had nothing better; and as a result of experience, they came to prefer
the smaller ships, under 100 tuns, to the bigger. Thus, Columbus found
his little *Niña* more serviceable than the big *Santa María*.

Methods of building were essentially the same in the Middle Ages
as those described in Longfellow's *Building of the Ship*, and as practised
in small-boat yards of England, France, Nova Scotia, and both American coasts down to 1945, when fibre-glass construction began to replace wood. Similar methods are still maintained in 1970 in other parts
of the world. The builder first selects a "slip" at the head of tide,
slightly inclined so the vessel will launch easily, and places big oak
blocks evenly spaced to support her when built. Some small vessels
were doubtless built by eye, but the larger ones, like those shown in the
Hastings Manuscript, were carefully planned with compass and divider,
the members "laid down" in a mould loft with chalk or charcoal, and
templates of them made with thin pieces of light wood. The English
builder, if he does not own an oak forest himself, arranges with another to take out the timber he wants. Oak is preferred, not only for its
strength but because limbs growing from the trunk at different angles

Edward Fiennes, Earl of Lincoln, Lord High Admiral, 1550–54 and 1558–85, holding a dry-card mariner's compass. From painting by unknown artist. Courtesy Ashmolean Museum, Oxford.

make natural crooks for the ribs or frames, the knees, and the curved stem piece. Builders would carry a wagon-load of templates into the oak grove, match them against standing trees, cut down those they wanted, and shape them with ax and adze. England then grew plenty of oak.

Venice, as Frederic C. Lane has vividly described, possessed shipyards which had many of the elements of a modern assembly plant, with gantry cranes and vehicles for bringing the component parts together. In comparison, the building yards of England and France seem to have been small and simple. The oak keel is laid with the keelson (the inside part of the keel) on top; all "scarfed and bolted straight and strong." Into the keelson are mortised the ribs or frames. Crossbeams tie them to the deck, and all must be adzed into shape. Pine is preferred for side-planking and deck. These were designed to shed water quickly by being given both sheer (fore-and-aft slope) and camber (transverse slope). Iron is used for fastenings, but such timbers as keel and stern piece are bolted by trunnels, long pegs of soft wood, which will swell in the water and hold as fast as iron or copper. Spars are almost invariably spruce fir, of which, surprisingly, there were large stands in England and Scotland at this time. Parts under water are covered with black tar or pitch, the best substance then known to discourage the growth of weed and barnacles. Topsides are gaily painted in longitudinal stripes of green, blue, yellow, and red.

Whether carvel- or clinker-built, topsides and decks had to be caulked. Oakum (shredded fibers of hemp) was driven into the seams and topped off with pitch locally distilled from pine tar or imported from the Baltic. The musical ring of the caulking iron driving home the precious stuff was evident in shipbuilding then as in the early twentieth century; and if a laboring ship "spewed her oakum," it was time for her crew to pray or abandon ship.

When the hull is complete, the launching takes place; that was always done with ceremony, as even today. A crowd of people attends to see it done, and lend a hand if necessary; one could have seen just such a community launching ceremony at St. Vincent, B.W.I., in 1969. If the vessel was not originally laid down on a cradle, one is now built under her keel, resting on greased "ways," two stout wooden rails leading down to water of sufficient depth, at high tide, to float her. A priest says a few prayers, sprinkles the bows with holy water, and pronounces her chosen name, usually that of a saint or an apostle expected to look after her safety and welfare.* At the moment chosen

* In England and northern France "Saint" was not often prefixed to the name; but, to familiar saints' names, the home or builder's port was added to distinguish her; e.g. *Mary of Guildford, Anthoine de Bordeaux*. Sometimes a northern ship had a nickname used instead of her real name: the ship *Sampson*, which started off with John Rut in 1527, was also called *Dominus Vobiscum*, reflecting a justified popular verdict on her safety. After the Reformation, English ships were

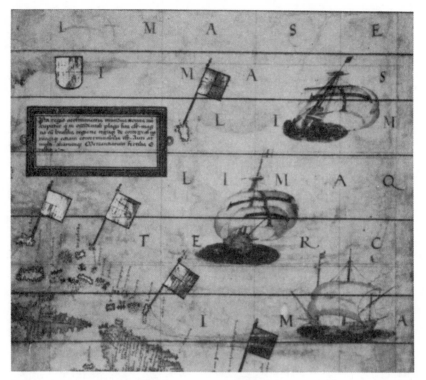

Long-course Portuguese ships from the Miller I Atlas of *c.* 1525. Courtesy Bibliothèque Nationale.

by the master shipwright, the "shores" which prevented the hull from toppling are knocked away by workmen with big mallets; and, if everything has been planned correctly,

> She starts,—she moves,—she seems to feel
> The thrill of life along her keel,

and she glides gracefully into her destined element, while the assembled multitude cheers.

After the hull is launched comes the ballasting, masting, and rigging. ·

Several important building and rigging innovations came about during the fifteenth century before Cabot set sail. Clinker-built gave way to

less often named after saints and angels, more often after qualities or things, such as *Delight, Aid, Sunshine, Mayflower;* and in the fifteenth century saints' names · become less usual for French ships.

carvel-built, with flush, smooth planking, edges laid just close enough to one another to admit caulking. That made a much tighter ship for deep-sea work than those of earlier centuries. Spars and rigging, too, were fundamentally changed. Down to 1400 the cog and every other sailing type in northern waters was one-masted; but by 1500 all but the smallest had become three-masters: (1) the foremast, which went through the forecastle and might even be stepped on the stem-piece; (2) the mainmast, which carried the principal weight, always stepped on the keelson; (3) the mizzenmast, which thrust through the sterncastle and was stepped on the deck. Later, around mid-century, the high-steeved bowsprit, by supporting a square spritsail spread on a yard, acted as a fourth mast, and the "bonaventure" mizzen, stepped on the taffrail, a fifth. Fore and mainmast each carried a square lower course, also called foresail and mainsail. Note in all contemporary pictures of around 1500 how long the main yard and how big the mainsail appear to be in comparison with the ship; but ship pictures from 1544 on suggest that designers had realized the advantage of dividing the sail area and putting more of it into the topsails. The seaman of 1480–1550 counted on his main course to provide the drive, just as a modern yachtsman depends on his genoa jib and spinnaker.

For the variables in the North Atlantic, a more balanced rig was preferable. The mizzen sail, always lateen, i.e. triangular, was valuable chiefly on the wind, and to kick the stern around when tacking. Sails were no longer made of wool, but of flax woven at home, or cut out of canvas imported from Oleron or Dieppe. All rigging was made of hemp, mostly imported from the Baltic, and properly laid in a rope walk. Bridport in Dorsetshire had the reputation of making the best sails and cordage in England. Standing rigging, the shrouds which held the masts in place, was tarred down and secured to the bulwarks by lanyards running through deadeyes, a method that lasted for merchantmen well into the twentieth century. Cordage was comparatively costly. The royal household books for 1501 show that the rigging of two "berkes" cost £46 13s. 4d.

Pictures or models of northern ships of this period are rare; time has disposed of most ex voto models in churches, and the occasional carvings of vessels on seals, corbels, and capitals are foreshortened and usually represent the crew as big as the ship. The best representatives of what Cabot's *Mathew* and other early exploring ships looked like are those we have reproduced from the Hastings Manuscript. The single vessel (with oversize mariners) is entering the English Channel with a fair wind aft, and a sailor is sounding from the sterncastle, which seems odd. Probably the lead was cast from the bow, but the line coiled aft, enabling the men to sound without coming up into the wind each time. The ensign, a big burgee with the red cross of St. George on a white field, flares out bravely, and shields of the same design are displayed topside to warn all and sundry that this is an English ship, not to be fooled with. The mizzen is furled so as to facilitate sailing before the wind; there is no spritsail, although Spanish ships as early as Columbus's day had one, bent to a yard slung from the bowsprit. Note the big anchor, of exactly the same design as those still used in the twentieth century, with cable bent onto the ring, ready for lowering. Halyards, braces, and clewlines are indicated on the forecourse and mainsail; and the shrouds are well "rattled down" (crossed with sections of tarred rope), so that sailors can nip up to the crow's nest quickly. All she seems to lack is bonnets on the main course.

The other painting from the Hastings Manuscript, a harbor scene, is even more explicit. The two ships at the top, and perhaps the big one in the center, have just entered harbor and are about to strike sail and anchor. The one at lower right is moored to two anchors (the general practice), and either the current makes her lie stern to wind or the artist has made her flags blow the wrong way. The one at the left is being towed by her longboat to a position where she may safely make sail and beat out. At lower left is one of the primitive lighthouses of the period—an iron cresset on a pole, to hold a warning fire. The ships' tops are bristling with weapons. Rigging is detailed and correct, assuming that the loops hanging from main yards in the two bottom ships are buntlines and clewlines that the crew has not had time to haul taut and belay. Puzzling features are the thing like a braided-up mizzen held by a sailor on the forecastle of the biggest ship, and the fact that all three under sail have their mizzens furled; one would suppose that they should have been set either for beating out or rounding into the wind to anchor. But we cannot expect—and seldom get—complete accuracy from artists in this era. They had a general idea of what a ship looked like but were not trying to paint portraits of individual vessels.

til þe come in to iiij fadmm deep and yf it be stremy
grounde it is beniene suspectant and aise in the entre
of the chanel of ffaundres and soo goo ȝoure course
til þe sane spyn fadmm deep. than goo est nortse est
a longe the see. + c.

Late fifteenth-century ship heaving the lead when entering the English
Channel. From the Hastings Manuscript. Courtesy J. Pierpont Morgan
Library.

English shipping in the late fifteenth century. From the Hastings Manuscript of *c*. 1480. Courtesy J. Pierpont Morgan Library.

Other ship pictures which we may presume to be accurate are on Portuguese charts from about 1510. Two excellent ones are on the section of the "Miller I" of *c.* 1525, which we illustrate near the end of Chapter VII below. The vessel at lower right is a much more sophisticated, blue-water type than those on the Hastings Manuscript, and may well be a delineation of the sea-going caravels that carried the Corte Real brothers and Fagundes to Newfoundland and Cape Breton. She is scudding before so strong a wind that the topsails and mizzen are furled. This sketch is remarkably accurate as to hull, profile, and rigging; the artist has depicted a fine, tall ship that any blue-water yachtsman would love to sail today. The vessel in the foreground is running free, her foresail and mainsail bellying to a fresh breeze. Portuguese cartographers, notably Ribero, loved to depict these ships in the trades, with their great square sails bellying like a modern balloon-spinnaker. Skeptical historians assert that such enormous mainsails, with bonnet and drabler (the second bonnet) lashed to the foot, are exaggerated; but I differ. We know from many sources that the *nef* or full-rigged ship carried a main yard as long as her over-all length and that the sail bent to it produced a surprising speed off the wind.

A *navicula* or little ship such as Cabot's *Mathew*, not less than fifty or over sixty feet long, would have had two decks, the main deck laid a few feet over the ballast, and the spar deck exposed to the elements; the head-room between them five feet or even less. On this main deck, against the bulwarks, were lashed the seamen's chests; here they slept, lapped in blankets or an old bit of sail, anywhere they chose; only the officers had bunks. These were in the after superstructure, the sterncastle, which also comprised the steerage. There the principal pieces of furniture were the tiller, shelves or lockers for charts, and traverse board, later superseded by a sea-journal kept on a slate. Here hung the half-hour glass, the ship's only timepiece; a boy was supposed to turn it every half hour (the origin of ships' bells which came later); if he forgot, he received from the bo'sun a few strokes of the "cat o'nine tails." Turning the glass not only served to keep the dead reckoning (as sailors still call navigation by time, distance, and direction), but at every eighth glass to call the new watch on deck.

Forward of the sterncastle, and between it and the forecastle, was the waist of the ship. Here were stowed the smaller ship's boats; the biggest one, the pinnace, or longboat, for which there was no room on

Long-course Portuguese ships of *c.* 1529 from the Ribero World Map
of that date. Reproduced from Nordenskjold's *Periplus*.

deck, had to be towed, and consequently was often lost in heavy
weather. In a rack around the masts or on the bulwarks were the be-
laying pins, of exactly the same design as in the twentieth century, to
secure running rigging. In the waist was a crude capstan for winding
in the hemp anchor cable by means of wooden pauls (handspikes) to
provide leverage.

The waist of the ship between forecastle and sterncastle was so near water level as to be constantly drenched. So a "waist-cloth," a long strip of canvas, was fitted to each side, to be lashed on to prevent too much water coming in, or to repel boarders. If noble or armigerous gentlemen were on board, they had their arms painted on the waist-cloths or attached their particular shields to them, a practice going back to Viking times. These purely decorative shields were called *pavesses.*

Tunnage in England and France at this period meant a ship's capacity in *tuns,* double-hogsheads in which they shipped wine. Usually this burthen was arrived at by a series of measurements which differed from one country to another. From this developed the modern standard for a maritime *ton* as 40 cubic feet.

I have often wondered how these ships of the early discoverers would have stood up in some of the strong gales and hurricanes described in Adlard Coles's classic *Heavy Weather Sailing.* Would they have hove-to and "laid a-hull" or "a-hold" as the boatswain ordered in *The Tempest?* Or would they have run before it under storm foresail or bare poles? We have almost no data to go on. Columbus on his homeward passage in *Niña* in 1493 logged a cyclonic storm so accurately that a modern meteorologist could map it, and the Admiral consistently drove the little caravel before it until he had no canvas left but a storm trysail with which to claw off the Rock of Sintra. One advantage those old ships had over modern yachts (too often designed for personal comfort rather than seaworthiness) is that they were really tight above and below, if the caulking had not been allowed to disintegrate. Their few hatches could be battened down watertight, they had no "self-bailing" cockpit to scoop up a big sea, and no companionway ladder over which the salt water could flow like a young Niagara into the cabin.

An officer on the highest and driest part of a sixteenth-century ship, the sterncastle, "conned" (directed) the helmsman through a small hatch. I was amused to learn that Bernard Moitessier, who successfully rounded Cape Horn in a forty-foot ketch in the 1960's, approximated a sterncastle by building aft a metal cupola, the "pilot's post," from which he steered. But one place which prevented these old ships from keeping completely tight and dry was the open port where the long tiller joined the rudder head, and which had to be kept open to allow for the rudder's play. When she was running free in a blow, every big wave must have sloshed through this port and drenched the helmsman ⸗ before flowing into the waist and out through a drain port.

In the seventeenth century high forecastles and sterncastles were abandoned in favor of flush-decked hulls with an uninterrupted sheer from bow to stern. Nineteenth-century steamships followed this basic deck plan, but the two high castles (now called superstructures) have been revived for small freighters. For it is more economical to have ⸗ your cargo holds run all the way fore and aft, and put the people, the galley, ward-room, etc. topside. When I saw a small Norwegian freighter depart from the Magdalen Islands in September 1969, laden with frozen fish for Boston, the thought occurred to me that if you masted and rigged her, she would closely resemble the ships depicted in the Hastings Manuscript!

Comparing those and other vessels of the late fifteenth and early part of the sixteenth century with those shown in our picture of London River in 1600, it is clear that the principal modifications in the course of the century were (1) square spritsail and sometimes spritsail topsail on bowsprit; (2) square topsail on mizzen, and (3) much larger fore and main topsails in comparison with the lower courses. As topsails increased in area the courses, especially the mainsail, were reduced, and the yards shortened radically. These changes required smaller crews and made the ships both faster and handier. Finally, with greater depth of hold dry compartments could be built between ballast and lower deck for cargo, dry stores, and powder.

In the meantime a new category appears, the "bark," or "barque." This is identified as early as 1552 as a "little shyppe," and an Act of Parliament of 1585 distinguishes between owners and masters of "any Ship, Bark or Boat." Shakespeare, in *The Merchant of Venice* (III, iv), has Gratiano say:

> How like a younker or a prodigal
> The scarféd bark puts from her native bay,
> Hugg'd and embraced by the strumpet wind!

Throughout the sixteenth century *bark* usually meant a ship of under a hundred tuns' burthen, but I have seen mention of one or two slightly over a hundred tuns. The bark was rigged exactly like the ship —fore and mainmast square, mizzen lateen.

In the last third of the sixteenth century there emerges a type called the *flyboat, fliebote,* or *flute.* Sir Walter Raleigh's 140-tun *Roebuck,* named from his family crest, is an example. The name came from the Dutch *vlieboot,* originally one of the small boats used on the *Vlie,* or Sleeve, the channel leading to the Zuyder Zee; but the English flyboat could be anything from 20 to 150 tuns' burthen, and to the English "fly" denoted speed, not sleeve. The late sixteenth-century flyboat was a small three-master, rigged exactly like the bark but built to sail faster and carry less, and requiring a much smaller crew. She was larger than the pinnace. One was described in 1590 as built "to take and leave, when the skyrmish is to hote for him to tarry," meaning that her speed enabled her at will to engage, or break off. Several flyboats were used in the voyages to America under Gilbert and Raleigh.

The smallest sea-going type, called *galion* in French and *pinnace* in English, was a small, shoal-draft, and presumably fast vessel, very useful for exploring bays and the like. Frobisher's pinnace had a crew of only four men. Not completely decked over, these tiny vessels were liable, like a modern yacht, to be pooped and swamped by a heavy following sea, as happened to Gilbert's *Squirrel.* The best practice was to carry a prefabricated pinnace in the hold and assemble it ashore at the first convenient place in the New World. Since davits had not yet been invented, the largest ships' boats were often towed across the Atlantic when there was no room for them on deck. These were called long-boats; or, as early as 1578, "gundalos." An account of Frobisher's third voyage says, "Towing our gondelo at stern, she did split therewith and so we were forced to cut her from the ship and lost her." The boat shown in our frontispiece is one of these. For the same reason, lack of deck space, the smallest boats, called "shallops" (*chaloupes* in French) were often towed, and so lost. John White in his account of the 1590 voyage to Virginia notes on 25 March, "At midnight both our Shallops were sunke being towed at the ships stearne by the Boatswaines negligence." Always blame "Boats"!

John Norden's *Description of the Moste Famous City of London* (1600) shows a number of different small craft in the Thames above London Bridge, types which are occasionally mentioned in the voyages of discovery. At lower left are moored three *tilt-boats* and three more are being rowed along the other bank. These were rowing boats with a lightly built cabin covered by an awning. They were, in effect, water

Shipping in London above the Bridge, 1600. From Visscher's *Londonium* (1616), reproducing John Norden's *Description of the Moste Famous City of London*, 1600. Other small craft will be seen in the second half of this engraving, at the end of the chapter. Courtesy British Museum.

taxis in which Thames watermen rowed paying passengers from Greenwich or even Gravesend to the City. Sir Richard Grenville took a tiltboat to Virginia in 1585, and had himself grandly rowed about Pamlico Sound. Between "South" and "Warke" is a wherry, a type of rowboat persistent to our own day, with fixed thwarts and square slots for the oars. These too were taken overseas. A shallop is being rowed out to the one-masted wood boat over FLUVIUS, and I daresay that even some of the barges, here floating haystacks down from the upper river, were carried to America. In a country where there were very few wharves, slips, or quays, boat service was exceedingly important; and even more so on returning home. We shall find two instances in the Virginia voyages of vessels battered at sea, with beat-up crews, having to anchor in or even outside a harbor and wait for someone to send them a boat.

Getting Under Way

Weighing anchor was an occasion for a chantey; and a Lowland Scots writer of about 1548 records one that he heard on an English galeass— a big ship with three masts and a bank of long sweeps:

> Veyra, veyra, veyra, veyra
> Wind, I see him!
> pourbassa, pourbassa
> haul all and one (*bis*)
> haul hym up to us (*bis*)

Having properly catted, fished, and secured the anchor, let us hear our complaining Scot tell us how a ship got under way.

The master orders "two men above to the foretop to cut the rib-bands"—meaning the gaskets or stops on the furled foresail, "and let the foresail fall." Then, "haul out the bowline," the line secured to the leach (edge) of a square sail to keep it taut on the wind; for want of a jib these vessels had to depend on the foresail to head them off the wind and gather way. The foresail yard is hoisted home to this chantey:

> Ho, ho, ho—
> Pull a', pull a'
> bowline a', bowline a'
> darta, darta,
> hard out stiff (*bis*)
> before the wind, (*bis*)
> God send, God send
> Fair weather, fair weather,
> Many prizes, many prizes
> God fair [wind] send (*bis*)
> stow, stow,
> make fast and belay!

"Then the master cried and bade renze [rein, i.e. lash on] a bonnet, veer the trusses [parrels that bind the yards to the mast], now hoist!" The mariners then perform their most arduous job, hoisting the heavy main yard and sheeting home the main course, to this chantey:

> heisa, heisa
> vorsa, vorsa

wow, wow
one long draft (*bis*)
more might, more might
young blood, young blood
more mude, more mude
false flesh, false flesh
lie aback, lie aback
long swack, long swack
that, that, that, that
there, there, there, there
yellow hair, yellow hair
hips bare, hips bare
tell 'em all, tell 'em all
gallowsbirds all, gallowsbirds all
great and small, great and small
one an' all, one an' all
heist all, heist all

"Now make fast the tiers [halyards]. Then the master cryeth 'set your topsails, haul your topsail sheets veer your lifters [clewlines] and your topsail braces and hoist the topsail higher. Haul taut the topsail bowline. Hoist the mizzen and change it over to leeward. Sway the sheets on the belaying-pins, haul the braces to the yard.' Then the master cryeth to the helmsman, 'Mate, keep her full and by, a-luff. Come no higher, hold your tiller steady as you are, steer from tip of the helm thus and so.' Then, when the ship is tacked, the master cryeth, 'Boy to the top. Shake out the flag on the topmast, take in your topsails and furl them, pull down the point of the yard dagger-wise. Mariners, stand by your gear and the tackling of your sails, every quartermaster to his own station.' "

All this makes sense to anyone who has sailed a square-rigger, but even to old shellbacks some of it needs explanation. The purpose of trimming a yard "dagger-wise," later called "cockbilling," was to spill the wind out of the sail when maneuvering. Changing the mizzen from one tack to another required many hands because this lateen sail, on a long diagonal yard, had to be shifted around the mast whenever the ship came about. This *Complaynt of Scotlande* (1548) indicates that many methods, words, and commands which lasted right through the age of sail, were already in use in the reign of Henry VIII. With allowances for greater simplicity and less yelling on a small vessel, we may apply them to the reign of Henry VII, and imagine John Cabot's crew on the *Mathew* sounding off like those that the Scots "Complayner" heard on the English galeass.

Food, Cooking, and Clothing

At the forward end of the spar deck, partly protected by the forecastle, was the galley, an eighteenth-century term; in our era it was called the cook-box. On the smaller ships this was merely a hooded box placed athwartship and carrying several inches of sand or earth as a base for the fire. A few pots and pans and a supply of firewood sufficed to cook everything for the crew of a 50-tun ship. Native sloops in the West Indies and Arab dhows in the Persian Gulf have similar cooking arrangements today; all very well for smooth seas and fair weather, but not for the rain, fogs, and variables of the Western Ocean. Thus, on every merchant ship or fisherman designed for transatlantic work, the cook-box was built directly on top of the sand, shingle, or rock ballast forward, below the spar deck, and became the "cook-room." This allowed cooking in almost all weather. A Spaniard who boarded John Rut's ship *Mary of Guildford* in 1527 reported that she also had an oven for baking bread. Smoke from the cook-room fire first emerged through the hatches, but by 1571 some sort of "charley noble" or smoke-pipe had been devised, since we hear of Frobisher's *Aid* catching fire from a defective one.

Sebastian Cabot, in his "Ordinances . . . for the direction of the intended voyage to Cathay" via the Northeast Passage (1553), required "the steward and cooke of every ship" to present the captain weekly with an account of the expenditure of victuals "as wel flesh, fish, bisket, meate, or bread, as also of beere, wine, oyle or vinegar." Nobody thought of drinking water until the wine, beer, and cider gave out or spoiled, and in northern latitudes one could usually depend on refilling water butts from rain. The pickled beef and pork, packed in brine, were what English sailors since time immemorial have called "salt horse"; and the "bisket," their main breadstuff, they called "hardtack." It was purchased from bakeries that specialized in ship chandlery, but despite being stored in the driest part of the ship, it always became mouldy and maggotty before the end of a transatlantic round voyage. Ferdinand Columbus relates of his father's fourth voyage, "What with the heat and dampness, our ship biscuit had become so wormy that, God help me, I saw many who waited for darkness to eat the porridge made of it, that they might not see the maggots; and others were so used to eating them that they didn't even trouble to pick them out because they might lose their supper had they been so nice." "Stock-fish," sun-cured codfish from Newfoundland, soon replaced salt herring on the menu for fast days. Potatoes were a gift of the New World, and both coffee and tea came from the Indies; a couple of centuries elapsed before sailors could enjoy either. Spanish ships, and probably northern ships too, carried a supply of salted flour which, kneaded with water into rolls, could be baked in the hot ashes as a relief from the tooth-breaking "bisket."

For Frobisher's second voyage in 1577 we are fortunate to have not only the total amount of each foodstuff, but the way it was calculated: One pound of biscuit and one gallon of beer per man per diem, one pound of salt beef or pork per man on flesh days and one dried codfish for every four men on fast days, with oatmeal and rice if the fish gave out; a quarter-pound of butter and half a pound of cheese per man per day, honey for sweetening (sugar was still an expensive luxury); a hogshead of "sallet oyle" and a pipe of vinegar to last 120 men for three or four months. Considering that they were able to catch all the fresh cod and salmon, and shoot all the wild fowl and game that they wanted, once they had reached the New World, this suggests that English sailors in the reign of Elizabeth I ate hearty. They drank hearty, too, unless the beer went sour or its container leaked.

The mariner's standard costume, which he usually provided himself, was a gown made of coarse serge with a hood attached to protect the neck from wind and rain, loose "trews" (trousers), and "shipmen's hose" (long woolen stockings). From our frontispiece it is evident that sailors' clothes were colorful—bright red or blue; or, if leather, buff. They had shoes, but most of the time went barefoot, as leather skids on a wet deck or spar. Petty officers might add to this simple costume a wide-sleeved belted jacket, with a dagger or knife in a scabbard. Masters and owners made no provision for foul- or cold-weather garb. Apart from Frobisher's ships, in which some mariners had up to six changes of clothing, there was no attempt until 1628, even in the Royal Navy, to provide seamen with spares. A writer to the Admiralty described changes as "necessary . . . for the preservation of health as to avoid nasty beastliness to which many of the men are subject by continual wearing of one suit of clothes." The Willoughby expedition of 1553 in search of the Northeast Passage carried a "slop-chest," so called because rough, cheap clothes were a specialty of Shropshire (abbreviated Salop). It was stocked, among other articles, with canvas breeches, doublets lined with cotton, petticoats (a short man's-coat worn under the doublet), and "rugg"—a coarse woolen cloth—"for sea gowns."

The hammock for sleeping, discovered by Columbus in 1492 in the Bahamas, was not introduced to the Royal Navy until 1596, but may have been used earlier in big merchant ships. Prior to the issue of hammocks, mariners slept any place they could find; bunks were provided only for officers and some petty officers.

The Sailor, His Wages and Division of Labor

In the early seventeenth century it became a literary fashion to describe the "character" of a lawyer, merchant, divine, etc. One such book, Richard Braithwait's *Whimzies, or New Cast of Characters* (1631), thus describes "A Sayler":

"He is an *Otter*, an *Amphibium* that lives both on Land and Water . . . His familiarity with death and danger, hath armed him with a kind of dissolute security against any encounter. The sea cannot roar more abroad, than hee within, fire him but with liquor . . . In a Tempest you shall heare him pray, but so amethodically, as it argues that hee is seldome vers'd in that practice. . . . Hee makes small or no choice of his pallet; he can sleepe as well on a Sacke of Pumice as a pillow of doune. He was never acquainted much with civilitie; the Sea has taught him other Rhetoricke. Hee is most constant to his shirt, and other his seldome wash'd linnen. Hee has been so long acquainted with the surges of the Sea, as too long a calme distempers him. He cannot speake low, the Sea talks so loud. . . . Hee can spin up a rope like a Spider, and downe againe like a lightning. The rope is his roade, the topmast his Beacon. . . . Death hee has seene in so many shapes, as it cannot amaze him."

The Laws of Oleron, the traditional laws of the sea, dictated the relative responsibilities of master, supercargo, and mariner, as well as sea discipline. We are informed, for instance, that "Yf the maister

Shipboard punishments for mutiny. From Olaus Magnus, *Historia de Gentibus Septentrionalibus*, 1555. One sailor's hand is impaled by a dagger to the mainmast, the one in the water is being keel-hauled, and the one aft is to be repeatedly dunked until almost drowned. Courtesy Harvard College Library.

smyte any of the maryners the maryner ought to abide the fyrst buffet, be it with fyste or flat with his hande. But if he smyte any more he may defend hym[self]."

Seamen in the Royal Navy during the reign of Henry VII were paid 1s. 3d. per week or 5s. per month on active service, and their food cost the government another shilling and a few pence weekly. The master touched 3s. 4d. per week, and the petty officers up to 1s. 8d. In the merchant marine the only figure so far noted is 10s. per month, for Frobisher's sailors. The "portage" or share system of compensating mariners—similar to the "lay" in American whalers and fishermen of the nineteenth century—was already obsolete in 1480, and money wages were the rule in the merchant marine, except in fishing vessels. Sailors were usually given some clothing by the owner, and received a bonus if they took the place of stevedores in unloading the vessel. Mariners had their own "Shipmen's gilds," corresponding to our unions, at Bristol, York, Hull, and elsewhere, to protect those that do business in great waters from being too much put upon by shipowners.

We have no hint as to how *Mathew*'s crew of eighteen divided their duties, except by comparison with Columbus's *Niña*, which had twenty-two men including the captain and the master-owner. *Niña*'s roster shows, among the officers, a pilot—who took charge of navigation—a surgeon, and a marshal, an office that existed in English vessels well into the seventeenth century. Captain John Smith wrote: "The Marshall is to punish offenders and to see justice executed according to directions; as ducking at the yards arme, haling under the keel, bound to the capsterne or maine-mast with a bucket of shot about his necke, setting in the bilbowes." We must never forget that in the great age of discovery a sailor's life was rough, hard, and perilous. Punishments for mutiny or refusing orders were cruel, and the punishment for inattention to his particular business was apt to be crashing a reef, broaching-to, and death for all hands.

Mathew and every English or French vessel had two essential petty officers, boatswain and carpenter. "Bo'sun" or "Boats" transmitted the master's orders with the aid of his whistle, and was responsible for the gear. He taught the boys how to tie knots, and the mysteries of splicing, whipping, worming, and parceling the cordage. "Chips" the carpenter and his mate performed all necessary repairs to the wooden fabric and spars, and saw to it that topsides and decks were properly caulked and the seams payed with pitch. Vessels larger than *Niña* or *Mathew* carried a cooper to see that the casks of wine and barrels of beer were kept in good condition, and that enough fresh water was collected from rainstorms for cooking, or, at a pinch, drinking. *Niña* shipped seven able seamen and seven gromets (the old name for ships' boys) who would graduate to ordinary seamen after one voyage; one of them doubled as the captain's servant. Most mariners in the age of discovery preferred nimble young boys, despite their tendency toward skylarking, to old salts who were always grousing and grumbling; but they had to ship a fair proportion of able seamen to see that the work got done and to teach the boys how to "hand, reef and steer." The lowest rating of mariners was known as the "swabber," since it was his duty to keep the ship clean; and a mop, when it goes to sea, still becomes a "swab."

Ballast and Bilgewater

One great problem on long voyages, especially if there were passengers, was to keep the ship clean. All hold space not used for ships' stores and cargo was filled with sand, shingle, or cobblestone ballast from the beaches of the West Country; and two square, wooden box-like pumps led from the spar deck to the keelson to suck up bilge water. That did not consist entirely of leakage, but of urine, vomit, and various foul food-leavings that lazy sailors discharged into the ballast contrary to orders, under the cheerful belief that the pumps would take care of it. They did, to some extent; and a passenger on an English vessel sailing to the Mediterranean complained of the "foul stinkes" from the pump, against which he was so unfortunate as to sleep. Sebastian Cabot, remembering conditions afloat early in the century, enjoined the 1553 Muscovy fleet, "No liquor to be spilt on the balast, nor filthines to be left within boord; the cook room, and all other places to be kept cleane for the better health of the companie." Despite threats and punishments, the ballast and bilge usually became so disgusting and emitted such "pestilential funkes," that the ship had to be "rummaged" before returning home. That meant heaving her down on some convenient beach, throwing all ballast overboard so that the tide would cleanse it, scraping the horrible gunk off the inside of the hold, spraying it with vinegar, and replacing the ballast with clean stones, sand or shingle. Sir Richard Grenville's *Revenge* was being rummaged at Flores in the Azores when he sighted the Spanish fleet and had to get under way in a hurry.

Some seamen in this era realized what disgusting smells they and their ship produced. This is indicated by Martín Cortés's explanation of the St. Elmo's fire which appeared on masts and yards in tempests or whenever the air was supercharged with electricity. As Englished by Richard Eden, Martín attributed the ghostly "corposants" to "the fumes and smokes of theyr Shyppe, with the heate of men couched close and neare together in a narrowe place, and when a tempest ryseth the sayde smoke is thyckned, prest together or beaten down by the windes," and virtually explodes into fire!

Such conditions bred vermin; rats were an even greater bane to seamen in those days than in ours. The laws of the sea, and charter parties, prescribed that every ship carry one or more cats to keep the rats in order. There was no means of dealing with cockroaches and other vermin except stepping on them; but as transatlantic voyages became more numerous, a tradition developed that shipboard insects remained coy until they reached the warmer parts of the Atlantic, when they came out in force to enjoy the tropics, and the crew.

Navigation

All ships of this era wanted the wind to be on the quarter, or dead aft, to make best speed and least leeway. If the wind came "scant," i.e. dead ahead, or less than four or five compass points from their course, they were forced, if the sea were very rough, to lay-to; or, in a moderate sea, to beat to windward, which they called "traversing." This meant zig-zagging with the wind first on one side and then on the other. Sir Humfry Gilbert on his 1583 voyage, when trying to make St. John's, Newfoundland (latitude 47°33'47" N), on a due west course, encountered "winde alwayes so scant" from west-northwest and west-southwest, "that our traverse was great," running south to latitude 41° and then north to 51°, missing the harbor he wanted but making northern Newfoundland. This meant that his fleet could not sail nearer the wind than five points—56 degrees.

Celestial navigation is another matter. Before the age of discovery, ships could coast along western Europe, the Mediterranean, and even West Africa with no more shipboard aids to navigation than the compass, a pair of dividers, and the "three L's"—lead, log, and lookout—and the log was not invented until around 1575. Transatlantic voyages stimulated masters and pilots to use celestial navigation to fix their approximate position, just as aviation stimulated scientists to invent quicker methods to get a "fix" than the old time-sight. We shall observe how assiduous Verrazzano, Cartier, Frobisher, and Davis were in taking "heights," i.e. latitudes, of places they discovered.

The art of navigation had been developed by 1497, so that we may assume Cabot, Verrazzano, and Cartier carried a crude, non-reflecting quadrant and a mariner's astrolabe to take altitudes. The only heavenly bodies that the average navigator knew how to use before the end of the sixteenth century were Polaris (the North Star) and the sun. All "rutters" or sailing directions included a crude design to indicate the correction to apply to the height of Polaris, according to the positions relative to it of the "guards"—the two outer stars of the Little Bear or Dipper. Declination tables for obtaining latitude from a meridional observation of the sun were already available. Neither method was accurate within a degree, when practised from a ship at sea; but, once ashore or in harbor, the navigator could get a reasonably good estimate of his latitude. He had no accurate method of obtaining longi-

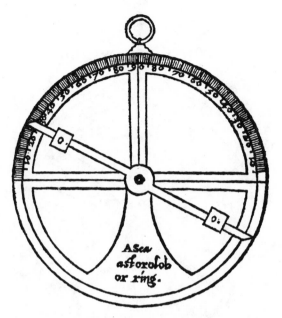

The mariner's astrolabe, or ring. From William Bourne's *A Regiment for the Sea*, 1574.

tude until "lunar distances" and the chronometer were invented in the eighteenth century. Navigators in the age of discovery simply guessed at a ship's speed and kept track of it in their sea journals. They did, however, know how to estimate speed "made good" when off course or beating to windward by a crude traverse board, or table. The rutters all charge the pilot to transfer data from traverse board, or table, to his "carde" (chart), a blank sheet of paper ruled for latitude and longitude. And he must "pricke the carde" for every noon or other estimated position.

The helmsman was directed by the officer on watch through a hatch or hole in the sterncastle deck, as the officer had the standard compass. That was a dry-card type on a pivot, floating in a bowl and enclosed in a waterproof binnacle which included a little whale-oil lamp. This, like similar binnacle lamps on nineteenth-century yachts, was always blowing out. On larger vessels, whose owners felt it a good investment, there was a second, steering compass just forward of the helmsman. Although ships of the period did a lot of rolling and pitching,

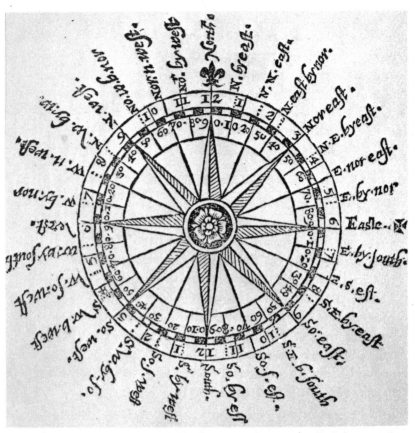

Compass card with both points and degrees. From John Davis's *The Seaman's Secrets*, 1594.

they were easy to keep on course if the sails were properly trimmed. As an aid to steering, prior to the invention of the wheel, a vertical beam called the whipstaff was riveted by one end to the deck, the middle loosely joined to the end of the tiller, and the top two or three feet used as a lever to pull it to starboard or larboard, as the port hand was called until the nineteenth century. This whipstaff did not become standard equipment in England until the second half of the sixteenth century, but the expert who constructed a model of Cartier's *La Grande Hermine* of 1525 gave her one.

The rutters (*routiers*), unofficial coast pilots of the period, were written primarily for finding one's way along European shores, but transatlantic voyagers were wise to have one on board for arrival and departure. Contrary to what most landsmen think, a shipmaster had a fairly easy time in blue water, where there were no obstacles; his troubles began when he arrived on soundings. That was when he snarled at his pilot, roared at the sailors, and aimed a kick at the ship's cat. Day and night he pored over his chart and his rutter, which might tell him from the depth of water, and the nature of the bottom, where he might be. Well did William Bourne, in his qualifications for a transatlantic captain, in 1574 write, "Also it behoueth him to be a good coaster, that is to say, *to knowe every place by the sight thereof.*" Fortunately an experienced seaman's memory of places he has passed but once, is phenomenal. The entire coast of western Europe is fraught with hazards to sailing vessels approaching from the sea; hazards which modern devices of lights, radio beacons, echo-sounders, etc. have mitigated but not removed. Consider, for instance, the problem of a master entering St. George's Channel in thick or strong weather, bound for Bristol, Dublin, or Liverpool. On one side Fastnet and the Smalls await his ship with greedy fangs; on the other are the Scillies and the multitude of rocks between them and Lands End, Cornwall, including Seven Stones, where the big tanker *Torrey Canyon* came to grief in 1967, drenching the Cornish shores with black oil. Or, supposing he were a man of Devon seeking the sanctuary of Plymouth. He had to sail well south of his destination to avoid the Eddystone's *scopulos infames,* as Camden called them; but if he sailed too far south he might strike the equally dangerous Casquets off Alderney.

Or, the master mariner returning from Newfoundland, after picking up familiar landmarks—a church steeple, a clump of trees, an odd house—and about to enter his home port, might be forced to sea again by a radical change in the wind. In the English Channel gale of July 1953, a well-built ten-ton yacht meeting a big wind funnelling out of Cherbourg head-on, could not enter, even with the aid of her engine. She was blown across the Channel and foundered off the Isle of Wight.

In these narrow seas local knowledge and a judicious use of the lead were essential. The heavy leads (as shown in the Hastings Manuscript) had a socket "armed" (filled) with sticky tallow to pick up samples of the bottom; and from them, as well as the depth, the experienced pilot knew where he was. For instance, Master Jackman on Frobisher's 1578 voyage "sownded and had 70 faddems, oosy sand, whereby we judged us to be northwards of Scilly, and afterward sailed south east all that night." The ship rounded Lands End safely, and three days later "had sight of the Start, 5 leags off, God be praysed!" A rutter like Bourne's made a point of giving the character of the bottom ("white sand, soft worms, popplestones as big as beans, cockleshells," etc.) at every crucial point.

Not all master pilots were as smart as Jackman. The *Hopewell* from Newfoundland, bound for London in August 1587, "drawing neere the coast of England," sounded and found seventy fathom, but nobody could agree on interpreting what the lead brought up; so through "evil marinership were fain to dance the hay foure days together," running northeast, southeast, east and east-northeast. Finally they sighted Lundy in the Severn estuary, whence they shaped their course around Lands End to London. Dancing the hey or hay was an old country reel in which the boys and girls danced in serpentine fashion, like beating to windward.

Once within the chops (entrance) of the Channel, the careful pilot bound for London, ticked off the prominent headlands as he passed. These are described in the old chantey "Spanish Ladies":

> Now the first land we make it is calléd the Deadman
> Then Rams Head off Plymouth, Start, Portland and Wight;
> We sailed then by Beachy, by Fairlee and Dungeness
> Then bore straight away for the South Foreland Light.

Deadman was what sailors called Dodman Island, Cornwall; Start Point you had to round to make Dartmouth; Portland Bill is a conspicuous point which makes a bad tide-rip; St. Catherine's Point, Isle of Wight, and Beachy Head are perfect landmarks; Fairlee meant Fairlight Hill just east of Hastings, and Dungeness is the last prominent cape before reaching the South Foreland.

There were none but dim local lights along this coast in the sixteenth century, and very few buoys or other navigational aids. The French coast was better marked. Biggest lighthouse in Europe was the forty-eight-foot stone Tour de Cordouan at the mouth of the Gironde, first erected in the ninth century and rebuilt by the Black Prince; a tower so famous that it became a point of reference in John Cabot's voyage. There were also lighthouses at La Rochelle (lighted only in storms), at Dieppe, and perhaps seven other ports in Normandy and Brittany. But "practically nothing is known for certain about any English lighthouses between the Roman occupation and the middle of the seventeenth century except that a few primitive towers did exist," states the historian of the then unmarked Eddystone. One such is shown in our illustration from the Hastings Manuscript of 1480. These were erected and maintained by private individuals or coastal towns; a fire of bituminous coal or resinous wood furnished the light. They were undependable since the owners usually considered it a waste of fuel to light up on a clear or moonlit night, and when most needed they might be quenched by rain or snow.

In the narrow seas one could not ignore the danger of collision. No running lights were required until centuries later, but masters were recommended to keep a lighted "lanthorn" in a bucket to show if they were in danger of being run down. Want of artificial lights made it desirable to begin a transatlantic voyage near the moon's first quarter, in order to have moonlight to clear the Channel.

For the master of a vessel which had no auxiliary power, a knowledge of tides was a necessity, especially in the English Channel and Bristol Channel where tides run swift and high. If he knows their times, and the direction and force of the currents they create, tides are a boon to the knowledgeable sailor, and a terror to the ignorant. There were then no government or private tide tables, but every rutter taught the pilot how to compile his own. Based on the changeless fact that high water on the day of new moon comes at noon or midnight, you figure that it comes forty-eight minutes later every day thereafter. But only experience, or information handed down from the Middle Ages, could teach one the flow of the currents at danger points like Eddystone and Ushant.

In discussing navigational methods, one is apt to ignore the gap between the invention of a device and persuading owners to supply it or sailors to use it. For instance, the chronometer, which first enabled a navigator to get accurate longitude, was invented in 1750; but the royal French navy in 1833, with 250 ships, had only 44 chronometers. To assume that once an instrument is invented or a rutter or nautical almanac published, every offshore shipmaster is familiar with them, is a complete fallacy. The very simple mathematical calculations involved in obtaining latitude from a meridional observation of the sun were too much for most sailors in 1550, and are still too much for many sailors in the present century. I had the experience of teaching a good down-east sailing master to take accurate sights with a sextant; but he could never get through his head that there are only sixty, not one hundred minutes, to the degree, hence his results were all wrong. And another of the same breed once remarked, "I don't know nothin' about chro-nometers and ba-rometers, but I can find my way around!" No doubt he could; there is a certain *feel* for a ship and the sea, possessed by men like Columbus, Cartier, Frobisher, John Davis, and by thousands of humble shipmasters unknown to fame, which is as good or better than scientific navigation.

In general, the navigational methods in effect around 1500 lasted, with many refinements but no essential changes, until 1920–30. Then radio beams, timers, echo-finders, and the like were first installed on warships and big steamships, replacing the navigator's dependence on his own efforts with shipboard instruments. But, woe betide the master who neglects the traditional Three L's! Remember the *Andrea Doria!*

Shipboard Religion

Sailors in the age of discovery were highly sensible of the danger of their calling—and why not? John Cabot was lost with four ships and all hands, the Corte Real brothers were lost with two ships and all hands, Sir Humfry Gilbert's pinnace was "devoured and swallowed up of the sea" within sight of her consorts. They were conscious of being in a special sense in the hands of the Almighty, and so made a point of public prayers to remind God and the Virgin Mary, "Star of the Sea," that they counted on heavenly protection against the cruel elements. For the same reason, to avoid affronting God to the point of His be-coming indifferent to a ship's fate, Sebastian Cabot charged "that no blaspheming of God, or detestable swearing be used . . . nor com-munication of ribaldrie filthy tales, or ungodly talke to be suffered in the company . . . neither dicing, carding, tabling nor other divelish games to be frequented, whereby ensueth not only povertie to the players, but also strif, variance, brauling . . . and provoking of God's most just wrath, and sworde of vengeance." Sebastian insists "that morning and evening prayer, with the common services appointed by the king's Majestie be read dayly by the chaplain or some other person learned," and "the Bible or paraphrases to be read devoutly and Christianly to God's honour, and for His grace to be obtained." As this indicates, every shipmaster provided himself with an Edward VI Book of Common Prayer. And the requirement of daily prayer lasted, as is shown by Captain John Smith's *Sea Grammar* of 1627, prescribing orisons and psalms at stated intervals. Similar injunctions against swearing and blasphemy are found in sailors' contracts in merchant marines right down to 1900.

Prior to Henry VIII's breach with Rome, English ships, and French ships later (unless owned by Protestants), probably followed the same ritual as did Columbus: a hymn, Our Father, and Hail Mary when changing the dawn watch; a little ditty each time the glass is turned; around sunset, when the first night watch is set, all hands repeating Our Father, Hail Mary, and the Creed, and singing the hymn *Salve Regina* to the Queen of Heaven. Frobisher held some sort of service at noontime; he records one day chasing Eskimo visitors off the ship at 11:00 a.m., "since we were to go to prayer."

Seamen were superstitious as well as religious, and still are. One must never sail on a Friday, because it was the day Our Lord was crucified. One must never lay a hatch cover upside down—goodness knows why. One must not destroy a printed page—it might belong to the Bible. In building a ship, a silver coin must be heeled below the mainmast. On the Isle of Man a burning brand had to be carried through every part of a new ship to drive out evil spirits. The ghost of an unbaptized infant buried at the foot of a tree whose wood was used to build a ship, would inhabit the vessel and bring her good fortune. This is the

> Sweet little cherub that sits up aloft
> To keep watch for the life of poor Jacke,

as wrote Charles Dibdin the sailor's poet.

Weapons, Sweeps, and Anchors

By mid-century, vessels built especially for war were designed differently from ordinary merchant ships, as you may see from our illustrations. But almost every merchant vessel mounted a few small cannon such as the lombard, which threw a stone cannon ball, and the smaller falconet, a swivel gun mounted on the bulwarks, which fired scrap metal. Verrazzano and Cartier, who sailed in kings' ships, probably

H.M.S. *Tegar*, 200 tuns, 100 "marrynars," and 20 "gonnars."

H.M.S. *Lyon*, 140 tuns, 100 men. From the Anthony Roll of the Navy, 1545 Add. Mss. 22047. Both have dressed ship for a holiday. Courtesy British Museum.

carried larger ordnance; but the only weapon mentioned in any Cabot narrative is the crossbow. Every ship carried a stand of swords, cutlasses, and pikes to be used in case natives or enemies endeavored to take her by boarding. The difficulty in keeping gunpowder dry on a small ship in rough weather, and the danger of its exploding if placed near the galley fire to dry, made steel more popular with sailors than firearms; pike and crossbow did well enough against enemies who had nothing more lethal than bows and arrows.

Cannon were always mounted on the spar deck prior to 1501, when a certain Decharges of Brest had the wit to place guns below on the

Ship in Dover Harbor, c. 1530–37. The Cross of St. George, the men at arms, and tier of guns (with two stern-chasers sticking out beside the rudder) show that she is one of the smaller units of the Royal Navy. From Cottonian Aug. Mss. I. i. 23. Courtesy British Museum.

Ships on the Thames below London Bridge, 1600. From Visscher's *Londonium* (1616), copying John Norden's *Description of the Moste Famous City of London*, 1600. Courtesy British Museum.

main deck and to pierce ports for them to fire through. The earliest picture that I have seen to show gun ports is on the war vessel here illustrated, in a view of Dover dated 1541. Incidentally, this is one of the best ship-pictures of that period for accurate detail of sails, spars, and rigging. Note the halberdier on the forecastle and another in her waist, and an archer on the poop. The projection under the bowsprit with the head of a fox was known as the beak head, and supposedly had been copied from Mediterranean galleys which used it for ramming. After informal war began with Spain, every English ship carried heavy ordnance. In our picture of Sir Richard Grenville's *Tiger* in 1585, the gun ports are prominent.

All vessels the size of Cabot's *Mathew*, and larger ones too, were provided with long ash sweeps so that they could be propelled in a calm. And they could also be towed by their longboat.

Iron anchors, of a design unchanged for over four centuries, were stowed in the forecastle during a voyage, and a hemp cable bent onto the ring for use in harbor or alongshore. The Hastings Manuscript ship shows one very plainly. The tackles securing the anchor to the cathead and the sides of the ship were called *stoppers* and *shank-painters* as early as 1577, in the inventory of Frobisher's flagship *Aid*. Every transatlantic vessel carried at least four anchors; and as ships often had to moor in an open roadstead, breakwaters being scarce even in Europe, and forced to get under way in a hurry, they were apt to lose two or three in the course of a long voyage. Columbus was once left with only one anchor for two ships, so he had to "raft" them together, as members of the Cruising Club like to do.

Almost every transatlantic voyage ended at anchor. In the ports of London, Bristol, Le Havre, Rouen, Dieppe, and a few others, local authorities provided stone quays or jetties alongside which a ship could lay and discharge cargo; but in the New World every stop meant anchoring. The prudent captain, before entering an unknown harbor, would send in a boat to sound and test the holding ground; the harbor might turn out to have a bottom of hard stone or slippery eel grass over which an anchor would skid like a sled on snow. No wonder that the anchor became the symbol of hope (Hebrews vi. 19) and of admiralty.

Many improvements were made in English rigging and ship design during the sixteenth century, but the blue-water merchantmen of 1500 and 1600 were essentially similar. Greater changes came in the following century, owing (as Hakluyt predicted) to overseas trade's requiring faster and more seaworthy ships, and accommodation for passengers.

As Buckminster Fuller pointed out in his *Ideas and Integrities* (1963), the building of a ship that could harness the wind, and by "traversing" sail where her master wished, is one of the greatest and most admirable achievements of mankind. The building alone involved many techniques of the modern assembly plant, and to sail successfully overseas drew on astronomy, meteorology, and dynamics, as well as courage, resourcefulness, and sound common sense. All the world's great geographical discoveries were made with no other power than oar and sail. As Edouard Peisson remarked in his *L'Aigle de mer*, "Le voilier était à la mesure de l'homme. Il n'écrasait pas l'homme, mais l'attirait, le séduisait, le gardait." And it still delights us and fortifies us against a mechanized culture which reduces man to a moron.

The men who manned these ships, or sailed in them as passengers, were those who enlarged the scope of Europe to embrace the whole world. Would that we knew far more than we do about life on board their wooden vessels, their only homes for a large portion of their lives.

Bibliography and Notes

GENERAL

The quotation at the head of this chapter is from Garcie's *Routier* as reprinted by D. W. Waters, *Rutters of the Sea*, p. 23. The quotation from Peisson is on p. 72 of his *L'Aigle de mer* (1941).

Mrs. Catharine Cooper has been of great assistance by searching out in the libraries and archives of greater London the bits and pieces from which this chapter has been constructed. The National Maritime Museum at Greenwich, and the manuscript and map rooms of the British Museum have been most helpful. Greenwich has a manuscript catalogue of ships which tells one what happened to those used by Frobisher, Davis, and others.

Anyone who wants accurate information on this subject, well presented, should first of all consult Gregory Robinson's illustrated booklet *Elizabethan Ships* in Longmans Then and There series (London, 1956).

The principal works in English are: Dorothy Burwash, *English Merchant Shipping 1460–1540* (Toronto University Press, 1947); R. and R. C. Anderson, *The Sailing Ship: A Thousand Years of History* (London and New York, 1947)—both good as far as they go; Maurice Oppenheim, *A History of the Administration of the Royal Navy and of Merchant Shipping from MDIX to MDCLX* (London, 1896; offprint 1961), with many data on the merchant marine. Frederic C. Lane, *Venetian Ships and Shipbuilders of the Renaissance* (Baltimore, 1935); and *Venice and History* (Baltimore, 1966), especially chap. xi: "Naval Architecture about 1550," chap. xvi; "Diet and Wages of Seamen in Early Fourteenth Century," and chap. xxi: "Tonnages, Medieval and Modern." There are also valuable articles by Pierre Chaunu and Paul Gille on tunnage in *Le Navire et l'economie maritime du XVe–XVIII siècle* (1956).

Chanteys are from *The Complaynt of Scotlande*, of which the best edition is that of the Early English Text Society, extra ser. XVII (London, 1872). This is conjecturally dated 1548 and attributed to Robert Semphill. The *Complaynt* is in "braid Scots" which I have had to translate to have it understood. *Veyra* may mean "veer" or "ware all," and *pourbassa*, "pull our best all," but they may be just nonsense like some of the early Spanish chanteys. Auguste Jal, *Archéologie navale*, II, 53, has the *Complaynt* in translation with useful notes.

DESIGN, RIGGING, AND DETAILS

Gregory Robinson's *Elizabethan Ships* is excellent as far as it goes, and includes a special study of Drake's *Golden Hind;* but not enough for us to extrapolate to the ships of Frobisher, Gilbert, and Davis. Auguste Jal, in his *Documents inédits sur l'histoire de la marine au XVIe siècle* (1842), p. 71, has this to say on the difference between clinker-built and carvel-built: "Carvel-built vessels differ from those *à clin* [clinker-built] in that their planks instead of overlapping, were placed over or beside each other, their edges touching. . . . The term *bordage à carvel* is no longer used in France but still is in England, where one says *carvel work*." The first carvel-built ship, he says, was constructed by the Dutch at Horn in 1460. R. C. Anderson, *The Sailing-Ship*, p. 124, states that carvel building started in Brittany.

Cogs and Hulks. Much information in Jacques Bernard, *Navires et gens de mer de Bordeaux* (1968), I, 295–304.

Flyboats. My information on this type comes almost entirely from *The New English Dictionary;* works on Tudor shipping such as Clowes and Burwash do not even mention it. R. M. Nance states that it was "an enlarged, ship-rigged barge, contrived to carry as much merchandise as possible with the smallest possible crew." An unnamed flyboat was very important in the Raleigh voyages to Virginia (see Chapter XX below).

Articles useful for details, though seldom for generalities, are the following in *Mariner's Mirror,* Journal of the Society for Nautical Research, London:

L. Arenhold, "Ships Earlier than 1500 A.D.," I (1911), 298–301.

C. N. Robinson, quotes from R. Braithwait's *Whimzies* on "A Sayler," I, 312–15.

M. Bloomfield, "Hammocks and Accessories," I, 144–47.

R. Morton Nance, "A Sixteenth Century Sea Monster," II (1912), 97–102.

Jules Sottas, "Guillaume Le Testu and His Work," II 65–75. Two of Testu's ship pictures are reproduced in Chapter VIII below.

Alan Moore, "Rigging in the Seventeenth Century," II, 266–74, 301–308. Illustrated. Superb!

H. S. Vaughan, "The Whipstaff," III (1913), 229–37 and IV (1914), 133–44. Illustrated.

R. Morton Nance, "Caravels," III, 265–71. Illustrated.

W. G. Perrin, "Seamen's Clothes," III, 178–79, 246–47; note on hose in VI (1920), 375.

L. G. Carr Laughton, "The Inventory of the Great Bark, 1531," V (1919), 21–22.

G. E. Manwaring, "Dress of British Seamen from the Earliest Times to 1600," VIII (1922), 324–33, and IX (1923), 162–73. Illustrated.

W. G. Perrin, "Bands in the Royal Navy," IX, 2–10. Illustrated.

R. C. Anderson, "Early English Three-Masters," XIV (1928), 84–85.

Sebastian Cabot's "Ordinance for the direction of the intended voyage to Cathay" (1583) is in Hakluyt (Everyman's ed.), I, 234. Henry L. Swinburne, *The Royal Navy* (1907), has a chapter on Naval Costume by C. N. Robinson.

See last note in this book on changes of design *c.* 1600.

Lighthouses. L'Abbé A. Anthiaume, *Les Méthodes de navigation en France au moyen-âge* (1924). Trinity House, chartered by Henry VIII in 1514, was authorized by Parliament in 1566 "to make, erect and set . . . beacons, marks and signs for the sea"; but more than two centuries elapsed before the Brotherhood of the Trinity obtained exclusive jurisdiction over lighthouses and seamarks, and in the meantime private persons received licenses to erect lights or beacons and to collect dues for the same from passing shipping.

Besides those ship pictures in the Hastings Manuscript and on various maps which we have mentioned or reproduced, there is an engraving of Dover of *c.* 1530–37 (British Museum Cotton Mss. Augustus, I, i, 22–23) from which we have taken a three-masted ship under full sail. *A Plan of the Harbour and Road of Calais* of about 1541–42 in Cotton Mss. Aug. I, ii, 57, also shows a multitude of ships, as does a view of Yarmouth "in the Elizabethan Period." See R. C. Anderson's article in *Mariner's Mirror,* VII (1921), 365.

RUTTERS

William Bourne, *A Regiment for the Sea* (1574), edited with introduction by E. G. R. Taylor (Hakluyt Soc., 1963); Roger Barlow, *A Briefe Summe of Geographie,* edited by the same (Hakluyt Soc., 1932); D. W. Waters, *The Rutters of the Sea; the Sailing Directions of Pierre Garcie* (Yale, 1967), including a translation of Garcie's *Grand Routier* (1542). Miss Alwyn A. Ruddock describes an earlier English rutter for Holland in Institute of Navigation *Journal,* XIV (1961), 409–31. The best collection of printed rutters in America is Henry C. Taylor's at Yale University Library.

As a sample of a good rutter, the paragraph of the Hastings Manuscript ending on the page where the ship is depicted entering the Channel reads as follows (with the archaic spelling modernized): "Course from C. Finisterre to England NNE—but if you want the Severn, go N and by E till you come on to soundings. And if ye be 3 parts [out of 4] over the sea and ye be bound in to the Narrow Sea and ye go NNE, then change your course and go NE by N till ye come in to soundings of 100 fathom deep, then go your course NE till ye come in to 40 fathom deep; and if it be streamy ground it is between Ushant and Scilly in the centre of the Channel of Flanders [an old name for the English Channel] and so go your course till ye have 60 fathom deep. Then go ENE along the sea." Lay that off on a modern chart, and you will find that, allowing a point either way for changed compass variation, it would get you there.

Early treatises on navigation are also valuable, and among the best is the Richard Eden translation of Martín Cortés, *The Arte of Navigation* (London, 1596). There is a copy in the Boston Athenaeum bound up

with Robert Norman, *The Safeguard of Saylers* (1612), and an early edition of Bourne's *Regiment*. All have interesting diagrams and profiles of
European landmarks. Norman's *Safeguard*, p. 66, has a table of the author's
record passages in European waters; to measure these on a chart would
indicate the speed of contemporary ships. His *Newe Attractive . . . of the
Magnes or Lodestone* (1581) is the classic on the magnet, with many useful
facts on compass variation. For instance, he tells you exactly how much
variation to allow on the favorite latitude route to America, from the
Bishop Rock (49°52′ N—Norman says 50°) to Cape Race (46°39′ N—
Norman says 46°20″). He concludes charmingly by putting this poem into
"The Magnes or Lodestone's" mouth:

Give place, ye glitteryng sparkes,
　Ye glimmering Sapphires bright,
Ye Rubies redde & Diamonds brave
　Wherein ye most delight.

. . .

No Shippe could Saile on Seas
　her course to runne aright
Nor Compasse shewe the readie waie
　Were Magnes not of might.

. . .

If this you can denie
　then Seeme to maike replie
And let the painfull Seaman iudge,
　the whiche of us doe lie!

NAVIGATION

Accurately copied from *The Mariners' Mirrour* (1588), this frontispiece
to Nordenskiöld's *Periplus* shows quadrants in the upper corners, with
mariner's astrolabes hanging under them; half-hour glasses on the edges of
the pediment; cross-staffs to left and right. Two well-dressed mariners are
heaving the lead. Compasses and dividers are in the lower corners. The
ship, of a post-1550 type, is sailing under mainsail only; the mizzen, fore
course, and main topsail are furled. The mainsail carries both bonnet and
drabler on its foot. These were cloths laced onto the foot of the mainsail;
unlacing them was the early equivalent to taking in one or two reefs.

William Bourne's directions for the use of the astrolabe are in the Taylor
edition of his *A Regiment for the Sea* (1963) p. 84. This process of applying sun's declination to sun's altitude can best be explained by a diagram.

Alidade and astrolabe are Arabic terms, western Europeans having obtained this instrument from Arab mathematicians. See Robert T. Gunther,
Astrolabes of the World (2 vols., Oxford, 1932). You took the altitude of
the sun in degrees, since the astrolabe of that era registered nothing less,
subtracted this altitude from 90°, the result being the zenith distance. You

then applied the sun's declination, plus or minus according to the season and hemisphere, and correct latitude should result. There were daily declination tables in every rutter. As an example, Christopher Hall, master of Frobisher's bark *Gabriel*, on 26 June 1576 found the altitude of the sun to be 53°, and its zenith distance 37°; adding the day's declination, 22°46', the resulting latitude was 59°46', within a few miles of correct (Stefansson, *Frobisher*, I, 150). This simple method is still widely in use.

Latitude from Polaris, the North Star, was even easier, except for the difficulty of catching so comparatively faint a star in the pinhole of the vane on an astrolabe's alidade, or in the pinholes of a crude quadrant (see diagram). To its observed altitude one applied corrections between +3.6° and −3.6° according to the position of Kochab, the brighter Guard of the Little Bear or Dipper, in relation to Polaris. In all books of navigation such as Pedro Medina's *Regimiento de Navigacion* you found a diagram of a little man for this purpose; the correction depended on whether Kochab was at head, feet, west arm, etc. In the early sixteenth century Polaris was about 3°42' from the celestial pole; precession has now reduced this to less than one degree.

The other instrument, besides quadrant and astrolabe, which Cabot must have had, is a *traverse board*. We know this because as early as 1436 a

Captain A. Fontoura da Costa and S. E. M. taking a meridional altitude of the sun with the mariner's astrolabe preserved in the Museum of Coimbra. Steadying the astrolabe between the knees is considered the better technique. We found the latitude to be 40° N; it is actually 40°12'.

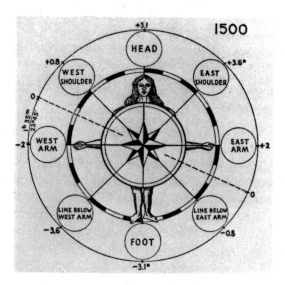

Diagram for obtaining latitude from an observed altitude for the North Star. The position of Kochab, the brighter "guard" of the Little Dipper, to Polaris, indicates the correction to apply. From S. E. Morison "Columbus and Polaris" in *American Neptune*, I.

Diagram for obtaining latitude from noon observation of the sun.

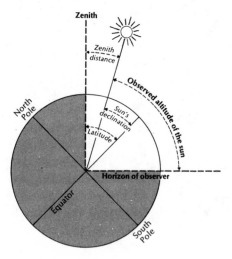

Nineteenth-century traverse board. Courtesy
Peabody Museum, Salem, Mass.

traverse table on the same principle is in the atlas of Andrea Bianco.*
Traversing, in the fifteenth to seventeenth centuries, meant what we call

* Reproduced, analyzed, and described in A. E. Nordenskiöld, *Periplus*, pp. 53–
54. Also by Eugenio Gelcich in his *Estudios sobre el Desenvolvimiento historico
de la Navegación* (Valencia, 1889), pp. 80–81.

tacking; and the traverse board was a device to help the seamen keep his dead reckoning when beating to windward or whenever forced off his intended course. The officer of the watch stuck a peg into the board every half-hour or hour, for each course that she sailed. The horizontal line of the holes at the foot were to record, again by pegs, the estimated speed on each course. Finally, the courses and distances were laid down on the chart. These traverse boards were in use well into the nineteenth century; *The Sailor's Word Book* (1867) recommends its use in "light and variable winds"—*Mariner's Mirror*, XVII (1931), 288–89. Gemma Frisius, about 1545, invented a diagram that he called the "nautical square," and others, "the sinical quadrant," which enabled anyone to find the course made good without calculations.

The best accounts of these and other instruments are in M. V. Brewington, *The Peabody Museum Collection of Navigating Instruments* (Salem, 1963); Charles Singer *et al.*, *A History of Technology* (Oxford, 1959); E. G. R. Taylor and M. W. Richey, *The Geometrical Seaman* (London, Institute of Navigation, 1962). I am indebted to Mr. Philip C. F. Smith, Curator of Maritime History at the Peabody Museum of Salem, for instruction as to the use of these old instruments. See notes that follow on later instruments that became available, and in later Chapters.

NAVAL ARMS AND ORDNANCE IN THE SIXTEENTH CENTURY

Cannon. 7¼" bore, firing a 50-pound iron ball.

Demi-cannon. 6¼" bore, firing a 32-pound ball.

Culverin. A long cannon of 5¼" bore, firing a 16¾- to 17½-pound ball.

Demi-culverin. 4¼" bore, firing a 9-pound ball.

Caliver. Hand-gun, a primitive light musket.

Falcon. A cannon of 2½" bore, firing a 2½- to 3-pound ball.

Falconet. A light cannon on a swivel, mounted on bulwarks or ships' boats; 2" bore, firing a 1¼- to 2-pound ball.

Minion. Next smaller than Saker. 3"-4" bore, 4-pound ball.

Saker. Next smaller than demi-culverin. 4" bore, 5-pound ball.

Serpentine. A small cannon of 1½" bore.

Reference: Michael Lewis, "Armada Guns," *Mariner's Mirror*, XXVIII (1942), 41–73, 104–47. See especially his discussion of ranges on pp. 70–72.

The best guns were of brass, but probably most of those in the merchant marine were of iron.

Of two Queen's ships that come into our narration (Lewis, p. 147): *Aid* in 1576 mounted 2 demi-culverin, 13 saker; total weight of shot, 83 pounds; *Tiger* in 1585 mounted 7 demi-culverin, 7 saker, 4 minion; total weight of shot, 88 pounds.

✳ VI ✳
John Cabot's Voyages

1497-1498

Kepe then the sea that is the wall of England:
And then is England kept by Goddes hande.
—A LIBEL OF ENGLISH POLICIE, *c.* 1436.

Who Was John Cabot?

In view of his importance as the first discoverer of North America
since the Northmen's voyages almost five centuries earlier, and as the
man who gave England her American title, it is amazing how little we
know about John Cabot. But not for lack of trying. During the last
century and a half, research into his life and voyages has been both
intense and assiduous, with results disappointingly meager. No portrait
or personal description of him, no letter, no scrap of his handwriting,
not even a signature, has been found. His momentous first voyage cannot be definitely traced. His fate, on his second voyage, is not certainly
known. Part of the historical muddle is due to the fact that John's son
Sebastian, who may have accompanied him on the first voyage, showed
a notable lack of filial piety in claiming the discovery for himself;
and as John disappeared in 1498 and Sebastian became a great man,
people believed him and forgot his father. So, to put John Cabot
together again from the bits and pieces excavated from archives and
muniments is like trying to construct a big picture puzzle from one
per cent of the original pieces, few of which can be fitted together.
We have no sea journal by Cabot himself as we have for Columbus,
nor did any of his shipmates leave an account of the voyage. All the
evidence is hearsay, mostly at third hand, and by people who made

wild guesses. It is no wonder that scholars disagree about Cabot. One has to discard part of the scanty evidence to make sense out of the rest.

To begin with, Who was John Cabot?

An Italian certainly; a Genoese probably. The name, common on the European littoral in various forms such as Cabotto, Kaboto, Chiabotto, Bagoto, Cabuto, Savoto, etc.—sometimes corrupted by writers who did not hear it correctly, to Babate or Talbot—means simply "Coaster" —one who engages in coastal shipping. The Spanish ambassador at the Court of St. James's in 1498 called John "another Genoese like Colón," but nothing about his family has been found in the Genoese archives. Our first trace of him is in Venice when he became a naturalized citizen. The Venetian senate confirmed his citizenship in 1476, stating that he had been a resident of the Republic for fifteen years. He must, therefore, have been born not later than 1453, and probably earlier, even in 1451, the same year as Columbus. They might have been boys together in Genoa. John's father took him to Venice when he was not more than ten years old. Soncino, the Milanese envoy in London, calls John "a very good mariner" and "of a fine mind, greatly skilled in navigation." He must have been, to have done what he did. And he must have possessed uncommon courage to set forth with only one small ship. Even the Pilgrim Fathers started with two.

The first known fact on Cabot's sea-going activities was told by him to Soncino: "In former times he was at Mecca, whither spices are brought by caravans from distant countries." Those who brought them thither knew not where spices originated, but Cabot incorrectly inferred that they came from *northern* Asia.

John Cabot was already married and living in Venice in 1484; documents prove that he was there engaged in buying and selling real estate, and there was some dispute about his wife's dowry. Next, in the archives of Valencia, it appears that a Venetian called "Johan Cabot Montecalunya" resided in that Spanish seaport between 1490 and 1493. He tried to interest King Ferdinand the Catholic in building a jetty; the project fell through in March 1493 because "matching funds" were not forthcoming. It cannot be proved that this John Cabot with the strange suffix was our John, but he may well have been; and it does not strain one's imagination to assume that he happened to be in Barcelona at the time of Columbus's triumphal entry in April 1493, that he met the Admiral of the Ocean Sea and decided to do him one better, reaching the Indies by a shorter route. He sought support in Seville and Lisbon, but failed.

It then occurred to him that England, being at the end of the spice line and paying the highest prices, would be interested in finding a short, high-latitude route to the Indies. Spices, especially pepper, cloves, and nutmeg, were household necessities in that era, for want of refrigeration; a liberal use of them disguised the flavor of spoiled meat. So to England went Cabot, and England was the one country where he was likely to gain support. Henry VII, in turning down the proposition of the Columbus brothers, had missed his chance to be "first"; he was not going to miss it this time, particularly since Cabot offered to sail on "his own proper charges," so it would not cost the crown a penny. And it is certain that Cabot went there not later than 1495, because the Spanish ambassador wrote to King Ferdinand in January 1496 that "Uno como Colón" (a man like Columbus) was proposing to King Henry VII "another business like that of the Indies." In reply the Spanish sovereign ordered his ambassador to protest; but his excellency, if he got around to it, did not succeed. On 5 March 1496 Henry VII granted letters-patent to "our well beloved John Gabote, citizen of Venice, [and] to Lewes, Sebastian, and Santius, sonnes of the said John . . . full and free authoritie, leave, and power, to sayle to all partes, countreys, and seas, of the East, of the West, and of the North, under our banners and ensignes, with five ships . . . and as many mariners or men as they will have with them in the saide ships, upon their own proper costes and charges, to seeke out, discover, and finde, whatsoever iles, countreyes, regions or provinces of the heathen and infidelles, whatsoever they bee, and in what part of the world soever they be, whiche before this time have beene unknowen to all Christians." They may govern these newly found lands as the king's lieutenants, monopolize their produce and enter them duty free, paying to the crown "the fifth part of the Capitall gaine so gotten." And no one may visit these discoveries "without the licence of the foresayd John, his sonnes, and their deputies." These letters-patent follow the form of the *cartas de doacão* that the Portuguese kings had been granting to navigators who wished to be lords of any new country that they found. Since in those days you wrote your own ticket for royal letters-patent, Cabot probably obtained a copy of a Portuguese charter, altered it to suit his case, and paid a court scrivener to engross and

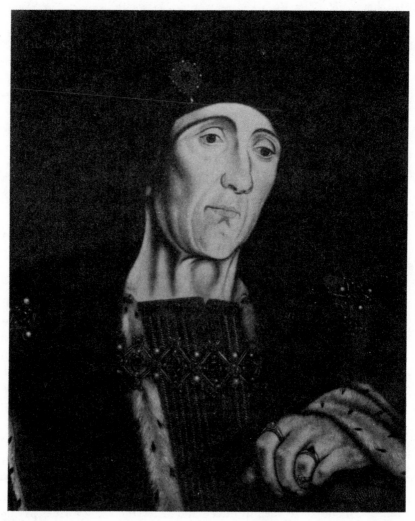

King Henry VII. By an unknown contemporary. Courtesy National Maritime Museum, Greenwich.

present it to Henry VII. And, as in the case of the Portuguese documents and of Columbus's contract with the Spanish sovereigns, nothing is said about a route to the Indies. Obviously a sovereign could not grant an ocean route, only the discoveries that the grantee might make while seeking it.

Bristol and the Transatlantic Passage

Bristol, where Cabot, his wife, and three sons settled shortly after they came to England in 1495, was the right place to gain local support. "Bristowe," as it was then pronounced and often spelled, is a truly extraordinary city. By making the most of its few natural advantages and surmounting every disadvantage, it had by 1400 become, and for four centuries remained, the second seaport in the kingdom. Bristol has never decayed. It welcomed the age of steam, built the first iron screw steamship *Great Britain* and hundreds of other steamships, created great industries out of its Spanish trade in sherry and its American trade in cacao and tobacco, survived some very severe bombing in World War II, and in 1969 enjoyed a trade not far short of £300 million per annum.

In the early Middle Ages, far-sighted Saxons chose a little peninsula between the junction of the Frome and Avon rivers, and there built a bridge and a town. Its original name, Brygstowe, means simply "Place of the Bridge." It lay eight miles from the Severn estuary, good insurance against surprise attack by pirates or other sea enemies. But the Avon, in comparison with the Thames below London, is difficult to navigate; a narrow, tortuous stream breaking through a rocky gorge up and down which tidal currents flow with tremendous force, the neaps having a rise and fall of twenty-one feet, and the springs forty feet, at Avonmouth. These are the highest tides in the world, excepting those in the upper Bay of Fundy; they rendered navigation between ocean and city both difficult and hazardous. In the last century an 800-ton steamship, running aground on the Horseshoe Bend at high water, rolled down the steep mud bank as the tide ebbed, and capsized. Just below the town the Avon is overlooked by green Brandon Hill, named for an otherwise unrecorded visit of St. Brendan. In 1497, there was an oratory on top dedicated to him; at the quatercentenary of John Cabot's voyage, this site was well chosen for the Cabot memorial tower, but the old name stuck. Men and boys of Bristol still play bowls there on spring and summer evenings, and several springs at the foot of St. Vincent's Rock, watered the Abbey of St. Augustine and the Carmelite Friary. Lower down the stream a hot well gushed out ten feet above the river at low water, but twenty-six feet below the high-tide level. This was drunk by homecoming sailors as a cure for

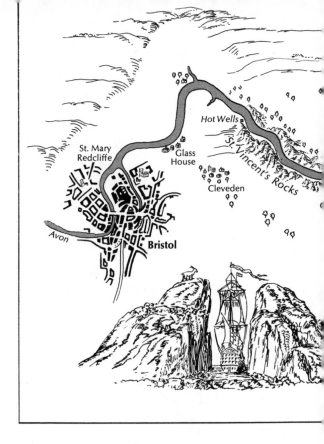

scurvy, and in the eighteenth century this Hotwell made Bristol a rival to nearby Bath. But that was long after Cabot's day.

The association with St. Brendan is not merely sentimental; at some time in the Middle Ages a group of Bristolians must have decided that if St. Brendan could make a voyage in a frail curragh, they could do better in stout wooden vessels built "shipshape and Bristol fashion," a phrase that went around the world. At any rate, that is what they did.

Two natural advantages Bristol possesses. It is the obvious outlet and shipping port for the Cotswold country, famous for sheep; and it lies about midway between Iceland and the Iberian Peninsula. Thus, by the twelfth century, there had grown up a profitable north-south trade of exporting woolens, some woven in Bristol, bringing back from Iceland stockfish (dried codfish), and from Spain and Portugal wine and olive oil—especially sherry, already called "Bristol milk." More wine and woad, the plant used to make a blue dye for woolens, came from Bordeaux and Bayonne in Gascony. The southern products were

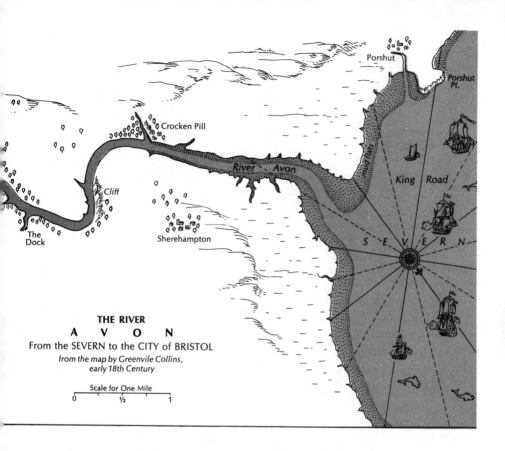

THE RIVER
A V O N
From the SEVERN to the CITY of BRISTOL
*from the map by Greenvile Collins,
early 18th Century*

Scale for One Mile
0   ½   1

mostly trans-shipped to Ireland, Wales, and Iceland; and the canny
men of Bristol kept profits in their hands by building their own ships
and manning them locally.

As early as the fourteenth century such prosperity descended on
Bristol that, sensible of "every good and perfect thing" coming from
God, the merchant-shipowners began to build superb churches. "Fairest
and goodliest parish church in all England" (as Queen Elizabeth remarked) was St. Mary Redcliffe, built in a suburb on the left bank
of the Avon where its noble spire could serve as a guide for any ship
floating up on the flood tide. Here one may see the magnificent tomb
of William Canynges (1400–1474), owner of ten ships and the first
Englishman to be called a "merchant prince." Here also are buried
John Jay who initiated an annual search for the elusive island of Hy-
Brasil in 1480, and sheriff Richard Amerike, traditionally one of Cabot's
backers and Bristol's nominee as the person after whom America was
named—*not* Amerigo Vespucci, if you please!

The central part of Bristol in 1673. From Miller's Plan of Bristol, original in City Museum; facsimile by Waterlow & Sons Ltd., 1950. Courtesy City Archives of Bristol.

St. Mary's was not the only landmark for sailors; Bristol merchants in the fifteenth century built a church on Dundry Hill south of the town, and upon its square stone tower erected one of the primitive lighthouses of that era, burning coal in an iron brazier. As early as 1245, in order to make a second harbor right in their city, the Bristolians diverted the little Frome River from its lower course to St. Augustin's Marsh and built a stone quay ("The Key" on our map) against which sea-going vessels could safely moor when grounded at low tide. This became the principal place for ships to lade and discharge, although there was also a stone quay at St. Nicholas' Back, on the Avon below Bristol Bridge, and a custom house at each place. Right on "The Key" there was built in the thirteenth century—and beautifully rebuilt in 1470—the church of St. Stephen. Here, according to local tradition, the Cabots worshipped at the time of John's first voyage. That very likely is true; for in the nearby Marsh Street lived the "masters and mariners" who in 1445 founded a fraternity to support a priest and twelve poor old sailors, who should pray for their brethren "when passing and labouring on the Sea." St. Mary Redcliffe, however, claims the Cabots as parishioners after the voyage of 1497, when they became more affluent, and points to the rib of a cow-whale alleged to have been brought back from Newfoundland by John as a thank-offering. After his return he rented a house in St. Nicholas Street near the bridge, for £2 a year.

The 1480's and '90's, when the Cabots came to Bristol, were prosperous. During the last twenty years of the fifteenth century Bristol exported more cloth, imported more wine, and handled more dutiable goods than any other English provincial port. This little city, with a population not exceeding 10,000, imported from Gascony in 1480 816 tuns of wine and £2450 worth of woad, and exported 2192 "cloths" to Ireland, Spain, Portugal, and Gascony; a "cloth," by act of Parliament, was 24 yards long. But her Iceland trade had been in trouble for years, owing in part to sailors' brawls with the Icelanders and in part to the enterprise of the Hanseatic League in exploiting this unpleasantness.

Bristol was also the right place to arouse interest in spices. Everyone remembered how, forty years earlier, Robert Stormy, merchant of Bristol, had sent two ships to the Levant in the hope of opening a spice trade at the end of the caravan route, and how one was wrecked on the coast of Greece and the other "spoiled by the Janneys" (the Genoese), who did not want Bristol cutting in on their middleman's profit. To discover a short, northern route to the land of spices would make a fortune for Bristol, and for England.

Bristol also needed new fishing grounds or a new fishing base; Hy-Brasil might well do; and from 1480 on, every few years one, two or three vessels sailed from Bristol in the hope of locating it. One in 1480, commanded by Master Lloyd, reported to be "the most knowledgeable seaman in the whole of England," hunted for months for the elusive isle but found it not; two ships went on a similar mission in 1481; and from 1491 on, Bristol sent from two to four ships a year "in search of the island of Brazil and the Seven Cities," wrote Ayala the Spanish ambassador. English historians who have joined their Portuguese brethren in search of "firsts" are now arguing that Lloyd "must have" discovered Newfoundland in 1480 but forgot to note its location; and that all the others were trying to rediscover it. This argues a very low intelligence on the part of the mariners of Bristol, and also makes the king's patents and rewards to John Cabot senseless. No doubt, after Cabot's voyage, many Bristolians were saying "He found nothing but that old island which we discovered years ago"; John Day, whose important letter will be found in the Notes to this chapter, evidently picked up this gossip.

Whilst Cabot's main object, and the king's in supporting him, was to discover a short ocean route to the Indies, he doubtless hoped to locate Hy-Brasil en route, just as Columbus counted on Antilia as a future staging point.

Whatever the reasons—timidity, dislike of the foreigner, or lack of funds—Cabot obtained but one vessel, a *navicula* (little ship) of fifty *toneles'* burthen, i.e. capable of carrying fifty tuns of wine. This was about the same as that of the *Niña* (60 tuns). Cabot's vessel probably spread the same sail plan as Columbus's sea-going caravels—squaresail on fore and main, lateen on mizzen, possibly a square main topsail. Her crew of eighteen included one Burgundian and a barber from Castiglione near Genoa—John did not intend to frighten the natives with a six weeks' beard! The rest we may presume to have been Englishmen.

The name of this ship, *Mathew*, so called in Toby's Chronicle of Bristol, has been challenged because Toby is under suspicion as a possible fabrication of Thomas Chatterton

> . . . the marvellous boy,
> The sleepless soul that perished in his pride,

the poet who supported himself by forgery. But William Adams's
"Pettie Chronicle," written in Bristol in 1625, states, "On the 24th of
June 1496"—his mistake for 1497—"was newfoundland fowend by
Bristol men in a ship called the *Mathew*."

Everything points to the fact that *Mathew* was a fast, able, and
weatherly craft. She performed a round transatlantic voyage of discovery in the astonishing time of eleven weeks, setting a record that
remained unbroken for almost a century. Quick to answer the helm she
had to be, to avoid crashing on a rocky headland when it suddenly
loomed up out of the fog; sea-kindly she had to be, to lay a-hull in
a heavy blow, with perhaps a small stormsail set, or run before it under
storm foresail. The model of her at the Bristol Museum, very carefully
worked out by local historians and based on the vessels depicted in the
Hastings Manuscript, is, in my opinion, excellent.

Mathew departed Bristol on her momentous voyage on or about 20
May. We do not know whether the city made a thing of it and the
rectors of St. Stephen and St. Mary Redcliffe blessed ship and crew; or
whether she slipped down the Avon with no other ceremony than
tender farewells by wives, sisters, and sweethearts. One can imagine
old codgers on the waterfront growling—There goes another voyage
to Brasil—God help the poor fools—there ain't no such island!—Why
do they think that furriner can find it when us men of Bristowe can't?

It was the spring of the year. Apple blossoms and the hawthorn were
out, and the sedgy banks of the lower Avon were white with great
drifts of *cochlearia officinalis*, which sailors called scurvy grass after
discovering that it was a better cure for scurvy than the water of the
Hotwell. Once safely around Horseshoe Bend, *Mathew* passed on the
port hand the village of Crockern Pill where lived a community of
river pilots and boatmen who made a living towing craft in a calm or
against headwinds. Bristol tradition affirms that a local pilot named
James George Ray accompanied Cabot. Possibly so; but it is more
likely that he piloted *Mathew* down river and went ashore at Avonmouth, where vast modern docks have enabled Bristol to keep her sea
supremacy.

Undoubtedly Cabot had pumped sundry master mariners of Bristol

Conjectural model of Cabot's navicula *Mathew* by Mr. N. Poole of Bristol.
Courtesy Bristol Art Gallery.

in the Iceland trade for information, and learned that in the spring of
the year he would have more easterly winds than at any other season.
April is now the best month for a westward passage. A westbound
vessel on this northern route could expect an easterly wind on only a
minority of days, but she would enjoy a good deal of due north and
due south winds too, which *Mathew* could take on her beam. Once
every so often—it happened last in the summer of 1958—a high-
pressure system between Norway and Greenland produces a strong
northeasterly in the region between latitudes 50° and 60° N, continuing from seven to twenty days. But as *Mathew* took 35 days Bristol to
America, which means 32 or 33 days from Ireland to Newfoundland,
she could not have enjoyed one of these lucky breaks. Nevertheless,
thirty-three days land to land—exactly the same as on Columbus's

first voyage although half the distance—was a good westward passage in latitudes north of 40°. Many, even in the last century, have taken two or three months to sail from England to North America. Peter Kalm in 1748 was delighted to have made Philadelphia in forty-one days from Gravesend; he noted that several vessels had taken fourteen to nineteen weeks for that passage.

Of *Mathew*'s Atlantic crossing we have provokingly few details. She sailed "north and then west," taking her departure around 22 May from Dursey Head, Ireland. That was a favorite point of departure for Atlantic voyages throughout the sixteenth century. This may have been because it was supposed to be the westernmost point of Ireland. It looks so as you approach from the south, and almost is; the Skelligs, the Blaskets, and Inishshark are only a few miles further west. The Irish coast between Dursey Head and Achill was reputed to be dangerous, and it behooved a prudent master to get sea room as soon as he rounded Fastnet. Day says that the wind blew from the east and northeast a good part of the way, but not all; and Soncino says that she "wandered about considerably"—a typical landlubber's interpretation of beating to windward. On the evening of the last day of May, a silver new moon hung in the western sky, and that moon would wax to full and wane to last quarter before *Mathew* made land. She enjoyed

Dursey Head and Bull Rock, Ireland. Photo in July 1969 by Captain H. K. Rigg of the Cruising Club of America.

smooth seas except for one gale two or three days before the landfall. Either on his outward or his homeward passage, Cabot noted a two-point ($22\frac{1}{2}°$) westerly variation of the compass.

Cabot's principle of navigation, the time-honored latitude sailing, is revealed by his latitude observations and by Soncino's statement that he kept the North Star on his starboard beam. Just as Columbus tried to sail due west along latitude $28°$ N, that of the Canary Islands, hoping to hit Cipangu; so Cabot tried sailing west on a high, short latitude, hoping to reach "Cathay," northern China. This crude method of navigation, later called running your westing—or easting—down, had been used even by Ulysses and by the Northmen without benefit of compass; uneducated sailing masters followed it up to within old men's memories. That explains why Cabot sailed northerly, around Fastnet and Cape Clear, to the west coast of Ireland and took his departure from Dursey Head, the northern entrance to Bantry Bay, at latitude $51°33'$ N. He might have sailed further north to seek a slightly shorter crossing; but he may have caught a good easterly off Dursey and then decided to make his westing on that latitude. Another reason for taking off from Dursey Head was the reported position of Hy-Brasil, due west of it; he might pick that up en route and have a good laugh on Bristol's Brasil-searchers.

Since Cabot had the benefit of compass, quadrant, and traverse table, all of which the Norsemen lacked, he did not need to stick closely to his chosen latitude; he could always find it again if a westerly wind forced him north or south. Two or three days before landfall, says Day, i.e. on 21 or 22 June, there was a gale of wind; and it is interesting that Findlay, who wrote the old "seaman's Bible" on the North Atlantic in the nineteenth century, warns his readers that ships are frequently compelled to lie-to for two or three days in a northerly gale when approaching Newfoundland.

Nothing is said about fog or ice in any Cabotian source, but anyone who has sailed in those waters in early summer will agree that *Mathew* must have encountered plenty of each.

The Landfall, 24 June 1497

We may imagine that by the time *Mathew* ran into the gale her seamen were becoming restless, muttering if that other Genoese had made it in 33 days, why can't we? Didn't you hear the Old Man promise that our route would be shorter? And, when the tempest blew, say-

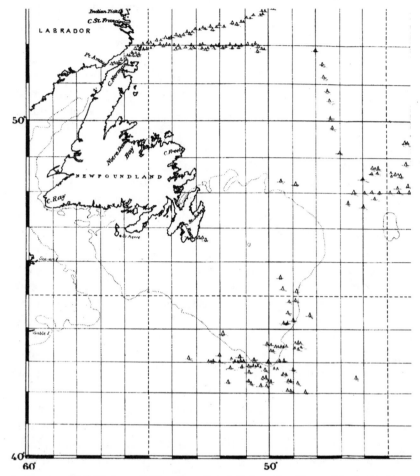

Icebergs and field ice off Newfoundland, July 1885. From Hugh Rodman
Report of Ice and Ice Movements in the North Atlantic Ocean (1890).
Note the dotted line indicating 100-fathom soundings. Inside of it are
the Banks.

ing—this is it—we'll never get back to old Bristowe—and the more
pious making vows to be performed at St. Mary Redcliffe if they ever
did return.

What a pity that we have no exact account of the momentous landfall! All we know is the inscription on Sebastian Cabot's Map of 1544,
at the wrong place, that it happened at 5:00 a.m., 24 June. So let us
supply a little imagination to bridge the few known facts.

After the gale the wind must have come off shore, blowing the fog away. Master Cabot makes all plain sail and shapes his course as near due west as possible. At nightfall 23 June, being an experienced mariner, he begins to *feel* "the loom of the land"—the odor of fir trees and other growing things floating out over the sea, low-hanging clouds, gannets, guillemots, and other non-pelagic birds flying and screaming. All that bright night—for it is never wholly dark in those lattitudes in June and they had a last-quarter moon—everyone keeps a sharp lookout, and the big bower anchor is unlashed and readied for use. Day breaks at three or four o'clock.

Now Cabot orders his little ship to shoot into the wind to check her headway, and lowers all sail, while the leadsman in the chains heaves the dipsy lead. It hits the bottom with a resounding thud—for the hundred-fathom line here approaches within twenty-two miles of the coast. "By the mark, eighty!" the sailor sings out, and with that reassuring depth of water under his keel, Cabot finds it unnecessary to lose time taking more soundings until he is close to land. Then comes the great moment. At 5:00 a.m. the rugged mass of Newfoundland's northern peninsula rises out of the sea, dead ahead, distant twelve to fifteen miles. Sailors are always delighted to make land in clear weather and early in the day, so that they may have plenty of daylight to work into a harbor. In the *Mathew*'s case, on a completely unknown coast, so early a landfall was particularly fortunate.

It is St. John the Baptist Day, 24 June, and Midsummer too; a date nobody was likely to forget, and a good omen for the rest of the voyage. A big island rose out of the sea fifteen miles to the northward. Cabot named it St. John's after the day; the French later called it *Belle Isle*, after an island off the Breton coast, and Belle Isle it still is.

The nearest rocky headland, as they approach, is framed in white foam from the ocean swells. Whether the day be fair or foul, breakers on that coast never cease beating in rhythmic strokes like an endless sword blade. It is the cape which the French later renamed Dégrat. Rising over 500 feet from sea level, it must have been sighted long before Cape Bauld (100 feet altitude), which marks the northernmost point of Newfoundland, appeared. The two capes, only one and a half miles apart, are on Quirpon Island, separated from the Newfoundland main by a narrow but navigable strait.

Mathew was now only five miles as the crow flies from L'Anse aux Meadows where Leif Ericsson had tried to establish a colony in 1001.

Cape Dégrat from the south. Belle Isle in the distance.

Capes Bauld and Dégrat from the north.

Cabot knew nothing of Leif's venture, and it probably would not have interested him if he had; but what an extraordinary coincidence! The first two Europeans to discover North America, half a millennium apart, hit that vast continent within a few miles of each other; and Jacques Cartier followed suit, 37 years after Cabot.

The master now starts his sheets, and with a fresh wind blowing off the land, skirts the coast to the southward, looking for a harbor. Why to the southward? Why not northabout, into the Strait of Belle Isle, considering that he was looking for a passage to Cathay? One may answer in one word—ice. Glance at the sketches of ice at the Strait of Belle Isle entrance in July 1885, by Lieutenant Hugh Rodman USN. Bergs and growlers enter the strait on the Labrador side, circulate within it, and pass out to sea on the Newfoundland side. Not very encouraging to Cabot! We don't know how thick the ice was in 1497, but in 1957 the eastern entrance to the strait was not open for shipping until 6/15 July (using both old and new style dates); and in 1964 it was not open until 13/22 July. Furthermore, "open" is now understood with respect to modern, high-powered shipping. Floating ice which any steamship could easily buck would have seemed forbidding to the master and crew of a little sailing vessel. Cabot naturally could not risk ending his voyage in a deep-freeze.

So, south he turned, to look for a harbor, and he had plenty to choose from: Quirpon (pronounced Carpoon) is the nearest, but the entrance is concealed and hard to find; Griquet (rhymes with cricket) Harbor, only four miles south of Cape Dégrat, comes next, and seems to me the likeliest spot. Wherever it was, John Cabot landed, formed a procession behind a ship's boy carrying a crozier, took formal possession for King Henry VII, and planted the banners of St. George for his sovereign, and of St. Mark as a reminiscence of Venice. Here too, at a quiet anchorage or ashore, he took a meridional altitude of the sun, and dawn and evening sights on Polaris, working them out as the approximate latitude of Dursey Head, Ireland, 51°33′ N. Considering that Cape Dégrat is on latitude 51°37′ N, and that Griquet Harbor is on latitude 51°33′, this must be considered one of the most accurate and successful bits of celestial navigation in the early era of discovery.

Any Cabot buff who reads the above will feel that I have assumed a lot—and I cheerfully plead guilty! In the appendix to this chapter other possible landfalls will be discussed. Here it will be enough to

Quirpon Passage and Harbor (top) and Griquet Harbor (middle), where
Cabot probably first landed. Air view, summer of 1948, from 20,000
feet altitude. The dark areas are spruce forest. Courtesy Air Photo Division,
Canadian Government.

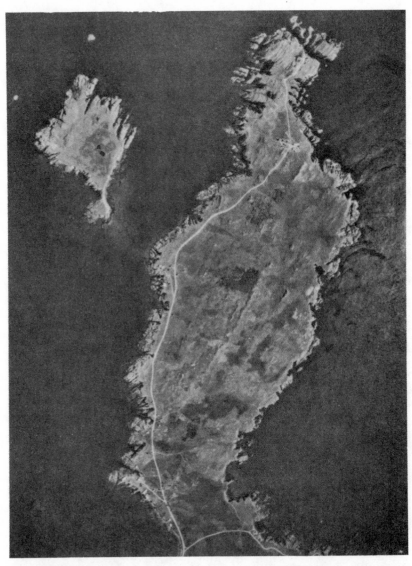

Cape Bonavista, Newfoundland. Taken 8 August 1965 from elevation of 8550 feet. Courtesy Air Photo Division, Canadian Government.

say that the Day letter—a translation of which will be found in the appendix—proves that the "official" Canadian landfall on Cape Breton is wrong on two counts: (1) Cabot himself reported his landfall to have been on the latitude of Dursey Head—51°33′ N; whilst the northernmost point of Cape Breton is latitude 47°02′ N. (2) In contrast to the inconstant winds, we must consider the constant factor of ocean depths. For any landfall south of Cape Bonavista, Newfoundland, *Mathew* would have had to cross the Grand Bank which extends some 220 miles east of the Avalon Peninsula, whilst the "Tail of the Bank" lies 250 miles southeast of Cape Race, with depths of twenty to forty-five fathom. This Grand Bank is a vast, balloon-like shoal embracing southeastern Newfoundland, with depths of twenty to eighty fathom, and a few isolated rocks that break in heavy weather. One may confidently assert that Cabot, like any experienced sailor, after striking soundings such as these, would have sailed as near due west as he could, feeling his way with frequent casts of the lead in dark or foggy weather, to the nearest point of land. A glance at the chart should convince any reasonable person that Cabot could not have sailed the five hundred or more miles from the eastern edge of the Bank to Cape Breton, missing Cape Race, Cape Pine, Cape St. Mary's, and Saint-Pierre. Also, for *Mathew* to have approached the coast far enough south to miss Cape Race and make first land on Cape Breton, one would have to assume that her navigator made a mistake of six degrees of latitude, 360 miles.

The Coastal Voyage

So, let us assume that Cape Dégrat was the 24 June landfall, and take *Mathew* on from there.

We learn from both Soncino and Day that Cabot went ashore shortly after his landfall to take possession. He saw no people, but observed signs of life such as snares and fish nets, and a stick painted red and pierced at both ends, probably a shuttle for weaving nets. He also noted dung which he supposed to mean that the natives kept cattle—moose or caribou were responsible. Why did Cabot never land again? Possibly because, with a small crew, he wished to avoid tangling with hostile natives; he admitted that he dared not explore inland further than the range of a crossbow from his ship. More likely, in my opinion, it was the mosquitoes. The rocky surface of eastern Newfoundland is full of small depressions which catch and hold the melting snow; swarms of mosquitoes breed therein and make life miser-

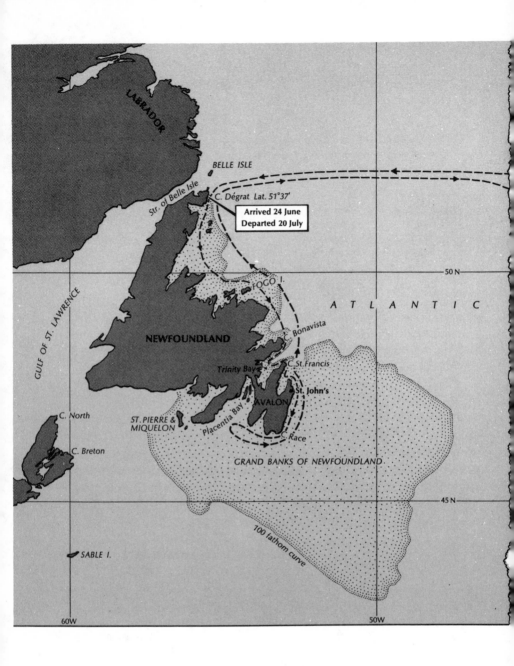

LABRADOR

BELLE ISLE

Str. of Belle Isle

C. Dégrat Lat. 51°37'

**Arrived 24 June
Departed 20 July**

50 N

FOGO I.

A T L A N T I C

NEWFOUNDLAND

C. Bonavista

C.St.Francis

Trinity Bay

St. John's

GULF OF ST. LAWRENCE

AVALON

C. North

ST. PIERRE &
MIQUELON

Placentia Bay

C. Race

C. Breton

GRAND BANKS OF NEWFOUNDLAND

45 N

100 fathom curve

SABLE I.

60W

50W

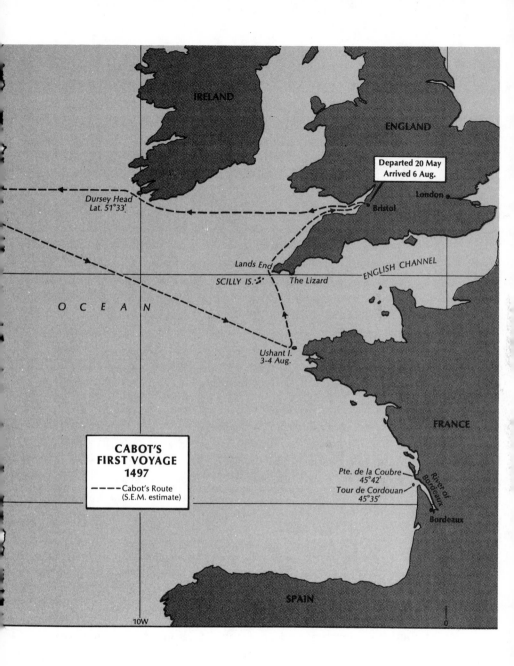

**CABOT'S
FIRST VOYAGE
1497**

– – – – Cabot's Route
(S.E.M. estimate)

Departed 20 May
Arrived 6 Aug.

IRELAND

ENGLAND

London

Bristol

Dursey Head
Lat. 51°33'

Lands End

SCILLY IS.

The Lizard

ENGLISH CHANNEL

O C E A N

Ushant I.
3-4 Aug.

FRANCE

Pte. de la Coubre
45°42'
Tour de Cordouan
45°35'

River of Bordeaux

Bordeaux

SPAIN

10W

0

179

able for all but the most hardened "Newfies." So huge, hungry, and notorious are the Newfoundland mosquitoes that one authority, reading in the *Navigatio* of St. Brendan that the fathers were attacked by insects the size of chickens, adduced this as proof that the Saint had sailed to Newfoundland!

Jumping ahead four years, the Beothuk Indians whom Gaspar Corte Real kidnapped in Newfoundland and brought to Lisbon in 1501, possessed a broken gilt sword of Italian manufacture, and silver earrings "made in Venice." These can only have come from Cabot. They may have been relics of an otherwise unrecorded fight between him and the Beothuk on his second voyage in 1498, but it is more probable that they were left behind at the landing place and there picked up by the Indians. If it be objected that people do not ordinarily abandon such valuable possessions, one may answer that all sailors remember a shipmate who, after the vessel is under way, finds that he has left behind his camera, false teeth, or what not; won't the skipper please stop the ship so he can go look for them? Lescarbot tells of a shipmate who left his sword ashore in Nova Scotia and, going back for it, got lost himself and all but perished.

Contemporary informants tell us almost nothing about Cabot's coasting. Pasqualigo, the Venetian in London, says that he coasted 300 leagues—954 nautical miles—but this was pure guesswork, as Cabot had no means of measuring distance. *Mathew*, like every later voyager to Newfoundland, must have encountered fog. Lescarbot, in his passage to Port Royal with Poutrincourt in 1601, made land somewhere about St. John's on 23 June, and from that time on "fell to the fogs again, which (afar off) we might perceive to come and wrap us about, holding us continually prisoners three whole days for two days of fair weather that they permitted us. . . . Yea, even divers times we have seen ourselves a whole sennight continually in thick fogs, twice without any show of sun." It took them twelve days to sail from Saint-Pierre to Cape Breton.

Cabot took plenty of codfish simply by letting down and drawing up weighted baskets. He saw tall trees suitable for masts, and what appeared to be cultivated fields—probably blueberry bushes and other low shrubs. With typical discoverer's optimism, he reported the country to be temperate enough for growing logwood and silk. At one point he saw two *bultos* (big objects or figures), one chasing the other, but so far away that without benefit of telescope he could not tell whether they were men or beasts.

Here is how I think that he proceeded after taking possession at Griquet or some nearby harbor on 24 June 1497. Please keep in mind that this is all an iron-bound coast—cliffs against which the ocean swells perpetually dash, but with many harbor openings. Leaving Groais and Bell Islands to starboard, *Mathew* crosses White and Notre Dame Bays to Fogo, making a wide sweep to avoid the foul ground off that reef-girt island. Off Cape Freels she turns south, passes Cape Bonavista, and (possibly after looking into Trinity Bay) rounds high, cliffy, three-mile-long Baccalieu Island, so named by the Portuguese after the swarms of codfish that abound in these waters. From here on she has the benefit of moonlight; a new moon on 30 June, full moon 14 July. Possibly she investigates the completely land-locked harbor which today nourishes St. John's, the Newfoundland capital. She whips around Cape Spear, a typical high, rocky headland with sparse vegetation, and resumes a southerly course. She passes Cape Broyle, 570 feet elevation, and the lower Ferryland Head, keeping a few miles off shore to avoid breaking rocks and islets. About fifty miles south of Cape Spear she reaches Cape Race, a long, flat promontory of slate cliffs 100 to 150 feet above the ocean. This conspicuous headland is where windjammers and steamships, sailing as near as possible the great circle course from northern Europe, tried to make land before squaring away for Halifax, Boston, or New York; pilots used to call passing Cape Race "turning the corner." Cabot turned the corner too, and after investigating Trepassey Bay, steered west for 200-foot-high Cape Pine, eighteen miles distant from Cape Race. That would have been his furthest south—latitude 46°37′ N—only forty-five to sixty-two miles north of the latitude of the mouth of the Gironde (45°35′ to 45°42′), which Day reported to have been Cabot's furthest south. And, since Cabot must have taken these latitude sights from *Mathew*'s deck in rough water, his estimate is not bad for the period. This "River of Bordeaux" latitude he undoubtedly knew from an earlier voyage, as the Tour de Cordouan lighthouse at the river mouth was one of the most famous seamarks in all Europe.

Cape St. Mary's, a 500-foot-high tableland, lies across the bay of the same name, about thirty miles west-northwest. It is the eastern promontory of Placentia Bay.

What Cabot Saw: Baccalieu Island and Grates Point; Cape St. Francis;
Cape Broyle.

182

What Cabot Saw: Cape Race; Cape Pine; Cape St. Mary's. The whiteness on a cliff in the foreground (center picture), and the white specks over the sea, are thousands of gannets. The lighthouses are of course later additions to the scene.

All this time, *Mathew* has been on soundings. But, continuing west from Cape St. Mary's, she soon finds herself over the 100- to 170-fathom trough that starts near Argentina and stretches through Placentia Bay well out to sea. My guess is that Cabot, after making several casts of the lead and finding no bottom at 100 fathom, chose here to turn back. The land on Burin Peninsula, next to the westward, is low, flat, and generally invisible from a point fifteen miles west of Cape St. Mary's. The wind may have blown hard from the west—it generally does at that season. Keeping in mind that Cabot was primarily looking for a passage to the Indies, he would now have thought that he had found it. Regarding this voyage as a mere reconnaissance to prepare for a big expedition later, he decided to turn back.

John Day is positive that the *Mathew* returned to her original land-fall before taking her departure for Bristol; and that makes sense, as doubling his course increased Cabot's knowledge of the coast and gave him, so he thought, an accurate latitude for running his easting down. On the return trip to Cape Dégrat he had time to look into harbors and bays which he had bypassed on the outward passage. He saw, says Pasqualigo, two islands that he had earlier missed: these could have been Great, Green, or Gull Islands off the Avalon Peninsula, or any two of a dozen islands further north; outlying islands are often sheathed in fog while the coast of Newfoundland itself is clear.

This coasting plan for Cabot is, of course, tentative; but the length of it—about 870 miles headland to headland (as I measure it on a modern chart)—fits a maximum cruise of twenty-six days, which no other hypothesis does, except the Cape Bonavista one. Still, there are several puzzling things about it. None of Cabot's reporters mentions fog, which he must have experienced. Nor do they refer to icebergs which he must have seen; they are most plentiful off the Newfoundland coast in July. I can only suggest that these omissions derive from the same motive as Eric's name Greenland for a country that is mostly rocks and ice; talk of fogbanks and icebergs would discourage further attempts to explore or exploit the "New Isle," as Henry VII named it. By 1502 the king was calling it "the newe founde lande" or "the Newfounded Island," and before long it became standardized as Newfoundland. With the English, once a thing is new, it always remains new, like Oxford's New College, and New York.

It is also odd that Cabot saw no Indians; but that fits Newfoundland rather than Nova Scotia. The Beothuk tribe which inhabited the big island were hunters and salmon fishermen, not particularly interested in the coast; but the Micmac of Nova Scotia, like the Abnaki of Maine, flocked to the shore in summer to fish and dig clams.

Another item that rings true is Cabot's report, through Pasqualigo, "that the tides are slack and do not flow as they do here" at Bristol. On the east and south coasts of Newfoundland the mean range is only 2.2 to 4.9 feet.

His Homeward Passage

Passing Cape Bonavista, Cape Freels, Fogo Island, and Cape St. John, Cabot picked up his landfall on Cape Dégrat and took his departure thence not later than 20 July, two days before a last-quarter moon. After a fast passage of fifteen days, *Mathew* made the Breton coast not later than 4 August. These calculations are based on Day's statement that *Mathew* crossed in fifteen days, made landfall in Brittany, and entered Bristol 6 August. The speed of this homeward passage is noteworthy, though not exceptional. Fifteen days was a passage which any yachtsman would be proud to make today; an average speed of about five knots. And this is calculated on the great circle course of 1720 nautical miles, without counting the dog-leg that *Mathew* must have made, at the instance of her sailors; for Day states that the mariners "confused" their captain and persuaded him to steer somewhat south of east, which explains why he missed England. Late July and August being a period of strong westerly winds in those latitudes, there is no reason to doubt Cabot's blue-ribband transatlantic passage. He had a new moon on 29 July, and it reached first quarter the day after his Brittany landfall. This we may assume to have been Ushant, which looms up conspicuously off the Breton coast; and, as *Mathew* is said to have been provisioned for a much longer voyage, Cabot had no reason to call at the nearest port.

Supposing she sighted Ushant at break of day 4 August, and that the brave westerly that brought her so far held good, she could have made Lands End—100 miles almost due north—at dusk, dodging the Longships and the Seven Stones; reached Lundy (80 miles more) by dawn, and on the 5th have begun picking up familiar landmarks in the Severn Estuary—the Welsh mountains, Flatholme and Steepholme, Denny

Island and Portishead. By evening she comes to an anchor in King Road off Avonmouth. There she had to await a fair tide to ascend the Avon, but messengers must have gone ahead on horseback to tell Bristol that the *Mathew* had returned with big news. If the wind fell or turned east, there were stout fellows with twelve-oared barges at the village of Crockern Pill inside the Avon entrance who could have passed her a line and towed her around Horseshoe Bend and through the narrow gorge of the Avon. Once past the site of the Clifton Suspension Bridge, the fair city bursts on her sight: green Brandon Hill looms up to port, and the tower of St. Mary Redcliffe appears dead ahead. She sails, or is towed, right up to the "Key," or the "Back," at Bristol Bridge. There she is met by wives, children, and sweethearts, and a delegation of the city fathers. It is 6 August 1497, a date of which we are certain.

Once customs formalities are over, friends greeted, and discovery of a "New Island" announced, John Cabot wastes no time in idle chatter. The same day he starts for London to see the king, tell his story, and claim his reward.

What Cabot thought he had found is less important than what he did find, but very interesting. Unfortunately the map that he brought home and showed to the king has long since disappeared. From his statement that he landed on *terra firma*, it is evident that he regarded northern Newfoundland as part of the Eurasian continent; and the Behaim globe of 1492 places "Cathay" in about the same latitude where Cabot thought he had hit the passage to China. But the language of his gift from Henry VII, "to hym that founde the new Isle," proves that Cabot regarded the major part of his discovery as insular, and that it was a *new* isle, not that tiresome old will o' the wisp Hy-Brasil, or the equally played-out Seven Cities. Obviously too, since Cabot had been given the right to "subdue, occupy and possesse" only "Isles, countryes, regions or provinces of the heathen and infidels . . . unknown to all Christians," and enjoy their "fruits, profits, gaines and commodities," he could not have made much out of a Hy-Brasil inhabited by Irish ghosts, or an Antilia with seven Portuguese cities. Newfoundland had to be new to be of any use to him or to the king. Now, the Avalon Peninsula looks like an island and almost is; most of the sixteenth-century maps show Newfoundland as an archipelago, to which its deep, narrow bays give credence; the Contarini-Roselli Map of 1506 which we have reproduced puts it at the tip end of a Chinese promontory called "Tungut Provincia Magna." As late as 1540, the commission of François-premier to Jacques Cartier defined Canada as *faisant un bout de l'Asie.*

The Contarini-Roselli Map of 1506 was evidently drawn from Portuguese sources, such as the Corte Real voyages. The Ruysch Map, which illustrated the Rome (1508) edition of Ptolemy, is more significant. Both Newfoundland and Greenland are eastern promontories of Asia, and the nomenclature is unique, as partly based on information derived from Cabot. *Terra Nova* is, of course, the English name for the "new isle," latinized; the "k" in *Baia de Rockas* suggests that Cabot appropriately called Notre Dame Bay the Bay of Rocks; *C. Glaciato* for Cape Bauld may record his finding ice and snow there on St. John's Day; and *Rio Grado* indicates that he investigated the mouth of the Gander River—but I do not claim that Gander is derived from Grado! South of that river are Baccalieu Island and the Cape of the Portuguese—Ruysch's concession to Cabot's rivals. Our old friend Antilia Insula is there, south of Newfoundland, complete with an inscription telling the story of the Seven Cities.

Mathew must have been quickly cleared at the Bristol custom house, for she brought back nothing except what was picked up at her one port of call. At any rate, Cabot lost no time in proceeding to London to lay his discoveries at the feet of the king. One of the main roads of England went from the West Country through Bristol to London; it was a narrow earth track some 130 statute miles in length, and the journey must have taken Cabot three days. He had no such impressive cavalcade as Columbus brought to Barcelona in 1493; no gold, no Indians, no parrots; there was only himself on a hired horse, accompanied perhaps by his three sons, and certainly by members of *Mathew's* crew to corroborate his story. The road led through Chippenham, Marlborough, Hungerford, Newbury, Reading (where it crossed the Thames), Maidenhead, Colnbrook, and Brentford. The Cabot party pushed ahead as long as daylight lasted, spent two nights en route, probably at travelers' inns, reached London by the night of 9 August, and rode to Westminster to see the king next day.

Henry VII knew a good thing when he saw it and, for a Tudor, responded generously. The royal household books record that on 10–11 August 1497 the king gave £10 "to hym that founde the new

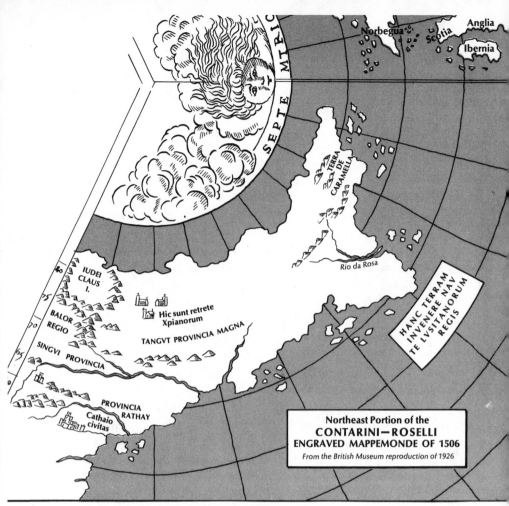

Within the map:

SEPTE MTRIC

Norbegua Scotia Anglia
Ibernia

TERRA DE CARAMELLA

Rio da Rosa

IUDEI CLAUS I.

Hic sunt retrete Xpianorum

BALOR REGIO

TANGVT PROVINCIA MAGNA

SINGVI PROVINCIA

HANC TERRAM INVENERE NAV TE LVSITANORUM REGIS

PROVINCIA RATHAY
Cathaio civitas

Northeast Portion of the
CONTARINI—ROSELLI
ENGRAVED MAPPEMONDE OF 1506
From the British Museum reproduction of 1926

The lower legend means: "This Land found by sailors of the King of Portugal." "Terra de caramella" means Land of Ice, and here is on Greenland. This entire land mass is assumed to be China, and "Zippon" is just off this part of the map, on the same longitude as "Magna."

Isle," and the following January a "rewarde" of 66s. 8d. "to a Venysian," probably Sebastian, who always made a good impression. On 13 December 1497 he settled on his "welbiloved John Calbot of the parties of Venice" an annuity of £20, at the expense of the Bristol customs. Two months later he issued a warrant for payment of the same to "the said John Caboote," who had been unable to collect owing to lack of funds in the Bristol custom house. The last payment of this pension was made at some time during the twelvemonth following

Michaelmas 1498. The discoverer's name then disappears from the books. He had gone to "the undiscover'd country from whose bourn no traveler returns."

Cabot's Second Voyage

Cabot's first voyage made a brief sensation. He spent the £10 that the king gave him "to amuse himself," says Pasqualigo, and swaggered about Lombard Street in gay silken apparel. Soncino says that the common people "run after him like madmen," that he regarded himself as an admiral of princely rank, and promised to bestow islands on his Burgundian passenger and his Genoese barber.

Nobody recorded what the sailors thought about *Mathew*'s voyage.

Outline of a portion of the Ruysch Map of 1508. Against the double island in the middle, the legend states, demons assaulted ships near these islands, which were avoided but not without peril. "CATHAY" is around the corner to the southwest. From Henry Harrisse, *Terre Neuve*, p. 58.

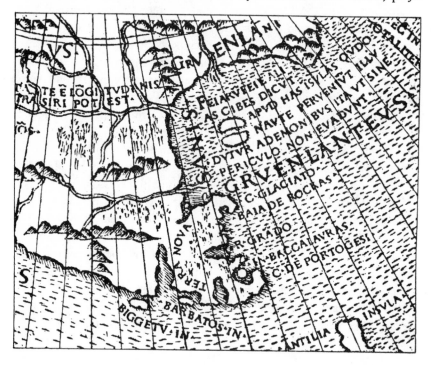

Cabot's Idea of His First Voyage

We can imagine their telling unbelievable fish stories in Bristol, and grumbling about the fog, the chill, and the mosquitoes; grousing that they found no women because the Old Man never gave them shore liberty. They did confirm the discovery, says Soncino.

Cabot probably flitted between London and Bristol the rest of the summer and fall of 1497, engaged in preparations for his second voyage. It was a bad time to get royal assistance. Perkin Warbeck the pretender was still on the loose, supported by Cornishmen marching on London to protest against war taxes. The siege of Exeter by the rebels was not raised until the end of 1497. Nevertheless Henry VII found time to promote what we might call his race for the Indies. He did not intend to let Spain and Portugal get away with everything.

On 3 February 1498, Henry VII issued new letters-patent for the second Cabot voyage, granting "to our well beloved John Kaboto, Venician," power to impress six English ships of 200 tuns or under, together with their tackle and necessary gear, "and theym convey and lede to the londe and Iles of late founde by the seid John in oure name," paying at the rate of government charters. Cabot also had the right to enlist any English sailors who sign on willingly. Thus "*Messer Zoane,*" says Soncino, "proposes to keep along the coast from the place at which he touched, more and more towards the East, until he reaches an island which he calls *Cipango*, situated in the equinoctial region where he thinks all the spices of the world have their origin, as well as the jewels." There he will "form a colony"; i.e. set up a trading factory, by which means London will become "a more important mart for spices than Alexandria." The king provided, manned and victualed one ship, in which divers merchants of London ventured "small stocks." Merchants of Bristol freighted four more vessels laden with "course cloth, Caps, Laces, points and other trifles," supposed to be the proper trading truck for natives, and all five ships departed Bristol together at "the beginning of May" 1498.

As to who accompanied Master John, we are as much in the dark as on the first voyage. We know the names of but two shipmates: a Milanese cleric in London named Giovanni Antonio de Carbonariis, and a Spanish friar named Buil who had been a leading troublemaker on Columbus's second voyage. The Spanish ambassador on 25 July 1498 informed his royal master that Cabot had departed with five ships and a year's provisions, and that the ship in which Father Buil sailed had put into an Irish port in distress. The other four were expected home the following month. They never returned.

Thus, the only known facts of John Cabot's second voyage are that it departed Bristol in May 1498, that one ship returned shortly, and that Cabot and the other four ships were lost. His pension was paid for the last time, probably to his wife (not yet known to be a widow) within the twelvemonth following Michaelmas 1498. Polydore Vergil, a contemporary English historian, wrote somewhat flippantly that Cabot "found his new lands only in the ocean's bottom, to which he and his ship are thought to have sunk, since, after that voyage, he was never heard of more."

The rest is silence.

Juan de La Cosa's mappemonde dated 1500 * shows a series of English royal standards planted along a coast which appears to stretch from the Labrador to Florida. A point usually identified as Cape Breton, but which may as well be Cape Bauld or Cape Race or Cape Cod, is named *Cavo de Yngleterra*. Stringing along to the westward are twelve names which make no sense and appear on no later map, and the inscription parallel to this coast reads, *mar descubierta por inglese* (sea discovered

* See Notes to Chapter VII.

by an Englishman). Certain historians consider this to be evidence that Cabot's second voyage ranged the coast of North America as far as Florida or even Venezuela, searching for a passage to Cathay. *But, if neither he nor any of his men returned, how did La Cosa get his facts?* Obviously, since the American half of this map has been post-dated at least five years, the English flags, if anything more than a whimsy, record a later voyage by the Bristol-Portuguese syndicate, to which we shall come in due course.

John Cabot and his four ships disappear without a trace. No report of them reached Europe. Anyone may guess whether they capsized and foundered in a black squall, crashed an iceberg at night, or piled up on a rocky coast. One remembers an old Irish proverb, "The waves have some mercy but the rocks have no mercy at all"; and God knows there are plenty of rocks both on and off the North American coast.

Nevertheless, John Cabot's first voyage was the herald and forerunner to the English empire in North America. Like Columbus, he never learned the significance or value of his discoveries.

Bibliography and Notes

GENERAL CABOT BIBLIOGRAPHY

Briefly, the most important of the sources are these:

1. *Documents in English and Foreign Archives:* Cabot's letters-patent of 5 March 1496 and 3 Feb. 1498; entries in royal accounts, copies of Bristol Chronicles; archives of Venice and Valencia.

2. *Pasqualigo Letter.* From London, 23 Aug. 1497, to his brothers, merchants of Venice.

3. *Milanese Documents.* Letters from London, 1497, to Ludovico *il Moro*, Duke of Milan. One by unknown writer, two from his envoy Soncino.

4. *Day Letter.* To Columbus, winter of 1497–98. Translation at end of these Notes.

5. *Ayala Letter.* From Spanish ambassador at London to the king of Spain, 25 July 1498.

6. *Maps.* Juan de La Cosa's dated 1500 but really later; and Sebastian Cabot's of 1544. See Notes to this Chapter and the next.

James A. Williamson, *The Cabot Voyages and Bristol Discovery under Henry VII, with the Cartography of the Voyages by R. A. Skelton* (Hakluyt Society, 1962), contains all known sources in translation, with interpretations by a scholar who studied the subject for half a century. Almost all my source quotations are from this book. It replaces Williamson's earlier *The Voyages of the Cabots and the English Discovery of*

America under Henry VII and Henry VIII (London, 1929) which, however, has additional data on Sebastian Cabot.

Translations of the Italian and Spanish letters, with valuable notes by Edward G. Bourne, are in his *Northmen, Columbus and Cabot* of the Original Narratives Series (1906); and also in A. F. Pollard, *The Reign of Henry VII* (1914), II, 329–31.

7. Name *Mathew*. D. B. Quinn in *The Times Literary Supplement*, 8 June 1967, tells the history of the Fust Manuscript of the Toby and other long-lost Bristol chronicles. William Adams's is in the Bristol City Archives.

George Parker Winship, *Cabot Bibliography* (1900), lists all earlier works, with sapient evaluations, states where original texts of the above letters may be found, and in his introduction untangles some of the puzzles about Sebastian. Of these earlier works the best, in my opinion, and the best illustrated by reproductions of old maps, are those by Henry Harrisse, *Découverte et évolution cartographique de Terre-Neuve* (Paris, 1900); *The Discovery of North America* (London, 1892), and *Jean et Sebastien Cabot* (Paris, 1882).

In September 1968, in a plane owned and piloted by Mr. James F. Nields, Señor Mauricio Obregón and I flew along the southern and eastern coasts of Newfoundland to "check up" on Cabot. I am greatly indebted to these gentlemen both for their company and their criticism.

The well-known Cabot family of Massachusetts is descended from John Cabot of the Channel Isle of Jersey, who emigrated to New England in 1671. The French family of Chabot is not related to the discoverer.

Cabot's landfall occurred on 24 June according to all contemporary authorities, and the outward voyage lasted thirty-five days according to Day, who says he left "toward the end of May," for which the 20th is near enough. Toby says 2 May, but the copyist probably dropped a zero. Remember that you add nine days to dates in the Julian calendar which Cabot used, to make the equivalent in the modern Gregorian calendar. Thus his 20 May was the 29th in our calendar, and his 24 June landfall would be 3 July 1497.

THEORIES OF WHERE CABOT SAILED IN 1497

The reader should keep in mind that English and Anglo-Canadian historians are desperately eager to prove that Cabot touched the American mainland, so that they can claim a "first" for him as discoverer of the continent, Columbus not having set foot on the mainland before 1498.

Williamson (p. 71 and ff.) to my astonishment, gives Cabot a Maine landfall in order to fit in with his identification of the "English Coast" on the La Cosa Map as Nova Scotia. Although second to none as a "Maine-iac" I cannot accept this. It ignores Day's evidence on latitudes, has Cabot missing not only Cape Race but Cape Sable on his outward passage, and adds many hundred miles to what he had to cover in 26 days.

Tryggvi J. Oleson, *Early Voyages and Northern Approaches* (Canadian

Centenary Series, Toronto, 1968), like most academic historians, is not interested in the navigational aspects; he introduces an "Icelandic Folk Tale" about Cabot visiting Iceland and getting information about the Labrador; and from Soncino's account of the outward passage, "Standing to the northward he began to sail toward the Oriental regions, leaving (after a few days) the North Star on his right hand," he makes the unwarranted conclusion that "Cabot was threading islands and called at Iceland and Greenland." Oleson's book, however, is useful for listing some of the biggest "whoppers" of Sebastian Cabot.

Among other odd theories about Cabot's first voyage is David O. True's in *Imago Mundi*, XI (1954), 11–25, where he insists on the 1494 date, together with miscellaneous nonsense. Father Lucien Campeau "Jean Cabot et la découverte de l'Amérique du Nord," in *Revue d'Histoire de l'Amérique Française* XIX (1965), 384–413, basing on an obscure reference to the Tanais (the River Don) in Soncino's letter (see note to E. G. Bourne, *Northmen, Columbus and Cabot*, p. 426), maintains that Cabot cheated, sailed to the northeastward, and never saw America! This is obviously a reflection of recent Quebec nationalism.

How do we know that Cabot had a 100-fathom sounding lead? Because Antonio Galvão, in his *Tratado* of 1563, repeating Sebastian Cabot's garbled account of his (i.e. his father's) first voyage, says that he found "no bottom in 70, 80 and 100 fathoms." Columbus's *Santa María* had two which he once spliced together and found no soundings at 200 fathom. So did Cartier and Frobisher.

Dr. Melvin J. Jackson of the Smithsonian, impressed probably by Soncino's statement that *Mathew* "Passed the western limits of Ireland before standing to the northward . . . toward the Oriental regions," assumes that Cabot took his departure from Achill Head in latitude 54°04′ N instead of Dursey Head on latitude 51°33′ N, and hit Cape St. Lewis, Labrador, on latitude 52°22′ N. "The Labrador Landfall of John Cabot," *Canadian Historical Review*, XLIV, No. 2 (June 1963), 122–41. He then sails *Mathew* all around Newfoundland, and, instead of returning to his landfall as Day said he did, which would have made a coastal voyage of 1027 miles, has him take off from Cape Freels. I insist that Cabot did not (and probably could not) enter the Strait of Belle Isle; and that, if he had, he would have sailed westward (as Cartier did later) in search of Cathay instead of hugging the Newfoundland shore.

G. R. F. Prowse in his pamphlets mimeographed at Winnipeg—*Cabot's Surveys* (1931), *Cabot's Bona Vista Landfall* (1946), and *Exploration of the Gulf of St. Lawrence 1499–1525* (1929), and in his book *Cartological Materials* I (1936)—argues for the Cape Bonavista landfall. He has no new facts to support it, but insists that Cabot must have had time to survey the coast from there to Cape Race, this survey having been stolen by the Corte Reals to appear on the Cantino Map! John J. Juricek "John Cabot's First Voyage," *Smithsonian Journal of History*, II (1967–68), 1–22, declares that the Juan de La Cosa Map (see discussion in Notes to Chapter VII), "unambiguously illustrates John Cabot's voyage of 1497," and squeezes up the English-flagged part of it to fit the south shore of Newfoundland. Juricek has to adopt the Cape Breton landfall to allow this, but as he cannot escape the implication of the Day letter that Cabot was steering due west to Cape Dégrat, he remarks that the gale two or three days before the landfall "makes it easy to imagine Cabot being swept past Cape Race without catching sight of it." Some sweep—275 miles! E. G. R. Taylor, "Where Did the Cabots Go?" *Geographical Journal*, CXXIX (1963), 339–41, places John's landfall on Cape Race and has him sail all the way to Cape Chidley, Labrador, before turning back. This adds about 618 miles to the distance covered by Cabot in twenty-six days.

SEBASTIAN CABOT AND HIS 1544 MAP

R. A. Skelton's section "Cartography of the Voyages" in Williamson, 293–325, is the best account of that aspect, but even Skelton, by ignoring such factors as winds and shoals, goes a little wild. He at least clears up the doubts about Sebastian Cabot's authorship of the 1544 World Map attributed to him. Since Sebastian is the original source for the Cape Breton landfall, unchallenged for three centuries, he and his map merit careful consideration. Henry Harrisse concluded that Sebastian was one of the greatest liars in the history of discovery, and I am inclined to agree with him; Charles Deane, in his excellent chapter on the Cabot voyages in Winsor's *Narrative and Critical History*, I, 11–58, will not go further than to call Sebastian "the sphinx of American history for over three hundred years" (p. 32). One might now add another century. The standard account of the Cabot voyages for the first three centuries is the "Discourse of Sebastian Cabot touching his Discovery of Part of the West Indies" in Hakluyt's *Voyages*.* He says that his father died in England after news arrived of Columbus's first voyage. This, says Sebastian, "increased in my heart a great flame of desire to attempt some notable thing."

> And understanding by reason of the Sphere, that if I should saile by way of the North-west, I should by a shorter tract come into India, I thereupon caused the King to be advertised of my devise, who immediatly commanded two Carvels to bee furnished with all things appertayning to the voyage, which was as farre as I remember in the yeere 1496. in the beginning of Sommer. I began therefore to saile toward the Northwest, not thinking to finde any other land then that of Cathay, & from thence to turne toward

* Everyman ed., V, 85; also in Hakluyt's *Discourse Concerning Westerne Planting* in Hakluyt Soc. ed. of his *Writings*, II,294. This is a paraphrase of the "Mantua gentleman's" account in Ramusio, *Primo Volume delle Navigationi et Viaggi*, I (1550), of which there is a translation in Williamson, pp. 270–73. Williamson remarks that "for sheer anachronistic nonsense this is hard to beat" (*Voyages of the Cabots*, p. 233).

A section of Sebastian Cabot's 1544 Map (Yeux Ouvertes reproduction)
compared with similar region on Nicolas Desliens's World Map of 1541
reversed. Photo of original in Sächsische Landesbibliothek, Dresden. Kindness of the Direktor, Dr. Burgemeister.

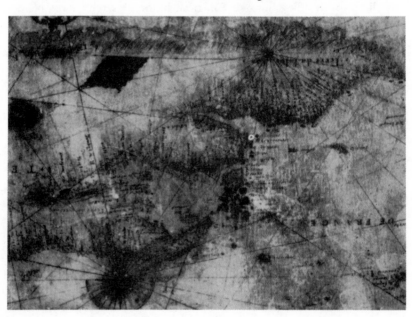

India, but after certaine dayes I found that the land ranne towards the North, which was to mee a great displeasure. Neverthelesse, sayling along by the coast to see if I could finde any gulfe that turned, I found the lande still continent to the 56. degree under our Pole. And seeing that there the coast turned toward the East, despairing to finde the passage, I turned backe againe, and sailed downe by the coast of that land toward the Equinoctiall (ever with intent to finde the saide passage to India) and came to that part of this firme lande which is nowe called Florida, where my victuals failing, I departed from thence and returned to England.

The Sebastian Cabot Mappemonde dated 1544 is a 4- by 6-foot engraved map of which but one copy now exists, in the Bibliothèque Nationale, Paris. A legend on it states that Sebastian Cabot, captain and *piloto mayor*, designed it in 1544. Sebastian certainly directed it (R. A. Skelton has found documentary proof), and his position as chief pilot of Spain, in charge of the *padron real* or standard chart, enabled him to supply a good part of the data. And he actually gives his father joint credit with himself for the discovery! The map is discussed in G. P. Winship, *Cabot Bibliography* (1900), pp. 13–26, and in Harrisse, *Jean et Sebastien Cabot* (1882), pp. 54–57, 64–66, and 151–56, with a good reproduction of the North American part in frontispiece. Full-size photographic facsimiles, made in 1882, are to be found in the Harvard College Library, the American Geographic Society in New York, and other institutions (see Winship, p. 13). A magnificent half-size colored-offset of the map, complete with the inscriptions and descriptions, by André Rossel and Roger Hervé, was published by Editions les Yeux Ouverts in Paris, 1968. It is the basis of my partial reproduction here.

This is the map that gives the date and hour of the landfall. Against a promontory obviously meant for North Cape, Cape Breton Island, is the legend *prima tierra vista*. North of it lies *Y. de S. Juan*, probably meaning Prince Edward Island. The legend (No. 8) states, "Esta tierra fue descubierta por Joan Caboto Veneciano, y Sebastian Caboto su hijo; anno M.CCCC.XCIIII a veinte y quatro de Iunio por la mannana." The year is evidently an engraver's error for MCCCCXCVII; later editions of the map correct it to 1497. The Latin version of legend No. 8 gives the hour as 5 a.m. "quam terram primum visam."

The rest of this Latin legend No. 8, translated, continues: "They called it *prima terra vista* and they called a great island near this land Isle of St. John for having discovered it the same day [of St. John Baptist]. The natives of these lands go clothed with skins of beasts, and in their wars they employ bows and arrows, spears & darts, and billets of wood, and slings. This land is very sterile, and therein are many white bears, stags as big as horses, and many other animals, and also an infinite number of fish—salmon, immense soles, and many other species of fish, the most numerous are called *baccalaos*. And there are in this land falcons, eagles, partridge, *pardillos*, and many other species of birds."

In my opinion, Cabot had before him, as he sent instructions for drafting the 1544 map, the Nicolas Desliens Map of 1541. Compare them here. Note close similarities—the fragmented Newfoundland, the shape of Cape Breton, the Magdalens, the Gulf nomenclature, the attenuated Labrador separated by a deep estuary (R. Dulce) from the false Labrador (Greenland). The Nova Scotia—New England (Norumbega) sections on both maps are taken from Ribero's 1529 map or a derivative. Cabot's nomenclature follows Desliens's in most instances. Note particularly the similarity between their depictions of Cape Breton.

Dr. Burgemeister, Direktor of the Sächsische Landesbibliothek, Dresden, kindly sent me this photograph of the Desliens Map. It is much better than the last reproduction (in 1903), although the Map was damaged by bombing in World War II. He writes as follows about the two flags, which come out black in the photograph. The easterly one shows in each of four quarters two interlaced capital C's; the westerly one shows three gold fleur-de-lys imposed on dark-blue lozenges. The New England coast, in the section here reproduced, ends with *Anoranbegue* (Norumbega, Penobscot Bay), taken (except for this name) from the Ribero Map of 1529.

It looks to me as if Sebastian Cabot, having only a vague notion of his father's landfall after forty-seven years but remembering that it was on a northward-facing cape on St. John's Day and that a big island was seen simultaneously, looked at Desliens's Cape Breton and Island of St. John and decided "These are them." Amusingly enough, his bad guess fixed John Cabot's landfall in the eyes of historians for over 350 years.

Note also that Cabot's *prima tierra vista* tails off, not from Cape Breton proper, but from Cape North on Cape Breton Island, which is even further from the open sea than Cape Breton itself, and so even less likely to have been a *prima tierra vista* for Cabot, or anyone. You may as well imagine Columbus threading his way through the Bahamas without seeing them and making his landfall at Miami.

This 1544 map places Cape Bauld on about latitude 54°30′ N, which is three degrees off, but *cavo rasa* (Cape Race) on about 47°30′—only fifty miles too far north. It is opposite the mouth of the "river of Bordeaux," an interesting agreement with the Day letter. See discussion of the Canadian part in W. F. Ganong, *Crucial Maps in the Early Cartography of Canada*, pp. 270–31, with parallel columns of nomenclature on p. 332; and Theodore E. Layng's "Commentaries," *ibid*. pp. 469–73.

Roberto Almagià, for whom an Italian-born discoverer could do no wrong, came to Sebastian's defense in several works, briefly in *Commemorazione di Sebastiano Caboto nel IV Centenario della Morte* (Venice, 1958); earlier, in a chapter of his *Gli Italiani primi esploratori dell' America* (Rome, 1937), and "Alcune considerazione sui viaggi di Giovanni Caboto" in *Rendiconti Accademia Nazionale dei Lincei*, 8th Ser., III (1948), 391–403.

OCEAN CROSSINGS AND METEOROLOGY

Information from the Hydrographic Office of the U. S. Navy (Rear Adm. O. D. Waters, Jr., USN), the Nautical Almanac Office, the American Meteorological Society, the Ice Forecasting Central of the Canadian Government at Halifax, has been very helpful, as have their several publications.

Williamson, pp. 225–26, quotes three passages from Hakluyt about the 1583 voyage of Sir Humfry Gilbert, which say some very interesting things about the winds in the North Atlantic: (1) one could count on fair winds sailing to Newfoundland from England between 15 January and 15 May, making the passage in thirty to forty days at most, and returning in twenty to twenty-four days. (2) "One wind suffiseth to make the passage," and (3) westward passages in March-May have been made "in 22 days and lesse." That was true of Cartier's in 1534—Saint-Malo to Cape Bonavista in twenty days; and Cartier started a month earlier than Cabot did. Referring to my chapters on his voyages, it will be seen that May was usually bad for a westward crossing.

Mathew's round voyage of seventy-seven days, including the exploration of an unknown and dangerous coast, was extraordinary. By way of comparison, A. G. Findlay in his *Memoir . . . of the Northern Atlantic Ocean* (14th ed., London, 1879, p. 519) boasts that brig *Ward* of St. John, N. B., "myself master," performed one round voyage to England in seventy-two days, and a second in ninety-two days.

LANDFALL AND COASTAL VOYAGE

It is hardly worth while to mention all the arguments for the Cape Breton landfall, now rendered untenable by information contained in the Day letter. In all landfall speculations we must keep in mind, first, that Cabot was trying to sail west to Cathay on a high latitude, and, second, his coastal voyage must be crowded into twenty-six days at most between 24 June and 20 July 1497, and bracketed between latitudes 51°35′ and 45°42′—the northern tip of Newfoundland and Cabot's somewhat faulty estimate of that island's southern extremity. And Cabot's coastal voyage may have been as little as 23, 24, or 25 days if *Mathew* raised Ushant on 1, 2, or 3 August. I am assuming her Breton landfall to have been on 4 August, giving her two days to cross the Channel, round Lands End and reach Bristol on the 6th, one of our few certain dates. But my friends at Bristol feel that I should have allowed at least three days.

One may well ask, How did Cabot know the latitude of Dursey Head and of the mouth of the Gironde? He had doubtless sailed to the latter and checked the latitude, and he could have shot the sun while passing Dursey Head; but editions of Ptolemy with latitude grids accurate within a degree were available in 1497, and Cabot may well have had one on board. Dursey Head continued to be, during the sixteenth century, a favorite point of departure for ships bound westward.

D. W. Prowse, *History of Newfoundland* (London, 1895), pp. 10–11, 105–6, is the principal protagonist for Cape Bonavista having been the landfall. His arguments are (1) an "unbroken tradition"; (2) the name *Bona Vista* is Italian for "Happy Sighting"; (3) John Mason's 1618 map of Newfoundland labels it as Cabot's landfall. In answer, (1) we do not know when that tradition started, as the English did not settle Newfoundland until the seventeenth century. (2) On the earliest map wherein this cape is named, the Martinez of 1580 in the British Museum (Prowse, p. 57), it is called *boavista*, and *bonavista* may be simply a translation of this Portuguese name. The argument against this hypothesis for Cabot's landfall is that it condemns Cabot to a 2°55′ (175 nautical miles) mistake in latitude, and makes no sense of Day's statement that he was steering too far *north* on the homeward passage.

I have consulted several members of the Cruising Club of America who have recently sailed along the coast of Newfoundland, and they all agree that *Mathew* would have had time to make the coastal voyage that I have sketched out, in twenty-six days. The nearest cruise to show what weather one may expect, is that of the thirty-three-foot Archer cutter *Direction*, with gaff rig and no power, rather topheavy and with poor windward ability, in June–July 1929. Her owner-skipper then was Arthur S. Allen; Rockwell Kent, one of the crew, described her voyage in his *N By E* (1930); and I have a copy of her log, thanks to its owner Mr. Charles S. Vilas. She rounded Cape Ray 22 June; next day, strong south wind and thick fog, lifting occasionally to reveal the shore, "a forbidding glamour, a terribleness, about the scene" (Kent); almost ran on the rocks off Bonne Bay June 24; into Bradore Bay (next Blanc Sablon, Labrador), on the north side of the strait dodging icebergs. 25–28 June, beating up the Strait of Belle Isle, full of ice; calm and so little progress that she accepted a tow back to Bradore by a fisherman. 29–30 June, kept in port by northeaster. 1 July, sail into dungeon fog with "18 interminable hours of blind man's buff with ice and rocks" (Kent). 2 July, pass out of Strait of Belle Isle and make Battle Harbor, Labrador, with the aid of a tow. Distance by chart measurement 380 miles, by taffrail log 408 miles, in fifteen days. Double this and you have 760 miles in thirty days. Compare this with my calculation of Cabot's 868 miles coastwise in twenty-six days, and you may conclude that Cabot never could have done it. But *Direction* had uncommonly bad luck as to calms and fogs.

Mr. George C. Whitely, Jr., who was brought up at Blanc Sablon, remembers seeing the Strait of Belle Isle covered with ice in early July. Yet in a small boat he has sailed from St. John's to Blanc Sablon through the strait without seeing any fog, and he has sailed in a brisk north wind from off Cape Freels to St. John's in one day. He saw no ice while circumnavigating Newfoundland in July 1951, and fog for only part of one day; but in 1952, twenty icebergs were in sight off White Bay. This shows how unreliable, for mapping any specific voyage, are "average" conditions taken from a modern chart or coast pilot.

Dr. Paul B. Sheldon, in a thirty-seven-foot ketch using his engine so little as not to count in the calculation, sailed in August 1948 from St. John's to Cape Race in seven and three-quarters hours with a strong north-northeast wind and fair current. It would have taken three or four days against a strong southwester. Other relevant runs by Dr. and Mrs. Sheldon were: Quirpon to St. John's, nine days in August 1948, spending every night in harbor except one at sea off Funk Island; St. John's to Quirpon, fourteen days in August 1952, spending every night but one in harbor; St. John's to St. Anthony, fifteen days in August 1964, with similar layovers. The Sheldons are positive that Cabot could have done it as I figure out, "and with a couple of good breaks could have done it easily."

The cruise of Mr. Joseph Field in the heavy thirty-six-foot yawl *Ventura*, with a crew of five in the summer of 1968, is relevant. He was bothered more by gale-force west winds than by fog. Starting from Port aux Basques 23 June, he reached Red Bay, on the Labrador shore of the Strait of Belle Isle, on 4 July, counting more than a hundred bergs and growlers in the strait. In Quirpon Harbor 6–8 July. Sailing close to shore, exploring small harbors and always passing the night in one, *Ventura* reached Fogo Island 20 July, rounded Cape Freels the 23rd and Cape Bonavista the 25th. Holed up in Catalina Harbor. On the 28th, rounded Baccalieu Island and reached Bay de Verde, spent two days, made St. John's in seven hours on the 30th. After spending about three days in harbor, rounded Cape St. Mary's at noon 6 August. Thus it took them twenty-nine days to do half of what I figure Cabot did in twenty-six. Mr. Field, however, thinks that Cabot could have done it with good weather, "which we did not have," and by sailing point-to-point in daylight (lasting about nineteen to twenty hours out of the twenty-four), instead of exploring practically every harbor. Mr. Edmund Cabot, determined to be "the first Cabot to circumnavigate Newfoundland," did so in 1970. In the forty-eight-foot auxiliary yawl *Avelinda* he departed St. Pierre 24 June, sailed around from east to north, and on 27 July departed Codroy on the Anguille Peninsula for the Bras d'Or. Sailed all night thrice. Only five foggy days after Cape Bonavista, but between Cape Freels and Quirpon spent every night in harbor owing to icebergs, plus two nights for repair of engine, which he used 10 to 15 per cent of the time.

All these yachts had the benefit of navigational aids which Cabot lacked, and all but one had power. But I am convinced that, given a fair chance, Cabot could have sailed the approximately 868 nautical miles from Cape Dégrat to Cape St. Mary's and back in twenty-six days. And we can cut his coastal voyage by 130 miles if we assume that he was satisfied by taking a peek around Cape Race, and started north from there.

Also, keep in mind fog, winds, and darkness—not much darkness in those northern latitudes in June–July but plenty of fog and head winds. No prudent and experienced mariner would sail along an unknown coast in fog or darkness, depending only on smell, sight, and lead. Cabot must have spent nights anchored in harbors even if he did not land. The official *Sailing Directions for Newfoundland* (1958 ed.) says that fog is most thick and frequent on the south and southeast coasts, and that they are the worst in July. "Cape Race has a monthly average of 22 days with fog in July" (p. 20); and 51 days out of 92 in May, June, and July! (p. 54).

On the homeward passage, assuming Cape Dégrat to have been the point of departure, Cabot probably shaped his course due east, following the same latitude sailing that he used on the westward passage; but the sailors persuaded him that there was no sense in touching at Ireland—they wanted home! He then altered his course too far to the southward, missed England altogether and raised Ushant. Actually, he would have done better to have run his easting down to Ireland and nipped around Fastnet into the Bristol Channel.

SUMMARY OF LATITUDE DATA

(all from Bowditch unless otherwise stated)

Ireland

Dursey Head, measured on chart as 51°33' N.
Bull Rock, about 3 miles off Dursey Head, 51°35' N.

Newfoundland

Cape Bauld, 51°33' N (to which I would add 45").
Cape Dégrat, 51°37' N, measured on chart.
Griquet Harbor, 51°33' N, measured on chart.
Cape Bonavista, 48°42' N.
Cape Race, 46°39' N.
Cape Pine, 46°37' N.

Mouth of "River of Bordeaux" (the Gironde)

Tour de Cordouan, 45°35' N.
Pointe de la Coubre, 45°42' N.

Thus, Cabot hit Cape Dégrat or Griquet Harbor "right on the nose," and he was only 45 to 62 miles off, depending on which Gironde landmark he meant, for the latitude of the southern point of Newfoundland.

Come on, Vikings, Portuguese, Bretons, and Normans: can you beat that?

THE GRATES COVE "INSCRIPTION" AND THE BACCALAOS FABLE

According to A. E. F. English, *Historic Newfoundland* (St. John's 1968), p. 15, there exists a rock at Grates Cove, Conception Bay (about thirty-three miles from Cape Bonavista), with an inscription which reads.

IO CABOTO SANCCIUS SAINMALIA

Sancio or Santius was one of John's sons, but who was Sainmalia? Possibly the barber!

There is a photo of the "Cabot rock" in the Newfoundland Museum at St. John's, on which it takes a great deal of imagination to see anything. My friends and neighbors the Raymond Hawtins visited Grates Cove on my behalf in June 1969 and report as follows: Local opinion differs as to whether (a) the stone is still there; (b) had been blown up or swept out into the harbor; (c) had been sent to the Museum, or (d) had had the Cabot inscription chiseled out of it, or (e) did not exist. The Hawtins found (a) to be correct. They saw the stone, identified it from the photo at the Museum, and examined it carefully for IO CABOTO or any such inscription. They found nothing of the sort, but numerous modern tourists' initials. The stone measures about four by five feet, is flat, hard, rectangular, and difficult to get at.

Bacailhaba, bacalhao, and baccala are respectively the Basque, Castilian, and Portuguese words for codfish, used long before the discovery of America (Harrisse, Jean et Sebastien Cabot, p. 75). Besides Baccalieu Island, which Cabot must have passed, there are now two other islands of the same name off Newfoundland. Peter Martyr, quoting Sebastian Cabot, started the story that Basque fishermen had been in Newfoundland years before Cabot, and named it "Codfish Land." He says (De Orbe Novo Decades, dec. iii, lib. vi, chap. i, of 1516 ed.) that Sebastian, who in 1513 was a frequent guest in his house, called the northern regions of the New World Baccalaos, "because in the adjacent waters he found a multitude of fish resembling tunnies, which the natives called by this name. These fish were so abundant as to slow up the advance of ships." * If you can believe that the Beothuk Indians of Newfoundland adopted a Basque name for codfish in lieu of their own name Bobboosoret or Bobbooshrat (J. P. Howley, The Beothucks or Red Indians, p. 304), you can believe anything. Cf. Justin Winsor, Narrative and Critical History, I, 147-49, 267, 274; and III, 12-16.

BRISTOL IN CABOT'S ERA

Captain R. A. Gibbons, Haven Master of the Port of Bristol Authority, sent me these official figures for tide ranges in the Avon, warning me that "Chart datum at Bristol is 9 ft. above chart datum at Avonmouth and accordingly the range of the tide is reduced." The appropriate heights of tide above chart datum are:—

---

* Williamson, p. 267. This tale obtained wide currency through Richard Eden's trans. of Peter Martyr (1555): "Sebastian Cabot him selfe, named those landes Baccallaos, bycause that in the seas therabout he founde so great multitudes of certeyne bigge fysshes . . . (which thinhabitantes caule Baccallaos) that they sumtymes stayed his shippes." Edward Arber, First Three English Books on America (1885), iii,vi,161.

The "Cabot Rock" at Grates Cove. Taken 1969 by Raymond Hawtin, who was unable to see even an "IO" on it.

	Mean High Water		Mean Low Water	
	Spring	Neap	Spring	Neap
Avonmouth	42.2 ft.	31.6 ft.	1.9 ft.	10.4 ft.
Bristol	33.4 ft.	22.6 ft.	2.4 ft.	2.4 ft.

"The level of low water at Bristol is, of course, very considerably affected by the amount of fresh water coming down from the catchment area and this fresh water does have to be taken into account in navigating the river following periods of heavy rain."

Among the useful pamphlets issued by the Bristol Branch of the Historical Association are J. W. Sherborne, *The Port of Bristol in the Middle Ages* (1965); D. B. Quinn, *Sebastian Cabot and Bristol Exploration* (1968); Vincent Waite, *The Bristol Hotwell* (1960); and E. M. Carus-Wilson, *The Merchant Adventurers of Bristol in the Fifteenth Century* (1962). This last is an abridgment from her *Medieval Merchant Venturers* (London, 1954). John C. G. Hill, *Shipshape and Bristol Fashion* (Liverpool, n.d.), and John Latimer, *History of the Society of Merchant Venturers of the City of Bristol* (Bristol, 1903), are excellent on later maritime developments. The popular Jackdaw Series of Clark, Irwin & Co. of Toronto has an excellent folder, No. 69, called *Bristol and the Cabots*, containing reproductions of documents, old ship pictures, etc.

There are articles on William Canynges's ships in *Mariner's Mirror*, III

(1913), 57 and 346-47. T. F. Reddaway and A. Ruddock in *Camden Miscellany*, XXIII (Royal Historical Society, 1969), print an interesting detailed account of the voyage of the ship *Trinity* of Bristol to Spain and the Mediterranean in 1480-81. As the journal mentions a donation to the monastery of La Rábida near Huelva, they throw out the suggestion that the mariners of Bristol told the monks about John Jay discovering Newfoundland in 1480, and they told Columbus; hence America was discovered! Miss Ruddock is more circumspect in her article "Columbus and Iceland," *Geographical Journal*, CXXXVI (1970), 177-89.

The plant with white flowers which I gathered on the banks of the Avon was identified for me as scurvy grass by the Arnold Arboretum—ever helpful in checking on the often puzzling botanical reports of the discoverers.

The Bristol-London road in 1497 was identical with that on the Gough Map of *c.* 1360, in the Bodleian. This map is studied in a Bodleian monograph of 1958 by E. J. S. Parsons, and by R. A. Pelham in H. C. Darby (ed.), *An Historical Geography of England before 1800* (1936), chap. vi. My thanks to Mr. Huddy of the Map Room, British Museum, and to Mrs. Cooper, for bringing this out.

I am greatly indebted to City Archivist Miss Elizabeth Ralph, to Mr. Graham Farr of Portishead, to Professors C. M. MacInnes, K. Gordon Davis, and P. V. McGrath of the history department, University of Bristol, for help on the Bristol background, and Mr. John Corin of the Bristol Port Authority; and to Captain Alan Villiers for help on the general maritime background of Bristol and the West Country.

JOHN DAY'S LETTER

Dr. Hayward Keniston, professor of romance languages at the University of Michigan, former cultural attaché to the American Embassy at Buenos Aires, found this document in the Spanish archives at Simancas in 1956, in a *legajo* labeled "Brazil." He called it to the attention of Dr. L. A. Vigneras, who saw its significance, transcribed and printed it with notes in the *Hispanic American Historical Review*, XXXVI (1956), 503-9. Vigneras published an English translation in his article "The Cape Breton Landfall: 1494 or 1497?" in *Canadian Historical Review* XXXVIII (1957), 219-28. Williamson, pp. 211-14, prints the same translation. The fresh one given here is the joint work of my friends James M. Byrne and Mauricio Obregón.

Although the recipient is not named but addressed as "El Señor Almirante Mayor," Columbus almost certainly was he. Only one other Spanish admiral, the Grand Admiral of Castile, then existed; and he not only had no interest in transatlantic voyages, but was occupied with court business during the winter of 1497-98 when (by internal evidence) this letter was written. The writer, John Day, was an English merchant who imported wine at Bristol in 1492-93 and later resided in Seville. Although a well-educated member of a London aldermanic family who had been respectable merchants for a century, John appears to have been a rather slippery character with many irons in the fire, who used the alias John Day after committing certain unspecified "wrongs." Dr. Ruddock's research into the Chancery Court of London in 1501 reveals that for several years past he had been trading in wine and woolens between England, Portugal, and Spain.* Having visited England about the time John Cabot returned from his first voyage, Day was a natural person from whom Columbus could seek information about a voyage which might impinge on his privileges and on the Spanish part of the New World.

The value of the Day letter lies not in his hint of a pre-Cabotian voyage to Newfoundland, but in its precise navigational data, such as a master mariner like Columbus would want to know.

John Day to the Very Magnificent and
Honorable Lord, the Lord Great Admiral

With your most revered Excellency's servant,[1] and considering what you instructed me therein, which I would wish to do in accordance with my desire and duty, I do not find the book *Invincio Fortunati;*[2] I thought I had brought it with my effects, and am greatly annoyed that I can not find it, because I sought very much to serve you. The other [book] by Marco Polo, and the copy of the *tierra* [globe or world map] which has been found I send you, and if I did not send you the chart, it is because, with my heavy schedule [*occupaciones*] it is not as I would like it to be, since I made it in a hurry at the time of my departure [from England], but with the help of the enclosed copy you will be able to ascertain what you wish to know, since the capes of *tierra firma* and the islands are therein named and you will also see there where the first landfall [*primera vista*] took place, because it

[1] The Vigneras translation opens, "Your Lordship's servant brought me your letter." This is probably what Day meant.

[2] Meaning, no doubt, *Inventio Fortunata* (or *Fortunatae*), written *c.* 1360, attributed to Nicholas of Lynn, a work mentioned by Ferdinand Columbus in his biography of his father (ch. ix), and by Las Casas (1951 ed., I,67) as having been known to Columbus. It has become a "ghost book": never printed, no manuscript known. For discussion see T. J. Oleson, *Early Voyages and Northern Approaches,* pp. 105–8, and B. F. De Costa, "Arctic Explorations" in *Journal* of American Geog. Soc., XII (1880), 159–92. The *Inventio* is known only through quotations on two maps. The Ruysch of 1508 quotes it as authority for there being a mag-

* Alwyn A. Ruddock, "John Day of Bristol and the English Voyages . . . before 1497," *Geographical Journal,* CXXXII (1968), 225–33, which includes a good presensation of the "secret voyage" theory.

was on the return [course] that was found the major part of the land depicted.[3]

Thus also your Lordship will see that the cape closest to Ireland is 1800 *millas* west of *Cabo Dursal*, which is in Ireland, and the lowest part of the Isle of the Seven Cities is west of the *Rio de Burdeos*,[4] and you will note that he did not go ashore save at one place of *tierra firma*, which is close to where they made the first landfall, in which place they went ashore with a crucifix and raised banners bearing the arms of the Holy Father and the arms of the King of England my lord, and they found big trees from which masts of ships are made, and other trees underneath them, and the land was very rich in pasturage; in which place (as I have already told your Lordship) they found a very narrow way leading into the land, and saw a spot where someone had made a fire, and found dung of animals which they judge to be tame, and they found a stick of elbow length perforated at both ends and painted with *brasíl*[5] and from these signs the land is judged to be inhabited; and as he found himself to be with few men he dared not enter the land beyond a cross-bow shot, and he took on fresh water and returned to his ship and along the coast they found many fish of the kind that in Iceland are cured in the air and sell in England and other countries and which in England are called *estoqfis;*[6] and also when coasting they saw running ashore two *bultos* [big objects], one chasing the other, but were unable to tell whether they were men or beasts; and it seemed to them that there were cultivated lands where they thought there might be villages, and they saw vegetation whose leaves appeared fair to them, and the time that he departed from England was in the end

netic rock 33 miles in circumference "under the Arctic Pole," surrounded by islands and depths into which the ocean flowed and was then regurgitated. The Mercator Map of 1569 tells how he heard from one James Cnoyen that "a certain priest in the King of Norway's Court" in 1364 reported that in 1360 "a certain English Frier" visited circumpolar islands and took their latitudes with his astrolabe. And, according to Hakluyt, John Dee stated that in 1360 "a frier of Oxford, being a good astronomer, went in companie with others to the most Northern islands of the world," and having returned, wrote the *Inventio Fortunata (aliter fortunae)* which he presented to the King of England. The book described the lands from lat. 54° N to the North Pole, which Nicholas visited five times[!] Hakluyt, *Voyages*, (Everyman ed.), I,100. See also Richard Hennig, *Terrae Incognitae*, III (1938), 261–67.

[3] This chart, alas, is not with the letter, and has long since disappeared.

[4] Dursey Head, and river of Bordeaux, the Gironde.

[5] Meaning, red in color. Probably a shuttle for weaving nets.

[6] Stockfish, dried codfish, a name still used in Europe.

of May and he was en route 35 days before he found land, and the
winds were east and northeast and the seas were smooth on the
outward as on the homeward passage, save one day when there
blew up a gale, and that was two or three days before he found
land; and being so far out, the north-seeking needle failed him
and varied two points down,[7] and he went exploring the coast one
month more or less and the abovesaid cape of *tierra firma* which
is closest to Ireland being [passed] on the return, they arrived off
the coast of Europe in 15 days. Carrying a stern wind, he arrived
in Brittany because the mariners confused [8] him, saying that he
was steering too far north; and from thence [Brittany] he came to
Bristol and went to the king to tell him all the abovesaid, and the
king gave him a grace of 20 pounds sterling per annum that he
might recuperate during the time when more becomes known of
this business, since it is hoped to launch an expedition of 10 or 12
ships to discover the said land more completely the coming year,
God willing, because on this said voyage he had but one ship of
50 *toneles* with 20 persons and victuals for 7 or 8 months, and
because he wished to get this [expedition] under way.

It is considered certain that this same point of land at another
time [9] was found and discovered by those of Bristol who found
el Brasil as you are already aware, which is called *Ysla de Brasil,*

[7] I.e., pointed to NNW instead of N.

[8] *Le ficieron desconcertar*—baffled, thwarted, or confused him.

[9] *En otros tiempos.* There is no English or other evidence of this alleged
pre-Cabotian discovery of America. The probability is that Day picked
up the usual post-discovery yarns about "Of course, we know all about
that, old So-and-So went there years ago," etc., and that he thought it
would please Columbus to report that Cabot's discovery was no part of
the Indies but had been discovered before. David B. Quinn, assuming
that *en otros tiempos* means "a long time ago" (whilst it may mean
simply a couple of years earlier), has built up a theory, based entirely
on this statement, that there was a "secret voyage" from Bristol to North
America which discovered Newfoundland before 1492. This puts Quinn
as a dialectitian in a class with the Cortesão brothers, and Henry VII in
the "keep it secret" category with João II! D. B. Quinn, "The Argument
for the English Discovery of America between 1480 and 1494," *Geographical Journal,* CXXVII (1961), 277–85; *The New Found Land*
(Providence, the J.C.B. Library, 1965) and "État present des études sur
la rédecouverte de l'Amérique," *Journal de la Société des Américanistes,*
LV, 2 (1966), 343–82. My comments are (1) that if America had been
discovered by men of Bristol before 1497, there would certainly have
been some record of it, somewhere; nor would that prudent prince
Henry VII have granted letters-patent to the Cabots in 1496 and rewarded John for discovering a *new* isle in 1497. And (2) if the men of
Bristol discovered Newfoundland and waters teeming with codfish in
1480, why did they have to send vessels out yearly to search for "Brasil"?

and is presumed and believed to be the *tierra firma* which those of Bristol discovered.

As regards the first voyage which Your Lordship wished to know about, the fact is that he [Cabot] went in one ship and the people whom he engaged disconcerted him [10] and he went ill provisioned and encountered contrary winds and decided to return.

Magnificent Lord, upon completion of other matters pertaining to the case, I would like to serve Your Lordship provided I am not impeded from so doing because of business obligations of great importance and by the proper preparation of documents and cargoes for shipment to England which I must expedite. Which matters greatly interfere with my serving of Your Lordship; but accept from me, Your Lordship, as a Magnificent Lord, the wish of my true intention, which is to be of service to you, and when I find myself in a position [so to do], when comparatively unencumbered by business, I will take up work which shall have for its purpose to be of service to you, and when I shall have had news from England touching on the above (and I know that everything [English] comes to my attention), I shall make known to Your Lordship everything that may not be prejudicial to the King [of England] my Lord.

In return for any services which I hope to perform on your behalf, I pray that your Lordship will be pleased to write to me a few words touching on those matters, since the kindness which in this matter you will be doing me will open many hints [11] wherewith to serve you with all the things of which you are aware. May Our Lord cause your Lordship's high estate to prosper in conformity with your merits. When your Lordship is through with it, please deliver the book or command that it be given to Mycer Jorge.

I kiss your Lordship's hands.

JOHAN DAY

[10] See note 8, previous page. This refers to Cabot's first attempt, in 1496, of which there is no other record.

[11] *Memoria;* perhaps "ways and means." The language of his concluding paragraph, flattering as if addressed to a king, suggests that Day wanted to get something out of Columbus, possibly the privilege of investing in his third voyage.

✻ VII ✻
Voyages to the Labrador
and Newfoundland

1500-1536

João Fernandes, *Lavrador*

After the excitement over John Cabot's first voyage and his disappearance on his second, there came a distinct letdown in northern voyages to America. The quarter-century after 1500 is a dark period in the history of North American discovery, faintly and doubtfully illuminated by old maps. The brilliant success of the southern voyages turned men's minds away from the northern region of ice, snow, and fog; only the fishermen kept coming, as did a few hopeful searchers for a strait to China. Gold from Hispaniola was already pouring into Spain. In July 1499 one of Vasco da Gama's ships returned to Lisbon with the news that this great Portuguese captain had finally reached India by sea. Columbus sailed on his third voyage in 1498, discovered the South American continent, and opened the pearl fisheries. Vicente Yañez Pinzón for Spain, and Pedro Álvares Cabral for Portugal, bracketed the great country of Brazil in the same year, 1500. After that, who cared for codfish, mast trees, and icebergs?

As a literary wit remarked, America was discovered by accident, not wanted when found, and early explorations were directed to finding a way through or around it. Columbus's fourth voyage, starting in 1502, was a search for a strait from the Caribbean to the Indian Ocean; Cabot died seeking a strait through North America; and for the next eight decades all recorded voyages thither, except those of farmer Fernandes and fisherman Fagundes, were, first and foremost, searches for the elusive Northwest Passage to fabulous Cathay.

Two places in Europe remained committed to this quest—Terceira and Bristol. Terceira in the Azores by 1500 had become an intensively cultivated island, and the chief town, Angra, a favorite port of call for Portuguese caravels returning from Africa. Angra already had splendid churches in the Manueline Gothic style, and paved streets lined with stone mansions. One of these belonged to Pedro Maria de Barcelos, a second-generation landowner, founder of a noble family which endures to this day. One of his friends and neighbors was João Fernandes, a *lavrador*, or small landed proprietor, who farmed out his land while he went voyaging; and it was humble Fernandes rather than noble Barcelos who received letters-patent from King Manuel, dated 28 October 1499, to search for and discover islands in the Portuguese half of the world.

A descendant of Fernandes's partner, Dona Maria Isabel do Canto de Barcelos Coelho Borges, whom I met at Angra in 1939, reminded me of an old Virginian lady, living in the tradition of pre-Civil War. When I referred to her as Portuguese, she remarked firmly, "I am not a Portuguese. I am an Azorean." She had portraits of the last five or six kings of Portugal in her salon; and, on each stair landing, a sedan chair; for, as she explained, in her youth no lady went out on foot in Angra. She gave me to understand that her Barcelos ancestor was a very great person indeed; but as for João Fernandes, he was "a nobody—no one ever heard of him!"

Nevertheless, João Fernandes *lavrador* has left footprints on the sands of time, and although information on him is scarce enough, it is more than we have on his aristocratic partner. João visited England while Columbus was abroad, for the Bristol customs records show that he shipped goods thence to Lisbon in January 1493. In October 1499, as we have seen, he received the letters-patent from D. Manuel "to go in search of and discover certain Islands of our sphere of influence," and be captain thereof. Barcelos possibly financed and certainly accompanied the voyage that followed, but he is not mentioned in the document.

All we know about this Fernandes-Barcelos voyage is from legends on maps, starting with the Cantino dated 1502. From these we learn that the partners made Cape Farewell, Greenland, in the summer of 1500 and that, since João Fernandes gave the *aviso* (which I take to be the "Land, ho!"), they decided to call it *Tiera del Lavrador,* Land of the Husbandman. It was doubtless a great joke on board that a farmer first sighted land. Greenland had been so completely forgotten in southern Europe that it could be renamed after an Azorean! A century later, after Frobisher had tried to call it West England, geographers learned of the old Norse name, revived it, and shifted the name "Labrador" to the continental area of eastern Canada, which still bears it. There is no doubt, however, that the first Land of the Labrador was Greenland. *Cauo Larbradore* appears at Cape Farewell on the Oliveriana Map of the first decade of the century; the Munich-Portuguese chart, also reproduced here, tells that the Portuguese rediscovered it but did not land; and the Wolfenbüttel Map of 1527, in a scroll next to Greenland, states, "Because he who gave the *aviso* was a *labrador* of the Azores, they gave it that name."

Although it has been argued that the partners were primarily interested in finding the passage to Cathay that John Cabot had missed, the letters-patent of 1499 distinctly state that their main object was to discover an island or islands, over which Farmer John could be donatory captain. The probability is that D. Manuel, having heard of John Cabot's discovery of Newfoundland, and believing that it lay on the Portuguese side of the Line of Demarcation, wished to forestall the English by settling the New Isle. From his point of view, the English had no proper title to it. The partners' landfall was probably unintended, but if the Oliveriana Map records their voyage and not those of the Bristol syndicate, they continued to Newfoundland and the continent. More probably, discouraged by the amount of ice encountered, they gave up their quest for the time being; hoping, like Cabot, to do better another year.

Returning to Terceira empty-handed after a voyage which yielded nothing but a view of Greenland's Icy Mountains, João Fernandes heard the bad news that D. Manuel had conferred a grant similar to his but wider in scope on Gaspar Corte Real. Offended and disappointed, he proceeded to Bristol where he had trading connections, and joined two other Azoreans and three local merchants in a petition to Henry VII for letters-patent, which were granted on 19 March 1501. Whether or not he accompanied the voyages that this Anglo-Azorean syndicate made in 1501–2 we do not know. João disappears from history after the granting of this patent.

Though soon forgotten, Fernandes is still commemorated in the common speech of those northern regions, whose inhabitants invariably use the article when speaking of the country named after him. They always say "The Labrador," never simply "Labrador." So, whenever you hear a fisherman speak of his "home in The Labrador," or a seaman say, "I'm bound to The Labrador," pray give a kindly thought to João Fernandes, the sea-going husbandman of Terceira.

Gaspar and Miguel Corte Real

Gaspar Corte Real was the youngest son of João Vaz Corte Real to whom a pre-Columbian discovery of America, in company with Scolvus, Pining, Pothorst, and God knows who, is still officially credited in Portugal. The Corte Real were a branch, probably illegitimate, of the great Portuguese family of Da Costa and used their same punning arms, six *costas* or ribs. They settled in the Algarve and honorably served the Aviz dynasty. João Vaz Corte Real, chamberlain to the Infante D. Fernando, showed such energy in obtaining colonists for Terceira that the king made him captain of that island in 1474, and within ten years added the island of São Jorge to his domain. He married a Spanish lady from Galicia after forcibly abducting her, and as ruler in the Azores he had the reputation of being greedy, cruel, and unjust. Dying in 1496, not greatly regretted, he left a family of three sons: Vasco Annes, Miguel, and Gaspar. The eldest inherited his father's Azorean properties, but never visited the islands after his father's death; the two younger, while maintaining the family connection with the royal court, grew up in the Azores, already a veritable hothouse for maritime discovery. And both lost their lives exploring the New World.

Gaspar, the youngest son, born in Portugal about the year 1450, served D. Manuel before that king's accession in 1481, and continued to be a *fidalgo* (a gentleman of the court) while residing at Terceira to look after his landed inheritance. Damião de Góis, in his *Crónica do Felicissimo Rei D. Manuel*, described Gaspar as "valiant and adventur-

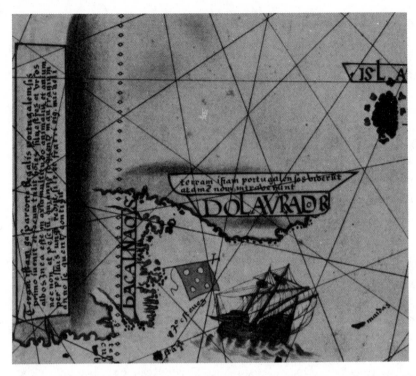

A section of the "Munich-Portuguese" Map. The legend on "Do Lavrador" (Greenland) reads: "This land the Portuguese sighted but entered it not." West of "Bacalnaos" (Newfoundland) the legend reads: "This land Gaspar Corte Real of Portugal first discovered and brought home men of the forest and white bears. Therein is a multitude of beasts, birds and fish. He was shipwrecked in the following year and never returned. His brother Michael next year went in search of him." From E. L. Stevenson's photographic facsimile.

ous and ambitious to win honor." Within a year of his father's death, he removed to Angra, as deputy captain of the island for his eldest brother, and on 12 May 1500 received an important donation patent from the king. In the preamble it states that Corte Real had already been on one voyage at his own expense, "to search out, discover and find . . . some islands and a mainland," and now wished to keep and govern whatever lands he might find on a subsequent voyage. Obviously a favorite of D. Manuel, Gaspar received unusually extensive privileges. He was guaranteed the property, jurisdiction, and trading monopoly of any lands he might discover for himself and his descendants. We know nothing of the earlier voyage, except that it was made at his own expense; he paid for this one too. Gaspar must have known about John Cabot's two voyages, yet was not dismayed by the Venetian's disappearance.

We have not the slightest hint as to the names, rigs, and burthens of the Corte Reals' ships. Since the brothers were men of means, they undoubtedly had the pick of the caravel fleet. This type, which the Portuguese had evolved for their voyages to the Western Islands and West Africa during the fifteenth century, was characterized by weatherliness. Owing partly to her lines, partly to her lateen rig on at least two of her three masts, the caravel could do better to windward than many a modern yacht. And weatherliness was the prime quality wanted in any vessel for North Atlantic discovery. The only certain item we have about Gaspar's outfit is that he received the privilege of drawing on the royal ship-biscuit bakery at Lisbon, and received 72½ quintals of hardtack in return for 7800 litres of country wheat.

More fortunate than Farmer Fernandes had been that very summer, Gaspar "discovered," says the chronicler, at about latitude 50° N, "a land that was very cool and with big trees," which he named *Terra Verde*. Newfoundland, undoubtedly.

Returning to Lisbon in the autumn of 1500, Gaspar obtained three ships, equipped them at his own expense, and departed in mid-May of 1501. His luck now ran out. Cantino, an Italian diplomat present at Lisbon when two of Gaspar's ships returned in October 1501, reports that the fleet had sailed due north for four months without seeing anything—obviously an exaggeration—ran into a huddle of icebergs, and a few days later into a field of pack-ice. They then sailed northwest and west for three months (but were away for only five!) and found a large and delightful country, well watered, covered with pines of mast-tree length, and "luscious and varied fruits." In the southern part of this *Terra Verde*, as they called Newfoundland, the Portuguese kidnapped fifty-seven Indians and brought them to the king at Lisbon. These were of the Beothuk tribe, who "live altogether by fishing and hunting animals, in which the land abounds, such as very large deer covered with extremely long hair, the skins of which they use for garments and also make houses and boats thereof. . . . Their manners and gestures are most gentle; they laugh considerably and manifest the greatest pleasure. . . . The women have small breasts and most beautiful bodies, and rather pleasant faces." To Cantino they appeared quite human, except for their costumes. "They go quite naked except for their privy parts, which they cover with a skin of the above-mentioned deer." Chronicler De Góis adds that the natives hunted, not with bow and arrow but with "pieces of wood burnt in the fire in place of spears, which when they throw them make wounds as if pointed with fine steel. . . . They live in rocky caves and thatched huts."

Although it is arguable that the Portuguese were the most thorough and successful European slave-traders of this or any other period, whether in Africa or America, they were not the only ones in that business. Columbus had shipped home thirty Indian slaves from Hispaniola in 1496, and many more followed; Ojeda began raiding the Bahamas for slaves in 1500. Everyone, including the early English and French voyagers, made a practice of "persuading" a few simple natives to sail home with them, as the best evidence that they had really discovered something, but few kidnapped for profit. The North American Indian slave trade never assumed the proportions of the African slave trade because the natives could not take it and would not endure it. In captivity or under forced labor they faded away. Pasqualigo, in his letter on Gaspar's voyage, said that the prospect of obtaining timber for masts and yards "and plenty of men slaves, fit for every kind of labor," was highly pleasing to D. Manuel, and evidence that "God is with his majesty."

After their first experiences with Europeans, the Beothuk retired to the interior. They were hunted like wild beasts and treated with the utmost cruelty both by the French and English settlers and eventually were exterminated.

The two ships of Gaspar Corte Real's expedition which reached Lisbon between 9 and 11 October 1501 reported that their commodore continued exploring southward, but Gaspar was never heard of again. He was lost, with all hands, and we have not the slightest hint of how it happened, any more than we have of John Cabot's fate.

It took more than shipwrecks to discourage maritime exploration in those days. In January 1502 D. Manuel assigned half the territory presumably discovered by Gaspar Corte Real to his next older brother, Miguel, who with two vessels embarked on a voyage toward Newfoundland in May. Again the flagship and all hands were lost. The other ship returned, but with no new knowledge.

The same Cantino who wrote about Gaspar's voyage caused to be made for his Lisbon master Ercole d'Este, Duke of Ferrara, a beautiful world map to illustrate the latest discoveries. This is still preserved in the Estense Library at Modena. Assuming that the American half of Juan de La Cosa's Mappemonde is no earlier than 1505, the Cantino Mappemonde, indubitably of 1502, becomes the first to incorporate the earliest voyages to the New World. Drafted in Lisbon, it expresses the Portuguese point of view, blithely ignoring the English voyages of Cabot and his followers, although Gaspar had found Cabot relics in Newfoundland. Against a deeply indented land studded with islands, west by south of a surprisingly accurate Greenland (here called "a point of Asia"), Cantino places the new *Terra del Rey de Portuguall*, and Portuguese flags are planted both there and on Greenland. The legend against the island states that it was discovered "by command of his most excellent majesty D. Manuel, King of Portugal, by Gaspar de Corte Real, a gentleman of the royal household, who sent thence a ship with both male and female natives, and stayed behind, but never returned. . . . There are many mast trees." The configuration suggests that Gaspar followed Cabot's course, ranging the coast from Cape Bauld to around Cape Race, breaking off near Placentia Bay.

When spring arrived in 1503 and Miguel Corte Real had not returned, the eldest brother, Vasco Annes, asked D. Manuel's permission to fit out ships and go in search of both his brothers. The king wisely refused his consent, on the ground that any such search would be useless.

Some day a lucky skindiver may come upon the wrecks of Cabot's ships, or the two Corte Real caravels that disappeared. Until then, their fate is a mystery.

All Gaspar's and Miguel's rights and privileges were transferred in 1506 to the surviving brother, Vasco Annes, and these were confirmed to his descendants by later kings over a period of seventy years. None of them did anything about Newfoundland, but the titular captaincy of the *Terra del Rey de Portuguall* remained hereditary in the family until 1578, when Manuel Corte Real, last in the male line, fell in battle fighting the Moors by the side of D. Sebastian, last Portuguese king of the house of Aviz.

The Anglo-Azorean Syndicate and Sebastian Cabot

João Fernandes *lavrador*, after his Greenland voyage of 1500—fruitless except for transferring his name to a vast territory—proceeded to
England, obviously to shake off Corte Real competition. At Bristol he
joined two other Azoreans, Francisco Fernandes (possibly his brother)
and João Gonsalves, and two English merchants named Thomas Ashhurst and John Thomas, in a petition to Henry VII for a grant. Letters-
patent were granted the same day, 19 March 1501. Unusually comprehensive, they authorized the partners "to sail and transport themselves
. . . under our banners and ensigns" to any part of the world, and take
possession for the crown of any place inhabited by "heathens and
infidels" still "unknown to all Christians"; to colonize and govern such
place and punish malefactors, notably those "who shall rape and violate
against their will or otherwise any women of the islands or countries
aforesaid." (This concern for the chastity of native women is unique.)
The partners will enjoy a trade monopoly for ten years, subject to the
royal customs; each and every one of them to be "Admirals in the
same parts"—i.e. to exercise admiralty jurisdiction over their colony;
and their heirs may inherit these overseas possessions. Apparently the
king's lawyers regarded his two earlier grants to the Cabots as having
lapsed, or, more likely, the syndicate bought off Sebastian and his
brothers.

Whatever voyages these five partners organized have left precious
little trace. On 26 September 1502 royal pensions of £10 a year were
conferred upon "Fraunceys Fernandus and John Guidisalvus, squiers,
in consideracion of the true service which they have doon to us to oure
singler pleasure as Capitaignes into the newe founde land." But
Fernandes the *lavrador* received nothing; he must have died, possibly
on the voyage. On 9 December of the same year, Franceys and John,
together with Hugh Elyot and Thomas Ashhurst, received fresh
letters-patent. This looks as if the partners had made a reconnaissance in
1501 or 1502, and claimed to be on the track of the Northwest Passage;
the king encouraged them in order to resist Portuguese claims and to
continue searching for *the* strait. They may well have entered some
northern strait where they certainly would have been stopped by ice;
no practicable Northwest Passage for a sailing vessel has ever been
found.

In my opinion, the highly controversial Oliveriana Map at Pésaro, of which the northwestern corner is reproduced in the Notes to this chapter, reflects the voyage of this Anglo-Azorean syndicate, as well as that of João Fernandes. The eastern promontory with the mountains, representing Greenland, contains six names that appear on no other map, together with *Cavo Larbradore* commemorating Farmer John. Next westward is a peninsula surely meant for Newfoundland, as it has the Portuguese names *bacalaos, del Marco, de la spera* (Cape Spear), and *Terra de Corte* [Real]. Finally, the western land mass which has but one legend, *costa fermoza* ("handsome coast"), vague as La Cosa's "Coast Discovered by the English," may well represent an extension of one of the Anglo-Azorean voyages to the North American mainland. This beautiful and little-known mappemonde, probably made in Florence for one of the Medici, as the Cantino had been for Ercole d'Este, cannot be dated earlier than 1504 or later than 1510. So it is not impossible that the cartographer gathered facts about the Anglo-Azorean voyages that have since been lost; the appearance of their former shipmate's nickname Labrador, both on Greenland and on a non-existent island replacing the mythical Antilia, as good as proves it. And the mysterious coast on the La Cosa chart may also be a record of the same voyages.

The rest of the evidence is from the household books of Henry VII, proving that he thought well of the Anglo-Azorean mariners. He gave £5 on 2 January 1502 to "men of bristoll that founde th' isle," tips to "a mariner that brought haukes" and "an other that brought an Egle"; and £20 in September to "the merchauntes of bristoll that have bene in the newe founde launde." In August or September 1505 the king gave £5 "to Portyngales that brought popyngais & catts of the mountayne with other stuf to the King's grace," and tipped a man 13s. 4d. for bringing said "wylde catts & popyngays of the New-found Island" to the king's grace at Richmond. Even more interesting gifts to Henry VII from overseas were three "men taken in the Newe Found Ileland" that the partners brought home. They were seen by Robert Fabyan the London chronicler, in 1502. These, the first Indians ever to be taken to England, were "clothid in beastys skinnys and ete Rawe Flesh," had the manners of "bruyt bestis," and spoke an unintelligible language. But they soon became civilized. Two years later Fabyan saw them in Westminster Palace, dressed like la-di-da English courtiers; but he couldn't get a word out of them.

The "Portyngales" who brought the wildcats and popinjays to Henry VII presumably were Fernandes and Gonsalves. "Popinjay" was then the common English name for a parrot, but here it must mean some noisy northern bird with bright plumage, such as the blue jay or the pileated woodpecker. A priest "that goith to the new Ilande" was given £2 in April 1504; this, as well as the popinjay entry over a year later, indicates that a third voyage of the Anglo-Azorean syndicate took place in the summer of 1504, and a fourth in 1505. Robert Thorne of Bristol and Seville claimed in 1527 that his father Nicholas, and Hugh Elyot, were the real discoverers of Newfoundland, but nobody has taken that claim seriously.

Thus the efforts of the Bristol syndicate, although persistently pursued for three or four years, seem to have had no result, not even attracting English fishermen to the Grand Bank. From maps of Newfoundland for the next quarter-century one would conclude that nobody but the Portuguese had explored these northern coasts.

Sebastian Cabot's supposed voyage in search of a Northwest Passage belongs in the doubtful class. We are still dependent on the accounts of sixteenth-century historians such as Peter Martyr, Gómara, and Ramusio, who built him up as *the* discoverer of North America. Sebastian, a pleasant and plausible fellow, impressed the great men of his day and, as *piloto mayor* of Spain (1518) who licensed all the deep-sea pilots, became one of them. As early as 1505, Henry VII granted an annuity of £10 to "our well-beloved Sebastian Caboot Venycian" in consideration of his "diligent service and attendaunce." What service could that young man have then done for the king?

Peter Martyr, the Italian humanist at the Spanish court who wrote the first history of the New World, stated that Cabot had often been his guest; and from Sebastian's lips he repeated an amusing tale. The codfish in Newfoundland, he said, swim up to shore in thick shoals to feed on the fallen leaves of certain tall trees overhanging the sea. Bears lie in ambush ashore, and when the codfish are busy feeding, they rush into the water, holding hands as it were, and surround the school of fish. Each bear then grabs a cod, which struggles to get free; the water is churned up, but in the end every little bear gets his codfish. As for the voyage, Peter Martyr and Gómara say that in 1508 Sebastian (then aged about twenty-six) fitted out two vessels with a crew of three hundred "at his own expense," sailed first to latitude 55° N, where, discouraged by great masses of ice, he turned south, passed "the Land of the Baccalai" (Newfoundland) and sailed as far as the latitude of Cuba. A certain "gentleman of Mantua" who claimed to have talked with Sebastian, reported to Ramusio, editor of the earliest published collection of voyages, that Cabot's search for the Northwest Passage took place in 1496; and in a later volume Ramusio said that Cabot had attained latitude 67°30' on 11 June of an unspecified year; the sea was open and he could have sailed right on to China, but the master and crew compelled him to return. Gómara's *Historia General* (1552) says that Sebastian took three hundred men in two ships and sailed to latitude 58° N; Thevet in his *Singularitez de France Antarctique* adds that all three hundred were landed so far north that they died of cold in July. Despite these wildly contradictory yarns, virtually every historian or commentator on the New World prior to 1830 accepted Sebastian at his own valuation as a great navigator, discoverer, and chart-maker.

Not every contemporary did so. In 1521, when he was trying to whip up support for a five-ship fleet "to be prepared towardes the Newefound Iland," Henry VIII asked the advice of the governors of two important London guilds, the Drapers and the Mercers. They turned the proposal down in an amusingly ill-spelled document:

> We thynk it were to sore aventour to joperd five shipps with men & goodes unto the said Iland uppon the singuler trust of one man, callyd as we understond, Sebastyan, whiche Sebastyan, as we heresay, *was never in that land hym self*, all [even] if he makes reporte of many thinges as he hath heard his Father and other men speke in tymes past." They further observe, "That if the said Sebastyan had bene there and were as connyng a man in & for thoos parties as any man myght be," he would be in but one of the five ships, and could not control the others. They clinch this argument with an "old proverb among maryners": "He sayls not surely that salys by an other mannys compas."

Methinks these worthy citizens of London had Sebastian's number! As a fifteen-year-old boy Sebastian may, as he asserted, have accompanied his father on the voyage of 1497, and he may have tried to find the Northwest Passage in 1508; several English historians accept this. The only voyage that Sebastian Cabot certainly commanded was one in 1525–28 under the king of Spain, which was supposed to follow

Magellan around the world. It got no further than the River Plate, and the voyage ended in disaster; but Sebastian landed on his feet as usual. He served under the kings of Spain and of England, receiving pay or pensions from both; and he also offered to sell his knowledge and services to the Venetian Republic. He took care to cultivate the "right people," especially those who were writing about voyages and discoveries; and so built himself up as to become the indispensable man to lead, or at least to advise, any new enterprise. In late life, Sebastian Cabot had his portrait painted. It shows an impressive old gentleman with a white forked beard, spreading a pair of dividers across the Arctic regions of a globe. Lest there be any doubt of who it was, he had a Latin inscription painted in the corner stating it to be the portrait of "Sebastian Cabot, Englishman, son of John Cabot, Venetian knight, first discoverer of Newfoundland under Henry VII, King of England." The Latin leaves it uncertain whether Sebastian intended to give his father credit or claim the discovery for himself; but he did give John a knighthood that he never had, so let us give him the benefit of the doubt.

One cannot help liking Sebastian. He was a genial and cheerful liar, devoted (insofar as it helped him) to the cause of oceanic discovery. See him at the age of seventy-four in 1556, pleasantly depicted by Stephen Borough, master of the pinnace *Serchthrift*, about to depart on a northeastern voyage of discovery:

> The 27 being Munday, the right Worshipfull Sebastian Cabota came aboord our Pinnasse at Gravesende, accompanied with divers Gentlemen, and Gentlewomen, who after that they had viewed our Pinnesse, and tasted of such cheere as we could make them aboord, they went on shore, giving to our mariners right liberall rewards: and the good olde Gentleman Master Cabota gave to the poore most liberall almes, wishing them to pray for the good fortune, and prosperous successe of the *Serchthrift*, our Pinnesse. And then at the sign of the Christopher, hee and his friends banketted, and made me, and them that were in the company great cheere; and for very joy that he had to see the towardnes of our intended discovery, he entred into the dance himself, amongst the rest of the young and lusty company: which being ended, hee and his friends departed most gently, commending us to the governance of almighty God.

Perhaps this caper at Gravesend proved too much for the old man. Philip II, when he came to England in 1557, tried to have his pension of 250 marks (about £166) annuled, and did; but Queen Mary (bless

Sebastian Cabot in his old age. From a copy of the original painting (since destroyed) made for the Massachusetts Historical Society in 1838. Translation of the inscription: "Portrait of Sebastian Cabot, Englishman, son of John Cabot, knight of Venice, First Discoverer of Newfoundland under Henry VII King of England." Courtesy Massachusetts Historical Society.

her for that!) restored it three days later. Even as he lay dying the old joker could still tell a good story. Richard Eden reported, "Sebastian Cabot on his death bed tolde me that he had acquired 'the knowledge of the longitude . . . by divine revelation.'" Eden concluded "that

THREE EARLY MAPS OF NEWFOUNDLAND'S EAST COAST
COMPARED WITH THE MODERN MAP (tilted 45°)

MODERN MAP (Shown tilted)

CANTINO, 1502

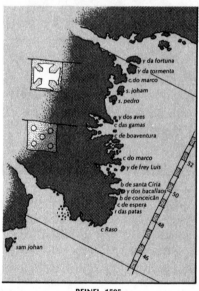

REINEL, 1505

MILLER No. 1, 1525

the good olde man, in that extreme age," was "somewhat doted, and had not yet even in the article of death, utterly shaken off all worldlye vayne glorie." In the late autumn of 1557 his pension payments stopped; and this, as in the case of his father almost sixty years earlier, is the only evidence we have of Sebastian's death. We know not the date, nor his burial place; nor was his will recorded.

Fishermen and Newfoundland Cartography, 1502–1524

The next quarter-century was an era of Portuguese supremacy in exploration of the north, and of other nations gradually getting on to the wonderful fishing to be had there.

Exactly how early the European fishermen resorted to the Grand Bank and the coastal waters of Newfoundland to take the cod we do not know, for fishermen leave few records, and their ordinary comings and goings were not noted. Judge Prowse, the historian of Newfoundland, asserted that West Country English were fishing off Newfoundland as early as 1498, but that is pure conjecture; he assumes that people rushed over to make a killing as soon as they heard Cabot's codfish stories. English fishermen are notoriously conservative, and I doubt whether any would have risked that long voyage until they had heard that the French and Portuguese were making apostolic hauls in American waters.

Although the Anglo-Azorean expeditions of 1501–5 may have done some fishing, the letters-patent point to exploration as their prime objective. And the earliest positive date we have for a French (Breton or Norman) fishing voyage is 1504. There were enough Portuguese doing it by 1506 to justify the king's clapping a 10 per cent import duty on their catch—the first European attempt to protect home industries from American competition!

After the Anglo-Azorean tentatives just noticed, prior to the voyage of Fagundes, we have only cartographic evidence about what was going on in northern waters. These early maps tell us a good deal. Suppose we tilt a modern map of Newfoundland about 40 degrees eastward so that the coast appears to run almost due north and south, and compare with it the delineations of the same coast on three old maps which took no account of compass variations, reducing them to the same scale. This will indicate a gradual unfolding and correction of the coastline, and a Portuguese nomenclature which, at least on the most conspicuous landmarks, endures to our day.

The first is the Cantino Mappemonde of 1502, still preserved in the Biblioteca Estense at Modena. The "Terra del Rey de Portuguall" (Newfoundland), the part we have reproduced, is placed much too far east in order to get it on the Portuguese side of the Line of Demarcation, which runs through the grove of pine trees. The west coast is vague, since nobody knew anything about it; but the east and south coasts indicate that Gaspar Corte Real had sent home an accurate chart of the points, bays, and islands from the Strait of Belle Isle to Placentia Bay. Newfoundland is out of scale, lengthwise, being twice as long as Ireland and longer than Great Britain. The label on it reads (in translation), "This land was discovered by order of the very high and excellent prince, King of Portugal D. Manuel, and the man who discovered it was Gaspar de Corte Real, gentleman of the court of said King; he who discovered it sent [home] a ship with . . . men and women who belonged to that land, and he [went off] with the other ship and never returned but was lost, and he [found] many mast [trees]."

The next outline of Newfoundland is on the Pedro Reinel Map, formerly (and perhaps still) in the State Library of Munich. Here the big island is not named but two Portuguese flags are planted thereon, and it occupies the same relative position (lat. 46° to 50° N) as on the Cantino Map. Although the date generally assigned to this Reinel Map is 1504/5, it cannot be earlier than 1521, as it incorporates some of the discoveries of João Alvares Fagundes, whom we shall consider shortly. Our third map, known as the Miller No. I, in the Bibliothèque Nationale, is (in my opinion) not earlier than 1525. Here Newfoundland is called *Terra Corte Regalis*, and Nova Scotia, *Terra Frigida*.

Note a little north of center on the three old maps, a deep bay containing three harbors. Comparing this with the modern map, it is evidently meant for Notre Dame and White Bays rolled into one, and the Reinel Map shows the two St. Barbe Islands as *y dos panes* (of the shields)—probably a reference to their peculiar rocks. Proceeding northward, we pass the high and conspicuous Grois or Gray Islands (*S. Pedro* and *S. Johan* on the Reinel) and reach the northern peninsula of Newfoundland. This peninsula, with an indentation meant for St.

Lunaire Bay, ends (on the Cantino) at Quirpon Island where Capes Bauld and Dégrat are situated.

West and north of these capes all the early maps show the Strait of Belle Isle, but it fades out in such a way as to suggest that the Portuguese navigators supposed it to be just another fjord. And the west coast of Newfoundland is always conventionalized as a straight line, half-moon, or series of scallops, proving it to have been as yet undiscovered.

Equally significant evidence of Portuguese supremacy on the outer Newfoundland coast are names which have lasted to the present, through corrupted English or French versions. Beginning at the southeast corner of Newfoundland, we have *c. raso* (shaved) which thereafter, and for all future time, will be Cape Race. About halfway from this cape to St. John's, the Miller I Map has *R. fremoso* (beautiful); this has become Fermeuse Harbor. Just south of St. John's Harbor (which Miller I already calls *Rio de Sam Joham*) is *c. de espera* (hope), now Cape Spear. Around Cape St. Francis, Conception Bay opens up; this is found, in various spellings, on all the early maps.

Off the next cape northward lies *y do baccalhao* or *y dos baccalaos*, celebrating the codfish that swarm about; this now is stabilized as Baccalieu Island. On the other side of Trinity Bay, which almost makes the Avalon Peninsula an island, is *C. de boa ventura*, the modern Cape Bonavista. Bonavista Bay is easily identifiable on the early maps by its depth; north of it every old map shows an *y do frey luis*, commemorating an otherwise unknown Fr. Luís, probably a ship's chaplain. The now forgotten friar's name has gone ashore and become Cape Freels; the island was either Stinkard (now renamed Cabot!) or Gull Island.

Next north of Cape Freels is Cape Fogo on the island of that name; we first find it as *y do fogo* (of the fire) on Miller I. Possibly some passing navigator saw a forest fire there. The name *Sam Joham*, attached to Groais Island in these early charts, has gone ashore, like that of Fr. Luís, and become Cape St. John. That takes us to Cape Bauld, which the Reinel and other early charts appropriately call *C. do Marco* (of the landmark); and off it lies *I. de la Fortuna* (Belle Isle), which Alonso de Santa Cruz says should rather be called the Isle of Ill Fortune, since a Portuguese fleet was wrecked there in the time of the Corte Reals.

An impressive record indeed of the Portuguese impact on Newfoundland, and of the growing importance of the Grand Bank fisheries. Local fishermen all along the Lusitanian coast must have been appalled by the competition when the first overseas vessels returned from the Grand Bank fairly bulging with enormous codfish all ready to cure; they obtained the 1506 protective tariff against what is nowadays called "dumping" of cheap goods.

It is a curious fact, yet unexplained, that around 1534–35, when Jacques Cartier sailed through the Strait of Belle Isle into the Gulf of St. Lawrence, mapmakers began to break up Newfoundland into five or more big islands separated by straits. It is as if they decided that since Cartier found the bay north of Cape Bauld to be a strait, all other deep bays must be straits too. Although a few Portuguese charts held out against that tendency, it was not until 1607 that the Stockholm Chart by James Hall shows Newfoundland properly, as a rough equilateral triangle, with no strait through it.

João Alvares Fagundes

At Viana do Castelo, a Portuguese fishing town near the Galician border, there lived a shipowner named João Alvares Fagundes, who took a keen interest in Codfish Land. In 1520, if not earlier, he made a voyage along the south coast of Newfoundland and into the Gulf of St. Lawrence, "apart from the land which the Corte Reals found to the northward." He named the principal places that he discovered, and we can identify most of them. *Isla de Pitigoen* means Penguin Island, for the "penguin" of that era was not the antarctic bird now so named, but the great auk, which also could not fly. The English were calling this Penguin Island as early as 1536; Lancaster, writing his account of Newfoundland for Hakluyt forty years later, said that the birds were so plentiful and helpless that you could lay your ship alongside the rocks at high water, drop a gangplank ashore, and drive as many waddling auks on board as you wanted. The fishermen used them for bait, and the Beothuk Indians made a cake out of their fat with wild strawberries. The island is still called Penguin, but the great auk has been extinct for over a century.

Fagundes's next discovery he called the Archipelago of the *onze mil virgenes*. He meant St. Pierre, Miquelon, and the numerous islets between them and the coast of Newfoundland. The story of St. Ursula, princess of Cornwall, and her eleven thousand sea-going virgins, who toured the waters of Europe for years but were murdered by the Huns at Cologne, was one of the most popular legends of the Middle Ages; and whenever an explorer found an extensive group of small islands he was apt to give them this name. Columbus so called the archipelago now known as the Virgin Islands of the United States and of Great Britain; and there is another group off the coast of Argentina. But this particular name of the Virgins was not honored by the French, except for Virgin Cove at Miquelon. On the early Portuguese maps, such as the Miller I which we have reproduced, they appear as a diagrammatic cluster of islets.

Fagundes mentioned an island called *Santa Cruz* "at the foot of the Banks," which may possibly have been Sable Island, and *Santa Ana*, which was "seen and not approached." Both appear on several early maps; St. Ann's became an overseas rival to Hy-Brasil. West of the Isle of Penguins he noted an island that he named after Saints John and Peter. This is probably the beautiful, rugged island later named after the Apostle Paul. It lies 130 miles due west from Penguin Island and 15 miles northeast of Cape North.

Upon returning from this voyage, Fagundes put all these facts into a petition to the king of Portugal for a captaincy, similar to those already granted to many navigators, pointing out that these places had not been discovered by the Corte Real brothers. D. Manuel complied, granting to Fagundes on 22 May 1521 complete property rights, jurisdiction, and privileges over this region—even to setting up soap factories! We do not know how or from what this enterprising Portuguese proposed to make soap, but he acutely observed that it would save time and labor for fishermen to cure their catch ashore instead of sailing every cargo the long distance to Lisbon or Viana; and, a century before the English, he set up a permanent shore establishment. Colonists were obtained in his native Minho and he even sent a ship to the Azores to recruit families who hoped to better themselves in the New World. They crossed the Atlantic in the summer, as early as 1521 or as late as 1525, and settled on a "beautiful harbor" on Cape Breton Island, which Fagundes called the Island of St. John. The harbor undoubtedly was Ingonish, which has everything that fishermen want: two bays, each with a protected harbor, and in each a sand beach where they

Part of "Miller I" Atlas world map. Courtesy Bibliothèque Nationale.

can draw up their shallops and a level area where they can cure the catch. No other place on Cape Breton has these advantages.

After a year or eighteen months at Ingonish, difficulties arose. As usual, the Indians turned hostile when they realized that the Europeans intended to stay instead of merely calling to fish and trade. Breton fishermen, from whom this island received its permanent name, cut the Portuguese fishing lines and destroyed their houses. Fagundes sailed along the coast of Nova Scotia, looking for a better spot, inadvertently discovering and mapping the Bay of Fundy. But his little colony could not continue without help from home, which it did not get. By 1526, perhaps before, this earliest (save the Norsemen's) of many vain attempts of Europeans to set up a colony in North America no longer existed.

Jean Alfonce, Roberval's chief pilot for his voyage of 1541–42, wrote an epilogue to these efforts in his *Voyages avantureux* (1559, but written 1544) when discussing Cape Breton Island: "Formerly the Portuguese sought to settle the land which lies the lowest, but the natives of the country put an end to the attempt and killed all those who came there."

The earliest cartographical record of Fagundes's voyages is on the so-called Miller I World Atlas at the Bibliothèque Nationale, by Jorge Reinel, of which we have reproduced the Newfoundland-Cape Breton sector. It shows no land connection between Cape Breton and Florida, proving that the map-maker knew nothing about the voyages of Verrazzano and Gomez in 1524–25; but it is clearly post-Fagundes. Note the archipelago of the 11,000 virgins, the southern entrance to this Gulf which Fagundes did not penetrate, and the uncharted back side of Newfoundland. Especially significant is the nomenclature of Cape Breton, *c. do bretoēs, R. de sam pablo, terra de mynta gente*, and *R. de saluago*, the last two being tributes to the natives. Below a herd of deer grazing on the future Nova Scotia appears the legend *Terra Frigida*. Reinel's Latin inscription records the discovery by Gaspar Corte Real, whose name is given to Newfoundland, and the nomenclature is purely Portuguese. The native Beothuk—whom other discoverers called "reds" from their lavish use of red ochre—are "of the same color as us," and "live like the ancient fauns and satyrs." Wild animals are listed but, strangely, no fish. South-southeast of Cape Race are the *ylhas de Johā Esteves*, shaped like two sausages. These, which one finds on earlier Portuguese maps, had been discovered by a fisherman from whom they were named, but could not again be located—more flyaway islands. This Miller I Atlas, a masterpiece of early Portuguese cartographical art, is also notable for its accurate drawings of animals and of ships. The two vessels on the part here depicted, barely one-twelfth of the whole, have already been discussed in Chapter V.

Whilst Reinel does not mention Fagundes by name, Diogo Homem's map of 1568 calls Cape Breton, *Cap Fagundo*, places Micmac Indian names along the outer coast, and inserts other names, none of which endured, along the Nova Scotian shore. Homem's definite delineation of the Bay of Fundy, with Grand Manan at its mouth, proves that either Fagundes or another Portuguese discovered that rough arm of the sea

The two harbors at Ingonish.

West coast of St. Paul Island.

where spring tides run up to sixty feet; and the cartographer's suggestion that he reached Penobscot Bay is supported by two French sources.

Posterity has been unkind to Fagundes. By 1600 his name had disappeared from North American geography. His countrymen long continued to come for fish, and their place names still remind us that these valiant seamen of a small nation helped to open up a new Western World.

Robert Thorne's Letter and John Rut's Voyage

The accession of Henry VIII in 1509 marks a notable falling off of interest by the English government and people in the New World. Postponing a discussion of the reasons, we shall here tell the brief and inglorious stories of English voyages, other than fishing trips, to Newfoundland and other northern regions during the half-century after Cabot's. The only ones known are the voyages of John Rut (1527) and Richard Hore (1536).

Robert Thorne of Bristol instigated Rut's voyage. This remarkable man, a precursor of Richard Hakluyt, was the son of Nicholas Thorne, who, with Hugh Elyot, had been a member of the Anglo-Azorean exploring syndicate of 1501–2. After representing the Admiralty at Bristol, Robert Thorne prospered as a merchant and resided in Seville, whence in 1527 he wrote "A Declaration of the Indies" to Henry VIII, and a "Booke" supporting the same, for Edward Lee, the king's ambassador to Charles V. "God and nature," he remarked, "both provided to your Grace . . . this Realme of England, and set it in so fruitful a place" as to be "free from foreign conquest," one cause being "that it is compassed with the Sea." Portugal and Spain had monopolized more than a fair share of the fruitful parts of the earth by sailing west, east, and south. Here "now rest to be discovered the sayd North parts, the which it seems to mee, is onely your charge and duety." And to Lee he made the astonishing suggestion that, there being "no land uninhabitable, nor sea innavigable," nothing prevented "sayling Northward and passing the Pole," then dropping down to the Equator on the other side of the world, so halving the distance sailed by Spaniards and Portuguese to the riches of Asia. He pointed out that in summer "perpetuall clereness of the day without any darkeness of the night" would help make this route safer than those of the king's rivals, which were fraught with "dangers or darkenesse." And to Lee he sent a world chart of his own making, with a latitude and longitude grid, to prove his point. Thus Thorne anticipated two leading airplane and submarine routes of our own day.

Henry VIII reacted promptly by setting up a voyage to discover the Northwest Passage. (His naval advisers evidently dissuaded him from trying the North Pole.) A fleet of "two fayre shippes," *Sampson* (nicknamed *Dominus Vobiscum*), commanded by Master Grube, and *Mary of Guildford*, John Rut, master, "well manned and vitailed, having in them divers connyng men," was quickly organized. Both were merchant ships owned by the crown; *Mary* (160 tuns, built 1524) had been employed by Henry VIII to fetch wine from Bordeaux for the royal household. Of Master Grube nothing seems to be known; but John Rut, of Ratcliffe, had served the king in war and peace for many years. The preparations acquired such fame that Lord Edward Howard, son of the Duke of Norfolk and an unemployed Captain R.N., begged Cardinal Wolsey "for the bittyr passion of Krist" to get him a berth and so relieve him from "as wretchyd a lyffe as ever dyd jentylman"; but he did not get it. Canon Albert de Prato of St. Paul's, "a great mathematician and a man indued with wealth, did much advance the action, and went therein himselfe in person." Under Grube's command they sailed from London River 20 May 1527, and from Plymouth 10 June, "to seke strange regions."

Rut's own letter states that he took final departure from the Scilly Isles, and on 1 July parted from Grube in "a marvailous great storme." Neither he nor anyone else saw *Sampson* again. On 21 July *Mary* made "Cape de Bas," Newfoundland, and entered a nearby harbor in latitude 52° N. No Cape de Bas appears on any known map; but as the Scillies are at latitude 50° N, and John Rut probably followed the time-honored latitude sailing; and as he rounded a big iceberg when returning to the same port in late July, it must have been north of Cape Bauld, Newfoundland (51°38′ N); probably near Battle Harbor, Labrador, at 52°15′ N. Rut's description of the place as having "many small Ilands," a "great fresh River going up farre into the mayne Land" fits that region best.

Master Rut evidently had no relish for northern exploration. According to his letter of 3 August to the king, he sailed only as far north as latitude 53°, that of Hawke Bay, Labrador. "There we found many great Ilands of Ice and deepe water, we found no sounding," (an obvious excuse, as that entire coast is on soundings), "and then we durst go no further to the Northward for feare of more Ice." So he "cast about to the Southward," took a sounding of 160 fathoms, which must have been at least twenty miles out, made land again at latitude 52° N, and, after passing a big iceberg, put in again at Cape de Bas. Tarrying ten days to water, and finding "all wildernesse . . . and no natural ground but all mosse and no inhabitation," only "footing of divers great beasts," he continued south, and on 3 August entered the harbor of St. John's. There he found ten fishing vessels: seven Norman, two Portuguese, and one Breton. Writing the same day to the king, he said he intended to return to Cape de Bas to look for *Sampson;* but whether he did or not we do not know.

What we do know is where he went next. *Mary of Guildford* ranged the coasts of Cape Breton and "Norumbega"—Nova Scotia and New England—frequently landing men to report on "the state of those unknown regions." And then she turned up in the West Indies.

A Spanish captain named Gines Navarro was loading cassava at Mona Island between Hispaniola and Puerto Rico, when a foreign ship of about 250 tuns' burthen sailed in and spoke him. The officers said they were Englishmen, that the vessel belonged to their king, and that when searching for a passage to "discover the land of the Great Khan," they had lost their consort. After various improbable adventures (such as entering a sea of hot water), they had sailed south along the coast that Ayllón had discovered, and now proposed to pick up a cargo of dyewood in Puerto Rico. Captain Navarro, entertained on board the English ship, reported that she had a crew of seventy, including artisans and shipbuilders with complete tool kits.

Spaniards reported the same ship—always unnamed—when she anchored off the Ozama River, the harbor of Santo Domingo, on 25 November 1527. The captain sent a boat ashore to ask permission to enter the harbor and obtain water and provisions. The authorities consented and sent out Diego Mendez, *alguacil mayor* of Hispaniola, with a harbor pilot to bring her in; but in the morning, when she lay just outside the bar waiting for a fair breeze, a trigger-happy commander of the fort fired a stone cannonball which made a near-miss. Master Rut, smelling "Spanish treachery," sent the alguacil and the pilot ashore and promptly made sail.

Oviedo, historian of the Indies, here picks up the story. Confirming

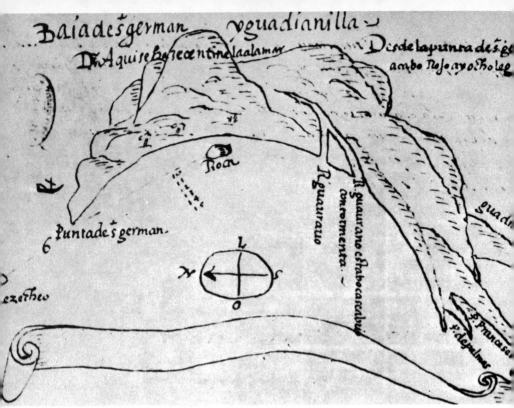

San Germán Bay, Puerto Rico. From the ms. *Derrotero* of Juan de Escalante de Mendoza, 1575, Real Academia de la Historia, Madrid. The soundings show the approach to the original town of San Germán, which by 1575 had been moved to its present site; at the time of Rut's visit, it lay a short distance inland. The ship indicates the *Aguada*, a river of sweet water which had been in use since 1493. To the south is Cape Rojo, the southwestern point of Puerto Rico, and Guayanilla Bay, where Sir Richard Grenville built a fort in 1585. Courtesy of Mr. Aurelio Tió.

the fact that the English ship was frightened away by a cannon shot, he says that she crossed the Mona Passage and entered the Bay of San Germán, Puerto Rico, now known as Añasco Bay. The town of San Germán had been moved inland for protection from pirates, but not far, so Rut was able to visit it and assure the alcalde that he had no intention to plunder, only to obtain provisions. These were furnished and, in addition, he bought some *estano de baxilla*, tableware made of marcasite from a nearby mine which, unlike those in Frobisher Bay, yielded a profitable amount of silver. The ship departed in peace, her conduct considered to be remarkably good manners for an Englishman, or any foreigner, in the Antilles. *Mary of Guildford* was back in England by the spring of 1528; and that autumn, still captained by John Rut, she sailed to Bordeaux to buy wine for the king's household.

Although Henry VIII bestowed an annuity of £20 on John Rut, it must be admitted that his voyage was a complete failure compared with the French voyages which preceded and followed his. Rut found nothing new, and left no trace on the nomenclature of the New World. Grube's ship had been lost with all hands; and Rut's, missing two chances (Strait of Belle Isle and Cabot Strait) to enter the Gulf of St. Lawrence ahead of Cartier, sailed south on what was little more than a pleasure cruise to the West Indies. Robert Thorne died in 1527; he did not suffer the mortification of learning about the frustration of his great design for superpolar sailing.

Master Hore's Tourist Cruise

Tourist cruises, with the pious excuse of a pilgrimage to Rome, the Holy Land, or some famous foreign shrine, were no innovation in the sixteenth century. For instance, in 1446, the cog *Anne* of Bristol carried to Joppa 160 pilgrims, who decided (fortunately for themselves) to return home overland; the cog on her homeward passage, laden with spiceries, crashed on the shores of Greece and lost all hands. Her owner, with another ship, then took fifty pilgrims to Santiago de Compostello. English curiosity about foreign countries was whetted by such books as Sanseverino's *Viaggio in Terra Santa* of 1458. But a pleasure trip to the New World was an innovation—much as if Thomas Cook or American Express set up an air trip to the moon in 1971— as they probably will do within a few years.

By 1536 Newfoundland was so well known that one Richard Hore, citizen and leather merchant of London, chartered two ships, *Trinity* and *William*, for the double purpose of catching codfish and giving certain gentlemen of London a pleasure voyage. This first tourist cruise in American history ended in misery, starvation, and even cannibalism.

Hakluyt, who traveled 200 miles to interview a survivor, says that Hore's "perswasions tooke such effect" that he signed on no fewer than "six score persons, whereof thirty were gentlemen." After attending mass at Gravesend they set sail near the end of April 1536. *Trinity* apparently was lost, but the *William* (which Hakluyt misnames *Minion*) passed Cape Race, and two months after leaving England anchored at Penguin Island, off the south coast of Newfoundland. There they killed a large number of "the foules" (the great auk) as well as "bears both black and white." Master Hore entered a small harbor on the adjacent Newfoundland coast and anchored. Provisions ran short even though they robbed an osprey's nest of the fish she brought to her young. The passengers first resorted to "raw herbes and rootes in the fields and deserts" and then took to cannibalism. Master Hore preached a sermon denouncing such ungodly and inhuman practice, and was rewarded by the arrival of a French ship "well furnished with vittaile" which the Englishmen promptly captured and "spoiled." By that time some of the tourists had died of starvation, and others had been killed and eaten. The survivors sailed for home, seeing "mighty Ilands of yce in the Summer season," and arrived at St. Ives, Cornwall, near the end of October 1536. One is glad to hear that Henry VIII compensated the Frenchmen; but why, in Heaven's name, could not the Englishmen have supported life from sea-fowl and fish?

That they did "make" (i.e. cure) codfish is evident from a lawsuit instituted by the owner of the *William* against Hore, complaining that the charterer defrauded him of his share of the fish. Next year, 1537, Master Hore procured another English vessel, named *Valentine*, sailed to Lisbon, and there shipped not only a cargo of salt and wine but a number of Portuguese passengers for London. Instead of taking them to their destination, he anchored at a small outport near Cardiff and tried to extort money from them. For that he was called to account by the lord lieutenant of the county, and subsequently he was sued by the crew of *Valentine* for £280. Master Hore seems to have been a rascal, and the gory details told by Hakluyt are credible.

Hore's voyage put an end to the tourist business, as far as the New World was concerned, for at least two centuries.

Bibliography and Notes

THE LA COSA MAPPEMONDE

The Juan de La Cosa Mappemonde is dated 1500. When discovered in a Paris antique shop in 1833 the English flags caused a sensation and aroused loud whoops of joy from historians of that nation, and of Canada. This map has been studied more intensively than any other on early discoveries. Theorists treat it like rubber—they squeeze, stretch, twist, and telescope it to fit anything from a hundred to a thousand miles, and even turn it sideways or upside down. Scholarly studies of the map have been made, especially by George E. Nunn, *The Mappemonde of Juan de La Cosa* (Jenkintown, Pa., 1934), and by G. R. Crone, *Maps and Their Makers* (1953); R. A. Skelton, in Williamson's *Cabot Voyages*, pp. 298–304, and in Bernard G. Hoffman's *Cabot to Cartier* (1961), pp. 93–96. These scholars have established that the New World half of the La Cosa is of a different scale, and a different date, from the Eurasian part, which contains no reference to discoveries subsequent to 1488. Admiral Guillén y Tato, curator of the Naval Museum in Madrid, who has custody of the original, has compiled a revised toponymy with the aid of infrared photography, for the Duke of Alba's *Mapas Españoles de America Siglos XV–XVII* (Madrid, 1951). His best estimate of the date of the American half is not earlier than 1505; Nunn says 1508. Hoffman thinks it is either post-1529 or a complete fake, a hypothesis I cannot accept in view of the accurate delineations of the Antilles and the Spanish Main—so good that Williamson (pp. 109–11, 233) argues that Cabot got down to Venezuela[!]

Ganong's and Guillén's lists of the names will be found in Williamson, p. 79; Harrisse's in *Discovery of North America*, p. 414. How reliable these are may be judged from the fact that Harrisse's *S. Nicolas* becomes Guillén's *S. Matias;* Harrisse's *Ansro* and Ganong's *Ansto* becomes Guillén's *gosfica*, and Harrisse's *Sastanatre* becomes Guillén's *c . . . slin*. Actually none of these names appear on any other map, nor do they make sense. English historians take comfort from the resemblance of C° *de lisarte*, the most legible, to The Lizard of Cornwall; but the English did not begin to name New World points after those at home until the seventeenth century.

It must not be forgotten that the early cartographers liked to invent coasts as well as islands. The world maps of Ortelius, Diogo Homem, and others, for instance, depict an imaginary Terra Australis, or Antarctica, running right around the world, extrapolated from Magellan's Tierra del Fuego.

Juan de La Cosa was definitely *not* the captain of the *Santa María*, as many have stated. He was a cartographer whom Columbus took on his second voyage of 1493–94, who actually saw the Leeward Islands and the Greater Antilles. Nobody knows how or whence La Cosa got his information about English discoveries, and the thirty-page discussion by W. F. Ganong in Part I of his *Crucial Maps* (the collected volume of 1964, chap. i) adds little, but T. E. Layng's "Commentaries" in the same volume, pp. 469–73, are suggestive. Nobody can explain why, after Spain had divided the New World with Portugal, a Spanish cartographer should give England a long coastline on North America.

Here is my sixpenny contribution to the discussion. The La Cosa Map was compiled around 1509, when Henry VIII married Catherine of Aragon, hence the compliment to England. I can imagine La Cosa conferring with Ferdinand the Catholic about his map. "What's this coast?" asks the king,

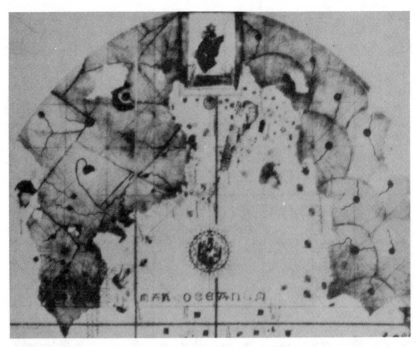

The Juan de La Cosa Mappemonde. The American part. Dated 1500, but certainly post-1505. The five flags on the northern coast are English.

"I never heard of any land between my West Indies and D. Manuel's codfish country." "Oh, I just put that in to balance the southern mainland; I don't really know whether it exists." "Good idea," says Ferdinand," but you can't leave it completely bare of names, or people will suspect you faked it." "So what shall I do with it, Sire?" "Oh, plant some English banners along that coast and think up some names to slap on—it will please that fine fellow Harry of England, my new son-in-law, and annoy my other son-in-law D. Manuel, who is getting much too big for his boots! Mind you don't mention that goddam codfish island he is always boasting about!"

And to continue this imaginary explanation, the Emperor Charles V, after Henry VIII had repudiated his aunt Catherine and broken with Rome, threw the map out of the royal library. But what happened to it between then and 1833, nobody knows.

THE BEOTHUK INDIANS

The best monograph on this tribe is James P. Howley, *The Beothucks or Red Indians* (Cambridge, 1915), to which may be added Allan M. Fraser, "Shanawdithit Last of the Beothuks," *Atlantic Advocate*, LVI, No. 3 (November 1965), 34–39, and John Gardner, "The *First* Atlantic Crossing?" *Atlantic Advocate*, LVII (October 1966), 36–44. Gardner compares the peculiarly shaped "humpback" Beothuk bark canoe with a drawing of a paleolithic boat in the famous Castillo cave, Spain, suggesting that those Indians either (1) crossed the Atlantic eastward in prehistoric times, giving

The "English coast" on the Juan de La Cosa Mappemonde. From E. M. Jomard, *Les Monuments de la géographie*, 1862. Courtesy Harvard College Library.

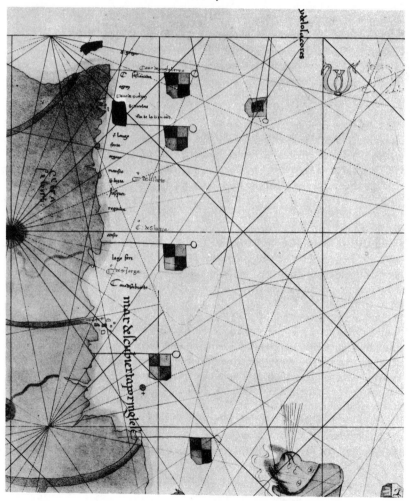

their canoe to the prehistoric Iberians; or (2) the Norsemen brought this design from Spain to Newfoundland! Beothuk burial sites are now being dug up by archaeologists, so we may expect plenty more crackpot theories.

JOÃO FERNANDES AND THE OLIVERIANA MAP

Several writers have followed the common practice of Portuguese historians in stepping up the Fernandes-Barcelos voyage to 1492, in order to beat Columbus. I tried to demonstrate in my *Portuguese Voyages to America* (Harvard University Press, 1940), pp. 51–68, that this theory cannot hold water.* Williamson, *The Cabot Voyages*, pp. 116–21, accepted these findings, but the Portuguese will have none of them. Manuel C. Baptista de Lima, the erudite librarian of Evora, has politely taken me apart and argued for the 1492 date in *Deux Voyages portugais de découverte dans l'atlantique occidental* (Lisbon, 1946). Theodore E. Layng, "Charting the Course to Canada," Congresso Int. de Hist. dos Descubrimientos, *Actas*, II (Lisbon, 1961), 255–67, is willing to settle for 1495, but makes our *lavrador* the prompter of John Cabot's voyage. Layng's thesis is based primarily on a statement in Alonso de Santa Cruz, *Islario*, written *c.* 1541, and first printed by F. R. von Wieser in 1908, that Greenland "was called Land of the Labrador because a *labrador* of the Azores gave the information and location (*aviso e indicio*) to the King of England when he sent *Antonio Gaboto*, English pilot and father of *Sebastian Gaboto* . . . to discover it" (H. P. Biggar, *Precursors of Cartier*, pp. 184, 190). The Canadian scholar regards this as credible because Alonso made a voyage to the River Plate with Sebastian; but in my opinion anyone who went to sea with Sebastian Cabot would hear so many contradictory stories as to be completely muddled; Santa Cruz does not even name Sebastian's father correctly. Layng also insists that the Fernandes patent of 1499 from D. Manuel indicates that he had "been there before." Arthur Davies, in the same volume of the *Actas*, pp. 135–49, disagrees; he points out that every such patent to a man who had "been there before" naturally mentions that fact as part of the reason for the grant. See also discussions by Quinn, Crone, Cortesão, and Skelton in the same *Actas*, pp. 267–344.

The Oliveriana map, at Pésaro, Italy, on which the name "Labrador" appears both on Cape Farewell, Greenland, and on a non-existent island south of it, is one of the most controversial early maps incorporating the New World. This map, which few scholars have taken the trouble to examine, but many write about very glibly, is best reproduced (American part only) in the Columbian *Raccolta di Documenti e Studi*, Parte IV, vol. II, 112, 166–218. Pohl in *Imago Mundi*, VII, 82, reproduces the entire map. It is discussed in Harrisse, *Terre Neuve*, pp. 53–55 and Planche IV. Bellio dates it 1501-2, but the South America part incorporates results of the Coelho-

---

* See also my article "The Date of the Fernandes-Barcelos Voyage to the Labrador," Congresso do Mundo Português Publicações, III, i (1940), 375–400.

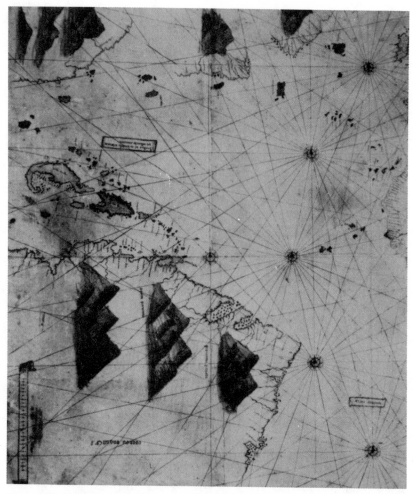

New World half of the Oliveriana Map, Pésaro. Giraudon enlargement of film kindly given me by Sr. Zicari, head of the Oliveriana Library, Pésaro.

Vespucci voyage of that date. The key to the date, I think, will be furnished by a study of the eastern half. MUNDUS NOVUS on South America doubtless refers to the title of Amerigo Vespucci's famous printed letter to Lorenzo Pietro Francesco de' Medici, the first dated edition of which is 1504 (but Harrisse assigns the undated ones to 1502–3); and this same Medici may well be the one for whom this remarkable mappemonde was prepared. Professor Giuseppe Caraci of Rome, who has given the map a

243

very careful examination, believes that it dates from 1503, is certainly Italian, and very probably Florentine. I agree. It is obviously pre-Magellan. The shrimp-tailed Cuba resembles La Cosa's Cuba; the Lesser Antilles are much more accurate than those on the La Cosa and Cantino maps.

Here, as well as I could make them out in my brief examination in April 1970, are the names on the two prominent northern promontories:

Newfoundland	Greenland
Lascerua	Terranoba
Cauo del Marco	Lentu
Bonaventura	Zafina
Terra de Corte[Real?]	Cauo Larbradore
Ponta del Pa[drone?]	Cauo Agrut
Riuo de los Bacalaos	Cauo de Mar Aserba
Riuo de Bosas	Cauo (& terra) de Spignus
Cauo (& Rio) de la Spera	Terra de Cabieri
Baia de Cos	Ponta de Sampaulo

OTHER EARLY MAPS OF NEWFOUNDLAND

Henry Harrisse, *Découverte et évolution cartographique de Terre Neuve* (1900), is by far the best general work.

Discussion of Reinel's oblique scale by H. Winter in *Imago Mundi*, II, 61–73.

For the Miller I Atlas, see H. Harrisse, *Terre Neuve*, p. 84 and Planche VII; cumulative toponymy of these and other old maps on pp. 359–66. The discussion by Armando Cortesão is in *Cartografia e Cartografos Portugueses*, I, 279–81.

THE CORTE REALS AND DIGHTON ROCK

Henry Harrisse, *Les Corte Real et leurs voyages au nouveau-monde* (Paris, 1883), is still the most comprehensive work on those unfortunate brothers, including a full discussion of their ancestry and descendants. He also wrote about them in his *Découverte de Terre Neuve*. No fresh facts have come out since, although Admiral Gago Coutinho imagined a "secret voyage" of Gaspar in 1499 which ranged the entire American coast from Cape Breton to the Gulf of Mexico—see his *A Nautica dos Descobrimentos* (Lisbon, 1952), II, chap. vi. Nansen, *In Northern Mists*, II, chap. xv, uses the facts available to very good purpose. H. P. Biggar, *Precursors of Jacques Cartier* (Ottawa, 1911), reprints the essential documents with translations. Relevant extracts with a detailed bibliography are in Hoffman, *Cabot to Cartier*, pp. 27–29. The reference to Damião de Góis's Chronicle is I 146 of the parte i, chap. 66 of the Coimbra, 1926 edition. For Gaspar's last and fatal voyage, our principal sources are: (1) a letter of Pietro Pasqualigo, ambassador of Venice to the court of Portugal and brother of the same Lorenzo Pasqualigo who reported on John Cabot's voyage from London; and (2) a letter by, and map prepared for, Albert Cantino, another Italian diplomat in Lisbon. Both are in Biggar, *Precursors of Jacques Cartier*.

Eduardo Brazão gives all facts and a lot of speculation in *The Corte-Real Family and the New World* (Lisbon, 1965), and *La Découverte de Terre Neuve* (Montreal, 1964). For Dr. Brazão, formerly Portuguese ambassador to Canada, John Cabot simply does not exist.

On the shores of the tidal Taunton River on Assonet Neck, in the township of Berkley, Massachusetts, there is a sandstone boulder with an inscribed face, measuring about four by ten feet. The inscriptions have puzzled observers since 1677, when English colonists seized the area from the Wampanoag Indians. To the casual observer the designs appear to be typical Algonkin petroglyphs, overlaid and supplemented by English inscriptions, recording the immemorial urge of mankind to leave a name or initials on historical monuments. The late Professor Edmund B. Delabarre of Brown University made an exhaustive search of everything hitherto written about Dighton Rock. The largest human figure has been identified as Astarte, the Oracle, Telsephone, and Gudrid, the wife of Thorfinn Karlsevni. The spotted quadrupeds near the base have been called horses, deer, leopards, a map of Europe, and the constellation Pegasus. The minor carvings have been described as Phoenician, Norse runes, Chinese or Mongolian characters, and finally, in Dr. Delabarre's hands, a memorial inscription to Miguel Corte Real, dated 1511.*

In the colonial era, John Danforth, Cotton Mather, Dean Berkeley, John Smibert, and Ezra Stiles were so intrigued by this rock as to send their crude drawings of the inscriptions to the Royal Society of London. Stiles thought the letters were "Phoenician 3000 years old"; Stephen Sewall, professor of Hebrew at Harvard, averred that they were Chinese or Japanese. Antoine Court de Gebelin (1724–84), author of *Le Monde primitif*, after studying some of these renderings, reported traces of three Phoenician navigators, an owl, a hawk, and a horse ("the symbol of Carthage"). In 1837 Carl Rafn published eleven different drawings of the rock in his *Antiquitates Americanae*, and these produced a flurry of theories. Finn Magnusen, an alleged runic expert, said there was "no doubt" of its being a picture record of the Thorfinn Karlsevni colony; can't you see Gudrid seated on the shore and beside her the infant Snorri, and the Skrellings attacking? Rafn even found runes meaning "Thorfinn and 151 companions took possession of the land." The sage Onffroy de Thoron casually translated the inscriptions into Phoenician. The Rev. John B. Lundy, most imaginative of all Dighton Rock readers, made a Chinese translation extending to some 2200 words (Col. Soc. Mass., *Pub.*, XX, 356). The imaginative

---

* Dr. Delabarre's History of Dighton Rock runs through Colonial Society of Mass., *Publications*, XVIII, XIX, and XX (1916–19); his final solutions are in his *Dighton Rock, a Study of the Written Rocks of New England* (New York, 1928), and in Rhode Island Historical Society *Collections*, XXIX (October 1936), 97–119.

Three photos of Dighton Rock with observers' interpretations of the inscriptions, chalked or painted on. Note, just to the right of feet of the big human figure, a little pot-bellied man (1875 and 1894), with a vertical stroke or two beside him, who becomes date "1511" at Delabarre's hands in the third photo. Photos by A. M. Harrison and W. B. Gardner, 1875; and Frank S. Davis, 1894; Edmund B. Delabarre, *Dighton Rock*, 1928.

eyes of Charles August Fernald (1842–1916) read on the rock that a captain of the Emperor Augustus had been there in A.D. 29, and that none other than Jesus Christ visited the Rock and carved His initials there in A.D. 15! After spending many years studying the subject, and compiling a bibliography of over 500 items, Professor Delabarre naturally began "seeing things" himself; and his findings were convincing when he chalked the letters and figures that he considered significant, leaving the rest in limbo. He found a Portuguese coat of arms, the date 1511, and the inscription

MIGVEL CORTEREAL V DEI HIC DUX IND
(Miguel Cortereal by Will of God, here Chief of the Indians)

Delabarre's theory is that Miguel, shipwrecked somewhere between Newfoundland and New England on his voyage of 1502, made his way to Assonet Neck, became chief of the Wampanoag, and, dying in 1511, was here commemorated by a faithful follower. Portuguese-Americans, numerous in that part of Massachusetts, have taken the Dighton Rock to their hearts as evidence that their ancestors were in New England more than a century before the *Mayflower*. As a result of their pressure the Commonwealth has had the rock removed from its half-tide position on the beach to a safe spot on the shore, and created a little state park to protect it from becoming a slate for still more inscriptions. Unfortunately, one can no longer get near enough to it for a careful examination, and, without its twice-daily bath in salt water, the inscriptions are disintegrating.

In the museum of the Sociedad de Geografia, Lisbon, there is a full-size model of Dighton Rock, with the Delabarre reading—and nothing else—inscribed on it. That, naturally, is very convincing. Most Portuguese historians, however, are skeptical. J. M. Cordeiro de Sousa, in *Arquivo Historico de Marinha*, I, 111–15, pointed out the discrepancies between this inscription, both in letter forms and language, from those of Portuguese discoverers' carvings elsewhere.

The latest contribution to Dighton Rock history is a book by George F. W. Young, to be published by the Old Colony Historical Society of Taunton, Mass. Professor Young sees in it all that Delabarre saw, and also several imperfect crosses of the Portuguese Order of Christ.

After examining the rock several times prior to 1935, under the amiable tutelage of Dr. Delabarre, I remain unconvinced that a Corte Real is there recorded. The "Portuguese arms" look to me like a crude Indian carving of a human face; the "5" of "1511" looks like a little man with thin legs; and the rest seems to me to be a complete hodge-podge into which you can read anything. In my opinion, the Dighton Rock is essentially an Algonkin petroglyph displaying crude human and animal figures, on which later visitors have overlaid their names. There are many similar examples done by the tribes of New England; several are depicted in the second half of Delabarre's 1928 book.

If the history of the Dighton Rock is nothing else, it is a remarkable demonstration of human credulity.

ANGLO-AZOREAN VOYAGES AND SEBASTIAN CABOT

All the essential documents and learned summaries are in J. A. Williamson, *The Cabot Voyages* (Hakluyt Society) and *The Voyages of the Cabots* (1929). Most are also in H. P. Biggar, *Precursors of Cartier*, and in Hoffman, *Cabot to Cartier*. Henry Harrisse, *Jean et Sebastien Cabot*, is indispensable. David B. Quinn does his best to rehabilitate Sebastian's reputation in *Sebastian Cabot and Bristol Exploration* (Bristol Branch of the Historical Association, 1968). Stephen Borough's account of the Gravesend caper is in Hakluyt; Richard Eden's relation of Sebastian's deathbed joke is in his *Very Necessarie and Profitable Booke Concerning Navigation* (London, c. 1575), quoted in Winship, *Cabot Bibliography*, pp. 45–46.

Sebastian married an English lady who did not live long; she bore him a daughter, Elizabeth, who married a merchant adventurer named Henry Ostriche. His second wife, a Spanish lady named Catalina de Medrano, predeceased him. Harrisse, pp. 135–36, states that his brothers Lewis (Ludovic) and Sancius (Santio), co-grantees with their father in 1496, had long before removed to Genoa and Venice. Nothing has been found by the antiquaries of Bristol as to when the widow of John Cabot left that city, or when she died.

THE PERIOD 1502–1525 AND FAGUNDES

Marcel Trudel, *Histoire de la Nouvelle-France, les vaines tentatives* (Montreal, 1963), is best for this period. Bernard Hoffman, *Cabot to Cartier* (1961), is a good guide to the cartography, for which the most thorough account (though full of fanciful conjecture) is W. F. Ganong (Theodore Layng, ed.), *Crucial Maps in the Early Cartography . . . of the Atlantic Coast of Canada* (Toronto, 1964). H. P. Biggar, *Precursors of Cartier*, prints all the documents. Comparison of maps, initiated by Nansen, *In Northern Mists*, II, 364, is carried out in vast detail by Hoffman. The rhymed *routier* by Jean Mallart, 1547, says, in describing Cape Breton Island,

> Les Portuglais l'ont quelque fois peuplée
> Mais ceux de L'Isle ont ces gens tuée.

George Patterson, "The Portuguese on the Northeast Coast of America," Royal Society of Canada, *Proceedings and Transactions*, VIII (1890), 127–78, is the only monograph on Fagundes. Harrisse, *Discovery of North America*, has a chapter on him and his voyages, which Harrisse believed to include the complete periplus of the Gulf of St. Lawrence. He places the colony near Halifax, N.S., which to me makes no sense; it would be too far from the Grand Bank. Samuel de Champlain, *Œuvres* (Champlain Society edition, I,468; III,418), noted that the Portuguese passed a winter on Cape Breton and were forced out by cold. But where on Cape Breton? My choice of Ingonish is based on sailing along Cape Breton Island years ago, flying over it recently, and trying to imagine which harbor would look best to Portuguese fishermen. Others say Sydney, or Spanish Bay whose only sand is an inconvenient bar at the harbor mouth, or the Bras d'Or Lakes, which would have been too difficult for fishermen to sail in and out of quickly. Patterson favors Louisbourg, but that site has been thoroughly bulldozed for the recent restoration of the French eighteenth-century citadel, and no Portuguese relics were found, so we may rule it out.

My Alfonce quotation is from Ganong, *Crucial Maps*, p. 365. There is on record a petition of João Alvares's only surviving daughter, stating that her father lost a fortune on his overseas adventure. Her descendant, the Conde de Bertiandos, was living in her father's old house at Viana do Castelo in 1911 (Biggar, p. 129).

"AN INTERLUDE OF THE FOUR ELEMENTS"

An anonymous play, *An Interlude of the Four Elements*, dated between 1512 and 1519, reprinted by the Percy Society, Vol. XXII (1848), indicates that certain Englishmen were bewailing the fact that other nations were pushing them hard:

> This see is called the Great Occyan,
> So great it is that never man
> Coude tell it sith the worlde began;
> Tyll nowe, within this xx. yere,
> Westwarde be founde new landes,
> That we never harde tell of before this
> By wrytynge nor other meanys,
> Yet many nowe have ben there;
> And that contrey is so large or rome,
> Muche lenger than all Cristendome,
> Without fable or gyle;
> For dyvers maryners had it tryed,
> And sayled streyght by the coste syde
> Above v. thousande myle!
> But what commodytes be wythin
> No man can tell nor well imagin,
> But yet not longe ago
> Some men of this contrey went,
> By the kynges noble consent,
> It for to serche to that entent,
> And coude not be brought therto; . . .

> O what a thynge had been than,
> Yf that they that be Englyshemen
> Myght have ben the furst of all
> That there shulde have taken possessyon,

And made furst buyldynge and habytacion,
A memory perpetuall!
And also what an honorable thynge,
Bothe to the realme and to the kynge,
To have had his domynyon extendynge
There into so farre a grounde,
Whiche the noble kynge of late memory,
The most wyse prynce the vij Herry
Causyd furst for to be founde. . . .

THORNE, RUT, AND HORE

Thorne's Letter and "Booke" are in Hakluyt's *Voyages* (Everyman ed.) I, 212–31, and *Divers Voyages* (Hakluyt Society ed.), pp. 33–54.

Rut's voyage is well covered by H. P. Biggar, with translations of the Spanish sources, in a chapter of *Mélanges d'histoire offerts à M. Charles Bémont* (1913), 459–72. The Spanish sources are printed in Biggar, *Precursors of Cartier*, pp. 165–77, with the exception of Oviedo's account of the visit to San Germán, Puerto Rico, which is in Oviedo, *Historia de las Indias,* lib. xix, cap. 13 (I, 611, of the Madrid 1851 ed.). My information about San Germán and the 1575 chart comes from my learned friend Aurelio Tió, author of "El Enigme del Descubrimiento de Puerto Rico," *Boletim de la Academia Puertorriqueña de la Historia* I, No. 3 (November 1969). Mr. Tió called to my attention a reference to Rut's visit in Antonio de Herrera, *Historia General*, III, the 1946 reproduction of the Madrid edition of 1726–30, III, bk. v., ch. iii, pp. 96–99. Herrera used the material in the depositions, and Oviedo's data, adding that the king of Spain, highly displeased with the leniency of his colonial officials toward Rut, ordered that the next English ship which violated Spanish territorial waters be captured. Méndez, the *alguacil* mayor, is the same man who effected the rescue of Columbus from Jamaica; see my edition of *Journals and Other Documents of Columbus* (1963), p. 398. Statements to the effect that Rut sailed as far as Hudson or Davis Strait and returned home in October 1527 are mere gossip, and false. Rut, by his own showing, sailed no further north than latitude 53° N.

Tourist cruises to the Holy Land are well described in R. J. Mitchell, *The Spring Voyage* (London, 1964); those from Bristol in E. M. Carus-Wilson, *Merchant Adventurers of Bristol* (1962).

Every historian of early Canada covers the Hore voyage in some fashion. The Hakluyt account, the principal source, is reprinted as Appendix I of Biggar's *Voyages of Jacques Cartier*, although Cartier had nothing to do with it and apparently never heard of it. Eva G. R. Taylor discovered additional details and published them in *Geographical Journal,* LXXVII (1931), 469–70.

THE BARCELOS BROTHERS' VOYAGE

Manuel C. Baptista de Lima, "Uma Tentativa Açoriana de Colonozacão da Ilha Demoniada 'Barcellosa' no Secolo XVI," in *Actas* do Congresso Int. de Hist. dos Descobrimientos, V, part i (Lisbon, 1961), 161–77, tells all that is known of a voyage by Diogo and Manuel de Barcelos, sons of João Fernandes's partner, around 1525–31. They claimed that their brother Afonso had discovered an island in the northern regions that he called *Barcellona de Sam Bordão* (St. Brendan), and obtained royal permission to colonize it; but what, if anything, they did about it does not appear. Señor Baptista de Lima identifies this island as the future Prince Edward.

✳ VIII ✳
The French Maritime Background

1453-1590

"Les français sont puissant sur mer, ils ont puissance partout
et s'accroissent toujours en nombre."
—PORTUGUESE AMBASSADOR TO D. JOÃO III, 17 FEBRUARY 1538

Emerging Normandy

In 1500 it was anyone's guess which European power would dominate
North America. Eliminating Spain and Portugal, both of whom had
little energy left for these supposedly poor and chilly regions of the
New World, we have France and England; and anyone estimating their
relative power in 1550 would have bet on France. She had sixfold
the population of England, double that of the Iberian peninsula, 50 per
cent more than the whole of Italy. France had a greater extent of
ocean-facing territory, as many or more seaports than England, an
equally enterprising maritime population, far greater wealth, and,
until her civil wars broke out, a government as much interested in
maritime affairs as that of the Tudors.

Why, then, did France not annex all America north of Florida? The
following chapters will provide part of the answer. In this we shall
briefly examine the maritime conditions and situation of France in the

* This chapter should be considered a supplement, insofar as France is concerned,
to Chapter V above, where the data on building, manning, and rigging English
ships, conditions of seafaring, etc., apply generally to France as well.

Jean Jolivet's two Norman ships and a galley from his map of Normandy,
1525. Courtesy Bibliothèque Nationale.

sixteenth century, especially preceding her first great voyages of discovery, those of Verrazzano in 1524 and of Cartier starting ten years
later.

Maritime France, so far as northern voyages are concerned, consists
of the ancient provinces of Normandy, Brittany, Saintonge, and
Guienne. Mediterranean France participated very slightly in transatlantic discovery and trade.

Normandy, above all, is the center of maritime France; it has been
ever since Rollo the Ganger and his merry men from Scandinavia took
over in the ninth century. As far back as the twelfth century the Arab
geographer Edrisi wrote, "Dieppe is a town where they build ships and
a harbor whence maritime expeditions depart." When Béthencourt
wanted colonists for the Canaries in the early part of the fifteenth
century, he found them in Normandy. Dieppe lay right on the sea, in

a perfect position to become at once the fulcrum for water traffic with England and the Netherlands and a leading center of the North Sea herring fishery. It was near enough to the mouth of the Seine to profit by exchanges with Rouen and Paris, and to vend its products through the center of France. In the Middle Ages, the Seine was to France what the Mississippi and the St. Lawrence later became to the United States and Canada: an axis of penetration. The Seine was navigable for small craft for many miles above Paris; a short carry took one to the headwaters of the Loire, and another to the Rhône; thus, salt herring directly from Dieppe figured at the breakfast tables of the popes at Avignon.

The end of the Hundred Years' War in 1453 found Normandy a devastated region. Under English occupation, Dieppe and Rouen had to live without their back country, farms were deserted, at least one-third of the population had evacuated, all maritime pursuits were feeble or dead. Almost complete anarchy prevailed on the narrow seas in the last decade of the fifteenth century, to such an extent that the king of France required his subjects before putting to sea, to sign a bond not to attack friendly craft. Honfleur had to fortify her main street leading to the sea, as defense against pirates; and no wonder, since our old friends Pining and Pothorst chased a convoy of twenty-five French *hourques* laden with salt for Danzig, selectively captured one that was charged with Madeira wine, and threatened to land and plunder every northern French seaport.

Normandy vegetated for about twenty-five years, after which so remarkable a revival set in that by 1503 bad times were forgotten. Profitable traffic with England and the Baltic was restored. In 1504 we have the first record of a Norman fishing vessel on the Grand Bank of Newfoundland, and in 1508–10 *La Pensée* of Dieppe and *La Jacquette* of Pléneuf were there; between the two dates, a third Norman vessel landed seven Indian slaves in Rouen from "Terra Nova." But the herring fishery in the North Sea was so profitable to Dieppe that she did not become really interested in the North American codfishery for several years.

D. João III, king of Portugal, complained to the king of France in 1510 that French ships had captured three hundred Portuguese sail in the last ten years. Jean Fleury, corsair of Dieppe, intercepted and spoiled a Spanish treasure fleet in 1523. But it would be a mistake to assume that Normandy's new prosperity came from piracy. Rouen was sending her locally woven cloth to Spain and the Mediterranean, in competition with the English clothiers; her *bonnetries*—hats and bonnets for gentlemen and ladies—found a ready sale in England where both sexes preferred French fashions to English. Instead of filching logwood and spices from homeward-bound Spanish and Portuguese ships, the Dieppois now cut their own logwood in Brazil; and Paris, formerly at the end of a lengthy land spice line, obtained her spices by sea via Rouen. A great churchman of Paris who wanted a pair of parrots, sent for them to Fécamp where a ship was just in from Brazil; Paris epicures who preferred smoked salmon from Scotland to their own from the Loire, could buy it at Rouen. The only European church or museum of the sixteenth century which has carvings or paintings showing natives of Brazil is Saint-Jacques at Dieppe, and natives of Brazil were the sensation of a fête given there to honor King Henri II.

The most important maritime section of Normandy was *le Pays de Caux,* which extends from the mouth of the Seine to that of the Somme, including Rouen, Dieppe, Fécamp, and Le Havre. This Pays de Caux resembles a big rounded cake of chalk, on the edge of which *le bon Dieu* with a giant cleaver made harbors; consequently they are short but deep—Dieppe means deep. A shipmaster sailing eastward up-channel might be tempted to put in at Fécamp, which had an excellent little harbor right on the sea, more conveniently situated for trans-shipments to the Seine. And Fécamp had a famous place of pilgrimage, an abbey with a magnificent church as big as Notre-Dame de Paris, and a monastic distillery which claimed to have given birth to the liqueur Bénédictine, distilled from aromatic plants growing on top of the chalk cliffs. Incidentally, Fécamp is one of the last strongholds of the French codfishery; it imported 22,000 tons of cured cod as late as 1961.

If in search of big business, the shipmaster would have been well advised to sail a few more leagues eastward to Dieppe. The excellent little harbor there owes its existence to the River Arques breaking through chalk to the sea and conveniently depositing silt outside the harbor on the modern *plage.* The river itself gave easy access for barges to the Forest of Arques, source of ship timber, and the mouth of the harbor was protected by a jetty, as early as the fifteenth century. Burghers of Dieppe maintained a primitive coal-fire lighthouse there, which made a range for entering with a second light mounted at Le Pollet, the suburb on the right bank of the Arques. Thus, with any northerly or westerly wind, and at any time of day or night, a sailing

A 1970 view of Fécamp harbor. The entrance is under the drawbridge to the right.

ship could nip into Dieppe, close-haul her sheets, and in fifteen minutes moor at the quai (later named Henri IV) right under the windows of the big merchants' establishments. There, within a quarter-mile, a ship-master could find everything he wanted: *douanes*, merchants, factors, building and repair yards, ship's charts and instruments, taverns, *filles*. For these and other reasons, this little place rose in the sixteenth century to surpass other Norman ports such as Harfleur and Honfleur.

Dieppe never eclipsed Rouen, despite the difficult access to that river city. Although the navigation of the Seine is more hazardous than that of the English Avon, and even dangerous when a tidal bore, the *mascaret*, sweeps up the river unexpectedly, hundreds of the little ships of the sixteenth century made the long passage from Havre de Grâce to Rouen with no other power than oar and sail. With a ten-knot current, three tides at least were required to make it either way, and you would see a whole fleet, like the *fragatas* of the Tagus a few years ago, strike sail and anchor when the ebb tide began, and wait until the flood set in. Pilots were available at Quillebeuf and Caudebec. There the Abbey of Sainte-Wandrille had the right to tax every passing ship in return for contributing to her safety by marking the edges of the mudflats (*battures*) with *balises* (perches). Ships of 100 to 120 tuns' burthen could easily get up to Rouen, where there were not enough quays to accommodate the traffic; vessels once discharged were ordered by the city council in 1520 to haul out into the stream, under penalty of having their lines cast off by the police.

Rouen was a great city, by sixteenth-century standards. Owing to its bridge, the lowest on the Seine, Rouen became the head of deep-sea navigation, where everything had to be transferred to small craft for

A plan of Dieppe in 1853, not very different from that of 1553. The Jetée de l'Est was the original jetty, where the fourteenth-century *phare* was located. From Eugène Chapus, *Dieppe et ses environs*, 1853.

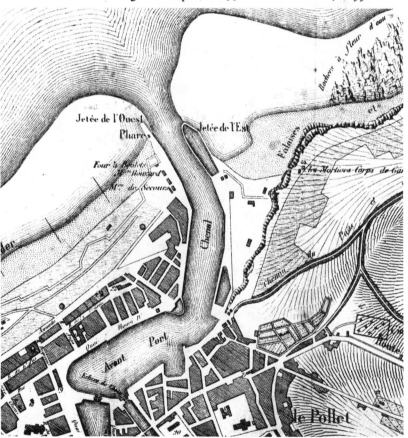

Dieppe and Environs, 1970: Harbor and quai Henri IV. Jean Ango's villa at Varengeville.

Rouen in 1526. Compiled from the manuscript album *Livre des fontaines de Rouen* of that date at the Bibliothèque Municipale, for an exhibition in 1845. The album pictures every church and almost every house in Rouen. Photo-Ellebé, Rouen.

passage to Paris or beyond; and a great deal of it was. In many respects Rouen was the French Bristol, with the additional advantage of being seaport to the capital. It lay up a difficult tidal river, it attracted foreign merchants (at Rouen, an Italian and a Spanish colony), the merchants built luxurious town houses and comfortable country manor-houses, and provided funds for magnificent churches—Rouen's cathedral, Saint-Ouen, and Saint-Maclou rival Bristol's cathedral and St. Mary Redcliffe. Finally, both towns have risen from their ashes. After terrific bombing in World War II they have repaired damage, rebuilt quays, shipyards, and dockyards, and Rouen is now the fourth port in France for tonnage.

Le Havre owes its existence as a great port to the interest of François-premier in creating a new deep-water naval harbor at the mouth of the Seine to replace silted-out Harfleur; no more could a "fleet majestical, holding due course for Harfleur," get into the harbor. On the site of a little fishing village on deep water, a long jetty was begun in 1517; quays and another jetty followed, and within three years the largest ships could moor there in safety. Nothing like this was ever done by the Tudors for any English port.

Norman shipmasters went to sea in the first half of the century better provided with printed and instrumental aids to navigation than (so far as we know) did any English captain prior to Frobisher. Pierre Garcie's *Routier* dates from 1483, and went through eighteen printings at Rouen before 1511.

In Chapter V we mentioned some of the difficulties that English ships experienced when approaching home ports after an Atlantic crossing. Those of the French were no less. *Haute Normandie*, extending from the Cherbourg Peninsula to the Seine, including the ports of Barfleur, Arromanches, and Honfleur, is very difficult to make out accurately from the sea, as the Anglo-American liberators of France found in 1944. A seemingly endless white cliff, with few church towers or other landmarks, confused mariners seeking the mouth of the Seine, which the Garcie rutter warned them not to enter at low water, owing to the numerous shoals and sand banks. For the Bretons, Ushant stretched out its ugly fangs and those with destination Saint-Malo not only had to avoid the Channel Islands and Les Minquiers but to thread the many off-shore reefs and rocky islands, like Cézambre, where the rise and fall of tide is almost equal to that of the Avon leading to Bristol.

Dieppe and Rouen were as famous as the cities of Flanders and Italy for great bourgeois families. Rouen boasted of three in particular—the Dufour, the Le Pelletier, and the Ango. The Dufours came from Geneva and had connections in Lyons; they were primarily drapers. The Le Pelletiers, who came from Provence, were merchants in almost "anything you can name or mention"; they so prospered that by 1550 some sixteen manors and châteaux in the Pays de Caux were theirs, and a few ships as well. They had connections with the Italian banker Bonacorso Rucellai, supporter of Verrazzano, and lent money to Charles VIII. The family that interests us most, however, is the Ango. Jean Ango, father and son, belonged to an old bourgeois family of Rouen and divided their time and interest between Rouen and Dieppe. The elder—known by popular acclaim as Le vicomte de Dieppe—financed a pioneer voyage to Newfoundland and was busily engaged in trade with the eastern Mediterranean, the British Isles, and the Low Countries; he helped to finance Verrazzano and Cartier. Ango owned great ships, small ships, and fishing vessels. His house flag, a Turkish crescent, adopted no doubt because of his Levantine interests (as did the nineteenth-century Boston families who traded with Smyrna), is flying from the mainmast of one of the Testu ships which we reproduce here, and the Norman cartographer Desceliers, whom Ango patronized, spread his crescent flag over the north of Canada as if he owned that too. In twenty years, 1520–40, his ships captured prizes worth a million ducats. The Portuguese condemned several Ango ships for trading with their possessions, and he retaliated by blockading Lisbon on his own account, with the approval of Admiral Chabot de Brion. François-premier did him the honor of visiting him at his manor at Varengeville. Under Henri II he fell out of favor, and in 1549, charged with withholding from the crown its due share of privateering profits, he was imprisoned and died soon after, a broken man. His family spent the next fifty years trying to recover his property.

Without the aid of Jean Ango, a veritable Renaissance merchant-prince, it is doubtful whether the voyages of Jacques Cartier would have been possible.

Dieppe by mid-sixteenth century had become a maritime metropolis where men not only built ships which established new trade routes, not only bought and sold seaborne merchandise, but studied cosmography, astronomy, and navigation. The proof of this is the appearance between 1542 and 1560 of a series of remarkable maps drafted by the Dieppe cartographers Roze, Desliens, Desceliers, and Vallard.* These Norman map-makers obtained their data fresh, at quayside, from master pilots such as Jacques Cartier, and produced charts of the northern regions equal to those of the Portuguese for accuracy and beauty. Why they did not undertake to chart Verrazzano's voyage we do not know; possibly the Florentine brothers refused to give out information so that Girolamo could keep it for his own purposes. Jacques Cartier, however, was generous with his information, which, incidentally, was more exact than that of any earlier navigator because he had broken out of the fish-and-salt class and learned all that Dieppe captains and Rouen rutters and instrument-makers had to teach.

The mariner's calling was as highly esteemed in Normandy and Brittany as that of the churchman, the physician, and the barrister. Jean Parmentier of Rouen, in his poem on the Marvels of God and the Dignity of Man, points out that to qualify as master pilot you need more time and training than to win a doctor's degree at a university:

* See Notes to and reproductions in Chapter XIII below.

WESTERN FRANCE
AND THE ENGLISH CHANNEL
IN THE SIXTEENTH CENTURY

London

Thames R.

NORTH
SEA

Str. of Dover
Calais
Boulogne
NETHERLANDS

Portsmouth
I. of Wight

Exeter
Dart R.
Plymouth
Dodman Pt.   Dartmouth
Falmouth   Start Pt.
Lands
End
SCILLY IS.   The Lizard

Portland Bill

ENGLISH   CHANNEL

Dieppe
Fécamp
PAYS DE CAUX
Arques R.
Harfleur
Le Havre   Rouen
Honfleur
Seine R.

C. de la Hague
Casquets   Cherbourg

CHANNEL IS.

Caen

NORMANDY

Paris
ILE DE
FRANCE

C. Fréhel
Granville
Ushant I.   C. Fréhel   Mt. St. Michel
(Ouessant)   Brest Landerneau   Ft. La Latte St. Malo
Le Conquet
Pt. du Raz   Quimper

B R I T T A N Y

Tours

BELLE ISLE

Nantes

Loire R.

I. de Yeu

VENDÉE

ILE DE RÉ   La Rochelle
AUNIS

ILE D'OLÉRON   Brouage
Pte. de la Coubre   Cognac
B A Y   O F   Charente R.   DORDOGNE

SAINTONGE

Tour de Cordouan

B I S C A Y

Gironde R.

Bordeaux

Garonne R.

GASCONY

Scale of Nautical Miles
0   50   100

S   P   A   I   N

West 0 East

Or pour certain on tient qu'ung bon pillote,
Ung marinier qui tout son cas bien note,
Bien entendu et bien exercité,
Est plus longtemps pour entendre sa note,
Parfaictement qu'il ne s'en faille iote,
Qu'ung docteur n'est en l'université.

Brittany

Brittany's geography differed greatly from that of Normandy. The ancient Armorica has the same sea outlook as the Norman duchy, only more so; in situation, Brittany is to Normandy what Portugal is to Spain. In geology, however, Brittany is very different from Normandy, between Caen and Cherbourg. Like the coasts of Maine and the Maritime Provinces, Brittany was solid rock underneath, with "drowned" river valleys which became tidal estuaries such as the Rance, leading from Saint-Malo to Dinan. But the prescience of the sea-going monk St. Malo (his real name was MacLaw or Maclou, a disciple of his contemporary St. Brendan) in founding this city on a rocky neck thrusting seaward made it unnecessary for Breton mariners to grapple with the tidal currents of the Rance. For all that, the rocks, reefs, and islets of Saint-Malo Bay make the town difficult of access; but it has always made its main business the training of mariners, and it is the last Breton harbor to send fishing vessels (now diesel-powered) to the Grand Bank.

Today, pastures as green as Normandy's come down to the edge of the Breton cliffs, but in the sixteenth century most of these grew only gorse and other wild stuff; and although Brittany lost less than Normandy in the Hundred Years' War, she had less to lose. As in Scandinavia, rural poverty made for maritime enterprise; and in the revival of the early sixteenth century we find Breton ships doing a large part of the French carrying trade. The aptitude of their crews in the New World fishing is proved by the large number of Breton pilots employed on Norman fishing craft. Saint-Malo seems to have prospered in good times and bad. Brest, which did not become *le boulevard de la marine* until after Louis XIV had built it up in the seventeenth century, was eclipsed by two little ports—Landernan, up river, and Le Conquet behind Ushant, a favorite port of call for north-south traders, or those coming from across the Atlantic in urgent need of water and provisions. And there were at least a dozen other tiny ports like Quimper and Paimpol where small vessels were built to take part in fishing or the carrying trade. Lower Brittany too had her axis of penetration— the Loire, flowing down past Nantes from the fat provinces of Anjou, Maine, Touraine, and the Orléanais.

"The permanent presence of Bretons in Norman ports is a prime factor," states the historian Mollat. They brought in woad for the Rouen and Paris dye-pots, wine and wheat from Gascony, and, above all, salt. Lower Brittany was the northernmost European country where salt could be made economically from ocean water; and in western Europe mineral salts had not yet been exploited. Enormous amounts of salt were used for seasoning and for preserving essential foodstuffs, and prior to the age of refrigeration all salt had to be supplied by evaporation from seawater. Brittany here had an advantage over Normandy, because when the duchy became part of France, through the marriage of its last duchess to Charles VIII, the French king agreed to exempt Bretons from the *gabelle*, the French salt tax. At that time Portuguese salt-pans at Aveiro and Setubal produced the best and purest salt, but they were too far away for imports, unless in small quantities for table use. The same applied even more strongly to Cadiz Bay, another major source of sea salt. Breton vessels mostly loaded at the salt-pans of the *marais* of Guienne, or at their own in Bouin, Brouage, and elsewhere. This copious, steady suppy of largely untaxed salt helps to explain the pre-eminence of the French in Newfoundland fisheries during the middle of the sixteenth century.

La Rochelle

The Biscayan coast of France south of the Loire is marshy, with long beaches open to the sea, and no harbor until you reach L'Ile de Ré. Behind that island rises the remarkable city of La Rochelle. One is now out of Brittany, in the old province of Aunis, or Saintonge, which became an eminent maritime region of France. Samuel de Champlain, her great captain-explorer of the next century, was born at the little salt-pan center, Brouage, in 1570, and in his writings described himself as *Xaintongeois*. Nobody has explained why La Rochelle (founded in the eleventh century) was placed where it is, fifteen miles north of the nearest navigable river, the Charente, and twice as far from the

Gironde mouth, gateway to rival Bordeaux. The harbor of La Rochelle is well protected, but only little streams suitable for small boats flow into it, and the salt marshes press in so close that the town lacked room for expansion. Only one road led out of it and that was impassable after a prolonged rain or during a high spring tide. The back country, too, was not fertile. It produced a white Aunis wine, and Cognac lies up the Charente; but there was nothing comparable to the vineyards of Bordeaux. Nevertheless, La Rochelle prospered, and in the late Middle Ages it became a semi-independent commune, like the city-states of Italy.

The real reason why this seaport flourished was the character of the people. A grim, determined race like the Scots, they found Calvinism to their liking and embraced the Reformed Religion with exceptional ardor. The Huguenot synod there in 1571 drew up a famous Confession of Faith, and in the religious wars La Rochelle successfully withstood a siege by the Catholic League in 1573. Since the city had become the chief Protestant stronghold in France, Cardinal Richelieu besieged and captured it in 1628. The siege reduced the population from 26,000 to 5000, most of those lost having died of starvation; but La Rochelle rose again. Years later, the Protestant cause was further damaged by the revocation of Henri IV's tolerant Edict of Nantes, and La Rochelle lost many of her most industrious citizens—hence New Rochelle, New York. Yet the city never gave up; in 1891 the construction of a new ship harbor, La Pallice, to handle big vessels, saved her foreign commerce, just as Avonmouth saved Bristol.

The merchants of La Rochelle, even before they went Calvinist, showed a great aptitude for finance. Whilst the oldest marine insurance policies issued in England are dated 1547, and they by Italian bankers, the Rochelais capitalists were insuring wine cargoes as early as 1489; and in 1563 no fewer than forty-five merchants of La Rochelle combined to underwrite two local vessels and one Portuguese for European voyages, at premiums of 7 and 8 per cent. Incidentally, I have found no instance of any transatlantic voyage, fishing or otherwise, being insured in the sixteenth century. They were considered much too risky.

By 1523 it is possible to name several fishing vessels from La Rochelle that were fishing on the Newfoundland Banks—*Marie*, *Catherine*, and *Marguerita*. And it is a good measure of Rochelais enterprise that Cartier, discovering (as he thought) the Gulf of St. Lawrence

et Haure de la Rochelle 5. Tour de S.t Sauveur
ur du Parre 6. Tour de S.t Nicolas
ur de la Chaisne 7. Tour de Morilles
uer de S.t Yon 8. Temple neuf

La Ville de la ROCHELLE, Capitale du Pays d'Aunis
fait par Aueline avec Priuilege du Roy

9. le Gabus
10. Marais Salans
11. Porte S.t Nicolas
12. Reduit du Dogn

Courtesy Musée de la Marine

in June 1534, found a fishing vessel from La Rochelle there ahead of him. Never, in this or any other century, did the Rochelais take back wind from anyone.

The historians of La Rochelle have not done justice to her fishing interests; but certain facts stand out on the sharing of expenses and profits. The industry was organized on the share or "lay" system, like almost all coastal fishing in England, France, and North America down to the twentieth century. A document of 1523–24 indicates that one-third of the profits of a voyage, in fish and fish-oil, went to the crew; but out of that they had to pay the master or pilot. The rest went to the owners, except for a *pot de vin*, a tip, to the fishermen, at signing on. This for the "dry" fishing; for the "wet," * the crew only got one-quarter of the profits, probably because "wet" took less time and two trips could be made a year.

As for quantity, the statistics collected by the local historians are impressive though contradictory. Departures from La Rochelle for Newfoundland or the Banks start with five in 1523 and jump to forty-

* See explanation of "wet" and "dry" fishing in Chapter XIV.

266

nine in 1559, an average of over ten annually for the twenty-six years covered by this table. Another table gives one hundred departures from La Rochelle for Terre-Neuve in the years 1534–65. Whichever is correct, it is evident that La Rochelle was one of the leading overseas fishing ports of France, and that this led directly to its heavy participation in the settlement of, and trade with, Canada. Roberval, as we shall see, fitted out and sailed from La Rochelle in 1541, and his celebrated pilot, Jean Alfonce, was a Rochelais.

Bordeaux and the Gironde

Jacques Bernard has rescued Bordeaux from the imputation of earlier French historians to the effect that the Bordelais did nothing but grow grapes and drink wine, leaving ships and shipping to others. But he does not deny that wine was the basis of the region's prosperity. By constant care and applied intelligence, the Bordelais transformed a region of poor soil and marginal agriculture into one where the vineyards yielded a quality of wine which all the world then wanted; it still does. Claret, as the English called the red wine of Bordeaux, became a favorite during their domination of Guienne and Gascony. The Falstaffs and Fluellens preferred the stronger sack from Spain, but your English country gentleman or merchant drank claret, or *vin d'Aunis* or German hock on the rare occasions when he wanted white wine. Only in the eighteenth century did the English merchant prefer port wine to claret.

Owing to the value of the medieval wine trade, the Cordouan lighthouse at the mouth of the Gironde, begun under Charlemagne and rebuilt by the Black Prince under the English occupation, became the biggest and most famous in Europe. We have already seen how John Cabot used it as a point of reference; he had doubtless sailed up and down the "river of Bordeaux" as he called it, many times. No spot in Europe, not even the Eddystone, needed a lighthouse more; Cordouan was surrounded by *battures*, sand or mud flats, like those later encountered by the French in the St. Lawrence.

Your typical Bordeaux shipbuilder in the sixteenth century was not a specialist. Primarily he was a peasant, owner of vineyards or of meadow and tillage, who took to shipbuilding as a seasonal occupation when farming did not require all his time. He always figured on getting his boats finished by Michaelmas, so as not to interfere with the vintage. Similarly, the eastern Maine farmers, many of whom this writer knew in his youth, took to shipbuilding and boat-building in the fall, as soon as their crops were gathered into the barn, and enough salt fish or pickled mackerel was "made" to last the family through the winter.

Bordeaux ship-carpenters had so good a reputation that English vessels needing repairs tried to plan their voyages to lay over there; and Bordeaux as a wine metropolis was a very pleasant place at which to linger. Most of the vessels built there were under 80 tuns' burthen; a bill of sale of 1515 gives the specifications of a 35-tunner; 35 *pieds* (11–12 meters) on the keel, 14 *pieds* beam. All vessels destined for the sea were completely decked over, with castles forward and aft. The sail plan of the *Marie Johan* in 1493, described as a *nabiu* (navire) of eighty tuns, has four masts (two of them lateen-rigged mizzens), a main course with three bonnets, a fore course with two bonnets, and a square main topsail. Fifty years later, one always finds a square spritsail under the bowsprit.

Shipbuilding

Had we been fifteenth-century sailors we would probably have been able to tell a French-built from an English-built ship at a glance. From the records one can see no difference between the hulls and rigging of French vessels and those we have described in England. Norman shipbuilding underwent a tremendous expansion after 1520, most of it owing to the demands of transatlantic commerce. For the New World was a graveyard of ships; count up the wrecks we have mentioned from Cabot's down, add the fishermen and unrecorded others who foundered off Newfoundland, and you will realize that never in the history of merchant navies, not even after the ravages of World War II, has there been so great a need of replacement shipping as in the years 1530–1600. By the latter date, western Europeans had learned many lessons in safety, both in sailing and construction, and the casualty rate began to fall. There is one difference between the French and the English: although Dieppe and Bordeaux obtained their oak locally (Dieppe from the Arques forest, Bordeaux from the Dordogne), and used largely local pine or beech for planking, they imported almost every-

The Cordouan lighthouse. From an engraving of 1612. Courtesy Musée de la Marine, Paris.

thing else: tar and pitch from the Pyrenees or the Baltic (Danzig was already an entrepôt for naval stores in 1500), cordage from England, anchors and other ironwork from Bilbao. The English, however, imported canvas sailcloth from Dieppe, which probably obtained her supply from the Baltic.

In general the French shipbuilders seem to have gone through the same evolution as that of the Low Countries and England. First the one-masted *cogge*, then the three-masted *houlke* which, with certain refinements, became the *nef, nau, vaisseau,* or ship. Dieppe shipbuilders may not have invented the carvel type of construction, but with them it had completely superseded clinker-built by 1500; whilst in England, John Davis (over the objections of his shipmates) took a "clincher" pinnace with him to the Arctic regions in 1587, and sailed her home. The medium-size ship, under one hundred tuns, was called *barque* in

France, *bark* in England; the smallest, without which no overseas expedition was complete, *galion* in France, *pinnace* in England. To add to the confusion, France had at least ten other types of vessels which we cannot now identify; and the *galion* grew and grew until it became equal to the Spanish galleon of 1588.

Practical seamen preferred small ships to big ones for overseas exploration; but certain merchant-shipbuilders built them of five hundred tuns up, not only for prestige but because the big ones could be converted to naval vessels or powerful corsairs. For instance, the royal French navy bought Harfleur-built *L'Hermine* of 500 tuns in 1517; *La Louise*, 780 tuns, flagship of Admiral Louis Malet de Graville, came from Dieppe; and, most extraordinary, between 1521 and 1527, at a little place near Le Havre, there was built *La Grande Françoise*, which had five masts and measured 1500 tuns. She even had a built-in chapel, ballroom, and tennis court, like a modern cruise ship! For six years *La Grande Françoise* resisted every effort to launch her; finally a tempest threw her on her beam ends and she had to be scrapped. This leviathan was much bigger than the pride of the Tudor navy, *Harry Grace à Dieu*, or Scotland's *Great Michael*, built in 1511, which cost £30,000, and, manned by three hundred sailors, was said to be capable of carrying one thousand soldiers.

Inauguration of the Grand Bank Fishery

Neither Dieppe nor any other French port had trading relations with Iceland in the Middle Ages; their famous *pêcheurs d'Islande*, immortalized by Pierre Loti, belong to later centuries. The reason is obvious—smoked and pickled herring of the North Sea and English Channel had saturated the French market. Hence it is not to be expected that Normans and Bretons would flock to the Grand Bank as soon as Cabot's news reached France of the plenty of codfish there, nor did they. The first authentic records of any French ship on the Newfoundland Banks are those of Jean Denys of Honfleur in 1504, who fished between Cape Bonavista and the Strait of Belle Isle, and Thomas Aubert in the *Pensée* of Dieppe, belonging to Jean Ango, two years later.

Once they had found this new source of fish, the French lost no time in exploiting it. In 1507 a Norman vessel brought from Newfoundland to Rouen an extra cargo of seven *sauvages;* they must have been

French *nefs* of 1555. From the Guillaume le Testu album in the Bibliothèque des Forces Armées, Paris. Note the *pavesses* (shields of gentlemen on board) on the waistcloths and along the poop on the one; and the house flag of Jean Ango on the other. Photo Giraudon.

Beothuk Indians. We know of an early Breton fishing voyage by *La Jacquette* of Dahouët (who sold her stockfish at Rouen) because of a shipboard brawl that led to trouble. The master, Guillaume Dobel, aged twenty-two, alleged that she was carrying too much sail. He qualified Skipper Picart as an *idiot*, and Quartermaster Garroche as a *veau*, apparently a serious insult, like *cochon* today. Garroche dropped the tiller, roared up to the quarterdeck in a menacing posture, and collected a sock in the jaw from Dobel, who then drew a dagger and chased him overboard. They tried to rescue him, using their small towed boat, but he drowned. Dobel made the best restitution he could to the widow Garroche (apparently by marrying her!); influence was brought to bear, and on the ground that he was a good mariner and a valuable citizen in peace and war he received a pardon from the king.

Another human touch is in Elegy XI of the poet Jean Doublet, who flourished in mid-sixteenth century. He writes on the age-old theme of a sailor's mother watching in vain for his return. *La bonne mère* burns candles to the saints to promote her son's return, watches every ship that comes in, hoping it be his, and queries every returning mariner for news of her dear boy.

We have indubitable evidence that these intrepid fishermen were accustomed to make two fishing trips annually to the Grand Bank. The first set out in late January or early February and, braving the winter westerlies of the North Atlantic, returned as soon as their holds were full; then discharged, started off again in April or May, and were home in September. This, of course, was the "wet" fishing, which required no call at a Newfoundland harbor. Saint-Malo set aside a rocky section of the shore called *Le Sillon* for curing the fish, as early as 1519.

Shipboard prayers, superstitions, and customs of the sea were similar in France to those in England. One difference I have noted is that the mainmast at Bordeaux, and presumably elsewhere, had a symbolic value, so that a religious ceremony took place when it was stepped.

Salt fish were sold wholesale in France by the thousand; and from ancient custom, a thousand fish meant twelve hundred. In 1515 Michel Le Bail, Breton merchant, sells 17,500 salt codfish to the local merchants at Rouen; and thenceforth no year passes without a record of one or more *terre-neuviens* discharging stockfish at Fécamp, Dieppe, or Rouen. By 1529 Normandy is re-exporting it to England. The

French Newfoundland fishery had become big business; sun-cured *morue* were pushing *hareng salé* hard in the salt-fish market, and Rouen had become the distributing center of it for the interior of France. Cured codfish, if properly cooked, is tastier than pickled herring and easier to handle. One can throw it about and stack it like cordwood, whilst herring has to be contained in a barrel full of brine. It was a great day for Rouen in 1542 when no fewer than sixty vessels departed the same day for the Grand Bank of Newfoundland.

This new transatlantic business, as well as earlier logwood traffic with Brazil, attracted to Rouen a group of Italian bankers; and in the sixteenth century, as in the twentieth, local prosperity was signaled by the need of credit and bankers moving in. To what good purpose these Italians came to Rouen and Dieppe we shall see in the next chapter.

Although the French seaports had every possible advantage for Atlantic exploration that the English had; although the French crown gave its merchant marine more support and encouragement than the Tudors ever did, there is one English asset which the French lacked— a Hakluyt. That English compiler of voyages not only published everything he could find on his own nation's voyages; he translated Verrazzano's report long before it was available in French, and even rescued the original accounts of two Cartier voyages from oblivion.

The fact is that seafaring was a central activity in England, a peripheral one in France. England had but one land frontier, with Scotland; whilst France had the House of Hapsburg on two fronts, the German Empire in the center, and Savoy in the southeast. The French kings from Louis XI through Henri II were far from indifferent to seaports and mariners, but their series of wars with the Empire and Spain made the army their chief concern. Then came the religious wars; and by the time they were over and Henri IV had brought internal peace to France, it was too late for his country to become the great North American power. His predecessors had ignored what Verrazzano found; he had to make do with what Cartier explored.

Bibliography and Notes

FRENCH MARITIME BIBLIOGRAPHY FOR THE FIFTEENTH AND SIXTEENTH CENTURIES

French maritime historians, unlike their brethren of England and Portugal, have not wasted time on what Mollat calls "the silly, stale discussion of the pretended priority of Dieppe in Discoveries." Arguments for French fishermen having been on the Grand Bank of Newfoundland fifty years before John Cabot, and for Jean Cousin having discovered Brazil long before Cabral and having trained one of the Pinzón family who showed Columbus the way, are based on nothing but wishful thinking.

French maritime historiography falls into three distinct epochs: (1) The reign of Louis Philippe, when French naval matters came to the fore after centuries of neglect. Auguste Jal then published *Archéologie navale* (2 vols., Paris, 1840), and *Documents inédits sur l'histoire de la marine au XVIe siècle* (Paris, 1842). (2) Around the turn of the century, Alfred Spont published a useful article, "La Marine française sous le règne de Charles VIII," *Revue Historique*, n.s., XI (1894), 387–454, and Charles de La Roncière began his magistral *Histoire de la marine française*, of which Volumes II, III, and IV (Paris, 1900–1910) cover our period. La Roncière, whom I was privileged to know, was *conservateur* of the Bibliothèque Nationale and an accomplished cartographer as well as historian. His scope was world-wide, his industry phenomenal, his judgment sound; very occasionally, enthusiasm led him astray. Coeval with these are the works—printed as small pamphlets and now difficult to obtain—of that sea-going priest, l'Abbé Anthiaume of Rouen. Here are some of his principal titles: *La Science astronomique et nautique au moyen-âge chez les normands* (Le Havre, 1919); *Les Méthodes de navigation en France au moyen-âge* (Paris, 1924); *Le Navire. Sa construction en France . . . chez les normands* (1922); *La Projection des cartes marines chez les normands aux XVIe et XVIIe siècles* (Académie de Marine, 1929). (3) Since World War II a new school of French maritime historians has arisen, of which Professor Michel Mollat (formerly of the University of Lille, now at the Sorbonne), Professor Pierre Chaunu of the University of Caen, and Charles-André Julien, Professor of Colonial History at l'École Nationale de la France d'Outre-Mer, Paris, are the leaders. Julien wrote the comprehensive *Voyages de découverte et les premiers établissements, XVe–XVIe siècles* (Paris, 1948), and edited a book of documents, *Les Français en Amérique pendant la première moitié du XVIe siècle* (Paris, 1946), Mollat, with an industry and perspicacity worthy of La Roncière, not only wrote *Le Commerce maritime normand à la fin du moyen-âge* (Paris, 1952), but organized several *colloques internationaux d'histoire maritime*, where real experts presented valuable papers. Particularly useful are: *Le Navire et l'économie maritime du XVe au XVIIIe siècle* (1957); *Le Navire et l'économie maritime du* *moyen-âge au XVIIIᵉ siècle, principalement en Méditerranée* (1958); *Le Navire et l'économie maritime du nord de l'Europe du moyen-âge au XVIIIᵉ siècle* (1960); and *Les Aspects internationaux de la découverte oceanique au XVᵉ et XVIᵉ siècles* (1966). These are all published in Paris by S.E.V.P.E.N., 13 rue du Four.

From the same publishing house comes another indispensable work: Jacques Bernard, *Navires et gens de mer de Bordeaux* (3 vols., 1968). The mass of data that Bernard has extracted from local records is phenomenal. He puts to shame the feeble attempts of English, Spanish, and Portuguese historians to record the history of their ports. His volumes are a veritable mine of information, and his diagrams help one to understand French terms for shipbuilding and rigging.

Another recent work of the highest scholarly standard is Charles de La Morandière, *Histoire de la pêche française de la morue dans l'Amérique septentrionale des origines à 1789* (3 vols., Paris, 1962–66).

For La Rochelle, E. Trocmé and M. Delafosse, *Le Commerce rochelais du début du XVᵉ au XVIIᵉ siècle* (Paris, 1952), is the best; but except for tables on page 72, this book has little on that city's fishing interests. Camille Vergniol, *La Rochelle et Bayonne* (1921), opens with a vivid description of the approach to the city, and Paul R. Fontaine, *Les Établissements maritimes rochelais* (La Rochelle, 1929), is also useful.

DETAILS

There are several biographies of Jean Ango of Dieppe, none equal to the data about him in Charles de La Roncière and G. Clerc-Rampal, *Histoire de la marine française* (one-volume ed., 1934), pp. 50–51, and Michel Mollat, *Commerce maritime normand*, pp. 497–511.

The *Jacquette* episode is in H. P. Biggar, *Precursors of Cartier*, pp. 116–18.

For the *Grande Françoise* leviathan, see La Roncière, *Histoire*, II, 250–57, 473–75, and Anthiaume, *Le Navire*, pp. 214–18, 376.

For the earliest Dieppe voyages to Newfoundland, see Julien, *Voyages de découverte*, pp. 24–26.

Other useful articles are: André Plaisse, "Le Commerce du port de Brest à la fin du XVIᵉ siècle," *Revue d'Histoire Economique et Sociale*, XLII (1964), 499–545; and, on shipbuilding, the chapter by Professor Malowist in *Le Navire et l'économie maritime du nord de l'Europe du moyen-âge au XVIIIᵉ siècle* (Paris, 1960).

Jean Parmentier's poem "Les merveilles de Dieu et la dignité de l'homme" is in Ch. Schefer, ed., *Le Discours de la navigation de Jean et Raoul Parmentier de Dieppe* (Paris, 1883).

FITTING OUT IN 1541

Details of fitting out vessels for northern voyages, with prices, are so rare that I have here printed two: the first, for 1512, is a victualing list for a sixty-tun vessel of the royal French navy, with a crew of sixty.* It was drawn up by Antoine de Conflans, the captain of Verrazzano's *La Dauphine*. This sixty-tunner stowed 1065 dozen *pain biscuit* (hardtack), 18 dozen loaves of fresh bread, a puncheon (two-thirds of a hogshead) of flour, 44 pipes (double hogsheads or tuns) of cider or beer, two pipes of wine, four pipes and one puncheon of salt meat, half a carcass of fresh beef and two fresh sheep, 90 chests of lard, 476 pounds of butter, a puncheon of peas, half a pipe of beans, six barrels of salt herring, 160 pounds of candles, 180 pounds of tallow, 211 logs of wood, a half-pipe of vinegar, a barrel of verjuice, a half-pipe of salt, and (as an afterthought) 12 pipes or barrels of water. Conflans explains that the herring, butter, peas, and beans are intended for fast days, and that French sailors preferred cider to beer, and North Sea pickled herring to Newfoundland stockfish. The wine, fresh meat, and bread were for officers only. Able seamen in the French navy, he says, were paid 6 livres 5 sous ($1.25 or 6 shillings in gold) per month.

The second inventory is for fitting out at Bayonne the caravel chartered by Charles V in 1541 at 20 ducats a month to pursue Cartier.** Noteworthy are 10 pipes of wine, 65 ducats; 18 empty pipes for water, 6 reals each; jugs, mugs, and dishes for the men, 6 reals; 1900 pounds of salt beef; 8 ducats 2 reals; and 50 bushels of wheat (to be baked in advance) for the crew for five months, 59 ducats; 20 oars for the caravel; 62 pounds of salt pork, and 24 gallons of oil, 45 reals; 120 dried codfish, 82½ reals; 13 gallons of vinegar, 100 pounds of candles, and 175 pounds of tallow "for paying the caravel," 87½ reals. The captain and pilot were each paid 10 ducats a month, the master and caulker 4 ducats, eight able seamen 3 ducats, five gromets 2 ducats, two pages 1½ ducats. A gold ducat weighed 4.55 grams and was equivalent to $2.32 in gold prior to the 1934 devaluation; there were about 17 reals to one ducat.

* Auguste Jal, *Documents inédits*, pp. 44–45.
** H. P. Biggar, who discovered this in the Spanish archives, prints it in his *Collection of Documents Relatng to Cartier* . . . (1930), pp. 356–61.

* IX *
The Voyages of Verrazzano

1524-1528

François-premier and the Search for a Northern Strait

While Fagundes and others were trying to make something out of Codfish Land and Cape Breton, mighty events were unrolling in the southern half of the hemisphere. Hernando Cortés won a Mexican empire for Spain in 1521. Ferdinand Magellan relentlessly pursued the greatest recorded voyage of all time. Victim of an ill-conceived amphibious attack, Magellan left his bones at Mactan in the Philippines, but his valiant subordinate Juan Sebastian del Cano carried on around the world. On September 1522 his ship *Vittoria*, sole survivor of the five with which Magellan started, anchored at Seville, carrying home but eighteen of the 239 men who had set forth three years earlier. The first printed account of this circumnavigation, *De Moluccis Insulis* by Maximilian of Transylvania, appeared at Rome in November 1523 and at Cologne in January 1524; and, just as the first voyage of Columbus sparked off that of John Cabot, so Del Cano's stimulated two attempts by major powers to find a better western route to Asia than the tempestuous Strait of Magellan.

François d'Angoulême, who succeeded his cousin Louis XII in 1515, ordered the first. François-premier, as he is generally called, dissipated a

Posthumous portrait bust of Verrazzano. Courtesy Samuel H. Kress Collection, National Gallery of Art, Washington, D. C.

good part of his energy on love affairs, and the major share of his revenue in fighting the Emperor Charles V; but he was not indifferent to things of the sea. By marrying his cousin Claude, daughter of Louis XII and of Anne, Duchess of Brittany, he united that province of ships and sailors to the French crown, and, at one stroke, doubled the maritime potential of his kingdom. And for his Norman duchy he began the fortification and reconstruction of Havre de Grace in 1516. The Queen Mother, Louise de Savoie, took such a keen interest in Magellan's voyage that Antonio Pigafetta, the Italian gentleman who made the complete circuit, visited her at court in 1523 and presented her with "certain things from the other hemisphere."

François-premier, one year younger than Henry VIII, resembled in many respects his English cousin, whom he met formally on the Field of the Cloth of Gold in 1520. Both were handsome, gallant, and courageous; both were arbitrary, arrogant, and intolerant; both patronized arts and letters. The French king differed from the English monarch in nourishing a strong pro-Italian bias. He invited Leonardo da Vinci, Cellini, Solario, and Primaticcio to his court; for army generals he chose a Pallavicini and a Montecuccoli; he had Italian ministers, bankers, mistresses, and chefs de cuisine; and, since the Spanish sovereigns had patronized an Italian navigator named Colombo, and Henry VII supported another named Caboto, the king of France must have one, too. Hence Verrazzano.

Spanish and Portuguese explorers, having covered the entire east coast of the Americas from Florida to Patagonia, could find no strait north of Magellan's; so the only two stretches left to investigate were Florida-Newfoundland and Labrador-Greenland. On every map of the New World hitherto drafted—always excepting Juan de La Cosa's and possibly the Egerton—Newfoundland floated aloof in the North Atlantic, or became a northern promontory of Asia. Between it and Florida lay a region extending over some thirteen degrees of latitude and covering the coast of the future United States from Maine to Georgia. Nobody yet knew anything about it, since nobody who crossed by the northern route, and returned, had pushed further south or west than the Bay of Fundy. Surely here, if anywhere, not in the frozen north which the English and Portuguese had failed to penetrate, would be found *the* Strait. Even better, one might find an open sea,

François Iᵉʳ, roi de France. Attributed to François Clouet. Musée du Louvre. Photo Giraudon.

which ships from western Europe could romp through to "the happy shores of Cathay," as Verrazzano called the coast of China.

Such was the opinion of a group of Italian bankers resident in Lyons, center of the French silk industry. They anticipated high profits from a discovery which would greatly lower the freight on silk. With royal patronage and approval they appointed as commander a master mariner of their own group, Giovanni da Verrazzano. One of the Lyons merchants, Bonacorso Rucellai, was not only a relative of the sea-going Florentine, but the banker for Jean Ango, the leading merchant-ship-owner of Rouen and Dieppe. Another, named Guadagni, was father or brother to Verrazzano's wife. The Guadagni were a leading Florentine family, banished in 1434; they settled at Lyons and became immensely wealthy. These Florentine bankers and merchants of Lyons formed a syndicate and, in March 1523, sent sums of money to some of their

Giovanni da Verrazzano. Late sixteenth-century copy of an earlier Florentine portrait. Courtesy of the Sig. Sindaco, municipio di Prato.

"De Guadagnis, Citizen of Florence," brother or father of Verrazzano's wife. Portrait Medal in Musée de Lyon. Photo Camponogara.

friends in Rouen to outfit the overseas expedition. Verrazzano also had a commission from François-premier, but it has not survived.

The Oliveriana Map (now at Pésaro), which we reproduced in part and described in the notes to Chapter VII above, may also have encouraged Verrazzano's search for a northern strait. As this map gives every indication of having been made in Florence for a princely individual, it is possible that Verrazzano, as a Florentine, had an opportunity to study it.

Giovanni da Verrazzano, Gentleman Explorer

In Tuscany, thirty miles south of Florence, one enters the Chianti country and a Tuscan landscape that has hardly changed since the painters of the *cinquecento* used it for backgrounds. Sparkling streams and rivers, bordered by conical hills, whose slopes are planted with vines almost to the summits; each hill-top crowned with a villa or a castle. By no means the least of these is the Castello Verrazzano, ancestral home of that noble family, whose arms are a six-pointed star.

It is a real castle with two stone towers for defense, but in the sixteenth century modern rooms were built, and a detached chapel, and a fish pond. Long has it been "comfortably accepted" (to quote Dr. Lawrence C. Wroth) that our Giovanni was born here in 1485. A recent French biographer denies this, giving Giovanni a new pair of parents, Alessandro da Verrazzano and Giovanna De Guadagni, and a Lyons birthplace. This is indignantly denied by everyone in the Chianti country, and ascribed to French chauvinism! Castello Verrazzano near Greve is indubitably the ancestral home, and as Giovanni and his brother were always referred to as Florentines, there is no sense quarreling whether they were born here or in the Florentine community of Lyons.

"This valiant gentleman," as Ramusio called him, differed from other heroes of northern exploration in that he was well born and well educated. All contemporary documents refer to him as such; some even call him a nobleman.

The Castello Verrazzano, Greve in Chianti. From a photo taken prior to recent "restoration." Courtesy Signor Carlo Baldini of Greve.

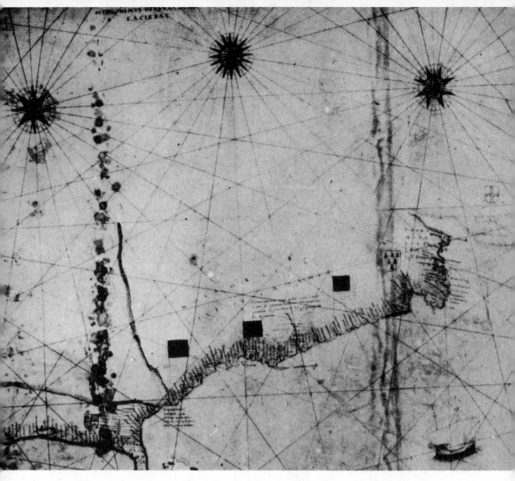

North American part of the Girolamo da Verrazzano World Map of 1529. Vatican Library. Note east shore of Pacific Ocean north and east of Florida. The three blacked-out flags are French; the arms of Brittany are north of Cape Breton, and the arms of England on the Labrador. The ship probably meant for *La Dauphine* is in the southeast corner. Photo by Giraudon.

If born in France, he was sent to Florence for his education, for the language of his Letter on the voyage of discovery and its literary allusions indicate that he received an upper-class Renaissance education. It also reveals that he knew more mathematics than most gentlemen of his time—or of ours.

The earliest actual fact that we know about him is that on attaining his majority, about 1506–7, he removed to Dieppe, in order to pursue a maritime career. A gossipy annalist of Dieppe, writing nearly three centuries later, stated that "Jean Verason," presumably our man, sailed in Ango's *La Pensée* to Newfoundland in 1508. In any case, the allusions to Carthage, Damascus, and the Saracens in the famous Letter prove that Verrazzano made voyages to the Levant, and there are hints that he was friendly with Magellan at Seville before the great circumnavigator's departure in 1517. A gentleman navigator, yes; but thoroughly professional.

None of the existing portraits of Verrazzano are contemporary with him, but as they all derive from one by Zocchi painted in his lifetime or shortly after, they may be assumed to be roughly correct. All show him with strong, confident features, black or dark brown hair, heavily bearded and mustachioed, with a prominent Roman nose; a thoroughly attractive and impressive figure.

By 1523, when he had attained the age of thirty-eight, Verrazzano had an impeccable maritime record, and as an Italian he appealed to the king. In the sixteenth century there was no hard-and-fast line between official voyages and privately financed voyages. Verrazzano borrowed *La Dauphine*, a ship of the royal French navy, and reported to the French king; but the Florentine bankers of Lyons and Rouen supplied most of the funds as well as the second ship, *La Normande*, which did not go far. *La Dauphine*, built in the new royal dockyard of Le Havre in 1519, was named after the dauphin François, heir to the throne, for whose birth the year before the great bell at Rouen tolled for twenty-four hours. She measured one hundred tuns and carried a crew of fifty; this was twice the burthen of Cabot's *Mathew*, and almost thrice the number of his crew. She probably flew the royal ensign of azure sprinkled with gold fleurs-de-lys. *La Normande* was a merchant ship chartered by the Lyons bankers from Jean Ango. In notes to Chapter VIII you will find the amount and kind of provisions then considered suitable for a ship with a crew of sixty for seventy days; multiply it by three, and we will have a fair picture of what *La Dauphine* carried as provisions for eight months. The vessel we have reproduced here as her possible portrait is depicted on Girolamo da Verrazzano's map, sailing west along the route he took, and one may hazard the guess that Girolamo meant her to represent Giovanni's ship.*

The outfitting took place at Dieppe, probably under the eyes of Jean

---

* One may object that the ship on the chart does not seem big enough for a 100-tunner; for what Norman ships of that burthen then looked like, see those reproduced in Chapter VIII from a contemporary map of Normandy.

A ship, probably *La Dauphine*. From the Vatican Verrazzano Map. This ship is sailing on a course from Madeira to Florida, and is the right burthen. Note the furled mizzen, as she is running free.

Ango, who owned *La Normande*. Spies reported to D. João III of Portugal that French mischief was afoot; this Florentine boasts that he is going "to discover Cathay," but his real objective may be a raid on Brazil. Be on your guard, Your Majesty!

Verrazzano should have had a fleet of four ships, but a tempest in the autumn of 1523 disposed of two, and only *La Normande* and *La Dauphine* were left. They put in for refuge at a Breton port, and after repairs started south in company, taking a number of prizes off the coast of Spain. For reasons unexplained, probably because she had to escort the prizes to France, *La Normande* peeled off, and *La Dauphine* alone continued to America.

We have not the name of a single shipmate of Verrazzano's, except that of his brother Girolamo, the map-maker. Giovanni, even less generous than Columbus in giving credit to subordinates, does not mention a single person in his official Letter to François-premier, and he refers to the crew as *la turba marittima*—the maritime mob. They had good reason to dislike him, as *La Dauphine* almost always anchored in an uncomfortable roadstead, and they had shore liberty but once in the entire voyage.

Before sailing, Verrazzano made his will: "Le noble homme Jehan Verrassenne, capitaine des navires esquippez pour un voiage des Indes," named brother Girolamo his heir and made him co-executor with Rucellai, his banker cousin. And in his official letter to François-premier he made the object of the expedition perfectly clear: "My intention on this voyage was to reach Cataia and the extreme eastern coast of Asia, not expecting to find such a barrier of new land as I did find; and, if I did find such a land, I estimated that it would not lack a strait to penetrate to the Eastern Ocean"—i.e. the Pacific.

We have no hint as to what navigational instruments Verrazzano had at his disposal. That he took a keen interest in scientific navigation is indicated by his keeping a day book or journal (which has not survived), and by making an honest effort to determine longitude. His latitudes, more accurate than any prior to Cartier's, suggest that he was not confined to Columbus's imperfect instruments, the triangular wooden quadrant, with its tiddly plumb-bob on a thread, and the mariner's astrolabe; that he had at least one of the newly invented *balestilas*, or cross-staffs. But we cannot be certain, for it took a long time for new inventions to be adopted by sailors. The Ribero World Map of 1529, made subsequent to the voyages of Verrazzano, Gomez, and Ayllón, illustrates the quadrant and astrolabe, but no cross-staff.

From Deserta to the "Isthmus"

Verrazzano's plan for his ocean crossing ran parallel to that of Columbus in 1492; but instead of dropping down to latitude 28°N and the Canaries, he chose to take off from Las Desertas in the Madeira group at latitude 32°30'N. French corsairs had already been preying on the Spanish treasure fleets, Spanish warships were looking for prowling Frenchmen, and Verrazzano obviously wished to avoid hostile confrontations in order to carry out his mission. The Madeiras were Portuguese.

On 17 January 1524 *La Dauphine* said farewell to the Old World. The latitude the Captain chose for the crossing lay well above the normal range of easterly trade winds, but for about three weeks *La Dauphine* enjoyed them: "Sailing with a zephyr blowing east-southeast with sweet and gentle mildness," as he puts it in his Letter. Like Columbus, Verrazzano appreciated the beauty of smooth seas and prosperous winds, and on the northerly edge of the trades he had them at their best.

On 24 February he ran out of luck, and encountered as sharp and severe a tempest as he or his shipmates had ever experienced. "With the divine help and merciful assistance of Almighty God and the soundness of our ship, accompanied with the good hap of her fortunate name, we were delivered," wrote Verrazzano. He altered course to west by north, and then turned west on latitude 34°N. Thus he made landfall on or about 1 March 1524 at or near Cape Fear, which is on latitude 33°50'47"N; Verrazzano said it was on 34°, "like Carthage and Damascus." Near enough—Damascus is on 33°30'.* Note that this navigator, like Cabot, compared latitudes of his discoveries with known points in Europe, which meant something to those who read his report.

Cape Fear, southernmost of North Carolina's three capes (Fear, Lookout, and Hatteras), is a long alluvial promontory where the Cape Fear River has been depositing detritus for many millennia. The tip is formed by Bald Island, a tract of still unspoiled dunes and wet marsh where birds, fish, and turtle breed, and a live-oak forest grows, and the Frying Pan Shoals extend some fifteen miles farther out to sea. Verrazzano did not tarry, as he wished to explore the coast between there and Florida before turning northward. His distances are difficult to follow on the map, because every unit is "50 leagues" (about 110 nautical miles),** recalling St. Brendan's "forty days."

So, from her landfall, *La Dauphine* sailed south for "fifty leagues,"

---

* But what did Verrazzano mean by Carthage? Nobody then knew the exact site of Rome's ancient rival, but many thought it was Tripoli, which is on 32°54'N.
** I assume that Verrazzano used the French *petite lieue marine*, equivalent to between 2.2 and 2.31 English nautical miles (see note to Chapter XI below); but his brother Girolamo's map has a scale showing four Italian miles to the league, which must have been the same league that Columbus used, equaling 3.18 nautical miles.

then turned north again "in order not to meet with the Spaniards." '
Since she had not found any "convenient harbor whereby to come
a-land," the turning point must have been short of Charleston; on
Girolamo da Verrazzano's map this point is called *Dieppa*, after *La
Dauphine's* home port. Returning to the place of her landfall, she
anchored well off shore, probably in the lee of Cape Fear. Unlike other
mariners of the period, Verrazzano liked anchoring in an open roadstead, provided he found good holding ground. However, he sent a
boat ashore on or near Cape Fear, and briefly consorted with a group
of natives who "came harde to the Sea side, seeming to rejoyce very
much at the sight of us; and, marveiling greatly at our apparel, shape
and whiteness, showed us by sundry signs where we might most com-
modiously come a-land with our boat, offering us also of their victuals
to eat."

Verrazzano here describes their manners and customs "as farre as we
could have notice thereof":

> These people go altogether naked except only that they
> cover their privy parts with certain skins of beasts like unto
> martens, which they fasten onto a narrow girdle made of
> grass, very artificially [i.e. artfully] wrought, hanged about
> with tails of divers other beasts, which round about their
> bodies hang dangling down to their knees. Some of them wear
> garlands of birds' feathers. The people are of color russet, and
> not much unlike the Saracens; their hair black, thick, and not
> very long, which they tie together in a knot behind, and wear
> it like a tail. They are well featured in their limbs, of mean
> [average] stature, and commonly somewhat bigger than we;
> broad breasted, strong arms, their legs and other parts of their
> bodies well fashioned, and they are disfigured in nothing, sav-
> ing that they have somewhat broad visages, and yet not all of
> them; for we saw many of them well favoured, having black
> and great eyes, with a cheerful and steady look, not strong of
> body, yet sharp-witted, nimble and great runners, as far as we
> could learn by experience; and in those two last qualities they
> are like to them of the uttermost parts of China.

This reference to China indicates that Verrazzano was familiar with
The Book of Ser Marco Polo.

Continuing some distance northward, the Frenchmen again landed,
noted sand dunes fronting the upland palmettos, and bay bushes and
cypresses "which yield most sweet savours, far from the shore"—even
a hundred leagues out. So he named this land *Selva di Lauri* (Forest of

Laurels), and *Campo di Cedri* (Field of Cedars). Like Columbus, Verrazzano had a genius for giving newly discovered places beautiful and appropriate names; but, unlike those given by Columbus, few of his names stuck. Unless an explorer is shortly followed by others, or by colonists of his nation, his names are quickly forgotten.

As laurel and cedar grow all along the coasts of Georgia and South Carolina, we cannot identify these places. Strange that neither the Florentine, nor the Englishmen who came here in 1585–90, mentioned the yucca palm, with its spiky fronds and great clusters of white blossoms. Possibly it did not grow that far north in the sixteenth century.

Continuing north-northeasterly, *La Dauphine* anchored again in an open roadstead and sent a boat ashore. Here is how Hakluyt translates Verrazzano's story of the encounter:

> While we rode on that coast, partly because it had no harbor, and for that we wanted water, we sent our boat ashore with 25 men; where, by reason of great and continual waves that beat against the shore, being an open coast without succour, none of our men could possibly go ashore without losing our boat. We saw there many people, which came unto the shore, making divers signs of friendship, and showing that they were content we should come a-land, and by trial we found them to be very courteous and gentle, as your majesty shall understand by the success. To the intent we might send them of our things, which the Indians commonly desire and esteem, as sheets of paper, glasses, bells and such trifles, we sent a young man, one of our mariners, ashore, who swimming towards them, cast the things upon the shore. Seeking afterwards to return, he was with such violence of the waves beaten upon the shore, that he was so bruised that he lay there almost dead, which the Indians perceiving, ran to catch him, and drawing him out, they carried him a little way off from the sea.

The young man, fearing to be killed, "cried out piteously," but these Indians had no sinister intention. They laid him down at the foot of a sand dune to dry in the sun, and beheld him "with great admiration, marveling at the whiteness of his flesh." They then stripped him down and "made him warm at a great fire," which caused his shipmates to expect him to be roasted and eaten.

> The young man having recovered his strength, and having stayed awhile with them, showed them by signs that he was

The Bailly Globe, 1530, with "Sea of Verrazzano" showing the Verrazzano concept of North America. About half actual size. Courtesy J. Pierpont Morgan Library, New York.

desirous to return to the ship; and they with great love clapping him fast about with many embracings, accompanying
him unto the sea; and, to put him in more assurance, leaving
him alone they went unto a high ground and stood there, beholding him, until he was entered into the boat. This young
man observed, as we did also, that these are of color inclining
to black, as the other were; with their flesh very shining, of
mean stature, handsome visage, and delicate limbs, and of very
little strength; but of prompt wit. Farther we observed not.

This spot Verrazzano named *Annunziata* because the day was 25
March, the feast of the Annunciation of the Virgin. It must have been
on the Outer, or Carolina, Banks between Capes Lookout and Hatteras,
or a few miles north of Hatteras. According to his own marginal note,
Verrazzano here committed his great geographical error. He found
"an isthmus a mile in width and about 200 long, in which, from the
ship, we could see *el mare orientale* [the Pacific Ocean], halfway between West and North"; i.e. northwesterly. This sea, he says, "is the
same which flows around the shores of India, China and Cataya. . . ."
To this isthmus the discoverer gave the name *Verrazzania*, and the entire land discovered was called *Francesca* after King François.

This passage has attracted a good deal of scorn to the Florentine
mariner, but without justice. You may sail for twenty miles south and
twenty miles north of Cape Hatteras without seeing the mainland from
the deck or mast of a small sailing ship. We flew Verrazzano's route
on a beautiful June day with high visibility at an altitude of two hundred feet, and for fifty miles could see no land west of the Banks. Even
from the modern motor road, which (spliced out with car ferries)
extends along the Banks, the far shore is commonly invisible. Verrazzano is, however, open to two criticisms. (1) In view of his preference
for open roadsteads, why did he not anchor off one of the inlets and
send in a boat to explore? These inlets are always shifting, but we
cannot imagine that there were none in 1524, since the flow of fresh
water always breaks out new ones when an old one closes. Sir Walter
Raleigh's colonists found at least three in the 1580's with two fathom
of water in each. (2) Verrazzano must have been familiar with a similar topography, on a smaller scale, in the Venetian lagoon; but there
you can almost always see foothills from outside the Lido.

The Letter continues: "We sailed along this isthmus," i.e. the Outer
Banks, "in continual hope of finding some strait or northern promon-

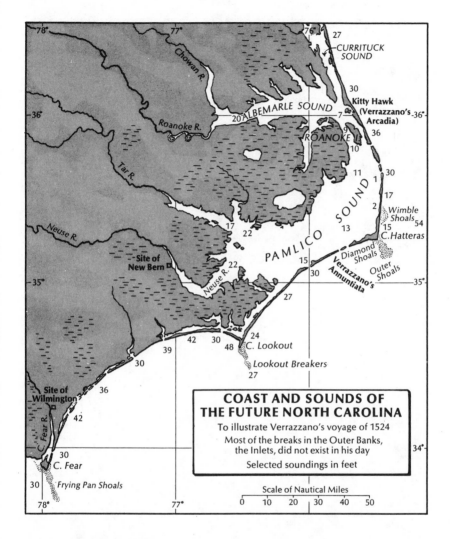

Map labels:

CURRITUCK SOUND
Chowan R.
Kitty Hawk
(Verrazzano's Arcadia)
ALBEMARLE SOUND
Roanoke R.
ROANOKE I.
Tar R.
Wimble Shoals
Neuse R.
PAMLICO SOUND
C. Hatteras
Site of New Bern
Diamond Shoals
Verrazzano's Annuntiata
Outer Shoals
Neuse R.
C. Lookout
Lookout Breakers
Site of Wilmington
C. Fear R.
C. Fear
Frying Pan Shoals

**COAST AND SOUNDS OF
THE FUTURE NORTH CAROLINA**
To illustrate Verrazzano's voyage of 1524
Most of the breaks in the Outer Banks,
the Inlets, did not exist in his day
Selected soundings in feet

Scale of Nautical Miles
0 10 20 30 40 50

tory at which the land would come to an end, in order to penetrate to
quelli felici liti del Catay" —those happy shores of Cathay.

Rather pathetic, is it not? Verrazzano and his shipmates straining
their eyes to find a bold, northward-looking promontory like Cape St.
Vincent or Finisterre, which *La Dauphine* could whip around in a
jiffy, and everyone on board would shout and yell, and the musicians
would strike up the *Vexilla Regis,* knowing that they had found the
long-sought Passage to India.

Verrazzano's "Pacific Ocean." The "Sea of Verrazzano" seen over the Carolina Outer Banks, each side of Cape Hatteras.

Thus Verrazzano assumed that he had sighted the Pacific Ocean
across an isthmus much narrower than that of Panama! This tremen-
dous error was perpetuated for a century or more by his brother
Girolamo and the Italian cartographer Maiollo. Their world maps give
North America a narrow waist around North Carolina, with the
Pacific Ocean flowing over some 40 per cent of the area of the future
United States. A good example is the Bailly Globe of 1530, which we
have reproduced here.

Et in Arcadia Ego

The next place where *La Dauphine* called, after the usual "fifty-league"
sail from Annunziata, "appeared to be much more beautiful [than the
other Outer Banks] and full of very tall trees." "We named it *Archadia*
owing to the beauty of the trees," recalling the Arcady of ancient
Greece.

The Arcadian concept, an ideal landscape inhabited by simple, virtu-
ous people, is derived from Virgil. In his *Eclogues* (x) he has the
lovesick Gallus say, "Arcadians, you will sing my frantic love for
Phyllis to your mountains, you alone who know how to sing; for you
have cool springs, soft meadows, and groves. Among you I shall grow
old, now that an insane love enchains me, and in the forest amidst the
dens of wild beasts carve the story of my loves on the tender bark of
trees: *crescent illae, crescetis amores;* as they grow, so shall my loves."
Virgil's story took a new lease on life in Jacopo Sannazzaro's fifteenth-
century novel *Arcadia*. This opens with a tribute to the tall, spreading
trees that grow wild on mountains, especially to the grove "of such
uncommon and extreme beauty," which flourishes on the summit of
Mount Parthenius in Arcadia. If not Virgil, Sannazzaro's novel, so
popular as to be printed at least fifteen times before *La Dauphine* set
sail, must have inspired Verrazzano to call this fair land after the fabulous province of ancient Peloponnesus.

After flying along the entire coast from Cape Fear River to Barnegat,
New Jersey, in search of a hilly section with big trees, I have no hesita-
tion in locating Verrazzano's Arcadia at Kitty Hawk, North Carolina,
the scene of the Wright brothers' pioneer flights in 1900–1903. Kill
Devil Hill, Kitty Hawk, although but 91 feet in elevation, is the highest natural eminence except Cape Henry (105 feet) on the coast be-

Arcadian landscape on Miller I Atlas. Courtesy Bibliothèque Nationale.

tween Florida and the Navesink Highlands. Already bare in the Wrights' day, as in ours, it was undoubtedly heavily wooded in Verrazzano's. Near by, under a high dune of tawny sand now called Engagement Hill, there is still a heavy forest growth of pine, live oak, red oak, bay, laurel, holly, and dogwood. Undoubtedly this was the most beautiful spot—to European eyes—that Verrazzano encountered on his voyage prior to New York Bay, and it is no wonder that he called there and spent three days, despite the lack of a harbor.

Moreover, Girolamo Verrazzano's map, immediately east of a misspelled Annuntiata, places *Lamàcra*—a misspelled L'Arcadia—and there are a dozen place names between it and New York Bay.

The doings of the Frenchmen were anything but Arcadian. Here is Verrazzano's account of a kidnapping:

> That we might have some knowledge thereof, we sent 20 men a land, which entered into the country about two leagues, and they found that the people were fled to the woods for fear. They saw only one old woman with a young maid of 18 or 20

Site of Verrazzano's Arcadia. Kill Devil Hill, Kitty Hawk, with the nearby forest, in June 1970.

years old, which, seeing our company, hid themselves in the
grass for fear; the old woman carried two infants on her shoulders, and behind her neck a child of 8 years old; the young
woman was laden likewise with as many. But when our men
came unto them, the women cried out; the old woman made
signs that the men were fled unto the woods as soon as they
saw us; to quiet them and to win their favor, our men gave
them such victuals as they had with them to eat, which the old
woman received thankfully; but the young woman disdained
them all, and threw them disdainfully on the ground. They
took a child from the old woman to bring into France, and,
going about to take the young woman (which was very
beautiful and of tall stature), they could not possibly, for the
great outcries that she made, bring her to the sea, and especially having great woods to pass through, and being far from
the ship, we purposed to leave her behind, bearing away the
child only.

Loud screaming, woman's first line of defense, here worked very well;
but one would like to know what became of the poor child, snatched
from his Arcadian people at a tender age.

"In Arcadia," continued Verrazzano, "we found a man who came
to the shore to see what [manner of men] we were. . . . He was
handsome, naked, his hair fastened in a knot, and of an olive color."
Approaching near a group of twenty Frenchmen, he thrust toward
them "a burning stick, as if to offer us fire." This must have been a
lighted tobacco pipe, and the poor fellow was simply making a friendly
gesture, offering the intruders a pipe of peace. They, having neither
seen nor heard of tobacco, took his intentions to be hostile and fired
a blank shot from a musket. At that the Indian "trembled all over with
fright" and "remained as if thunderstruck, and, like a friar, pointing a
finger at sky, ship and sea as if he were invoking a blessing on us."

Verrazzano describes the dugout canoes which the Indians constructed by burning out the interior of a hardwood log, and wild
grapevines that climb trees "as they do in Lombardy"; "roses, violets,
lilies, and many sorts of herbs, and sweet and odoriferous flowers, different from ours." The Indians wore leaves for clothing, and lived
mostly by fishing and fowling; but they offered him pulse (beans)
"differing in color and taste from ours, of good and pleasant taste."
La Dauphine remained in Arcadia for three days around 10 April,
anchoring, as usual, off shore; and the captain states that he would
have stayed longer but for the absence of a harbor.

Arcadia is one of three place names of Verrazzano's which have survived, but later map-makers continually moved it eastward until it became *L'Acadie*, the French name for Nova Scotia, New Brunswick, and part of Maine. Verrazzano must have been very bored, as he sailed northward, to find the same long, thin, sandy islands fronting lagoons, with only two breaks—the Virginia Capes and the Delaware Capes. He missed these entrances to Chesapeake and Delaware bays, which he surely would have explored as possible straits to Cathay. Prudently avoiding shoal water, he evidently sailed *La Dauphine* so far out to sea that these great bays were not visible.

After Barnegat, New Jersey, he closed the shore and began observing places more to his liking. He anchored every night off shore; named one promontory *Bonivet*, after the grand admiral of France; and a river *Vendôme*, after Charles de Bourbon, duc de Vendôme; but it is impossible to locate these from his vague directions. A coast "green with forests" which he called *Lorraine*, after one of the titles of Jean Cardinal Guise, was probably New Jersey.

Verrazzano was the first North American explorer to name places newly discovered after personalities and beloved spots at home. His predecessors generally confined themselves to descriptive names, such as codfish, grapes, boldness, or flatness, adding a few saints' names appropriate to the date of the landfall. The Florentine set a precedent which most of his successors honored; Cartier, for instance, used some of the same names, and a few of them have survived.

One thing is certain: *La Dauphine* was favored by extraordinarily good luck in weather. To sail along the coast from South Carolina to New York, in the turbulent spring of the year, and anchor off shore without mishap, is an exploit that any merchant captain under sail, and some steamship masters too, might well envy. The United States Coast Guard estimates that there are six hundred wrecks off the Carolina Outer Banks. On the *National Geographic's* map of them, the names of known wrecks in historic times are so close together as to seem continuous. When Verrazzano's Letter was published in 1841, many a practical seaman said, "It cannot be—the fellow is a fraud and a fake!" But there the record is, in black and white, from an honest captain; and who are we to deny it? But for his tragic end, we might conclude Verrazzano to have been especially favored by the gods of the sea and the winds.

Four personages of the French court, for whom Verrazzano named places on the American coast: François le Dauphin; Louise de Savoie, duchesse d'Angoulême and Queen Mother; la duchesse de Vendôme, née d'Alençon; le seigneur de Bonnivet, amiral de France. From Gower, ed., *Three Hundred French Portraits*, 1875; Moreau-Nélaton, *Les Clouet et leurs Émules;* and Originals in Dêpot des Étampes, Bibliothèque Nationale.

Angoulême and Refugio

"In space of 100 leagues sailing," continues Verrazzano, "we found a very pleasant place, situated amongst certain little steep hills; from amidst the which hills there ran down into the sea a great stream of water, which within the mouth was very deep, and from the sea to the mouth of same, with the tide, which we found to rise 8 foot, any great vessel laden may pass up."

This description well fits New York Bay; the hills, the first he had seen since Kitty Hawk, might have been the Navesink Highlands, Staten Island, or Brooklyn Heights. The day was 17 April, *La Dauphine* sailed gently before a soft southwest wind, and New York Bay never looked fairer than on this very first day when European eyes gazed upon it.

The rest of Verrazzano's brief account indicates that he anchored in the Narrows, now renamed after him and spanned by the Verrazzano Bridge:

> But because we rode at anchor in a place well fenced from the wind, we would not venture ourselves without knowledge of the place, and we passed up with our boat only into the said river, and saw the country very well peopled. The people are almost like unto the others, and clad with feathers of fowls of divers colors. They came towards us very cheerfully, making great shouts of admiration, showing us where we might come to land most safely with our boat. We entered up the said river into the land about half a league, where it made a most pleasant lake about 3 leagues in compass; on the which they rowed from the one side to the other, to the number of 30 of their small boats, wherein were many people, which passed from one shore to the other to come and see us. And behold, upon the sudden (as it is wont to fall out in sailing) a contrary flaw of wind coming from the sea, we were enforced to return to our ship, leaving this land, to our great discontentment for the great commodity and pleasantness thereof, which we suppose is not without some riches, all the hills showing mineral matters in them.

Verrazzano showed good judgment in weighing anchor and standing out to sea, rather than risk dragging ashore in the Narrows. But we wish he could have spent more than one day at the site of the future city, and not confined himself to this brief description of it and the feather-clad natives. His short boat tour indicates that he regarded the

New York Bay

Narrows as part of the river, and that the "pleasant lake" about ten miles in circumference was the Upper Bay. Of the Hudson River he viewed only the mouth; and if he noticed the East River he probably figured that it flowed from the same source as the "Great" (Hudson) River, verdant Manhattan Island dividing the river's lower course so that it emptied into the sea by two mouths. He named this part of the country *Angoulême*, the title of François-premier before he became king, and the bay *Santa Margarita* in honor of the king's sister, Marguerite, duchesse d'Alençon, who (he explains), "surpassed every other woman for modesty and intelligence." (She is best known as the authoress of the *Heptaméron*, which she wrote after she had become queen of Navarre.) He also named a promontory *Alençon* after her, somewhere on the Jersey coast.

"We weighed anchor," continues the Letter," and sailed toward the East, for so the coast trended, and always for 80 leagues,* being in the sight thereof, we discovered an island in the form of a triangle, distant from the mainland 10 leagues, about the bigness of the Island of the Rhodes. It was full of hills covered with trees, well peopled, for we saw fires all along the coast. We gave it the name of your Majesty's mother, not staying there by reason of the weather being contrary." From the fact that La Dauphine immediately scudded into Narragansett Bay to escape foul weather making up, it is clear that this triangular island, which recalled Rhodes to Verrazzano, and which he named Luisa after the Queen Mother, was Block Island. The French later called it Claudia after the queen of France, and the Dutch renamed it after one of the navigators in the early seventeenth century.

Here, inadvertently and astonishingly, Verrazzano named a future State of the Union. Roger Williams, founder of the colony and state to which Block Island has always belonged, wrote a letter in 1637 dated "at Aquednetick, now called by us Rode Island." On 13 March 1644 the colonial assembly declared, "Aquethneck shall be henceforth called the Ile of Rhods or Rhod-Island." And in 1663 the name Rhode Island was applied to the colony. Roger Williams, a well-read gentleman and scholar, must have brought to New England a copy of either edition of Hakluyt which contains a translation of Verrazzano's Letter, and interpreted his island "about the bignesse of the Ilande of the Rodes, . . . full of hilles, covered with trees" as Aquidneck. That is the big island in Narragansett Bay, the future seat of Newport; and its shape does resemble that of Rhodes in the Aegean. Thus, the smallest state of the Union owes her name to Roger Williams's mistaken notion of the island which Verrazzano compared to Rhodes!

The natives who flocked around La Dauphine in canoes as she anchored a few miles outside Narragansett Bay on a hard, boulder-strewn bottom were so friendly that Verrazzano (doubtless to the joy of his crew) decided to make an exception to his practice of mooring in the open. Piloted by an Indian he sailed La Dauphine into the bay. Leaving the future Point Judith and Beaver Tail to port, he noted the little rocky islands now called The Dumplings as a suitable place for a coast-defense fort; the American patriots of 1775 agreed

---

* I.e. 176 miles, if I have the right factor for the French league, and that is not far off. From the Narrows outside Long Island to Block Island is about 150 nautical miles.

Verrazzano's *Petra Viva*. The Dumpling Rocks off Conanicut Island, Brenton Point in the background. Photo of about 1885, courtesy Mr. Wm. King Covell.

with him and fortified the biggest islet. Verrazzano punningly named this cluster of rocks *Petra Viva* after the wife of Antonio Gondi, one of his banker promoters; her maiden name was Marie-Catherine de Pierre-Vive. The native pilots conducted *La Dauphine* to a completely sheltered anchorage, the present Newport Harbor, behind the highest point of Aquidneck. There he spent a fortnight palavering with the natives—but he never did hear about a Portuguese, Miguel Corte Real, having been their chief only thirteen years earlier.

These Indians were the Wampanoag, whose domain extended over the eastern side of Narragansett Bay and southeastern Massachusetts. They had lately taken Aquidneck from the Narragansett tribe and were apprehensive about a comeback. This in part accounts for their friendliness to the Frenchmen and, almost a century later, to the Pilgrim Fathers.

Verrazzano's description of the Wampanoag corresponds closely to what Roger Williams later wrote about them. They came on board fearlessly after the Captain had caused a few "bells and glasses and many toys" to be tossed into their canoes. Among the visitors were two "kings," one about forty and the other about twenty years old. Each was clothed in a deerskin artistically embroidered with dyed por-

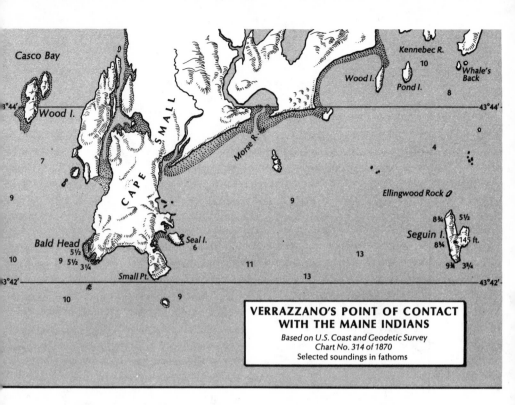

Map labels:

Casco Bay

Kennebec R.

Wood I.

Whale's Back

Pond I.

Wood I.

43°44'

43°44'

CAPE SMALL

Morse R.

Ellingwood Rock

Bald Head

Seal I.

Seguin I.

145 ft.

Small Pt.

43°42'

43°42'

**VERRAZZANO'S POINT OF CONTACT
WITH THE MAINE INDIANS**
Based on U.S. Coast and Geodetic Survey
Chart No. 314 of 1870
Selected soundings in fathoms

cupine quills, and, as an emblem of office, "a large chain garnished with divers stones of sundry colors." "This is the goodliest people, and of the fairest conditions, that we have found in this our voyage," wrote Verrazzano; "they exceed us in bigness," are comely, "with long black hair, which they are very careful to trim"; their eyes are "black and quick," and their color, various shades of "brasse." Their bodies are well proportioned, "as appertaineth to any handsome man." The women, too, are "very handsome and well favored," and "as well mannered and continent as any women of good education. They are all naked, save their privy parts, which they cover with a deer's skin, branched or embroidered, as the men use." Some "wear on their arms very rich skins of leopards." They use elaborate head-dressings "like unto the women of Egypt and Syria," and ornaments made of their own hair hang down on both sides of their breasts. "When they are married, men as well as women wear divers toys, according to the usage of Asiatics." For "toys" we should read trinkets or gewgaws; and for leopard skins, those of wildcats or lynxes.

Verrazzano particularly noted the Wampanoags' most valued possessions, "plates of wrought copper, which they esteem more than gold."

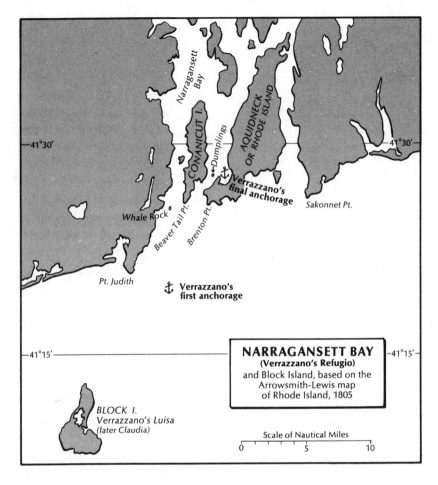

Inside the map:

Narragansett Bay

CONANICUT I.

Dumplings

AQUIDNECK OR RHODE ISLAND

41°30'

Verrazzano's final anchorage

Sakonnet Pt.

Whale Rock

Beaver Tail Pt.

Brenton Pt.

Pt. Judith

⚓ Verrazzano's first anchorage

41°15'

NARRAGANSETT BAY
(Verrazzano's Refugio)
and Block Island, based on the
Arrowsmith-Lewis map
of Rhode Island, 1805

41°15'

BLOCK I.
Verrazzano's Luisa
(later Claudia)

Scale of Nautical Miles
0   5   10

These copper plates, which they obtained by trade from tribes of the Great Lakes region, were the native jewelry; they were mistaken for early Norse on the Indian remains which Longfellow celebrated as "The Skeleton in Armor." The bells which Verrazzano gave them, and which he says they "esteemed most" after copper, were tiny spherical hawks' bells, which Columbus found to be greatly prized by natives of the Caribbean; and the blue crystal beads next in favor were no doubt Venetian. These were used as earrings or necklaces. Strangely enough, the Wampanoag had no use for cloth—peltry suited them better—nor did they want iron or steel implements to replace their stone axes.

The one disappointing thing about these natives, from the crew's point of view, was the men's concern for the chastity of their women. Every day, when anchored in the future Newport Harbor, "The people repaired to see our ship, bringing their wives with them, whereof they are very jealous." While they came on board and stayed "a good space," their poor wives had to sit stolidly in canoes. If it was a royal visit, the queen and her ladies stayed in a canoe at Goat Island "while the king abode a long space in our ship, . . . viewing with great admiration all the furniture," and demanding to know its use. "He took likewise great pleasure in beholding our apparel, and in tasting our meats, and so courteously taking his leave departed." Landing on the island, "The king drawing his bow, and running up and down with his gentlemen, made much sport to gratify our men."

During the fifteen days that *La Dauphine* tarried in Newport Harbor, parties of sailors explored the interior for some thirty miles. They noted plains near the present Pawtucket, fertile soil, and woods of oak and walnut; they flushed game such as "luzernes" (lynxes) and deer, which the Indians took in nets or shot with flint and jasper arrowheads; they admired the native houses covered with mats, and the cornfields; and they undoubtedly found means to frolic with Indian girls when their lords and masters were away hunting.

Verrazzano also wrote that the Wampanoag were "very pitiful and charitable towards their neighbors, . . . make great lamentations in their adversity," and at their death "use mourning, mixed with singing, which continueth for a long space." These prolonged bouts of mourning were a characteristic of the Algonkin and other Indian nations of the northeast. Roger Williams recorded that Wampanoag families went into mourning for "something a quarter, halfe, yea a whole yeere," during which time they considered it "a prophane thing" to play, or "to paint themselves for beauty." As bad as English court mourning in the reign of Queen Victoria!

Following Cabot's practice of noting comparative latitudes, Verrazzano adds, "This land is situated in the parallel of Rome, in 41 degrees and 2 terces"; i.e. 41°40′ N. The center of Newport is on 41°30′ N, and the Vatican is on 41°54′ N. This proves, even better than his earlier comparison of his landfall with Damascus, that the Captain was a competent celestial navigator. He must have "taken" the sun and Polaris frequently and averaged them; Rome's latitude he could have obtained from any printed Ptolemy or rutter.

This fortnight at the site of Newport must have been the most en-
joyable part of the voyage, from the point of view of *La Dauphine*'s
sailors.

Maine—"Land of Bad People"

On 5 or 6 May, *La Dauphine* resumed her voyage eastward, passing
Sakonnet Point, which Verrazzano named *Jovium Promontorium* after
his friends, the Giovio family of Como. The Captain sailed through
Vineyard Sound, Nantucket Sound, and Pollock Rip (which daunted
the *Mayflower* in 1620) rather than around Martha's Vineyard and
Nantucket. The treacherous shoals where, in spots, there was only
three feet of water, he called *Armellini*, possibly by way of a crack at
Francesco Cardinal Armellino, a prelate much disliked for his avarice
and his success at collecting papal taxes. Next, the ship rounded *un
eminente promontorio*, which Verrazzano named *Pallavisino* after Pallavicini, one of the king's Italian generals. This must have been Cape
Cod; *eminente* means "outstanding," which that Cape certainly is.

Stretching across Massachusetts Bay, *La Dauphine* hit the coast of
Maine at or near Casco Bay. Verrazzano described the land as fair,
open, and bare, with high mountains (the White Mountains) visible far
inland. But the Abnaki natives, although they looked like the Wampanoag, were "of such crudity and evil manners, so barbarous, that
despite all the signs we could make, we could never converse with
them. They are clothed in peltry of bear, lynx, 'sea wolves' and other
beasts. Their food, as far as we could perceive, often entering their
dwellings, we suppose to be obtained by hunting and fishing, and of
certain fruits, a kind of wild root." These were ground-nuts, which
the early settlers of New England found to be a good substitute for
bread.

Wherever the crew came ashore, these Indians raised loud war-
whoops, shot at them with arrows, and fled into the forest. But they
consented to trade meagerly with a French boat crew from a rocky
cliff on the seashore, letting down in a basket on a line "what it pleased
them to give us . . . taking nothing but knives, fishhooks, and tools
to cut withall." The latitude of the place where this happened, says
Verrazzano, was 43°40′ N, and the only two spots in that area whence
one could let down a basket on a line into a small boat are Seguin Island

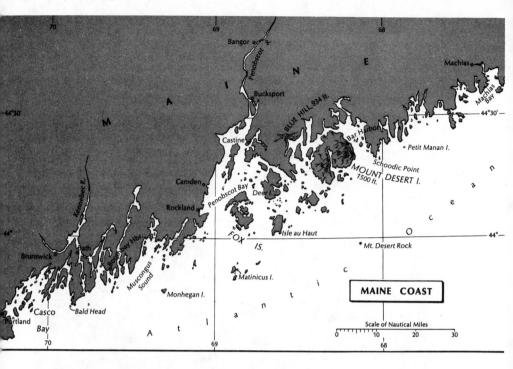

Map labels (reading around the map):

70 · 69 · 68

Bangor

Penobscot R.

N · E

Bucksport

Machias

44°30′ — Machias Bay

I

A

M

BLUE HILL, 934 ft.

Castine

Bar Harbor

Petit Manan I.

Schoodic Point

MOUNT DESERT I. 1500 ft.

Camden

Penobscot Bay

Deer I.

Rockland

n

a

e

c

Kennebec R.

FOX IS.

Isle au Haut

O · 44°—

Mt. Desert Rock

Brunswick

Bath

Boothbay Hbr.

Muscongus Sound

Matinicus I.

c

Monhegan I.

i

MAINE COAST

Casco

Bald Head

Portland

Bay

t

n

a

Scale of Nautical Miles

0 · 10 · 20 · 30

A

70 · 69 · 68

(latitude 43°42′) and Bald Head, at the tip of Cape Small (latitude 43°43′ N), the eastern entrance to Casco Bay. Both are cliffy and steep-to; Bald Head is the more probable place, as it is on the mainland. What displeased the Frenchmen more than the awkward method of trading were the Indians' uncouth manners; at parting they used "all signs of discourtesy and disdain, as was possible for any brute creature to invent, such as exhibiting their bare behinds and laughing immoderately." One can well picture this scene—glowering Frenchmen in the boat, braves exhibiting bare buttocks, little boys urinating, and men, women, and children raising just such an unholy clamor of whoops, laughs, shouts, and yells as only Indians could make. Since North American natives were usually friendly to the first Europeans they encountered, and hostile only after being abused or cheated, this attitude of the Abnaki suggests an earlier visit by foreigners raiding the Maine coast for slaves. However that may be, Verrazzano gave this coast a bad name, *Terra Onde di Mala Gente* (Land of Bad People), as it is called on his brother's map.

La Dauphine continued northeasterly along the Maine coast, counting in the space of fifty leagues some thirty-two islands "lying all near the land, being small and pleasant to the view, high, and having many turnings and windings between them, making many fair harbors and

Isabeau d'Albret, vicomtesse de Rohan. Portrait by Clouet in Musée Municipal de Lille. Photo by Giraudon. Courtesy of the Musée and of Professor Michel Mollat.

channels, as they do in the gulf of Venice in Illyria and Dalmatia." A very apt comparison: the Dalmatian coast always reminds one of Maine, and Maine of Dalmatia.

May on the Maine coast is a joy to all seamen—when the fog does not roll in. Verrazzano not only admired the excellent harbors but appreciated the beauty of this region—white fleecy clouds, turquoise sea flashing in the sunlight, islands where the shad-bush flings out masses of white blossoms among somber evergreens. He named the three biggest islands that he passed after three young princesses at the French court—*le tre figlie di Navarra*, "the three daughters of Navarre." These were Anne, Isabeau, and Catherine, daughters of Jean, duc d'Albret, and Catherine de Foix, queen of Navarre. They were then between fifteen and eighteen years old, celebrated for their beauty, and as orphans spent much time at the French court. The islands thus honored were Monhegan, Isle au Haut, and Mount Desert. These stand out above all others as one sails wide along that coast, and all have a natural beauty worthy to be compared to that of the lovely daughters of Navarre.

Here Verrazzano added another word to American nomenclature. Near the Daughters of Navarre, on his brother's Vatican map, appears *Oranbega*. This is obviously Norumbega, which in the Abnaki language means a stretch of quiet water between two falls or rapids. That fits in well with the spot on the Penobscot River which later writers magnified into the capital of a region. Its appearance on the Verrazzano

Monhegan Island. Photo by Augustus Phillips.

Mount Desert Island, from Mount Desert Rock. Photo by Augustus Phillips.

map is puzzling; his brother's relations with the Abnaki were brief and brusque, yet it is the only native Indian name on the map. After the voyage, map-makers and writers began to expand Norumbega to cover the entire region between the Hudson and the St. Lawrence, complete with a rich and noble city of the same name on the Penobscot River, and in the first printing of Verrazzano's Letter, by Ramusio, it is captioned as "Della Terra de Norumbega." *

La Dauphine now ran into easterly winds and had to beat to windward, making good an east-northeast course. This neatly covered the rest of Maine. After sailing for 150 leagues, missing the Bay of Fundy and most of the future Nova Scotia, she "approached the land that in times past was discovered by the British, which is in fifty degrees." There, says Verrazzano, "Having spent all our naval stores and victuals, and having discovered 700 leagues and more of new country, we topped off with water and wood and decided to return to France." In view of his remarkable accuracy in taking latitudes, we may conclude that Verrazzano sailed along the east coast of Newfoundland and took his departure from Cape Fogo or Funk Island (latitude 49°50'). Both his brother's and the Maiollo map cover Newfoundland. They use

* See Chapter XIV for further consideration of Norumbega.

the old Portuguese place names instead of applying new French ones, suggesting that they had a Portuguese chart on board and claimed no new discovery.

The ship made a speedy passage, a little more than two weeks, and had safely anchored at Dieppe by 8 July 1524, the day that Verrazzano dated his Letter to François-premier. It concludes with the gallant Captain's prayer that God and his majesty may help him to bring this initial step to a perfect end, so that, in the holy words of the evangelist (Romans ix. 18), *in omnem terram exivit sonus eorum*, . . . "Their sound went into all the earth, and their words unto the ends of the world."

End of the Voyage, and of Giovanni

Near the end of his Letter Verrazzano makes some interesting observations on the longitude of his discovery. He states that if a degree on the equator is 62.5 miles (as he was using Italian miles of 1480 meters, or 1619 yards, this was an underestimate), a degree of longitude at latitude 34° N, upon which he endeavored to cross the Atlantic, is fifty-two miles. He and his officers kept careful estimates of distance, making daily meridian elevations of the sun, and decided that they had sailed 4800 miles, land to land. This, divided by fifty-two, assured Verrazzano that *La Dauphine* had crossed 92 degrees of longitude. But the true difference in longitude between Deserta and Cape Fear is about 61.5 degrees! This 50 per cent overestimate was due in part to the Captain's underestimate of the length of the degree, and in part to exaggerating the speed of his ship. Columbus erred similarly; any sailor will condone a mistake of that nature.

Nevertheless, this miscalculation enabled Verrazzano to state emphatically what his predecessors had said less firmly, that the coast between Florida and Newfoundland belonged to a completely New World. It might, he admitted, be joined to northern Europe in the Arctic regions, but the land he had coasted was no promontory of Asia, as many map-makers had depicted it, and would long go on doing. This insistence on the newness of the New World cancels Verrazzano's earlier mistake about the false isthmus. Unfortunately, Ramusio omitted this from his early version of the Letter, so it did not circulate. Verrazzano and Cartier were not the last navigators to look for

"Cathay" just around the corner. Frobisher, as we shall see, thought that the north side of his bay in Baffin Island was part of Asia. As late as 1638, when Jean Nicolet was sent as envoy to the Winnebago tribe, he provided himself with an embroidered robe of Chinese damask, just in case he should meet Chinese mandarins!

Verrazzano sounded a note of reasoned optimism. Although he had not found the Northern Strait and had written it off as non-existent in those latitudes, he had discovered a vast continental mass which could be of immense value to France. He hoped to be allowed to follow it up. Unfortunately for France, he returned at the very worst time for organizing a second voyage. François-premier, preparing to resume his interminable war against Charles V and to carry it into Italy, gave the discoverer an audience at Lyons and, in a moment of enthusiasm, allotted him four ships for a second voyage; but he decided that they were needed for coastal defense and canceled the order. His Italian campaign ended disastrously in the battle of Pavia on 26 February 1525; the king lost his army and for a year his freedom, and would have lost his throne but for the sagacious regency of his mother, Louise of Savoy. Nor did Verrazzano impress his banker supporters; the samples of drugs, gold ore, and "aromatic liquors" that he brought home proved to be spurious or worthless, and the bankers were not interested in a long view of future values. They missed the chance to obtain Manhattan Island for even less than the traditional $24 worth of goods.

The discoverer, after considering (it was rumored) and rejecting good offers from Henry VIII and D. João III of Portugal to enter their service, turned for support to Jean Ango of Dieppe and Philippe de Chabot, sieur de Brion and admiral of France. Giovanni received the command, and the right to one-sixth of the profits. In the spring of 1527 the fleet sailed from Dieppe. Off the Cape Verde Islands one ship separated in a gale and the sailors of the two others mutinied, insisting on returning home; but as they knew nothing of navigation, Verrazzano fooled them, nipped across the Atlantic Narrows to Brazil, cut and loaded a cargo of logwood, and returned to Dieppe in mid-September of the same year. The fourth vessel eventually made the Brazilian coast and she too loaded logwood. This "Brazil wood," in great demand for dyeing cloth, sold well to the clothiers of Rouen.

Verrazzano had never renounced his ambition to find a new strait through the Americas. The dyewood profits suggested to him and his backers a means of combining exploration with profit—seek the strait in a region where, if you failed to find it, you could cut a cargo of logwood. Accordingly they arranged a third voyage, consisting of two or three ships, with Verrazzano's flag in *La Flamengue* of Fécamp. They departed Dieppe in the spring of 1528. Our sole knowledge of what happened on this voyage, which ended fatally for the Captain, is derived from a few words in Ramusio's collection of voyages, and a poem by Giulio Giovio, nephew and disciple of the humanist Paolo Giovio. Girolamo the map-maker, who survived, told the tragic tale to both Giovii, and Giulio wrote of it in a long narrative, *Storia Poetica*.

This fleet crossed the Atlantic by a route slightly north of Columbus's. First raising the coast of Florida, Verrazzano sailed to the Bahamas and then shaped a course for the Isthmus of Darien, intending probably to investigate the Gulf of Darien for a possible strait. En route he changed his mind and followed the chain of the Lesser Antilles. There he made the mistake of anchoring well off shore, as he customarily did. Unfortunately, the island where he chose to call—probably Guadeloupe—was inhabited by no gentle tribe of Indians, but by ferocious, man-eating Caribs. The Verrazzano brothers rowed shoreward in the ship's boat. A crowd of natives waited at the water's edge, licking their chops at the prospect of a human lunch; but the French as yet knew nought of this nation of cannibals. Giovanni innocently waded ashore along while Girolamo and the boat's crew plied their oars far enough off the beach to avoid the breakers. The Caribs, expert at murder, overpowered and killed the great navigator, then cut up and ate his still quivering body whilst his brother looked on helplessly, seeing the "sand ruddy with fraternal blood." The ships were anchored too far off shore to render gunfire support.

Questo infelice fine hebbe questo valente gentilhuomo, wrote Ramusio. "To so miserable an end came this valiant gentleman."

From subsequent lawsuits we know that *La Flamengue* continued her voyage to Brazil, and in March 1529 brought back a cargo of logwood to Brittany. Girolamo, after finishing his chart showing the 1524 voyage, sailed back to Brazil in 1529 as master of the ship *La Bonne Aventure* of Le Havre.

Verrazzano may have opened for France a lucrative trade with Brazil, but the results of his voyage along the North American coast were largely negative. The "Isthmus" and "Sea" of Verrazzano, his only positive contributions, turned out to be pure fantasies—but they influenced North American cartography for over a century. By reporting the absence of any strait between Florida and Nova Scotia, he turned the exploratory efforts of France and England northward; Jacques Cartier took up the quest where Verrazzano left off, and Frobisher continued it, further north. Neither discovered "the happy shores of Cathay," but empire followed in their wakes, whilst France completely ignored that of *La Dauphine*, which subtended a land of riches immeasurable—the Carolinas, Virginia, New York, New England. But it was not Verrazzano's fault that the French government remained indifferent to the opportunities that he opened.

There is no blinking the fact that Verrazzano missed many important places, and that he was singularly incurious. His habit of avoiding harbors caused him to miss great bays such as the Chesapeake, the Delaware, and the Hudson estuary, leaving them for the English, Dutch, and Swedes to explore and colonize in the following century. His failure to take a good look at the mouth of the Hudson River is perhaps the greatest opportunity missed by any North American explorer. But no sailor will blame him for missing things, since most of them have done so themselves. The great Captain Cook missed Sydney Harbor. Drake and all the Spanish navigators missed the Golden Gate and San Francisco Bay, which were discovered by an overland expedition. Why, even Des Barres's Royal Navy team of surveyors in 1770 missed Northeast Harbor, Maine!

Let us, however, judge Verrazzano by what he tried to do, rather than by what he accomplished. If he failed to find the strait "to the happy shores of Cathay," it was because it was not there; his attainable vision of a New France stretching from Newfoundland to Florida faded because king and country were not interested. His greatest ambition, as his brother told Ramusio, had been to people the regions he discovered with French colonists, to introduce European plants and domestic animals, and to bring the "poor, rough and ignorant people" of North America to Christianity. When one contemplates the fate of the North American Indians, one cannot be very enthusiastic over these benevolent gestures of European pioneers; but at least they tried.

Bibliography and Notes

SOURCES AND SECONDARY WORKS

There are four versions of Verrazzano's Letter to the king, all in Italian and dated 8 July 1524.

Number 1 was printed in G. B. Ramusio, *Terzo Volume della Navigationi et Viaggi* (Venice, 1556). Translated by Hakluyt, it appears in his *Divers Voyages* (1582) and in the second (1600) edition of his *Principal Navigations, Voyages . . .* , but not in the first edition. I have used Hakluyt's translation of the Letter whenever possible.

Number 2, a garbled and inferior version, is in the National Library of Florence. It was translated by George Washington Greene, an early champion of Verrazzano, and published in New-York Historical Society *Collections* for 1841 (2nd ser., I, 41–51). Since certain local pundits could not suffer the idea of New York's being discovered by an Italian, this publication precipitated a silly dispute as to whether Verrazzano was a real person or a disguised pirate who met his death on the gallows. The curious may read about this in Justin Winsor, *Narrative and Critical History*, IV, 19–28.

Number 3, the most detailed yet found, is known as the Cellère "Codex." (For the uninitiated, a "codex" is a European manuscript sold to an American for a sum written in five or six figures.) Originally in the Como library of Paolo Giovio, friend of the Verrazzano family, this manuscript turned up in the collection of Count Giulio Macchi de Cellère in Rome and was purchased by the J. Pierpont Morgan Library of New York. Alessandro Bacchiani printed the original, with an introduction and a translation by Edward H. Hall, as Appendix A of the American Scenic and Preservation Society's *Fifteenth Annual Report* (Albany, 1910). This Cellère manuscript, as I write, is about to be reprinted by Yale University Press with a fresh translation and voluminous notes by Lawrence C. Wroth. He, with a gesture of singular scholarly courtesy, allowed me to read the proof and to quote his translation whenever it seems to be the most accurate, as it generally is. Dr. Wroth's *The Voyages of Giovanni da Verrazzano 1524–1528* will render earlier texts obsolete, but his learned introduction on Verrazzano's background, early life, geographical knowledge, etc. is far better than any existing biography of the explorer. The Cellère manuscript is in a contemporary scribal hand, with numerous marginal additions and annotations which most authorities believe to be Verrazzano's own.

Number 4, a sixteenth-century copy known as the Ottoboniano manuscript, is in the Vatican Library. There is a photographic transcript in the J. Pierpont Morgan Library, New York. It has only minor variations from the Cellère manuscript.

A list of notarial documents about Verrazzano at Rouen and Dieppe will be found in Michel Mollat, *Le Commerce maritime normand* (1952), p. 253, n. 16. Charles de La Roncière prints important documents in his *Histoire de la marine française*, III (1906), 260–61, and has the names of all known backers of Verrazzano. See also, Charpin-Feugerolles, *Les Florentins à Lyon* (Lyon, 1893).

Jacques Habert, *When New York Was Called Angoulême* (New York, 1949), is really a biography of Vérrazzano. The three best accounts of the voyage, prior to Wroth's, are in Mollat, Ch.-A. Julien, *Les Voyages de découverte* (Paris, 1948), and Marcel Trudel, *Histoire de la Nouvelle-France*, I, *Les Vaines Tentatives* (Montreal, 1963), chap. i. W. F. Ganong, in *Crucial Maps* (Toronto, 1964), pp. 99–203, goes into maps in vast detail, but his attempts at identifying localities are hopelessly wild, as he knew nothing of the coast. I have followed Verrazzano's course from New Jersey to Newfoundland under sail, and have flown along the coast from New Jersey to Cape Fear; but that should be covered from a sailing vessel, with the Letter and the early charts in hand.

The late Roberto Almagià, in a twenty-page pamphlet *L'Importanza geografica delle navigazioni di Giovanni da Verrazzano* (Florence, 1962), told almost everything known about the Florentine and closed with an eloquent plea for more research.

DETAILS

Influence of Magellan. This question is thoroughly ventilated by R. A. Skelton in his Introduction to the Yale manuscript of that voyage (1969), pp. 14–18, 148. The story that Simon de Coline dedicated his French translation of Pigafetta's narrative (Paris, 1525) to Louise de Savoie is not true; but the chronicler himself states that after his return he visited Madame la Régente in France and gave her souvenirs "from the other hemisphere." See the William L. Clements Library reprint of the 1525 edition of Pigafetta (Englewood Cliffs, N.J., 1969).

Antoine de Conflans, master of *La Dauphine*, has been played up by "patriotic" French historians as being the real hero of this expedition. But it is very doubtful whether he sailed. The only evidence of any connection between him and Verrazzano is a receipt signed by Conflans for six months' salary from the crown (1 January–30 June 1524), 100 livres tournois, as captain of the *barche Daulphine*. Even for that era, 16⅔ livres per month (roughly $3.33) was a beggarly salary for a master mariner of Conflans's age and reputation; this must have been a mere retaining fee for the captain during Verrazzano's absence. The Florentine had no need for a flag captain when his fleet was reduced to one ship. In view of the many instances in early history—even today—of friction between a captain or commodore and his next in command, I suspect that Verrazzano had a row with Conflans on the first leg of the voyage and let him go home in *La Normande*.

New York Bay. Lino S. Lipinsky's booklet *Giovanni da Verrazzano, the Discoverer of New York Bay* (1958) is lavishly illustrated, including facsimiles of maps and globes. Lipinsky, by counting the number of days' sail from the last firm date that Verrazzano gives, 25 March at Annunziata, figures that his day in New York was 17 April. Verrazzano named a little hill in the Navesink Highlands *Saint-Pol*, after François, comte de Saint-Pol, brother to Charles, duc de Vendôme.

Rhode Island. For the story about Roger Williams, see the article in Rhode Island Historical Society *Collections*, XX (1927), 81, and *Newport History* (Bulletin of the Newport Historical Society, No. 113, January 1964). The operative sentence in the Cellère manuscript is "Lontana da continente leghi *dieci* de grandeza simile a la insula di Rhodo, piena di colli." Block Island is only some fifteen miles from the continent; but Martha's Vineyard, which also claims to have been Verrazzano's *Luisa*, is even nearer.

As for the *Petra Viva* fort, the American revolutionists paid unconscious homage to Verrazzano by erecting crude earth works there in 1775 to protect Newport. The stone one which we have depicted replaced it about 1798 and was demolished a century later when a hideous summer "cottage" was built on the site. Information from Mr. William King Covell of Newport.

MAPS

These are analyzed, point by point, by Lawrence C. Wroth in his forthcoming *The Voyages of Giovanni da Verrazzano 1524-1528*. To these maps we owe most of the Verrazzanean nomenclature, of which he was sparing in his Letter to the king. So it is possible that these names were put in after the voyage, just to fill in.

The four crucial maps are that of Vesconte Maiollo, or Maggiolo, 1527, formerly in the Ambrosian Library, Milan, but destroyed by bombing in World War II, and three planispheres by Giovanni's brother Girolamo (Hieronymo): (1) at the Vatican, (2) in the Greenwich Maritime Museum, and (3) in the Library of the Hispanic Society in New York. These are the maps that set the tradition of an "Isthmus" and "Sea" of Verrazzano. Every source or book about Verrazzano reproduces them—usually very badly—but there is a good one of the Maiollo in Harrisse, *North America*, p. 217. The Greenwich map (2) is identified as Verrazzano's and reproduced by Marcel Destombes in *Imago Mundi*, XI (1954), 57-66.

The glamour of Verrazzano's name has led people to overlook the fact that his brother's and Maiollo's maps are very poor maps indeed, even in comparison with others of that decade, such as the Ribero and the Miller I. Their coast is conventionalized, prominent capes and bays are barely indicated, and the latitudes are in error as much as ten degrees. For instance, Maiollo gives the latitude of Luisa (Block Island) as 35° N, and Girolamo gives it as 45° N; correct latitude is 41°09'. I believe that both maps were prepared after Giovanni's death, and without consulting the log that he kept.

A map by Juan Vespucci (nephew of Amerigo) dated 1526 belongs to the Hispanic Society of America, which reproduced it in 1925 as *Vespucci World Map MDXXVI*. This is examined exhaustively by William P. Cumming, *The Southeast in Early Maps* (Princeton University Press, 1958). This is the earliest general chart to show the influence of the 1524 voyage; it has a *r. da sa terazanus* (error for Verazanas?) about where Cape Fear River should be.

The Robertus Bailly Globe of 1530, which we have reproduced, is described in E. L. Stevenson, *Terrestrial and Celestial Globes*, I (New Haven, 1931), 106–8. The Michael Lok Map, based on a long-lost one given by Verrazzano to Henry VIII, is in Hakluyt's *Divers Voyages* (1582).

The "Sea of Verrazzano" concept died slowly. The John Farrer Map of Virginia (1651) states that the Pacific lies ten days' march from the head of the James. Governor Spotswood of Virginia expected to see it in 1716 when he led his gay cavalcade over the Blue Ridge. The English government's colonial sea-to-sea charters reflect the narrow-continent concept. For other maps and globes that show Verrazzanean influence, the reader is referred to Wroth's forthcoming magistral work. See also notes on the maps based on Gomez's voyage at the end of Chapter X below.

My statement that the Maiollo and Verrazzano maps are the earliest, except La Cosa's, to show a continuous coast between Newfoundland and Florida, will be challenged in the name of the Portolan Atlas at the British Museum, known as Egerton Ms. No. 2803. This is reproduced by E. L. Stevenson as *Atlas of Portolan Charts, facsimile of ms. in British Museum* (Hispanic Society of America, 1911), and discussed by Arthur Davies in *Imago Mundi*, XI (1958), 47–52. The one dates it 1508, the other 1510. The North American part is very sketchy and contains but three names (Labrador, Bacalaos, and *Septem Civitates*), suggesting that it was hastily dubbed in. In my opinion the Egerton is post-Verrazzano; the artist had heard of his voyage but knew no details. It is a mistake to assume that a manuscript atlas was done all in one swoop; many of the sixteenth-century ones show signs of having been worked on over a number of years.

PORTRAITS

No portrait made in Verrazzano's lifetime, or within a century of his death, is known to exist. There are several posthumous ones, all derived from a portrait by Galleaggo Zocchi of Bologna, who was painting at Rome in 1573; and he could hardly have seen Verrazzano. The marble bust (here reproduced) with GIO · DA · VER · incised on the plinth, now in the Samuel H. Kress Collection in the National Gallery of Art in Washington, is thought by the authorities there to be an Italian work, by Romeo Pieratti, c. 1601–50; but those of the Museo de Storia de Scienza, Florence, who have a replica, assign it to the eighteenth century. A full-length canvas attributed to Orazio Fidani (1610–56), owned by Signora Cesaroni Favi, Villa di Vitigliano, Greve, shows the hero in plate armor to the thighs,

VESCONTE DE MAIOLLO CONPOSUY
HANC CARTAM IN JANUA ANNO DÑY 1527
DIE XX DECENBRIS

-60
-55
-50
-45
-40
-35
-30
-25
-20
-52
-50
-48
-46
-44
-42
-40
-38
-36
-34

F R A N C E S C A

F R A N C I A

MARE
INDICUM

MARE OCEANUM

N O V A   G A L L I A   S I V E   IV   C A T A N E T

VERRAZANA SIVE NOUA GALLIA
quale discopri 5 anni fa Giovanni
da Verrazano fiorentino per ordine
et Comandamlo del Christianissime
Re di Francia

Laurocostia
silva de serui
costa Vadosa
pia de calmi
costa de lauroreno
longa Villa
C. de germano
Anguileme
G. S. margarita
normani Villa
polmar Villa
S. lodovico
C. de S. Joam
p. reale
C. de S. fransc
Refugio
Corte maiore
Iouium pormtorium
firloi
Sauleum pormtorium
Caregi
La trinita
C. S. gallo
La lartossa
C. S. Jeorgi
Iflora
Virdanus pormtorium
Costa de S. Jeorgi
Saminico
le paladiso
orto de rucelay
quoachi
le panche
Gibercas
Cressuy pormtorius
palatius pormtorium
ponta de diamante
C. de bertom

la de
S. Joan

le figole de navarin

Carpoes pormtorium
Monicelli

Armelines Siltes

Isola Maiolla Jenoesa
la Scarides
baduaria

C. de S. Maria
luisa

R. de
la foresta
p. de diluuio
Una Flor
Valleunarosa
anaflor
p. delisola
c. codira
diepa
palma
TERA
FLORIDA

dorius pormtorium
Lanunciata

Da questo mare
orientale sive de
il mare occidentale
sono 6 miglia da terra
infra l'uno e l'altro

punta de cervi
Santiago
Comara
P. daraflor
palavisina
pta de luiuo
Dieppa
livotimo
punta de calami
TERRA
FLOR
ID
A

C. do limpo
olimpo
la victoria
gosuma
Santanna
la macra
la nutiata
San Franc.
palavisina
Lanunciata
palavisina
San germano
La Victoria
Santana
lan puntieta
angolemme
tolovilla
palavisin
Vendomo
m. morello
g. del refugio
m navara
Palavisin
San Severino
Iouim pormontorium
La foresta
C. de la basse
seluade
cervi
palaia
San giorgio
Santana
Santanna
C. di pani
C. di monta
morella
La foresta
C. di morello
belvedera
longvilla
Vendomo
bonivetto
San Severino
Le figle
di navarra
oranbega
La pescania
Santania
C. grosso
Rio della
pescania
La foresta
terra onde
he mala
gente
Rio formose
San migh
plaia

lunga Villa
Luisa
C. do limpo
C. del refugio
armalline Sirtes
C. di san luisi
C. de bretton

Tracings of Verrazzano's Course on the
MAIOLLO (1527)
and
GIROLAMO VERRAZZANO (1529)
Maps

From Wm. F. Ganong: Crucial Maps of Canada

200   400   600   800   miglia
50   100   150   200   legha

but bare legs (for wading ashore, presumably) and carrying a baton of command.* At the town archives of Penzano, near Greve, is the half-length which I have reproduced. The most popular portrait is a copperplate engraving, of which the J. Pierpont Morgan Library in New York has the only extant strike, inscribed, "F. Allegrini inci:1767, G. Zocchi del." Allegrini, a well-known Italian engraver of the eighteenth century, evidently did this from the Zocchi portrait, which may then have been in the Giovio gallery of worthies at Como. The De Guadagni portrait-medal that I have reproduced was found when the site of the De Guadagni mansion in Lyons was being excavated.

Other busts and portraits alleged to be of the explorer are simply portraits of contemporary gentlemen to which some enterprising dealer has attached the name Verrazzano. Consult appendix to Dr. Lawrence C. Wroth's forthcoming work.

It is impossible, with our present knowledge, to identify the tribes encountered by Verrazzano in the future Carolinas. The historians who deal with the Indians of that region (Rights, Lee, and Mooney), do not even mention Verrazzano's visit; their interest begins when the English in the seventeenth and early eighteenth centuries contacted the Waccamaw, Pedee, Cape Fear, and other Siouan tribes. The Indians whom Verrazzano met in 1524 may have been exterminated by disease or driven elsewhere by war, long before the first attempts at English settlement under Walter Raleigh.

For the Wampanoag, see Roger Williams, *Key to the Indian Language*, the Bradford and Winslow Journal generally known as *Mourt's Relation*, Thomas Lechford, *Plain Dealing*, Thomas Morton, *New English Canaan*, and William Wood, *New Englands Prospect*. There are recent editions of all these. Relevant quotations may be found in *Newport History* (January 1964), pp. 26–31.

The wild roots that Verrazzano says that the Maine Indians ate were ground-nuts. He added, "They have no grain," which is correct; east of the Saco River the Indians did not clear the forest to make cornfields, and a century later the Pilgrim Fathers made a good thing out of selling maize to the Eastern Indians.

For the origin and use of this phrase, see Erwin Panofsky, *Meaning in the Visual Arts* (1955), pp. 295–320. Sir Philip Sidney's *Arcadia* and Poussin's celebrated painting *Les Bergers d'Arcadie* were inspired by the same source. Ernest H. Wilkins, "Arcadia in America," American Philosophical Society *Proceedings*, CI (1957), 4–30, reproduces maps exhibiting the progress of

* Reproduced in Lino S. Lipinsky's booklet, and elsewhere.

Verrazzano's Arcadia to Nova Scotia. Longfellow's *Evangeline*, and the Acadia National Park on Mount Desert Island, which the French claimed as part of their *L'Acadie*, perpetuate this romantic association with the classic Arcadia. Although others have spotted Verrazzano's Arcadia elsewhere (H. V. Covington, "Verrazzano's Visit to the Eastern Shore," *Maryland Historical Magazine*, X, 1915, 199–217), I insist on its being at Kitty Hawk, because there is the only hill Verrazzano encountered prior to New Jersey. Kill Devil Hill, although stated to be 100–103 feet high in McFarland's *Papers of Wilbur and Orville Wright* (1953), I, 68, II, 863, 1025, is stated by the National Park Service to be only 90 feet. C. Henry is about 105 feet high; but Verrazzano cannot possibly have sighted C. Henry or he would have turned into Chesapeake Bay.

THE DAUGHTERS OF NAVARRE

These are identified by Habert, and by Nancy Roelker, *Queen of Navarre: Jeanne d'Albret* (1968), as Catherine, Isabeau, and Anne, daughters of Jean, duc d'Albret, and Catherine de Foix. At this time they were about sixteen to eighteen years old and renowned for their beauty, according to the connoisseur Brantôme. Jeanne d'Albret was their niece. Anne died *en fiancailles;* Isabeau, whose portrait we reproduce, married the vicomte de Rohan; and Catherine took the veil and became abbess of l'Abbaye aux Dames, Caen. Wild guesses have been made to identify the three islands that Verrazzano named after them; but having sailed along the Florentine's course at least a hundred times, I insist that he meant Monhegan, Isle au Haut, and Mount Desert, the last two so named by Champlain in 1604. Mount Desert looks like an island afar off, as in our photo; but near-to it looks more like a peninsula, hence the Ribero Map of 1529, reflecting Gomez's voyage of 1525, shows only the fjord-like Somes Sound, which almost bisects the island, as *Rio de las Montañas.*

CARTIER AND VERRAZZANO

Gustave Lanctot, in his *Jacques Cartier devant l'histoire* (Montreal, 1947), pp. 108–36, and *History of Canada* (Hambleton trans., 1963), argues that Cartier sailed with Verrazzano in *La Dauphine* and also on his next voyage, and took command after Giovanni's death. His evidence, largely negative or trivial, has been answered with devastating irony by Marcel Trudel in *Histoire de la Nouvelle France* (1963), pp. 58–60. French Canadians generally exalt Jacques Cartier at the expense of the Italian; but can they deny that the French cause in North America would have prospered more had colonization been directed to Verrazzano's Arcadia, Angoulême, or Refugio, rather than to Cartier's St. Lawrence?

Verrazzano's only name for the region he discovered was *Francesca*, a compliment to François-premier; but *Nova Gallia* appears on his brother's Vatican map. Père Biard, missionary and historian of the attempted French settlement at Mount Desert in 1613, correctly wrote: *"Jean Verazan* was godfather to the name of *La Nouvelle France;* for Canada . . . is only that part which extends along the banks of the great River of Canada."

THE GEOGRAPHICAL CONCEPT

Although Amerigo Vespucci got the credit for calling South America *Mundus Novus,* his concept was no different from that of Columbus's *Otro Mundo.* Both meant that South America was a continent unknown to Ptolemy which tailed off from southeast Asia, much as Indonesia actually does. George E. Nunn in a significant monograph, *The Columbus and Magellan Concepts of South American Geography* (privately printed, Glenside, 1932), demonstrates that even Magellan sailed with the same idea, which was only disproved by the width of the Pacific. Several maps incorporating this concept are sketched in J. G. Kohl, "Asia and America," *American Antiquarian Society Proceedings,* n.s., XXI (1911), 284–338. The Nicolet story is in Francis Parkman, *La Salle,* p. 4.

EXPENSE OF THE 1524 VOYAGE

The figures in *livres tournois* (five to the gold dollar) have been preserved and are printed in Mollat, *Le Commerce maritime normand,* p. 417. Admiral Chabot, sieur de Brion, contributed a *galion* and 4000 livres. The following contributed 2000 each: Verrazzano himself, Guillaume Prudhomme (général de Normandie), Jean Ango, Jacques Bourdier "de Paris," and Pietro Spinola. Ango also gave a *nef,* a full-sized ship.

DEATH

For Verrazzano's voyages after the one of 1524, Wroth has sifted the often contradictory evidence and come to sensible conclusions. Michel Mollat has a valuable article on the Verrazzano brothers' Brazilian ventures in *Revista de História,* XXIV (São Paulo 1967), 343–58. Wroth prints the Giovio poem. Its ninth *strofa,* on the *giorno lacrimando,* reads:

Da gente cruda fur a un tratto presi
Ch'a l'improviso gli saltorno adosso.
Occisi fur et per terra distesi
Fatti in più pezzi sin al minimo osso
Da quelli fur mangiato. E in quei paesi
Gli fu il fratel del Verezan che rosso
Vede il terren del sangue del fratello
Nè puote in barca stando aggiutar quello.

Alberto Magnaghi, in his article on Verrazzano in *Enciclopedia Italiana* (1937), challenges this tale as spurious, largely on the ground that Girolamo failed to note the murder on his 1529 map. But he may have had good reasons to omit it.

Giovio's meager account does not help us to locate the place of the murder. Off the Lesser Antilles, where Carib rule was then still unchallenged, there are few places where one can anchor a mile or more off shore, as Verrazzano liked to do. Guadeloupe, however, has two big shoal areas on each side of its narrow waist, the Grand and the Petit Cul-de-Sac Marin; and near by, around Les Saintes, is another shoal area. Guadeloupe, chief stronghold of the Carib and the most heavily populated, where Spaniards had ceased landing after several experiences like Verrazzano's, is the most likely scene of this tragedy.

✻ X ✻
Gomez and Ayllon

1524-1530

Estévan Gomez

Spain now put in a bid for discovering the North American Strait by sending a Portuguese mariner in search of it, sailing a reverse course from Verrazzano's. Estévão Gomes, a native of Oporto, after a creditable career in the Portuguese marine, emigrated to Spain, where his name was hispanicized as Estévan Gomez. Charles V seriously considered appointing him commander of a round-the-world fleet, but then decided on Magellan. So Gomez shipped in that armada as pilot of the ship *San Antonio*. In the Strait of Magellan, after an outlet to the Pacific had been discovered, Gomez decided he had had enough, mutinied, captured the ship, deserted his commodore, and sailed home. Upon arrival in Spain, he was clapped in jail for mutiny. He asserted, in defense, that the Strait of Magellan was too far south and too intricate and tempestuous to be practicable, and that he, Gomez, could find a better one for his royal master. After Sebastian del Cano's *Vittoria* arrived home in 1522, and Charles V had digested the official account of the great circumnavigation, he let Gomez out of jail, adopted his plan, and even had a ship specially built for him to try to find a passage through North America.

Unfortunately we have no journal or report by Gomez of his voyage; only the brief, contradictory accounts of it, written many years later by Spanish historians. We now know the name of his ship, *La Anunciada*, a caravel of fifty tuns. But we have a good documentation of the preparations, which are of great interest since they show how voyages of discovery were then organized.

Charles V considered this voyage very important, hoping it would disclose a short cut, preferable to the Strait of Magellan, to the Philippines and the Moluccas. In March 1523 the king-emperor contracted with his *piloto* Estévan Gomez to "go and discover *el Cathayo oryental* . . . as far as our isles of Malucca; and whereas on the said route to eastern China there are many undiscovered islands and provinces, very rich in gold, silver, spices and drugs," he is licensed as captain "to sail in a 50-tun caravel, fitted out and provisioned for a twelvemonth by me the King, at an expense not exceeding 2500 ducats"—about $5800 in gold. The king will advance two hundred ducats of Estévan's salary, which he may invest in a part of the caravel's cargo. Everyone who shares in the cost of outfitting may have a piece of the outward lading. And, after the royal goods and those of the outfitters have been traded off to the natives, all petty officers, mariners, and even the gromets or ship's boys, can share in the business. They may barter their *caxas é quinteladas* (the stuff in their sea-chests) to the value of two hundred ducats each, and enter the proceeds in Spain duty free.

Here one can see the beginnings of the "privilege" and "primage" system. These were encouragements to masters and mariners to make a little bit on the side, which endured as long as sailing vessels engaged in the China trade. "Privilege" was the master's share, and "primage" that of the seamen. And (to continue this set of royal documents) the value of prize ships shall be divided thus: the major part for the crown and the "partners" who helped equip the caravel, and about 25 per cent for officers and crew. Not a very generous division, but it didn't matter as they made no prizes.

On the same day, 27 March 1523, Gomez received his royal commission as captain. Charles V really meant business. Ordinarily the commanding officer of a merchant ship would be a mere master pilot, but Gomez as a royal officer ranks as captain. The king promises him a reward upon his return, but cannily leaves the amount to be determined by the value of his discoveries. Cristóbal de Haro, a Dutch merchant and outfitter who had transferred his counting-house to Seville and had taken a leading part in outfitting Magellan's armada, is ordered to go to Corunna to hasten the building of the caravel, toward the cost of which the king will pay half (750 ducats). Alcaldes of three other towns in Galicia are ordered to supply Gomez with all the timber, nails, tackle, and other gear that he may need for building, at current prices, and to find for him the master carpenters, caulkers, and other workmen that he may require.

All this in March and April 1523. One can guess the reason for the royal haste: Charles V had heard through his foreign intelligence of Verrazzano's projected voyage and wished to find the Northern Strait ahead of his hated rival, the king of France. But in spite of imperial injunctions to hurry, the building and fitting out of this caravel took far longer than anyone expected. It always does: why should a workman make haste when his worshipful monarch, or Uncle Sam, pays the bills? So far as one can judge from conflicting accounts, Gomez's caravel did not depart Corunna until September 1524—an odd time to leave for a northern voyage. And—that was two months after Verrazzano had returned to Dieppe!

The choice of Corunna for departure point is significant. It is on latitude 43°23′ N, exactly the same as Cape Sable, Nova Scotia; no sense hitting America further north, as the Portuguese knew all about that region already. Gomez intended to cross by that latitude and start his search for the Strait to China somewhere near the point where Verrazzano left off.

From her tunnage, Gomez's ship must have resembled the handsome Portuguese caravel in the Miller I Map (reproduced in Chapter VII above). She raised the North American coast in February 1525, after a long, rough passage, made land at or near Cape Breton, and in spite of cold weather and ice entered the Gulf of St. Lawrence. Had Gomez holed up for the rest of the winter at Ingonish, the site of Fagundes's deserted settlement, and continued westward in the spring, he might have anticipated Jacques Cartier as discoverer of the St. Lawrence River. But (according to Alonso de Santa Cruz, writing around 1545), Gomez concluded that any possible strait at the western end of the big gulf would be too full of ice to be practicable; he wanted south. After sighting Prince Edward Island, which he called

St. John, and discovering the Gut of Canso, which he named St. Julian, he followed the coasts of Nova Scotia and Maine.

The 1529 Portuguese World Map of Diogo Ribero, and the clearer 1545 map of Alonso de Santa Cruz, offer the best evidence of what Gomez did next. He must have shaken off winter somewhere between Cape Breton and Passamaquoddy, for he experienced the spicy odors, brisk offshore breezes, and warm sunshine of a Maine June. He sailed close to the beautiful island of Mount Desert that Verrazzano had just named after one of the daughters of Navarre, believed it to be a promontory, and named its fjord-like and mountain-bordered Somes Sound *Rio de Montañas*. The maps indicate that he crossed Blue Hill Bay (named simply *golfo*), threaded the future Eggemoggin Reach, observing sands (*medaños*) and ledges (*arecifas*), and entered Penobscot Bay and River. There he found a vast number of deer, which caused him to name it *Rio de las Gamas*, River of Deer, and he also found (according to Ribero's inscription) Abnaki Indians who came there in summer to catch salmon and various other fish. Apparently these Indians were friendly, unlike those who taunted Verrazzano with unseemly gestures the year before. The Spaniard's visit cannot have been earlier than June, as the Indians came to the coast for summer fishing and clam-digging after planting cornfields in their winter villages, and they never planted corn until the leaf of the oak was "as big as a mouse's ear."

Estévan sailed up the Penobscot, hoping it to be the Strait, but on reaching the head of navigation at the site of Bangor he decided that this was only a "famous river with a great flow of water." The country is temperate, he wrote, well forested with oak, birch, olive (!), and wild grape, and he saw much *margarita*—iron pyrites—which glittered like gold; but the map inscription is positive, *no hay alla de oro*, no gold. Thus he was much more realistic than Sir Humfry Gilbert's men half a century later, or than the natives of Maine who were selling gold-and-silver-mine stocks on the banks of the Penobscot in the 1880's. Another credit line goes to Gomez because he never mentioned Norumbega, the alleged city on the Penobscot which had all England by the ears long after his death.

The rest of Estévan's discoveries are easy to identify, following the Santa Cruz and Ribero maps, for anyone who knows the Maine coast.

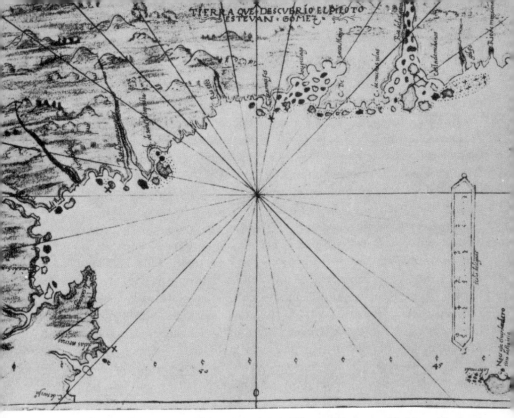

"The Land which the Pilot Estévan Gomez Discovered," New England from Cape Cod to Mount Desert Island. From the *Islario* of Alonso de Santa Cruz, *c.* 1545, the 1908 edition.

At the mouth of the Penobscot are several big islands, evidently meant for the Fox Islands, Isle au Haut, and Deer Isle. Then comes *C. de muchas islas,* an appropriate name for Owls Head, as one can count some thirty to forty islands when sailing by. Next come *C. de Santa Maria* (Whitehead), an *Archipelago* (which I believe to be Muscongus Sound, although others say Casco Bay); *C. de Arrocifes* (Pemaquid); and *Rio Seco,* which may be any of the numerous streams in that part of Maine. There follow *R. de Juan bautista* (Boothbay); *Rio de buena madre* (the Kennebec), with Seguin Island off it. These names indicate that he passed them on 24 June and 2 July. *Montañas* on the mainland suggests that Gomez sighted the White Mountains when crossing Casco Bay; a beautiful experience in early summer when their summits are still covered with snow.

Rio de Sant'Antonio is probably the Merrimac; *Baia de S. Xpoual*

(St. Christopher) I take to be Ipswich Bay, and *C. de Santiago* (St. James), Cape Ann; these identifications are supported by the feast days of the saint and the apostle coming on successive days, 24 and 25 July. Next comes *C. de las Arenas*, which cannot be other than Cape Cod. Beyond that is a *C. de San Juan*. Every cartographer for the next century imitated Ribero's thick-waisted *C. de Arenas*. Santa Cruz's map ends here, but the earlier one by Ribero continues the coast to Florida, with nomenclature possibly derived from the next voyage, Ayllón's. We do not know from what point he took his departure for Spain; it was not later than early August, because *La Anunciada* arrived Corunna on the 21st.

We do not know exactly where Gomez went ashore; but at some point, disgusted with his failure to find a lucrative trade for the goods so abundantly supplied, he kidnapped a load of Indians for slaves. This probably happened at Newport, R.I., where the Indians were friendly and off their guard. According to the historian Peter Martyr, Gomez had been forbidden by Charles V to do just that; nevertheless, "so as not to return with empty hands," he "filled his ship with innocent people of both sexes, half naked." When the ship reached Corunna on 21 August 1525, an officious person, hearing that her cargo consisted of *esclavos* (slaves), misunderstood it to be *clavos* (cloves), mounted a horse, and spread the news that she had brought a load of valuable spices! When the people learned the truth they treated Estévan with scorn and contempt, and the government forced him to liberate such wretched Indians as had survived the Atlantic crossing.

Peter Martyr concluded that since Gomez had discovered only lands with products similar to those of Europe, there was no sense in Spain's bothering with them. "It is to the southward, not the icy north, that everyone in search of a fortune should turn, for below the equator everything is rich."

Through Ribero's map Gomez had a strong influence on North American cartography. The Riberan concept of the New York–New England–Nova Scotia coast lasted until Samuel de Champlain and Captain John Smith in the early seventeenth century brought out far more accurate charts, with new French and English names.

Luís Vasquez de Ayllón

One more attempt of this sort, and Spain suspended North American exploration until she was virtually forced to do something, in order to protect her treasure fleets on their homeward passage. This attempt set a new precedent; it was a northern voyage from a southern colony, Spanish Hispaniola. The Licentiate—i.e. lawyer—Luís Vasquez de Ayllón, justice of the supreme court of Santo Domingo, developed an itch for exploration. In 1521 he sent a vessel commanded by Francisco Gordillo along the coast north of Florida. Gordillo, joining his forces with those of a professional slave trader, and for want of anything more profitable, loaded seventy Indians at a point on the Carolina coast which he believed to be on latitude 33°30′ N. Judge Ayllón, to do him credit, liberated the slaves, but he did not lose interest in the territory. In 1523 he obtained a patent from the king to explore some 2500 miles of the coast, follow any oceanic strait he might find, and set up a colony. After sending two caravels to make a preliminary reconnaissance in 1525, Ayllón fitted out at Santo Domingo an ambitious armada. The flagship was a big *nef* called *La Bretona;* there were two smaller ones, *Santa Catalina* and *Chorruca;* a *bergantín* (a light craft like the English pinnace, suitable for exploring shoal waters), and a lighter, or barge. Altogether they carried five hundred men, women, and children, including a number of friars and black slaves, and eighty to ninety horses. They sailed to the mouth of a river where the slave-snatching had taken place earlier, and which they called *Río Jordán.* Verrazzano may have called there the previous year; it appears on his brother's maps.

Ill luck pursued the Ayllón expedition from the start. Upon entering this river (which nobody has certainly identified), the flagship ran aground and became a total loss. The others sailed upstream a certain distance, but finding no place suitable for settlement stood out to sea again and sailed to another river forty to fifty leagues away. Henry Harrisse, who knew the North Carolina coast, decided that this second river was the Cape Fear, and that Ayllón's colony, which he named *San Miguel de Guadalupe,* lay somewhere on its banks below Wilmington. The surrounding country Ayllón named *Chicora,* and that name appears on maps of the Carolina region for about a century.

Cape Fear and Frying Pan Shoals (above). Probable site of Ayllón's
Colony on Cape Fear River (below).

Everything went wrong at San Miguel. The settlers were undisciplined, the terrain malarial, the Indians (suspicious owing to the previous kidnapping) refused to provide food; cold weather set in early, and Ayllón died of a fever on 18 October 1526. His colony broke up, one ship foundered on the return passage, and only 150 survivors reached Santo Domingo.

Thus Ayllón, like Gomez and Verrazzano, merely accomplished a negative. All three helped turn the attention of mighty Spain away from North America, leaving it to France and England to exploit and colonize.

Gomez in 1533 submitted to the Council of the Indies a detailed proposal for establishing a drydock on the Guadalquivir River above Sanlúcar by damming one of its tributaries. Nothing of the kind was done, but Charles V next day made him a *cavaleiro* "in recognition of the distinguished services which he had performed for Magellan's fleet" —which he had deserted! That was typical of the era—notable mariners were rewarded, but usually for the wrong thing.

The Ribero Maps of 1529

A fair monument to Gomez and Ayllón is the magnificent Diogo Ribero Mappemonde of 1529, of which there are two versions: one at the Landesbibliothek of Weimar, the other in the Vatican. Along a fairly well-drawn coast of North America from Florida to Labrador are two important inscriptions. The southernmost reads, "TIERA DE AYLLON," and records the tragic end of his colony; the northwestern inscription states that the Indians on that coast are taller than those of Santo Domingo, and live on maize and fish, of which there is a great abundance. When the Spaniards arrived, the natives fled into the interior, so the colonists could obtain no food; and "when winter set in many died of cold and hunger, and those surviving decided to return to Hispaniola." The Land of Ayllón covers the region from Florida to Cape Cod. It contains thirteen names, which it would be hopeless to identify, except *Bahía de Santa María*, the Spanish name for Chesapeake Bay in the second half of the century, and the *Rio Jordán*, probably the Cape Fear River. The coast is conventional, but much more accurate and detailed than the Maiollo and Verrazzano maps.

North and east of the Ayllón country, covering the New England

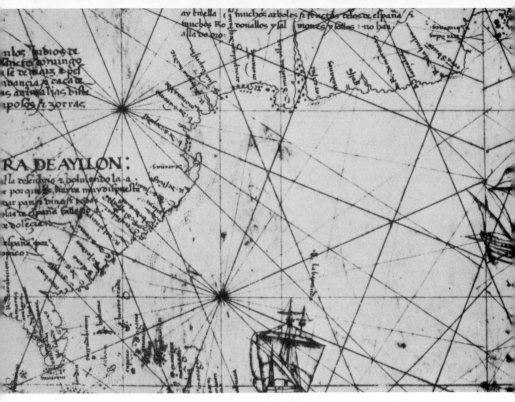

"Lands of Estévan Gomez and of Ayllón." The coast of North America from the Gulf of St. Lawrence entrance to Florida. From Diogo Ribero's World Map of 1529. Stevenson photograph of the Weimar copy.

COAST IS TIERA DE ESTEVAN GOMEZ, "discovered by command of His Majesty in the year 1525, in which there are many trees and fruits like those of Spain, and many *roduallos* and salmon and sole, but no gold." Gomez, having returned from the Strait of Magellan with a map of his own making, knew how to map strange coasts and must have provided Ribero with his information.

East of Mount Desert Island with its Rio de Montañas, Ribero relies partly on Portuguese sources. There is no Bay of Fundy, despite the earlier discovery of it by Fagundes, and Nova Scotia is squeezed onto Maine. There is a *tiera de los bretones* (Cape Breton), followed by a small gulf with a scalloped northern margin, the convention for a coast unknown, or only suspected to exist. Apparently nobody had reported the Gulf of St. Lawrence to Ribero. His Newfoundland is a peninsula attached to Nova Scotia, with the already familiar Portuguese nomenclature. The Strait of Belle Isle is a mere fjord, north of which is *Tiera de Llabrador,* inscribed "Discovered by the English of the town of

Bristol. Nothing therein of any value." A tardy and grudging bow to John Cabot! But in the Vatican copy, Newfoundland bears the inscription "*Tiera Nova de Cortereal,* wherein there is nothing of value except the fishery of *bacallaos* and much pine timber."

The date of Ribero's maps, 1529, is a good one to take stock of the northern voyages from Europe to America in the previous thirty-two years. There is no denying that their results were disappointing to performers and promoters alike. Nobody foresaw, or at least publicly predicted, the brilliant future of these temperate lands. In current estimates the constant refrains were "found nothing of profit," "no strait to Cathay." Codfish apparently interested only the fishermen, not the governments. During this third of a century, the east coast of North America from the Labrador to Florida had been discovered, mapped, and named; but as yet nobody had explored its major estuaries and rivers such as the Chesapeake, the Delaware, the Hudson, the Merrimac, Kennebec, the St. John, or even the Gulf of St. Lawrence; the only exception being Gomez's sail up the Penobscot. Although Spain had occupied the Greater and Lesser Antilles, founded posts from Florida to Texas, and conquered the empire of the Aztecs, no other European country had even made a start of an American empire.

France, in the person of Jacques Cartier, was about to change all that.

Bibliography and Notes

GOMEZ

The only monograph on Gomez is by the great Chilean historian J. Toribio Medina, *El Portuguès Estéban Gómez al servicio de España* (Santiago, 1908). Most of the sources are printed, in original and translation, in H. Harrisse, *The Discovery of North America* (1892), chap. iv. H. P. Biggar found some documents about the outfitting in the Archives of the Indies and printed them in his *Precursors of Cartier* (1911), pp. 146–59; he also gives in full the account in the *Islario* of Alonso de Santa Cruz (1545), first printed in whole in 1908. B. G. Hoffman, *Cabot to Cartier* (Toronto, 1961), reprints the essence of both. Ganong, *Crucial Maps* (1964), chap. iv, and Wroth, in his forthcoming book on Verrazzano, go into the maps derived from this voyage in great detail. One of the most interesting is the Ulpinus copper globe of 1542, in the New-York Historical Society. Ulpinus, a Florentine, wished to be fair to his fellow citizen and so put in the Sea of Verrazzano and the nomenclature of that voyage, in addition to names from Cape Cod eastward which must have come from Gomez or Ribero. L. A. Vigneras has fresh material in *Terrae Incognitae*, II (1970), 25–28.

For Gomez's ignoble part in the Magellan armada, see Charles McKew Parr, *So Noble a Captain* (New York, 1953), Visconde de Lagóa, *Fernão de Magalhâis*, Vol. II (Lisbon, 1936), and J. Alexander Robertson (ed.), *Magellan's Voyage Around the World by Antonio Pigafetta* (Cleveland, 1906), I, 237–38. Armando Cortesão, who despises Gomez as a double traitor to Portugal, tells of his 1533–34 activities in *Cartografia . . . dos seculos XV e XVI* (1935), II, 203.

Gomez's discoveries are mentioned on the Desceliers's Harleian, or Dauphin, Map of 1542 in the British Museum, part of which is reproduced in Chapter XI below, and the rest of the North American part in Biggar, *Voyages of Cartier*, p. 128. Desceliers's coastline is based on Ribero's but his nomenclature differs. The Penobscot is here called *R. dos yslas;* and Cape Cod, *Cavo St. John.* West of the Penobscot is *Archipel de Estiene gomez,* the island-studded bay that I have identified as Muscongus Sound; others believe it to represent Casco Bay. Desceliers digs a convenient channel through the Carolina Banks to the Sea of Verrazzano; but he uses none of the Florentine's nomenclature. Next to this strait is the *R. de jordan,* scene of Ayllón's ill-starred colony.

AYLLÓN

The sad story of Ayllón, the sea-going judge, is found in greatest detail in H. Harrisse, *The Discovery of North America*, pp. 198–213, and, briefly, in Edward G. Bourne, *Spain in America* (1904), pp. 138–40. The sources (except for the text of Ayllón's patent and documents in a suit against him at Santo Domingo) are all secondary, starting with Peter Martyr; and, to my knowledge, nothing fresh has been found since John G. Shea in Justin Winsor, *Narrative and Critical History* (1886) II, 238–41, brought out the gory details of Ayllón's attempted settlement on the Rio Jordán. Shea located that inside Chesapeake Bay, but Harrisse's location on the Cape Fear River is much more reasonable.

SAINTS' DAYS IN NOMENCLATURE

Some of the names on the Santa Cruz and Ribero maps, as we have noted, indicate that Gomez followed the practice of other Portuguese and Spanish navigators in naming a prominent point after the saint on whose feast day it was discovered. St. John the Baptist's day is 24 June, and the Visitation of Our Lady (*La Buena Madre*) on 2 July. But Columbus named half a dozen islands after the Virgin without any reference to the days on which she is particularly honored. Saints' days vary from country to country and century to century; I have checked from the calendar in the early sixteenth-century *Regimento do Estrolabio e do Quadrante*, published in facsimile by my esteemed and regretted friend Dr. Joachim Bensaude (Lisbon, 1924). Gomez may well have had a copy of the original edition on board. This method of dating a voyage is far from infallible; some who have tried it arrive at the absurdity of sailing along the Labrador and Newfoundland coasts in the dead of winter, and others have postulated imaginary voyages simply from a series of saints' days on a map. As Skelton says, identifying discoveries from saints' names is "a hazardous proceeding."

✳ XI ✳

Cartier's First Voyage

1534

Now brothers, for the icebergs
Of frozen Labrador
Floating spectral in the moonshine
Along the low, black shore,
Where like snow the gannet's feathers
On Bradore's rocks are shed
And the noisy murre are flying
Like black scuds overhead.

J. G. WHITTIER "THE FISHERMAN"

Le Maître-Pilote Jacques Cartier

In southern Normandy near the border of Brittany there stands out the remarkable island and abbey of Mont-Saint-Michel. Of old it could be reached only by sea at high water or over the sands at low water; a dangerous procedure because the flood tide roars in with the speed of a galloping horse, overwhelming any man or beast it overtakes. The monastery, built in the Dark Ages and rebuilt or enlarged by the piety of Norman dukes and French kings, has been a place of pilgrimage for a thousand years. Pilgrims still go there to pray, make vows, and be shrived; tourists come to admire the site and the architecture—and also to consume omelettes *chez* Madame Poulard *ainée*. Madame and her rival daughter-in-law are long since gone; but (judging from what their successors did for us) at any hour a fire of crackling thorns will be kindled on an open hearth, eggs broken into a heavy iron skillet, and a delicious omelette produced.

Since omelettes are a traditional delicacy of Mont-Saint-Michel, we

Saint-Malo from Saint-Servan, by Louis Garneray, *c.* 1820. Musée de Saint-Malo. Photo Philippot.

permit ourselves to imagine that they figured in the hospitality afforded to François-premier at a moment when the history of France in the New World began. The king, performing a pilgrimage in 1532 in company with his son the Dauphin, was received by the very magnificent Jean Le Veneur de Tilliers, abbot of Mont-Saint-Michel, grand almoner of France, bishop and count of Lisieux. He there presented to the king a relative of the abbey's treasurer, Jacques Cartier by name, master mariner of nearby Saint-Malo. This man, said the bishop, in consideration of his voyages to Newfoundland and Brazil, is capable of commanding ships "to discover new lands in the New World" for France; and if the king would consent so to employ him, the bishop promised to furnish chaplains for the voyage, and even contribute to the cost.

François-premier did consent, Cartier sailed, and Canada was born. But many voyages had to be performed and many false starts made before the fleur-de-lys could be firmly planted on the Rock of Quebec by Samuel de Champlain.

The first obstacle was the bull of Pope Alexander VI dividing the New World between Spain and Portugal. Clement VII, pope in 1532, was a Medici and an ally of François-premier against Charles V; one of the king's sons, the future Henri II, married the pope's niece Catherine de' Medici. That made it easy, when king, pope, and Bishop Le Veneur met at Marseilles to celebrate this union in 1533, to persuade the Holy Father to declare that the Alexandrine edict applied only to lands already discovered, not to those later found by other sovereigns. Thus François-premier had the green light from the Vatican, and passed the word to Jacques Cartier.

Who was this master mariner of Saint-Malo, destined to become the founder of New France? We know a little more about him than we do of Verrazzano, and far more than we do of John Cabot. He was born in 1491, at "the ancient town of Saint-Malo, thrust out like a buttress into the sea, strange and grim of aspect, breathing war from its walls and battlements of ragged stone, a stronghold of privateers, the home of a race whose intractable and defiant independence neither time nor change has subdued." Thus Francis Parkman happily described this ancient seaport and the Bretons. After a destructive bombardment in 1944 the town rose from its ashes, and was rebuilt in the old style with Breton granite, gray with flecks of gold.

Cartier in legal documents is called a bourgeois. Born to a respectable family of mariners, he improved his social status in 1520 by marrying Catherine des Granches, of a leading Malouin ship-owning family. For aught we know they were a faithful and loving couple, but they had no children. His good name in Saint-Malo is proved by its frequent appearance in baptismal registers, as godfather or witness. And we have more than the bishop's word that he had made voyages to Newfoundland and Brazil. In his narratives of the Canadian voyages he makes several allusions to the people and products of Brazil, and in Newfoundland he seemed to be at home.

We do not really know what Cartier looked like. The portrait with which the public is most familiar, showing a stern-visaged man looking glumly out to sea, was painted by a Russian artist in 1839 for the city of Saint-Malo. It might as well have been labeled "Dostoevski Communing with his Soul." Other portraits have been "discovered" or

Sketch by M. Dan Lailler, Conservateur du Musée de Saint-Malo, of an early portrait of Cartier. Owned privately.

produced by obliging antique dealers of Paris from time to time, but none can reasonably be accepted as genuine. The Desceliers-Harleian Map of 1542, here reproduced, shows on the Gaspé peninsula a cloaked figure, featureless except for a forked beard, handing something to a man with a huge pointed nose, behind whom a horse team harrows a patch of ground outside a French-style farmhouse. The one we have used, from a sketch by M. Dan Lailler, is not strictly contemporary, but nearly so; and I believe it to be a portrait of the navigator in his old age.

Since no contemporary has left us a word on Cartier's personality, it has to be inferred from such sources as we have. They indicate that Champlain's later description of the character of "a good and perfect navigator" applies to him:

> Above all to be a good man, fearing God, not allowing His sacred name to be blasphemed on board his ship, . . . and careful to have prayers said morning and evening. . . . He had better not be a delicate eater or drinker, otherwise he will be frequently upset by changes of climate and food. . . . Be continually on his guard against scurvy, and be provided with remedies against it. He should be robust and alert, have good sea-legs and be indefatigable . . . so that whatever accident may befall he can keep the deck and in a strong voice order everyone to do his duty. He must not be above lending a hand to the work himself, to make the seamen more prompt in their attention. . . .
>
> He should be pleasant and affable in conversation, absolute

Section of the Harleian-Desceliers-Dauphin Map of 1542, with alleged portrait of Cartier. Courtesy British Museum; photo Giraudon.

in his commands, not too ready to talk with shipmates, except the officers; otherwise he might be despised. He should punish ill-doers severely, and reward good men, gratifying them from time to time with a pat on the back, praising them but not overdoing it, so as to give no occasion for envy—that gangrene which corrupts the body and if not promptly quenched leads to faction and conspiracy among the crew. . . . He should never let himself be overcome by wine, for if an officer or seaman becomes a drunkard it is dangerous to entrust him with responsibility; he might be sleeping like a pig when an accident occurs . . . and be the cause of loss of the vessel. . . . He should turn night into day, watch the greater part of the night, always sleep clothed so as to be ready to come on deck promptly if anything happens. He must keep a private compass below and consult it frequently to see if the ship is on her course. . . . He must be . . . cognizant of everything concerning ship handling, especially of making sail. He should take care to have good food and drink for his voyage, and such as will not spoil, to have good dry bins to keep bread or hardtack; and, especially for long voyages, to take too much rather than too little. . . . He must be a good economist in issuing rations, giving each man reasonably what he needs, otherwise dissatisfaction will be created, . . . and entrust the distribution of victuals to a good and faithful steward, not a drunkard but a good manager; for a careful man in this office is above all price.

Considering that Cartier made three voyages of discovery in dangerous and hitherto unknown waters without losing a ship; that he entered and departed some fifty undiscovered harbors without serious mishap; that the only sailors he lost were victims of an epidemic ashore, and that he performed everything that a good seaman could for king and country, we may assume that he conformed to these rules later dictated by his great sucessor Champlain. They were as applicable in the following centuries as in the sixteenth; in fact, a modern naval officer or master of a merchant ship would do well to heed them today.

Fishermen from Saint-Malo and other Breton ports, as we have seen in earlier chapters, were already doing well on the Grand Bank and inshore. Cartier must have sailed in one or more of these vessels; possibly the one which discovered that the Strait of Belle Isle led to a great gulf. For, in the court order organizing Cartier's first voyage, he is authorized to sail "beyond the strait of the Baye des Chasteaulx," the earliest name of the Strait of Belle Isle.

Cartier's title, in all these documents pertaining to his first voyage, is

"Capitaine et Pilote pour le Roy." This means that he was captain by the king's command, but a master pilot by experience. In all European languages *pilot* then had two meanings: (1) a local river or harbor pilot who guided ships in and out, as today; and (2) a seagoing officer, corresponding roughly to first mate, next under the captain and master. He took charge of navigation, kept the reckoning, and usually (unless the master insisted on taking charge) ordered making and taking in of sail. Cartier was the second kind of pilot, and in his American voyages he took on the responsibilities of captain and master as well. Moreover, in all three fleets he was senior captain, what we would call commodore.

Cartier's First Voyage Gets Under Way

Even in want of any surviving copy of Cartier's royal commission, we can infer from the narratives of his voyage that his main charge was to find a passage to China; and his second, to discover sources of precious metals. Verrazzano had insisted (without adequate evidence) that these were to be found in northern regions. Preparations for the first voyage were not too easy. The king's treasurer for his navy granted Cartier on 18 March 1534 the sum of 6000 livres tournois (roughly equivalent to the same number of gold francs) for the equipment, provisioning, and seamen's wages of "certain ships . . . which should in company with and under the command of Jacques Cartier make the voyage from this kingdom to *Terres Neufves*, to discover certain isles and countries where there is said to be found a vast quantity of gold and other rich things." And in a local court order of next day, he is described as "*Maistre Jacques Cartier, capitaine et pilote pour le Roy*, in charge of voyaging and going *aux Terres Neuffves*, beyond the strait of the *baye des Chasteaulx*." Terres Neuffves in this instance means all lands to be newly discovered in that region.

As Columbus had wryly observed, royal orders are not promptly obeyed in outports; and the merchants of Saint-Malo, fearing a scarcity of hands for their fishing vessels, were so successful in preventing mariners from signing on with Cartier that he had to persuade the *procureur* of Saint-Malo to clap an embargo on the Banks fishing vessels until such time as the "Captain and pilot for the king" had obtained a full complement. That did it; and on 20 April 1534 Cartier was able to sail from Saint-Malo in command of two ships, each of "about" sixty tuns' burthen and each manned by a crew of sixty-one men. This means that they were of about the same burthen as Verrazzano's *La Dauphine*. Regrettably, no record of their names or those of their officers has survived.

The voyage began with a ceremony at Saint-Malo. Charles de Mouy, vice-admiral of France, swore in the captain and crew, in the presence of wives, sweethearts, and parents, "well and loyally to conduct themselves in the service of the king and under command of the said Cartier." The two vessels sailed 20 April under a first-quarter moon—good for clearing the English Channel—and on 10 May, in the dark of the moon, made landfall on Cape Bonavista, Newfoundland—an Atlantic passage of only twenty days. Cartier must have been favored by a rare prolonged burst of easterly wind. It is evident that he was using the old method of latitude sailing, and to a known objective. For the latitude of Saint-Malo is 48°39' N, and that of Cape Bonavista, 48°42'. Cartier's *Première Relation* of this voyage called it 48°30'—near enough; any yacht navigator of today would be pleased to do as well. Cape Bonavista had obviously become a favorite landfall of French fishermen.

Nevertheless, Cartier ran risks in arriving so early in the year. The 10th of May (19 May in our calendar) is a bad time for ice on the east coast of Newfoundland, and he encountered plenty of it—so much indeed that he found it necessary to enter "un havre nonmé *saincte Katherine*" five leagues to the southeast. Distance and bearing are correct for the harbor now called Catalina, a snug little port where the English later established a flourishing fishing village. Here the two ships tarried for ten days, making repairs; the fast ocean passage must have been rough on sails, spars, and tackle.

On 21 May when the wind came west, blowing away icebergs that were hammering the coast, and the new moon had passed its first quarter, "We departed the said harbor," says Cartier's *Première Relation*. He shaped a northerly course to *L'Isle des Ouaisseaulx* (Isle of Birds), as he named it, 80 miles distant. For reasons obvious to the nose it became *Puanto* (stinking) island on the Testu map of 1555, and is Funk Island today. This islet, hardly more than a rock, lies 32 miles north-northeast of Cape Freels, the nearest land. As Cartier doubtless remembered from his earlier visit, it was covered with nesting birds, under a feathered umbrella of thousands more, flying and screaming. The biggest species, unable to fly, was the great auk, the original penguin, which Cartier called *apponatz*. His crew in half an hour killed enough to fill two boats. They ate some fresh, and salted down ten or twelve barrels for future consumption. In addition they saw multitudes of birds that they called *godez* (either the murre or the razorbill auk) and the snow-white *margaulx* (gannet) "which bite even as dogs" when one disturbs their nests. The Beothuk Indians used to paddle their canoes to Funk Island for the sake of great auk meat, and it is said that bears swam from Cape Freels to gorge themselves on wild fowl. Cartier's ships met a swimming bear on 24 May after they had left the island, "as big as a cow and white as a swan." The men took to their boats and killed this enterprising polar bear; "its flesh was as good and delicate to eat as that of a two-year-old steer." Sebastian Cabot had set the fashion for bear stories about Newfoundland.

From Funk the two ships stretched northwest some 140 miles, and on the day of full moon, 27 May, made Cape Bauld, which Cartier calls *Dégrat;* this is the first appearance of the name of Cabot's probable landfall. Cartier observed that the cape was on an island with two good harbors—*Karpont* (now Quirpon) and *L'Anse Dégrat*—on the eastern side of Quirpon Island. How strange that three distinguished discoverers, Leif Ericsson, John Cabot, and Jacques Cartier, were drawn to this remote and lonely spot at intervals of five hundred years and more! Cartier well observes that Quirpon Harbor may be entered from the east or the west, and that the western entrance is the better; he gives the latitude as 51°30′ N, which is almost correct, the eastern entrance being only five miles north of that.

Cartier or one of his men must have climbed 500-foot-high Cape Dégrat, since he writes that from it one sees clearly two *Belles Iles* "which are near Cap Rouge," well to the southward. He could not have meant the present Belle Isle, which lies 18 miles *north* of Cape Dégrat, and was not so named until after Cartier's day, but two "fair islands," the pair now known as The Gray, or Grey, Islands, Groais and Bell. The former, a high island, could easily have been seen from Cape Dégrat. The real Belle Isle, Cartier never mentions, outward or homeward; but it is so named and described in *La Cosmographie* of Jean Alfonce, Roberval's pilot.

South Shore of The Labrador

Cartier was delayed several days at Quirpon by contrary winds and ice. During the first week of June, sailing west by north from Cape Bauld, he passed two islands to port. These must have been the bigger Sacred Island, which in the eleventh century screened Leif Ericsson's settlement from the sea, and Schooner Island. This he well describes as flat, low, and appearing to merge with the mainland; he named it *Saincte Katherine*, after his wife's patron saint. Then, sailing fifteen miles due north across the Strait of Belle Isle, he entered *le hable des Chasteaulx*, Labrador, already so named by French fishermen and still called Château Bay. The island at the entrance, with a sheer cliff of vertical columns of basaltic rock two hundred feet high, and a flat top like the glacis of a castle, gave the harbor its name. The official Sailing Directions for Newfoundland dismisses Château Bay thus: "Little grass grows in the vicinity but moss is plentiful and there is considerable cranberry growth. Mosquitoes and flies are troublesome in summer." The back country here is to the last degree rocky and barren, but the harbor is excellent and in the colonial era it rivaled Blanc Sablon as a fishing rendezvous. Considered to be the key to the northern fisheries, it was fortified in the eighteenth century by both the French and British.

As Cartier turned southwest up the Strait of Belle Isle to follow the mountainous south coast of the Labrador, he began the most difficult, as well as the least profitable, leg of his voyage. The entire north coast of the Gulf, as far as the Bay of Seven Islands, is studded with outlying islets and reefs; and these waters are opaque, unlike those of the Caribbean where one can see bottom through six fathom or more of water. Cartier, however, had threaded all the murmurous passes of the sea into iron-bound Brittany, and he sailed so carefully that not once on this voyage did either of his ships touch bottom.

Steering southwesterly through the Strait of Belle Isle, Cartier named two small harbors *des Buttes* (of the knolls) and *de la Baleine* (of the whale). The first, now Black Bay, with two conspicuous hillocks, is recommended by the Sailing Directions as a temporary summer anchorage only; the second, now Red Bay, with red granite cliffs and

Château Island, Château Bay, Labrador.

marked by a 550-foot hill with white boulders on top, was formerly a favorite anchorage for fishing vessels. It was here that Dr. Wilfred Grenfell founded his first Labrador hospital. Alas, there was not a sailing fisherman to be seen in the entire Gulf of St. Lawrence when we flew around it in 1969. But there were still plenty of icebergs.

Thirty-five miles further, Cartier reached the harbor of Blanc Sablon, already named by French fishermen and still so called today. Cartier well describes it as "a *conche* [shell] where there is no shelter from the south or southeast," to which he might have added the southwest. At the head of it is a gray sandy beach and dunes, which when sunstruck look white. Despite its exposed anchorage and being closed in by ice from December to mid-May, Blanc Sablon became a famous fishing port. The fishermen liked the beach, where they could haul up their boats, and the dunes, on which they dried their catch; sheltered anchorage for their ships lay around the corner.

Lying off Blanc Sablon to the south-southwest, says Cartier, are two islands which he calls *Bouays* and *des Ouaisseaulx;* they are now Isle au Bois and Greenly Island. On Greenly, marked by two hillocks, Cartier

349

Black Bay and Red Bay, Labrador. Cartier's *Port des Buttes* and *Port de la Baleine*. Taken 26 August 1967 from elevation of 30,000 feet. The dark areas are dwarf spruce; light areas, bare rock. Courtesy Air Photo Division, Canadian Government.

first encountered great flocks of puffin, which he describes as having red beaks and feet, and nesting in holes in the ground like conys. Multitudes still nest there, now that Greenly has become a Canadian bird sanctuary. The French named this bird *perroquet* (parakeet) because of its parrot-like beak, and a little island around Long Point is so named. Greenly Island figures in the history of aviation, because in April 1928 three aviators, Fitzmaurice, Koehl, and Von Huenefeld, one Irish and two German, attempting a transatlantic flight from Dublin in the W-33L *Bremen*, made an emergency landing there. It was the first east-west crossing by air, and took 36½ hours. Although the *Bremen* was smashed, the aviators survived. Floyd Bennett died on a flight to rescue them from Greenly.

Cartier, passing island-studded Bradore Bay and safely threading

Greenly Island off Blanc Sablon.

The beach that gave Blanc Sablon its name.

The natural rock road from Blanc Sablon village to the harbor.

another archipelago with the aid of alert masthead lookouts, entered on 10 June a harbor that he named after Brest in Brittany. There the two ships took on wood and water. This was the harbor now named Bonne Esperance, which the Sailing Directions for the Gulf of St. Lawrence describe as "excellent." Cartier took the sun and recorded the latitude as 51°55'. This was not one of his best efforts—about thirty miles out.

Next day, 11 June, was St. Barnabas's day, which in the Julian calendar was the longest of the year, and it was also the day of new moon. English children used to sing:

> Barnaby bright—
> Longest day and shortest night.

Cartier, after hearing mass, organized a boat party and had himself rowed westward, discovering innumerable islands which he called *Toutes Isles*. The crew spent the night on one, where they found and cooked fresh eider ducks' eggs; these were also greatly relished by Canadians in the nineteenth century.

On 12 June, the boat party having returned, the ships resumed their voyage, and at twilight entered a good harbor which Cartier named *Saint-Antoine*, it being the feast of that much-tempted saint. He investigated another harbor a mile distant, which he called *Saint-Servan* after the old town adjoining Saint-Malo. One league southwest of Saint-Servan he landed on "an islet round as an oven" and set up a cross with the arms of France. Saint-Antoine has been identified by H. F. Lewis as the now unnamed space between Dog Islands and the mainland, Saint-Servan as Rocky Bay, and the islet as the present Le Boulet. Lewis found there a cairn of stones which may well have been a base to Cartier's cross.

Two leagues beyond (assuming that *dix* of the narrative is a mistake for *deux*), they entered a bay—either the Shekatika (now renamed Jacques Cartier) or St. Augustine River, which they named *Rivière Saint-Jacques*, after their Captain's patron saint. Here they took many salmon. In the offing, becalmed, they saw the only ship encountered on this voyage: a big fishing craft from La Rochelle, whose seamen (said Cartier) did not know where they were; a remark perhaps dictated by annoyance over his being second on the scene. But he sent his long boats to tow the vessel into a nearby harbor. The Rochelais joined

Dog Island and Le Boulet, "round as an oven," where Cartier set up the Cross.

Lobster and Rocky Bays.

Cartier, and in company sailed to one of the several harbors in the St. Augustine estuary, probably the one now named Cumberland, which the Captain named after himself, *Havre de Jacques-Cartier.* He observed that it was "one of the best harbors in the world"—an exaggeration, of course; but the official *Sailing Directions* concede it to be "one of the best harbors along this coast." At that point, apparently, the fishermen parted company and sailed home, with a good fare of fish, it is to be hoped.

Cartier in his *Première Relation* is very uncomplimentary about this land. "Were the soil as good as the harbors, it would be fine; but this [coast] should not be called *Terre Neuve*, being composed of stones and frightful rocks and uneven places; for on this entire northern coast I saw not one cartload of earth, though I landed in many places. Except for Blanc Sablon there is nothing but moss and stunted shrubs. To conclude, I am inclined to regard this land as the one God gave to Cain."

Such candor about a newly discovered country, well justified in this case, is very rare among discoverers. For most, a scrawny wood is a noble forest, every stretch of open country the richest soil in the world, every glittering stone a precious gem. Even Cartier, as we shall see, was seduced into the belief that he had discovered diamonds. Audubon, who called this a "poor, rugged, miserable country," endorsed Cartier's description. The desolation is the same today: granite hills smoothed by a glacier, stunted spruce in the valleys the only green, and all extending northward as far as the eye can see.

The natives, whom Cartier had met somewhere between Blanc Sablon and Rocky Bay, he describes thus: "The men are well enough formed but untamed and savage. They wear their hair bound on top of their heads like a fistful of twisted hay, sticking into it a pin or something and adding some birds' feathers. They are clothed in peltry, men and women alike, but the women shape theirs more to their figures and gird their waists. They paint themselves with tan colors. They have boats in which they go to sea made of birch bark, and from which they catch a great quantity of seal. Since seeing them I have ascertained that they are not natives of this place, but come from warmer regions to take seal and other things to eat."

From this brief description, and the vocabulary which he added to the *Première Relation*, some ethnologists conclude that these were an Iroquoian tribe from the St. Lawrence valley; others identify them as the Newfoundland Beothuk, who are known to have been great seal hunters. Seal-bone heaps are as common along the Newfoundland coast as clamshell heaps in Maine.

West Coast of Newfoundland

Returning to New Brest (Bonne Esperance Harbor), Cartier caused mass to be held on Sunday, 14 June, and next day shaped a new course to explore the west coast of Newfoundland. Nobody knows why he made this radical change of course instead of continuing right on to "Cathay." A change of wind, perhaps, or mere curiosity to discover the back side of Newfoundland, which all earlier maps had left blank.

Sailing south twenty leagues (46 nautical miles), he came into his first Newfoundland thick o'fog. It lifted in time to sight a cape where there was a long, low point and behind it one small hill and a big one; so he named it *Cap Double*. This may easily be identified as Point Rich; the profile in Captain Cook's chart of 1770 shows the two hills very clearly.

After spending the night in a small harbor near by, Cartier's fleet on 16 June sailed southwest by south thirty-five leagues (80 miles) along a range of mountains that he named *Monts des Granches* because one of them resembled a barn—*grange* in French. It does look like a huge stone barn as you pass it today. The mountains, now called the Long Range, have an even altitude of some 2500 feet. In the evening the Captain observed a break in the coastline and approached a promontory, which he called *Cap Pointu*. He described it as rugged on top but pointed where it enters the sea, and to the north of it, a flat islet. This cape is the modern Cow Head, and the islet is now Stearing Island. He spent the night in a very beautiful harbor just south of the point, now St. Paul's Bay and Inlet.

On 17 June a northeast gale blew up. They clewed up the mainsail, housed the topmasts, and scudded southwesterly until the following morning, when they found themselves off a bay "full of round islands like dovecotes, and for this reason gave them the name *Coulombiers*" and the bay, *Sainct Jullian*. This was the beautiful Bay of Islands, opening between two gray, rocky headlands covered with spruce trees. Two or three islets, with a little imagination, may be compared to dovecotes.

High Land of S. *John*

Sketch of the scenery from Ferolle Pt. to Point Rich (Cartier's *Cap Double*). From Captain James Cook's Chart of Newfoundland, 1770.

From here southward the scenery becomes more spectacular, a high, bold coast with reddish cliffs and waterfalls cascading directly into the sea. Cartier noticed 1255-foot-high Bear Head and named it *Cap Royal*. Off that cape, on a twenty-fathom bank marked on the modern chart, his men found the best fishing of the entire voyage; in

St. Paul's Inlet.

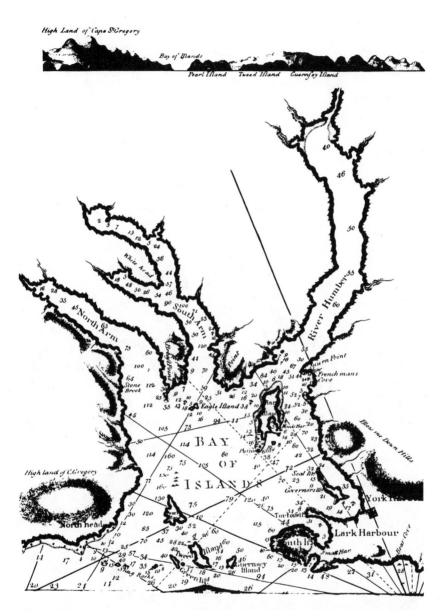

Bay of Islands (Cartier's *St. Julian*), from C. Gregory to Bear Head
(*Cap Royal*). Capt. Cook's Chart of Newfoundland, 1770.

Cape St. George (Cartier's *Cap de Latte*), Newfoundland. Note the castle-like point. Photo by Dr. Paul Sheldon, 1970.

Fort La Latte, Brittany, from Cap Fréhel.

Fort La Latte, close-up.

less than an hour, while waiting for the other ship to catch up, they pulled in more than a hundred *grosses morues*, big codfish.

The next prominent point, off which lay a low island at a distance of a mile and a half, Cartier called *Cap de Latte*, after Fort La Latte near Saint-Malo, with which he was familiar. The Breton fort is a medieval castle on a lonely promontory. The ruins, when first I saw them in 1913, might well have inspired the last act of Wagner's *Tristan und Isolde;* but the fort has since been restored. Cartier's Cap de Latte is magnificent, and so sheer as to suggest castle walls rising directly from the edge of the sea, as they do in the Breton fort. The English changed the name to Cape St. George; and the low island which Cartier noticed is now named Red, from the color of the rocks.

"The next day, the 18th of the said month" (June), states the *Première Relation*, "the wind blew strong and contrary so we returned to find shelter," and put into a great bay between Bear Head and Cape St. George, now called Port au Port. The latitude he gives as 48°30', which is correct for Cape St. George. A boat party sent ahead to explore reported so much foul ground that Cartier decided not to enter: a sound decision and a good instance of the care with which our *maître-pilote* reconnoitered a new harbor. One could not risk being entangled in foul ground or suffer the inconvenience of being embayed by a wind blowing directly into a narrow entrance. The current Sailing Directions give a forbidding picture of the rocks and shoals within this entrance; the only secure anchorage is in Head Harbor, twelve miles above Fox Island, which Cartier noted but did not name, and Fox Island is six miles inside the entrance. Probably the boat party penetrated that far and reported adversely to their commander.

Accordingly they put out to sea, shaping a westerly course. From 19 to 26 June they had contrary winds and stormy weather and did not sight land again until "the day of St. John," when they sighted Cape Anguille—which Cartier accordingly named *Cap Sainct Jehan*. Even with a full moon, it was too risky to close the coast and seek a harbor; and actually there was none. Codroy, now an active little port, had to be made snug by a breakwater.

Cape Anguille, briefly glimpsed through the mist, was the last point of Newfoundland that Cartier sighted on this voyage until he turned homeward. He had found nothing but fish "to write home about" on the west coast of Newfoundland. Presently he would discover islands and harbors to arouse his enthusiasm.

The Magdalen Islands
Bird Island (Cartier's *Ile de Margaulx*). The white dots in the air are
gannets, and so are the white places on the cliffs.

Ile de Brion.

Beach connecting two parts of the Magdalen Islands.

Brion, Magdalen, and Prince Edward Islands

From Cap Saint-Jean on 25 June, Cartier sailed west-northwest close hauled in "foul weather, overcast and blowy," and in the evening he hove-to. The two ships made sail again at midnight, when the wind shifted to northwest as it usually does after an easterly gale. A southwest traverse on 26 June brought them to "three islets, two of them as steep as a wall, so that you cannot climb up." These are the Bird Rocks; the biggest is 105 feet high and less than a quarter-mile long. Cartier named them *Isles de Margaulx* after the gannets which, together with auks, murres, puffins, and kittiwakes, were "as thick ashore as a meadow with grass." Or, as Captain Charles Leigh described them half a century later, "as thicke as stones lie on a paved street." Even after four centuries of indiscriminate slaughter they still do; the gannets sit so close as to look like icing on a cake, and their whiteness renders these rocks visible seven miles away on a moonlit night. Cartier's men landed on the biggest islet and killed more than a thousand murre and great auk; in an hour they could have filled thirty boats with birds had they wished.

"Five leagues west from the said islets," says Cartier, "was another island, . . . about two leagues long and as wide. We spent the night there to take on wood and water. . . . This island has the best land that we have seen; one *arpent* of it is worth more than the whole of Newfoundland. We found it full of beautiful trees, meadows, fields of wild wheat and pease in flower as fair and abundant as I ever saw in Brittany, and appearing to have been sowed by farmers. There are plenty of gooseberries, strawberries and roses of Provins, parsley, and other good sweet-smelling herbs. And around this island, several big beasts, big as oxen, with two teeth in their mouth like the elephant, and which live in the sea"—the walrus. "We also saw bears and foxes." The island he named *L'Ile de Bryon* after his supporter, Philippe de Chabot, seigneur de Brion and admiral of France. Cartier's description seems ecstatic for an island only one mile by five; but he did not exaggerate— much. A French writer who visited the island about 1878 wrote: "Brion has lost its air of terrestrial paradise. Its great trees have disappeared. . . . Its incarnadine roses are dead, suffocated by the bitter kisses of the north wind. But the island's soil has preserved its fertility;

Southern part of the Magdalen Islands in 1969.

Entry Island, Magdalen Group. The red cliffs with huge white blotches make it an ideal landmark for fishermen.

its meadows are famous throughout the Gulf of St. Lawrence. . . .
The cattle pastured there are superb, and the sheep of Brion meet the
requirements of our most finicky Canadian butchers at Eastertide."
When we visited Brion Island in 1969, it was about half open-pasturage
and half spruce forest; nobody appeared to be living there but the
lighthouse keeper, and no cattle were visible.

At this point Cartier interjects in his *Première Relation*, "I rather
think, from what I have observed, that there exists a passage between
Newfoundland and the Land of the Bretons; if so, it would be a great
time and distance saver if this voyage [to China] succeeds." Of course
there was such a passage—Cabot Strait between Cape Ray and Cape
Breton; and why Cartier did not investigate it before returning home
is a puzzle.

"Four leagues from the said island to the west-southwest," says
Cartier, "there is a *terre firme* which appears to be an island, surrounded by sand islands. It has a fair cape which we called *Cap du
Daulphin*, as it marks the beginning of good land." This name, the
title of the king's eldest son, has since been attached to the eastern
point of the Magdalen Islands. Cartier did not name these islands
because he considered them to be mainland. He sounded the eight-
mile channel between Brion Island and Cape Dauphin and found
"fine sandy bottom and even depth." The modern chart agrees. "We
struck sail and lay-to" for the night, says Cartier, because he wished
to gain a more ample acquaintance with these waters.

"On the 27th of the said month of June" with a full moon, "we
ranged this land, which runs east-northeast—west-southwest, and
seems to consist of sand dunes. . . . We could not go thither or land,
because the wind made up from off shore," which made it too difficult
for a rowing boat. Next day, 28 June, having apparently lain at hull
all night, he resumed his sail along the Magdalens, noting a cape of
bright red earth (Hospital Point, Grindstone Island) which he named
Cap Saint-Pierre, it being the feast of Saints Peter and Paul. He observed the sand bars, the numerous lagoons, and the curve of the coast.

The Magdalen group is a curious chain of islets, each with a fairly
high hill, and most of them connected by sand causeways which every
big gale threatens to wash away; over the centuries it has been the
scene of very many wrecks. The English captain George Drake
in 1593 found the harbors occupied by Bretons from Saint-Malo and

Basque whalers from Saint-Jean de Luz, and when Leigh tried to obtain a footing there he was repulsed by two hundred French and three hundred Indians. After the expulsion of the Acadians from Nova Scotia, they effected a permanent settlement on the Magdalens, and their descendants are still there. Admiral Sir Isaac Coffin R.N., a native of Nantucket, received a grant of the islands from the crown as a reward for saving his frigate under their lee during a furious gale, when conveying Lord Dorchester to Quebec in 1786. He established a feudal tenure and made a good thing out of the dues. His heirs were bought out by Quebec and, owing to the rich cod and other fisheries in the surrounding waters, which have given them the name *le royaume des poissons* among the French, the islands in 1969 boasted a population of over 10,000, have a lively export trade in frozen cod fillets, and are beginning to attract tourists.

Noting the 300-foot-high Southwest Cape on Amherst Island, Cartier sailed west, and, eight miles beyond, observed a high, pointed rock, which he named *Allezay*, an old French word having something to do with an anvil. Later the French called it *Corps-Mort*, which the English translated as *The Deadman*. Tom Moore, in a poem that he wrote about it when sailing by in 1804, explains the name. A shadowy bark, wraith of a wreck on the "cold and pitiless Labrador,"

> To Deadman's Isle, in the eye of the blast,
> To Deadman's Isle she speeds her fast,
> By skeleton shapes her sails are furl'd,
> And the hand that steers is not of this world!

Cartier seems to have been fascinated by this group of islands, which he evidently regarded as mainland until his return from the second voyage in 1536. This is borne out by the Desceliers Harleian Map of 1542 (which we have reproduced) showing *C. de Daulphyn* on a mainland near *Yle de brion* and *isles de Margaux*—the Bird Rocks.

On 29 June, with wind south by west, Cartier left these waters, ran west all night, and next day at sunset sighted what appeared to be two islands. These were the heights of land on Prince Edward Island around New London Bay. He reached this big fertile island at about its middle and coasted northwest to a "very beautiful cape" which he named *Cap d'Orléans* after Charles, duc d'Orléans, youngest son of the king. This was probably Cape Kildare. "All this land is low and uniform," wrote Cartier, "the fairest one could possibly see, and full of

Allezay, The Deadman.

Cap des Sauvages, Cape North, P.E.I.

View on the north shore of Prince Edward Island. Courtesy Canadian Government Travel Bureau.

fine trees and meadows; but we could find no harbor there," only shoals and rocks. They landed several times from their boats and entered a beautiful but shallow river, "where we saw the savages' boats, and for that reason called it *rifvière de Barraques*." This figures conspicuously on the Harleian Map, in a shape that suggests Malpeque Bay. Sailing as he did, from point to point, Cartier never realized that Prince Edward was an island, although Gomez and probably Fagundes had done so before him. He did, however, have the good sense to put out to sea when an easterly wind blew up, making that coast a lee shore. Clawing off on the starboard tack, he cleared the land safely, and at 10 a.m. on 1 July sighted the cape he had just named d'Orléans and another, seven leagues north by east, which he named *Cap de Sauvages*, because an Indian appeared on the shore, making friendly gestures. Although the distance is exaggerated, the course is almost correct, and this "wild men's cape," as Hakluyt translated it, must have been Cape North of Prince Edward Island; Cartier observed the dangerous shoal off it on which the sea was boiling. Apparently he rounded the cape and coasted for about thirty miles toward Egmont Bay without finding a harbor, landing in four places "to see the trees, which are marvellously beautiful and sweet smelling; and we found them to be cedar, yew, pine, white elm, ash, willow, and several others unknown to us." The open country he found "very fair and full of pease, white and red gooseberries, strawberries, raspberries, and wild wheat like rye, which looks as if it had been sowed and cultivated"—Leif Ericsson's lyme grass again. "It is the most temperate land that one could ask for, and of great heat; and there are many turtledoves, wood-pigeons, and other birds; only good harbors are wanting." This is a fair description of that part of Prince Edward Island, now intensively cultivated by the industrious inhabitants. As Cartier observed, there is nothing more de-

John Rotz's "Boke of Idrographie," 1542, folios 23–24. Rotz had information of Cartier's first voyage only, as proved by Cape Gaspé being joined to Anticosti, and the Magdalen and Prince Edward Islands being joined to the mainland. The V-shaped bay on the west is the Penobscot. Courtesy Map Division, Public Archives of Canada.

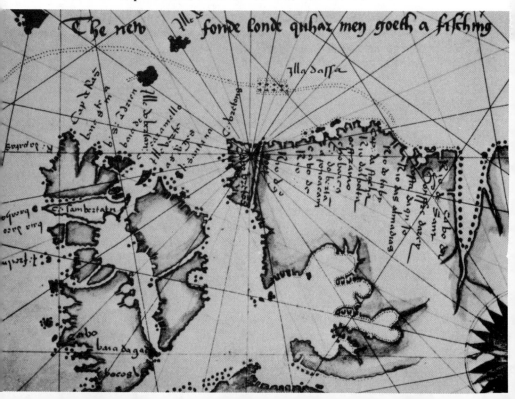

lightful than sailing along a wooded coast in the early summer, close enough to hear bird-song and smell the green herbage.

Gaspé

Sighting the cliffy Richibucto Head ten miles across Northumberland Strait on 2 July, Cartier crossed the strait with a last-quarter moon, turning northward as the land opened up, and discovered the present Miramichi Bay. He named it *Baye Sainct Lunaire* after a Breton saint whose festival fell on the first of the month, and which also was the title of his patron, the abbot of Mont-Saint-Michel. Sending his long-boats into this bay, outlet of a famous salmon river, he observed its triangular shape, but the boats reported so many rocks and shoals that he did not attempt to bring in his ships. Ten leagues off shore, he says, the depth was twenty fathom—exactly what the modern chart gives on a line ten miles from each cape.

Foul weather and strong wind that night (2–3 July) forced the two ships to heave-to off the coast, but on the morning of the third the wind came fair and they rounded North Point on Miscou Island, the southern entrance to Chaleur Bay, and entered that bay. Cartier, who named it, waxed more enthusiastic over this beautiful sun-drenched bay, with its warm air and water, than over any other place discovered on this voyage. He admired the land and the spruce trees, tall enough to mast a ship of three hundred tuns. These amenities must have been a joy to his sailors after experiencing the ice and fog of the eastern Gulf. Cartier reported the climate to be more temperate than that of Spain, the soil rich, "fairest you could see anywhere," the flora like that of Brion Island and the waters teeming with salmon.

As at the northern entrance to Chaleur Bay, mountains were visible to the north, and one could see no land at the head of the bay. Cartier hoped that he had found a strait like that of Belle Isle, which would lead him to *the* passage to China. For that reason, he said, he named the present north point on Miscou Island *Cap d'Esperance*. The lati-tude at midbay, he said, was 47°30′, half a degree short of correct; and here he attempts a longitude, 73° W. But as usual he does not tell us what prime meridian he counted from. The head of this bay is 68°45′ W of Paris, but Cartier more probably counted from Saint-Malo, which would be a few degrees less, or Ferro, which would have made the correct longitude 50°25′ W. Thus he was no better at guessing longitude than Verrazzano. Both navigators, like Columbus, hopefully placed America on the globe much nearer to Asia than it really is.

The rich soil, teeming fisheries, and warm climate (temperature often passing 90°F. in summer) have made Chaleur Bay one of the most thickly populated parts of the Gulf littoral. All along the northern shore are farms of uniform shape and size—so many *arpents*—which were parceled out to *habitants* in the colonial era; a neat little house near the shore, vegetable garden, hayfield, and pasture behind it in that order, and usually ending in a woodlot. Cartier on 4 July put in at a little harbor that he named *Conche Sainct Martin*, it being the feast of the translation of the relics of St. Martin of Tours. Cartier always called an open, shell-shaped harbor like Blanc Sablon, a *conche* (shell). St. Martin is now Port Daniel, seat of a huge wood-pulp mill. And there the ships rested for eight days, part of which was taken up with exploring the bay in one or more longboats.

The village of Paspebiac, whose inhabitants were nicknamed "Paspy Jacks," used to be the Canadian headquarters of the famous Jersey firm of Robin & Cie. In the 1870's they were exporting $300,000 worth of fish annually to the Mediterranean, Brazil, and the West Indies, and schooners from Cape Ann took home as much more. "The annual yield of the Bay of Chaleur is estimated at 26,000 quintal (each 112 pounds) of dry codfish, 600 quintal of haddock, 3000 barrels of herring, 300 barrels of salmon, and 15,000 gallons of codliver oil," states the standard guidebook of 1875. "The fisheries, the bay and gulf are valued at $800,000 a year, and employ 1500 sail and 18,000 men. . . ."

On 6 July, somewhere on the north shore of Chaleur Bay, probably near the site of Paspebiac village, Cartier had his first meeting with the Micmac tribe. This first encounter was not encouraging. Two fleets of forty to fifty canoes, loaded with natives, approached from the south shore of the bay, and a large number landed close to the French boat, yelling their loudest and brandishing peltry on sticks—a sure sign that European fishermen had been there before. "We having only the one boat," wrote Cartier, "did not care to land there but rowed toward the other lot, still at sea. They [of the first fleet], seeing that we fled, manned two of their biggest canoes to catch up with us, joined five others of the second fleet, then at sea, and came alongside our boat,

dancing and making divers signs of joy and of wanting our friendship.
. . . Not trusting them, we made signs to them to sheer off, which
they didn't like, but paddled with such great strength that with their
seven canoes they completely surrounded our boat. So, since they
wouldn't obey our signs, we shot over their heads two *passevolans*,"
small pivot-guns mounted on the gunwale. The natives retired momen-
tarily but returned, and the Frenchmen had to hurl two *lanses à feu*
among them before they could frighten off the importunate visitors.
They obviously meant well, and the next encounter may be said to
have inaugurated three centuries of friendship between French Canada
and the Micmac.

That came next day, 7 July. Nine canoes full of savages appeared at
the mouth of Port Daniel, the paddlers making a hideous racket but
again displaying peltry for sale. "We made them signs that we wished
them no harm," wrote Cartier, "and sent two men ashore to deal with
them, bringing knives and other cutlery, and a red cap to give their
chief." Some Indians then landed, and a profitable traffic took place,
the natives dancing, making amicable gestures such as pouring seawater
over their heads, and selling the very clothes off their backs—furs, of
course.

On 8 July, Cartier resumed his exploration of Chaleur Bay by boat.
It was now the dark of the moon, but at that season the nights are always luminous if there is no fog. They rowed, he says, 25 leagues (80
miles) up to the head of it, and that is nearly accurate. On the morning
of the 10th "We had cognizance of the end of said bay, which gave
us grief and displeasure," he writes. The magnificent scenery at that
point, the mountains at the mouth of the Restigouche, were no compensation for finding this bay a dead-end instead of a passage to China.
Upon turning back, at the site of the present Carleton behind Tracadigash Point, the boats encountered some three hundred Micmac men,
women, and children, who brought them strips of broiled seal meat on
wooden platters; the French responded with gifts of "hatchets, knives,
paternoster beads, and other merchandise." This started a brisk trade
of peltry "and what else they had." The women came freely to the
French, rubbing their arms—a friendly gesture—selling the furs they
wore, and retiring completely naked. Cartier remarked that these
sauvages were nomads who lived largely on fish, that they were ripe
for conversion. Near by were fields of "wild wheat with a head like

barley and a seed like oats"—lyme grass again—ripe berries, sweet-smelling white and red roses, and a pond full of salmon. He recorded the words that the savages used for hatchet and knife, which gave proof that they were of the Micmac nation.

With regret at leaving the warmth, both human and climatic, of Chaleur Bay, Cartier on 12 July resumed his search for Cathay, under the new moon. He sailed east along the coast "some 18 leagues" to *Cap de Pratto* where "we found a wonderful range of tide, little depth, and a very high sea. We found it best to hug the shore between the said cape and an island about one league to the eastward, and there we dropped anchors for the night." Although this is a matter of contro-versy, I believe that Cap de Pratto (Cap du Pré on the Desceliers Map of 1546) is the present White Head, or Cap Percé, where in Cartier's time there may have been enough open grass to be called a meadow; and that the island was Bonaventure, with 250-foot red cliffs. Between this and the main is an anchorage in fifteen fathom which the modern Sailing Directions recommend, except in bad weather. But why did not Cartier mention the extraordinary Ile Percé, with its natural arch? For the simple reason that the sea had not yet broken through the soft sandstone isthmus that connected that island with the point; one may also conjecture that the famous hole or tunnel had not yet been pierced. Early in the nineteenth century Ile Percé had two holes, but one collapsed in 1843.

These now peaceful shores have echoed cannon fire many times in the past. Sir William Phips dropped in on his way to Quebec in 1690, and burned all the houses and churches on Cap Percé and Bonaventure Island. Hovenden Walker, in 1711, cut out two French ships from the roadstead where Cartier anchored, but in the great storm of 22 August three of his own ships were wrecked and all hands were lost. Local tradition insists that a phantom ship crowded with men in uniforms of the old régime appears off shore in foggy calms, crashes on the cliffs, and disappears. The last scene of violence, apart from wrecks, was in 1776, when H.M.S. *Wolf* and *Diligence* sank two American privateers off Ile Percé.

Cartier's fleet now encountered a spell of foul weather; the ships set forth but could make no progress. This is a place where the north and the south winds meet and make either a calm or a disturbance. He anchored in the outer roadstead for two days while his boats explored

Mouth of Miramichi Bay.

Cap Percé and Bonaventure Island.

View in Gaspé Bay. Courtesy Canadian Government Travel Bureau.

the spectacularly beautiful Gaspé * Bay, then selected Gaspé Harbor near the head of the bay and tarried there from 16 to 25 July.

Cartier here made a new and important contact with a party of about two hundred Huron Indians in forty canoes—who with their chief, Donnaconna, were on a mackerel fishing trip—from the site of Quebec. As they seemed friendly like the Micmac, he let them paddle close to the ships, and issued the usual trading truck of cheap knives, combs, and glass beads. These people, wrote Cartier, "could well be called savages, for they are the poorest people that can be in the world; all their possessions, apart from the canoes and fishing nets, were not worth five sous." They wore nothing but a G-string and a few furs that they threw over their shoulders like scarfs. Unlike the natives encountered before, their heads were shaved "except for a topknot that they leave as long as a horse's tail, which they bind and tie to their heads in a knot with strips of leather"—the scalp lock. They eat both fish and meat almost raw, and their only huts are their canoes, reversed. Naturally, as this was a summer fishing party, the natives brought noth- with them but bare necessities.

On St. Mary Magdalen's day, 22 July, the French rowed ashore to where the natives had assembled and mingled with them, dancing and singing. Prudently, the Indians had sent all their young girls away ex- cept two or three; to each of them the Captain gave a little tin hawk's bell, which so delighted the damsels that they rubbed his arms and chest, their mode of expressing appreciation. Suddenly Cartier was al- most overwhelmed by twenty more girls rushing out of the forest whither their menfolk had banished them, all trying at once to massage him and earn a bell; and he amiably gave one to each. One assumes that French sailors followed the girls back into the discreet thickets where they could celebrate the Magdalen's day appropriately if not sacerdo- tally.

Cartier noted a kind of wild grain "like the pease of Brazil" that they ate in lieu of bread and called *kagaigo*—this probably was maize—and plums which they dried for winter use and called *honnesta;* both are Huron words. "They will never eat anything with a salty taste," he says, and "they are wonderful thieves, filching anything they can lay hold of."

---

* This name, of Micmac origin, was first used by Champlain in 1603 in the form *Gachepé*. Cartier consistently used a form of *Honguedo,* the Huron name for the region.

On 24 July the master pilot caused a cross thirty feet tall to be raised on a point of this harbor, inscribed VIVE LE ROY DE FRANCE, and attached to it a carved panel displaying three fleurs-de-lys, the arms of François-premier. The Indians followed this proceeding with interest. As soon as the cross was set up, the sailors knelt and with joined hands adored it, making signs toward Heaven that their redemption lay aloft. The Huron obviously could not make much sense out of the doctrine of the redemption, but they did gather that this was a formal taking possession. Their chief, Donnaconna (of whom we shall hear more), came on board dressed in an old black bearskin and conveyed by signs that this was his country and nobody should erect a cross without his permission. But he was placated by gifts, and acquired such confidence in Cartier that he allowed him to carry off two of his teen-age sons, Domagaya and Taignoaguy, on the promise that they would be returned. The boys were promptly dressed European fashion, in shirts, livery jackets, red hats, and brass necklaces, which pleased them greatly; their cast-off furs were bestowed on their friends who stayed behind. Next day some thirty Indians came out in canoes to say goodbye.

Political reasons explain Donnaconna's desire to make friends with the visitors. His tribe, which dominated the St. Lawrence River from Quebec down, was being pressed hard by the Etchemin of Maine, and he needed a powerful ally.

Anticosti and Home

Departing Gaspé Bay 25 July, the day of full moon, Cartier rounded Cape Gaspé and ran into a wall of fog. Skirting the fogbank, he sighted the great island of Anticosti. Assuming that the part he saw of it was a peninsula jutting out from Gaspé, Cartier did not attempt to penetrate the fogbank but steered for the island's nearest point, and made it on the 27th. He then ranged the southeast coast of the big island and named East Cape *Cap Saint-Louis* because it was the feast of a local Breton saint of that name. He gives its position as latitude 49° 15' N, longitude 63° 30' W. The latitude is correct within five miles, and the longitude was not too bad; East Cape is 61° 40' west of Greenwich— but no Frenchman for centuries would use the Greenwich meridian, and Cartier never tells us which meridian he used: Ferro, Saint-Malo, or Paris. Cartier was a fairly good guesser at longitude, for the first half of the sixteenth century, but no more.

Cartier's *Cap St. Louis*, East Cape, Anticosti.

Cap Rabast, Anticosti. Off here Cartier turned back on his first voyage.

Anticosti, an island singularly devoid of charm—except to salmon fishermen—is now almost completely covered with spruce forest and peat bog; but Cartier found the south coast "flat, and the most bare of timber of any place we have seen, with beautiful fields and marvellously green meadows." From its position in the mouth of the great river, and its fringe of reefs, Anticosti is a menace to navigation. "This hideous wilderness," wrote George Warburton in 1846, "has been the grave of hundreds, by . . . starvation. Washed ashore from maimed and sinking ships . . . they drag their chilled and battered limbs up the rough rocks"—but there is no shelter, no food, and if not frozen by the winter cold they are eaten by immense swarms of black flies and mosquitoes. Five stout fellows of Sir William Phips's invading Yankee army, sole survivors of a ship wrecked there in 1690, built themselves a skiff and rowed all the way to Boston, the passage taking forty-four days. I heartily agree with a modern yachtsman, Oliver Green, who observed, "The sight of land is usually welcome, but this had an eerie look. . . . It seemed to have remained since the creation and had certainly never given any welcome to man."

On Wednesday, 29 July, the two ships rounded Cap Saint-Louis and ranged the northern coast of Anticosti, naming Table Head as they passed after Anne de Montmorency, grand constable of France. They sounded some twenty miles off shore and found clean bottom at 100 and 150 fathom—which agrees with the modern chart. Incidentally, this proves that Cartier carried good long dipsey lead lines. On 1 August the highlands of southern Quebec were sighted across *le Détroit de Saint-Pierre* (St. Peter Strait). They made such slow progress along the coast against head winds and the strong ebb current that Cartier ordered both longboats manned to row ahead and investigate a prominent Anticostian cape. The Captain's boat, when trying to benefit from counter-currents near shore, struck a rock "which was immediately cleared by dint of the whole crew jumping overboard to shove her afloat." Good evidence of a loyal crew, as the last thing a sailor cares to do is to go over the side in cold water; one hopes that the Captain issued a tot of brandy to all hands after the salvage. Even with thirteen oars manned, the longboats could make no progress, so they were left ashore under guard while Cartier and a dozen men scrambled along the rocks to the cape, which on his second voyage he named *Rabast*. Having ascertained it to be the narrowest part of the strait, and that the Anticosti shore fell off thence to the southwestward, they returned to the longboats and rowed to the ships. These, though under sail, had drifted over twelve miles to leeward of the spot where the boats had been hoisted out.

Once back on board, Cartier summoned "all captains, pilots, masters and *compagnons* [gentlemen volunteers]" to his cabin to consult them "as to the best to be done." After everyone had had his say, they decided. "Considering that heavy downstream winds had set in, and that the tidal currents were so strong that they did nothing but lose ground, and that it was impossible to gain beyond this season; and also that tempests begin at this season in Newfoundland, that we were even now very far [from home] and knew not what dangers lay ahead; it was high time either to turn back or to stay right there; and moreover, if a succession of east winds caught us, we might be forced to stay. These opinions, once taken, we decided, almost unanimously, to return [to France]."

A very sensible decision, and it was just like Cartier to take the others into his confidence and solicit their views. Very few captains did that, especially in the age of discovery. This conference took place on 1 August 1534, in the Détroit de Saint-Pierre, which has been renamed Jacques Cartier Passage.

So, homeward turned the two ships on 2 August, the day of the moon's last quarter. Thenceforth and until Wednesday 5 August, a prosperous gale of wind blew them eastward at high speed. They paused only once, at Natashquan Point, where they received on board a party of Montagnais Indians engaged in fishing for a certain Captain Thiennot, whose ships were lying in Natashquan harbor. Cartier apparently knew Thiennot, as he named the cape after him; that name has vanished from the maps but there are still some famous codfishing banks a few miles off the point. After passing Cape Whittle on 8 August, Cartier steered due east for the west coast of Newfoundland and made it between Cow Head and Point Rich. When the wind blew up furiously from the east-northeast, they sailed north to Blanc Sablon, spent six days there, and with a first-quarter moon on 15 August, after hearing mass, made sail for the homeward passage. On that, as on the outward one, Cartier is reticent. Mid-passage they were "tost and turmoyled three days long with great stormes coming from the East," as Hakluyt's translation tells it; but "with the help of God we suffered and endured it," says Cartier, "and arrived at the haven of

Limoïlou. The farmhouse, the well, the nearby cross (with M. Lailler and Mrs. Morison), and close-up of the Cartier arms.

Saint-Malo whence we had departed, on the 5th day of September"
1534, only three weeks from Blanc Sablon.

Since Jacques Cartier probably regarded this voyage only as a reconnaissance, he had every reason to be pleased with himself. In the
space of five months he had sailed completely around the Gulf of St.
Lawrence and, although no passage to Cathay had miraculously opened
up, he had a good idea where to start looking for one—in St. Peter
Strait—next time. He had discovered the beginning of the great axis
of penetration of the North American continent. This was the Gulf
and River of St. Lawrence and the Great Lakes, which French explorers in the next century would follow west to the Dakotas and down the
Mississippi to the Gulf of Mexico.

This first voyage enhanced Cartier's status at Saint-Malo. He adopted
a coat of arms, and had it carved on the entrance gate of a farm that
he acquired outside Saint-Malo. Since his town house has long since
disappeared, and his ships have crumbled to dust, this farm, still named
Limoïlou, and still a working farm, brings us closer to the great Captain than any other place short of Canada. Located in the parish of
Saint-Ideuc, it is within sight of the sea, and near enough to Saint-Malo
for the Captain to ride there in an hour's time. A short distance away is
a cross-roads with a typical Breton granite cross, where he is said to
have prayed before his last two voyages; and in the nearby village
of Rotheneuf is a tiny chapel where he worshipped when spending
a Sunday or saint's day at Limoïlou. Like many another sailor, Cartier loved the land, and between voyages as in old age he spent all
the time he could at Limoïlou.*

Cartier's sailors spread stories that enhanced his popularity. They had
lived off the fat of the land—auk meat, salmon, and other fresh fish,
goose eggs, and wild strawberries. The savages were gentle and kind,
and their Captain was not only an expert mariner but a just man, who
gave them opportunities to enhance their pay by trading knickknacks
for peltry. They were ready to sign on for a new voyage under Maître-
Pilote Cartier, and soon they had their opportunity.

* Also spelled *Limoelou;* pronounced as a four-syllable word. I am deeply indebted
to M. Dan Lailler, conservateur du Musée de Saint-Malo, for his sympathetic and
intelligent guidance there, and wish him well in his efforts to have Limoïlou classi-
fied a *monument historique.*

Bibliography and Notes

SOURCES

Cartier's fame has suffered almost equally from former neglect by his compatriots as from recent over-enthusiasm of French Canadians. His account of his first voyage was known for three centuries only by an Italian translation by Ramusio in his *Navigationes*, Vol. III (1556), translated into English (London, 1580), and in the second edition of Hakluyt's *Principal Navigations, Voyages*, etc. (1600), and thence *re-translated* into French! Considerable garbling and serious omissions resulted; for instance, the cape Cartier named *Cap de Latte* becomes *Lait*, causing a frantic search for a cape with milk-white rocks. In the last century, however, a contemporary French manuscript of this narrative was found in the Bibliothèque Nationale. A facsimile is reproduced in Baxter's *Cartier* (see below), and a printed version will be found in H. P. Biggar, *The Voyages of Jacques Cartier* (Public Archives of Canada, *Publications*, No. 11, 1924), with valuable notes and a running English translation. It is also in Ch.-A. Julien *et al.*, *Les Français en Amérique pendant la première moitié du XVIe siècle* (Paris, 1946). Students of this document agree that it is not in Cartier's handwriting; and that, although the narrative is in the first person, someone made an *abrégé* for him, as Las Casas did of Columbus's Journal. The manuscript has no title, so is generally called *La Première Relation de Jacques Cartier*.

Biggar, in *Collection of Documents Relating to Jacques Cartier and the Sieur de Roberval* (Public Archives of Canada, *Publications*, No. 14, 1930), published everything found in French and other archives, apart from what is in his *Voyages*. For the works of Alfonce and Thevet, see notes to Chapter XIII.

SECONDARY ACCOUNTS AND QUESTIONS OF IDENTIFICATION

Since French Canada adopted Jacques Cartier as her discoverer, godfather, and founder, there has been a vast amount of trash written about him, and pious theories built up, which Gustave Lanctot has wittily demolished in his *Jacques Cartier devant l'histoire* (Montréal, 1944). The classic biography, however, is that by Charles de La Roncière, *Jacques Cartier* (Paris, 1931). The best in English is James Phinney Baxter, *Memoir of Jacques Cartier* (New York, 1906), valuable for documents in translation, but dull reading. Of general secondary works, Marcel Trudel, *Histoire de la Nouvelle-France*, Vol. I. *Les Vaines Tentatives* (Montreal, 1963), and Ch.-A. Julien, *Les Voyages de découverte et les premiers établissements* (Paris, 1946), are the best. Bernard G. Hoffman covers the voyages in his peculiar fashion, with special reference to ethnology and ecology, in *Cabot to Cartier* (Toronto, 1961). Champlain's *Traitté de la marine et du devoir d'un bon marinier*, is in the Champlain Society edition of his *Œuvres*, VI, 257–66.

Cartier himself left us ample courses, distances, and a fair amount of description, making it comparatively easy to follow in his wake and identify the places that he named or mentioned. Many Canadians have applied themselves to the task, and there has been much amiable wrangling as to where he set up the first cross, etc. Most of these articles are good examples of library geography; and this applies even to W. F. Ganong, "Voyages of Jacques Cartier" in his *Crucial Maps* (omnibus edition, Toronto, n.d., but post 1964), pp. 254–413, and to Bishop M. F. Hawley, "Cartier's Course—a Last Word," in Royal Society of Canada, *Transactions*, 1st ser., XII, part ii (1895). Ganong did everything in identifying these places that a scholar could do without viewing them, and his parallel columns of names from the maps are particularly useful. He was at it from 1884, at the age of twenty, until his death in 1941; for almost forty years he served as professor of botany at Smith College. He has subjected every map to a vigorous analysis, but apparently visited only a small number of the places that Cartier did. Nevertheless his work is indispensable. He admits that such problems cannot be settled until some "well provided historian-yachtsman of leisure could follow Cartier's course throughout, with the narrative in hand, viewing his described places from the same positions that he did, and photographing them" (p. 273). This is what your author has tried to do by air, admittedly inferior to sailing, but at least better than the usual procedure of looking at a cape on a modern map and deciding, "This is it."

To my knowledge, the only writer who has literally followed Ganong's advice is Harrison F. Lewis. He made a dozen or more yachting trips along the Labrador shore and other parts of the Gulf, with Cartier's voyages in mind, and described them in Royal Society of Canada *Transactions*, 3rd ser., XXVIII (1934), part ii, 117–48, "Notes on Some Details of the Explorations by Jacques Cartier in the Gulf of St. Lawrence." Notes from this article appear in Julien's and Biggar's editions of the *Première Relation*. A detailed study of Cartier's course along the Gaspé Peninsula appears in E. B. Deschênes, "L'Apport de Cartier et de Jean Alfonse dans l'onomastique de la Gaspésie," *Bulletin des Recherches Historiques*, XL (July 1934), 410–30. Father Deschênes follows Ganong's methods in even greater detail.

Cartier has been accused of exaggerating distances, on the assumption that he used the Spanish league which equals 3.18 nautical miles. Actually, like Verrazzano, he used the French *lieue marine* which, according to a comparative table of distances in the Petrus Plancius Planisphere of *c.* 1604 engraved by Josue van den Ende, plate 11 (Bibliothèque Nationale), equaled 2.2 English nautical miles. The *Grande Encyclopédie* states that a *lieue marine* equals 5.55 kilometers or 2.98 nautical miles and other authorities state that the *petite lieue* marine equals 2.31 nautical miles. I have used 2.2 nautical miles for the conversion figure, believing that Plancius has it correct for the sixteenth century.

Cape Dégrat, from *dégras* (fish oil), is another proof that French fishermen were there before Cartier. It became such a common landfall for

September iceberg on Cartier's route. Photo by James F. Nields, 1969.

Some of Cartier's *Toutes Iles*.

French fishermen bound to either coast of Newfoundland, that *dégrat* came to mean a vessel's departure for the codfishery (Larousse).

Groais, Cartier named after an island off L'Orient, and *Karpont* after a tiny harbor behind Ile Bréhat, which he had to weather after leaving Saint-Malo.

Belle Isle and *les Belles Isles*. My interpretation of Cartier's "Belles Isles" is confirmed by the *Cosmographie* of Jean Alfonce, Roberval's pilot in 1541. Describing the east coast of Newfoundland from south to north, he puts *les Belles Isles* on latitude 51°40′ (correct for the northern one), and adds: "Les Belles isles et le Carpon sont NNW et SSE. . . . Et entre les deux est le baye de la Cramaillère [Cremaillere Harbor on lat. 51°20′] et le cap Rouge," 50°55′ N (Biggar, *Voyages*, p. 281). Alfonce, writing in 1544, calls the big Belle Isle by its modern name (pp. 282–83) and gives it the latitude of 52°30′ N; the northern cape is on 52°02′. Groais was named after an island in Brittany, as this region became "le petit nord" to French fishermen.

Greenly Island and the *Bremen*'s Non-Stop Flight. See Kenneth McDonough, *Atlantic Wings 1919–39, the Conquest of the North Atlantic by Aeroplane* (London, 1966), pp. 52–57.

Brest. The name first appears at Bonne Espérance harbor on the Desliens, S. Cabot, Vallard, Mercator, and other maps (Biggar, *Voyages*, p. 17*n*) but later was transferred to a fishing settlement on Bradore Bay. In 1600 this second Brest reached the height of its prosperity with 200 houses and 1000 people.

Jacques Cartier, river and harbor. Ganong, pp. 179–81, discusses at great length the claims of various places to be those named by Cartier after himself.

Brion and Magdalen Islands. Philippe de Chabot, sieur de Brion, a childhood friend of François-premier, the most powerful figure at the French court when Cartier sailed, signed his commission for the second voyage. By the time Cartier returned from his third voyage, Chabot was in trouble owing to various accusations against his loyalty and honesty. The king pardoned him, he retired, and died in 1543. He is the "Byron" of George Chapman's *Byron's Conspiracy*. The Leigh quotation, together with useful data on the birds, is in Biggar, *Voyages*, pp. 30–31, who also explains Cartier's *rossez de Provins*. These must have been the ordinary wild rose, but they reminded him of the red rose of Provins which, imported into England by Edmund Crouchback, became the badge of the Lancastrians in the Wars of the Roses. The name *Magdalen* is not found earlier than 1663; before that the group was known as *Ramea*. Vivid description in G. Peabody Gardner, *Ready About* (1959); earlier ones in Narcisse H. E. Faucher de Saint-Maurice, *Promenades dans le Golfe Saint-Laurent* (Québec, 1879), and, by J. M. Clarke, in N. Y. State Museum, *Seventh Report of Science Division* (15 April 1911), pp. 121–55.

Prince Edward Island. The local historians are not much help in identify-

Philippe Chabot, sieur de Brion, amiral de France. Sixteenth-century engraving. Courtesy Bureau des Étampes, Bibliothèque Nationale.

ing Cartier's landfalls. North Point, like Greenly Island, made aviation history. Two Russians, General V. Kokkimaki and Major M. Gordienko, made a crash landing there in April 1939 in a two-engine Moskeva bomber, after being airborne from Moscow only four minutes short of twenty-three hours.

Chaleur Bay and the Micmac. The account of the fisheries is from *The Maritime Provinces: A Handbook for Travellers* (Boston, 1875), pp. 240–

42. The *Première Relation* states that the Micmac saluted them with *Napou tou daman asurtat,* which Father Pacifique, missionary at Restigouche, translated as *Ami, ton semblable t'aimera.* With all due repect to the Reverend Father, Indian slogans are not likely to be recorded accurately by Europeans, especially if a fight has followed; and the sentiment seems more natural to a converted native than to a *sauvage.* Fire-lances, described in Biggar, *Voyages,* p. 305, were sticks with one hollow end stuffed with a mixture of gunpowder, resin, and other combustibles. To set off these and the small cannon the men had to bring a burning slow match with them in the boat.

Cap de Prato, or Pratto. There is a terrific local controversy, both over what Cartier meant by the name, and over which cape it was. Ganong argues with some cogency that it was Cap Percé on White Head, off which are Ile Percé, with its spectacular natural arch and crowded rookeries, and Bonaventure Island. H. F. Lewis (*op. cit.* pp. 132–35) agrees. Others, notably Biggar, prefer Cap d'Espoir, further south. I cannot attempt to enter Cartier's mind to decide why he used an Italian name, but regard the theory that he named it after Alberto de Prato, that alleged canon of St. Paul's who accompanied John Rut in 1527, as utterly fantastic. Father Deschênes argues with some cogency (op. cit. pp. 426–30) that the name is older than Cartier's voyage, representing some earlier Spanish voyage; this too was the opinion of Charlevoix. But if so, where did Cartier get it? One can hardly assume that one of the Indians he met remembered the Spanish name and told it to the *maître-pilote.* Our air tour of the Gaspé convinced us that Cap de Pratto was Cap Percé, and nothing else.

The Gaspé Cross. Julien (*Voyages de découverte,* p. 121) calls the cross-raising on the shores of Gaspé Bay "L'acte de naissance du Canada français"; Lanctot asks, "What's the matter with the earlier cross-raising on the Labrador coast?" He places Cartier's cross at Pointe Penouille on the north shore, but the Quebec government chose the village of Gaspé on the south shore to place their replica of the cross in 1934. La Roncière has a pleasant theory (*Jacques Cartier,* pp. 57–60) that these Hurons remembered the cross from knowing Norsemen four centuries earlier.

Anticosti. Cartier named it *Ile de l'Assomption* on his second voyage, but it reverted to its Indian name, which means "place where you hunt the bear." The feast day of the local Breton saint, St. Louis or St. Leobatius, is 28 July. My disparaging quotation is from George Warburton, *Hochelaga* (1846), p. 19. Oliver Green's impression is in Alastair Garrett (ed.), *Roving Commissions No. 8* (London, 1968). *Détroit de Saint-Pierre* was named by Cartier "because it was St. Peter's Day." A second St. Peter's day, "A Cadeira de Sam Pedro," in my Portuguese almanac for 1 August 1509, means, I suppose, the anniversary of his chairing as Bishop of Rome.

PORTRAITS OF CARTIER

These are discussed in Lanctot, *Cartier devant l'histoire,* pp. 137–57, and in Ganong, *Crucial Maps,* pp. 258–60. The Saint-Malo portrait by a Russian artist, painted in 1839, is a work of pure imagination. Various miniatures of leading figures on early maps of Canada are allegedly of Cartier, but I doubt whether any were intended to be portraits. Cartographers of that era, unlike Champlain and Captain John Smith in the next century, made no attempt to put accurate portraits on their maps. The figure on the Desceliers-Harleian Map of 1542, reproduced in the text of this chapter, having no features but a forked beard, has lent itself to imaginative popular illustrators. A souped-up version with glowering features inspired by the Russian portrait is used as frontispiece to Biggar's *Voyages*. Nicholas Vallard's Map of 1547, which we have reproduced in Chapter XIII below, shows a full bearded person carrying a spear and pointing out a group of natives to a huddle of well-dressed French colonists. Ganong accepts this as an authentic Cartier portrait; in my opinion it is meant for Roberval because it was he, not Cartier, who brought out high-class colonists. See Note to Chapter XIII.

The most convincing portrait of Cartier existing is the one I have reproduced from M. Dan Lailler's sketch of a privately owned (and closely held) portrait which he believes to be contemporary. The features are similar to those on a sixteenth-century portrait reproduced in *Les Explorateurs célèbres* (Geneva: Mazenod, 1947), p. 60. See Lailler's *Jacques Cartier 1491–1557* (Saint-Malo, 1957). This catalogue comprises a list of all known portraits of Cartier, including several twentieth-century statues, some of which are figures of fun (e.g. Cartier grasping the tiller of *La Grande Hermine* and sighting land—but this statue has been so placed that he is looking at the nearest restaurant of Saint-Malo!)

CARTIER'S MILE AND LEAGUE

There is no doubt that Cartier and Roberval used the *petit mille marin*, three of which made the *petite lieue marine*. The *petit mille* measured 1440 meters, or 0.77 English nautical miles; the *petite lieue*, therefore, measured 4320 meters or 2.31 nautical miles—other authorities say 2.2. Information kindly furnished by Professor Michel Mollat, who refers to the *Composo da Navigare* of *c.* 1250. The difference between this mile and a minute of latitude worried navigators; so that in 1585 some French authority, probably the Admiralty, after a careful measurement of latitude, declared that the *mille marin* equaled the equivalent of 1620 meters (0.87 nautical miles); but it was not until 1633 that a correct measure was made, 1854 meters, which is exactly one nautical mile. L. Denoix in *Le Navire et l'économie maritime . . . du moyen-âge au XVIIIe siècle* (Mollat's 3rd *colloque* of 1958, S.E.V.P.E.N., 1960), p. 137.

✳ XII ✳
Cartier's Second Voyage
1535-1536

En un bon vaisseau il n'y a à craindre que la terre et le feu.
SAMUEL DE CHAMPLAIN

To Sea with Royal and Episcopal Blessing

Did Cartier go to court and talk with the king? We do not know, but his friends and supporters lost no time in providing him with the means and the authority to make a second voyage of discovery and exploration. He arrived home on 5 September 1534, and as early as 30 October 1534 received a commission from his patron, Philippe Chabot de Brion, who uses his full titles: "Compte de Buranczoys et de Charny, baron d'Aspremont, de Paigny et de Mirebeau, seigneur de Beaumont et de Fontaine-franczose, admiral de France, Bretaigne et Guyenne, governeur et lieutenant-général pour le Roy en Bourgougne, aussi lieutenant-général pour monseigneur le Daulphin ou governement de Normandie."

The recipient, described as "le capitaine et pillote maistre Jacques Cartier de Sainct-Malo," is

> by royal command, to conduct, lead and employ three ships equipped and victualed for fifteen months, for the perfection of the navigation of lands by you already begun, to discover beyond *les Terres Neufves;* and on this voyage to endeavor to do and accomplish that which it has pleased the said Lord King to command and order you to do. For the equipment

thereof you will buy or charter ships at such price as people
of means know to be reasonable, and such as you think good
and proper for the said navigation. For these ships you will
engage the number of pilots, masters and mariners as you
think to be requisite and necessary for the accomplishment
of this voyage. . . . We give you power and special command over the total charge and expense of these ships, the
voyage and navigation, both out and home. We order and
command all the said pilots, masters, gentlemen, mariners,
and others who will sail in the said ships to obey and follow
you in the service of the King . . . under pain of suitable
punishment if disobedient.

Cartier, despite his popularity at Saint-Malo, had the same trouble as
before in obtaining a full complement, and for much the same reason.
Most of the available seamen owed money to shipowning merchants
and were prevented by them from signing on for a non-fishing voyage.
Of expenses, the king contributed only 3000 livres tournois; the rest
was probably furnished by Cartier's local friends and supporters. The
master pilot did, however, obtain three ships from the royal French
navy, whose names we know, as well as those of their officers.

Here was what we might call Capitaine Jacques Cartier's task organization:

LA GRANDE HERMINE, *nef généralle* (flagship), 100 to 120 tuns and 12
guns; Thomas Fromont, master. Several *compagnons* (gentlemen volunteers) such as the dauphin's cupbearer Claude de Pontbriand, as well
as the two Hurons, Domagaya and Taignoagny, sailed in her.

LA PETITE HERMINE, about 60 tuns and 4 guns; Macé Jalobert, captain
and pilot; Guillaume le Maryé, master.

L'ÉMERILLON, galion of about 40 tuns and 2 guns; Guillaume Le
Breton, captain and pilot, Jacques Maingard, master.

Total complement, 112 officers and men.

Hermine (weasel) had a special significance for Brittany; *hermine
enchainée* was an important part of the arms of Anne de Bretagne,
queen of Louis XII. The little one, formerly called *Courlieu* (the
curlew) was renamed for this voyage. *Émerillon* means a merlin, or
sparrowhawk. Both "weasels" were larger than the two ships Cartier
sailed on his first voyage, but *L'Émerillon* was smaller than either, a
galion, what the English called a pinnace. Galions at that era were not
big, lumbering warships like the Spanish galleons in the Armada of
1588, but small maneuverable vessels which carried oars as well as sails

La Grande Hermine sailing past Saint-Malo. Rendering by Commandant Denoix for his full-sized model of her, built for Expo 67.

and had a one-to-four or one-to five ratio of beam to length as compared with one-to-three for the *nef*, the standard three-masted ship. The French employed them extensively for coastal voyages and Grand Bank fishing. Cartier agreed with what Columbus learned from *Niña*, that a small, handy ship is the most suitable for coastal exploration and equally capable of crossing the ocean. Henceforth we shall find no fleet for northern discovery complete without one.

The only models I have seen of *L'Émerillon* are inaccurate, but Commandant Denoix of the French navy, the leading authority on French ships of the sixteenth century, designed a full-sized one of *La Grande Hermine* for the Montreal exposition of 1967 which, in my opinion, is correct. There are cabins for officers and gentlemen volunteers in the sterncastle. Petty officers bedded down in the forecastle, and the men shared the 'tween decks (headroom four feet or less) with the cooking arrangements, and even some of the smaller cattle and poultry. However, most of them were Bretons who lived in one-room, dirt-floor *chaumières* with a cow or goat, so they probably didn't mind.

About two-thirds of the 112 names on the *rôle d'équipage* indicate that Cartier had a home-town crew. No fewer than twelve were his relatives. Captain Jalobert of *La Petite Hermine* was the son of Catherine Cartier's sister, and the masters of the other two were her nephews or cousins. There were seven carpenters—very necessary for repairing hull and gear; a barber who doubled as surgeon, an apothecary, corresponding to our modern pharmacist's mate, and a trumpeter. The last was a required rating on sea-going vessels for at least two hundred years. With a "noise of trumpets" passing ships were hailed, boats recalled, the men summoned to general quarters, or the watch changed. And there is evidence in the *Brief recit* that other musical instruments were shipped, and an informal orchestra organized to amuse both sailors and natives. The rest of the crews, whose names do not appear on the list, were probably gromets, or ship's boys, the lowest rating in European merchant marines.

Two men on the crew list were entitled "Dom," and mass was said on board; but, as on the first voyage, this may have been a *messe blanche*, and it seems significant that Cartier refused baptism to the Huron chief Donnaconna on the ground that he had nobody competent to do it, and that he directed divine service himself. These *doms* were probably bachelors of arts, who, like Portuguese kings, were so entitled in that century.

The objects of this voyage, as stated in Cartier's commission and in a royal order to pay him 3000 livres tournois, were *descouvrir outtre les Terres Neufves* (explore beyond Newfoundland) *pour aller descouvrir certaines terres longtaines*, (to discover certain far-away countries). There was to be no fooling around with straits north of the Labrador, or with isthmuses reported by Verrazzano. Neither missionary efforts nor gold nor precious stones are mentioned; but every discoverer expected to play apostle to the Indians, and to find quantities of gold, silver, and gems. Apparently the two Huron boys had not told anyone in France about the marvelous Kingdom of Saguenay, which Cartier hoped to be the first to exploit.

On Whitsunday, 16 May 1535, the Captain and every crew member confessed and received holy communion in the cathedral of Saint-Malo, and the bishop blessed all hands, and their ships and mission.

Retracing First Voyage

We are fortunate to know about this voyage from Cartier's own *Brief recit*, printed at Paris in 1545.

The "second voyage made by wish and command of the Most Christian King of France, François-premier, for the achievement of discovery of western lands parallel to the territories of the said prince," began on 19 May 1535, with a moon two days past full. That being the time of Cabot's departure in 1497, Cartier should have enjoyed a prosperous crossing. Up to a point he did; but on 26 May, foul weather and contrary winds set in, tossing them about for a full month; and on 25 June each of the three ships lost sight of the other two. After fifty days at sea, the flagship sighted Funk Island on 7 July. It made an excellent landfall in the fog; screaming sea-fowl (as I have observed in the Bay of Fundy) are as good as a modern diaphone to warn mariners of their approach to land. The men gathered two boatloads of great auk here, as Breton sailors relished their meat.

Without calling at any Newfoundland harbor, the Captain shaped a course for Blanc Sablon, arriving 15 July, again under a full moon. Eleven more days elapsed before the two smaller ships turned up. Necessary repairs and loading wood and water took three days more, so it was not until 29 July at break of day that the voyage of exploration really began.

The three vessels romped up the Strait of Belle Isle with an east wind, and were not much bothered by icebergs. Unless the Indians had thrown it down, Cartier had the gratification of seeing the cross he had erected on the little island "round as an oven," but he did not tarry. After two or three days, sailing right through the luminous nights, they reached "two islands further off shore than the others, which we named *les ysles sainct Guillaume.*" It was the feast of St. William, bishop of Brieux. Cartier's description fits Great Mecatina Island and several offshore islets which stand out conspicuously from the mainland. Whittier, in "The Fisherman," writes:

> Hurrah! for Meccatina
> And its mountains bare and brown!

We found no cheer in this high, gray granite island, with its sparse vegetation; nor did Cartier.

Cormorant Rocks and Cape Whittle.

Mont-Saint-Pierre, Gaspé Peninsula, Notre Dame range in distance.

The westward voyage continued at a good pace; Cartier well described the coast as "bordered by islands, all cut-up and rocky, with no good land or wood, save in a few valleys." Islands which he named in passing *ysles saincte Martre*, after St. Martha whose feast was on 29 July; must certainly have been the Harrington Islands. Centuries before they acquired that English name they were called, in Alfonce's *La Cosmographie* (1544), *les isles de la Demoiselle*, obviously in memory of Marguerite de La Roque, whom Roberval marooned there in the summer of 1542 (see Chapter XIII). Next came *Les ysles sainct Germain*, the Cormorant Rocks off Cape Whittle, named on 30 July after Saint-German l'Auxerrois, since it was the vigil of his feast. Others, such as the St. Mary group, Cartier noted but did not name. The islands here are so numerous, and so confusing even with a modern chart in hand, that it is a wonder that none of the Captain's three ships struck; but he had the benefit of a waxing moon.

After spending a night hove-to off Cape Whittle, the fleet resumed course west by south on the last day of July. The land became low and fair, covered with tall spruce trees, in sharp contrast to the "land of Cain" to the eastward; but there is no such contrast today. Recognizing Cape Thiennot, named on his previous voyage after a French fisherman, and with clear weather and a fair wind, Cartier ventured to sail westward all night. He then turned for shelter to a "neat little harbor" which he named *Saint-Nicolas;* the date, 7 August, was correct for a local St. Nicholas of Brittany. With the Captain's accurate description, Lewis has identified it as Mascanin Bay. Cartier raised "a big wooden cross" on the nearest island as a landmark to help other vessels enter. "One must bring this cross bearing northeast, then head for it and leave it on the starboard hand; and, avoiding the shoals, anchor in the said harbor in four fathom." At Saint-Nicolas he tarried until Sunday, 8 August.

With a waxing moon, Cartier crossed the channel to Cap Rabast on Anticosti, which again he found to be harborless and unattractive. He then returned to the mainland and entered a harbor well protected by two islands (Sainte-Geneviève and Hunting), which he named *La baye sainct Laurins*. The day, 10 August, was the feast of St. Lawrence, the Roman martyr who was grilled alive. Here is the first appearance of the name which Cartier's successors applied to the great gulf, to the mighty river that he discovered, and to the mountain range northward. Never, since the Roman empire, have two local names received such a vast extension as Canada and St. Lawrence.

On 13 August, the day of full moon, Cartier again crossed obliquely the strait that he had named Saint-Pierre (now renamed after him), and doubled West Point, Anticosti. Now recognizing it to be an island, and on the vigil of "Our Lady's Day of August," he named it *L'Isle de l'Assomption*. He then turned southwest across Gaspé Passage to the mainland, which he called by its Huron name, *Honguedo*. His aiming point must have been the highest peak (altitude 4160 feet) of the range now officially called Monts Jacques Cartier; he named these "marvellously high mountains" *Les Monts Notre Dame*. For some twenty miles he sailed along that beautiful coast where every few miles a fertile river valley bursts through the mountain chain to the shore, and on 17 August turned north, having sighted mountains on the Quebec shore. Upon arriving at the Bay of Seven Islands, Cartier consulted his two captive savages, who well knew the country from there to Quebec. They informed him that "this was the beginning of the Saguenay and inhabited country, and that thence came the red copper that they called *caignetdaze*," an Iroquoian name for any metal other than gold. And the great river they had just crossed where it is sixty miles wide, was "the great river of Hochelaga and *chemyn de Canada*."

Thus, almost inadvertently, Canada entered the stream of history.

Le Chemyn de Canada

The *Brief recit* reflects Cartier's excitement over being at the gates of the fabulous Kingdom of Saguenay, which the two Huron boys were already building to the status of a northern Peru. As they further asserted, he was at the mouth of "the grand river of Hochelaga . . . which, always narrowing, leads to Canada, where one finds fresh water in the said river, which comes from such a distance that no man has been to the end, so far as they had heard say; and no other passage was there except for boats."

Unwilling as yet to trust the young savages, Cartier insisted on sailing eastward along the coast between Seven Islands and Saint-Laurent to make certain that the way to Saguenay and Canada did not lie there. This took him four days, 18–21 August, with the moon waning to last quarter. All they saw were the barren Mingan Islands and the Moisie

(PROVINCE OF QUÉBEC)

52

66   64   62   60

(Moisie R.)

18-21 Aug. 1535

B. St. Laurins
10 Aug. 1535

St. Nicolas
(Mascanin Bay)
7 Aug. 1535

C. Thiennot

(C. Whittle)

50

Baie des Sept Isles

(Mingan Is.)

(Hunting I.)

(Natashquan Pt.)

Is. St. Germain
(Cormorant Rks.)

C. Rabast

(West Pt.)

Détroit de St. Pierre

x Cartier
turned back
2 Aug. 1534

(R. St. Lawrence)

Mont St. Pierre
14 Aug. 1535

(Salt Lake Bay)

I. DE L'ASSOMPTION
(ANTICOSTI I.)

C. de Montmorency
(Table Head)

C. St. Louis
(East Cape)

(South Pt.)

HONGUEDO
(GASPÉ PENINSULA)

Gaspé Hbr. and Bay
16-25 July 1534

(C. Gaspé)
15 July 1534

C. Pratto
(White Hd.)

(Percé)

(I. Bonaventure)

Gulf of St. Lawrence

Conche St. Martin
(Port Daniel)

(Tracadigash Pt.)
10 July 1534

Paspébiac Pt.
6 July 1534

48

Baie de Chaleur

C. Espérance
(Miscou I.)

I. de Margaulx
(Bird Rocks)

Ile de Bryon
1 June 1536

Cap du Dauphin

(MAGDALEN I.)

(Grindstone I.)

C. St. Pierre

(St. Paul I.)

B. St. Lunaire (Miramichi Bay)
2 July 1534

Allezay
(Deadman I.)

C. de Lorraine
(C. St. Lawrence)

C. St. Paul
(C. North)

C. des Sauvages
(North Pt.)

Cap d'Orleans (Kildare)

(Ingonish)

(Richibucto Hd.)

R. des Barraques
(Malpeque B.)

(Egmont Bay)

(Scutari I.)

(PRINCE EDWARD I.)

(CAPE BRETON)

46

(Northumberland Strait)

(C. Breton)

(Bay of Fundy)

NOVA SCOTIA

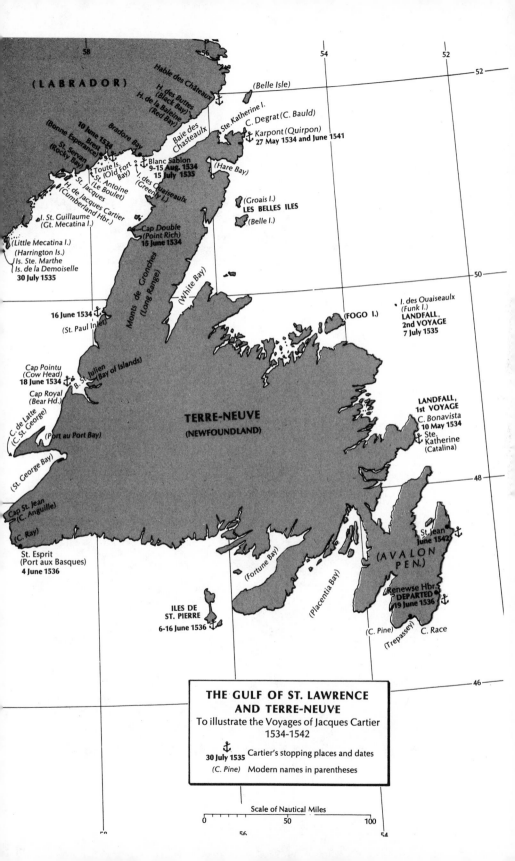

Entrance to Bay of Seven Islands.

The Moisie River. Cartier thought this might be the strait to China.

River, up which they made a boat trip to make sure that it was not *le chemyn de Canada*. This beautiful river, flowing like a miniature Saguenay between high, wooded, rocky banks, with frequent rapids where you may see bears fishing for salmon, was not named by Cartier. At the entrance his boat party marveled over the walruses, which they described as "fish with the shape of horses, which spend the night ashore and the day in the sea." "And as soon as we were convinced that we had ranged the entire coast," wrote Cartier, "and that there was no passage [to China,] we returned to our ships which were at the said *Sept Isles* where there are good anchorages in 18 and 20 fathom, sandy bottom."

Indeed there are. The modern chart agrees; one can almost see the spots where the two *Hermines* and *L'Émerillon* dropped their hooks. Sept Iles is now humming with activity, since it has become the shipping point for iron ore which comes by railway from the mines of Knob Lake, 350 miles to the northward. Six, not seven, high and wooded islands protect this bay from the sea, but Cartier's name, Seven Islands, has stuck. In the nineteenth century it became a famous rendezvous for fishermen, and the title of a romantic poem by Whittier. The Yankee skipper of fishing schooner *Breeze* falls in love with one of the twin daughters of a French Canadian family on the Bay. Her parents forbid the match; but the night before *Breeze* sails the skipper finds the girl, as he thinks, on board. She turns out to be the other twin and such a termagant that on his next summer's visit the skipper hopes to "turn her in," as it were, for the girl he loves. But she, alas, had died of a broken heart.

This site of blighted love lies many miles beyond Cartier's furthest western stop on his first voyage; and, although it was now later in the year than that day in 1534 when he decided to go home, he had no intention of turning back.

The Captain, concluding that his Huron passengers were speaking the truth, decided to continue up the main stream, which he calls the *La Grande Rivière* or *La Rivière de Hochelaga*. On 24 August, states the *Brief recit*, "we made sail and stood along the coast." They passed Egg Island off Pointe-aux-Anglais—a name commemorating the worst shipwreck in Canadian history, that of eight out of fifty-five ships in the invading fleet of Admiral Sir Hovenden Walker in 1711; almost nine hundred men were drowned. The Coast Pilot still warns ships of the foul ground between here and Pointe des Monts, and the modern chart calls

The Bic Islands, Cartier's *Iles St. Jean.*

Old Bic Harbor.

the reach between that point and Cap Chat on the Gaspé shore the most dangerous part of the lower river for sailing vessels. Here tides from the Gulf meet the river current, and a two-knot or more set during the flood runs due south cross-river, tending to throw ships onto the Gaspé shore. "Vessels inward bound should not attempt to take advantage of westward currents sometimes found close inshore with rising tide," warns the modern chart. Domagaya and Taignoagny, their navigational experience limited to the birch-bark canoe, may have tried to persuade their captain to do just that, but Cartier refused to take the risk. He probably anchored east of Pointe des Monts in sixteen fathom until the current or the wind turned. The middle of the river here, and for many miles upstream, is two hundred fathom deep. He passed and described, but did not name, the Manikuagan River which flows into the St. Lawrence between two headlands, one high and the other low, and fringed by dangerous shoals.

On 29 August, the day after new moon, the three ships anchored behind "three flat islands, which stand right out in the stream." These Bic Islands—Bic, Bicquette, and what is now a mere reef—Cartier named *Ysleaux sainct Jehan* because it was 29 August, "the day of the decapitation of the said saint"—John the Baptist. That name did not stick—there were already too many St. John capes, islands, and bays. The Captain's statement that his chosen harbor dries out on the ebb, that the rise and fall of tide is two fathom, and that the best anchorage is "to the south of an islet, near another islet," well fits Old Bic Harbor. He also observed Barnaby Island, six miles eastward, so long and narrow that it looks like a breakwater. Next day they reached the mouth of the Saguenay.

In Parkman's vivid prose, "To ascend this great river, and tempt the hazards of its intricate navigation with no better pilots than the two young Indians . . . was a venture of no light risk. But skill or fortune prevailed; and, on the first of September the voyagers reached in safety the gorge of the gloomy Saguenay with its towering cliffs and sullen depth of waters." Cartier called it "a very deep and rapid river, which is the . . . *chemyn du royaume et terre du Saguenay*, as our men of Canada have told us." Off its mouth lies a very dangerous part of the St. Lawrence, with a sandbank in midstream, tide-rips, currents up to seven knots, and a narrow entrance between shoals. But the fleet weathered it safely and anchored off the site of Tadoussac. Here, four

Mouth of the Saguenay, Tadoussac, Red Island and reefs.

The Saguenay, a few miles above Tadoussac.

canoes of Hurons on a fishing party "from Canada" (Quebec) were so frightened by the sight of the ships that only one came near enough to be hailed by Domagaya, who named and identified himself, and persuaded them to board. "This river," noted Cartier, "flows between high mountains of bare rock, which nevertheless support a vast quantity of trees of various kinds, which grow on said bare rock as if on good soil; we saw a tree suitable for masting a ship of 30 tuns, and as green as it could be, growing out of a rock without a trace of earth." Spruce trees apparently growing out of solid rock are a common sight along the shores of Maine and the Maritime Provinces; it is odd that Cartier had not noticed one before. The tree actually seeds itself in a small accumulation of dead needles, but can only survive by thrusting a root into a crevice leading to water and better nourishment.

On 2 September, leaving the Saguenay for future exploration, Cartier got his three vessels under way "pour faire le chemin vers Canada." The tide was running swift over Red Islet Bank, with (he correctly noted) "a depth of only two or three fathom" and a bottom of boulders as big as hogsheds; *L'Émerillon* was only saved from grounding by the other ships' sending boats to tow her clear.

Five leagues up-river the fleet reached a long island in midstream (on their return named *Ile aux Lièvres*, Hare Island) and the Captain decided to anchor there to await flood tide. Steamships are still advised so to do if they wish to avoid wasting fuel bucking the current. Cartier notes that his fleet tried sailing upstream, made no progress, and, finding no bottom at 120 fathom a bowshot from shore, returned to Hare Island "where we anchored in 35 fathom with fine holding ground." One can see that spot on the modern chart, a mile or two west of Hare Passage. Cartier's ships must have carried cables at least a hundred fathom long to anchor in so great a depth. The business of getting in that length of sodden hemp rope, several inches in diameter, must have been the most back-breaking of all tasks for the mariners.

Upon leaving this Hare Island anchorage on 3 September, Cartier was too busy admiring a school of beluga, or white whale "with head like a greyhound," to notice Murray Bay and Pointe au Pic. The beluga is still caught in those waters, largely for its edible inner skin, which is marketed under the Eskimo name, muktuk. Not until the 6th could the fleet make *L'Ile aux Coudres*, so named by Cartier because his men found there a grove of trees bearing hazel nuts "bigger and of better

Hare Island, Cartier's *Ile aux Lièvres*.

Baie de Saint-Paul.

Cartier's anchorage off *Ile d'Orléans* or *de Bacchus*.

flavor than ours" in France. They anchored between the island and the mouth of Baie Saint-Paul; saw an "inestimable number" of snapping turtles and more beluga. The currents, up to five knots on the modern chart, reminded him of the Gironde at Bordeaux.

On 7 September, "jour Nostre-Dame," says the *Brief recit* (it was the vigil of her birthday), "after hearing mass, we left the said isle to go up the said river, and we came to fourteen islands." This archipelago begins with Goose Island and extends to Madame Island; there are more than fourteen if you count the islets. These "mark the beginning of the land and province of Canada."

They did indeed. Cartier had really arrived.

Stadaconé—Quebec

After a hard pull upstream, all ships manning their sweeps, they anchored the same day between the north shore and "a great island," where were camped a great number of natives engaged in fishing. Cartier landed with a large company, including his Huron guides, who convinced their fellow tribesmen, after an initial panic, that the Frenchmen were not to be feared. These jolly Hurons "made good cheer, dancing and making several 'talks'; and some of the chief men came to see our boats, bringing us a heap of eels and other fish, with two or three loads of maize, the bread that they live on here, and several big melons." This delegation bearing gifts was followed by another of both sexes. They were "well received" by Cartier, who regaled them with "what he had" and gave them little gifts of slight value, "with which they were well content." Cartier found the island richly wooded, with such masses of wild grapevines clinging to the trees that he named it *Ile de Bacchus*. Thinking perhaps that this would not go well at home, he renamed it *Ile d'Orléans*, after Charles, duc d'Orléans, son of François-premier.

Next day, 8 September, "The seigneur of Canada, named Donnaconna, whose title was Agouhanna," came on board *La Grande Hermine* with a suite of sixteen warriors, in twelve canoes. After talking with his two sons, whom he had not seen for over a year, and learning of the good usage they had received in France, Donnaconna asked Cartier to extend his bare arms to be kissed and wrapped around his neck "which is their way of greeting in that country." The English called this "colling." As soon as he had performed the ceremony (not too pleasant, as the Indians were well greased), Cartier treated the delegation to bread and wine, "with which they were much pleased." He then manned his ships' boats to explore upstream with the flood tide and find a good harbor. After passing the mouth of the Montmorency River—without noting the waterfall—there burst on them a magnificent view—again, no comment. A high scarped promontory thrust between the Great River and its tributary the St. Charles; and at its foot nestled a dirty, squalid native village called Stadaconé. This promontory was the great Rock of Quebec, now fraught with historic memories—Samuel de Champlain, Bishop Laval and Count Frontenac, Montcalm and Wolfe, the death of General Montgomery, Sir Wilfrid Laurier, Mackenzie King, and the Quebec Conference which gave the signals for victory in September 1944. For Cartier, however, a good anchorage was the only subject of immediate interest; and, exploring in *Grande Hermine*'s longboat, he found "at a forking of the waters, fair and pleasant, where there is a little river [the St. Charles] which he named *Sainte-Croix*, and a harbor with a bar and two or three fathom, which we found suitable for placing our ships in safety." Upon his return the people of Stadaconé flocked to the waterside, a leading man gave a "preachment"—a typical Indian talk, while the women danced and sang, standing in water up to their knees. Cartier distributed a few trinkets; and, as his men rowed him back to the flagship downstream, they could hear the people singing miles away. This was indeed the golden age of race relations in North America.

With a good eye to geography, Cartier realized that Stadaconé was the focal point of the Great River. On 14 September he brought all three ships up from Ile d'Orléans, preceded by Donnaconna, and twenty-five canoe-loads of subjects. Two days later he warped *Grande* and *Petite Hermine* into the fork of the two rivers, anchoring at spots which he had sounded and buoyed, and where they would ground out at low water. *L'Émerillon*, the little pinnace, he anchored in the roadstead right under the Rock of Quebec, ready to take him upstream. As soon as the *Hermines* were moored, canoes full of Indians swarmed about them, and Donnaconna with his two boys and members of his council boarded.

Domagaya and Taignoagny, who had promised to pilot the French up-river to Hochelaga, now began to sulk and stall, and Cartier soon found out what ailed them. Their father did not wish Cartier to go to Hochelaga. The chief there, also a Huron, claimed dominion over Donnaconna, who did not relish the relationship; but their respective positions would be reversed if the chief of Stadaconé could gain such powerful allies as the French, with their ships, firearms, and iron tools. He feared that if Cartier reached Hochelaga he would be persuaded by the chief there to be his ally, not Donnaconna's. Taignoagny told Cartier that his father was displeased with the projected visit to Hochelaga and would not let him serve as pilot; the Captain answered that he was determined to push on, and would make it worth while for the lad to accompany him. But he failed to move him.

Donnaconna now tried another tack. Inviting Cartier ashore, he made a speech and then presented the Captain with his niece, a little girl of ten or twelve years, and two younger boys, one his own son. Taignoagny explained that these were a gift to dissuade him from going to Hochelaga. Cartier answered that, in that case, he would have to return them. Domagaya then took up the dialogue, declared that Donnaconna made these gifts out of pure affection and that he, Domagaya, would pilot the pinnace. Two swords and two brass wash basins were then presented to the chief, at whose request a salute of twelve guns was fired from the flagship. Consternation among the natives! "They howled and yelled so loud you would have thought that hell had broken loose," says the *Brief recit*.

Next day, 18 September, with the moon at last quarter, Donnaconna emptied his bag of tricks. Three medicine men dressed as devils—blackened faces, long horns, and dogskin pelts—paddled out and around the flagship, one making a harangue. Presently Taignoagny and Domagaya came on board crying *Jesus! Maria! Jacques Cartier!* and explained that their god, *Cudouagny* by name, was warning the Frenchmen by means of these black-faced actors that there would be so much ice and snow up-river that they would all perish. Cartier and his men laughed them off and said that their priests had consulted Jesus, who predicted fair weather! Donnaconna then affected to regard the whole thing as a joke, and the day ended pleasantly with more dancing, singing, and shouting of *Ho! Ho! Ho!* Cartier decided that the two boys were a choice pair of rogues who would probably try to run him aground if taken as pilots, and that he would dispense with their services.

MER DES ETILLES:

TROPIQVE DE CANCER:

LA MER OCCEANE:

MER DESPAIGNE:

MER DE FRANCE:

CANADA

QVE: LA TERRE DV LABOVREVR.

orth America in the Desceliers Mappemonde of 1546. The top is south;
e bottom, north. Photo of original in John Rylands Library, Manchester,
England. Courtesy, Map Division, Public Archives of Canada.

Everything was fair at this season around the Rock of Quebec. Cartier admired the trees, the cornfields, the wild grapes; and he might well have called it a day and gone into winter quarters. Ambition, curiosity, and a sense of duty to his king forced him on.

Hochelaga

So, on 19 September 1535, *L'Émerillon* made sail and started upstream with the flood tide and a last-quarter moon, towing the two longboats of the bigger ships. Cartier and several gentlemen volunteers were on board, together with Captain Jalobert of *La Petite Hermine*, who came to help Le Breton and Maingard. They did a very good job getting the pinnace upstream and down without mishap, for this was the most difficult part of the entire voyage. Fortunately, the river was nearing its annual low, which meant that the currents were at least strength; but, even so, there must have been many times when the crew of the pinnace had to man their sweeps to make progress or keep her from grounding.

Passing between wooded shores festooned with wild grape, and encampments of friendly Indians who approached to trade; and hearing the song of the blackbird, the thrush, and (as they imagined) the nightingale, the expedition in one day proceeded about thirty-two miles, to a place the Indians called *Achelacy*. This has been identified as the modern Notre-Dame de Pontneuf. Here a local chief came on board, warned them against the rapids ahead, and presented Cartier with another little girl, eight or nine years old. There is no blinking the fact that these Indians, like primitive tribes in other parts of the world, considered the gift of a fresh young virgin to be a compliment to a distinguished visitor, and that Cartier accepted them as such. The little girl previously presented by Donnaconna ran away, complaining that she had been abused by the ship's boys when their captain was absent. Captured and returned, she was taken to France, where she and all but one of the other Indian children died.

It took the pinnace nine days to get seventy-three miles up the great river, "without losing a day or an hour," states the *Brief recit*. First, and without benefit of pilot, she had to get through the Richelieu Rapids, where the ebb current runs 5½ knots in a channel less than a quarter-mile wide, between *battures*, banks of boulder-covered shale, bare at low water. After these rapids came five channels, even narrower, but with less swift currents. Cartier must have anchored during the ebb, sent his boats ahead to sound, and proceeded during the flood. It became a little easier after passing the site of Trois Rivières at the mouth of the St. Maurice. On 28 September (having made an average of only 8.2 miles a day), the pinnace arrived at the outlet of Lac Saint-Pierre, a widening of the river twenty miles long. This lake is very shoal; *L'Émerillon*'s leadsmen found no depth greater than two fathom.

After more or less feeling their way across Lac Saint-Pierre, the Frenchmen were puzzled how to get on, for the St. Lawrence flows into this lake by five different channels separated by islands. Anchoring the pinnace, Cartier explored the islands with his boats, incidentally encountering a friendly group of five savages. One of them, when the boat grounded, picked up the Captain in his arms and carried him ashore "as if he had been a six-year-old child." These natives were hunting muskrat, of which they had accumulated a great number, and gave Cartier all he and his men wanted to eat; the French found them good. The Indians also indicated which channel to follow to Hochelaga, and said it would be a three-day journey. It took Cartier exactly that; the distance is sixty-five nautical miles.

The Captain wisely decided to leave *L'Émerillon* moored at the west end of Lac Saint-Pierre, and to proceed upstream in the longboats. He provisioned them with as many dry and liquid stores as they could hold, and, accompanied by masters Le Breton and Jalobert, four gentlemen volunteers,* and twenty-eight sailors to do the work, set forth on 29 September, with the new moon two days old. The longboats, each manned by seven oarsmen (three to each side and a coxswain), pushed along in perfect weather, trading knives and other trifles for fish, with the natives encountered en route.

On 2 October the boats arrived before Hochelaga, the present Montreal. This was a more impressive place than Stadaconé, Quebec. More than a thousand natives came to the edge of the river to greet the

---

* These four, who deserve mention as members of the first European party to reach Montreal, were Claude du Pontbriand, *eschanson* (cupbearer) to the dauphin; Charles de La Pommeraye, nephew to a canon of the cathedral of Saint-Malo; Jean Guyon, seigneur de Thaumetz; and Jean Poullet of Dol, who probably edited for publication the *Brief recit*. It is a curious coincidence that Pontbriand's father was seigneur de Montréal (Gers), a little place just east of the Landes, as well as governor of the château de Bergerac, Cyrano's home.

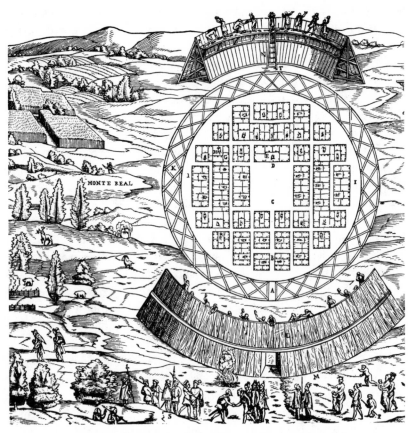

Ramusio's plan of Hochelaga. Courtesy Harvard College Library.

Ramusio's key, translated, is as follows:
A   Gate to City of Hochelaga
B   Principal street, which goes to the Plaza
C   The plaza
D   House of the king Agouhana
E   Courtyard of said royal house, and his fire
F   One of the ten streets of the City
G   One of the private houses
H   Courtyard with fire, where the kitchen is
I   Space between the houses and the City, where one can go around it
K   The palisade, made of boards around the City in lieu of wall
L   Palisades outside the City
M   Space outside the city circuit (Cartier greeting the Agouhana)
N   Palisade behind the city circuit
O,P Gallery where men stand to defend the City
Q   Space between one palisade and the other
R   Indian men, women and children outside the City to see the Frenchmen

412

S Frenchmen who enter the City, and who take the hands of the Indians who come outside the City to see and caress them.

T Ladder to the platform

The main thing wrong with this picture is the boards; they should have been logs and poles with the bark on, erected vertically. This way of constructing a fort was universal among the Iroquois tribes. See note at end of this Chapter on The Huron.

Frenchmen. They bore gifts, especially corn bread, of which "They threw so much into the boats that it seemed to fall from the air." When Cartier and his chosen companions landed, the people crowded in and the women brought their children for him to touch. This spot may confidently be identified as the beginning of the Sainte-Marie *sault*, which runs five knots on the ebb. Opposite is L'Ile Saint-Hélène, site of the famous Expo 67, and the river is now crossed at that point by a bridge named for Jacques Cartier. All night these Hurons "remained on the river bank, keeping fires burning, dancing, and calling out *aguyase*, which is their term for a joyful welcome."

Between a conspicuous hill and the river were well cultivated cornfields and a wooden citadel such as Eastern Indians generally built for defense. The Hurons who dwelt here, and the name of whose *Agouhana* (chief) we do not know, were in a far more vulnerable position than Donnaconna's subjects, being situated on one of the favorite warpaths of the Five Nations. The picture-plan of Hochelaga, which we owe to Ramusio's curiosity, must have been based on a sketch or description brought home by Cartier, whose *Brief recit* agrees with it perfectly. Hochelaga citadel was situated some three miles from the river bank, partly on the present grounds of McGill University, but mostly southeast of them.

On Sunday, 3 October, Cartier donned his dress cloak and, with his gentlemen and twenty sailors armed with pikes, marched through a beautiful oak grove to a point where he was greeted by a head man and several Indians. They passed open fields where maize was ripening, and reached the citadel, overshadowed by a hill which the Captain named *Mont Royal*. This eventually became *Montréal*. His description, which Ramusio's picture follows closely, states that the town was protected, not only by a wooden wall but by two redoubts, "garnished with rocks and stones, for defense and protection." Inside the wall the town contained some fifty bark and wood dwellings, each with several rooms, an open fireplace in the middle, and lofts where braided sheaves of corn were hung for winter provision. He even gives us a recipe for the corn bread with which the French were showered on arrival: the maize is brayed in a mortar, mixed with water into dough, and separated into cakes which are cooked on a hot stone and covered with hot pebbles. They also smoked fish and eels for winter use. The Frenchmen disliked the Huron food, not because of the dirt but for absence of salt. Cartier describes their most precious possession as *esnoguy*, or white wampum, beads made from shells of river clams, which they used as currency. These clams were obtained by planting in the river the dead bodies of criminals or enemies, with buttocks and thighs cut. The clams worked into these incisions and were pulled off when the bodies were withdrawn.

The Frenchmen were conducted into the central plaza, where the women flocked around to touch and stroke them. A bark mat was brought in for the guests to sit on, and the "chief lord of the country, whom they call in their language *Agouhana*" was carried in by ten braves on a deerskin litter. A partly paralyzed man of about fifty years of age, his rank was displayed by a red headband of porcupine quills. This he presented to Cartier after the Captain had obliged by rubbing the royal arms and legs. Numerous blind and crippled Indians then came to be touched; "One would think that God had come down there to cure them!" wrote Cartier. He read the opening words of the Gospel according to St. John—*In principio erat verbum*—making the sign of the cross "and prayed God to give them knowledge of our holy faith and of the passion of Our Lord." He capped this by reading the gospel account of the passion in John xviii and xix. It is difficult to imagine what the Hurons got out of this, but at least they were impressed; and after the Captain had distributed gifts and let the children scramble for handfuls of pewter rings and little tin representations of *agnus Dei*, they evinced "a marvellous joy." Finally, Cartier caused his trumpets and other musical instruments to sound off, which put the people in ecstasies.

Now the Captain and his party climbed to the top of Mont Royal, where they were rewarded by a magnificent view—the Laurentians on the north, outspurs of the Green Mountains and the Adirondacks to the south, and the Great River flowing through the picture from west to east like a long band of silver. To his dismay, Cartier saw, just above the point where he had left the boats, a series of rapids which no boat bigger than a canoe could pass. These were the Lachine rapids around which Canada eventually built a canal. In the *Brief recit* he simply calls them "a *sault* of water, the most impetuous one could possibly see." Tradition states that Cartier named these sardonically *La Chine*, as the nearest he was able to get to China; but they were so named by Robert Cavelier de La Salle, who had a seigneurie there in the next century, and the sarcasm is his.

Before leaving the site of Montreal, Cartier acquired from the local Indians a second installment of what we may call the Saguenay dream. After a canoe journey up the Great River, one would reach another river flowing from the west—the Ottawa, obviously. This waters the Kingdom of Saguenay, inhabited by "bad people" armed to the teeth, armored in wood, tough fighters; but a country rich in precious metals. That concept the Hochelaga Indians conveyed by touching Cartier's silver whistle chain and a sailor's gilt dagger handle, pointing north-westerly and crying *Saguenay! Saguenay!* The Hurons, like Verraz-zano's Wampanoags, wore copper ornaments, and when Cartier asked if these too were products of Saguenay they answered truthfully, "No," and pointed west to the Hiawathan "Land of Gitche Gumee" —Lake Superior.

After this excursion the Frenchmen returned to their boats, some being carried piggyback by obliging natives, as shown in Ramusio's picture of Hochelaga. Cartier had sailed or rowed almost a thousand miles from the open ocean; enough for one voyage.

The current being favorable, and the moon waxing daily, they took off at once in their boats and reached their pinnace in Lac Saint-Pierre on 4 October. Next day they made sail in *L'Émerillon* and started downstream for "the province of Canada," explored the lower reaches of the St. Maurice, one of the Three Rivers which give that town its name. On Monday 11 October, the day of full moon, the pinnace joined her consorts at "the port of Sainte-Croix," the mouth of the St. Charles, at Quebec.

Here the sailors of the two *Hermines* had built a fort on the shore, close to where they lay, constructed of vertical logs and mounted with ships' guns so as to cover all possible approaches. Donnaconna, evi-

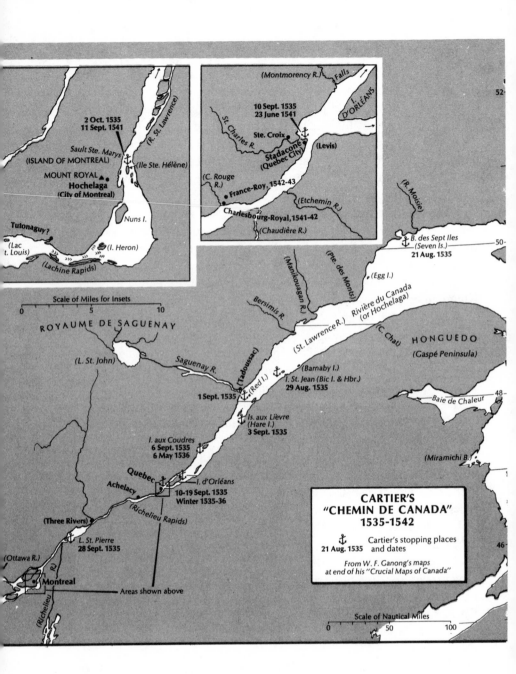

(Montmorency R.) Falls

10 Sept. 1535
23 June 1541
Ste. Croix

St. Charles R.

I. D'ORLÉANS

Stadacone
(Quebec City)

(Levis)

(C. Rouge
R.)

• France-Roy, 1542-43

(Etchemin R.)

Charlesbourg-Royal, 1541-42

(Chaudière R.)

2 Oct. 1535
11 Sept. 1541

Sault Ste. Marys
(ISLAND OF MONTREAL)

(R. St. Lawrence)

(Ile Ste. Hélène)

MOUNT ROYAL ▲ •
Hochelaga
(City of Montreal)

Nuns I.

Tutonaguy?

(Lac
t. Louis)

(I. Heron)

(Lachine Rapids)

Scale of Miles for Insets

0   5   10

ROYAUME DE SAGUENAY

(L. St. John)

Saguenay R.

(Tadoussac)

(Red I.)

1 Sept. 1535

Bersimis R.

(Manikouagan R.)

(Pte. des Monts)

(Barnaby I.)
I. St. Jean (Bic I. & Hbr.)
29 Aug. 1535

(St. Lawrence R.)

Rivière du Canada
(or Hochelaga)

(C. Chat)

HONGUEDO
(Gaspé Peninsula)

B. des Sept Iles
(Seven Is.)
21 Aug. 1535

(Egg I.)

(R. Moisie)

52—

50—

48—

46—

Is. aux Lièvre
(Hare I.)
3 Sept. 1535

Baie de Chaleur

I. aux Coudres
6 Sept. 1535
6 May 1536

Quebec

Achelacy

(Miramichi B.)

I. d'Orléans
10-19 Sept. 1535
Winter 1535-36

(Three Rivers)

(Richelieu Rapids)

L. St. Pierre
28 Sept. 1535

(Ottawa R.)

Montreal

Areas shown above

(Richelieu)

**CARTIER'S
"CHEMIN DE CANADA"
1535-1542**

⚓   Cartier's stopping places
21 Aug. 1535   and dates

*From W. F. Ganong's maps
at end of his "Crucial Maps of Canada"*

Scale of Nautical Miles

0   50   100

dently convinced that he had better not try any more funny business, invited Cartier "to visit him the following day at Canada," i.e. Stadaconé. After the usual song-and-dance and presentation of gifts—Cartier must have had barrels of small wares—the chief showed the Captain some scalps of his enemies, whom he called *Toudamans*, which his braves had obtained that summer. This was in revenge for one of his fishing parties in the Gaspé having been ambushed two years before, and all but five out of two hundred people slaughtered. Whether these Toudamans were Micmac, Etchemin, or Seneca is disputed; but it does not much matter since, apart from the Iroquois confederation, every North American Indian tribe was in a perpetual state of war with its neighbors.

First Winter in Canada

Exactly when Cartier decided to spend the winter of 1535-36 in Canada he does not say; but he must have done so before he returned to Stadaconé, for it was then too late to depart. It would have taken him a least another month to reach the open sea, and he did not care to risk a winter passage of the Atlantic. Also, he wished to experience a Canadian winter. And that he did!

It was now October, the fairest season of the year in that northern region. All along the Great River and on every side of Stadaconé the fall foliage was at its height, and the hunter's moon was full. There is nothing more superb in nature than this autumnal pageant in Canada. Yellow birch leaves, brilliant scarlet, gold, and crimson maple, bronze ash and walnut, flash their colors against a background of green conifers, of which alone the larch, or hackmatack, turns its needles to gold before snow falls. During the halcyon days of autumn the colors are reflected in the river; then a line gale strips the leaves from the branches and, when the wind drops, they float on the calm water like a stippled painting. Cartier never mentioned this; but neither (to my knowledge) did any of his successors refer to autumn foliage prior to the romantic eighteenth century. Could the sight of this splendor have been repulsive to men used to the muted colors of the European autumn? One remembers the story of Matthew Arnold's being taken to see fall foliage near Boston and exclaiming, "I say! Are your trees infected with some sort of *disease?*"

Cartier and his men, oblivious to the beauties of nature, prepared for winter, strengthening their fort, bringing in great stacks of firewood, and salting down fish and game. Cartier compiled for his *Brief recit* a sort of gazetteer of the St. Lawrence which must have been very useful to his successors. He included several pages on the manners and customs of his savage hosts, at whose habit of going almost naked in the dead of winter, except for moccasins and leggings, he never failed to marvel. One custom rather shocked him, although it must have pleased his men; nubile girls were placed in a common brothel, where all men of any age could take their pleasure, and no girl could leave until she had hooked a fellow to marry her; but as a Huron could have two or three wives, the girls really had a chance. If they failed to secure a husband, they became community drudges. Cartier wrote that he and his friends visited several of these establishments "and found these houses as full of girls as schoolrooms in France were of boys." The same *maisons de plaisir* served as gambling houses, where the men, using a crude dice game, staked their all, even to their G-strings, and emerged naked as their mothers bore them.

Cartier also made the earliest recorded mention of tobacco in these northern parts. The natives carried in a pouch the sun-dried leaves of a plant that they called *kiyekta*, crumbled them into powder which they crammed into a pipe made of baked clay with a reed stem, lit it with a live coal, and alternately sucked in and blew out great clouds of smoke. "They say it keeps them warm and in good health, and never go abroad without it." The Frenchmen tried a few drags from a lighted pipe but found the smoke too hot to bear, "like powdered pepper."

The most favorable impression of the Gulf and River that Cartier carried away was the vast number and variety of fish, fowl, and game, especially the fish, in which "this river is the most abundant in all varieties that in the memory of man have been seen or heard of." He mentions twelve varieties, as well as seal, walrus, porpoise, and beluga. Canadian economy was long based on fish and fur.

From mid-November 1535 to mid-April 1536 the French fleet lay frozen solid at the mouth of the St. Charles, under the Rock of Quebec. Ice was over two fathom thick in the river, and snow four feet deep ashore. "All our beverages," says the *Brief recit*, "froze in their casks. And on board our ships, below hatches as on deck, lay four fingers' breadth of ice." To add to their discomfort, scurvy broke out, first among the Huron of Stadaconé and then among the French. Considering the plentiful game, fish, fruit, and berries that Cartier boasts about, it seems strange that either race should have been so afflicted; but the symptoms that Cartier relates are unmistakable—teeth falling out, gums rotting, swollen limbs, acute pain. By mid-February, "out of the 110 men that we were, not ten were well enough to help the others, a thing pitiful to see"; in addition, some fifty savages had died. Cartier put on a brave front to conceal his plight from the natives when only three or four of his men were still healthy, making a great noise behind the fort's palisade as if scores of hearty fellows were brawling. Then, "God in His holy grace took pity on us, and sent us knowledge of a remedy." This happened after Cartier had made a vow to go on pilgrimage to Rocomadour, and staged a service of intercession to Our Lady; if she heard, she chose a strange instrument for the cure.

Domagaya, who had suffered a bad case of scurvy, came to the fort for a friendly call, and appeared to be cured. What had healed him? The juice and concoction from a certain tree which he called *annedda*. He sent two women with Cartier to gather it. "They brought back from the forest nine or ten branches and showed us how to grind the bark and boil it in water, then drink the potion every other day and apply the residue as a poultice to swollen and infected legs." The sailors gagged at something new, said they'd rather die than drink that stuff; but a few bold fellows tried it, felt better at once, and after two or three days were completely cured. This miraculous tree, a specimen of the common arborvitae (*Thuja occidentalis*) was pulled to pieces by the Frenchmen, and every leaf and piece of bark consumed in a week by sailors frantic for relief. Even some who had suffered for five or six years from *la vérole* (syphilis) said they were cured of that! Cartier, before he left Stadaconé, dug up some young arborvitae which were successfully transplanted in the royal garden at Fontainebleau. He remarked that if all the doctors of Louvain and Montpellier (the leading medical schools of western Europe) had been there with all the drugs of Alexandria, "They could not have done as much in a year as this tree did in a week." Everyone who took it recovered, leaving the total company at eighty-five men.

After the turn of the year, Donnaconna and some of his pals went off on a hunting expedition on snowshoes and were gone two months. They returned with several score natives whom the French had not seen before, causing Cartier to suspect that the chief was plotting to overwhelm and massacre the French. On the contrary, Donnaconna was bringing in what modern politicians would call "mattress voters" to support him in the forthcoming election! A strong faction of the local Hurons wished to depose him in favor of a brave named Agona; but the temporary voters, from a village called Sitadin on the Beauport shore, were for him. Taignoagny even suggested that Cartier seize candidate Agona and carry him to France. But the Captain, as he admits, had already made up his mind to take Donnaconna to France.

A clever spinner of tall tales, Donnaconna embroidered on the fancied wealth of that mythical Kingdom of Saguenay, which (he said) could be approached either by the Saguenay River or the Ottawa. He had been there himself! It had immense quantities of gold, rubies, and other valuable things; the people were as white as Frenchmen and went clothed in woolens. Cartier did not realize that Indians were not only great liars and story-tellers but yes-men, eager to please. They noticed that the Frenchmen's eyes sparkled and fingers twitched when gold was mentioned, so Donnaconna let Cartier have it. The Captain even swallowed a yarn that his host had been in a land of pygmies who were unipeds (like Thorfinn Karlsevni's alleged murderer), and in another region where the people had no anus, hence subsisted on liquids which they could void as urine.

Donnaconna paid heavily for his fun. Cartier decided to kidnap him so that he could tell François-premier convincingly about the wonders of Saguenay. For this outrage—a violation of his royal instructions—Cartier executed a ruse as carefully planned as a bank robbery. With no sense of inconsistency, he set Holyrood day (3 May), the feast of the Holy Cross, for the treacherous act. After raising a wooden cross with a Latin inscription and the arms of France as an excuse for important tribesmen to attend, a band of well-rehearsed sailors seized and bound the chief, his two sons, and two leading subjects, and whisked them on board ship. The others, alarmed by gunshots, "scampered off like sheep before a wolf, some across the river and some to the forest, each for himself." All night on the river bank they "cried and howled like wolves" for their beloved chief, but Cartier was implacable. In all he carried to France ten natives, including the little girls and boys given to him as gifts. Not one ever returned to Canada.

Donnaconna's subjects were somewhat appeased by the chief showing himself to be alive, and by Cartier's promising to return him in "ten or twelve moons," loaded with gifts after seeing the king. Also he presented the hull of *La Petite Hermine* to the intruders from Sitadin who wanted it to extract the iron. He abandoned her as the least valuable of his fleet, because after the epidemic he had only enough men to handle two vessels; but he saved her sails and other gear for which the natives had no use. After a final exchange of gifts, *La Grande Hermine* and *L'Émerillon* set sail for France on 6 May 1536.

The river was so high and swift as to be dangerous, so Cartier anchored behind Ile aux Coudres until 16 May when the spring floods abated, and he had a new moon. He then anchored off Ile aux Lièvres (Hare Island), so named because his men snared a large number of hares. Next day a strong east wind blew up-river and they had to return to the Ile aux Coudres anchorage. Wind came fair on 21 May, and they sailed downstream through the passage between Anticosti and the Gaspé Peninsula, which had been solid with fog on the first voyage, "passed cap de Pratto, beginning of the Baie de Chaleur," carried on day and night "because the wind was both full and fair" and the moon was waxing. On the 24th they sighted Brion Island. This, the *Brief recit* explains, "was just what we wanted to shorten our route." Cartier wished to try the strait between Cape Breton and Newfoundland which Fagundes had discovered, but the French, apparently, had never used. It has subsequently been named for John Cabot, who never saw it.

On 25 May, Ascension Day, they sailed ten miles to East Island of the Magdalen group, found no good anchorage, so returned to Brion Island and there remained until 1 June, enjoying the beautiful groves and meadows seen on the first voyage. They then sailed around the Magdalens, ascertaining that they were islands indeed; and, sighting mountains above the horizon to the southeastward, steered for them. These were on Cape Breton Island. Cartier named the northwestern point, now Cape St. Lawrence, *Cap de Lorraine* after an important cardinal of the house of Guise-Lorraine. He noted the strong shoreward set of current against which mariners are warned today. Cape North, the next promontory, he named *Cap de Sainct Paoul*. On 4 June he sighted Newfoundland, and entered a harbor named *Sainct Esprit* because it was Whitsunday. This must have been Port aux Basques, about seven miles east of Cape Ray. There they rode until the 6th, when they coasted eastward to *Les Iles de Saint-Pierre*, a

Cross on Ile aux Coudres, looking toward the north shore of the river.
Courtesy Canadian Government Travel Bureau.

name which had replaced the Portuguese Eleven Thousand Virgins.
This was the only place that Cartier visited on his voyages which is
still under French sovereignty. There on St. Barnaby's day, 11 June,
they met the first ships encountered on this long voyage—fishermen
from Brittany and other parts of France.

Sailing from Saint-Pierre 16 June, Cartier rounded Cape Race, Newfoundland, and entered Renewse Harbor (which he calls *Rougnouse*),
to top off with wood and water. This place served French fishermen as
a second-hand boat exchange. Since shore fishing was done mostly
from small boats, it was convenient to pick up *chaloupes* in Newfoundland and turn them in before returning home, rather than encumber the
deck and risk losing the lot in a storm. Cartier left behind one of his.

From Renewse, *La Grande Hermine* and *L'Émerillon* took their departure on 19 June, the day after new moon. Favored by fine weather and fair westerlies, they crossed the Atlantic in three weeks, reaching Saint-Malo on 15 July "by grace of the Creator, praying him at the close of our voyage to grant us his grace for paradise hereafter."

So ended the second and most profitable of Cartier's voyages, lasting fourteen months, Having already located the entrance, he now opened up the greatest water route for penetrating North America. He had made an intelligent estimate of the resources of Canada, both natural and human, despite considerable exaggeration on the mineral side. Whilst some of his actions with respect to the "savages" were dishonorable, he did his best, according to his lights, to establish friendship with the Huron up and down the Great River, an indispensable preliminary

Tip end of Cape Breton Island; Cape North, Cartier's *Cap de Saint-Paul*, in background. Courtesy Canadian Government Travel Bureau.

to French settlement. And on his third voyage he made a serious attempt to found a colony.

Bibliography and Notes

BRIEF RECIT

Cartier's own account of his second voyage was printed in Paris anonymously in 1545 under the title *Brief recit, & succincte narration, de la navigation faicte es ysles de Canada, Hochelage & Seguenay & autres.* . . . The British Museum owns the unique copy of this little tract. Ramusio translated it into Italian for his Volume III (Venice, 1556), and Hakluyt had John Florio translate the Italian translation into English as *A Shorte and Briefe Narration* (London, 1580). Hakluyt used the Florio version, with a few changes,* for his own *Voyages,* ed. 1598–1600. H. S. Burrage reprinted the Hakluyt version in his *Early English and French Voyages* (1906), pp. 37–88.

In the meantime, three contemporary manuscript copies of the *Brief recit* had been found in the Bibliothèque Nationale and were printed at Paris in 1841 and Quebec in 1843. Ms. No. 5589, the most accurate and probably nearest to the lost original, is printed with many annotations in Ch.-A. Julien, *Les Français en Amérique pendant la première moitié du XVIe siècle* (1946), pp. 115–83, and H. P. Biggar, *Voyages of Jacques Cartier* (Public Archives of Canada *Publications,* No. 11 (1924), pp. 83–246. Biggar has a fresh English translation and copious notes. These authorities agree that Jean Poullet of Dol, who sailed with Cartier, edited the Captain's original sea journal (now lost) to make the *Brief recit* and added, for publicity's sake, a florid introduction castigating "wicked Lutherans, apostates and imitators of Mahomet." Marcel Trudel, *Histoire de la Nouvelle-France,* I, 72–73, has a résumé of the authorship problem, Rabelais being among those mentioned. For this wild hypothesis see Note to Chapter XIII below.

LA GRANDE HERMINE

Commandant Denoix's full-sized model is now (1970) located at the Cartier-Brébeuf park in Quebec. As described in a pamphlet issued by Expo 67, this model is a two-decker, 78'9" long, 25' beam, and with a 12' depth of hold. The three masts, fore, main, and mizzen, are respectively 82'8", 101', and 45'6" tall, including the parts below deck; the bowsprit is 42'6" long. The rudder is so designed that the man at the tiller, or whipstaff, can really see ahead. The rendering of this model by Cdt. Denoix is shown at the

---

* Dr. Thomas R. Adams, librarian of the John Carter Brown at Providence—a library noteworthy for its helpfulness to scholars—has kindly compared for me the Florio text of 1580 with that in Hakluyt's *Voyages,* 1598–1600 ed., III, 202–32, and found few differences other than spelling, and corrections of printer's errors. For instance, Florio's *gallion* becomes *pinnesse, New land* becomes *newfoundland,* and *greene fish* becomes *cod fish.*

✒Brief recit,&

ſuccinᣦe narration, de la nauiga-
tion faiᣦe es yſles de Canada, Hochelage & Saguenay & autres, auec
particulieres meurs,langaige, & ce-
rimonies des habitans d'icelles:fort
deleᣦable à veoir.

Auec priuilege.
On les uend à Paris au ſecond pillier en la grand
ſalle du Palais , ᵹ en la rue neufue noſtredame à
l'enſeigne de leſcu de fräce,par Ponce Roſſet diᣦ
Faucheur,ᵹ Anthoine le Clerc freres.
1 5 4 5.

Title page of Cartier's *Brief recit*, 1545.
Courtesy British Museum

beginning of this chapter. There is a miniature model (shown here) of the
ship in the Musée de la Marine, Paris, differing from the full-sized one in
several details, especially in having a bonaventure mizzen and a lower
stern-castle.

IDENTIFICATIONS

Cartier's compass bearings are generally correct within a point, but are magnetic and we do not know what the westerly variation was in the waters he explored. Thus his W by S (259°) from the Cormorant Rocks to Natashquan Point is 269° true on the modern chart—near enough. Ganong has tabulated the variations on the Desceliers and other maps, and thinks that the mean was about 14° W. See Biggar, *Voyages*, pp. 315–16.

North Shore of the Gulf. Harrison F. Lewis's article (see notes to Chapter XI above) and his wife's illustrated "Along the North Shore in Cartier's Wake" in *Canadian Geographical Journal*, VIII (1934), 209–21, are indispensable. Alfonce says it is 36 leagues from Blanc Sablon to the Demoiselles, which are in lat. 50°45' N; and from the Demoiselles to Cap Thiennot is twenty leagues. The correct latitude of the Harrington Islands is 50°29' N; they are about 110 miles from Blanc Sablon, which seems to pinpoint them as the place where the unfortunate Marguerite de La Roque was marooned (see Chapter XIII below), although there is a modern Demoiselle Island far to the eastward.

The Saguenay. Francis Parkman, *Pioneers of France*, part ii of 1909 ed., pp. 205–6, is the source of this description. Bayard Taylor mentions "firs of gloomy green," water "black as night with a pitchy glaze on its surface" (quoted in the Osgood *Maritime Provinces* of 1875, p. 297). But the Saguenay, with its green-muffled banks, looked neither gloomy nor sullen on the bright September day of 1969 when we flew up it to the first rapids. At each stream that falls into it there is now a little village, such as Sainte-Rose du Nord. For the Kingdom of Saguenay see Notes to Chapter XIII below.

Gaspé. Father Deschênes in *Bulletin des Recherches Historiques*, XL (1934), 416–17, argues cogently that Cartier named the Notre Dame range, and that he reached Gaspé from Anticosti at Rivière Claude, where Mont St. Pierre rises directly from the sea.

Whittier's "Bay of Seven Islands" was first published in 1882. The poet had many contacts with New England fishermen who lived on the lower Merrimac River.

Cartier's costume at Hochelaga. The word is *se accoustra;* that is, he put on the cloak and hat in which he is shown in the Hochelaga picture and the Desceliers-Harleian Map. Biggar translates it, "Put on his armor." It is doubtful whether Cartier owned a suit of armor, not being a nobleman; or that, had he owned one, he would have carried it upstream in a boat. The man in armor shown on the other Desceliers Map which we have reproduced is captioned Roberval, who as a nobleman should have owned a coat of mail. Armor by 1535 was of no use in warfare, only in tournaments; but possession of one or more suits was a status symbol. As we shall see in Chapter XX, Governor John White took one to the Virginia wilderness.

La Grande Hermine. Miniature model in Musée de la Marine, Paris.
Courtesy Musée de la Marine.

The French never called the natives of North America *Indians,* a term first applied by Columbus and largely used by Spaniards. Cartier always called them *sauvages;* later they were called *peaux-rouges* (redskins); or, if one wished to be polite, *indigènes* (natives). Even Chateaubriand in the eighteenth century, when he met a comparatively civilized tribe in New York State, called them *sauvages.* The same term is used by the English writers of the Raleigh colony.

Games. See articles "Games" and "Huron" in F. W. Hodge, *Handbook of American Indians,* I (1907). Gambling was universal among the natives of America, and dice games have always been popular. The dice were made of all sorts of materials—stone, bone, horn, hide, wood, seeds, clay, and shell (Letter of Dr. J. Otis. Brew). One version, *pawpaw* or *props,* was adopted by the settlers of New England, and "prop-houses" existed in Boston as late as 1850. In this game the "bones" were cowrie shells filed flat, the openings filled with sealing wax.

Hochelaga's location in Montreal is disputed; references to the principal articles will be found in Ganong, pp. 312–14, and Biggar, *Voyages,* pp. 154–55. W. D. Lighthall, in Royal Society of Canada *Transactions,* XXVI (1932), ii, 181–92, challenges the authenticity of the Ramusio picture, unconvincingly to me. Gabriel Sagard-Théodat, *Histoire du Canada* (Paris, 1636), describes the Huron towns of his time in terms that meet the picture, even to the stone-throwing galleries.

Tobacco. Roland B. Dixon discussed the Huron words for tobacco and smoking in "Words for Tobacco in American Indian Languages," *American Anthropologist,* n.s., XXIII (1921), 28–29. The Huron name was *kyekta* or *quiecta.* This was the northern leaf, *Nicotiana rustica;* very hot smoking it was, and is. Smoking of the southern leaf, *Nicotiana tabacum,* in cigars (*cigarros*) had already been brought from Cuba to Spain; Columbus observed the practice on his first voyage. Cartier's surprise at smoking indicates that it had not yet reached France, nor did it reach England until 1565, when John Hawkins brought some home from Florida, where the natives, like other North American Indians, used pipes. Hawkins described it thus: "The Floridians when they travell have a kinde of herbe dried, who with a cane and an earthen cap in the end, with fire, and the dried herbs put together, doe sucke thorow the cane the smoke thereof, which smoke satisfieth their hunger, and therwith they live foure or five dayes without meat or drinke, and this all the Frenchmen used for this purpose," H. S. Burrage, *Early English and French Voyages* (1906), pp. 125–26. Later French accounts of Canada, such as Lescarbot's, indicate that the northern Indians cultivated and cured their own tobacco. Thevet, author of *Les Singularitez de la France antarctique,* introduced the herb to France, along with its Brazilian name *petun.*

What became of them? By the early seventeenth century, when Frenchmen returned to the St. Lawrence, Donnaconna's people had vanished, and it is still a mystery what became of them. Champlain in 1603–8 found no trace of Stadaconé, Hochelaga, Charlesbourg-Royal, or France-Roy, and the river banks were inhabited by Montagnais, an Algonkin tribe whose pitiful remnants are still around in 1970. Probably the Hurons found their river too exposed to Iroquois raids and removed to Lake Huron, where the Iroquois followed and almost exterminated them.

The Epidemic. A little book published at Montreal in connection with the 19th International Congress of Physiology, *Jacques Cartier et "La Grosse Maladie"* (1953), has everything necessary to identify the malady and the healing tree *Thuja occidentalis.* The author tested an infusion of the leaves and found them to be rich in vitamin C. So, don't despise Indian herb doctors!

THE NAMES Canada AND St. Lawrence

The name *Canada* has given rise to endless speculation, some by people trying to prove that Spaniards, Portuguese, Vikings, or whatnot were there before the French. I believe it to be a form of the Iroquois-Huron word *Cannata,* meaning a village or settlement; and, specifically, the village Stadaconé at the site of Quebec. The Eastern Indians never named regions, only towns, villages, and natural features; but, as in the case of *Norumbega,* Europeans expanded a mere place name to that of a region. See Parkman, *Pioneers,* p. 205, Baxter, *Cartier,* p. 135, and Ganong, *Crucial Maps,* 308–9. Cartier used *Canada* both as a synonym for Stadaconé and for the region between the Saguenay River and Quebec. I suggest that the popularity of this name is due to the fact that vowels repeated in one word, like the river *Oronoco,* and *Outourou,* the Tahitian whom Bougainville brought to Paris, appeal to the French ear. I remember how the marketwomen of Paris, wheeling barrows of apples of doubtful origin, used to cry them as "Canada! des vraies Canada!"

The St. Lawrence River to Cartier was *La Grande Rivière* or *La Rivière de Hochelaga.* The projection of *Saint-Laurent* from the little river so named by Cartier to the Great River and the Gulf was due to a misunderstanding of the *Brief recit* by Ramusio and others, as Biggar has demonstrated in his *Voyages of Cartier,* p. 108 n. 91. Mercator called the Gulf *S. Laurentii* on his 1569 map. Hakluyt used it frequently for both river and gulf, but Champlain really established the name.

✳ XIII ✳
The Search for Saguenay
1538-1543

Preparations for Cartier's Third Voyage

On 16 July 1536, Capitaine et Maître-Pilote Jacques Cartier brought *La Grande Hermine* and *L'Émerillon* safely through the many rocks and other hazards of Saint-Malo Bay and into L'Anse de Mer Bonne, the harbor. He had lost some twenty-five shipmates, victims of scurvy; but, partly to balance, he brought to France ten Hurons—Chief Donnaconna, his two unstable sons, two little girls, two little boys, and three adults. None ever saw their own country again. By the time Cartier set sail on his third voyage, all had died except one ten-year-old girl, and what became of her we know not. Domagaya and Taignoagny merged into the Paris underworld and came to no good; but Donnaconna enjoyed four years of glorious life as publicity agent for the mythical Kingdom of Saguenay. Cartier brought him to court where he was baptized, given a pension, and eventually a Christian burial.

François-premier regarded Saguenay as a means of re-establishing the balance of power in his favor. Apart from England there were only three great powers in western Europe—France, Spain, and Portugal; and England apparently had forgotten about John Cabot's discovery. Spain drew immense wealth from the mines of Mexico and Peru and financed her wars against France with American gold. Portugal waxed rich from her slave and spice trade with Africa and the Moluccas. Now, at an easy distance north of the Great River of Canada, lay another horn of plenty waiting to be emptied by France. Donnaconna, noting the king's interest in spices, added clove, nutmeg, and pepper to the products of Saguenay, and besides repeating the stories of unipeds and anus-less people, invented more yarns, with which the king loved to regale his friends. For instance, Saguenay grew oranges and pomegranates, and nourished a race of men who had wings instead of arms and flew like bats from tree to tree. To one skeptic the king replied testily that Donnaconna never varied in his stories and, under pain of death for blasphemy, had even sworn to their truth before a notary

Marguerite, reine de Navarre. By François Clouet. Courtesy Dépôt des Gravures, Bibliothèque Nationale.

public! Moreover, Cartier brought back and showed to the king some sparkling rocks which he believed to contain diamonds, and some iron pyrites—"fool's gold"—as samples of the mineral wealth of Canada.

So, a third voyage to Canada there must be—this time with no hope of getting through to China, but of conquering (like a northern Cortés or Pizarro) the curious, fabulous, glorious Kingdom of Saguenay.

That took time. Cartier's third voyage did not begin until almost five years after his return from the second. For two years the delay was due to a fresh war between France and Spain, which ended in the Treaty of Nice, June 1538. Preparations then began; but they were so elaborate and encountered so many diplomatic difficulties that three more years elapsed before the third voyage took off.

What was Cartier doing in the meantime?

Apparently he was fairly well off. He owned a small house and garden in Saint-Malo and the farm at Limoïlou. The king made him a gift of his former flagship, La Grande Hermine, and the Spanish ambassador complained that he used her to capture and pillage Portuguese and Spanish ships. Cartier had something to do with the attempt of Lord Gerald Fitzgerald to become king of Ireland, which failed, like all enterprises of that nature. An English spy at Rouen reported that the defeated Fitzgerald had arrived at Saint-Malo in March 1540 "conducted by sea by one Jackes Carter pylot of St. Mallow," but French historians believe that all Jacques did was to show Gerald the honors when he came ashore. Cartier probably fulfilled a vow made during the scurvy epidemic to make a pilgrimage to the famous shrine of Rocamadour. The early navigators, starting with Columbus, were always getting themselves involved in these pious journeys as a fair return to Our Lady for bringing them safe home.

It is a mark of the long neglect by France of Canada and of Cartier, that, of his third voyage and the first of Roberval, there have survived only the English translations of the sea-journals, summarized in Hakluyt. These abbreviated accounts have been augmented in the present century by the discovery of scores of documents in French and foreign archives on the preparations. We know ten times as much about the preliminaries as we do of the voyages themselves.

Not long after the Treaty of Nice, a few inconclusive preparations were made. The king repaid Cartier 3500 livres tournois (about $700 in gold) for expenses of his second voyage, plus 100 l.t. more for his care of the *gens saulvaiges,* the Hurons he brought home. And the royal archives preserve a detailed list of what Cartier, in September 1538, considered necessary to establish a colony on the banks of the Great River, as a base from which to discover Saguenay. He wants at least six ships with full crews, and 120 extra mariners to man boats for exploring rivers, and to remain in Canada. He wants forty *arquebuziers* (musketeers), thirty carpenters (both ship carpenters and sawyers), and ten master masons. He should also have from three to twelve each of tile-makers, charcoal burners, blacksmiths, metallurgists, vine-dressers, and farmers; barbers and apothecaries "who know about herbs"; jewelers who know precious stones and metals; tailors, cobblers, ropemakers, gunners, and priests; a total of 274. They should be provided with clothes and victuals to last two years, allowing five livres per man per month. Knocked-down boats to be assembled in Canada are wanted for exploring rivers; naval stores for repair and caulking of the ships; and one thousand francs a month for the people's payroll until the expedition starts. Also, a variety of seeds, domestic animals, and poultry should be taken to make the colony partly self-supporting. Quantities of iron and tile, and materials to build a water mill and a windmill, were a "must."

François-premier probably took one look at this and exclaimed, in effect, "Sacré nom d'un nom! trop cher!" Anyway, he paid no attention to Cartier for more than two years. Then, in August 1540, he alarmed the courts of Spain and Portugal by inviting all and sundry of his subjects to go, as the Spanish ambassador wrote to Charles V, to *las tierras nuevas.* On 17 October of the same year, the king issued a new commission to "*nostre cher et bien amé* Jacques Cartier, who having discovered the great country of the lands of *Canada* and *Ochelaga,* constituting a westward point of Asia," is to return thither "and to Saguenay if he can find it . . . to mingle with their people and live among them, the better to fulfil our aforesaid intention to do something agreeable to God." To that end, having confidence in the said Cartier's "good sense, capability, loyalty, prudence, courage, great diligence and good experience," the king appoints him Captain-General and master pilot of all ships embarked in said enterprise, and commander of all who engage therein. He may break up the "already old and obsolete" galion *L'Émerillon* to repair other ships. Royal officials in the north and west of France are ordered to let him recruit fifty convicts from the prisons, provided they had not been condemned for heresy, lèse majesté, or counterfeiting coins.

This permission to recruit convicts may mean that Cartier's popularity had waned at Saint-Malo, or merely that the word had gone around the waterfront that Canada was a lonely, frigid place which gave you nothing but scurvy. From a sailor's point of view there was far more fun and profit to be had in a fishing voyage to the Grand Bank, with a chance to trade with the Indians for valuable furs. Actually, twenty-four French ships went a-fishing to Newfoundland that very year. Similarly, after Columbus's first voyage, everybody wanted to go to the Indies; but after his second voyage nobody wanted to go, and Spain had to rake the jails to obtain settlers for Hispaniola. It is difficult for Americans, north or south, to accept the fact that for a century after Columbus's discovery, the ordinary sort of European had to be bribed, drugged, or beaten to go out to this "land of promise," unless to fish.

Roberval and Diplomatic Snooping

In January 1541 François-premier put a new face on his Canadian enterprise by placing Roberval over Cartier. Offspring of the high nobility, Jean-François de La Roque, sieur de Roberval and of a dozen other feudal fiefs, was the offspring of a royal ambassador who came from Provence and a noblewoman of Picardy. Born in or about 1500, a decade after Cartier, he had been a soldier in the Italian wars, a courtier, a friend of the poet Clément Marot, and, like that poet, a Protestant. Marot dedicated to Roberval two of his worst poems. Both men had to flee from the persecutions of 1525; but Roberval soon returned to court, protected by the king and his sister Marguerite de Navarre, authoress of the Heptaméron. Nobody knows why this Protestant nobleman, who had never been to sea, should have been promoted over Cartier.

Roberval's royal commission of 15 January 1541, more than twice as long as Cartier's, made him lieutenant-general, chief, commander, and captain of the said enterprise, including both ships and people; and conferred on him viceregal powers. The king gave him complete authority over the new lands, and over every Frenchman who went thither, with the privilege of granting lands in feudal tenure to gentlemen volunteers. Cartier became definitely a subordinate; his authority henceforth could be exerted only when Roberval was not around. Happily for the Captain, he almost never was.

At the same time, paradoxically, the enterprise entrusted to this Protestant gentleman now received a distinctly Catholic missionary flavor. Nobody before had said much or done anything about converting Canadians; Cartier had missed one opportunity, and only three of the ten natives he brought home were even baptized. But his new commission put conversion of the heathen on a par with discovering Saguenay; Roberval's is even more explicit. From now on the enterprise, on paper though not in fact, is fraught with apostolic zeal to bring thousands of *les sauvages* to embrace the Catholic faith. The obvious reason for all this beating of the religious drum was to placate the new pope, Paul III. At Rome, Emperor Charles V was again invoking the bulls of Alexander VI that divided the New World between Spain and Portugal; and the pope was no longer the complaisant Clement VII. François-premier cannily estimated that if he made a great noise about adding thousands of souls to the Catholic fold, the pope would not interfere. And probably the only reason the pope did not is that his nuncio at Paris informed him that the king had determined to send this expedition whether Rome liked it or not. To a Spanish grandee who remonstrated, François-premier replied with a phrase that made the rounds of Europe: "That the sun shone for him as for others, and he would like very much to see Adam's will to learn how he divided up the world!"

The king's earlier invitation to all and sundry of his subjects to emigrate to *les terres neufves* soon set every rumor mill a-grinding and all diplomatic bees a-buzzing. "Stop Cartier" letters fly to and fro like the diplomatic cables of 1939 on stopping Hitler. Spanish and Portuguese spies infest Paris and the seaports, seeking out and passing along to their sovereigns alarming information as to the scope of the expedition. The Emperor Charles V needs to know how many ships are involved, when they will sail, and what is their destination (maybe Canada is just a blind—may they not intend to raid Brazil or West Africa?). One report says there will be three fleets of forty sail each! The Emperor tries to stir up his brother-in-law João III of Portugal, who has an equal interest to keep the French out of Brazil and the codfish country. D. João replies he cannot be bothered; but he did send a fleet to defend Malagueta (the future Liberia) and lost it en route. More to the point, D. João sent a special envoy to the court of France, a lusty young man, the former lover of the duchesse d'Estampes, now the royal mistress, with valuable presents for her, in order to obtain knowledge of her bedroom confidences from the king. João III is not one of the most famous kings of Portugal, but he certainly had sense; to the Spanish ambassador who at Christmastide 1541 brought up the matter of a combined fleet to stop Cartier, he replied that he cared to hear no more of the subject; suppose he and the king of Spain did equip a fleet, it would have little effect, "since the ocean is vast," and the French destination unknown, "so there was no certainty where to encounter them."

The cardinal archbishop of Toledo, originally an advocate of a preventive war against Cartier, now advises the king to forget him; the French will find nothing of value up north, will get sick of it and go home—as indeed happened. His Eminence of Seville points out that Canada is too remote from New Spain to become a base for piracy. The Spanish ambassador at Paris consults Orontius Finus, a celebrated cosmographer, who assures him that the French can never get through to the Pacific via Canada, as the Emperor Charles V feared they might. Even the English, quiescent about America for years, take notice; Henry VIII's ambassador writes from Paris, "The French king sendythe certayne shippes to seeke the trayde of spicerey by a shorter waye than the portingallez doth use with a nombre of fyve or six hundred fotemen intending to passe by *mare glasearum*. Theire pilate ys one Jacquez Cartier a britton." Just what Robert Thorne had recommended, and what Frobisher and Davis would attempt. Charles V orders several key points in the Antilles to be fortified, stations 150 musketeers at Nombre de Dios, fifty each at the Havana and San Juan de Puerto Rico, and a hundred at Santo Domingo, to protect those towns from being plundered by Cartier! He is so apprehensive as to send two caravels to search for Cartier in the summer of 1541; both vessels crossed the Atlantic and sailed from Newfoundland to Florida without finding hide or hair of the French. In November 1541 the Spanish ambassador to France learns that Cartier had been seen in Newfoundland, icebound, and that Roberval intends to plunder the West Indies before joining him. Even after the entire French enterprise had been liquidated, Charles V caused a number of Spanish fishermen who had met the explorers in Newfoundland to be interrogated at Fuenterabbia, and only then did he feel secure in his American possessions.

Cartier's Third Voyage

Captain-General Cartier, as we should now style him, was ready to sail in April 1541; Roberval, arriving on the 21st, found five ships riding at anchor in the harbor of Saint-Malo. Crew, colonists, and animals were on board, yards crossed, and sails bent. The squadron consisted, first, of two gifts from the king to Cartier, his old flagship *La Grande Hermine* under a new master (Thomas Fromont having died in Canada), and the sprightly pinnace *L'Émerillon*, Macé Jalobert, master. Cartier evidently liked *L'Émerillon* too well to break her up. In addition, he had ships *Saint-Brieuc* and *Saint-Georges* and a third whose name we do not know. According to a Spanish spy's report written from Saint-Malo in the same month of April, Cartier and Roberval had a combined fleet of ten sail. The total complement, according to the spy, was 400 mariners and twenty master pilots, obviously an exaggeration.

Cartier himself had recruited only twenty colonists from the jails, but on 19 May there marched into Saint-Malo a gang of chained convicts secured by Roberval. These were of both sexes ranging in age from eighteen to forty-five, who had been condemned for everything from homicide to "stealing bronze to make bells." For romantic interest there was an eighteen-year-old Manon Lescaut, engaged to prisoner Gay, who insisted on accompanying her fiancé; and five "persons of quality" —a mint master who had juggled the currency, a man who had beaten up a royal prince's maître d'hotel, a fugitive from justice, and two murderers. Roberval turned all these over to Cartier because he was not ready to sail himself and did not wish to pay for their keep until he did. So, not only were 'tween decks congested with convicts but the spar decks were uncomfortably crowded with horses, cattle, swine, sheep, goats, and poultry.

The Spanish spy took a very dim view of the alleged 150 members of the nobility and gentry who were supposed to accompany Cartier. Apart from Pierre du Plessis, sieur de Savonnières, they were a sorry lot, and no more than twenty-five "so-called gentlemen" actually sailed. That may well be; but Roberval recruited many for his squadron, and Cartier's brother-in-law the vicomte de Beaupré certainly went with him.

On 19 May Cartier made his will, describing himself as *capitaine & maistre pillote du Roy ès Terres Neuffves . . . bourgeois en Saint-Malo*, and leaving to his wife Catherine all his property, including the Limoïlou farm and a "petite maison et jardin derrière" in Saint-Malo. Next day he is on record as quelling a street brawl over money between his trumpeter Pierre and a local cobbler. The trumpeter drew a sword on his adversary, whose wife slapped Pierre in the face. Cartier broke it up, but the trumpeter's brother-in-law, a carpenter, grabbed the cobbler by the hair, threw him down, and punched him, "and would have done more but for the said Cartier."

Roberval now informed Cartier that he was not yet ready to sail, having received neither artillery nor ammunition nor other important supplies. But he ordered Cartier to get going. This the Malouin was only too glad to do, for there is nothing more exasperating than being delayed when one is ready for sea. What happened to Roberval we shall see in due course; we may now follow Cartier to Canada for the third and last time.

The fleet of five departed Saint-Malo 23 May 1541, with a two-day new moon. Although but three days later in the season than John Cabot's start, they had a very rough crossing, with not thirty hours of fair wind; and all but one other vessel parted from flagship *La Grande Hermine*. Water ran short, and goats and swine had to be given cider to survive. It took the flagship a month to make the familiar Quirpon Harbor behind Cape Dégrat, Newfoundland. Cartier spent some time there, awaiting the rest of his fleet, taking on wood and water, and buying or borrowing bread and wine and *chaloupes* from the French fishing vessels he found there. The fishermen were loath to part with their *chaloupes*, but Cartier had lost several small boats during the crossing and had to have replacements.

We have no details of the passage between Quirpon and Stadaconé (Quebec), where the fleet anchored 23 August 1541, three months out. The Huron received Cartier with the usual "show of joy." Agona, who had taken Donnaconna's place, seemed not displeased with the news that his predecessor had died. He placed his leather coronet edged with wampum on the Captain-General's head, gave him two wampum bracelets, and subjected him to the usual "colling," or embrace. Cartier lied about the other deportees, asserting that they stayed in France "as great Lords, and were married." His intuition told him that all was not well between the two races—and no wonder! Hence he decided not to seat his colony at Stadaconé.

Leaving his ships at the St. Charles anchorage near Quebec, Cartier took two boats and had himself rowed eight or nine miles upstream, past the mouth of the Chaudière, to the present Cap Rouge. There, on a spot he had observed on his previous voyage, he decided to settle, and so brought up all five ships. The convicts and other colonists were landed, the cattle which had survived three months on shipboard were turned loose, earth broken for a kitchen garden, and seeds of cabbage, turnip, and lettuce planted. The men also began collecting quartz crystals ("diamonds") and iron pyrites ("gold"). Ships *Saint-Brieuc* and *Saint-Georges* were dispatched home on 2 September under charge of Macé Jalobert and Cartier's great-nephew Etienne Noël. They made a fast passage, arriving Saint-Malo 3 October 1541, and Jalobert proceeded directly to Paris to bedazzle the court with his samples of spurious mineral wealth.

The Captain-General now directed the building of a palisaded and fortified settlement. This he named Charlesbourg-Royal after Charles, duc d'Orléans, son of the king; and he also built a fort on the falaise overlooking Charlesbourg, as additional protection.

Cartier's idea in settling on Cap Rouge rather than at Stadaconé was to establish a base for discovering Saguenay that was not cheek-by-jowl with the Huron capital. Moreover, it was nearer the Ottawa River which he had been lead to believe was one of the two routes to Saguenay. He felt that the Indians were not so cordial as they had been at his departure; and he was right. American natives, usually friendly and hospitable to newcomers from Europe, inevitably turned hostile when they learned that their visitors intended to settle. Furthermore, Cartier and his men had not given the Huron uniformly good usage; he had kidnapped several, including their chief, and some of his young men (according to Jean Alfonce who had it straight from Donnaconna in France) made a practice of helping themselves to any poor savage's possessions that took their fancy, and trying their sword blades on the natives' limbs.

Having set everyone to work at Charlesbourg-Royal, and leaving his

Charles, duc d'Orléans. For whom Ile d'Orléans and Charlesbourg-Royal were named. Portrait by François Clouet. From Gower, ed., Clouet's *French Portraits*.

brother-in-law the vicomte de Beaupré as governor, Cartier took the longboats with sundry "gentlemen, masters and pilots" to make a Saguenay reconnaissance. They departed 7 September with a moon two days full and called on the "Lord of Hochelay" (Achelacy, near Pontneuf), by whom the French had been well received on the previous voyage. Cartier presented the chief, on unfriendly terms with the Stadaconé Hurons, with a "cloake of Paris red" trimmed with "yellow and white buttons of tinne and small belles." The chief consented to receive into his household two French boys to learn his language— Domagaya and Taignoagny having proved wanting as interpreters. This new method of bridging the language gap became standard in Canada throughout the colonial period. What became of the French lads we do not know; presumably Cartier took them home next year.

On 11 September, within sight of Mont Royal and Hochelaga,

Cartier's boats reached the first *sault*, Sainte-Marie, which had blocked his way in 1535. Leaving one boat ashore, he double-banked the other but could do nothing against the current, so returned to the first boat (which he had left near the site of the modern Jacques Cartier Bridge) and followed an Indian portage along shore. This led him to a village of friendly natives called Tutonaguy, where he obtained four young men as guides to Saguenay. These lads led him to another village situated on the north bank of the Lachine rapids, which fall forty-two feet in two miles. The boys made him a sort of map with sticks, but told him that there was another big *sault* to pass; meaning, no doubt, the Long Sault. And here Cartier quit. It was as near Saguenay as he ever got. It seems strange that the natives did not direct him up the Ottawa River—but perhaps they were trying to put him off.

Returning downstream to Charlesbourg-Royal, Cartier missed the chief of Achelacy, who had gone to Stadaconé to confer with Agona; and when the Frenchmen arrived at their new settlement they were apprised by Beaupré that things looked ominous. The Hurons no longer made friendly visits or peddled fish and game, but prowled about in a sinister manner; it seemed likely that Agona was organizing a concerted attack to wipe out the colony. If so, he did not plan it well, and most of the French escaped. These savages now realized what all other North American natives learned sooner or later, that co-existence with Europeans meant death for them. If you accepted the palefaces, they tilled, built, shot, and pillaged you out of land, game, possessions, house, and home. If you attacked and succeeded in wiping them out, others came back with more ships and greater fire power. Had some Indian genius invented the sea-going ship and gunpowder by 1500, native empires might have withstood predatory Europeans for centuries, just as Japan did. But their inveterate defect, lack of organization, would probably have been their undoing.

Hakluyt's, the one surviving narrative of Cartier's third voyage, abruptly ends with his return to Charlesbourg-Royal. All we know of what happened there in the winter of 1541–42 comes from bits of gossip picked up when the sailors reached home. The Indians attacked, killing first some carpenters who were out cutting wood, and more than thirty-five people all told. It would be interesting to know how the colonists took this, but not a word has survived. Scurvy broke out but was cured by the magic arborvitae. The impression one gets is one of general misery and of Cartier's growing conviction that he had insufficient manpower both to protect his base and go in search of Saguenay. Roberval never having turned up, Cartier assumed that he had been lost at sea and that the game was up.

At any rate, Cartier raised camp in early June 1542, and with his three remaining ships (*La Grande Hermine, L'Émerillon,* and the nameless one) carrying all surviving colonists and (according to gossip) eleven barrels of "gold," a basket of "precious stones such as rubies and diamonds," and seven barrels of "silver," he entered the harbor of St. John's, Newfoundland, before the end of the month.

And there, lying at anchor, as pretty as you please, were Roberval's three big ships!

Cartier Meets Roberval and Goes Home

And what had the king's Lieutenant-General and Governor for Canada been doing all this time? It took him the better part of a year after Cartier's departure to get going. He sold one of his estates to raise the wind, but that was not enough to pay all the "land sharks" to whom he owed money; so, desperately, he armed his ships and practised piracy in the English Channel, capturing several Portuguese and English merchantmen. Henry VIII complained vigorously through his ambassador at Paris, who wrote back that François-premier (tongue in cheek) professed to be profoundly shocked and threatened to hang Roberval. Nothing, of course, was done; and on 16 April 1542, almost one year after Cartier, Roberval sailed. He commanded three new merchant ships that he had bought at Honfleur, named *Marye* of Saint-Malo (nicknamed *Lechefraye*) of 80–100 tuns, *Sainte-Anne* (80 tuns), and *Vallentyne* of Jumièges, 92–100 tuns. Alonce de Civille, the leading Italian merchant-shipowner of Rouen, largely financed Roberval's expedition and guaranteed the cost of these ships.

According to the Spanish spy, Roberval embarked three hundred soldiers, sixty masons and carpenters, ten priests, three physicians, and ten barbers. This is doubtless an exaggeration, but his ships were well armed and provisioned. Each carried knocked-down *charretes,* the two-wheeled carts of the period, two mills, and a quantity of ironware.

Marye, Sainte-Anne, and *Vallentyne* sailed from La Rochelle 16 April 1542, with a new moon. After spending several days anchored under the lee of the Breton Belle-Ile awaiting a fair wind, they put to sea, enjoyed an easy crossing, and anchored in St. John's Harbor, Newfoundland, on 7 June 1542. Twenty-seven fishing vessels were already there. Roberval had engaged as pilot, Jean Alfonce, evidently experienced in latitude sailing. Belle-Ile, off Quiberon Bay, is on latitude 47°23′; St. John's, on 47°34′ N.

A few days later, Cartier's three ships entered the harbor of St. John's, Newfoundland. Although the Captain-General now came legally under the orders of the Lieutenant-General, he refused to admit it. When his efforts to persuade Roberval to give up and go home failed, and the younger man ordered him to return to Canada, Cartier refused, and the following night "stole privily away" with his three ships and set a course for Saint-Malo, where he arrived about mid-October, 1542.

This flight home looks like a black mark on Jacques Cartier's record; another instance of desertion at sea, too common in that century. He rightly warned Roberval that it would be impossible for the French to defend themselves at Charlesbourg-Royal; but he refused to assist his legal commander, who was determined to try. Roberval ascribed it to Cartier's "ambition" to cash in on the "diamonds." On the other hand, Roberval's failure to join him earlier had caused Cartier to assume that the Lieutenant-General was never coming, and he had made up his mind to return to France. This had been announced to his passengers and crew, who probably would have mutinied rather than spend another winter in Canada. In any case, Cartier's reputation at home did not suffer. The Malouins, obviously glad to have their sailors safe home, treated the Captain as their most prominent citizen; the government consulted him on maritime matters, and the *Brief recit* of his second voyage was published in 1545. He never received a patent of nobility for his efforts, to be sure; but neither did any other early navigator, not even Columbus; and the king repaid almost all that he was out of pocket for the voyage, as well as presenting him with *La Grande Hermine* and *L'Émerillon*.

"The good captain must know his ship, and have sailed in her, whence he will learn the trim that she demands, and the speed she can make according to the strength of the winds, and what leeway she makes with the wind abeam, or hove-to with only the topsail or main course set, so as not to labor. . . ." So wrote Samuel de Champlain

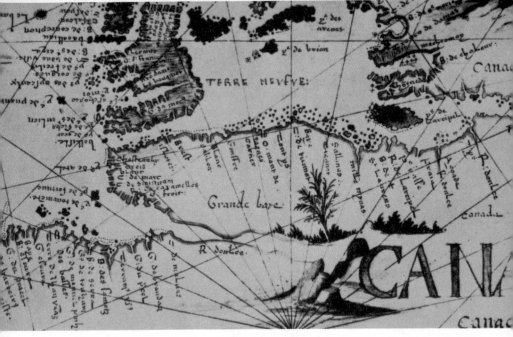

West Canadian part of Desceliers Planisphere, 1550. Original in British Museum, Add. Mss. 24.065. Courtesy of Map Division, Public Archives of Canada.

after thirty-eight years' experience at sea. Cartier, after two trans-atlantic voyages in *La Grande Hermine* and *L'Émerillon*, must have known them as well as any master ever knew any ship; and he now owned both, a royal gift. The pinnace he appropriately renamed *Canadie*, and both vessels were employed in the merchant marine, under other masters. Considering their performance in 1535–36 and 1540–41, they belong in the maritime hall of fame along with *Mathew*, *La Dauphine*, *Santa Maria*, and *Vittoria*.

Among the numerous entries in local church records of Cartier's apparently favorite recreation, attending baptisms, there is one which suggests that his last years were anything but sad. The name of Jacques Cartier "avec d'aultres bons biberons" (with other good drinkers), appears as a witness. This allows one to imagine old Master-Pilot Cartier as a jolly *bon-viveur* spending his time between farm, town and tavern, and perhaps visiting his relative at Mont-Saint-Michel to eat an omelette with him and the abbot. He had a neat little house and garden on the rue de Buhen in Saint-Malo, and enjoyed his farm at Limoïlou. Jacques doubtless regaled young Malouins with tales of storms, rapids, savages, and the fabulous Kingdom of Saguenay which he would certainly have

444

East Canadian part of same map. Top is south.

found had he been given more time, and thus made every Breton sailor richer than a conquistador of Mexico. Around 1550 he entertained in the town house some distinguished visitors—André Thevet the sea-going monk, a Swedish navigator named Bayarni, and the aged Sebastian Cabot. What would we not give for a tape-recording of their conversations! Cabot seems to have held the floor, as usual, telling about a voyage to Florida that he never made.

Jacques Cartier died at Saint-Malo from an epidemic then raging, on 1 September 1557, aged 66. His wife survived him by several years. Although the English Hakluyt did more for his reputation than any Frenchman, his compatriots both in France and Canada have more than made up for his neglect during the last hundred years. Rightly so, for Cartier ranks among the most expert seamen and careful explorers in the era of discovery.

The Valiant Demoiselle

Roberval's official narrative of this voyage, like Cartier's, is known only through Hakluyt's translation, but we have another valuable source in *La Cosmographie* written by his pilot Jean Alfonce. According to him, Roberval (whom he refers to as "the General") spent about three weeks at St. John's after Cartier's departure, and entered the Gulf of St. Lawrence by the Strait of Belle Isle.

The atmosphere in Roberval's ships, apart from the barnyard odors of the cattle, sheep, swine, and horses, was one of youth and gaiety. Most of the gentlemen volunteers, and all the lady colonists, had embarked with him. Jacques Cartier doubtless displayed some of his "gold" and "diamonds" before parting from Roberval at St. John's; thus the General's ladies and gentlemen continued the voyage with high expectations of profit as well as fun. Monsieur de Roberval had royal authority to grant fiefs in Canada; wouldn't it be nice to own a piece of land which included a mine of gold or diamonds? A few of these passengers of noble blood are named in Roberval's narration; Paul d'Aussilon, seigneur de Sauveterre; Nicholas de Lépinay, seigneur de Neufville-sur-la-Wault; a son of Jacques de Frotté, president of the parlement de Paris; the sieurs de Noirefontaine and La Vasseur de Coutances; the sieur de Longueval, a cousin of the General.

A master mariner likes a cheerful atmosphere among his passengers; but one couple in the flagship were too gay for Roberval. His own niece or cousin, a damsel named Marguerite de La Roque, was accompanied by her old nurse, a Norman peasant named Damienne, and—as it later appeared—by her lover. Damienne played the classic maid's part in covering up her mistress's gallantry; but on a crowded ship the dalliance of lovers could not forever escape notice. When brought to Roberval's attention, his Calvinist principles were so outraged that he marooned Marguerite and Damienne. The place of their exile was one of the Harrington Islands, which Cartier had passed and named St. Marthe on an earlier voyage. Roberval set the two women ashore with a few provisions and arquebuses for defense, and left them to their fate.

With despair they saw the ships weigh anchor, make sail, and depart; but see! What is this? A man swimming ashore! This was the gallant, whom Roberval intended to keep on board as prisoner but had not got around to putting in irons. He leaped overboard during the confusion of the ship's getting under way, and swam ashore bringing two more guns and a supply of ammunition.

With such an expert swimmer for companion, Marguerite fared well enough for a time. Until winter set in, the lovers lived an idyllic life. The gentleman built a cabin for his mistress and her maid, chopped

The Harrington Islands.

wood, caught fish, and shot wild fowl; but before winter ended, he died. Marguerite, unable to dig a grave in the frozen ground, guarded his body in the cabin until spring, to protect it from wild animals.

In the ninth month of exile a child was born to her and promptly died. Another winter passed, and Damienne died, leaving Marguerite alone. The intrepid demoiselle gathered enough food to keep alive and defended herself not only against the bears (she killed three, one "white as an egg"), but against spirits of another world. Demoniac voices shrieked about her cabin, howled the louder when she fired a gun, but were stilled when she read passages from a New Testament which she had brought ashore.

It seems incredible that she survived, but the evidence that she did is conclusive. In the early spring of 1544, after she had been two years and five months on the island, smoke from her fire was observed by passing French fishermen. They landed, found Marguerite emaciated and in rags; but, more charitable than Roberval, gave her passage back to France. She returned to her home at Montron in Picardy, became a schoolmistress, and told her story to Jean Alfonce. He in turn told it to Marguerite, queen of Navarre, sister of François-premier, and patroness of Roberval; and she, in turn, used it as Nouvelle No. LXVII in her famous Heptaméron. Marguerite proved the Pauline doctrine that "God hath chosen the weak things of the world, to confound the

447

things which are mighty" (1 Corinthians i.27). This poor, weak woman on a desert island protected the corpse of her man against wild beasts and exorcised the powers of darkness by reading the Word of God; and God saw to it that she survived. Thus Marguerite was presented to the public by this intelligent Protestant queen as a shining example to womankind.

France-Roy and Search for Saguenay

Cartier, before sailing for home from St. John's, must have left with Roberval's pilot Alfonce his own sailing directions for Canada. The Roberval fleet departed St. John's at the end of June 1542, passed through the Strait of Belle Isle, and a few days later marooned poor Marguerite. They then sailed up-river, passed Stadaconé without stopping, and toward the end of July came to an anchor off Cartier's Charlesbourg-Royal at the mouth of the River Rouge.

According to Spanish spies, Roberval had hundreds on board—585 men and women. Even if you cut this down to 150 (which is my guess), he had plenty of people to build a fortified camp, and he had time to plant vegetable seeds to provide vitamins for winter diet. Cartier's Charlesbourg-Royal, which possibly had been taken apart by the Huron, is not mentioned; and, disdaining Cartier's names, Roberval renamed this place *France-Roy*, and the river *France-Prime*. The site of the *habitation*, he says, was "upon an high mountain," probably the spot where Cartier had his lookout post; but "there was also at the foote of the mountaine another lodging" with "a great Towre of two stories high," used largely for storage. The main building on the hill, enclosed by a palisade, had towers from which an enemy's approach could be observed, barracks for the soldiers, a central building with hall, kitchen, and offices; places for everyone to sleep, one or more mills for grinding corn, and an outdoor oven.

The general appearance of this building we may infer from Champlain's drawing of the *habitation* built by him and Poutrincourt at Port Royal in 1605; or still better, by visiting that beautifully restored building at Lower Granville a few miles from Annapolis Royal, Nova Scotia.

Nicholas Vallard's Map of 1547 is probably as near as we can get to a contemporary picture of France-Roy. The number of ladies, gentle-

Restored Port Royal *Habitation* of 1605. Courtesy Canadian Government Travel Bureau.

men, and soldiers indicates that this depicts Roberval's company, not Cartier's The bearded figure pointing to the natives must be intended for Roberval, and the little stockade armed with cannon, which the artist had to make small for lack of room, was the defense.

On 14 September, Roberval sent home two of his ships, commanded by Paul d'Aussilon, who had been tried for killing a sailor, and acquitted. His object was to carry news of the voyage to the king, inquire what the experts thought of Cartier's gold and diamonds, and bring out more supplies next year.

The trees shed their brilliant leaves. Dark November days followed, and then the brief Indian summer—St. Martin's summer it was called in Europe—when the winds were hushed and the sun shone bright and all nature seemed to be taking a deep breath before winter set in. Then drear December, snow and more snow; one could not venture out without *raquettes*, as the French called the savages' snowshoes. There were clear, cold days when ice in the river sent chords of unearthly harp music ringing in one's ears. At night the northern lights threw up white and rosy flashes almost to the zenith, and only Orion and the Bear and a few other constellations reminded the French that they were on the same globe as Paris. Apparently the kitchen gardens did not yield much, as everyone went on short rations for the winter; each mess—five to eight people—had two loaves of bread for breakfast, bacon and half a pound of butter for dinner, and half a pound of beef, with beans, for supper. Wednesday, Friday, and Saturday were fast days when they had nothing but dried or fresh codfish, porpoise meat, and beans. The Indians helped them by bringing "great store of *aloses*" (shad); but this must have been in the spring shad-run. We would dearly love to know more about that winter at France-Roy. Did the gentlemen and ladies organize theatricals, or something like *l'ordre du bon temps* which kept everyone cheerful at Port Royal more than a half-century later? Did the men go hunting on snowshoes? Or did they mope by the fire, complaining and begging Roberval to take them home? We simply do not know. Not one person brought overseas by Cartier and Roberval, unless an obscure mariner, ever cared to return to Canada.

Although Cartier must have warned Roberval of the winter disease and told him about the arborvitae cure, the colony suffered greatly from scurvy, and "about fifty people" died. Roberval kept strict discipline; men and women were flogged, others put in irons, and one man hanged for theft, "by which means they lived in quiet." There is no reason to accuse the General of undue severity. As Columbus found in Hispaniola, and the English learned at Jamestown, a colony consisting of all sorts and conditions of people, planted in a remote country, must have strict discipline to survive.

So far as we can learn from the meager records, the Indians never attacked France-Roy; it had more formidable defenses than Charlesbourg-Royal, as they doubtless observed. Yet, all in all, it must have been a very unhappy winter for the French.

The river ice began to break up in April, but it was not until

6 June, when the white birch was shaking out its tender green leaves and the shad-bush gleamed white among the stately conifers, that Roberval began his search for the Kingdom of Saguenay. Probably he had waited for the river current to abate. An upstream expedition set forth in eight boats carrying seventy people, leaving thirty behind at France-Roy. The numbers indicate that Roberval had lost more than fifty from scurvy and other causes. He left as deputy governor one Sieur de Royeze, but most of the gentlemen volunteers accompanied him upstream. After one boat had been wrecked and eight men drowned, Roberval turned back, at the Lachine rapids.

Here the one existing narrative of Roberval's voyage breaks off; we have to carry on as best we can with that of his chief pilot. Jean Alfonce probably explored the Saguenay River while Roberval was up the St. Lawrence. In his *La Cosmographie* he had this to say about it: "The entrance is between two high mountains. The point of the Saguenay is a white rock" (actually it is a light-colored clay) "and the entrance of the said Saguenay is at 48°20', and it is only a quarter of a league wide." That measure is accurate, and Alfonce's latitude is less than twelve miles out. He adds that the mouth is difficult and dangerous to enter, as the river current meeting the tide "makes a terrible *raz*"—the Breton word for a violent tidal current. "Inside the entrance," he continues, "the river widens after two or three leagues, and begins to take on the characer of an arm of the sea, for which reason I estimate that this sea leads to the Pacific Ocean or even to *la mer du Cattay*." There he leaves us flat. It seems probable that Alfonce, using one of Roberval's long boats, rowed up the Saguenay and turned back short of the Chicoutimi rapids which, had he seen them, would have taught him (as the Lachine did Cartier), that this was no arm of the sea. His own map shows Lac Saint-Jean, from which the river issues; but he may simply have been told about it by the natives.

Although Roberval had written to the king asking for a relief expedition, he decided some time in the summer not to await it but to abandon France-Roy and return to France. We have no record of the time of his departure. It was probably at the end of July, as he had arrived in France by 11 September 1543. On that date he ordered the sale of *Sainte-Anne* and the other unnamed ship which had brought him home. The only explanation of this decision is on one of Desceliers's maps, where there is an inscription stating, "It was impossible to trade

North American section of Nicholas Vallard Map, 1547. (T

C.º ftorijha jnco

p of this map is south.) Courtesy Henry E. Huntington Library.

with the people of that country because of their austerity, the intemperate climate of said country, and the slight profit."

So ended this valiant French enterprise, and so died the dream of the rich, glorious Kingdom of Saguenay, a new Mexico in the Laurentian wilds. Saguenay lasted for over a century on maps, even one dated 1677, then quietly disappeared, except as the name of the river. For the Kingdom had never been anything but an *ignis fatuus*, a will-o'-the-wisp, with no basis in fact, not even in Indian folklore; it was simply a collection of tall tales made up to fool the French. Since nothing in history is too foolish to be wholly discarded, the Kingdom of Saguenay has been revived in recent years both as a tourist attraction and to support the theory that Norsemen, Irishmen, "Quii," and whatnot were wandering about the interior of North America in the Middle Ages.

François-premier died in 1547. His son and successor Henri II cared nothing for American exploration, and before his death France fell into the religious wars that exhausted the energy of her adventurous sons. Roberval, a cousin of Diane de Poitiers, the king's mistress, frequented the court of Henri II and received a royal concession to search for and exploit mines of iron or precious metals. Herein, too, he failed. The former Lieutenant-General for the king in Canada was killed in a religious riot in Paris in 1561.

These efforts were not entirely wasted. For half a century Canada was left to her native inhabitants (which was all to their good), but Cartier's voyages brought about a revolution in North American cartography. Not only French maps, but those of the Spaniards, the Portuguese, and Sebastian Cabot show in detail the Gulf of St. Lawrence, the Great River of Canada, and the Lachine rapids beyond which no European had penetrated.

Many, many years elapsed before any French expedition comparable with Cartier's and Roberval's came in this direction; for Canada had, as it were, been laughed off the map. As all things in France end in jest, so here; it became a popular saying, applied to everything that glittered and was not gold, or sparkled and was not diamond; *C'est un diamant du Canada!*

Bibliography and Notes

SOURCES ON THIRD VOYAGE *

Two source books which contain everything known about the third voyage of Cartier and the first and only of Roberval, are H. P. Biggar (ed.), *Voyages of Jacques Cartier* and *Collection of Documents Relating to Jacques Cartier and the Sieur de Roberval;* these are Publications Nos. 11 (1924) and 14 (1930) of the Public Archives of Canada. The Spanish examination of fishermen at Fuenterrabia in Sept. 1542 is in *Documents,* pp. 447–67. Hakluyt, when attached to the English embassy in Paris, apparently received the original French account from Jacques Noël, a great-nephew of Cartier who had been on this voyage, and Hakluyt prints a letter from him, dated 1587, in his *Voyages* (1600 ed.), II, 236.

All biographies of Cartier are unsatisfactory on this voyage; but Marcel Trudel has an excellent critical account in his *Histoire de la Nouvelle France,* I, 119–75.

Roberval always signed himself by his family name La Roque, Roberval being one of the many estates that he owned; but Canadian historians, fearing perhaps to confuse him with the later De La Roche, insist on calling him plain Roberval. His genealogy will be found in an article by La Roque de Roquebrune, "Roberval, sa Généalogie, son Père," *Revue d'Histoire de l'Amérique française,* IX, No. 2 (September 1955), 157–75.

NOTES ON VARIOUS POINTS

The Gold. Certain Canadian historians insist that Cartier brought samples of real gold, given to him by the chief he encountered between Quebec and Montreal. It is true that gold has been extracted from quartz crystals in eastern Canada, with a maximum of $56,661 in 1881—J. Arthur Phillips, *Treatise on Ore Deposits* (1896), p. 832; but the Huron were not metallurgists like the Indians of Central America, and they had no use for gold. The precious metal which they used for jewelry was copper, which they got from Lake Superior by way of trade.

Cartier's List of "Wants" for this voyage is in Biggar, *Documents,* pp. 70–74. Denials of Cartier's authorship of this list because his name is not attached to it seem to me finicky. Nobody but he or someone on his first voyage would have known what was wanted, and the king would certainly not have consulted a subordinate when Cartier was available.

The king's cogent phrase is in a letter from the Cardinal Archbishop of Toledo to the Emperor, 27 January 1541. The original reads, "Sino que

---

* Of 1541–42. A few historians have assumed that Cartier commanded the relief expedition of 1543 asked for by Roberval; but it has been proved that he was at Saint-Malo collecting more *dragées* when that expedition (of which we know next to nothing) was at sea.

tanbien le calentava a él el sol como a los otros y que deseava mucho ver el testamento de Adam para saber como rrepartió él el mundo." Biggar, *Documents*, p. 190.

The Convicts. Gustave Lanctot, in his witty book *Filles de joie ou filles du roi* (Montreal, 1952), p. 26, states that the total number of convicts shipped with Cartier and Roberval numbered about thirty-nine, including five women, and that most of these went with Roberval. Marcel Trudel, *Histoire de la Nouvelle France*, I, 140–41, names twenty-eight of Roberval's lot, admittedly incomplete, and states that about twenty more went with Cartier. Other authorities place the total number of convicts sent to Canada at this time as high as 150, which I believe to be excessive.

The Spanish Spy's Report of the Cartier-Roberval fleet, in April 1541, gives no names, only tunnages which are difficult to fit in. He says Cartier's fleet consisted of two *navires* owned by himself, each 90 tuns; a third owned by a merchant of Saint-Malo, 80 tuns, and three king's ships: a *galion du port* of 70 tuns and two *navires*, one of 110 and the other of 120 tuns. Roberval had four ships being fitted out at Rouen and Honfleur, each of 90 to 100 tuns and carrying in all 300 *hommes de guerre*. The Cartier fleet, he says, shipped 1500 *lardz* (salt pork?), 800 salted and air-dried beeves, 100 tuns of grain (some for seed); 200 pipes of flour, 20 of oil, 20 of mustard and 20 of butter, a great quantity of biscuit, 200 tuns of wine, 100 of cider; and for livestock 20 cows, 4 bulls, 100 sheep, 100 goats, and 10 swine for breeding; also 20 horses and mares to draw carts for building purposes. They carry 18 or 20 boats for exploration, each armed with six light pieces "especially made for them," and the ships are bristly with deadly weapons—arquebusses, *rondelles*, crossbows, and "more than a thousand pikes and halberds." Biggar, *Documents*, pp. 275–78.

Tutonaguy. The site is a matter of dispute; see Biggar, *Voyages*, p. 257, and Ganong, *Crucial Maps*, pp. 356–57. As Cartier does not mention Hochelaga on the voyage, although he passed the site, one infers that it had burned down and that Tutonaguy was a new native citadel nearer the river.

Date of Cartier's return, and his accounts. In his statement of accounts dated 21 June 1544, Cartier declares that his voyage lasted seventeen months (Biggar, *Documents*, p. 483) which would bring its close to the latter part of October. In the same document he claimed that he had been advanced 31,360 livres tournois (about $6270 in gold) before the voyage; and, including that sum, had dispensed (the court ascertained) 39,988 livres 4 sous 5 deniers; consequently he had 8688 livres (about $1738 in gold) coming to him. The crown paid up all but 88 livres, which was still owing to his heirs in 1587.

France-Roy. Cartier mentioned a spring being at or just outside his fort, and Roberval's narrative mentions "a well before the house." As a soldier he doubtless had a better eye for fields of fire than Cartier. Champlain's drawing of the Port Royal *habitacion* is reproduced in the Champlain Society edition of his *Works*, I,373; my quotation about a good captain knowing his ship is in VI,267. The photograph that we have used was supplied by the Canadian Government Travel Bureau, Ottawa. We hear of only one chimney, however, at France-Roy.

André Thevet's account of his visit with Cartier is in his manuscript *La Grande Insulaire* at Bibliothèque Nationale, fonds francais, 15,452 f. 176. Professor D. B. Quinn kindly gave me a photostat of this passage.

ALFONCE, THEVET, AND SAGUENAY

The complicated bibliography of Jean Alfonce can best be followed in Justin Winsor, *Narrative and Critical History*, IV, 68–72. Alfonce's not very helpful sketch maps in his *La Cosmographie* are reproduced in Ganong, *Crucial Maps*, pp. 366–80. The only good modern edition of *La Cosmographie*, by G. Musset, was published at Paris in 1904. The Canadian part is reprinted in Biggar, *Voyages*, Appendix II. Alfonce states that this work was completed 24 May 1544, so shortly after Cartier's third voyage as to be regarded as an original source. The Canadian parts of his *Voyages avantureux* (Paris, 1550), as well as *La Cosmographie*, are analyzed in Ganong, *Crucial Maps*, pp. 364–84.

The story of the marooned Marguerite de La Roque is told in a different *Cosmographie Universelle* (Paris, 2 vols. fol., 1575) by a sea-going monk named André Thevet who describes himself as *cosmographe du roy* (for bibliography see Winsor, IV, 30–32). Thevet also wrote *Les Singularitez de la France antarctique* (Paris, 1551; Gaffarel ed., 1878). He was a five months' house guest of Cartier, whom he calls *mon grand et singulier ami*, and of Roberval whom he calls *mon familier;* and he heard the tale from Marguerite's own lips. The monk is not much liked by Canadian historians, who show a curious reluctance to tell the dramatic story. Two classic historians, Charles de La Roncière in his *Cartier*, and Parkman in his *Pioneers*, made the most of it. It is true that Thevet is a teller of tall tales—he built up Norumbega to a castellated city on the Penobscot—but in that respect he was no worse than his contemporaries who swallowed Saguenay, and there is no reason to discredit his story of the marooning. The tradition of an Isle of Demons precedes Roberval's voyage by many years; an *Isla Tormenta* appears on early Portuguese maps of Newfoundland-Labrador near the Strait of Belle Isle. The scene of Marguerite's marooning can be definitely placed on one of the Harrington Islands on the north shore of the Gulf, since after this episode they were called *Les Iles de la Demoiselle* in Alfonce's *La Cosmographie*, and on later maps.

Joseph E. King, "The Glorious Kingdom of Saguenay," *Canadian Historical Review*, XXXI (1950), 390–400, has that subject well wrapped up. Anne Wyman, "Kingdom Without a Palace," *Boston Sunday Globe*, 27 July 1969, reports that Msgr. Victor Tremblay of the seminary at Chicoutimi maintains that Lac St. Jean, from which the river issues, had been a center of a native confederation which "kept peace in that area for over

300 years"; but their descendants have mostly disappeared. The Lake is now a depressing region of ghost towns, deserted summer resorts, and a big aluminum plant which has desolated the country and killed the fish. At St. Gedeon where Louis Hémon wrote *Maria Chapdelaine*, there is a shrine to that Canadian classic.

CARTIER AND ROBERVAL IN LITERATURE

Marguerite de Navarre *L'Heptaméron des Nouvelles* first appeared in 1559. The story of Marguerite de La Roque is Nouvelle No. LXVII. She makes the episode more respectable by marrying the lovers, and stating the cause of the marooning to have been an act of treason against Roberval on the man's part.

Ch. A. Julien, *Voyages de Découverte*, pp. 351–62, has a good account of the controversy whether or not Rabelais drew from Cartier. Marius Barbeau, "Cartier Inspired Rabelais" in *Canadian Geographical Journal*, IX, No. 3 (September 1934), 113–25, is fantastically far-fetched and sentimental. The only facts are these: a canon of the cathedral of Saint-Malo, writing in 1628, asserted that Rabelais learned from Cartier the correct maritime words and phrases "to point up his silly Lucianisms and impious epicurianism," and that Cartier's *Brief recit* came out before Rabelais's *Tiers Livre*. See also A. R. Wood, "Jal versus Rabelais," *Mariner's Mirror*, III (1913), 81.

After re-reading Rabelais I can find no trace or hint of Cartier's voyages in his comic history of Pantagruel's travels to "Thohu Bohu" and other imaginary places. In his account of the storm at sea in *Le Quart Livre* chaps. xviii–xxii, he is merely throwing words and phrases around as he loved to do on any subject; and the editor of his *Œuvres Complètes* (Bibliothèque de la Pléiade ed., pp. 591, 602, notes) well observes that Rabelais's maritime vocabulary is provençal and applies, if at all, to Mediterranean, not Atlantic, sailing. The account of the storm is most amusing—Pantagruel being seasick and declaiming, "Thrice happy they who plant cabbages!" But it is an insult to Cartier's seamanship to ascribe this mish-mash to him. Rabelais did pick up some choice seaman's cuss words, but Panurge's orders and those of his pilot Jamet Brayer in *Le Quart Livre* (chap. xx) make no sense; they remind me of a story by Alphonse Daudet in which he tries to create a maritime atmosphere by having the sailors continually shout *bâbord! tribord!*

MAPS BASED ON CARTIER

Although a number of European mapmakers went right on depicting a continuous shore south from the Labrador to Florida, as though Cartier had never existed, his voyages revolutionized the conception of North America on the part of the principal French, English, and Portuguese cartographers. Here are listed and briefly described only the earliest. Starting points are (1) a pamphlet by Justin Winsor, *The Results in Europe of Cartier's Ex-*

Title page of *L'Heptaméron*, 1560 edition. Courtesy Harvard College Library.

plorations, reprinted from Mass. Hist. Soc. *Proceedings*, 1892; and (2) H. Harrisse, *Terre-Neuve* (1900), ch. v, "La Cartographie Americano-Dieppoise." Comprehensive are Marcel Trudel (ed.), *Atlas historique du Canada français* (Quebec, 1961) and *Sixteenth-Century Maps Relating to Canada* (Ottawa, Public Archives, 1956). Cartier made his own maps, all of which have disappeared, but he obviously allowed the Dieppe cartographers to redraw them.

1541

The Desliens, signed and dated "faicte à Dieppe par Nicolas Des Liens 1541." Damaged in World War II but still in the Royal Library of Dresden (now Landesbibliothek) of Dresden; reproduced above, Chapter VII in connection with Sebastian Cabot's of 1544. Absence of natives, flora, fauna, or any embellishments except flags proves that this was meant to be a sailors' chart. The Great River starts just above Ile d'Orléans. Discussed by Ganong, pp. 226–28 and 331–41.

1542

John Rotz's manuscript, "Boke of Idrography"; a ms. atlas in the British Museum prepared for Henry VIII, dedicated to him, and signed "Made by one John Rotz in the yer I^mV^cXLII." Justin Winsor found this among the Royal Mss. in the British Museum in 1884. Rotz was a Dieppois of Scots ancestry. The sheet entitled "The new fonde londe quhar men goeth a fisching" is reproduced in Chapter XI above. It shows results of Cartier's first voyage only; no St. Lawrence River, and Nova Scotia coasts follow Ribero. Discussion in Harrisse, *Terre-Neuve*, pp. 170–77 and Ganong, *Crucial Maps*, pp. 179–80.

The Desceliers-Harleian Mappemonde of 1542, now in the British Museum. Signed by Pierre Desceliers, the eminent Dieppe cartographer. Description in *Geographical Magazine*, XXIV (1951), 103–10. Biggar, who has a pull-out reproduction of the American part in his *Voyages*, p. 128, dates it 1536; Ganong (pp. 327–28) dates it *c.* 1537, *but it cannot be earlier than 1542 as it contains data from the third voyage.* In Chapter XI above we have reproduced the section showing the Gulf, the River, and Newfoundland, together with the vignette of a cloaked and fork-bearded figure receiving natives; see discussion of Cartier's portraits in Notes to Chapter XI above. The extension southward (cf. Note to Chapter X above) shows the mythical Isthmus of Verrazzano with a canal running through it to the Pacific. Desceliers's west coast of the Gulf of St. Lawrence follows Rotz, but he uses Cartier's names. He depicts a remarkably accurate St. Lawrence River, right up to "Ochelaga," but does not make much of Saguenay; it is represented by a figure in European clothes at the top of our reproduction. CANADA, on the other hand, appears thrice on this map, which probably helped to make the name popular. Several imaginary islands are south of Newfoundland. Best reproduction of Canadian part is in Harrisse, *Terre-Neuve*, p. 208.

1544

The Sebastian Cabot Mappemonde, already discussed in notes to Chapter VII above, and the Canadian part there reproduced. This, as Roger Hervé observes in his introduction to the excellent reproduction by Editions des Yeux Ouverts (Paris 1968), is based largely on the 1541 Desliens, Cabot adding a few names from other maps and rendering them into Spanish.

15.46

The Desceliers Mappemonde dated 1546, formerly owned by Jomard the geographer and by the Earl of Crawford and Balcarres, now in the John Rylands Library, Manchester, incorporates information of all three Cartier voyages. Photo of northern part in Chapter XII, above. CANADA appears on the north shore Gulf of St. Lawrence and, less conspicuously, on the south bank of the river. Many animals and human figures including "Roberval" in full armor addressing a muster of soldiers in "Sagne" (Saguenay), a fork-bearded priest holding forth to natives, a nude nymph in a grotto; bears, wild boars, deer, and caracoling cavalry in Labrador. Reproductions: Harrisse, *Terre-Neuve*, p. 230; C. H. Coote autotype reproduction of the whole as an album, by the British Museum, 1898. C. A. Borland, *A Note on the Desceliers Mappemonde of 1546 in the John Rylands Library* (Manchester, 1951). Discussed also in Ganong, pp. 232–33 and 328–31. Cartographically, this is a distinct improvement over the 1542 Desceliers.

1547

Nicholas Vallard of Dieppe, World Map dated 1547. Formerly in the Phillipps Collection, now in the H. E. Huntington Library. Oriented with south at the top. Photo in Chapter XIII above, of North American part. Good colored reproduction in *Illustrated London News*, 11 August 1934. See our note on Portraits of Cartier at end of Chapter XI above; this is the one with the full-bearded person acting as guide to a group of ladies and gentlemen. Vallard took much more trouble than Desceliers to depict Indians accurately; dressed them in furs. The "Rio do Canada" (strange that he should use Portuguese), starts at *Totamagy*, the village named as the terminus of Roberval's navigation. Newfoundland is solid except for insular Avalon Peninsula. The real Belle Isle is so named for the first time, but a nonexistent island blocks Cabot Strait, and some new fictitious islands—*argua, zanna, breta*, and two *Ste. Croix* lie southeast of Newfoundland. The coast between Cape Breton and Florida follows Ribero's Map of 1529 rather loosely, and Penobscot Bay has the name which he bestowed, *Rio de las Gamas* (of the deer); hence the stag hunt depicted near by.

1550

The Desceliers Planisphere, signed and dated by him 1550, British Museum, Add. Mss. 24,065 Reproduction of Canadian part in this chapter, in Lord Crawford *Bibliotheca Lindesiana* and (in miniature) in Ganong, p. 342, where it is discussed (also on p. 363). This is the one showing a turbaned figure frightening away people by his gestures, pygmies attacking cranes which look like ostriches, beehive-like "maisons des sauluages," polar bears eating fish on an ice floe, a couple of unicorns, and a stone martello tower at *Sagne*, up the Saguenay River. CANADA appears thrice on the north coast of the Gulf and once on the south. The nomenclature shows little difference from that of the earlier Desceliers except that on the upper St. Lawrence, just above *Totomagy*, is the inscription "iusques icy a este monsr. de roberval." A long inscription tells how François-premier sent "the honest and clever gentleman M. de Roberval with a great company of intelligent people, both gentle and common, and with them a great company of degraded criminals to people the country." After brief mention that Jacques Cartier discovered this country, the cartographer remarks that its *austerité, intempérance,* and *petit proffit,* caused it to be abandoned. Another inscription describes the pygmies' war on the cranes, doubtless one of the Saguenay yarns of Donnaconna. The interesting ship may have been meant for one of Roberval's; but a whale spouting from two blow-holes does not create much confidence in this cartographer's pictorial accuracy. Desceliers had quite an establishment, and I suspect that he did the actual cartography himself and told some clever boy to put a ship here and a whale there, to fill up space.

1569

Mercator's earliest world map, an engraved one dated 1569, is a good example of this great Flemish cartographer's art, and the first to incorporate his Projection, a boon to mariners which we still use today. Pull-out in Biggar, *Voyages*, p. 240; discussed in Ganong, pp. 415–25. The atlas to which it belonged is reproduced by the Prins Hendrik Maritime Museum, Rotterdam, 1967. Engraved and widely disseminated, this map had a greater influence on future cartography of this region than any other. Only three copies of the original have survived, at the Bibliothèque Nationale, the British Museum, and Breslau. But, for Canada, Mercator is inferior to some of his predecessors. Zeno's phony Drogeo, Friesland, etc., are put in. Newfoundland again is fragmented, and reverts to the name *Terra de Bacallaos.* The *Estroit de St. Pierre* is on the wrong side of Anticosti. The islands of the marooned demoiselle are too close to Cartier's *Brest. Sinus S: Laurentii* here appears for the first time on the great Gulf, but *Honguedo* is on the wrong side of it. The entire Laurentian region is called *Nova Francia* whilst *Canada* is both the region above the St. Charles River and a turreted town near its mouth. On the whole, a sailor making for the St. Lawrence for the first time would have done better with any of our earlier charts—except Rotz's—than with Mercator's.

Many more early maps of the Laurentian region could be cited here; but they are all listed in Dr. Layng's excellent checklist *Sixteenth-Century Maps Relating to Canada* (Ottawa, Public Archives, 1956). The important fact is that Cartier's discoveries, even before his death, had joined the mainstream of American cartography.

✳ XIV ✳
England, France, and the Northwest

1553-1600

The Glorious Kingdom of Norumbega

At about the same time that the Cartier and Roberval voyages put a
quietus on the Kingdom of Saguenay, another myth began building
up concerning the City and Kingdom of Norumbega on the Penobscot
River. Although it received no countenance from the Ribero and other
maps derived from the voyages of Gomez and Ayllón, it had already
been mentioned as *Oranbega* on Girolamo da Verrazzano's map of his
brother's voyage of 1524. There is this difference from the Saguenay
myth: that was based on the tall tales of Donnaconna, magnified by the
Frenchmen's greedy expectations. Norumbega, apart from the name,
which means "quiet place between two rapids" in Algonkin, was
wholly created by European imagination.

The myth grew quickly. Pierre Crignon, in his *Discourse of a Great
French Sea Captain of Dieppe* (Jean Parmentier) wrote as follows "of
the Land of Norumbega" in 1545: "Beyond Cape Breton is a land
contiguous to that cape, the coast of which travels south-southwest-
ward, toward the land called Florida, and for a good 500 leagues. This
coast was discovered fifteen years ago by M. Giovanni da Verrazzano
in the name of King François and of Madame la Régente. . . . The in-

464

habitants of this country are docile people, friendly and peaceful." (He can hardly have derived that opinion from Verrazzano!) "The land overflows with every kind of fruit; there grow the wholesome orange and the almond, and many sorts of sweet-smelling trees. The country is called by its people Norumbega."

Jean Alfonce, Roberval's pilot, improved on this description in his *La Cosmographie*. He reported that coasting south from Newfoundland he had discovered the *Cap de Norombègue* and a mighty river of that name, "more than 40 leagues wide at its entrance and retains its width some thirty or forty leagues. It is full of islands, which stretch some ten or twelve leagues into the sea, and is very dangerous for rocks and reefs. Said river is on latitude 42° N. Fifteen leagues within this river there is a city called *Norombègue* with clever inhabitants and a mass of peltries of all kinds of beasts. The citizens dress in furs, wearing. sable cloaks. . . . The people use many words which sound like Latin and worship the sun, and they are fair people and tall." In his *Voyages avantureux* (1559, but written 1544), Alfonce attributes the discovery of this river to the Portuguese, and the rhymed *routier* of 1547 by Jean Mallart agrees:

> . . . la rivière Norembergue
> Laquelle fut découverte naguères
> Des Portugais avec plusières carrières
> Et d'Espagnols . . .

As for the inhabitants,

> Ils ont châteaux et villes qu'ils décorent
> Et le soleil et la lune ils adorent.

In the Desceliers, Desliens, and other French maps based on Cartier's voyages, Norumbega, variously spelled, appears always at the same spot on the Penobscot River. Like Cartier's Canada, it is at once a region and a place. Mercator's Map of 1569 has both—*Norombega* is an inland country extending across the forks of the Penobscot and a city on the east bank just above the head of navigation, with a high tower at one end and a little turret at the other.

André Thevet, the sea-going monk, returned to France in 1556 from Florida. In his *Cosmographie universelle* (1575) he places the Grand River or *Norumbègue* next after Florida; but he gives the latitude as 43° N, which is only one degree south of the entrance to Penobscot

Norumbega on the Mercator World Map of 1569. Courtesy Bibliothèque Nationale.

Bay. At said entrance, he says, appears "an island surrounded by eight very small islets, near a land of green mountains and *le Cap d'Isles.*" The mouth of the river "is dangerous from the great number of big, high rocks" and, three leagues up, you encounter an island running north-south, four leagues in circumference, "inhabited only by fishermen and birds," shaped like a man's arm, and called by the natives *Aiayascon.* This description fits Long Island (Islesboro), which is depicted on the Mercator Map; and the green mountains suggest the Camden hills, muffled in fir trees to this day. Thevet makes the unsupported statement that the French formerly built a fort on the banks of this river, and he is very contemptuous of pilots who confuse Norumbega with Canada—the one is on latitude 43° and the other between 50° and 52°. "Thus you see what it is to lack experience, mistress of everything," he concludes smugly.

Norumbega's next alleged visitor was David Ingram, an English sailor who, set ashore with two others in October 1567 on the Gulf coast of Florida, managed to walk by Indian trail all the way to the Maine coast. After a couple of years' tramping, he hailed a French ship at the mouth of the St. John River, New Brunswick, and returned to Europe. Once home in England, David made a living telling in sundry taverns the tale of his incredible journey—a profitable sort of pub-crawling. Since his story seemed to be authentic, it was taken down officially about 1582 when Sir Humfry Gilbert began preparing an expedition "for the discovery of Norumbega." From this rough sailor's lips, the Norumbega legend reached its apogee. In "a towne half a myle longe" which "hath many streets farr broader than any street in London" the men go naked except for skins about their middle, and wear on their arms and legs "hoopes" of gold and silver . . . "garnished with pearls, divers of them as big as one's thumb." The women wear plates of gold like armor and gold leaves about their middles, and on their limbs bracelets and leg ornaments like the men's. Their houses are round like a dovecote and are upheld by pillars of gold, silver, and crystal. Their country has a "great aboundance of gold, sylver and pearl"; he himself found gold nuggets as big as his fist in springs and small brooks. When queried about Norumbega's wild life, Ingram reported a beast like a horse, but with tusks, which chased him up a tree; sheep with red wool and red meat, and "a beast farre exceydinge an ox in bignes," with floppy ears like a bloodhound and long hair. This possibly was his impression of a moose.

After Ingram had been embroidering this tale for some ten years, two voyages of reconnaissance visited the Penobscot estuary in 1579–80. Their object was to find out whether Norumbega would be a suitable site for Sir Humfry Gilbert's colony. His own pinnace *Squirrel*, commanded by Simon Ferdinando, went first. Simon was a former Portuguese pilot in the English service who, a few years later, conducted the first English colony to Virginia. John Walker, in a vessel unnamed, came next. Walker, described as "Sir H. Gylbert's man" in a document that relates his findings, returned with a reasonably accurate description. "The River of Norambega," said he, was ten leagues broad and twenty-five fathom deep at the mouth, without a bar. This fits the entrance to Penobscot Bay, either measured between Whitehead and Isle au Haut, or between Two-Bush and Swans Islands. Twenty-seven miles from the mouth, where the river was twenty-one miles wide and eighteen fathom deep (which fits the site of Camden, Maine), he climbed a nearby hill and "did discover a silver mine." The rocks on the Camden hills are charged with sparkling mica which, as late as the 1880's, caused many people to sink their savings in silver mining. He noted that north of Camden, as far as he could see, the narrowed river was of the same breadth; and, seven miles from the sea, he saw an Indian lodge where four hundred dry hides, some of them eighteen feet square (meaning probably measuring 18 square feet) were stored. He brought home some of these hides, which probably were deer or moose. And he made a fast passage of seventeen days from the Penobscot to England. Both visitors were too honest to describe a City of Norumbega that was not there; but Walker alleged the country to be "most excellent both for the soyle, diversity of sweete woode and other trees."

Very similar was the report of a French voyage by Hakluyt's friend Étienne Bellinger, merchant of Rouen. Departing in January 1583, he "discouvered [explored] very diligently 200 leagues" from Cape Breton westward and returned home in four months with a rich load of furs, giving Hakluyt "a diligent description of the coaste." But he found no city and probably got no farther than the Bay of Fundy.

Sir Humfry Gilbert never saw the Penobscot, but England claimed the country of Norumbega by virtue of the Cabot voyages, and many English and other fishing vessels must have caught codfish on the Maine banks during the last decade of the sixteenth century. Norumbega became the generally accepted name of the region between the Bay of Fundy and the Hudson until replaced by Virginia in 1606, and New England in 1620.

It remained for Samuel de Champlain to spike the legend of a City of Norumbega, storied like a New Jerusalem, where natives, clad in expensive furs and displaying gold and pearl garters, lived in stately mansions pillared with silver and crystal. In September 1604, after passing Mount Desert and Isle au Haut, Champlain sailed boldly up the Penobscot to the head of navigation at the site of Bangor. He reported no city, no precious metals, nothing. "This river," he wrote, "is that which several pilots and historians call *Norembègue.* . . . They also assert that there is there a big town inhabited by skilled and clever savages, who use cotton. I am convinced that the greater part of those who mention it never saw it, and speak of it only by hearsay. . . . That anyone ever entered the river is unlikely, or they would have described it differently."

Thus, Norumbega vanished along with Saguenay—but not immediately. It took a long time for the fabled city to disappear from maps, and it has never dropped out of literature or legend. Milton, combining the classical names of northerly winds with that of this region, wrote:—

> . . . Now from the North
> Of Norumbega, and the Samoed shore
> Bursting their brazen dungeon, arm'd with ice
> And snow and hail and stormy gust, and flaw,
> Boreas and Caecias and Argestes loud
> And Thrascias rend the woods, and seas upturn.

In the nineteenth century, Professor Eben Horsford, equating Norumbega with Norsemen, located the fabled city in Massachusetts, created a Norumbega Park, and built a stone tower to nail the myth to the banks of the Charles. But Maine clings to the legend as one of her folk tales, and within her ample borders Norumbega has become a favorite name for hills, yachts, and villas. Sailors along the Maine coast, when the summer sun makes fantastic figures in a lifting fog, may even now imagine that they see the towers and battlements of a shimmering dream-city; and someone who knows the story will sing out, "Norumbega!"

The Newfoundland Cod Fishery

It is still a mystery why so little attention was paid to North America by the northern European governments and nations for a generation after 1542. Apparently all felt that it was well enough to let the fishermen alone. This neglect is easier to explain for France than for England. The kings of France were not only at war with Spain from 1532 to 1559, and at times with England too, but also subjected to a cruel civil war between Catholics and Protestants. That lasted until 1594 when Henry of Navarre "bought Paris with a mass" and was crowned Henri IV.

Cartier's and Roberval's reports on the Laurentian region were so disappointing that the only French efforts at colonization prior to 1588 were directed to Florida. Gaspard de Coligny, admiral of France, whose French colony in Brazil had broken up, sent the first group of settlers to Santa Elena (Port Royal, South Carolina) under Jean Ribaut of Dieppe. Ill led, unenterprising, discouraged, they returned home two years later. A second attempt, Protestant like the first, was made by René de Laudonnière in 1564. He built Fort Caroline near the mouth of the Floridian St. John's River, so near the homeward route of treasure fleets that Spain could not ignore it, and in 1565 Philip II sent Menéndez de Avilés to destroy it. That he did very successfully, taking Fort Caroline by assault and massacring the French who, with promise of good treatment, had surrendered; an act of treachery which even then shocked Europe. A French corsair named Dominique de Gourges avenged his countrymen by recapturing the fort from the Spanish garrison in 1568 and appropriately murdering all prisoners.

Postponing a detailed account of these futile French attempts to establish themselves in Florida, as belonging properly to Southern Voyages, let us return to Newfoundland and adjacent coasts. For no part of the world has ever been so rich in edible fish and other products of the sea as the Newfoundland Banks, the coast of the Labrador, and the Gulf of St. Lawrence.

England's indifference to northern exploration and colonization after

the Cabot era has never been satisfactorily explained. Unlike France,
England enjoyed internal peace under the House of Tudor. Henry VII
and his successors claimed sovereignty over America by virtue of John
Cabot's voyage, but did nothing to "nail it down." Bristol supported
Cabot and the Anglo-Azorean syndicate, partly to find new fishing
grounds; but when found, they were neglected. Rut found not one
English fisherman in St. John's in 1527; and Roberval, if any of the
fishing fleet he encountered there were English, did not admit it. An
act of Parliament of 33 Henry VIII (1542) indicated that too many
English fishermen were buying codfish from "Pycardes, Flemynghes,
Norman and Frenchmen," sometimes "half the sea over" and even in
foreign ports, instead of catching fish themselves. This practice Parliament forbade under severe penalty, since "the craft and feate of
fishing" gave "great strenthe to this Realm by bringing up and encreas-
ing of Maryners . . . but also a great welthe to the Realme." But the
situation changed in the next thirty-five years, for in 1578 Anthony
Parkhurst wrote to Hakluyt that the English fishermen were lording it
over all others in Newfoundland harbors. Edward Hayes, in his narrative of Sir Humfry Gilbert's voyage of 1583, found that to be the
situation in St. John's Harbor.

What had happened in the meantime? We simply do not know, for
lack of records; or, more likely, failure of historians to comb local
records sufficiently. It has been argued that England's going Protestant
lessened the demand for fish by reducing radically the 160 fast days
in the Catholic calendar; but Elizabeth's Parliament in 1563 passed a
law declaring both Wednesday and Saturday to be fish days in order to
"mayneteine fisshermen." A list of Frobisher's provisions for his 1578
voyage indicates that an average of fourteen days a month were still
fast days. In any case, England became a very good customer for the
stockfish, crammed full of vitamins and a boon to poor people who
could not afford fowl or red meat.

There were plenty of other fish on the Banks—haddock, pollock,
halibut, deep-sea flounder—and all can be cured. But your sixteenth-
century fisherman would have none of them simply because he could
not sell them. "Fish" meant codfish, *morue*, *baccalaos*. All others were
thrown away or cut up for bait—the voracious cod would snap at
anything. In coastal waters of Newfoundland north of Fogo, the codfish were on the small side, easily cured in the sun, and in special de-

The entrance to St. John's Harbor, Newfoundland. Courtesy Canadian Government Travel Bureau.

mand in the Mediterranean and, in the next century, the West Indies. Elsewhere, and on the Banks, they ran up to 100 and 200 pounds' weight.

One thing is certain: the Spanish Newfoundland fishery out of Biscayan ports such as San Sebastian, which began to be noticeable in 1540, and which in 1553 was earning 200,000 ducats a year, declined during the Spanish wars with France and England and never recovered. Too many Spanish fishermen were captured. Sir Bernard Drake's attack on Spanish ships in Newfoundland waters in 1585 netted hundreds of fishermen and thousands of quintal of fish. This process was fur-

thered by stupid policies of the Spanish crown: impressing fishermen and commandeering their ships for the navy, and taxing salt. In
consequence, the English and Dutch could buy salt from the La
Rochelle salt-pans for two reals per *fanega*, but San Sebastian had to
pay six times that. As soon as peace was concluded with Spain by
James I in 1603, England began supplying a large part of the Spanish
market with codfish, and it became a toast of English fisherman at St.
John's, "The Pope and 10 shillings per quintal!"

English or not, hundreds of fishermen, whose names we do not even
know, by mid-sixteenth century were exploiting the Banks and the
shore fisheries of Newfoundland. Not only the Grand Bank, which lies
like a big buffer to the southeastward, but little banks south of Newfoundland such as Burgoo, St. Pierre, and Banquereau. The waters off
southern Labrador and around the Magdalen Islands were almost
equally fecund.

In general, there were two methods of codfishing in American waters, the "wet" or "green," and the "dry." Spaniards, Portuguese, and
Frenchmen on the Bay of Biscay, having plentiful and cheap supply of
salt from the salt-pans of the Aunis, Cadiz, the Gironde, and the Algarve, made a practice of heavily salting their catch on the Grand
Bank, sailing directly home, and curing the *baccalaos* ashore. English
and Irish fishermen, having to import salt (their own climate being too
cool and foggy for the sun to evaporate it from seawater), found it
more profitable to pursue dry fishing. Normans and Bretons had plenty
of cheap salt and pursued both kinds of fishing.

For dry fishing, the vessel brought out double crews, one to fish
and one to work ashore. In order to be first in the chosen harbor or
"tickle" of Newfoundland, French and English fishing vessels sometimes braved the winter gales in order to be the "admiral" or commander of others who arrived later, but there was no use arriving before May when the capelin swarmed inshore and the cod followed
them. From the time the ship anchored, her crew was never idle. After
mooring her well, and harbor-furling her sails, barrels were lashed
along the topsides, and a mariner in each barrel started pulling in codfish and throwing them on deck to be gutted. Most of the fishing, however, was done from the fleet of small boats—shallops, or *chaloupes*—
that each ship brought out, hauling in the fish by handline. Each ship
carried an average of seven shallops with five men for each, and each

"Making fish" at Petty Harbor, near St. John's. Note the "stages" (wharves), the brushwood "flakes," and the "tilts" (sheds). Courtesy Canadian Government Travel Bureau.

shallop's crew expected to fill her to the gunwales with cod by noon.

The shore crew, in the meantime, felled trees and put up a fish stage (*chaufaud*), a wharf projecting into the harbor, onto which the fishermen threw the codfish from the boats, to be gutted and split. Most important, on the rocky shore behind this wharf were built the flakes (*vignots*). These were platforms of brush and small boughs raised some three feet above the ground, on which the cod were cured. Each fish had to be washed, split, and slack (lightly) salted; it was then spread on the flakes for a series of exposures to the sun. The French

Dr. John Dee, by an unknown artist. Courtesy Ashmolean Museum, Oxford.

used no fewer than ten *soleils,* in which the fish were shifted about or stacked in different patterns.

Every night and in foggy or rainy weather, the split fish had to be covered with wood or sailcloth; and even in Newfoundland, upon occasion, they had to be protected from too hot a sun. This went on for several weeks, after which the fish were left, insides up, for several days before being pronounced cured. They were then stored in a shed, which the fishermen called a "tilt." The final sun-cured codfish, called stockfish or poor-john in English, *morue* in French, *baccalao* in Spanish—hard, stiff, and almost indestructible—became a delicious, savory morsel when soaked out and properly cooked. Try a dish of *baccalaos vizcaína* or one of the hundred other ways the Portuguese cook salt cod, and you will understand why the Banks fisheries were so important to that country, and still are. Don't be put off by the favorite Newfoundland method of frying it in cheap grease!

The "wet" or "green" fishermen from France and the Iberian peninsula mostly frequented the Grand Bank as the nearest to home; they knew when they had arrived there, not only by the sudden shoaling of the water from hundreds of fathom to sixty, forty, and twenty-five, but by the flocks of birds which came out from land to get their share of the fish. As described by Lescarbot early in the following century, wet fishing was all done with hook, three-pound sinker, and twenty- to twenty-five-fathom line. The gutted fish were thrown into barrels with a liberal supply of salt between layers; and "in this way they work continuously," at anchor, "for the space of about three months, with sails down, until the fare is complete." Incredible as it may seem, the fishermen of Brittany, Normandy, and Saintonge often sailed from Rouen, Dieppe, Saint-Malo, or La Rochelle as early as January or February, braving the winter westerlies; they brought home a full fare of fish in April or May, and after landing them to be cured on shore, sailed again to the Grand Bank wtih a fresh load of salt, returning not later than October. It was not only a tough voyage to reach the Grand Bank; it was a bad place to spend your time at any season. The ocean swells are enhanced by the shoal water, and there is absolutely no shelter. In a steamer I once passed through the French *Terre-Neuve* fleet on a relatively calm day in June 1900. The little schooners and brigs, no bigger than those of the sixteenth century, were all at anchor, rolling scuppers-under and pitching bows-under.

Rudyard Kipling's *Captains Courageous* and James B. Connolly's *Out of Gloucester* describe the green-fishing method as used by Gloucester fishermen in the 1890's, but it has since completely disappeared (and so have the fish) before the competition of power-dragging and instant refrigeration. One wonders why some enterprising green fisherman in the 1500's did not think of hacking off sections of icebergs to save the expense of salt.

Whilst wet fishing demanded no American shore lodgment, the French dry fishermen, by trading on the side, founded colonial Canada's second most lucrative business, the fur trade. All kinds of furs, especially marten and beaver, were in great demand in Europe; men as well as women wore fur linings and trimmings on their garments, and the broad-brimmed felt hats which every lady and gentleman sported indoors and out, were made from pressed beaver hair, shorn from the pelt. Styles and shapes changed, but the demand for furs increased, far exceeding the local supply from trappers in eastern Europe. Here the dry shore fishermen came in. With the friendly Micmac at the Gaspé, and Montagnais in southern Labrador, they traded beads, hatchets, knives, and all manner of ironmongery for peltry, enabling every fisherman who brought out a bundle of trading truck to make a neat little profit. This had two important consequences in the long run. Toward the end of the sixteenth century, enterprising Frenchmen began organizing trading companies primarily to engage in the fur trade, and it was one of these which sent Poutrincourt and Champlain to begin the permanent settlement of Canada in 1604–8. The natives preferred a fur-trading European to a land-grabbing European, as the former did not immediately disrupt their economy. This did not apply to Newfoundland, where the Beothuk were too shy to trade. Richard Whitbourne in 1580 obtained at Trinity Harbor, Newfoundland, not only a fare of fish but deer, bear, beaver, otter, and seal skins which he sold to good advantage in Southampton. But, says he, "*We* killed" these animals; they could obtain none from native hunters.

The French called the northern peninsula of Newfoundland *le petit nord*, and frequented it for dry fishing because the codfish caught there were of a uniform medium size, suitable for the Mediterranean or West Indies market. Once he had accumulated a cargo of cured fish, the *petit nord* fisherman sailed with it directly to one or the other of these markets.

The English, who concentrated on dry fishing, were often so successful as to "make" two or three shiploads of stockfish in one season. Hence the practice grew of sending from England so-called "sack ships" in midsummer to St. John's and other harbors in order to buy, take home, and sell the results of the fishermen's labors. The men who fished, as well as the shore parties, were not rewarded by wages but by the "lay" system, which lasted among New England fishermen and whalers into the twentieth century. This meant that the profits were divided up into shares. The owner of the ship took one-third to one-half, the rest was divided among the men by agreed-upon fractions, the master getting the biggest.

Parkhurst in 1578 has an amusing sociological argument for English support of Newfoundland dry fishing. Not only did the fishermen make about double what they could get on a summer's coasting voyage; they were free of temptation from wine and women, unobtainable in Newfoundland. Thus, damsels of the West Country looking for a husband much preferred a fisherman to an ordinary mariner! He might have added that the dry-fishermen in Newfoundland ran tenfold the risks of European coasters. They had to make, through fog and ice, an ironbound coast on which the slightest mistake meant disaster. But with the aid of the "three L's," Lead, Log, and Lookout, they usually made their chosen harbor, caught and cured their fish, and returned, eager for another voyage.

The Gulf Whale and Walrus Fisheries

Whale fishing was pursued in the Strait of Belle Isle and the Gulf. This was a specialty of the Basques of the old Kingdom of Navarre, who had been whaling for centuries in the Bay of Biscay. They extended their operations to Newfoundland as early as 1527 and the business grew continually. Whaling ships anchored in north shore harbors between Blanc Sablon and Tadoussac, adjacent to waters where the right whales spouted and sported. They pursued their quarry in a big pulling boat, harpooned the whale, and towed his carcass ashore where it was "rendered" into oil in big iron cauldrons. Parkhurst states that twenty to thirty Basque vessels were so engaged in 1578. Their crews were reported to be so tough that other fishermen avoided the harbors that they frequented.

Somewhat similar was the walrus killing around the Magdalen Islands, where Cartier had reported them to be in great numbers. Hakluyt prints several narratives of this specialized fishery for "morsses or sea oxen," which the English first tried in the last decade of the century. They found that the Bretons and Basques had got there ahead of them; "we arrived the day after the fair," explained one in a homely metaphor. Walruses were valued for oil, hides, and tusks. A physician of Bristol prescribed for patients suffering from impotency, powdered walrus tusk, "as soveraigne . . . as any Unicorne's horne."

Grace, a thirty-five-tun bark of Bristol, got her "train" (whale) oil at second hand, salvaging full casks from the wrecks of two big Basque whalers in the Bay of St. George, Newfoundland. She continued to "the Isle of Assumption, or Natiscotec" (Anticosti), where she found "wonderfull faire and great Cod fish," but nary a walrus or whale. The Englishmen then sailed up Placentia Bay, Newfoundland, where they found more than threescore sail of fishermen, including eight Basques from Saint-Jean de Luz and its neighbor "Sibiburo" (Ciboure) "of whom we were very well used and they wished heartily for peace betweene them and us." The Basques even gave them two boats to help their fishing. After a brush with the Beothuk Indians, hostile as usual, the *Grace* rounded Cape Race to Ferryland, where she found twenty-two sail of English fisherman and completed her cargo with stockfish, arriving at Bristol 24 September 1594.

When we consider that as early as 1560 more than thirty fishermen sailed from Saint-Malo and Cancale for Newfoundland and that the same number sailed next year from three minor ports of Normandy; that Parkhurst in 1578 reported 50 English, 150 French and Breton, and 100 Spanish in Newfoundland ports, exclusive of the whalers; and that Thevet puts the total number (including the Dutch, who had just got onto it) at 300 in 1586; one can appreciate that European sailing craft had become common every summer in Newfoundland and Gulf waters. A brave sight they must have been, as if a yachting regatta were on. We have no details whatsoever of these many hundreds of northern voyages, since fishermen kept no journals and published no narratives. For the most part they had no aid to navigation more modern than the compass, and performed latitude sailing by eye altitudes of sun and North Star. Even a mariner's astrolabe would have been beyond their means or skill. Thus, long before the coast-dwelling natives of Norumbega and the region between the Hudson and Florida had seen any European sail save those of an infrequent explorer, one could say of the Gulf of St. Lawrence and the outer coast of Newfoundland as did Wordsworth of English waters in the eighteenth century: "With ships the sea was sprinkled far and nigh, like stars in Heaven."

A French Colony on Sable Island

Sir Humfry Gilbert's taking possession for England of Newfoundland in 1583 must have suggested to the French that they had better lose no time establishing permanent bases in what they considered to be theirs. But the first effort in this direction was on the highly unsuitable Sable Island, where Gilbert's flagship foundered later the same year.

Sable Island, a bow-shaped strip of sand twenty miles long and a mile wide, ninety miles south-southeast of Cape Canso, Nova Scotia, has even a better claim to the dubious title "graveyard of the Atlantic" than the Outer Banks near Cape Hatteras. Since the lighthouses were established in 1801–2, no fewer than 187 sailing vessels and 20 steamships have been wrecked on Sable Island; and there probably were as many more in the colonial period, since this island lies close to the well-traveled ship lanes.

The one asset of Sable Island was a herd of wild cattle. This had been started by Fagundes or another early Portuguese mariner; for both they and the Spaniards adopted the charitable practice of leaving horses, cattle, and swine on islands they discovered, in the hope that they would increase and multiply for the benefit of later explorers. Lescarbot, the merry lawyer and early historian of New France, asserted that the cattle on Sable Island had been left there by a certain Baron de Léri et de Saint-Just, vicomte de Gueu. That is all we know about this benefactor; the baron, never identified, may well have been a creation of Lescarbot's ever fertile imagination.

Be that as it may, a very persistent nobleman of Brittany, Troïlus de Mesgouez, marquis de La Roche, actually tried to colonize Sable Island with convicts. Two unsuccessful attempts were made in 1578 and 1584. The English captured his first flagship and the second was wrecked. But in 1598, armed with a commission from Henri IV conferring upon him the same viceregal powers that Roberval had enjoyed, he sent *Catherine* (160 tuns), belonging to a Norman captain named Thomas

Chefdhostel, and *François* of ninety tuns, to reconnoiter his domain. They picked up salt at Brouage, then sailed for Sable Island in March 1598. The Marquis combed the prisons for colonists, but took only sixty with him. His curious choice of Sable Island for a colony, from all his vast domain which extended from Cape Chidley to Cape Cod, seems to have been due to a fear that the convicts would run away if settled on the mainland—which doubtless they would have done. La Roche returned to France in October 1598, leaving his settlement to its own devices for five years. The ex-convicts hunted cattle, wolves, seal, and fox, fished, built huts from the timbers of a wrecked vessel—possibly Gilbert's—and quarreled among themselves. La Roche having sold out, it was Chefdhostel who annually brought provisions to Sable Island and returned to France with peltry and fish oil. During his visit of 1603 he found only eleven colonists, all men, alive. Those he repatriated, and Henry IV summoned them into his presence. Clothed in shaggy skins and with beards of prodigious length, they looked like ancient river gods. Chefdhostel had robbed them of the peltry that they had accumulated, but the king forced him to disgorge and also gave each man a generous gift.

Thus "another New France came to a tragic ending," writes Trudel, and for the same reason as several others, the obsession of early colonizers for islands. But Sable Island did have important consequences. La Roche sold his grant to a Dieppe captain named Chauvin, who in 1600 founded the fur trading post of Tadoussac at the mouth of the Saguenay; and it was his successor, the sieur de Monts, who formed the company which founded Sainte-Croix, Port Royal, and Quebec.

"If Canada were cultivated and peopled, it would be as warm as La Rochelle," wrote Jean Alfonce, Roberval's pilot. Very few French as yet were willing to make the experiment; but Canada as a province of France, a British colony, commonwealth and, finally, a nation, evolved from these little fur-trading and fishing outposts. England, on the contrary, while not neglecting the fisheries, followed whither Sir Humfry Gilbert pointed on his last voyage, to New England and Virginia, which eventually became the twin nuclei of the United States.

English mariners had a long way to go before founding Virginia.

English Voyages "Around the Clock"

While the English government virtually ignored these northern regions of America for fifty years, English mariners and merchant adventurers were busy in other parts of the world. They tried trading with one region after another where they were not likely to tangle with Spain. A steady Tudor policy, reluctantly abandoned by Elizabeth I, was to keep on friendly terms with Spain, even after England went Protestant. According to certain English historians, respect for Spanish power is the principal reason for the crown's making no effort to realize on the Cabot discovery for so very long. But it would seem that Charles V's failure to do anything about Cartier might have encouraged the English to try something on their own in northern regions, much earlier than they did.

The Spanish alliance was severely strained in 1544–45 by the Emperor's making peace with France, expelling English merchants from Seville, and prohibiting trade between England and his dominions, which included the Netherlands and part of Germany. Although the alliance was temporarily restored and supposedly cemented by Queen Mary's marriage to Philip II, that did not last long.

Out of these misfortunes and restrictions came a new English policy of trade expansion—but to the northeast, not the northwest, to the Mediterranean rather than to Newfoundland, and to Africa rather than to America. Finally, the English came full circle to the Northwest Passage, Newfoundland, and Norumbega.

In 1548 the Duke of Northumberland, who ran the government under the boy king Edward VI, succeeded in persuading Sebastian Cabot to shift his allegiance from Spain to England. Cabot had a hand in the equipping of a ship in 1551 to trade with Morocco by a group of London merchants including one Henry Ostriche, who had married Cabot's daughter. They made two successful round voyages to Morocco, led by Captain Thomas Wyndham, and established factories (agencies) at Santa Cruz and Safi. The same people, with royal support, sent Wyndham with a Portuguese pilot in 1553 to trade along the Grain Coast of Africa, the future Liberia. Only one ship returned, with forty survivors, the rest being victims of yellow fever; but the gold, ivory, and pepper brought back in her hold made the investors' fortunes. One of the survivors was a teen-ager named Martin Frobisher.

In the meantime, about two hundred English merchant-adventurers had started a more elaborate project, with a capital of £25,000. Styled ambitiously "The Merchants Adventurers of England for the Discovery of Lands, Territories, Isles, Dominions and Seignories Unknown," they received a royal charter from two successive sovereigns in 1553 and 1555, and elected Sebastian Cabot their governor. For a time the directors debated whether to take another crack at the Northwest Passage or to try a Northeast Passage to Asia.

John Dee recommended the eastern course. This extraordinary Welshman was only ten years older than Richard Hakluyt; but his portraits, showing a long white beard and a black skull cap, make him seem permanently aged. Born 1527, he went up to Cambridge, became early famous as a "polymath"—one who knew every branch of mathematics, astronomy, and astrology—and was appointed by Henry VIII one of the original foundation fellows of Trinity College in 1546. To Louvain he went next year, and there became friends with Gemma Frisius, and was impressed by his globe which showed a northwest passage called *Fretum Trium Fratrum* (Corte Reals or Cabots?). Other friends he made in his travels were Gerard Mercator, Ortelius, and Petrus Nonnius, one of the Portuguese galaxy who so greatly contributed to the art of navigation. His lectures in English at the University of Paris made a sensation; so that when he returned to England in 1551 he received a pension and a benefice from Edward VI, and his acquaintance was cultivated by the Dudleys, Leicesters, Gilberts, and everyone interested in navigation and discovery. He also brought from Europe the cross-staff, or *balestila*, as an improved method of taking altitudes of heavenly bodies. Dee seems to have been generous with advice to the Muscovy Company, and to navigators such as Frobisher, Drake, and Davis. All the world, including Queen Elizabeth, came to his house at Mortlake on the Thames, to admire his library and collection of instruments. Certainly no intellectual did so much for English discovery as John Dee. He was one of those "stern men with empires in their brains," like Peckham, Carleil, and Hakluyt, who laid the intellectual foundations of the British Empire, an expression which Dee is said to have coined. Unfortunately, he seems to have been regarded with suspicion as a devil's disciple ever since college days, when he rigged too spectacular a display of pyrotechnics in St. John's hall. His unashamed dabbling in alchemy and astrology supported the charge, and holy orders did not protect him from charges of practising the black art. He did practise crystal-gazing; and Prince Lasky of Poland was so impressed by this at Mortlake that he invited Dee to accompany him to Poland in 1583. In his absence a local mob gutted his house. Ironically enough, his name in America was given only to "Dee's Pinnacles," rough crags in Greenland, and "Dee River" (Narragansett Bay); but in neither place has it survived.

To get back to the corporation with the long name. Since the immediate object of this Muscovy Company (as it was generally called for short) was to find new markets for English woolens, the northeast-men prevailed; Cathay and the "Indies" had no use for woolen cloth. The company's first expedition, three ships under Sir Hugh Willoughby, departed in 1553. The flagship and one other wintered off Lapland, and their entire complement died; Russian fishermen next spring found their emaciated bodies on board, frozen stiff. The third ship, commanded by Richard Chancellor, entered the White Sea and landed at Archangel. Chancellor then traveled overland to Moscow, obtained permission from Ivan the Terrible for his company to trade with Russia, and opened up a new line of commerce. It remained profitable for a few years, until the Hanseatic League's overland enterprise undermined it. On return from a second expedition to Archangel, in the autumn of 1556, Chancellor's ship was wrecked on the coast of Scotland. That summer the Muscovy Company sent out a third attempt, in the *Serchthrift*, Captain Stephen Borough, to probe for the Northeast Passage. At his send-off party at Gravesend, Sebastian Cabot joined the dance, as we described in Chapter VII above. Borough got as far as Vaigats Island and contacted the Samoyeds.

Anthony Jenkinson, who succeeded Chancellor as spearhead of the Muscovy Company, traveled overland to the Caspian Sea in 1557, crossed it, and penetrated to Bokhara, finding conditions in the Middle East too chaotic to offer possibilities for English trade expansion. In 1562 he visited the Shah of Persia and opened a trade there; but that ended a few years later when the Turks invaded Iran. He then, as we shall see, turned to the Northwest.

Another important African voyage was made in 1554–55 under Captain John Lok, one of whose officers was sixteen-year-old Martin Frobisher. They brought back a rich cargo, including a hundred pounds' weight of pure gold. Portugal protested that this was poaching on her territory, but Lok claimed he had never seen a Portuguese on the coast and had traded only with independent black sovereigns. For two thousand miles Portugal maintained only the one pre-Columbian fortress of El Mina, and a fort at Cape Puntas. The English Privy Council insisted that there must be a more effective occupation than that to claim sovereignty over an undeveloped country, a doctrine they would soon apply to Spain in North America. English trading voyages to the West Coast of Africa, notably the three under William Towerson, continued well into the reign of Queen Elizabeth I, who acceded in 1558.

In that glorious reign, when the spirit of "freeborn Englishmen" asserted itself in every walk of life, things began to move. But not right away, or toward North America.

John Hawkins of Plymouth in Devon had to be heard from first; we may make brief mention of him here, postponing to our volume on Southern Voyages a detailed account of his exploits. Well educated and mannered, Hawkins made valuable contacts in Spain, and talked to Philip II when he landed at Plymouth in 1554. He conceived the idea of sailing to the Caribbean with shiploads of black slaves to sell to the Spanish planters, perhaps doing some privateering on the side. There was nothing new about this; French corsairs had been raiding the Spanish islands and treasure fleets since 1521, smuggling slaves on the side, and the Spanish crown had even licensed foreigners to import slaves.

With three ships Hawkins sailed from Plymouth in the autumn of 1562. He spent the winter slave-catching and slave-buying on the West Coast of Africa and, next spring, with the connivance of the Spanish authorities of Hispaniola, disposed of his cargo amicably and profitably at three outports. Already respectable, Hawkins returned rich and was smiled upon by Queen Elizabeth, who even lent him a naval vessel for his next slaving voyage and allowed him to fly the royal ensign. There seems to have been no twinge of the European conscience, north or south, Catholic or Protestant, that there was anything wrong about the slave trade. It seemed to be the order of nature and the will of God that the "blackamoors," who had been enslaving each other since time immemorial, should work for Christians. One of Hawkins's slave ships was named *Jesus*, and he enjoined his mariners to "love one another" and "serve God daily." Hypocrisy if you will, but all Europeans flattered themselves that they were doing a favor to benighted Africans in bringing them to civilized lands where their souls might be saved. When Hawkins adopted coat armor, he chose "a demi-Moor proper bound with a cord" as his device.

Hawkins's second slave-trading voyage of 1564–66 went not so smoothly as the first, as the Spanish colonial authorities had been warned not to deal with him. Nevertheless, under threat of force, those on the Spanish Main allowed him to vend his blacks for gold, silver, and pearl. Next he called on the French colony in Florida, lent them a ship to go home in, visited Newfoundland to top off with stockfish, and returned to England. Incidentally, he had learned to smoke from the French and was the first to introduce tobacco to England, in 1565. The profits of this voyage, according to the Spanish ambassador, were 50 per cent; but the Queen expected double. Hawkins, when received by Gloriana, excused himself thus: "Paul might plant and Apollos water, but only God can give the increase." At this Elizabeth burst out with, "God's wounds! This fellow went out a sailor and is come home a divine!"

The "third and troublesome voyage" to the West Indies, as Hawkins called it, sailed from Plymouth in October 1567, with 408 men in six ships, one commanded by his twenty-two-year-old kinsman Francis Drake. After connived-at trading and numerous adventures on the Spanish Main, they put in at the Mexican seaport of San Juan de Ulua in order to grave and repair the flagship. Here they were jumped, as it were, by the Spanish treasure fleet. The Viceroy of Mexico agreed to let the Englishmen depart in peace, but Hawkins and Drake had to cut their way out and returned home in January 1569, eager to avenge this act of bad faith.

One may well regard this event, rather than the Queen's accession ten years earlier, as the true beginning of the Elizabethan age. It ended the long period of Tudor alliance with the House of Hapsburg and began a state of quasi-war in the New World that outlasted Elizabeth's reign, although war was not formally declared until the Great Armada threatened England. The English explored North America at will, and not a score of years elapsed before we hear of a Colony of Virginia and, within thirty years, the smashing defeat of the Spanish Armada. Throughout these years Englishmen were acquiring experience of deep water and long voyages which qualified them to contest empire with mighty Spain.

According to George Best's *True Discourse* (1578) of Frobisher's voyages, "two speciall causes" account for England's long slumber while other countries explored and founded colonies. One was "lacke of liberalitie in the Nobilitie" and the other, "want of skill in Cosmographie, and the Art of Navigation." England might have waited forever, had she depended on the nobility, not merchants, to adventure their money; but during the quarter-century previous her mariners had made great advances in scientific navigation.

Coeval with these round-the-clock voyages that we have mentioned briefly, came an increased production of English works on navigation, astronomical tables, and nautical instruments. Whilst Cartier and Rut did business in great waters with no instruments except quadrant, astrolabe, and declination tables, Frobisher and Gilbert had the cross-staff (also called Jacob's staff and balestila) introduced from the Low Countries by John Dee; translations of the classic tomes on navigation by Pedro de Medina and Martin Cortés, and a number of new instruments. Richard Eden (the same who took down Sebastian Cabot's amusing "last words" on longitude) brought out a series of translations from Spanish, Italian, and Latin books such as Peter Martyr's *Decades of the New World*, and Casteñada's *Voyages to India*. Humfrey Cole, who flourished in London between 1560 and 1580, made nautical instruments second to none in beauty and perfection. John Dee studied the theoretical aspects of navigation, searching in vain for a ready method of ascertaining longitude. Stephen Borough visited Seville to study the Spanish system of training pilots. By 1570 England had caught up with the Latin countries in celestial navigation; her mariners in the last quarter of the century were better equipped to cope with conditions in the North Atlantic than Cartier, Rut, and Verrazzano had been.

The one department in which they were still deficient was cartography. As the reader may see from our reproductions, the maps carried by Frobisher and Gilbert, or (like Lok's and Molyneux's) made in consequence of their voyages, were primitive in comparison with those that the Portuguese had been drafting of North America since 1500, and the French since 1540. The English produced nothing comparable to the early Portuguese charts, especially of outer Newfoundland. Apparently they were ignorant of what Desceliers and other Dieppe cartographers had done for the Gulf of St. Lawrence. One English chart telescopes everything between Narragansett Bay and the Penobscot, placing Verrazzano's Block Island off the River of Norumbega; Gilbert's 1583 grant of land to the Peckhams confuses the Penobscot with the Hudson.

George Best in his *True Discourse* has this to say about the then state of navigation: "The making and pricking of Cardes, the shifting of Sunne and Moone, the use of the compasse, the houre glasse for observing time, instruments of Astronomie to take Longitudes and Latitudes of Countleys, and many other helps, are so commonly knowen of every Mariner now adayes, that he that hathe bin twice at Sea, is ashamed to come home, if he be not able to render accompte of all these particularities." That is a great exaggeration. Even Frobisher did not try to determine longitude, as Verrazzano had done more than fifty years earlier, nor did he use to advantage the instruments that he had. The vast majority of shipmasters were still crossing the ocean "by guess and by God."

Bibliography and Notes

NORUMBEGA

The name, spelled *Oranbega*, first appears on Girolamo da Verrazzano's map dated 1529, next to *Le Figlie di Navarra*, which we have identified (see Chapter IX above) as Monhegan, Isle au Haut, and Mount Desert Islands. Thus, Oranbega must be the Penobscot, which had already been named *Rio de las Gamas* (of deer) by Estévan Gomez. Ganong, *Crucial Maps*, pp. 130–32, supported by Ch.-A. Julien, *Les Voyages de découverte*, p. 85n., argues that Verrazzano picked up the name at Newport, R. I., and that his statement in his Letter to the king to the effect that the Wampanoag, given European technique, were capable of constructing magnificent edifices "since their entire coast abounds in blue stone, crystal and alabaster" is the nucleus of the Norumbega legend. Ganong asserts that the name was later applied "by a cartographical quirk" to the Penobscot. I regard this hypothesis as unsound because (1) North American Indians never knew anything about tribes or regions remote from where they dwelt; and (2) *Nolumbeka* in the Abnaki tongue means either a stretch of quiet water between two rapids, or a succession of rapids interspersed by still waters. This exactly fits the Penobscot River above Bangor. Father Vetromile, a missionary to the Abnaki at Old Town, noted that Indians were still using that name for their region in 1866. Ganong, pp. 215–17, prints a parallel table of names on maps from 1529 to 1569, and Norumbega, under varied spellings, is always in the same position. Nor can I accept the theory of the learned Abbé Anthiaume that the name is Dieppois in origin, applied by Verrazzano to please a shipmate from that Norman seaport.

In my opinion, Fagundes visited the Penobscot, heard the Indian name *Norumbega* prior to the Verrazzano voyage of 1524, and Girolamo da Verrazzano picked it up from him or some other Portuguese sailor in time to put it on his 1529 map.

A few articles tell all that is known about Norumbega: John H. Wiggins, "Norumbega, the Lost Empire of New England," Ellsworth (Maine) *American*, 27 September 1967; Benjamin F. De Costa, *Ancient Norumbega or the Voyages of Simon Ferdinando and John Walker to the Penobscot River, 1579–1580* (Albany, 1890); Sigmund Diamond, "Norumbega: New England Xanadu," *American Neptune* XI (April 1951), 95–107; F. W. Hodge, *Handbook of American Indians* (1910), II, 84. De Costa also wrote the chapter "Norumbega and Its English Explorers" in Winsor, *America*, III, 169–218, valuable for cartography. The Crignon account is in Ramusio's *Terzo Volume* (1556), f. 423. Thevet's is in *Cosmographie universelle*, II (1575), 1008.

David Ingram's narrative is in Hakluyt, *Voyages*, 1589 ed., 557–59; his answers to "certayne questions" are reprinted in De Costa, *Ancient Norumbega*, pp. 5–7. Hakluyt evidently decided that Ingram was a liar and left him out of his next edition. We should remember that Ingram, like all Sinbads, had to tell marvels in order to live, and that not all he says is pure imagination. But he so mixes things up—penguins next to flamingoes, tropical plants next northern pines—that it is difficult to sift out his Norumbega data from those about Florida and the country between.

A more flamboyant account of Norumbega, allegedly by Ingram, with a description of the "palace of the Bashaba" who sat on a pearl-studded throne, engaged David in conversation, gave him wine in golden goblets, and told him he was "in the land of Norambega . . . known as Arembec," is a palpable modern forgery. It is printed in Herbert M. Sylvester, *Maine Coast Romance. The Land of St. Castin* (1909), V, 71 ff. Bellinger's brief account is in Hakluyt, *Discourse Concerning Westerne Planting*, Leonard Wood, ed. (Maine, 1877), p. 84, and Hakluyt Society edition of Hakluyt's *Writings*, II (1935), 266. Bellinger probably got home too late in 1583 to be of any assistance to Gilbert. Essential documents are in D. B. Quinn (ed.), *Voyages of Sir Humphrey Gilbert* (see notes to Chapter XVI below), I,52; II,278, 287, 309–10. See also Trudel, *Nouvelle France*, I,220.

For the Horsford hypothesis that Norumbega was derived from the Leif Ericsson Norse colony and was located on the Charles River near Boston, see notes to Chapter III above. This theory was not original with Horsford. Philip Cluwer (Cluverius), a popular German geographer of *c.* 1600, stated in his *Introductio in Universam Geographiam* (first published 1629; this quote is from 1667 ed., p. 615): "Norumbega urbs ad fluvium qui Rio

Grande vulgo dicitur" is situated between Nova Francia and Virginia; "Caeterum Norumbegam dictum portant quasi Norvvegiam, sed Coloniam e Norvvegia eo deductum." Hjalmur R. Holand (the Kensington Rune Stone man) has improved on Horsford. Assuming in chap. xxii of his *Explorations in America Before Columbus* (1956) that the *Nor* in Norumbega means Norsemen, he places the fabled city on Narragansett Bay, the Newport stone tower being vestigial remains of the turreted city. Holand makes a great deal of the name *norman villa* which appears on the Maiollo (1527) map of Verrazzano's voyage; but this occurs at Angoulême (New York) rather than Refugio (Newport). It probably was intended to compliment one of Verrazzano's noble friends. There are two places called Normanville in France, one near Evreux in Normandy which would naturally be it. West of it, conjecturally on the Delaware or New Jersey coast, is a *Longa Villa*, which Verrazzano certainly named after François d'Orléans, duc de Longueville.

Champlain's description of the Penobscot is in *Les Voyages du sieur de Champlain* (1613) and his later *Voyages* which are reprinted in the Champlain Society edition of his *Œuvres*, I,284–86, 293; III,353–63. The story that he discovered a moss-covered cross in the forest, subject of a poem by Whittier, happened on the Bay of Fundy.

Alfonce's descriptions are in his *La Cosmographie*, 1904 ed., p. 504, and *Voyages avantureux* (1559); Thevet's in his *Cosmographie universelle* (1575), II,1008. Lescarbot, the early historian of New France, said that there was "no truth" in Jean Alfonce, who "never saw the hundredth part of the places he described." That I believe to be too harsh; he certainly complemented our meager accounts of the Cartier-Roberval voyage. Lescarbot would more justly have called Thevet a congenital liar. The best account of Alfonce is still Winsor's in his *America*, IV,69–73. Jean Mallart's rhymed *routier* is in Harrisse, *Jean et Sebastien Cabot*, pp. 225–29. Dr. Jaime Cortesão in *Congresso do Mundo Portugês*, III, pt. i (1940), pp. 42–43, invents a Portuguese guard-post at Norumbega to protect the Gulf of St. Lawrence from an incursion by Columbus!

Some of the quartzite rocks on Mount Beatty and around Camden show an unusual amount of sparkling mica, which has fooled hundreds of people long after John Walker into believing they had struck gold or silver; there was a distinct gold and silver rush there in the 1880's. My classmate John W. Webber and Captain Leon O. Crockett of Camden, Maine, have sent me information about the local "gold mine"; and Frank W. Hatch of Castine tells me he owns a stock certificate of the "Castine Silver-Mining Company." I mention this to show that the Elizabethans like Walker and Frobisher were not more dumb about gold ore than Americans of a century ago.

There is no doubt that Gilbert's colonizing plans were directed to Norumbega and thwarted only by shipwreck. The shortest course from England to New England takes you to the Penobscot. Throughout the colonial period, English shipmasters aimed for the Grand Bank and Cape Race, sailed well off the shore of Nova Scotia to avoid Sable Island, and, once past Cape Sable, picked up the Mount Desert hills which guided them to the Penobscot, unless they were destined for Boston. In that case their next landmark was Mt. Agamenticus near York, Maine.

THE NEWFOUNDLAND AND GULF FISHERIES

Charles de La Morandière, *Histoire de la pêche française de la morue dans l'Amérique septentrionale*, I (Paris, 1962), has replaced every earlier work, even H. P. Biggar, *The Early Trading Companies of New France* (Toronto, 1901), where, fifty years ago, I learned the relation between fishing and fur trading and the distinction between wet and dry fishing. The description of processes in D. W. Prowse, *History of Newfoundland* and Adolphe Bellet, *La Grande Pêche de la morue à terre-neuve* (1902), pp. 64–73, apply only to the eighteenth century; but owing to the conservatism of fishermen, they may probably answer for earlier centuries. I have not found a single description of how the earliest English did it; but in our times "making fish," as the Maine people call curing cod, haddock, and pollock in the sun, is simple enough. My sailing master Enos Verge and I used to do it with great pleasure and success in the days before the draggers had ruined the coastal fisheries of Maine. You simply soak the gutted, split, and washed fish in brine for two or three days, slack-salt them, and spread them on home-made flakes to be cured in the sun, covering them in foggy weather, rain, and at night. A deluxe variant, called dun fish because the flesh of the fish so treated acquired a golden-brown color, I confess never to have practised; you cured big split cod in a manure pile. "Dunning" gave the fish a delicious ripe, rich flavor, which delighted the gourmets before they learned about the process. It could also be done more delicately by piling the split fish in a dark building and covering them with eel-grass and salt hay; or, as old men have told me, simply shoving the fish into their hay-mow, where they matured like bottles of wine in a cellar and could be pulled out by the tail when wanted. Dun fish, a specialty of the Isles of Shoals (which used the eel-grass and salt-hay method, cow manure being in short supply), sold for a guinea a quintal when ordinary stockfish was worth less than half a guinea, says W. D. Williamson in his *History of Maine* (1832), p. 24. And there is a tradition that the kings of Spain in the eighteenth century insisted on an Isles of Shoals dunfish for their Good Friday dinner.

The Act of Parliament of 1563 declaring Wednesday and Saturday to be fish days, in order to help the fisheries, is quoted from Hakluyt's *Discourse Concerning Westerne Planting*. That tradition endured. A Saturday salt fish dinner was a regular institution in New England Protestant households when I was a boy. But few Yankee housewives learned to cook salt cod deliciously as the Portuguese did, and still do.

Hakluyt (Everyman ed., VI, 91–114) has several narratives of walrus-hunting voyages to Ramea (the Magdalens). Comparison of walrus tusks with the unicorn horn is significant; the unicorn's horn had been a reputed aphrodisiac for centuries, hence the search for a substitute. Cf. also Frobisher's valuable narwhal horn, below. All other horns have been replaced in the Far East by the rhinoceros horn, and the demand in China today is so great that the rhino is threatened with extinction.

The quotation "With ships . . ." is from Sonnet xxxiv of Wordsworth, *Miscellaneous Sonnets*.

Since the Beothuk were forest people, living largely on game and river salmon and visiting the coast only to kill the great auk, almost all European trading for fur was done in the Gulf of St. Lawrence with Huron, Micmac, and Montagnais, and the bulk of it by the French.

H. A. Innis, "Rise and Fall of the Spanish Fishery in Newfoundland," in Royal Society of Canada *Transactions*, 3rd ser., XXV (1931), 50–70, is of prime importance. He says nothing of the Portuguese fisheries. Since Philip II took over Portugal in 1580, they probably followed the fate of the Spaniards; and it may be significant that Portugal did not even protest against Gilbert's taking possession of her old *Tiera de Baccalaos* in 1583. Innis makes a suggestive comparison between the results of a rigid central control of her fisheries by Spain, and those of Anglo-French laissez-faire: "The strong political power contributed to the decline of the fishery and suggested a striking contrast to the strength of economic power in England and in New England. The British Empire became possible with the overriding of political power by economic power, but Spain, as illustrated in the fishery, was limited by the overwhelming strength of political control." By mid-seventeenth-century, Yankee fishermen were supplying Spain with their best grades of codfish, caught and cured in North America.

Flake and tilt. Flake comes from the medieval word for a wattled hurdle, *Tilt* from the flimsy cabins on "tilt-boats," the water taxis of the Thames.

LÉRI, LA ROCHE, AND SABLE ISLAND

Francis Parkman wrote the classic account of this short-lived enterprise in his *Pioneers of France*, Part II, chap. ii; but more material has since been found; Gustave Lanctot, *L'Établissement . . . à l'Ile du Sable* (Ottawa, 1933; Marcel Trudel, *Histoire de la Nouvelle France*, I (1963), 228–35, with map of the island. Ch.-A. Julien, *Voyages de découverte* (1948), 78–79, mistakenly identifies Ile de Sable with the Magdalen group. Baron de Léri is not to be confused with Jean de Léry, one of the French discoverers of Brazil. For a copy of D. Johnson's map of the wrecks on Sable Island I am indebted to Mr. Kenneth Tripp.

"ADMIRAL," "ADVENTURER," AND JOHN DEE

In Tudor and Stuart England, "Admiral" generally meant the flagship of a fleet, and "Vice Admiral" and "Rear Admiral" meant the two ships next in seniority. But all three terms were occasionally applied to the respective commanders of these ships. The Lord High Admiral of England, however, was always "the Admiral."

"Adventurer" in the same era meant a capitalist, an investor, not one who sailed the ocean. Alfred Noyes's line in his *Tales of the Mermaid Tavern*, "marchaunt adventurers chanting at the windlass," is an anomaly; merchant adventurers stayed comfortably shore and left the sailing to their paid hands.

Dee's phrase "British Empire" is in a memoir on navigation dedicated to Sir Christopher Hatton in 1577; R. P. Bishop in *Geographical Journal*, LXXII (1928), 240. The best account of Dee is still that of Isaac D'Israeli, "Dizzy's" father, entitled "The Occult Philosopher, Dr. Dee"; it is in *Amenities of Literature*, II, 216–37, of the Paris, 1842 edition.

✳ XV ✳
Queen Elizabeth and
her Master Mariners

The glittering fleece that he doth bring, in value sure is more
Than Jason's was, or Alcides fruite, whereof was made such store . . .
And bringes home treasure to his land, and doth enrich the same,
And courage gives to noble heartes, to seek for flight of fame.
THOMAS ELLIS'S POEM TO FROBISHER.

Gloriana

The age of Elizabeth, in which English genius burned brightly in almost every aspect of life, now reached its acme. Shakespeare's "happy
breed of men," living on a "precious stone set in the silver sea," awak-
ened to a feeling of exuberant life. They reached high achievement in
arts and letters, in music and in science, in exploration and warfare,
such as few people had attained since ancient Greece. This was an age
when the scholar, the divine, and the man of action were often one and
the same person; for the Elizabethans well knew that life is empty
without religion, that the tree of knowledge bears no fruit unless
rooted in love, and that learning purchased at the expense of life and
liberty is a sorry bargain. Man in those days was not ashamed to own
himself an animal, nor so base as to quench the divine spark that made
him something better; but above all he exulted in the fact that he was
a man, "What a piece of work is a man!" declaims Hamlet. "How
noble in reason! how infinite in faculty! in form, in moving, how express and admirable! in action how like an angel! in apprehension how
like a god! the beauty of the world! the paragon of animals!" Christopher Marlowe's Tamburlaine declares that Nature

Queen Elizabeth the First. From a portrait by an unknown artist. Courtesy of Trustees of National Maritime Museum, Greenwich.

Doth teach us all to have aspiring minds; .
Our souls, whose faculties can comprehend
` The wondrous architecture of the world,
And measure every wandering planet's course,
Still climbing after knowledge infinite,
And always moving as the restless spheres
Will us to wear ourselves and never rest.

Which is about what has happened to us in the present century.

Queen Elizabeth, in her forty-fifth year in 1578, had not lost her charm for men; and twenty years on the throne had taught her statecraft in the school of experience. She was excommunicated by the pope in 1570, and in *de facto* war even before the declared war with Spain, whose ambassador financed an unsuccessful plot to assassinate her. Elizabeth found security only in the hearts of her subjects. They rendered to their queen a love and loyalty that no English monarch had yet received or would receive for centuries to come. "Gloriana," as the poets named her, called the wisest men in the kingdom to her council, but she was wiser than some and shrewder than any. More than any European prince she encouraged with her patronage and supported from her privy purse the overseas voyages of her subjects. She had a "good liking" to all, not only Frobisher's, and showed her approval both of Drake's circumnavigation and of his despoiling a Spanish treasure ship by knighting him on the deck of the *Golden Hind* when he returned in November 1580. In this queen England found her identity.

All England in her reign was insecure. Unfriendly Scotland lay on her northern border; hostile Spain, Portugal, and often France confronted her on the Continent. She stood constantly on the verge of disaster at the hands of Spain, just as she has been twice in our times on the edge of bitter defeat at the hands of Germany; but then as now she came through gloriously. Everyone knew that once Spain got rid of Elizabeth, the fires of Smithfield would be relighted and the Reformed Religion stamped out in a series of St. Bartholomew massacres. Then as now, her first line of defense was the Royal Navy, with its merchant auxiliaries; ships and sailors were the main factors that enabled England to break through her encompassing enemies.

Elizabeth had a genius for compromise, but she remained uncompromisingly Protestant in religion, refusing offers of marriage from several Catholic princes. Her Protestantism enhanced the insecurity and isolation of her realm, but stimulated national pride. Englishmen now felt a spiritual urge to adventure, and expansion; it was their duty to see that American savages got the Gospel straight and pure, and that Protestant colonies were planted in the New World to counterbalance the overwhelming power of Spain.

Enter Gilbert and Frobisher

The English record of northern voyaging in 1575–1600 is a series of glorious failures which left experience as a foundation for the English colonies of the seventeenth century. With Martin Frobisher, in 1576 a thirty-seven-year-old mariner of abounding courage though with a shady past, English discovery comes full circle. Muscovy Company, Morocco, West Africa, West Indies, and now back to the Northwest Passage, the short cut to the Indies that inspired John Cabot. Neither then, nor for centuries, could the English get that concept out of their heads; and only when the objective was shifted from gold and spices to exploration was the goal finally reached in 1905, by a Norwegian, Roald Amundsen in *Gjøa*.

Mariners and cosmographers of at least four nations had been working on the Passage to Cathay idea for some eighty years, starting with John Cabot's first voyage. John Dee's German friend Gemma Frisius had produced a map calling the Passage *Fretum Trium Fratrum*. At the Pacific end, Spaniards produced a mythical Strait of Anian through North America to the Atlantic; Drake searched for it on his circumnavigation. Antonio Urdaneta, a Spanish friar, claimed to have sailed through it from west to east; and Humfry Gilbert adduced these "facts" and many more, in his *Discourse*, to prove that the passage existed and was practicable. Everybody said you could do it from east to west, but who would try? Martin Frobisher would, and did.

First, however, a word on Humfry Gilbert, born to a Devonshire family of substance in 1537. In a petition that he made to Elizabeth I in 1565, Humfry began, "Whereas of longe tyme, there hath bin nothinge saide or donne concerning the discoviringe of a passage by the Northe to go to Cataia, & all other east parts of the worlde," he wishes "to make tryall thereof" at his "owne costes & charges." He only asks for a monopoly of trade through the Passage for his lifetime, and a 25 per cent cut of the customs duties all goods brought through it to England. Anthony Jenkinson of the Muscovy Company, disillusioned with the Northeast Passage and impatient over the meager results of trade with Russia and Persia, joined Gilbert in petitioning the Queen for Northwest Passage privileges. Next year, during his leaves from fighting in Ireland, Sir Humfry wrote *A Discourse of a Discoverie for a New Passage to Cataia*. Although it was not printed for ten years, this tract made a great impact on English opinion. Gilbert threw in quotations from ancient and modern writers to show that "any man of our country that will give the attempt, may with small danger passe to Cataia . . . and all other places in the East, in much shorter time than either the Spaniard or the Portingale doth." His appended map (here reproduced) makes it deceptively easy: Choose a wide passage between "Baccalaos" and "Canada," and you enter an immense sea which will lead you by the fabled Strait of Anian to Quivira and the Sierra Nevada (known from the Spaniards), where you are on the edge of the Pacific and a short sail from Japan, China, and the Moluccas. Gorgeous prospects are painted of the rich commodities England could obtain by this route: "Gold, silver, precious stones, cloth of gold, silks . . . grocery wares"—which last, in that era, meant spices, sugar, raisins, and other foreign products.

In the matter of export, he holds out hope that the shortness of the passage will enable England to vend her products in the Far East far cheaper than the Spaniards can sell theirs. And he holds forth the possibility of settling the Strait with "such needie people of our Countrie, which now trouble the common welth, and through want here at home, are inforced to commit outragious offences, whereby they are dayly consumed with the Gallows." Gilbert concludes with a fine flourish: "That he is not worthie to live at all, that for feare, or daunger of death, shunneth his countrey service, and his own honour, seeing death is inevitable, and the fame of vertue immortall."

Gilbert's *Discourse* was published in 1576 as promotion literature for a company that had been formed to send Martin Frobisher to discover the Northwest Passage.

Frobisher, coeval with Humfry Gilbert, belonged to a very different breed. He was a dour Yorkshireman, not a jolly man of Devon; a professional sailor rather than a part-time writer and soldier; a man incapable of writing a good letter, but of speaking very expressively: on one occasion, we are told he "swore no smale oathes," including "God's wounds!" One of three children born to a family of country gentry in Pontefract, Yorkshire, near the end of 1539, he and his rela-

Martin Frobisher. From a portrait by an unknown artist, dated 1577.
Courtesy Bodleian Library, Oxford.

tives spelled the name some fifty different ways, but historians in desperation have settled on *Frobisher*. His father having died, his mother sent him at an early age to be raised by her brother Sir John York of London, a merchant adventurer in African voyages. Martin did not take to letters; all his life he spelled even more abominably than the nobility, and so phonetically that we may be sure he talked with a rough North Country accent. Sir John, observing that his nephew was a lad "of great spirit and bould courage and naturall hardnes of body," got him a berth on the almost completely fatal Wyndham expedition of 1553 to West Africa; Martin, aged fourteen, was one of the survivors. After fighting in Ireland, where he probably met Gilbert, he shipped on John Lok's African voyage of 1562. The captain left him as a hostage with the Portuguese, who imprisoned him at their Mina fortress for several months and then shipped him home. Apparently the lad did not enjoy this stretch in jail, as he next figures in a scheme to capture the Mina; and when that failed he became captain of a privateer which brought in both French and Spanish prizes. The first were legitimate since England was then at war with France, but the second got him into trouble, since the Queen was not yet ready to break with Spain. He then became a professional sea-rover, accepting commissions from French rebels and the Prince of Orange, or anyone, and for a time doing very well. But, on account of having seized a London merchant's cargo of wines, he enjoyed another short stretch in jail, this time in England. There are records of Frobisher's being involved in a dozen enterprises of questionable legality down to the year that he signed on for the series of voyages that made him famous.

The contemporary full-length portrait of Frobisher grasping a petronel or horse-pistol in his right hand suggests that he was not a person to be trifled with. For seamanship, courage, and experience, no man could have been better qualified than Frobisher for the voyages he now undertook; no earlier voyage of discovery was so well equipped, and few were so unfortunate.

Martin Frobisher's First Voyage, 1576

Martin had been dreaming of this for fifteen years, and he was now only thirty-seven years old. As shipmate George Best wrote of Frobisher, he was "persuaded of a new and nearer passage to Cataya, than by Cape d'buona Speranza, which the Portugallas yeerley use. He began first with himselfe to devise, and then with his friends to conferre, and layde a playne platte unto them, that that voyage was not onely possible by the Northwest, but also as he coulde prove, easie to bee performed."

And who were these friends? Advocates, of course, of the Northwest Passage—Sir Humfry Gilbert, merchant-shipowner Michael Lok, Stephen and William Borough, and, most important, the famous John Dee, who had brains, and Ambrose Dudley Earl of Warwick, who had money. The noble earl brought Frobisher's project to the notice of Lord Treasurer Burleigh; and it was he and Michael Lok who "perceavinge the corrage and knowinge the aptnes of Martine Furbusher" persuaded the Muscovy Company to relinquish their yet unused right to northwestern exploration, to a group of merchant adventurers of London. These included, principally, Michael Lok, Sir Thomas Gresham founder of the Royal Exchange, and two others who subscribed £100 each; five who put in £50 each, and a number who paid £25 each; total, £875. That proved to be not nearly enough, and Lok had to pay the balance, some £739. The same group organized the Company of Cathay for Frobisher's second voyage, but for the first they were only a partnership.

The task organization was as follows:—

Bark GABRIEL, 15–30 tuns,* Christopher Hall, master, specially built for this voyage at a cost of £152, including the pinnace. Crew of 18, including George Best.

Bark MICHAEL, 20–25 tuns, Owen Gryffyn, master, purchased all equipped for £120. Crew of 17.

Pinnace, unnamed, 7–10 tuns, 4 men.

The "tackeling" for all three cost £172 extra.

Nobody has yet found even a crude sketch of any vessel of Frobisher's three fleets. Both participants on this first voyage are described as "barks," then a generic name for a small three-masted ship under 100 tuns. At the highest estimate neither *Gabriel* nor *Michael* had the burthen of Cabot's *Mathew*, Verrazzano's *Dauphine*, or Cartier's *La*

---

* Where I give two figures for tunnage, they are from different sources and there are intermediate estimates too.

Grande Hermine. Neither had room on board for the indispensable pinnace, even if knocked down and stowed below. Frobisher's pinnace had to sail on her own bottom, and she did not sail far.

More impressive than the ships was the equipment. Some £ 100 was paid to Humfrey Cole, the leading instrument-maker of London, for nautical instruments and books. The literature included two works by André Thevet: his *Cosmographie universelle,* just out, and *Singularitez de la France antarctique;* and Medina's *Arte de Naviguar,* one of the best available treatises on navigation. Strangely enough, Frobisher did not carry William Bourne's more recent *Regiment of the Sea* (1574). Probably more for amusement than anything else, he had a copy of Sir John Mandeville's famous book of whoppers. Also, for good measure, a "great" English Bible. This was probably the "Bishop's Bible" of 1572, whose title page includes a portrait of the Queen, useful to show the natives. Navigational instruments on board were impressive in number and quality. They included a cross-staff (also called Jacob's staff, jackstaff, and balestila), an instrument for taking celestial altitudes recently brought by John Dee from the Netherlands; a "ring of brasse" (mariner's astrolabe), and a regular astrolabe; but no quadrant. The cross-staff was more efficient than the wooden quadrant with its plumb-bob hanging by a silken thread, but both continued to be made and used for centuries. George Best records that Polaris was so faint in the high northern latitudes that you could not catch it in the peep-holes of an astrolabe. They found meridional altitudes of the sun with the cross-staff the best means of determining latitude.

There were no fewer than twenty "compasses of divers sorts," and eighteen half-hour sand glasses. The other instruments included an *armilla tolomei* (armillary sphere); a *horologium geometricum,* a sundial adjustable to any latitude; a *compassum meridianum,* a compass with an attachment for recording the sun's shadow at high noon, thus determining the variation at that point; and a *holometrium geometricum,* a version of the French surveying instrument called *holometre.* John Dee spent many days in the spring of 1576 on board *Gabriel* and *Michael* instructing the pilots in navigation, and in the use of these instruments. It is difficult to see what use the armillary sphere and the holometer could have been to Frobisher; but the rest, with declination tables from Medina and a traverse board, certainly helped him to obtain his remarkably accurate latitudes.

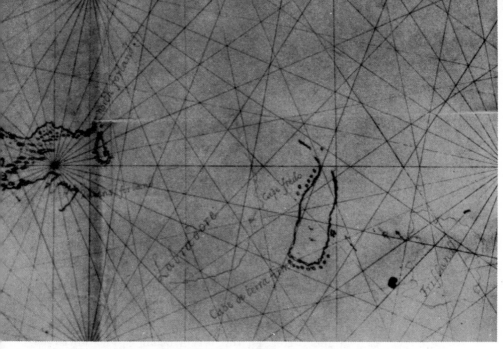

William Borough's Map furnished to Frobisher for his first voyage, and inspired by John Dee, who was responsible for the odd Greenland (western half only). The faint outlines and names were inserted by Frobisher on his first voyage, as well as the snub-nosed Greenland and Frobisher Bay. The arrows record his observations of compass variation. From the photo in Miller Christy, *Silver Map of the World* (1900), from the original in Hatfield House.

The most significant piece of Frobisher's equipment was a "carta of navigation . . . ruled playne," prepared especially for the expedition by William Borough the Muscovy Company commander. As one may see by our reproduction, Borough took a blank parchment, crossed and recrossed it with rhumb lines, dubbed in the British Isles and Norway (in the eastern half which we have not reproduced), and gave it to Frobisher to add what he found. He did just that, spotting in very faintly "Friesland," "Cape de terra firma" (at Cape Farewell), "Labradore," and "Cape fredo"; and, firmly, Greenland, his own strait, and Hall's Island. The arrows are Frobisher's record of compass variation; one of them, under his own strait, explains why it is oriented E-W instead of SE-NW. This is the kind of map-making which every explorer did, starting with Columbus; but Frobisher's is the only one prior to 1600 that is extant.

Frobisher's geographical contributions would have been more valuable had he not included in his sea-going library, and trusted, a copy of the Zeno brothers' fictitious voyages and map. These, as we have seen, made a sensation when printed at Venice a few years earlier. They even misled Mercator, who introduced Zeno features into his 1569 map, the best chart that Frobisher had on board. The English believed the Zeno map to be authentic, and it continued to befuddle northern navigators and cartographers for at least a century.

Besides books, charts, and instruments, we have a complete list of "furniture" for this voyage, including pots, pans, kettles, gridirons, and trivets for cooking over the open grates; grates rather than fire boxes, since Frobisher wisely brought "sea coal," guessing that firewood would be hard to come by in the north. The most expensive item, £13 18s., was for three hogsheads of aquavitae to give internal warmth when the external was wanting. For daily drink there were five tuns of beer which the Admiralty supplied for ten guineas. "Mr. Captayne Frobiser" paid an upholsterer £3 16s. 5d. for bedding. The other officers evidently supplied their own, and the common sailors, as usual, could expect no bed but a "soft plank," and brought their own blankets.

Frobisher was too sophisticated a navigator to depend on old-fashioned latitude sailing to attain his objective. Sailing 7 June 1576, he shaped a course well north of west. The ironical thing is that if he had followed the old system and taken his departure from northern Ireland at about 55° N, he could have followed the Labrador coast north for another five degrees, rounded Cape Chidley and entered Hudson Strait where no one had earlier penetrated. As it was, by deciding beforehand to hit the coast of America at around 63° N, he discovered only the dead-end Frobisher Bay; and when by accident he entered Hudson Strait on his third voyage, he had neither time nor inclination to press through.

Despite all these precautions and preparations, the fleet was fraught with misfortune from the start. It sailed 7 June from Ratcliff on the Thames, with a first-quarter moon. Off Deptford the pinnace collided with an anchored ship and had to be fitted with a new foresail and bowsprit. That done, they sailed past Greenwich, firing a royal salute, and in return receiving a gracious wave from Queen Elizabeth as she watched them from a window of the palace. She followed this up by sending "a Gentleman abbord of us, who declared that "her Majesty had good likings for our doings, and thanked us for it."

Foul winds forced the fleet to put in at Harwich and Yarmouth. Thence they had a good run to "St. Tronions" (St. Ninians) in the Shetlands, arrving 26 June. The wind now made up to a heavy gale that lasted eight days and proved too much for the pinnace. She disappeared, and her crew of four was never heard of again.

Christopher Hall's log indicates that *Gabriel* was a fast sailer, and that she enjoyed a prosperous wind from the Shetlands to Greenland. There were few four-hour watches in which she did not reel off nineteen or twenty knots; and in one, on 4 July, she made an average of seven. During the twenty-four hours between 7 June and noon on the 28th she made, by Hall's reckoning, 136 to 137 nautical miles before a "good gale," with forecourse, main topsail, and square spritsail set. On 1 July, "We had so much winde that we spooned * afore the sea Southwest 2 leagues." Hall's log indicates careful and skillful navigation, frequently working out compass variations from the new instrument.

On 11 July, in a full moon, the two ships sighted a land which Frobisher thought to be the mythical Friesland of that precious pair of fakers, the Zeno brothers. It was the east coast of Greenland. They could not even approach the shore because of pack-ice. Here, says Best, the master and men of bark *Michael*, "mistrusting the matter, conveyed themselves privilie away from him and returned home." *Michael* reached London 1 September where her cowardly master spread the lying excuse that *Gabriel* had been "cast awaye."

Far from it! Frobisher, after consulting his officers, decided to press on. Off or near Cape Farewell *Gabriel* ran into "an extreme storm which cast the ship flat on her syde"—on her beam ends as sailors usually express it. The water poured down an open hatchway, and she almost foundered; but "In this distress, when all the men in the ship had lost their courage, and did dispayre of lyfe," Frobisher "like himself with valiant courage" ran along the ship's exposed and almost horizontal topside, cutting or casting off lines and braces to relieve the pressure; he then ordered the mizzenmast to be cut away, and that

* To spoon, properly spoom, means to send your ship scudding before a heavy wind and sea. "Spoom her before the wind, you'll lose all else!" cries the jailer's daughter in John Fletcher's *Two Noble Kinsmen*, Act III, scene iv. Good advice!

righted her. But he forbade his men to sacrifice the mainmast, which they wanted to do.

This incident may well have inspired an outburst which George Chapman in one of his plays, *Byron's Conspiracy*, puts into the mouth of Chabot de Brion, Cartier's friend:

> Give me a spirit that on life's rough sea
> Loves t'have his sail filled with a lusty wind
> E'en till his sail-yards tremble, his masts crack,
> And his rapt ship runs on her side so low
> That she drinks water, and her keel plows air;
> There is no danger to the man that knows
> What life and death is: there's not any law
> Exceeds his knowledge; neither is it lawful
> That he should stoop to any other law.

Frobisher would certainly have agreed with the last four lines of this Elizabethan extravaganza; but like every other real sailor he preferred fair weather to foul, and calm seas to rough water. In his one recorded poem, Frobisher praises "An easie passage, void of loathsome toil." He never enjoyed such a one himself.

Gabriel, once righted, spoomed south before the wind until she could be pumped dry and a new mizzen rigged; she then turned westward and on 20 July, with a last-quarter moon, sighted what Christopher Hall first supposed to be Labrador, "a new land of marveilous great heith" with "a good store of Yce." This was Resolution Island off the southeastern cape of Baffin Island; Frobisher named it Queen Elizabeth's Foreland. Sailing north, he "descried another forlande, with a great gutte, bay, or passage, deviding as it were two mayne lands or continents asunder"—America and Asia. The Passage to Cathay! The ice parted and Frobisher "determined to make proof of this place, to see how farre that gutte had continuance . . . and so entred the same" on 21 July and sailed up it for some 150 miles. He persuaded himself that the high land to starboard was "the continente of Asia" and the equally lofty land crowned with glaciers on his port hand to be America. So he named that body of water "Frobishers Streytes, lyke as Magellanus at the Southwest ende of the Worlde, havying discovered the passage to the South Sea, . . . called the same straites Magellanes streightes."

Alas, Martin, this was no strait, and you were some thousands of miles from the South Sea; yet this dead-end sound or bight shall forever bear thy gallant name, as the real strait bears that of the noble Portuguese captain.

One calm day Frobisher had his men sound all around an iceberg, which fell apart while they were so engaged, making a terrifying noise "as if a great cliffe had fallen into the Sea." Returning to the mouth of the bay, they landed on an island which Frobisher named Hall after his competent sailing master Christopher Hall.* Here they began to see "sundry tokens" of people. Frobisher on 19 August climbed to the top of a hill and saw "a number of small things fleeting in the Sea a farre off, whyche he supposed to be Porposes, or Ceales, or some kinde of a strange fishe." They turned out to be Eskimo in kayaks. Elizabethans never called these natives Eskimo; that is a corruption of the Abnaki word for them, meaning "eaters of raw flesh," which the English and French colonists picked up in the next century. Frobisher and Davis referred to them simply as "the savages" or "the countrey people." Hall noted, "They be like to Tartars, with long blacke haire, broad faces, and flatte noses, and tawnie in colour, wearing Seale skinnes . . . the women are marked in the face with blewe streakes downe the cheekes, and round about the eies." That was, and still is, the fashionable beauty treatment for the females.

These Englishmen seem to have been as ill prepared as the Norsemen had been some five centuries earlier for dealing with the jolly but wily Eskimo. This group tried to cut Frobisher off from his boat, but he was too quick for them. By signs he invited a number on board, and cautiously bartered furs, fresh meat, and salmon for the usual trading truck. The natives showed that they were no strangers to European ships by doing gymnastic exercises in *Gabriel's* rigging, proving that they were "verie strong of theyr armes, and nimble of their bodies."

One Eskimo who came on board was engaged, by sign language, to pilot *Gabriel* through the supposed Strait by paddling ahead in his kayak. Frobisher sent him ashore in one of his boats with a crew of five, whom he strictly enjoined to land the man at a good distance from his fellows and return on board at once. The first part of this order they carried out literally; but "their wilfulnesse was such" that they rowed to a point crowded with natives, hoping, sailor-like, to do some private trading. No Englishman ever saw them again. Frobisher waited for

* Hall's is now Loks Land, the north foreland to Frobisher Bay; but the islet off Loks is still called Hall.

them several days, tried without success to get his hands on some natives to force an exchange, but they eluded him, laughing contemptuously. Gunshots and trumpet blasts availed naught; the Eskimo simply folded their sealskin tents and stole away to the interior of Baffin Island.

Stefansson, who should know, insists that these actions of the Eskimo prove that they had had experience dealing with Europeans. In all probability, some vessels of the Newfoundland fishing fleet had sailed this far north, or missed the Strait of Belle Isle and made Baffin Island, and from them the Eskimo had learned to keep out of their clutches and to move inland if the Europeans became too obnoxious.

Frobisher was now on a spot. "Being thus maymed," he "dispayred how to procede furder on his voyage toward Cathay." Presently a fleet of kayaks approached the ship. Clearing for action by stretching canvas cloths across the open waist, covering the chain plates where an enemy might climb on board with canvas nailed to the ship's side, and shotting every gun, Frobisher succeeded in frustrating the probably intended attack. Next, having learned that the Eskimo loved bells, "He wrought a pretty pollicie" (strategy) by ringing a small one to make known "that he would give him the same that would come and fetch it." As the Eskimo still held off, he rang a louder bell, which attracted to the ship's side in his kayak the native who had agreed to be his pilot. The Captain, being a man of resource and of prodigious strength, "caught holde on the man's hand, and with his other hand caught holde on his wrest; and suddenly by mayn force of strength plucked both the man and his light bote out of the sea into the ship in a tryse." Frobisher gave the Eskimo to understand that he would be set free in exchange for the five Englishmen; but, although the man was given a chance to communicate with his fellows, they did nothing.

The loss of these five left *Gabriel* with only thirteen men and boys, "so tyred and sik with laboure of their hard voyage," that Frobisher decided to return home forthwith. First, however, he took formal possession of the land. Then he sent most of his reduced company ashore in relays to pick up what they could, "living or dead, stocke or stone," as souvenirs or tokens of possession. One brought from Hall's Islet a piece of coal-black stone which, by its weight, seemed to be metallic. This little lump of marcasite or iron pyrites set off a chain reaction in London.

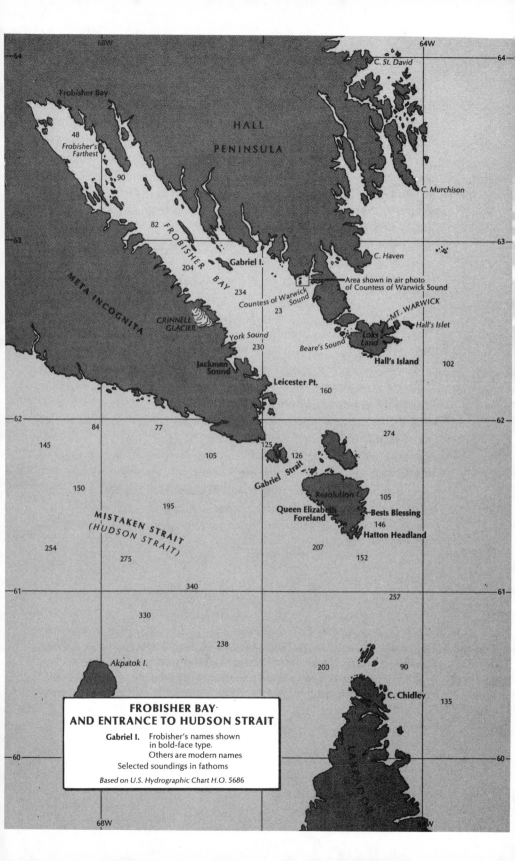

64W · · C. St. David

Frobisher Bay

HALL

48
Frobisher's
Farthest

90

82 F R O B I S H E R

204 · Gabriel I.

234

Countess of Warwick Sound

GRINNELL GLACIER

York Sound

230

Jackman Sound

Leicester Pt.

160

META INCOGNITA

B A Y

PENINSULA

C. Murchison

C. Haven

Area shown in air photo
of Countess of Warwick Sound

MT. WARWICK

Hall's Islet

Loks Land

Beare's Sound

Hall's Island

102

84   77   274

145

105   125   126

150   Gabriel Strait

195   Resolution I.

MISTAKEN STRAIT
(HUDSON STRAIT)

Queen Elizabeth
Foreland

105

Bests Blessing

146

Hatton Headland

254   275   207   152

340   257

330

238   90

Akpatok I.   200

C. Chidley   135

FROBISHER BAY
AND ENTRANCE TO HUDSON STRAIT

Gabriel I.   Frobisher's names shown
                 in bold-face type.
                 Others are modern names
           Selected soundings in fathoms

Based on U.S. Hydrographic Chart H.O. 5686

LABRADOR

68W

Departing 26 August with the new moon, and continually enduring "extreme storms of weather but the wynde still in their favour homewards," *Gabriel* made the Orkneys a month later, Harwich on 2 October 1576, and London on the 9th. There they were "joyfully received with the great admiration of the people, bringing with them their strange man and his bote, which was such a wonder onto the whole city and to the rest of the realm that heard of yt." The Queen herself named the mainland they had found, *Meta Incognita*, the unknown bourne. It is still so called today.

The Eskimo died shortly of a pulmonary complaint.

Frobisher, confident that he had "discovered the passage to the South Sea," now submitted to supposed experts the "peace of a blacke stone" from Hall's Islet. Two different assayers declared it to be marcasite, the old name for iron pyrites, which undoubtedly it was; but a third, an Italian named Agnello, insisted it was gold ore, and in three trials produced a speck of gold dust. To skeptical Michael Lok, inquiring how he found gold after the others reported none, Agnello remarked, *"Bisogna sapere adulare la natura"*—nature needs a little coaxing! Possibly the Italian had been bribed; possibly he had "salted" the stone himself, a practice not unknown in the nineteenth-century gold rushes; but iron pyrites, though well deserving the name "fool's gold," do sometimes contain small quantities of the precious metal. A German mineralogist named Jonas Schultz supported Agnello's opinion, the word went around that Frobisher had discovered a real gold mine, and a firm conviction to that effect, which is what all England dearly wished to believe, spread through the city and the court. Another Saguenay!

Bibliography and Notes

GENERALITIES

J. A. Williamson, *The Age of Drake;* the works of A. L. Rowse, especially *The English Spirit, The Expansion of Elizabethan England,* and *The Elizabethans and America;* D. B. Quinn's introduction to his Hakluyt Soc. ed., *Voyages and Colonising Enterprises of Sir Humphrey Gilbert* (1940); E. G. R. Taylor (ed.) *The Troublesome Voyage of Capt. Edward Fenton* (Hakluyt Soc., 1959); Boies Penrose, *Travel and Discovery in the Renaissance 1420–1620;* Ernest S. Dodge, *Northwest by Sea.*

SOURCES FOR FROBISHER'S VOYAGES

Although Justin Winsor in his *Narrative and Critical History*, III (1884), 97, disclaims any intention to give "a complete bibliography of the northwest explorations," his account that follows is the most comprehensive for those of Frobisher prior to Vilhjalmur Stefansson, *The Three Voyages of Martin Frobisher* (2 vols., London, 1938). Stefansson, with the help of Eloise M. Caskill, wrote a 130-page introduction which contains a good biography of Frobisher, and he reprints accurately the original narratives of the three voyages, together with sundry documents from other sources. The eminent bibliographer Wilberforce Eames compiled a Frobisher bibliography which appears in Stefansson, op. cit. II, 224–25, but this does not include secondary works which are listed in vol. I, pp. cxxix–cxxx. Nothing remains to be done about Martin Frobisher except to search the Spanish archives. As one on Philip II's "little list" of Englishmen to be hanged if he could lay hands on them, there should be data at Simancas or Seville on his "piratical" activities.

The original narratives are:

1. George Best, *A True Discourse of the late Voyages . . . Under the Conduct of Martin Frobisher, Generall* (London, 1578). Written after the third voyage. Reprinted with meticulous accuracy in Stefansson, I, 4–134. This first appeared in Hakluyt's *Voyages*, III (1600), 47–96; also in Everyman ed., V, 177–281.

2. Christopher Hall (master of *Gabriel*) "The First Voyage of M. Martin Frobisher," Stefansson, I, 149–54. First printed in Hakluyt's 1589 ed., II, 615–22. Hall's is the nearest we have to a bare ship's journal, and the more valuable for that. I have generally followed his dates when they differ from Best's and Lok's.

3. Michael Lok, Frobisher's principal promoter, compiled shortly after his return from the first voyage a manuscript called "East India by the Northwest," Stefansson, I, 157–66. First published by the Hakluyt Society in 1867.

Exasperatingly, four contemporary works on the voyages are known to exist only by their titles. These include a *Farewell to Master Frobisher* pub. by John Jugge (1577) and an anonymous *Thing Touching Fourboyser* of the same year.

Of biographies, William McFee, *The Life of Sir Martin Frobisher* (1928), written by an old sailor, is the only one worthy of the subject.

IMPROVEMENTS IN NAVIGATION

The best book on the new navigational instruments and methods is D. W. Waters, *The Art of Navigation in England in Elizabethan and Early Stuart Times* (Yale, 1958). Eva G. R. Taylor, *The Haven Finding Art* (London, 1956), also has details on instruments.

The list of instruments that Frobisher took on his first voyage is printed in Stefansson, *Voyages*, II, 77–78. These are identified in R. T. Gunther, "The Great Astrolabe and Other Scientific Instruments of Humphrey Cole," in *Archaeologia*, LXXVI (1927), 273–317, and Miller Christy, *The Silver Map of the World* (1900), App. A, pp. 47–49, and plate ix. Of these new instruments the most important was the cross-staff (Jacob's staff, jack-staff, or *balestila*) because it permitted a careful observer on a not-too-rolly ship to catch the altitude of a comparatively faint star like Polaris. For the formula of working out latitude from Polaris altitudes, see Chapter V, Notes, above. The more sophisticated cross-staffs (and people went on making them until 1800), had several cross-vanes to fit different altitudes of the celestial body, with an altitude scale for each on one of the four faces of the staff.

Hall's Journal, earliest detailed log of any northern voyage, and Best's and Sellman's narratives of later Frobisher voyages, enable us to check on their latitudes. Here is a table of them, culled from accounts of all three voyages:

	Frobisher	*Correct Latitude*
Gravesend	51°33′ N	51°27′N
Harwich	51°54′ N	51°55′ N
"St. Tronions" (St. Ninians)	59°46′ N	59°59′ N
"Fowlay" (Foula Island)	59°59′ N	60°07′ to 60°10′ N
"Friesland" (Greenland)	Hall 61°00′ N Best 60°30′ N	Cape Farewell is 59°45′ N; we don't know how far N of it Frobisher made land.
Sighted land, first voyage	62°02′ N	Entrance to Frobisher Bay is between 62° and 62°20′ N.
Hall's Islet	63°08′ N	62°30′ N
Due E of Queen's Foreland	61°40′ N	Resolution I extends from 61°18′ to 61°42′ N.

Comparing these with the table of Cartier's and Alfonce's latitudes in W. F. Ganong, *Crucial Maps*, p. 292, it will be seen that Frobisher was somewhat more accurate than they.

Sellman's statement (Stefansson, II, 59) that latitude 62°10′ proved they were *south* of the Queen's Foreland makes no sense. Possibly a printer's error for 61°10′.

The Borough Map, the earliest actual chart used by a navigator that has been preserved, is in Hatfield House, seat of the Marquess of Salisbury,

From Pedro de Medina *Regimento de Navigacion* (1964 reprint).

Shooting Polaris with cross-staff.

From Justin Winsor, *Narrative and Critical History of America*, II (1886).

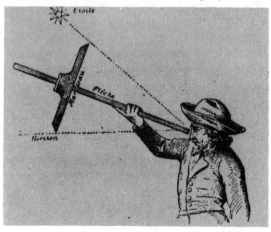

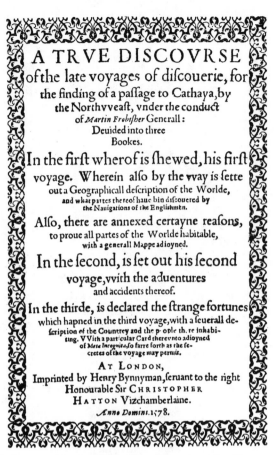

Title page of George Best's *True Discourse* (1578). Courtesy Harvard College Library.

descendant of Frobisher's backer Lord Burleigh. Reproduced in Stefansson, I, p. xcix. And (better) in Christy's *Silver Map*. Stefansson (I, cxiv) superimposes the Zeno map on a modern chart, and (II, 212) reproduces maps of 1664, 1675, 1728, and 1740 still showing the Strait in Greenland. See also Justin Winsor, *Narrative and Critical History*, III, 190. It is strange that Frobisher, despite having an instrument to measure compass variation, orients his "Streighte" almost due east and west; but he shows the variation by an arrow, and his depiction of the islands therein is more accurate than Hall's of 1865.

See also notes on navigation and navigational instruments to Chapter V above and Chapter XVIII below.

Sophus Ruge, *Fretum Anians* (Dresden, 1888), and J. G. Kohl, "Asia and America," American Antiquarian Society *Proceedings* for October 1911, pp. 284–338, really wrap it up. George E. Nunn, *Origin of the Strait of Anian Concept* (privately printed, 1929), is a brief summary of everything anybody wrote about the relation of Asia and America to 1700. He follows Ruge in believing that the name Anian comes from a Chinese province called *Ania* by Marco Polo. The Zalterius Map (1566) was the first to show the Strait of Anian. Search for this non-existent body of water went on almost as long as the one for the Northwest Passage; Russians were working on it in the eighteenth century. A Spanish character named De Fuentes or De Fonte claimed to have found it in 1640 and to have sailed through to Hudson Bay, where he encountered a vessel owned by "Señor" Gibbons of Boston, Mass.! Benjamin Franklin, of all people, fell for this hoax; see L. W. Labaree (ed.), *Papers of Benjamin Franklin*, X (New Haven, 1966), 85–100, with photo of De Fonte's map.

✳ XVI ✳
Frobisher's Second and Third Voyages

1577-1578

Second Voyage Begins

O Frobusher! thy bruit and name
    shall be enrold in bookes,
That whosoever after comes
    and on thy labour lookes,
Shall muse and marvell at thyne actes,
    and greatnesse of thy minde.
I say no more, least some affirme
    I fanne thy face with winde.
THOMAS CHURCHYARD, "A WELCOME-HOME TO
MASTER MARTIN FROBISHER" (1578)

Optimism about gold and the expectation that "Frobisher's Strait" really was a strait, reigned so high that the Captain's original backers now joined with others to form the Company of Cathay. By receiving a charter from the crown (17 March 1577), this company became a respectable joint stock corporation. Meeting in London, the stockholders elected Michael Lok governor for life, and Frobisher "High admiral of all seas and waters, countries, lands and isles, as well of Cathay as of all other countries and places of new discovery." The precedent was Columbus's appointment as Admiral of the Ocean Sea and of the Indies. Queen Elizabeth subscribed £1000, several others paid up to a total of £4275, and Lok levied a 20 per cent assessment on the stockholders. The crown furnished a fine tall ship, the *Aid*, and both *Gabriel* and the recreant *Michael* of the previous voyage were available. George Best gives us the task organization as follows:—

"Generall of the whole Company": MARTIN FROBISHER

Ship AID, 200 tuns, Christopher Hall, master; also on board, the General's deputy George Best. Complement: 115 to 120, "whereof 30 or more were Gentlemen and Souldyers, the rest sufficient and tall Saylers." Among the gentlemen were members of the Carew, Stafford, Lee, Kinnersley, and Brackenbury families, and Dionyse Settle, who wrote one of the two extant accounts of this voyage.

Bark GABRIEL, 15–30 tuns, Edward Fenton, captain; William Smyth, master. Complement: 10 mariners, 3 soldiers, and about 5 more.

Bark MICHAEL, 25 tuns, Gilbert Yorke, captain; James Beare, master, who doubled as fleet surgeon. Complement: 10 mariners, 2 soldiers, and about 4 more.

Thirty of the ships' companies were miners, refiners, and other appropriate civilians. Also there were six criminals to be set ashore on "Friesland" (Greenland) to civilize the natives (!). Provisions included hardtack, flour, pickled beef and pork, dried peas and codfish, butter, cheese, oatmeal, rice, honey, "Sallet oyl," and vinegar. For drink, eighty tuns of beer (calculated to give every man one gallon a day for six months) and five tuns of sack and malmsey for the officers. For clothing there was a slop-chest of "wollinge clothe for jirkens, breche and hose, canvas and lynnenge clothe for dublets and sherts." The Company intended its men to eat hearty and dress warm. On the third voyage we find that some mariners owned five changes of clothing.

Among those on board *Aid* was a young man named John White, a member of the Painter-Stainers' Company of London, who would win posthumous fame centuries later as the artist of the first Virginia colony. Owing to him we have the first European pictures of the Eskimo.

Frobisher's orders from the Company of Cathay were, (1) to set his sappers and miners to work collecting "gold ore" on Hall's Island or elsewhere; (2), in one of the barks, to sail no more than 100 leagues up his "Strait," but not so long as to jeopardize returning home the same year; (3) to leave some of his company to winter on the Strait, with a pinnace and supplies; and (4) if no more promising ore were forthcoming, to send the flagship home and go on to China with the two barks.

The inventory of flagship *Aid*, which has survived in the Public Record Office, includes enough detail to enable a fairly accurate model to be constructed—if only someone would do it! Built for the Royal Navy prior to 1571, she was bought by the Company "of the Queenes

Majestie" in 1577 especially for Frobisher's second voyage. Stepping three masts and a bowsprit, she flew the St. George ensign (red cross on white field with arms of England at the crossing). She carried a square spritsail on bowsprit, spread lower courses and topsails on the foremast and mainmast, and a lateen mizzen; a mizzen topmast also is mentioned, on a short yard. All her blocks (still called "pulleys") were brass-bound with brass sheaves. Her "skyffe" shipped twelve oars and mounted Rotherhithe ironwork; her longboat, which she probably towed, had its own mast, sail, and windlass. On *Aid*'s deck were mounted a main capstan with iron "collor and paull" and four bars, and a fore capstan with two bars. She carried four great anchors complete with stoppers and shank painters, and three ordinary ones, and their cables were of twelve-inch hemp. There were many spare rodes and hawsers down to five-inch. The only items mentioned below deck are "a bed sted and a table in the captaines cabbine, the table broken."

Of brass ordnance, *Aid* mounted five minions and falcons; of cast-iron guns, 14 sacres, minions, and falcons. She was well furnished with iron and stone balls, crossbar shot and chain shot; and, in addition, whole racks and chests of calivers, long bows and arrows, partisans, pikes, and arrows tipped with "wilde fyer," presumably like Cartier's fire lances. Those who took the flagship's inventory judged her to be worth £838 16s. 8d., including the equipment.

The fleet weighed at Blackwall, London, 25 May 1577 with a first-quarter moon. It called at Harwich on the 28th to take on "certayne victualles," and tarried until the 30th. Frobisher there received orders from the Privy Council reminding him that his official complement, 120 persons, had been exceeded; he was reported to have shipped some fifty more. Tongue in cheek, the General put on the beach the six criminals designated to civilize Greenland, and enough other "proper men, whych with unwilling myndes departed," to bring the number down to 120. Hearing that the Queen was staying at the Essex seat of his supporter Ambrose Dudley, Earl of Warwick, Frobisher had the tact to call on her "with diverse resolute and forward gentlemen . . . to take their leaves." "Kissing her highness's hands" and receiving her "gracious countenance & comfortable words," they "departed towardes their charge." If anything were needed to increase Frobisher's resolution, this royal interview did. Whatever happened, he could not let his Queen down.

The fleet next called at the Orkneys on 7 June and traded old shoes and junk rope with the natives for fresh provisions. Departing with "a merrie winde by night," and a last-quarter moon, they steered west-northwest and soon lost sight of land. The wind turned scant and forced them to beat, or, as Best called it, to "traverse on the Seas." They spoke three sail of fishermen returning from Iceland and sent letters home by them. Twenty-six days of beating or lying-to followed, and they saw "many monsterous Fishe and strange Fowls." Then, "God favoured us with more prosperous windes," and a full moon on the last day of June. *Michael*, in the lead on 4 July, fired a gun and struck topsails as a signal she had sighted land. At 10 p.m. they "made the land perfect, and knew it to be Freeseland"; the latitude they found to be 60°30'. Greenland again, of course. Men on the becalmed flagship caught a "hollibut" big enough to feed all hands and to make some sick who overate. Twice Frobisher tried to land but could not get through the ice floes, and "having spent 4 days & nights sailing alongst this land, finding the coast subject to such bitter cold & continuall mistes," he decided to bear away for his own Strait. En route the fleet had to "lay a-hull" a couple of days, and *Michael* broke her "steerage" and lost a topmast. On 17 July, with a new moon, they made the North Foreland "otherwise called Halles Iland, and also the small Iland bearing the name of the saide Hall, whence the Ore was taken uppe." The latitude, says Best, was 62°30' N; correct. "Happie landfall" indeed!

Frobisher Bay Again

Frobisher and "goldfiners" landed on Hall's next day to look for more gold ore. They found a bit of marcasite no bigger than a nut, but collected a quantity of "Egges, Fowle, and a yong Seale." The flagship, in the meantime, spent most of the night dodging "monstrous and huge yce, comparable to great mountaines." They never could have escaped, wrote Dionyse Settle in his account of this voyage, "If God . . . had not provided for this Our extremitie a sufficient remedie, through the light of the night whereby wee might well discerne to flee from such imminent dangers, which we avoided" by tacking fourteen times in one four-hour watch. He credits master's mate Charles Jackman the temporary commander, and pilot Andrew Dyer, "men expert both in navigation, and other good qualities." Frobisher returned on board 19

Little Hall's Island, "Whence the Ore was taken uppe." Photo taken
31 August 1959 from 30,000 feet elevation. The white objects off shore
are icebergs. Courtesy Air Photo Division, Canadian Government.

July 1577 "with good newes of great riches . . . in the bowels of
those barren mountains." This brought "a sudden mutation" from
black despair to extravagant delight. "We were all wrapt with joy,
forgetting both where we were, and what we had suffered." The northwest wind having blown the icebergs out to sea, disclosed "a large
entrance into the streight." In they sailed, and on the 20 July "founde
out a faire Harborough for the shippe and barkes to ride in and named
it after our Master's mate Jackman's Sound." This was on the southwest
shore of Frobisher's Strait, which the Queen had named Meta Incognita.
Gabriel nipped in behind Queen's Foreland, finding a strait that is still
named after her. Frobisher still thought the eastern shore, part of
Baffin Island, to be a far-thrusting cape of Asia.

The "Generall" now held a special service of thanksgiving for their safe arrival, praying "that by our Christian studie and endeavor, those barbarous people trained up in Paganrie and infidelitie, might be reduced to the knowledge of true religion, and to the hope of salvation in Christ our Redeemer." * He exhorted the ships' companies to obey

* In the silly controversy whether Virginia or Plymouth had the "first Thanksgiving," nobody has mentioned this, much the earliest English thanksgiving service on American soil that has been recorded.

Jackman Sound, Frobisher Bay, and part of Grinnell Glacier. Photo taken 2 September 1959 from elevation of 30,000 feet. Courtesy Air Photo Division, Canadian Government.

Part of Hall's Island (now Loks Land). Photo from elevation of 30,000 feet, 31 August 1959. "Mount Warwick," which Frobisher climbed and named, is almost in the middle. Courtesy Air Photo Division, Canadian Government.

Fenton, Yorke, and Best while he landed with Settle and some forty gentlemen and soldiers on the big Hall's Island, to explore and take possession of the supposed continent of Asia. The company erected "a Columne or Crosse of stones" on the highest hill of this island, planted an ensign, named the hill Mount Warwick after their noble patron, and, with noise of trumpet and "certain prayers" said on their knees, took possession in the name of the mighty princess Elizabeth, Queen of England, France and Ireland, Defender of the Faith.

After they had come down the hill, some Eskimo appeared and made signs of friendship; and each side sent two men to do a limited trade in "pinnes and pointes and such trifles." Frobisher and his partner, hoping to secure hostages to trade for the five sailors captured on the previous voyage, tried to grab two "salvagies," but the maneuver failed; the greasy Eskimo slipped out of their clutches, recovered their weapons, and chased the two Englishmen ignominiously back to their boat, Frobisher suffering an arrow wound in the buttock. One of his boatmen, Nicholas Conger, "being a Cornishman, and a good wrastler," grappled with an Eskimo and showed him "such a Cornishe tricke, that he made his sides ake . . . for a moneth after." All had to spend the night in the open, "keeping verie good watche and warde . . . upon harde cliffes of Snowe and Ice, both wet, cold and uncomfortable."

This was not the best way to "allure them to familiaritie" or get word of the five men abandoned the year before; nor did the next episode help. The landing force, rowing around the opposite side of Hall's Island, suddenly came upon a group of Eskimo who "fiercely assaulted our men with their bowes and arrows." The Englishmen replied with arquebuses whose reports so terrified the natives that they either fled to the hills or leaped off the rocks into the sea. We are fortunate to have a colored sketch of this scene, made on the spot by John White, and which we have used as frontispiece. In a ship's longboat containing seven or eight men, two are shooting at three Eskimo on a cliff, who reply with bows and arrows; one Englishman, an officer, is trying to fend off arrows with sword and target. The scenery is correct for Frobisher Bay, and the royal ensign on the boat is right for a Queen's ship. Note in the background a fleet of kayaks, angry natives, and sealskin tents; in the foreground, ice floes, and space filled up by depicting an Eskimo in his kayak.

Frobisher's men landed and managed to capture two women. One was so old and ugly that the sailors took her to be a witch, "had her buskins plucked off, to see if she were cloven footed." Disappointingly she had normal feet, so they let her go. The other, a young mother carrying a baby, they kept and brought on board. The Englishmen

John White's painting of the Eskimo mother and baby captured by Frobisher in 1577. Courtesy British Museum.

then "made a spoyle" of the Eskimo tents, where they found old clothes which must have belonged to the five missing men.

The rest of their stay in Frobisher's Strait that summer was devoted to two objects: recovering the five lost sailors and loading ore. A party of Eskimo conveyed by signs that three missing Englishmen were living up-country and wished to communicate. Frobisher gave them pen, ink, and paper to deliver to his shipmates, with a letter remarkable for its Biblical diction and patent sincerity:

> In the name of God in whom we all beleve, who, I trust, hath preserved your bodyes and souls amongst these Infidels, I commend me unto you. I will be glad to seeke by all meanes

you can devise, for your deliverance, eyther with force, or with any commodities within my Shippes, whiche I will not spare for your sakes, or anything else I can doe for you. I have aboord, of theyrs, a Man, a Woman, and a Childe, which I am contented to delyver for you, but the man which I carried away from hence the last yeare, is dead in ENGLAND. More- over you may declare unto them, that if they deliver you not, I wyll not leave a manne alive in their Countrey. And thus, if one of you can come to speake with me, they shall have eyther the Man, Woman, or Childe in pawne for you. And thus unto God whom I trust you do serve, in hast I leave you, and to him we will dayly pray for you. This Tuesdaye morning the seaventh of August. Anno. 1577.

Yours to the uttermost of my power,
MARTIN FROBISHER.

John White's painting of the Eskimo captured by Frobisher in 1577. Courtesy British Museum.

I have sente you by these bearers, Penne, Incke, and Paper,
to write back unto me agayne, if personally you can not come
to certifye me of your estate.

No word, no reply came, and the mystery of the Englishmen's fate
lay hidden for nigh three centuries. Around 1862 it was solved when
an American explorer named Charles F. Hall stayed for two years in
Frobisher Bay, mingling with the Eskimo and learning their language.
An ancient woman named Ookijoxy Ninoo, and other old people, told
him this story. Long, long ago, *kodlunas* (white men) came to their
country in three successive years; first year two ships, second year
three ships, third year a great many ships (Frobisher's three visits, almost exactly). Five Englishmen, captured by the Innuit (as these
Eskimo called themselves), went to the island now called Kodlunarn
(White Men's Island), dug a sloping trench in the rock close to the
water's edge, built a boat with timber that Frobisher had left behind,
and sailed away, only to perish from the cold.

What an amazing example of the reliability of oral tradition among
primitive, unlettered people! We can now see what happened. The
Eskimo kept the five Englishmen prisoner until after Frobisher's final
departure in 1578. Then, either because they had no further use for
them, or from feelings of compassion, the hosts turned them loose. The
wretched men went to the island where Frobisher had abandoned
plenty of materials, built a boat, put to sea, and perished.

Hall, and in 1943 my late friend Dr. Alexander Forbes, visited Kodlunarn Island and found trenches where Frobisher dug out "ore" on
his third voyage, the dock they excavated to help loading, and where
the five Englishmen probably built their boat, and foundations of the
Englishmen's houses, together with fragments of brick, glass, and iron.
On our reproduction of Forbes's air photograph, the rectangular loading dock is conspicuous on the east side facing the mainland, and off it
the fleet anchored. West of the dock can be seen one of the deeper
trenches where they excavated "ore," and, in the center of the island,
a little round thing marks the stone foundations of the house that Frobisher built on his next voyage.

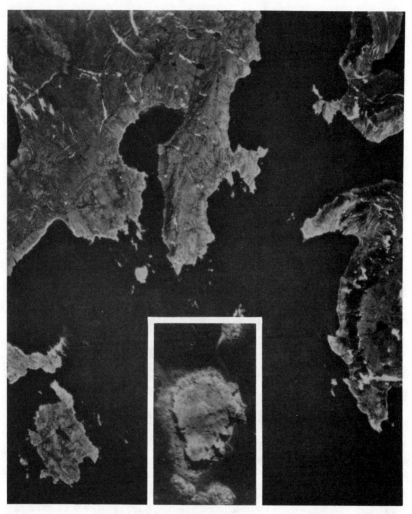

Countess of Warwick Sound. Photo from 30,000 feet elevation, 4 August 1959. Courtesy Air Photo Division, Canadian Government. Insert: Low-altitude photo of Kodlunarn Island (800 feet long), taken by Alexander Forbes in 1943.

Conclusion of Second Voyage

A find that aroused almost as much interest as the female captive was that of a dead narwhal on the shore. George Best, who made a sketch of it, called it a sea unicorn, and described it as about twelve feet long, "havyng a horne of two yardes long, growing out of the snoute or nostrels . . . wreathed and strayte, like in fashion to a Taper made of waxe." The horn they took home and presented to the Queen, who kept it in her wardrobe, handy for bringing out to exhibit "as a Jewel," and to stimulate the art of bawdy conversation that she is said to have loved.

"Having now got a woman captive for the comforte of our man," wrote Best, the two were brought together, surrounded by a circle of Englishmen curious to see what would happen. The Eskimo behaved with exemplary dignity and, although forced to bunk together on the voyage home, "did never use as man and wife." Best marveled at their modesty: "The man would never shift himselfe, except he had first caused the woman to depart out of his Cabin, and they both were most shamefast, least anye of their privie parts should bee discovered, eyther of themselves, or any other body."

John White depicted the Eskimo man twice, and the woman with her baby peeking out of her hood. Both are done in watercolor and in great detail, showing the hair on the sealskin, exquisite needlework on jacket, boots and breeches, and narrow fur edgings. Since these Eskimo had worked out a way of life suited to their boreal environment and available food, their fashions did not change; not only Hall but Amundsen in 1905 found them wearing the same styles as those of 1577, including the dorsal flap to the jacket—a very useful appendage when you had to sit on ice or frozen ground.

Having secured these hostages, Frobisher concentrated on obtaining a quantity of "ore" to take home. On an island (the modern Kodlunarn) which he named *Anne Warwick* after the Countess, he dug out some 200 tons of worthless rock and stowed it in the three ships. Other interchanges with the "craftie villains" led to nothing, but the captured Eskimo showed them how to harness the dogs to sleds. Settle concluded that here "there is nothing fitte, or profitable for the use of man" except the supposed minerals "couched within the bowels of the earth."

George Best's narwhal. From his *True Discourse.* Courtesy Harvard College Library.

By 21 August, when the holds of the three ships were crammed with supposed gold ore, and a first-quarter moon hung in the sky, it seemed "good time to leave." Nature gave warning by surrounding the ships with fresh ice every night. Next day "We plucked downe oure tentes" on Anne Warwick Island, and after lighting bonfires, marching with ensigns displayed, and firing a volley in honor of the Countess, the company departed for home. They took meridional latitude sights daily from the sun with the cross-staff, says Best; and of Polaris too.

On 17 September, approaching England cautiously with frequent casts of the lead, and lighted by a first-quarter moon, the fleet made Lands End. The flagship put in at Padstowe roads in Cornwall, then at Milford Haven in Wales, and finally at Bristol. *Gabriel,* too, made Bristol, whilst *Michael* sailed northabout to Yarmouth. And so ended Frobisher's second voyage to his "Streightes" and the Meta Incognita.

At Bristol the three Eskimo made a great sensation; a local chronicler described how the man put on an exhibition shoot in the Back (the upper harbor), carrying his kayak to the shore and hitting ducks on the wing with his spear.

Fortunately, there happened to be living at Bristol, Lucas de Heere, a refugee artist from the Low Countries. He produced, for the French edition of Dionyse Settle's account of Frobisher's second voyage, the picture that we have reproduced. The Eskimo hunter, like those of other primitive tribes, used a throwing-stick to enhance the speed and deadliness of his spear. He is shown both bringing his kayak to the shore and using this weapon; a dead duck lies in the water, and other fowl are trying to escape. The woman and her baby are interested observers. In the background, instead of Bristol, De Heere has depicted what he supposed to be a native Eskimo scene, complete with dog har-

Lucas de Heere's drawing of the Eskimo's demonstration at Bristol, with a native background. Note the spearthrower, the kayaks, the dogsled, and the sealskin tent. From Dyonyse Settle's *True Report* (1577). Courtesy British Museum.

nessed to sled. He exhibits the usual European inability to depict Indian or Eskimo faces correctly; John White was the exception.

Although the English catered to these captives by feeding them raw meat and not trying to replace their sealskin clothing with wool, they died within a month.

Part of the supposed "ewer" (as the English often spelled "ore") was landed at Bristol, where Jonas Schultz built a "furnace" to smelt it next the house of Sir William Winter, an investor in this voyage to the tune of £500. The other part was smelted at Dartford on the Thames where a rival German "expert," known as "Doctor" Burcot or Burchard, took charge. This plant cost the Company of Cathay £1105.

On one occasion, it is said, Frobisher became so furious with Jonas's double-talk that he pulled a dagger on him when attending the Bristol furnace "naked," but no harm was done.

Third Voyage

The second voyage cost the Cathay Company some £6410; and as only £2500 had been subscribed before sailing, the 200 tons of "ore" brought home just *had* to be pay dirt. Remembering how the Paris assayers had shown up Cartier's worthless gold and diamonds thirty-five years earlier, one wonders whether the two Germans employed by the Company were corrupt or just plain stupid. Their final estimate accepted by the Cathay Company was this: one ton of Meta Incognita ore yielded gold worth £7 15s., and silver valued at £16, at a cost of £10 for refining. Since this meant a profit of £5 per ton, the Cathay Company cheerfully accepted it as correct and proceeded to organize an ambitious third voyage for 1578. Sixteen persons subscribed £6952 10s. to finance it, the Queen giving more than half. The Warwicks stuck by Frobisher, and the names of Knollys, Suffolk, Pembroke, Sydney, and Walsingham appear on the list; all subscribers except Michael Lok were of the nobility and gentry. Canny merchants kept "hands off."

Mariners and soldiers were paid 10s. per month; officers as high as £6 13s. 4d.

The task organization, from Best and other sources, was as follows:

CAPTAIN GENERAL: MARTIN FROBISHER

AID: "Admirall" (flagship), 200 tuns, Frobisher, captain; Charles Jackman, master.

THOMAS ALLEN (vice admiral), Gilbert Yorke, captain; one Gibbes, master; Robert Davis, master's mate; Christopher Hall, chief pilot.

JUDITH, rear admiral, Frobisher's lieutenant general, Edward Fenton, captain

ANNE FRANCES, George Best, captain; John Gray, master

HOPEWELL, Henry Carew, captain; Andrew Dyer, master

BEARE of Leicester, property of Michael Lok, Richard Philpot, captain

THOMAS of Ipswich, William Tanfield, captain; Cox, master

EMANUELL of Exeter (also called ARANELL or ARMONELL), Courtney, captain

FRANCES of Fowey, Moyles, captain

Buss MOONE of Fowey, Upcot, captain; John Lakes, master

Buss EMMANUELL of Bridgewater, commonly called "The Buss of Bridgewater," Newton, captain; James Leech, master

SALAMON or SALAMANDER of Weymouth, Thomas (or Hugh) Randall, captain

Bark DENNIS or DIONYSE, Kendall, captain

Bark GABRIEL, Edward Harvey, captain; William Smyth, master

Bark MICHAEL, Kinnersley, captain

Frobisher's instructions from the Company ordered him to depart not later than 1 May. He may call at "Fryzeland" en route to Countess of Warwick's Sound. He will put men to work on the Countess's island, look for other mines and minerals and search for the lost men with his two barks. He must keep a written record of all metal, ore, etc. removed from the country and pack them "in apte and peculiar boxes." When he has accumulated 800 or more tons, the fleet may sail for home. But he is to provide for forty able seamen, shipwrights, and carpenters, thirty soldiers, and thirty "pyoners with sufficient vittalle for 18 monthes" to be left behind at Meta Incognita under Captain Fenton, together with ship *Judith* and the two old barks. Absolutely nothing is said about pursuing the northern waters further west; in their greed for gold, the adventurers seem to have forgotten about that passage to Cathay. Miners were requisitioned from Cornish towns which, as few real miners accepted, impressed anyone they could lay hands on. Poor devils, they had a rough time at sea and ashore, and many died before returning home.

Now in command of a fleet of fifteen sail, Frobisher felt obliged to issue a set of general orders: No swearing, dice, card-playing, or filthy communications to be allowed; serve God twice daily "with the ordinary service" according to the Church of England. The Admiral to lead the fleet, and none to part further than a mile from her. Each ship to speak the Admiral every evening between seven and eight o'clock to receive night orders from chief pilot Hall. If weather grows thick or wind contrary, forcing *Aid* to tack or lay at hull, she shall fire one or two guns, and the *Thomas Allen* and *Judith* must reply in kind. When sailing in a fog, every ship to "keepe a reasonable noyse with Trumpet, Drumme or otherwise." If any ship "lose company by force of weather," she must rendezvous at "Freeseland" or the Strait. If attacked by an enemy, four designated ships "shall attend upon" *Aid* and *Thomas Allen*.

Frobisher obviously knew how to conduct a fleet, although he asked too much to expect a sailing vessel to keep station within a mile. Even steamships found that difficult in World War II convoys.

In November 1577 Francis Drake's fleet, including the *Golden Hind* in which he circumnavigated the globe, sailed from Plymouth. The court and the public expected much less of Drake than they did of Frobisher, who must later have wished that he had shipped with his great contemporary. That opportunity would come later.

Frobisher's fleet, collected from ports as far apart as Yarmouth and Bristol, assembled at Harwich, sailed 31 May 1578 with a last-quarter moon and shaped a course through the English Channel. Just before taking their departure from that favorite jumping-off place, Dursey Head, Ireland, they spoke a derelict vessel manned by "poore menne of Bristowe" who had been "spoyled" by French pirates. Most of the crew, wounded, had been left on board with nothing to sustain them but "olives and stinking water." Frobisher (wrote Best), "who well understandeth the office of a Souldioure, and an Englishman, and knoweth well what the necessity of the sea meaneth . . . relieved them with Surgerie and salves, to heale their hurts, and with meate and drinke to comfort their pining hartes."

First stop, as usual, was the east coast of Greenland. Frobisher, seeing signs of people, had himself rowed ashore, but by the time he landed the Eskimo had fled, leaving some forty dogs to guard their possessions. The Englishmen captured two puppies which, if they survived the voyage, were the first huskies to reach England. The Captain General, imagining that he and his were the first "Christians that ever set foote upon that ground," took possession of Greenland in the name of their Queen, and even named it "West England."

On 20 June the fleet "having a fayre and large wind" and a full moon, departed for Frobisher's Strait. *Salamander* bumped a whale which "thereat made a great and ugly noise" and stopped her dead in

A fair June day in Frobisher Bay. From foot of Grinnell Glacier looking toward Baffin Island. U. S. Navy Photo of 20 June 1946.

the water. Approaching the coast in the dark of the moon, they sighted on 2 July Queen's Foreland (now Resolution Island) off the southern entrance to the Strait, and there their troubles began.

That summer of 1578 was abnormally cold and stormy. Frobisher's Strait was "combred with Ise," "enclosing us, as it were, within the pales of a Parke," and those little ships, like the mammoth tanker that made the Northwest Passage in 1969, had to watch for a passage through the floes and among the bergs, "looking everie houre for death . . . our ships so troubled and tossed among the yce." *Judith* and *Michael* disappeared and were given up for lost; actually they had nipped ahead to Countess of Warwick Sound, where the rest later joined them. Bark *Dennis*, "being but a weake shippe & brused afore among the yce," was so damaged that she came apart and sank within sight of her consorts "which so abashed the whole fleete, that we thought verily we should have tasted of the same sauce." They manned their boats in time and despite the icy obstacles rescued every man jack of her crew. Those men were mariners, no doubt about it.

While the fleet lay "compassed . . . on every side with Ise," there arose a "sodaine and terrible tempest" from the southeastward, which worsened the ice problem and prevented all but four ships (*Anne Frances, Moone, Frances* of Fowey, and *Gabriel*) from recovering sea room. Some set sail to take advantage of every opening, others took in sail and drifted, others anchored to the lee side of a big berg; all buttressed their topsides with old junk, spars, fenders, spare spars, and even bedding to protect them "from the outragious sway and strokes of the said Ise." As extra precaution, mariners stood by with poles, pikes, oars, and three-inch plank to sheer off threatening floes and bergs. Some ships were so squeezed as to be "heaved up" a foot or more, resulting in bent and broken knees and beams. George Best commended the captains for encouragement of the men, and the "poore Miners unacquainted with such extremities," who toiled "to the everlasting renowne of our nation."

After two days and nights of extreme peril, the wind veered to northwest, "which did not only disperse and dryve forthe the Ise before them, but also gave them libertie of more scope and Sea roome." The fleet, rejoining the four sail which earlier had sought safety at sea, spent several days off shore, effecting repairs and hoping (in vain so it turned out) that sun and offshore wind would melt the ice.

The "Mistaken Straits"

Alas, more woe lay ahead.

On 7 July, Frobisher, with twelve of his fifteen sail, again closed the shore. The General, making South or Queen Elizabeth's Foreland on 7 July in a snowstorm, judged it to be Hall's Island, the North Foreland, and so left it on the starboard hand. When the sun came out and a meridional altitude was taken from the flagship's deck, the resulting latitude, 62° 10′ N, proved that *Aid* was on the wrong side of Queen Elizabeth's Foreland. She was sailing up what Frobisher called "the Mistaken Straites." After another great explorer had resolutely sailed through, these would be named Hudson Strait.

High summer in Frobisher Bay, 1864. Meta Incognita and Grinnell Glacier
in background. From C. F. Hall, *Arctic Researches* (1866).

For twenty days the fleet sailed cautiously up Hudson Strait, with
a waxing moon, which for most of the time was shrouded in fog. The
currents were so strong as to turn a ship around "after the manner of
a whirlepoole." Captain Yorke of *Thomas Allen*, with chief pilot Christopher Hall on board, and *Anne Frances* commanded by the narrator
George Best, peeled off and sought the open sea. There they ran into
another press of ice so thick that the men made plans to save themselves in boats and on hatch covers. The rest of the fleet, "following
the course of the Generall whyche ledde them the waye, passed up
above 60 leagues within the sayd doubtfull and supposed straytes, having
alwayes a fayre continente uppon their starreboorde syde, and a continuance still of an open Sea before them."

After he had realized his mistake, Frobisher looked for an opening
on the north that would connect with his own "strait." When he had
given up hope of that, he debated whether to sail on, in the expectation
that this would prove to be *the* passage to "the ritch Countrey of
Cataya" (since he had observed that the flood tide ran three hours to
the ebb tide's one, indicating a great body of water to the westward);
or return to fulfill his duty of gathering ore. Duty won; but in the
meantime some of Frobisher's men landed on the shore of the Ungava

Peninsula, found it to be far better stocked with fauna and flora than Meta Incognita, and did a little trading with the local Eskimo.

It was no small task to get out of Hudson Strait, with its headwinds, baffling currents, and a "furious overfall" (tide rip) at the entrance, which one could hear roaring afar off, like the tide race at London Bridge. Frobisher at times had to anchor in more than 100 fathom, bending two long cables together, and on other occasions sailed over rocky reefs with only six inches to spare. When all seemed lost, the men would cry out, "Lorde, now helpe or never; nowe Lorde looke down from Heaven and save us sinners, or else oure safetie commeth too late!" Then, "at the very pintch one prosperous breath of winde" would waft them past the threatened danger. Nobody in Frobisher's fleet doubted the efficacy of prayer, or that he owed his life to the compassionate help of His Divine Majesty.

By 24 July the fleet again united in harbor, except for *Gabriel* which had just got through the strait named after her on "the backside and Western point of the Queen's Foreland." There are two entrances to Frobisher Bay behind this big cluster of islands. Captain Bob Bartlett in 1942 conned schooner *Morrissey* through the narrower, to the admiration of Alexander Forbes. "Next morning," wrote Dr. Forbes, "we entered our first ice floes, a picture of rare and thrilling beauty, the ice pans either of clear blue or snow white, in strong contrast against the calm water." But Frobisher's men had neither taste nor time to admire the beauty of this scene. Buss *Emmanuell* reported ice so thick and dangerous that, despite all efforts to sheer off the floes, she was holed in many places and could only be kept afloat by pumping 250 strokes an hour. Sailors and even some officers now "beganne privily to murmure against the Generall" for his "wilful manner of proceeding," saying that they had better seek a safe harbor in the Queen's Foreland, or go home; and they would rather stand their chance of being hanged in England for mutiny, than freeze to death. Master Frobisher would hear none of it. He determined to return to his port in Countess of Warwick Sound, and load up.

A Summer's Ore-Gathering

While Frobisher lay to seaward of the Foreland, still debating what to do, "There arose a sodaine and terrible tempest," making the headland

Frobisher Bay.
Photos by Alexander Forbes, July–August 1942. Meta Incognita, from
Frobisher Bay. Delano Bay, on southwest shore. *Morrissey* at anchor
among the islands. Courtesy of Dr. Forbes's heirs.

a lee shore and driving back the ice which had floated seaward. Every ship inside Frobisher Bay furled her sails and drifted; *Anne Frances*, *Moone*, and *Thomas* "plyed oute to Seawarde, holding it for better policie and safetie to seeke Sea roome." The General and others managed to weather the Foreland and get inside the Bay. Before all did, on 26 July, came "an horrible snowe," which "laye a foote thicke upon the hatches," and "did so wette thorowe oure poore Marriners clothes, that he that hadde five or sixe shifte of apparell, hadde scarce one drie 'threede to his backe." And many now fell sick.

Once inside the bay named after him, Frobisher rallied his fleet, "and where he saw the Ise never so little open, he gat in at one gappe, and out at another." Dr. Forbes described the same procedure in the *Morrissey* exactly 364 years later. The lookout picks the open lanes and cons the ship; and if ice closes in she rams the pans with a terrific crunch and opens a new lead. *Morrissey*, however, was a specially built vessel, bigger than any of Frobisher's, sheathed with ice-resisting greenhart, and having a powerful auxiliary engine. The best method that Frobisher's vessels could apply to clear a lane was to hook onto one ice floe with two anchors, and with all sail set push it ahead to butt other ice floes out of the way.

"The 28 day" of July, wrote Ellis, "we passed the dangers, by day light. Then night falling on the face of the earth" (it was the dark of the moon), they hove-to "in the cleare, till the chearefull light of the day had chased away the noysome darknesse of the night: at which time wee set forward towards our wished port; and by the 30 day we obtained our expected desire." In Countess of Warwick Sound they found riding at anchor behind Kodlunarn Island, Fenton's *Judith* and bark *Michael*, "which brought no small joy unto our Generall, and ' great consolation to the hevie heartes of those wearied wightes." The fleet chaplain, Master Wolfal, now conducted a service of thanksgiving. George Best praised this parson for having left a pleasant country parish, "a good honest woman to wife, and verie towardly Children," to save pagan souls and minister to the mariners. *Judith* and *Michael* had been in constant danger for the month of July, often so encompassed by ice that the men could walk ashore or from one vessel to another, and shot seals on the ice to eke out their rations. On one berg, estimated to be half a mile in circumference and 1200 feet high, the ' water fell down in "sundry streames." They only survived by hooking anchors to the leeward side of these monsters, or by driving a sizable floe before them to crush another.

Troubles with ice were far from ended. Frobisher had not been two hours at anchor, on 30 July, when big ice floes began driving toward the flagship. *Aid* hastily weighed, but the ice struck her before the anchor could be catted, and it drove one fluke right through the bows of the ship, under water. The people had to pump and bail all night; next day they heeled her until the hole came out of water, and covered it with a sheet of lead.

Frobisher, after appointing an advisory council of his captains, began mining on Anne Warwick (Kodlunarn) Island on 1 August. He drew up a set of remarkable sanitary regulations for these operations: 1. No washing of hands or clothes in the spring set aside for drinking water. 2. "Easement" only to be permitted "under the cliffes where the Sea maye washe the same awaye." 3. No garbage to be cast overboard from the ships. In view of what we are struggling with in 1970, these regulations appear highly significant; on pollution problems, Frobisher was almost four centuries ahead of his time. Houses were erected ashore, and everyone not specially employed was put to work digging up the worthless rock from long trenches. Ships occupied the rectangular dock dug the previous voyage, so they could load easily. Gentlemen set the example to "the inferiour sorte" in these futile labors.

"Mining," as they called it, was not confined to this tiny island. As the rocks there were very hard and difficult to break up with no better tool than a pickaxe, Frobisher sent the smaller ships and pinnaces along the shores of his Strait looking for similar marcasite or iron pyrites that would be easier to dig out and load. One mine was named after the Countess of Sussex—Frances, daughter of Sir William Sydney of Penshurst and founder of Sydney Sussex College, Cambridge. The others were called Beare's Sound, Queen's Foreland, Dyer's Passage, Fenton's Fortune, and Winter's Furnace. Out of 1350 ton of so-called ore loaded in thirteen ships for the return passage, only 65 tons came from Kodlunarn Island. George Best in his *True Discourse* (1578) had a crude map of the "Straights," indicating the other mines; all they produced was equally worthless. Best's general conception of the area, based on the Zeno brothers' map, he and Frobisher later rejected.

Gabriel and the three ships which had sought sea-room joined within a week. When the entire fleet had assembled, except *Thomas* of Ips-

Inside portrait oval: FORBISHERUS ◆ MARTINUS ◆ Foauratur

FÖRBISHERVS ruans NEPTVNIÆ regna frequentat
Pro Patria at tandem glande peremptus obit

Sir Martin Frobisher. Posthumous portrait by the Dutch engraver Crispin
de Passe, *c.* 1595. Courtesy of Trustees of National Maritime Museum,
Greenwich.

wich, Captain Tanfield (who, "compelled by what furie I know not,"
said Ellis, had sneaked off home), Frobisher held a council to decide
future action. He had already planned to return shortly with such ore
as could be collected in a few weeks, and to leave behind, under Captain
Fenton, three ships and a hundred men to accumulate a quantity for
shipping home next year. Many objected. If this be summer, with water
freezing nightly in the Strait, what would winter be? How could any
man or ship survive? Captain Best of the *Anne Frances,* to whom we
owe this account, denounced any cut-and-run plan as dishonorable; he
would have none of it, and urged everyone to search for a better harbor. He was allowed to do just that, and on the outer shore of Resolution Island found a harbor with such a "plentie of blacke Ore" (marca-

site) "that it might reasonably suffise all the golde gluttons of the
worlde." Reporting this to Frobisher on 9 August, Best was honored
by having the place named "Best's Blessing." Captain Fenton, too, un-
deterred by "the cruell nipping stormes of the raging winter" or "the
savagenesse of the people," wished to remain, and a hundred men including Master Wolfal volunteered to stay with him, desirous "to have
profited their countrie."

Either at this conference, or when Best was absent, Frobisher and the
other captains decided to cancel the wintering plan. Lucky for all that
they did! Among the decisive factors were the "many straunge Meteors"—the aurora borealis which are particularly brilliant and blind-
ing as seen from Frobisher Bay. The General took them to be a warning to leave.

"Nowe, whilest the Marriners were romaging theyr Shyppes," continues Best, "the Miners followed their laboure, for getting togither of
sufficient quantitie of Ore," and the carpenters assembled *Anne Frances's* prefabricated pinnace. In her Captain Best, Captain Upcot of
Moone, and a crew of twenty-eight went on an exploring expedition,
starting 19 August with a full moon. They "shot up about 40 leagues
within the straites," named a big island after bark *Gabriel* and met
another pinnace from the *Thomas Allen* whose crew was excavating
supposed gold ore from the Countess of Sussex Mine. Eskimo occasionally appeared but were too wary to be spoken to, much less kidnapped.

The stone house intended for Captain Fenton's winter residence on
Kodlunarn Island was finished, in order to "prove against the nexte
yere, whether the snowe could overwhelme it, the frosts breake uppe,
or the people dismember the same." To "allure and entice" the Eskimo
"against other years," Frobisher garnished it "with many kinds of
trifles," such as dolls on foot and horseback, besides fresh bread "for
them to see and taste." Hopefully, he made a winter sowing of grain
and peas. The Captain-General made a final exploration of Hall's Island
in his pinnace, and returned to Countess Anne's sound. On 22 August
his company "plucked downe" their tents ashore, built bonfires at the
highest point of Kodlunarn Island, marched about with ensign displayed and trumpets sounding, and fired a farewell volley "in honour
of the right Honourable Lady Anne, Countesse of Warwicke, whose
name it beareth." Master Wolfal offered a mass on shore, and on the

last day of August, in the dark of the moon, Frobisher left his Strait for the last time.

Homeward Bound

Their toils and troubles were not yet over. Frobisher set a fleet rendezvous at Beare's Sound between Hall's Island and the mainland, as he wanted to top off some ships' cargoes there with ore. At a time when men were ashore or in boats transferring stone from beach to ship, there made up the most "outragious tempest" of the voyage, "beating on our ships with such vehement rigor, that anchor and cable availed naught; for we were driven on rockes and Islandes of yce." Not one ship escaped without damage or loss of ground tackle and boats. Many men, caught ashore by the sudden storm, were lucky to board any ship when their own had been blown out to sea. Frobisher himself, going ashore in the prefabricated pinnace to pick up some of his men, almost lost his life. "Chips" warned him that she was held together only by nails, since oaken knees had not been provided by the builders and none could be cut in the Strait; but he insisted on taking her ashore for want of anything better, since the alternative was to leave his mariners stranded in that barren land with no provisions. Upon being rowed back, the pinnace leaked so badly that the General ordered the rowers to hasten to the nearest ship, *Gabriel*. He had barely stepped on board when the boat fell apart and sank. So Frobisher returned to England in *Gabriel*.

At last, on 2 September 1578, they dropped the desolate shores of Hall's Island and Meta Incognita, never to return. The passage home was boisterous. *Aid* cracked her main yard and was pooped by a following sea. The ships were unable to keep together, and the barks were so "pestered with men" from other ships that provisions ran short. Whether from exposure, ship fever, or from what cause we know not, men died almost daily. Thomas Ellis, with unusual compassion, mentions every death by name, thus: "The 7th, God called to his mercy George Yong, myner." Altogether about forty members of the fleet never reached home alive.

The most memorable incident of the homeward passage was the pretended discovery of a new island by the buss *Emmanuell*, familiarly known as "the Busse of Bridgewater." After an almost miraculous escape from shipwreck in the "outragious tempest" of 1 September, she raised "Frisland" (Greenland) on the 8th, and departed two days later, steering southeast. At 1100 she fell in with a hitherto unknown island at latitude 52°30′ N. Sailing along the coast for twenty-eight hours, the captain observed two harbors and much ice, of which they were never free. But the land looked fruitful, full of woods and open meadows. Passenger Thomas Wiers in the buss, a man of vast imagination, told this to Hakluyt.

The "Island of Buss," as they named this phantom, became a favorite of cosmographers who wanted something to fill vacant spaces southeast of Greenland. It acquired a shape, a toponymy, and a wreath of whales and walruses, although nobody could ever locate it. As late as 1675 John Seller's *Atlas Maritimus* places it on latitude 57°30′ N, "not yet fully discovered," and our map is from one of the editions of his *English Pilot*. Even after a century of searching had failed to locate Buss, the cartographers, loath to give it up, introduced a "Sunken Land of Buss" which, like Hy-Brasil, hung on into the nineteenth century.

Almost all the way home the wind blew "large" and fair for England. *Gabriel* lay off the Scillies on the day of full moon, 24 September, an ocean passage of twenty-two days; the other twelve made port by the first of October. Most of their worthless cargoes were shipped to Bristol or London where Schultz, Burcot, and perhaps other "experts" got to work on the sacks of rock. Best and Sellman rushed into print with their narratives of the third voyage before a final report had been made. In the meantime there was wrangling and jangling among the seamen for their pay, and adventurers demanded their money. Thomas Allen, owner of the like-named ship, wrote to Walsingham on 8 December 1578 begging him for funds to pay off her crew: "Crystmas beynge so nere, every man cryyeth out for money!"

Attempts to smelt precious metal out of the 1350 tons of rock that Frobisher brought home went on for five years. The Company turned from one expert to another in the vain hope of finding "pay dirt," assessing the stockholders some £9270 for the heavy expenses. Michael Lok, furious, drew up a list of "The Abuses of Captayne Furbusher against the Company." The ore brought home on the first voyage was full of gold, but on the next two, instead of getting more of the same, Frobisher had loaded up with "not one stoane therof." His refusal to let the men winter at Countess of Warwick's island was due to jealousy of Fenton. He should have sent the two barks ahead to find the passage to Cathay. He wasted supplies and provisions, and allowed his officers to pilfer them. Men in the *Aid* died from being forced to eat "evill fishe" four days in the week, and "all the way homewards they drank nothing but water." Horrible, horrible! Lok even held the exploration of Hudson Strait against Frobisher. "Arrogant in his governement . . . and imperious in his doeings," the General drew a dagger against Captain Fenton, and raised "sclannderous reportes against Mr. Lok," author of this bill of complaints. Frobisher replied that Michael Lok 'was "a bankrupt knave" who had "cozened" the Company out of £3000 without investing one groat; Lok replied that he had ventured £2600 of his own money, and that the assayers should be punished for their false reports on the ore, as well as Frobisher for his conduct of the expedition. In the end, the Company of Cathay went broke; and (wrote the historian Camden in his *Annals*) the stones, "when neither Gold, Silver, nor any other metall could be drawne" from them, "we saw them throwne away to repayre the high-wayes."

To so inglorious an end came this great enterprise.

Conclusion

Frobisher's revised ideas of his geographical discoveries may presumably be represented by the interesting world map in George Best's *True Discourse* of 1578. "Frobussher's Straights," covering a greater area than the Great Lakes, end in the Pacific where the "Straight of Anian" feeds into them. "Cathaia" is now relegated to its true position instead of extending into Baffin Island; Meta Incognita, instead of being the south side of Frobisher Bay, is divided into six islands and a four-part *Terra Sep-ten-triona-lis* (Greenland apparently represents the *ten* section) balances *Terra Australis*.

When everyone had to admit that the ore was worthless, recriminations such as those that we have quoted passed back and forth. Sellman, Lok's agent on board the flagship, probably produced most of the "scandell" about Frobisher; for, by his own account, Sellman intervened twice in disciplinary matters in which he had no business, and was promptly slapped down by the General.

In view of their objectives, all three voyages, which cost the stockholders about £20,160, were complete failures; and there is no use try-

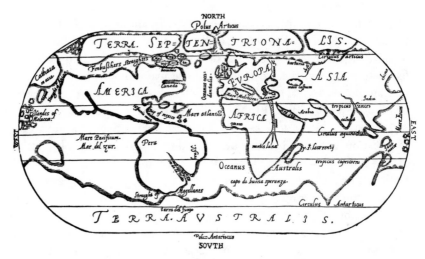

George Best's map of the world in his *True Discourse* (1578). Courtesy Harvard College Library.

ing to blame anyone except the "goldfinders" for their dishonest or incompetent reports on the ore. Why could not the Company of Cathay have imported French assayers, who had showed up Cartier's gold and diamonds? Why did the English fiddle around with it for five years? Possibly mere stupidity; but one suspects skulduggery—investors trying to hold back the truth so they could unload.

Frobisher's reputation declined, as it were, with the market; but for a year or more it remained very high. Shipmates Best, Settle, and Ellis praised his conduct of the voyage in their printed accounts. The Queen gave him a gold chain. Besides Thomas Churchyard, one stanza of whose poem we have quoted at the head of this chapter, several bards unknown to fame contributed poetical effusions to Ellis's *True Report.* John Kirkham, for instance, called Frobisher "a martial Knight," whom "no chaunces dire could dismay, no doubt could daunt his hart." "He ventred not to knowen coastes, nor lands devoid of feare," but sought boreal lands of storms and snow and "mightie mountaines huge of cold congealed yce."

> A Hector stout he is on land, Ulysses on the seas,
> Whose painfull pilgrimage hath brought unto his countrie ease.

All this adulation was based on the conviction that Frobisher "the way to golden Fleece to Britane had made plaine." When it became clear that he had brought home nothing more valuable than paving stones, [1] his reputation fell under a cloud.

Frobisher's petition to the Queen in 1579 for financial relief or employment was not answered. His old bark *Gabriel* for which (as McFee wrote), "Frobisher seems to have had an affection more durable than any woman could command," was knocked down by the Cathay Company's creditors for a mere £80, and Martin was too poor to cover that bid. Of necessity, he took up his former occupation of piracy or privateering. Once more in the money, he subscribed £300 toward a projected expedition in 1582, hopefully financed in part by still affluent members of the Company of Cathay, to reach those "happy shores" via the Cape of Good Hope. Frobisher was to have commanded it, but when the adventurers placed his former lieutenant Edward Fenton, whom he detested, next in command, he gave it up. Fenton sailed in May 1582 but mismanaged things badly and got no further than Brazil.

Although Frobisher did not participate in the Virginia voyages, he highly approved of them; as may be seen by his prefatory poem in Sir George Peckham's *True Report* of Sir Humfry Gilbert's exploits.

> A pleasant ayre, a sweete and firtell soil,
> A certain gaine, a never dying praise:
> An easie passage, voide of loathsome toile,
> Found out by some, and knowen to me the waies,
>   All this is there, then who will refraine to trie:
>   That loves to live abroad, or dreads to die.

In 1585 Frobisher obtained the highly honorable command of vice-admiral in Drake's expedition against the Spanish West Indies, and fought both well and profitably. When the *felicissima armada* threatened to invade England, the Lord High Admiral, Howard of Effingham, gave him command of the Channel fleet. After Lord Henry Seymour had relieved him from that command, Frobisher was given sixty-gun galleon *Triumph*, biggest ship in the Royal Navy. After covering himself with glory, twice beating off four great Spanish galleasses in the fight off Portland Bill, he was rewarded by knighthood, and by being given command of a division of fighting ships under Lord Howard.

After the Spanish defeat there broke out an altercation between Frobisher and Drake because Sir Francis tried to keep for himself and his own sailors the entire prize money from the Spanish galleon *San*

Charles Howard of Effingham, Lord High Admiral, 1585–1618. By D. My-
tens. Courtesy of Trustees of National Maritime Museum, Greenwich.

Luís, leaving none for the ships and men who had covered him and so made that capture possible. Sir Martin declared that Sir Francis behaved in the battle "like a cowardly knave or a traitor—I rest doubtful which!" The hero Drake "thinketh to cozen us of our shares of 15,000 ducats, but we will have our shares, or I will make him spend the best blood in his belly!" After the dispute had been adjudicated by the privy council, Sir Martin was awarded £4979 as his share of the prize money—a small fortune for that era.

Next summer Sir Martin commanded a task force of five naval vessels which captured two Spanish treasure ships off the Azores. He repeated this exploit in 1592; and two years later commanded an amphibious operation in support of Sir John Norris to expel the Spanish garrison from Brest. For his conduct there he received a complimentary letter from the Queen.

In his last letter, a report to the Lord High Admiral, Sir Martin told about the assault on the fort named Crozon ("Croydon" was the nearest he could get) on 7 November 1594. "It was tyme for us to goa through with it," he said, as a Spanish relief force was advancing. He and Sir John personally led the assault; they took the fort and put all Spaniards to the sword, but Frobisher received a bullet in his leg. Provisions running short (as usually they did in the Queen's navy), the victors had to sail home or starve, and the mariners vowed they would not leave without Sir Martin. En route the infected wound festered, and on 22 November 1594, aged fifty-five, the gallant seaman, already old by standards of the time, died at Plymouth. His body was taken to London and buried at St. Giles's, Cripplegate.

Frobisher's first wife having died shortly after his return from the Arctic in 1578, he married Dame Dorothy Widmerpole, daughter of Lord Wentworth, and she survived him. They lived as country gentry in Altofts, Yorkshire, where he became a considerable landowner. His first wife bore him a son who predeceased him, and a spendthrift nephew inherited the fortune that Sir Martin had accumulated from prize money.

Frobisher's character was based on simplicity and integrity. Every shipmate except Fenton and Lok's man Sellman paid high tribute to him, praising his humanity in dealing with his own men and the poor natives. He suffered, no doubt, from lack of learning, and of the courtly manners which make Raleigh and Gilbert so attractive to romantic historians. Reading between the lines of his shipmates' narratives, it is clear that the old sea-dog was impatient, irascible, and incapable of concealing his rage when once aroused, as it always was by injustice. But he was endowed with "a singular faculty for leadership." He "had in him not only greatness, but a human quality which made men curse him and love him, grumble at him and toil for him," wrote McFee, an old sailor himself. Sir Martin was a sailor's sailor of the same breed as John Paul Jones, Collingwood, and the Perrys. For my part, I conclude that Frobisher was a very great seaman indeed, that his courage and resource enabled him and his ships to survive adversities of ice and weather which would have ruined anyone else, and that he fully deserves his reputation as one of the English mariners who paved the way for England's greatness.

It was tyme for us to goa through with it. That sentence in the last letter that he wrote is typical of Frobisher. What he undertook he went through with; no turning back like Gilbert, no sliding off like John Rut to something easy and pleasant.

Futile as they were, unsuccessful in immediate results, we would not erase those three voyages from the roll of maritime history. There were high moments, when all men of the fleet pitched in to protect one another from the ice, "to the everlasting renowne of our nation." No higher quality of seamanship and devotion to duty has been shown anywhere than among the officers, the "paynefull Mariners" and the "poore Miners" embarked in those sailing vessels, all so small, weak and comfortless in comparison with the giant icebreakers of our day. England and her offspring have every reason to cherish the records of the "late voyages of discoverie . . . under the conduct of Martin Frobisher, General." If nothing else, they taught England to "goa through with it" to glory, dominion, and empire.

Bibliography and Notes

SOURCES

Every known source is reprinted in Vilhjalmur Stefansson, *The Three Voyages of Martin Frobisher* (2 vols., London, 1938); see Notes to Chapter XV. George Best's *True Discourse* covers all three voyages. Richard Willes, "For M. Cap. Furbisher's Passage by the Northwest" in Richard Eden, *History of Trauayle in the West and East Indies* (London, 1577), is a learned argument for their practicability. Thomas Ellis, *A True Report of the Third and Last Voyage into Meta Incognita* (London, 1578), is also by a participant. In his preface Ellis apologizes for being "a Sailer more studied and used in my Charde and Compasse . . . than trayned up in *Minerva's* Court," but his English is the most vivid of any Frobisher narrative. Dyonyse Settle, *A True Report of the Laste Voyage into the West and Northwest Regions* (London, 1577), is by "one of the companie . . . and servant to the Right Honourable the Earle of Cumberland." Edward Sellman's account of the Third Voyage "delivered to Michael Lok, the 2 October 1578, in London," remained in manuscript until 1867. Sellman is best for tracing Frobisher's erratic courses in and around his "strait," and for latitudes; a person acquainted with that country could, from his data, lay down *Aid's* course.

Several of the above are in various editions of Hakluyt.

William R. Scott, *Constitution and Finance of . . . Joint-Stock Companies to 1720* (Cambridge, 1910–12), I, 76–82, II, 342, III, 464, for the Company of Cathay, whose official name was "The Adventurers to the North-West for the Discovery of North-West Passage, or, the Companye of Kathai." I have followed Scott's figures, based on an intensive study of the Company's affairs, rather than Stefansson's.

TRACES OF FROBISHER AT KODLUNARN ISLAND

Frobisher Bay or Sound has seldom been visited since 1578. The Rawson-MacMillan Sub-Arctic Expedition was there in 1927 and made some photos of traces of Frobisher on Kodlunarn Island. Charles Francis Hall, *Arctic Researches and Life among the Esquimaux in the Years 1860, 1861 and 1862* (1866), pp. 281–85, tells Ninoo's story, and on pp. 290, 305–6, 361–66, 379–81, 426–30, 433–38, 594–95, describes localities and the Frobisher remains on Kodlunarn Island. Hall's visit in 1860–62 is responsible for the curious modern nomenclature of Frobisher Bay, part Elizabethan and part after heroes of the American Civil War. He brought back sacks full of Frobisher relics and gave them to the Royal Geographical Society, the Smithsonian Institution, and other museums, which have managed to mislay every one, as Stefansson (op. cit. II, 240–49) found when he tried to see them. In World War II the Bay suddenly acquired strategic importance as on the northern air route from Canada to Great Britain. Alexander Forbes's *Quest for a Northern Air Route* (Harvard University Press, 1953), covers his observations in 1942–43. Two airfields were built, one on an island and one, called Frobisher Bay, at the head of the Sound. The Canadian government in 1969 was planning to spend $13 million to construct a government center there for administering the Eastern Arctic. God help the Eskimo!

MARCASITE AND IRON PYRITES

These two minerals are very similar in appearance, having the same chemical composition (FeS_2), and were generally considered identical until the nineteenth century. H. N. Stokes, *On Pyrite and Marcasite* (U. S. Geological Survey, Washington, D.C., 1901), states that the color of pyrites is "pale brass yellow," and that marcasite can be brass yellow, bronze-yellow, grayish-white, or greenish. That leaves us guessing just what Frobisher's sample "black as sea coale" was. Stefansson devotes two appendices (*Voyages of Frobisher*, II, 119-51, 248-52) to examining the relevant documents, without any clear conclusion as to what kind of rocks constituted the two worthless loads.

The 140 tons of it brought home on the second voyage was deposited in Bristol Castle, and a furnace built in Sir William Winter's house by Jonas Schultz the German mineral man. He pretended to have extracted £40 worth of pure gold from every hundredweight of "ore," and repeated this twice. Charles F. Hall in 1860 found great lumps of a black rock on Kodlunarn Island that he supposed to be bits of the "ore" that escaped loading. The geologist of the Rawson-MacMillan Sub-Arctic Expedition of 1927 found the same, and as Frobisher's ore was said to be the color of coal, that is probably it. The Rawson-MacMillan report, with photos, is in Stefansson, II, 245. T. A. Rickard, a mineralogist quoted in Stefansson, II, 249-50, observes that both Frobisher and the Cornish miners were "lamentably ignorant," as were the assayers and concludes, "the story of the Arctic gold mine is a compound of ignorance and knavery." So, the question of just what kind of stone Frobisher brought home is still unresolved. Anyone by examining Kodlunarn Island and the nearby "mines" could dig out samples of stone from the holes left by Frobisher, and bring them home for analysis.

The smelting was done both at Winter's house in or near Bristol, and at Dartford on an estuary of the Thames (Stefansson, II, 144, 249). Some rocks of foreign origin, unearthed there in the present century, are possibly remains of the "ore" not used for road metal.

"ISLAND OF BUSS"

The Bus or Buss, apparently Dutch in origin, was used mostly in the herring fishery. Brindley and Moore in *Mariner's Mirror*, VII (1921), 194-205, describe a herring buss of 1575 as "narrow, bluff-bowed, needing less canvas than a vessel with greater overhang," square-rigged with either two or three masts. There is a good modern model of one, *c.* 1584, in the Science Museum, South Kensington. When the seamen of the "Buss of Bridgewater" asked for their pay, they were told to take it out of the "gold ore" in her hold. But even though robbed of their wages, they obtained a certain fame by telling stories of "discovering" the non-existent island of Buss. It first appears on the Borough Map that Frobisher had with him (reproduced in Chapter XV) as a little bean-shaped island east-southeast of Cape Farewell. The brief inscription on it is read "Ise" by R. A. Skelton, "bo" or "no" by me. The Molyneux Globe of 1592 places Buss at latitude 59° N, longitude 30° W. Captain Thomas Shepherd in the *Golden Lion* of Dunkirk claimed to have found it in 1671, as John Seller describes in his *English Pilot* (1673 and later editions), from which we take

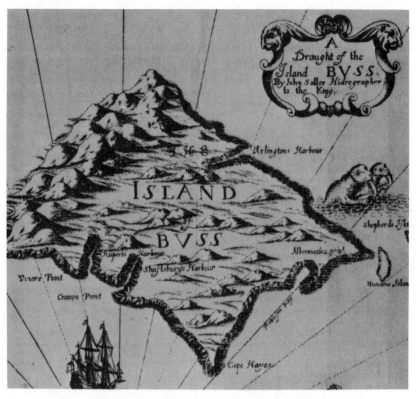

John Seller's map of Buss, from his *English Pilot* (1673).

In this Elizabethan view of Great Yarmouth (British Museum MS 2207) the ship anchored is a buss. Courtesy British Museum.

our map. James Hall, Henry Hudson, and Sir William Parry in 1819, searched for Buss; when nobody could find it, the spot was honored on maps as "The Sunken Land of Bus." Even W. H. Babcock in *Legendary Islands of the Atlantic* (1922), pp. 173–78, does not try to identify Buss with any real island; but a credulous "Bluenose" named H. S. Poole insists that it sank, and locates it at a place where a cable ship reported a sounding of 8000 fathom in 1903 (Nova Scotian Institute of Science *Proceedings*, XI, 193–98).

* XVII *
Hakluyt and Gilbert

1578-1585

I marvel'd how this Knight could leave his Lady here,
His friends, and pretty tender babes that he did hold so dear,
And take him to the Seas where daily dangers are.
Then weighed I how immortal fame was more than worldly care.

THOMAS CHURCHYARD'S COMMENDATION OF
SIR H. GILBERT'S VENTROUS JOURNEY. 1578.

Richard Hakluyt

We have been quoting Hakluyt as a source ever since the days of John Cabot, although he was born more than half a century after Cabot's death. His *Voyages*, in their several editions, have well been called the prose epic of the English nation. Not only was English literature enriched with hundreds of pithy sea narratives; they accomplished their author's purpose of firing his countrymen to worthy deeds overseas. Nor were his labors confined to a narrow national groove. We have seen how he rescued two Cartier voyages from the oblivion to which the French had consigned them. To exhibit and praise what other nations had done overseas, rather than denigrate their exploits, Hakluyt believed to be one proper means to arouse England from her lethargy.

Hakluyt was not the first to attempt a literary support to navigation. John Dee applied his mathematical knowledge to help seekers of the Northeast and Northwest Passages. Humfry Gilbert's *Discourse* came out in 1576; Richard Willes's *History of Trauayle in the West and East Indies* (a new edition of Eden's Peter Martyr) the next year; Thomas Nicholas and John Frampton, English merchants who had survived tortures by the Spanish Inquisitors, printed translations of Monardes

Sir Humfry Gilbert. From a contemporary portrait at Compton Castle. Courtesy of the owner, Commander Walter Raleigh Gilbert, R. N.

(*Joyfull Newes out of the New founde World*) and of Gómara (*Pleasant Historie of the Conquest of the West Indies*) in 1577 and 1578. That year no fewer than five Frobisher narratives were in the market. The subject only awaited a master mind, and that Richard Hakluyt had. He tells his story memorably in the "Epistle Dedicatorie" to Sir Francis Walsingham, in the 1589 edition of *The Principall Navigations, Voiages and Discoveries of the English Nation.*

Right Honorable, I do remember that being a youth, and one of her Majesty's scholars at Westminster (that fruitfull

nursery) it was my hap to visit the chamber of Mr Richard
Hakluyt my cousin, a Gentleman of the Middle Temple, well
known unto you, at a time when I found lying open upon his
board certain books of Cosmography, with an universal Map:
he seeing me somewhat curious in the view thereof, began to
instruct my ignorance, by shewing me the division of the
earth into three parts after the old account, and then according to the latter and better distribution, into more: he pointed
with his wand to all the known Seas, Gulfs, Bays, Straights,
Capes, Rivers, Empires, Kingdoms, Dukedoms, and Territories
of each part, with declaration also of their special commodities
and particular wants, which by the benefit of traffick and
intercourse of merchants, are plentifully supplied. From the
Map he brought me to the Bible and turning to the 107th
Psalm, directed mee to the 23th and 24th verses, where I read,
that 'they which go down to the sea in ships, and occupy
[their business in] great waters, these see the works of the
Lord, and his wonders in the deep,' &c. Which words of the
Prophet together with my cousin's discourse (things of high
and rare delight to my young nature) took in me so deep an
impression, that I constantly resolved, if ever I were preferred
to the University, where better time, and more convenient
place might be ministered for these studies, I would by God's
assistance prosecute that knowledge and kind of literature, the
doors whereof (after a sort) were so happily opened before
me.

According to which my resolution, when, not long after,
I was removed to Christ-church in Oxford, my exercises of
duty first performed, I fell to my intended course, and by
degrees read over whatsoever printed or written discoveries
and voyages I found extant either in the Greek, Latin, Italian,
Spanish, Portugal, French, or English languages, and in my
publick lectures was the first, that produced and shewed both
the old imperfectly composed, and the new lately reformed
Maps, Globes, Spheres, and other instruments of this Art for
demonstration in the common schools, to the singular pleasure,
and general contentment of my auditory. In continuance of
time, and by reason principally of my insight in this study, I
grew familiarly acquainted with the chiefest Captains at sea,
the greatest Merchants, and the best Mariners of our nation:
by which means having gotten somewhat more than common
knowledge, I passed at length the narrow seas into France
with sir Edward Stafford, her Majesties carefull and discreet
Ligier [ambassador] where during my five years abroad with
him in his dangerous and chargeable residency in her Highness's service, I both heard in speech, and read in books, other
nations miraculously extolled for their discoveries and notable
enterprises by sea, but the English of all others for their slug-
gish security, and continual neglect of the like attempts, espe-

cially in so long and happy a time of peace, either ignominiously reported, or exceedingly condemned. . . .

Hakluyt, at the time he wrote this, had already taken his master's
degree and holy orders, but clerical duties rested lightly upon him,
other than supplying an income to pursue further studies. He was still
attached to Christ Church in 1582 when he brought out his first book,
Divers Voyages touching the discoverie of America. Dedicated to
Philip Sidney, it was small and cheap enough to be bought and read by
anyone. Opening with Henry VII's letters-patent to John Cabot, as if
to nail down North America for England, Hakluyt translated Ramusio's chapter on Sebastian Cabot's Northwest Passage attempt, Robert
Thorne's writings urging a circumpolar voyage, Verrazzano's Letter,
and added notes on the value to England of colonizing northern regions, "commodities" to be expected thence, and goods proper to be
shipped thither.

Secretary Walsingham appointed Hakluyt chaplain to the English
embassy at Paris in 1583. Next year, on a visit to London, he wrote for
the Queen's eyes and "at the request and direction of the righte worshipfull Mr. Walter Raghly nowe Knight," *A Discourse Concerning
Westerne Planting.* It was not printed for almost three centuries—and
then in the State of Maine, one of the regions that the author had
wished to "plant." The *Discourse* is an eloquent plea for English settlements in America for these objects:

> To extend the Reformed Religion.
> To replace other English trades which, thanks to Spain, have
> grown "beggarly or dangerous."
> To supply England's wants from her own dominions, instead of
> from foreign countries.
> To employ "numbers of idle men."
> To provide overseas bases in the event of an open war with Spain.
> To enlarge the Queen's revenues, and increase the Royal Navy.
> And, finally, that hardy perennial, to discover the Northwest Pas-
> sage.

Hakluyt had to fall back on Verrazzano's description of Arcadia and
Cartier's of Canada, to convince the Queen that those shores were
temperate, fruitful, and suitable for an English colony. He went in
great detail into the English woolens trade, which he asserts to have

Christ Church, Oxford, in Hakluyt's day. Tom Tower has not yet been built, nor the north range of Tom Quad. Canterbury College and Peckwater's Inn, later annexed, became Canterbury and Peckwater Quads. "South Streate" is now St. Aldate's. The two Colleges partly shown on the left are Corpus Christi and Oriel. From Agas, *Plans of Oxford* (1578–88; this from facsimile ed. of 1899).

been worth more than half a million pounds as early as 1550; he rightly predicted that England could support fivefold her then population if she had colonies to absorb the unemployed—and colonists to buy woolens. Very eager to increase England's "great shippinge," vessels of 200 tuns upward, he predicted that through colonial trade "This Realm shall have by that meane shippes of great burden and of great strengthe for the defence of this Realme." (Lucky for her that she had them in 1588!) Be not content with piddling little cross-channel voyages in 20-30-tun barks; "wee are to passe over the breste of the maine Ocean and to lye at sea a moneth or sixe weekes together." Thanks to Sir Humfry, England can soon obtain the naval stores that she needs in Newfoundland, and build big ships of 500 to 1000 tuns, as the "Portingales and Spaniardes" have done. Colonial trade "will breed more skilfull, connynge and stowte pilotts and maryners than other belonging to this land: For *it is the longe voyaiges . . . that harden seamen and open unto them the secretes of navigation.*" The Emperor Charles V, as Hakluyt reminded the Queen, had set up a course on navigation at Seville, and required every master sailing to the West Indies to pass it; had we done so in England, "Such grosse and insufficient felowes as he that caste away the Admirall of Sir Humfryes company with 100 persons" would not have been given so important a command.

Here, one may say, are the blueprints for the British Empire in America from 1606 to 1776.

Queen Elizabeth accepted the *Discourse* but ignored its sound advice; relations with Spain were already too sticky to launch a big state-sponsored colonial enterprise. Raleigh was left alone to make his colonizing effort in Virginia, and the strategy of Philip II, bringing the war home to England, caused the mighty effort that Hakluyt wanted, to be shelved for nigh thirty years.

We are running ahead of the story of voyages of discovery; but before going on with them, you may wish to know more of Richard Hakluyt. He returned to Paris, collected more accounts of voyages there and in England, and in the Great Armada summer completed his most famous work: *The Principall Navigations, Voiages and Discoveries of the English Nation.* The massive quarto of 825 pages appeared next year, and an enlarged three-volume edition in 1598–1600. He put John White's drawings into the hands of the Dutch engraver De Bry, whose illustrated works helped to inform the European public about

English voyages. Hakluyt should have gone to Virginia in 1607 as rector of Jamestown, but age or infirmity prevented. Beneficiary of several comfortable ecclesiastical livings, he married twice, enjoyed a tranquil life, died in 1616 at the age of sixty-four, and was buried in Westminster Abbey. But neither portrait nor monument exists to give us the features of this "clerke of Oxenford" who did more than any man of his generation to invigorate the efforts which eventually bore fruit in Virginia and New England.

Sir Humfry Gilbert and His First Voyage

South Devon is an enchanting country. The River Dart, rising in the rugged tors of Dartmoor, flows gently to the sea between high banks, almost all cultivated; afloat one is constantly in the sight of green pastures divided by hedges, and red tilth sloping to the horizon, with many copses of beech and great isolated oaks spared by the ship builders of old. Within a mile of the mouth lies the ancient town of Dartmouth, and the tide ascends to Totnes, ten miles up. The mouth itself, barely 400 yards wide, is guarded by two ancient stone castles; from the sea it is difficult to find, and, for sailing vessels, almost impossible to enter in a north wind and ebb tide. Thus, it was comparatively safe from enemy attack. At the time of which we write, this West Country was coming up; a national survey of shipping in 1571–72 gives 162 vessels to London, 124 to Exeter (including Dartmouth), sixty-nine to Plymouth (which lies several miles to the west of Dartmouth around Start Point); and fifty-three each to Southampton and Bristol. All out of a grand total of 1383 English vessels.

Dartmouth lost its relative importance in the following centuries, but has become a leading yachting center. Overlooking the harbor is the magnificent Britannia Royal Naval College, which in 1943 became the amphibious force training center for the United States Navy. Just before D-day 1944, some four thousand American sailors were quartered at Dartmouth in tent cities, and over four hundred landing and beaching craft sortied on 4–5 June from the same river mouth which, four centuries earlier, had seen square-rigged fishermen and merchantmen set forth for the New World.

Three families remarkable in the history of English discovery lived in the valley of the Dart—Gilbert, Raleigh, and Davis. About three

Minesweeper leaving Dartmouth Harbor. Courtesy Gill of Plymouth.

The River Dart at Stoke Gabriel.

miles upstream from Dartmouth, on the left bank, is Greenway House, birthplace in 1539 of Sir Humfry Gilbert, and later one of the Devonshire residences of Sir Walter Raleigh. Another three miles upstream takes one to the charming village of Stoke Gabriel, where the parish register of the Church of St. Mary and St. Gabriel for October 1543 notes "Wm. Davis had a child christened named John." The Davises were yeomen farmers, and their farm, Sandridge Barton, is still operated as a farm, like Jacques Cartier's Limoïlou. Inland nine or ten miles, in a dell, rises the magnificent Compton Castle, seat of the Gilberts since the fourteenth century. Sir Humfry lived there later with his elder brother Sir John; but his parents were living at the demesne farm of Greenway when he was born.

Humfry's parents were Otho Gilbert and Katherine, daughter of Sir Philip Champernowne of Modbury, about halfway from Dartmouth to Plymouth. Katherine, left a widow when son Humfry was eight years old, married Walter Raleigh of Fardell, Devon, and moved into one of the Raleigh properties at Hayes Barton in Budleigh, a few miles east of Exmouth. There her eldest son by this second marriage, the future Sir Walter, was born in 1552. The two families were always intimate, and John Davis after he became a famous navigator married Faith Fulford, a relation of the Gilberts. Thus all three families were connected by blood as well as profession.

Katherine Champernowne must have been a remarkable woman. Four of her five sons, two Gilberts and two Raleighs, attained knighthood, and these four were primarily men of action, with a strong intellectual and artistic bent. They loved music and wrote poetry. They were proud, rash, impetuous, and quarrelsome. Their ideas, as A. L. Rowse has well said, "went to their heads, were liable to carry them away. They were speculators, projectors, bent not only on voyages across the sea, but voyages of the mind." Their sea-going ambitions may have been aroused in childhood by visiting Dartmouth, whither seamen were returning from voyages to Africa, Morocco, and Muscovy. In any case, all (as one of them wrote) longed to go to sea, "purchasing renown both to themselves and their country."

Humfry Gilbert, eldest of this band of brothers, born in 1539, went up to Oxford at an early age. Through the influence of a fond aunt, he found a place in the household of Princess Elizabeth during the dangerous reign of Queen Mary, and continued to be an habitué

Compton Castle. Photo by Nicholas Horne Ltd. Courtesy of Commander
Walter Raleigh Gilbert, R. N.

of her court after Elizabeth became queen in 1558. Four years later
she commissioned him captain in the army under the Earl of Warwick
that she sent to Le Havre to help the French Protestants against the
Catholic League. Humfry was a man whom everyone noticed. His
stature was above ordinary, his complexion sanguine, his conversation lively, and his constitution robust. Warwick reported to the
Queen, "There is not a vallyanter man that lyveth." But valor was not
enough; the little expeditionary force had to surrender next year, and
Captain Gilbert and his company were shipped home.

We find him arguing before the Queen and her Privy Council in
1566 against Anthony Jenkinson of Muscovy fame, for a Northwest as
against a Northeast Passage "to go to Cataia and all other the east partes
of the world." He would undertake it himself, at his own charge, if
given the usual discoverer's monopoly rights. The same year, to sup-

port this very ambitious scheme, he wrote *A Discourse of a Discoverie for a new Passage to Cataia, Written by Sir Humfrey Gilbert, Knight. Quid non?* (Why not?—the Gilbert motto). This *Discourse*, when printed ten years later made a small sensation. Even earlier than Hakluyt, Gilbert stressed the argument that English colonies should be established in the New World, both for trade and to open new opportunities for the unemployed.

After a summer's campaign in Ireland in 1566, Gilbert interested Elizabeth's adviser Sir William Cecil (Lord Burleigh) in his project, and presented a petition for royal support asking for territorial and viceregal privileges such as Columbus had obtained in 1492. Muscovy Company influence at Whitehall defeated him, and Gilbert returned to Ireland where, intermittently for four years, he fought and planned for English domination. His colonizing views shifted temporarily from America to Ulster; he may be called the progenitor of the "English Plantation in Ulster," so disastrous in its long-run effects. He then became interested in a similar plan for Munster. The Irish lords of that region resisted violently; and in 1569 Humfry Gilbert, promoted colonel, crushed the Munster rebellion with a savagery and cruelty unusual even in the tragic annals of Ireland. For these services the Lord Deputy of Ireland, Sir Henry Sidney, knighted him in 1570.

Back in England, Sir Humfry was elected a burgess for Plymouth in the Parliament of 1571. Next year he commanded over a thousand men in the Queen's expedition to help the Dutch rebels against Spain. He indulged in blistering rages, quarreled with his associates, and won no battle of any consequence. Recalled, he employed what he called his "loytering vacation from martial stratagemmes" in compiling a document which has given him a place among the reformers of education—that phase of life which is always being reformed and ever in need of more.

Gilbert's contribution to the endless controversy was, at least, constructive. He proposed "The Creation of an Achademy in London for Education of her Majesties Wardes and others, the youth of nobility and gentlemen." Disgusted with the scholastic curriculum at Oxford and (wisely) not venturing to reform the medieval universities, he advocated a new one with a course specially adapted for country gentlemen and men of action "relevant" (as latter-day reformers would say) to the needs of his class and time. There would be practical as well as theoretical instruction in mathematics, ballistics, navigation, and naval architecture; enough law to enable a gentleman to function properly as justice of the peace; modern as well as ancient languages (even Hebrew, surprisingly), equitation, sword-play, dancing, and music. This academy, once founded, would certainly have siphoned off gentlemen's sons from Oxford and Cambridge, and left the two ancient universities mere feeders to the church, as their founders intended. But nobody did anything about Gilbert's plan.

Sir Humfry had already written off losses from an alchemical speculation to turn iron into copper and lead into quicksilver. The one get-rich-quick scheme he did not go in for was the Frobisher series of voyages. No Gilbert held stock in the Company of Cathay; as Sir Humfry had something else in view. One plan was to mop up the fishing fleets of Spain, Portugal, and France in Newfoundland waters, and plant a colony on "St. Lawrence Island," by which he meant the utterly unsuitable Anticosti.

Queen Elizabeth did not think much of this, but she loved Sir Humfry. Both red-heads, they had a certain physical affinity, and both indulged in sudden rages, though not in each other's presence. But the Queen never supported any of his schemes until 11 June 1578, when she granted him letters-patent of such wide scope as to deserve the title of the first English colonial charter.

The letters-patent, granted a fortnight after Frobisher had departed on his third voyage, are of the form later called a proprietary charter. They allow her "welbeloved servaunte Sir Humfrey Gilberte of Compton" "to discover, searche, finde out and viewe such remote heathen and barbarous landes countries and territories not actually possessed of any Christian prince or people." He may make a settlement with any English subjects who "shall willingly accompany him," expel intruders, and (like Roberval in Canada) enjoy viceregal powers of government as well as the right to dispose of lands "in fee simple or otherwise according to the order of the lawes of England." The extent of his jurisdiction is left vague; he may take possession anywhere between the Labrador and Florida, but wherever he does take possession, Sir Humfry has the right to "take and surprise" all vessels found "traffakinge into any harbarowe . . . within the lymittes aforesaid."

This document is, in a sense, the Magna Carta of colonial England, for it guarantees to all Englishmen and their descendants who might

Captain Thomas Lee
By M. Gheeraedts, 1594. The Captain is depicted in the standard uniform
of the Elizabethan army in Ireland, adapted to bog campaigns. He is armed
with sword, partisan (pike), and petronell (horse pistol). Courtesy of
Tate Gallery and the owner, Captain Loel Guinness.

inhabit the American colony the rights and privileges of Englishmen
"in suche like ample manner and fourme as if they were borne and
personally residaunte within our sed Realme of England." And it re-
quires that the Proprietors' laws and edicts be "agreable to the forme of
the lawes and pollicies of England." Those points were being argued
in the Thirteen Colonies as late as 1776; in Canada even later.

During the summer of 1578 there was a great deal of scampering
about England, planning, issuing colonial propaganda, getting informa-

tion from Richard Hakluyt, the polymath John Dee, and others. Sir Humfry kept his mouth shut, but everybody speculated as to what was on his mind, and the Spanish ambassador almost went wild trying to get the correct answer for Philip II. Was his destination Newfoundland, the St. Lawrence, Norumbega, the West Indies, or even *Terra Australis* in latitude 45°–50° S, as he coyly hinted to the French ambassador? We shall never know, since this first voyage of Sir Humfry never left soundings. It was financed principally by the Gilbert family and friends.

The fleet sounds formidable on paper: "Sir Humfry Gilbart, Generall" in 250-tun *Anne Aucher* (the name of Lady Gilbert); *Hope of Greenway*, "vice admiral" of 160 tuns captained by Cary Raleigh (Sir Humfry's half-brother); *Falcon*, a Queen's ship of 100 tuns, Captain Walter Raleigh (his other half-brother); *Red Lyon*, 110 tuns; an unnamed "gallion" and *Swallow*, 40 tuns each, and "the lytell Frigat or *Squerrill* of viii Tunes" with a crew of eight.* Total, 365 "gentlemen, solgiars and mariner" in this Fleet, including a flag band consisting of a drummer, a trumpeter, and six "Musitians." These ships do not include the squadron of Henry Knollys, Gilbert's second in command, which consisted of the ship *Elephant*, 150 tuns; bark *Denye*, "a Frigat in leangth the kele 72 foote"; and a French bark of 70 tuns named *Frances*. All were heavily armed so as to be able to give a good account of themselves in battle, and all were provisioned for a year.

Gilbert was always a tardy sailer; he lacked the ability to get things ready on time. His fleet sailed from Dartmouth 26 September 1578 and soon experienced the hazards of so late a start—as the *Mayflower* did some forty-two years later. The ships were hurled back by westerly gales, and a second start more than a month later was equally unpropitious. So much friction had developed between Sir Humfry and his second in command that Knollys slipped away with his three ships a day before Gilbert left Plymouth with the main body on 19 November. Gilbert wrote two long letters to Sir Francis Walsingham relating the many "outragious words and acts" Knollys had used toward him, and the riotous insubordination of his men. What hurt him most was his cousin Edward Denye, owner and captain of the like-

---

* Another instance of the unreliability of names of ship types; "frigate" in 1578 meant a small, handy vessel, synonymous with pinnace, but the seventy-two-foot bark *Denye* is also called a frigate. The Gilbert family crest was a squirrel.

named bark, taking off with Knollys, alleging as an excuse that Gilbert had rebuked him for striking an unarmed sailor "with his naked sworde" and told him if he could not keep his temper he was "not fitt for the voyage"; Denye retorted "outragiously and with verey unsemely terms." English gentlemen of Elizabeth's era were very different from their tight-lipped, reticent descendants of the twentieth century; few were capable of "keeping their cool" under provocation. One only regrets that no more of their rich language of obloquy has been preserved.

Gilbert's first voyage never really "got off the ground," to use aviation language. Knollys's squadron sailed south, capturing ships off the coasts of France and Spain. Gilbert's put in at certain Irish ports to revictual, since during his long detention in England the men had already consumed a great quantity of sea stores. And they never got any further. The fleet returned that autumn to Dartmouth, whence Gilbert intended to make a fresh start in 1579. But the privy council forbade him to leave, owing to the piracies of Knollys and even his own men. For instance, while Sir Humfry was enjoying liberty at Greenway, his sailors seized a Spanish ship laden with oranges and lemons in Dartmouth Harbor and made off with her. As the English government was not yet ready for a complete breach with Spain, there was a great hue and cry after the pirated fruiter, and both Gilbert and Raleigh were warned that they would never again be allowed to sail until and unless she was recovered. Fortunately the captors put in at Lynn early in June, the owner recovered his ship, and was allowed to export grain as recompense for the oranges and lemons, which had rotted.

Gilbert's Second and Last Voyage

For this and other reasons, Sir Humfry attempted no second voyage in 1579. Flagship *Anne Aucher* and frigate *Squirrel* were employed in the perennial war with Ireland that summer, causing their owner financial loss. Undiscouraged, he then began preparations for a real colonizing expedition.

Gilbert's principal problem was to raise money. One means was to sell American land grants, as his royal patent allowed him to do; but so far as I can judge, he found no paying customers. In August 1580 he made an oral gift to the polymath John Dee of all land above latitude 50° N—practically the whole of Canada. And in 1582–83 Sir Humfry deeded to Sir George Peckham and his son a modest patrimony of 1,500,000 acres. Guided by Verrazzano's Letter (which Hakluyt had printed), the grant begins at "Dee River" (Narragansett Bay) with its five islands, and extends sixty English miles "along the sea coast westwarde towardes the ryver of Norumbeague." This was the wrong direction from Newport to the Penobscot; why such a mistake was made is not apparent. Laid down on a modern map, the Peckham grant covers about half Rhode Island and half Connecticut; but the only consideration was that after seven years the Peckhams should pay five shillings for every 1000 acres "actuallie possessed and manured." Gilbert also granted three million American acres, and two-fifths of all precious metals and pearls to be discovered, to Philip Sidney "to have, holde and enjoye forever," on condition that after seven years he pay a quitrent of 15d. per thousand acres, and after ten years a halfpenny an acre toward maintaining a navy and army for the defense of the colony. A few grants of a mere 100,000 acres each were also made.

What, if anything, Gilbert realized from these dubious land grants we do not know; but it was more than he obtained from the other extraneous source that he counted on, the English Catholics. The recusants, as they were called, since they refused to attend divine service according to the Book of Common Prayer, were very unhappy. They were not massacred as the Huguenots were in France, or tortured as Protestants were in Spain; but the £20 a month fines to which each family was liable were ruinous, and they dearly wished to combine loyalty to the Queen with the practice of their own religion. Gilbert, precursor in this respect of the Calverts and Maryland, offered to give them (for a consideration) a colony of their own with complete religious liberty; but the Queen would not let them go unless they paid up long overdue fines, which would have stripped most of them clean. Furthermore, the Spanish ambassador vetoed the scheme, threatening English Catholics that if they settled anywhere near Florida they would "have their throats cut" as had happened to the French Protestants under Ribault. For, just as the Soviets now wish communists in capitalist countries to stay at home as foci of propaganda and, in due time, of revolution; so Philip II wanted the English Catholics to stay put, conceal refugee priests, hold secret masses, and prepare to act as a fifth column in the Spanish invasion of England which Philip II was already planning. The ambassador concluded his report to the king by stating it to be necessary "for the reduction of this kingdom" (the conquest of England) that the Roman Catholics stay at home.

So, in the end, Gilbert and his friends did most of the financing for this voyage. On 2 November 1582 he signed an agreement with a group of local capitalists, calling themselves the Merchant Adventurers of Southampton. That town was then losing trade to Bristol, and hoped by this means to recoup; for Gilbert agreed to make it the "staple town" through which all his colony's trade would pass, as Seville served the Spanish Empire. For that and other privileges, fifty citizens of Southampton subscribed a total of £500. From others not of that city, including Sir Francis Walsingham, Gilbert raised about as much more; Walter Raleigh put in £2000, including a ship. This was not nearly enough, and there was no provision for supporting the colony once established.

That the populace was enthusiastic for Gilbert's second voyage may be inferred from a Londoner's diary. One Ashley, preparing beads and other trading truck for the voyage, was so confident of Sir Humfry's finding the Northwest Passage that he hoped to see the day when a letter dated London on 1 May would be delivered in China before midsummer. He would have had to wait some three centuries for that!

If there be any doubt of Gilbert's intention to found a real colony in Norumbega, a document he signed on 8 July 1582 should resolve it. He appointed brother Sir John, brother-in-law William Aucher, and Sir George Peckham, executors in the event of his death. They were to set up a government in the colony, consisting of a governor appointed by themselves, and thirteen councillors to be "chosen by consent of the people." Owners of four thousand or more acres must build a house in the "cheif Cittie." Free homesteads were to be given to poor emigrant families, provided each bring a pickax, a hand saw, a spade, a hatchet, and a certain amount of seed corn and peas. The Church of England is to be established and to assign 5 per cent of church lands for support "of maymed soldiars and of learninge, lectures, scholers and other good and godlye uses"—a foretaste of the famous provision for education in the Northwest Ordinance of 1787. Gilbert's executors are reminded that his colonists are to enjoy all the rights of native-born

Englishmen and that the colonial government's "lawes and ordinaunces may be as nere as convenyently may be agreable to the forme of the lawes and pollicie of England."

Now a fresh obstacle loomed up. The Queen informed Walsingham, who passed it on to Gilbert, that she did not wish Gilbert to go with the expedition, "as a man of not good happ by sea." How right she was!

Gilbert, not to be denied, wrote a vigorous reply to Walsingham. If her Majesty objected to his long delay, "It hath proceeded by Southwest wyndes of Godes making." The winter of 1582–83 had been very rough; ships had been blown from the Azores to England under bare poles. If he be accused of want of skill, he appeals to the best navigators and cosmographers of England. If it be "suspition of dayntines of dyett or sea sickness," he insists he is second in toughness to no man living. Unfortunately, Elizabeth relented. On 16 March she sent Sir Humfry, by his half-brother Walter, a piece of jewelry showing an anchor guided by a lady, and she asked for his portrait and wished him and his ship "great good hap and safety."

Stephen Parmenius, a learned Hungarian roommate at Oxford of Richard Hakluyt, asked Gilbert to take him as chronicler, and by way of testimonial presented him with a turgid Latin poem. And he got the job.

Here is the task organization for Sir Humfry's second and last voyage:

CAPTAIN GENERAL: SIR HUMFRY GILBERT, KNIGHT

Ship DELIGHT (also called GEORGE), 120 tuns; owned and commanded by William Winter, who was relieved at St. John's by Captain Browne of *Swallow;* Richard Clarke, master.

Bark RALEIGH, 200 tuns, owned by Sir Walter. Commanded by one Butler; Robert Davis of Bristol, master.

GOLDEN HINDE (also called SAMUEL) of Waymouth, 40 tuns, owned and commanded by Edward Hayes; William Cox, master.

Frigate SWALLOW, 40 tuns, Captain Maurice Browne. Gilbert had arbitrarily seized her from John Callis after catching him in an act of piracy.

Frigate or pinnace SQUIRREL, 10 tuns, owned by Gilbert. Captain William Andrews.

The total complement was about 260 men, including masons and carpenters, "minerall men" and refiners. "Besides, for solace of our people, and allurement of the Savages, we were provided of Musike in good variety not omitting the least toyes, as Morris dancers, Hobby horsse, and Manylike conceits to delight the Savage people, whom we intended to winne by all faire meanes possible. And, to that end, we were . . . furnished of all petty haberdasherie wares to barter with these simple people." So wrote Edward Hayes, captain of the *Golden Hinde*, in the most moving of all narratives printed by Hakluyt.

The fleet sailed together from Cawsand Bay, the outer part of Plymouth Sound, on 11 June 1583, two days after new moon. It was late in the season for a northern crossing, but Gilbert decided to go that way instead of following the southern route, probably for fear of running into a West Indian hurricane. The "course agreed upon," says Hayes, was to steer WSW from Scilly (about latitude 50° N) until they were in latitude 43° or 44°, "because the Ocean is subject much to Southing windes in June and July"; then try to head up to latitude 46° or 47° in order to make landfall on Cape Race (46°39' N) and rendezvous in Renewse or Fermeuse Harbor, Newfoundland. Very good advice, "if God shall not Enforce the contrary," wrote Hayes. Unfortunately He did. Bark *Raleigh* quit only two days out. The other four kept together for a month of head winds and foul weather. *Swallow* and *Squirrel* dropped out of sight of the *Delight* in a fog-mull. The wind blew from WNW and WSW, so that their "traverse" (beat to windward) "was great," running on the starboard tack down to 41°, the latitude of Montauk Point, then coming about to the port tack and sailing up to 51°, missing Cape Race. They hit the Newfoundland coast at the Grois Islands on 30 July, after crossing the Grand Bank. Then, "Forsaking this bay and uncomfortable coast, nothing appearing unto us but hideous rocks and mountains, bare of trees, and voide of any greene herbe," says Hayes, "we followed the coast to the South, with weather faire and cleare." Fortunately they started their coasting with the moon almost full.

Sighting (and scenting) Funk Island (which he calls Penguin Island after the great auk), they rounded Baccalieu Island and Cape St. Francis, and in Conception Bay on 3 August picked up the *Swallow*. Captain Browne had indulged in a little piracy since parting from the fleet. On the same day they arrived off St. John's, and there found

Squirrel lying at anchor. Gilbert, having taken this northern route, decided to derive some profit from it by taking formal possession of Newfoundland for England. Cabot had done so in 1497, but everyone had forgotten about that, and there was no record of it. There were thirty-six sail of fishermen "of all nations" (twenty Spanish and Portuguese, sixteen French and English) in the harbor of St. John's. After General Sir Humfry Gilbert had displayed his commission, they fired a salute in his honor; and when *Delight* struck a rock beating into the narrow harbor, all sent their longboats to tow her free. Gilbert raised a wooden pillar ashore with "the Armes of England ingraven in lead" fixed to it, and formally took possession for the Queen. The foreigners offered no objection, and all the fishermen observed a time-honored custom of presenting Sir Humfry with a turf and a twig of that soil as acknowledgment that they were now under English sovereignty. This was on 5 August 1583, which Newfoundland regards as the birth of the British Empire or Commonwealth—in which she intends to remain.

The General now promulgated the first three laws of the English overseas:

1. Public worship to be according to the Church of England.
2. Any attempts prejudicial to her Majesty's "right and possession" to be punished "according to the lawes of England."
3. Anyone uttering words "to the dishonour of her Majesty" to "loose his eares, and have his ship and goods confiscate."

The Captain General, now actual governor of Newfoundland, laid out lots "convenient to dresse and to drie their fish," to the shipowners without distinction of nationality.

A fortnight at St. John's passed merrily enough; this was the high point of the voyage. Finding that the three dozen fishing crews were living on friendly terms, electing a new "admirall" every fortnight as an occasion for a feast, Gilbert and his officers joined their social gatherings, and they furnished his messes with plenty of fish, flesh, fowl, and lobster. Ashore the morris dancers, hobby horses, and jack o' the greens cavorted, to the delight of the fishermen, many of whom joined in; there was bowling on the little green of the fishermen's "garden," and the learned Parmenius poked about with his hammer, knocking off samples of rock which might contain precious metals. He found time to write a rather gloomy letter in Latin to Hakluyt: *praeter soli-*

tudinem nihil video. Piscium inexhausta copia. "I see nothing but solitude. Inexhaustible supply of fish."

Before leaving this happy haven, the captains of *Delight* and *Squirrel*, alleging ill health, refused to go further. Gilbert accordingly took command of the pinnace himself, replaced the captain of *Delight* by Browne of the *Swallow*, and also annexed *Swallow*'s crew, to prevent their perpetrating further "outrages" on peaceful fishing vessels. She took on masters and mariners "sicke of fluxes," who recovered sufficiently to sail her home.

On 20 August the fleet, now reduced to *Delight*, *Golden Hinde*, and *Squirrel*, departed St. John's. Sir Humfry elected to sail in the pinnace as "most convenient to discover upon the coast, and to search into every harbor or creeke, which a great ship could not doe." He made the mistake, says Hayes, of overcharging *Squirrel* with ordnance "to give a shew," and thus encompassed his ruin.

Gilbert's first objective was Sable Island off Nova Scotia, to stock up with fresh meat—the Portuguese or French having left swine and cattle there many years before, to breed.* This was not a bad idea; Gilbert had expended so much pickled beef and dry provisions entertaining the fishermen at St. John's that he had little enough to keep his intended colony at Norumbega through the winter. They shaped a course for Sable Island from Cape Race. It took the three vessels eight days to reach Cape Breton. There they fell into "flats and dangers." On Tuesday 27 August, *Squirrel* sounded and found white sand at thirty-five fathom, being then in latitude 44° N. Wednesday the wind came south, and the two ships followed *Delight*. "The evening," (moon four days past full) "was faire and pleasant, yet not without token of storme to ensue, and most part of this Wednesday night, like the Swanne that singeth before her death, they in the Admiral, or *Delight*, continued in sounding of Trumpets, with Drummes and Fifes; also winding the Cornets, Haughtboyes: and in the end of their jolitie, left with the battell and ringing of dolefull knels." That night "strange voyces" were heard by the helmsmen.

Thursday the 29th, the wind rose and "blew vehemently" southward, bringing rain and thick fog. The fleet, led by Sir Humfry, fell in with the shoals around Sable Island. *Delight* (which, says

* See Chapter XIV.

master Clarke, drew fourteen feet) struck hard and fast. Everyone who put off in shallops and rafts was drowned, many within sight of *Golden Hinde* and *Squirrel* which went beating up and down for two days "if by good hap we might espie any of them." "But all in vaine, sith God had determined their ruine." Her towed pinnace, built in Newfoundland, "the bignes of a Thames barge," was boarded by master Clarke and about 15 other mariners. They, having but one oar, drove before the wind for seven days and nights to the coast of Newfoundland. Twelve of them survived, and only by drinking their own urine. They rowed along shore for five days, keeping alive by eating wild peas and berries, and were rescued by a vessel of Saint-Jean de Luz; she took them to a port on the Bay of Biscay, whence they made their way home. These were the only survivors of the *Delight*. The rest of the ship's company, some eighty-five men in all, including Captain Browne and Parmenius the learned Hungarian, perished.

The sailors in *Golden Hinde*, buffeted back and forth, their provisions "waxing scant" and winter drawing on, became discouraged and surly. What sort of a colony could so few establish that late in the season, and in so wintry a climate? Drawing near to one another, master Hayes discussed returning with Sir Humfry, who promised to turn home in these words: "Be content, we have seen enough, and take no care of expence past: I will set you foorth royally next Spring, if God send us safe home. Therefore I pray you let us no longer strive here, where we fight against the elements."

So, homeward they turned, and on the last day of August shaped their course for England. "Even in winding about" they sighted a horrid sea monster resembling a lion, which made an "oughly demonstration of long teeth, and glaring eyes," and bellowed at them ominously. Monday afternoon 2 September, with wind "large for England . . . but very high and the sea rough," they roared by Cape Race. That day Gilbert boarded the *Golden Hinde* to have the surgeon dress his foot, infected by a rusty nail, and argued about night signals with Hayes. In telling of his losses of charts, notes, and mineral samples in the wreck of the *Delight*, he "beat his boy in great rage" for having forgotten days earlier to fetch these samples from the flagship when so ordered. Sir Humfry left for the *Squirrel*, "willing us to be of good cheere," since he was confident that the Queen would lend him £10,000 so that next year he could send out two expeditions, one to the northern parts and one southward. The master and company in vain entreated him to stay with them in the *Hinde;* he said, "I will not forsake my little company going homeward, with whom I have passed so many storms and perils." "And so," writes Hayes, "we committed him to Gods protection, & set him aboord his Pinnesse," the *Squirrel.*

North of the Azores they "met with very foule weather, and terrible seas, breaking short and high Pyramid-wise." They were going through a weather front, the worst possible ordeal for a small sailing vessel. The corposants, St. Elmo's fire, blazed ominously from the mainyard, and seamen "which all their life time had occupied the Sea, never saw more outragious Seas." On Monday, 9 September, "In the afternoone, the Frigat was neere cast away, oppressed by waves, yet at that time recovered; and giving foorth signes of joy, the Generall sitting abaft with a booke in his hande, cried out unto us in the *Hinde* (so oft as we did aproch within hearing), 'We are as neere to heaven by sea as by land.' Reiterating the same speech, well beseeming a souldier, resolute in Jesus Christ, I can testifie he was."

The book, we may be certain, was Sir Thomas More's *Utopia,* which says, "The way to heaven out of all places is of like length and distance." Gilbert, moved by More's description of a peaceful, happy society in the New World, had resolved to start one next year. Too late!

Hayes continues: "The same Monday night, about twelve of the clocke, or not long after, the Frigat being ahead of us in the *Golden Hinde,* suddenly her lights were out, whereof as it were in a moment, we lost the sight, and withall our watch cryed, 'The Generall was cast away,' which was too true. For in that moment, the Frigat was devoured and swallowed up of the Sea."

She had been pooped and swamped, the fate of so many small vessels in a heavy following wind and sea. Sadly the *Hinde* continued eastward, reaching Falmouth 22 September, and a few days later Dartmouth, where Sir Humfry's kindred heard the sad news.

So died in the forty-eighth year of his age Sir Humfry Gilbert, knight.

What shall we say of him? An attractive and even fascinating figure (as we could have learned from the Queen who loved to engage him in conversation), Sir Humfry was more full of sound ideas on English expansion and colonization than any man of action of his day, or of any other man except Richard Hakluyt. He regarded a colony, not as a place to exploit the natives and get rich, but as a social experiment to cure unemployment at home and realize the Utopian dream outlined in the last book that he is known to have read. Long did he entertain these ideas, never did he give them up, and after his death they were in part attained. But the Queen sized him up correctly as a man of "no good happe at sea." He lacked the know-how, the "feel" of a ship; his fleets always started late; he quarreled with subordinates. Men could love and hate him at the same time; Sir Thomas Smith, the Queen's secretary of state, described him in one letter as fickle, boastful, and vain, but in another that he was as good-natured as any English gentleman "as sone as he is owt of his stormes." We all revere the memory of a man of charm whose brain teemed with fresh ideas, rather than that of pure men of action like Davis and Frobisher. But England needed both kinds to lead her toward glory and empire.

But for the wreck of the *Delight*, Gilbert might have kept on to Norumbega and established his little colony on an island of Penobscot Bay. It would have been the glorious fall of the year, when the hardwood trees fling out their brilliant colors against a background of sapphire sea and emerald evergreen. But no such tiny colony could have lasted—witness the French settlement on the St. Croix River and the English one on the Kennebec established by Sir Humfry's son Adrian in 1607.

"Though he be extinguished," concluded Hayes's account of Gilbert's last voyage, "some sparkes of his vertues may alwaies appear, he remaining firme and resolute in a purpose by all pretence honest and godly, as was this: to discover, possesse, and to reduce into the service of God and Christian pietie, those remote and heathen Countreys of America." Pathfinder of the English empire, too intelligent to stop at Newfoundland, or to contest France in the Gulf and River of St. Lawrence, Sir Humfry Gilbert pointed the way to New England and Virginia.

Bibliography and Notes

HAKLUYT'S VOYAGES

The best biography is by J. A. Williamson in Edward Lynam (ed.), *Richard Hakluyt and His Successors*, the centennial volume of the Hakluyt

Society (1946). More detail in George B. Parks, *Richard Hakluyt and the English Voyages* (American Geog. Soc., 1928), and in Quinn's Introduction to the 1965 reprint of the *Voyages* (No. 2, below).

In Justin Winsor, *Narrative and Critical History*, III, 199–208, there is a very useful chronological list "Earliest Publications on America, 1509–99." Hakluyt's *Discourse Concerning Westerne Planting* (1584), most important expression of his ideas, remained unpublished until 1877, when the Maine Historical Society, having procured a copy of the manuscript in the Phillipps Collection, brought it out as Vol. II of *The Documentary History of Maine*. This Phillipps ms., now in the New York Public Library, became the basis of the first English edition, in E. G. R. Taylor, *Original Writings and Correspondence of the Two Richard Hakluyts* (Hakluyt Society, 1935) II, 211–327. Included in these two volumes are numerous letters and documents elucidating Hakluyt's life.

Of the work commonly called *Hakluyt's Voyages*, the first three editions, published in his lifetime, are cumulative:

1. *Divers Voyages touching the Discovery of America and the Islands adjacent unto the same, made first of all by our Englishmen and afterward by the Frenchmen and Britons* (London: imprinted for Thomas Woodcocke, dwelling in paules Church-Yard, at the sign of the blacke beare, 1582, 120 pp.) Reprinted by the Hakluyt Society in 1850 with Introduction and Notes by John Winter Jones. See Justin Winsor, *America*, IV, 204–5.

2. *The Principall Navigations, Voiages and Discoveries of the English Nation, Made by Sea or over Land, to the most remote and farthest distant Quarters of the earth at any time within the Compasse of these 1500 yeeres.* . . . By Richard Hakluyt Master of Artes, and Student sometime of Christchurch in Oxford (London, George Bishop and Ralph Newberie, 1589), 825 pp. Facsimile edition with introduction and notes by D. B. Quinn and R. A. Skelton, published by the Hakluyt Society (2 vols., 1965).

3. Same, three-volume edition, 1598–1600. First volume contains *Discoveries &c of the English toward the North and Northeast by Sea* . . . (4to, London, George Bishop, Ralph Newberie, and Robert Barker, 1598, 619 pp.). Vol. II: *The Second Volume of the principall Navigations, Voyages, Traffiques and Discoveries* . . . *to the South Southeast parts of the world* (4to, London, same, 1599, 516 pp.). Vol. III: *The Third and Last Volume of the Voyages, Navigations, Traffiques, and Discoveries of the English Nation, and in some few places where they have not been, of strangers* . . . *to all parts of the Newfound world of America, or the West Indies* . . . (4to, London, same, 1600, 868 pp.)

Of modern editions, these are the best:

4. *The Principal Navigations, Voyages, Traffiques & Discoveries*, etc. (12 vols., Glasgow: J. MacLehose & Sons, 1903–5).

5. The Everyman's Library edition: *The Principal Navigations, Voyages, Traffiques & Discoveries*, etc. (8 vols., London: Dent; and New York: Dutton, 1907). Reasonably complete and accurate, with a fine introduction

by John Masefield. I tardily express my gratitude to Messrs. Dent and Dutton for bringing out this cheap but good edition of the classic which has been my constant companion "these fifty year,"; and also to the Hakluyt Society, whose volumes in the Boston Athenaeum, bound in light blue and fading to brown in the harsh Boston sun, were to me as a boy what his cousin's "bookes of Cosmographie" were to Richard Hakluyt.

The cousin, incidentally, acted as an information center for far-off lands and long voyages when the author was otherwise occupied. *Divers Voyages* includes (Hakluyt Soc. ed., pp. 132–38) his "Notes . . . for a discoverie," which Quinn (Gilbert, I, 116–22) reprints and dates 1578. Lawyer Hakluyt, who lived in the orchard country of Herefordshire, concludes by offering to furnish the discoverer (presumably Gilbert) with "five dry fats" (cheese tubs) of young apple trees, which will "yield you great store of strong durable good sider to drink."

The great desideratum now is an annotated, critical edition of the *Voyages.*

Almost everything of any consequence on Gilbert, his plans and his voyages, will be found in David B. Quinn (ed.), *Voyages and Colonising Enterprises of Sir Humphrey Gilbert* (Hakluyt Society, 2nd ser., Vols. LXXXIII, LXXXIV (1940). The editor's introduction is better than any existing biography. He does not include Gilbert's scheme for an "Achademy," text of which will be found in *Archaeologia*, XXI (London, 1827), 506–20.

William G. Gosling, *Life of Sir Humphrey Gilbert* (1911) is the best of the separate biographies; Conyers Read, *Mr. Secretary Walsingham* (3 vols., Oxford, 1925), the best for the Elizabethan background. R. P. Bishop, "Lessons of the Gilbert [Dee] Map." *Geographical Journal*, LXXII (1928), 235–43. Two articles on "Dee River" and the Peckham grant are in Rhode Island Historical Society *Collections*, XXVII (1934), 38–50, and XXVIII, 97–100.

Edward Haie (Haye or Hayes's) account of Gilbert's end is found in every edition of Hakluyt's *Voyages*, and in most selections. Gilbert, although well known in London literary circles, was rather unhappy in the quality of poetry dedicated to him; Churchyard's poem which I have quoted at the head of this chapter is perhaps the best. The learned Stephen Parmenius, *De Navigatione illustris & magnanimi equitis aurati Humfredi Gilberti ad deducendam in Novum Orbem Coloniam suscepta*, has not been reprinted since 1804, when the Massachusetts Historical Society brought it out in Vol. IX, 49–75, of its *Collections*, but D. B. Quinn and N. M. Chesire are shortly bringing out a new edition with translation (U. of Toronto Press). The poem is over 300 lines long, and I doubt whether anyone for a century or more has read it through. As a sample, America begs sister England to rescue her from being overrun by the cruel

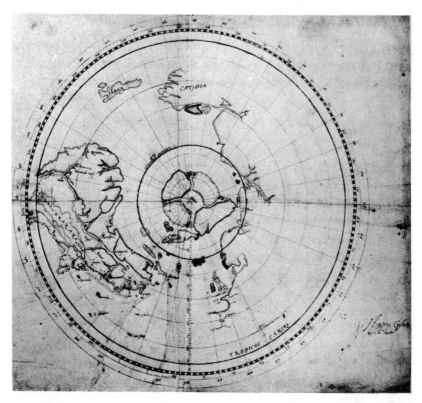

"Sir Humfray Gylbert knight his charte," by John Dee, 1583. From the original in the Free Library of Philadelphia. Originally in the library of Henry Percy, 9th Earl of Northumberland (1564–1632), "the wizard earl." It bears the personal symbol of John Dee and is described in the ms. list of his writings in the British Museum. Supposedly drafted as propaganda for his voyage of 1583. Note the Sea of Verrazzano, the city of Norumbega, the St. Lawrence running from sea to sea, and the Penobscot flowing out of it. Greenland is too far north. The four big islands around the north pole are one of Mercator's ideas said to have been derived from Lopo Homen. Zeno's "Estotiland," shaped like a rabbit, is off Labrador, north of which a Northwest Passage lies open for a sail to "Iapan" and "Cathaia." Courtesy Free Library of Philadelphia.

Spaniards, reminds her that Cabot *proximus a magno ostendit sua vela Columbo*—"next after the great Columbus showed his sails" in the temperate region, and begs Elizabeth "stretch thy sceptre where its regal sway befits thine honour."

There can be no doubt that the *Delight* came to grief on Sable Island. Hayes prints her log from Cape Race, kept by master's mate John Paul and which, laid down on a chart, leads directly to the north end of Sable Island. See Gosling's biography, p. 258n. Master Clarke's vivid narrative of the boat journey is in Gosling, pp. 261–64, and Quinn, II, 423–26.

✳ XVIII ✳
The Northern Voyages of John Davis

1585-1587

I desire that it may please his divine Majestie to shew us such mercifull favour that we may rather proceed then otherwise; or if it be his wil, that our mortall being shal now take an ende, I rather desire that it may be in proceeding then in returning.

JOHN DAVIS'S SPEECH TO HIS MEN OFF THE STRAIT OF MAGELLAN.

John Davis, Master Mariner

The reader must have concluded by this time that the story of English voyages is one of repeated failure; and that in a sense is correct. No amount of hero-worship can conceal the plain fact that the voyages of John Rut, Martin Frobisher, and Humfry Gilbert were failures, if we compare their objectives with the results. And before we take up another failure, which stemmed from Gilbert's, that of his half-brother Raleigh's first Virginia colony, we must take a look at the series of searches for the Northwest Passage by John Davis. They at least eliminated one dead end, and indicated where a successful search might begin.

Failure and success are not absolutes, and the historian should attempt to understand the one as well as the other. Of overseas expeditions, only one like John Cabot's second, lost with all hands, may be accounted a complete failure. Cartier failed to find the "passage to Cathay," but he vastly increased European knowledge of North American geography. Frobisher, with his pitiful cargoes of worthless rock, at least turned the gold-seekers away from northern regions. Sir Humfry Gilbert blew to a high flame the torch of colonization which Richard Hakluyt had lit, and at his death it passed to Walter Raleigh. And now comes John Davis, with three voyages in fruitless search of the Northwest Passage. Why bother with him? Because his voyages are highly interesting in themselves, and because he "lighted Baffin into his bay," whence the first successful traverse of the Northwest Passage started in 1903. And also because his gallantry, persistence, and enthusiasm are examples to sailors and space explorers for all time to come.

John Davis was born to a yeoman family at Sandridge Barton, a farm on the right bank of the Dart, near Stoke Gabriel, where he was baptized in October 1543. Sandridge Barton is as unchanged as Cartier's Limoïlou farm in Brittany. At the end of a narrow, steep lane bordered by hawthorne hedges, one comes upon a cluster of buildings, now a dairy farm, overlooking a bend in the Dart. The farmer's house is not more than two centuries old; but the stone-walled fowl house and cow barn might have been there in Davis's lifetime. A typical Dart valley farm, it is all uphill and down dale, the only level spots being the house and a notable feature which dates from even before 1500. This is a great hollow elm embracing a well of sweet water, which keeps cool in the hottest weather. Davis's biographer imagines him paddling and fishing salmon with the Gilbert boys, and rowing downstream to wonder at the sea-going ships anchored off Dartmouth; but the distance socially and also in miles, between their respective houses, renders that improbable. They certainly became intimate in the late 1570's after Davis had qualified as a master mariner. He married Faith, daughter of a neighboring magnate, Sir John Fulford; this raised him in the social scale and allied him with the Gilberts, but the marriage was not happy. During one of Davis's voyages, Faith took a lover, one Milbourne, who had her husband clapped into jail on a trumped-up charge after his return, and the eminent navigator had to use influence to get free.

The earliest definite fact that we know about Davis subsequent to his christening, is at the age of thirty-six when, apparently, he had retired to Sandridge Barton after a successful career as a privateersman and shipmaster. The Gilberts now interested him in undertaking a fresh search for the elusive Northwest Passage. Davis and Adrian Gilbert (Humfry's younger brother) called on John Dee the philosopher at his Mortlake home in October 1579 to talk it over, and again in June of the following year. In January of 1583, wrote Dee, he met Secretary Walsingham, Adrian Gilbert, and John Davis at Mortlake. "And so

Sandridge Barton: The farm and a view of the Dart with the great elm.

talk was begone of the North-west Straights discovery." In March these four, together with Thomas Hudson (probably an uncle of Henry), Sir George Barnes, a leading director of the Muscovy Company, and a member of the Towerson family noted for African voyages, held a colloquy on this subject. Dee argued that there were five passages from Europe to Cathay—the two that Spain and Portugal had pre-empted, the Northeast which the Muscovy Company had in vain pursued, the route right over the Pole (as Thorne had advocated fifty years earlier), and the Northwest. The last two, he thought, were worth looking into.

Thus it came about that in February 1585, when Queen Elizabeth granted a patent to Adrian Gilbert and associates, they were empowered to sail "Northwestward, Northeastward or Northward," using as many ships, barks, and pinnaces as they chose. They were given a monopoly of trade with any newly discovered region, and, if they elected to plant a colony on its shores, they would enjoy the same governmental powers as had earlier been conferred on Adrian's brother Sir Humfry.

It was under this authority that Davis made three voyages, which enlarged English knowledge of the Arctic but brought nothing profitable to him.

Since by this time very little money was available in the Gilbert and Davis families, the partners appealed for funds to "divers worshipful merchants of London." Of these, the principal was William Sanderson, who had married a niece of the Gilbert and Raleigh brothers, and signaled his interest in them and maritime affairs by naming his first three sons Raleigh, Cavendish, and Drake. Sanderson was a noted merchant adventurer, who had traded to all European countries and acted as Sir Walter Raleigh's business manager—he once had to raise £16,000 in a hurry to keep Sir Walter out of jail. He also made, or helped others to make, celestial and terrestrial globes; that pursuit probably explains his interest in and knowledge of Davis. For it was Sanderson who persuaded the associates to appoint "one Mr. John Davis, a man well grounded in the principles of the arte of navigation, for Captaine and chief Pilot of the exploit."

This language, as well as the lack of earlier records about Davis, suggests that he was not too well known in 1585. But there is no doubt that the partners made the right choice. No portrait of John Davis, or description of his person, has yet been found; no research into the life of this great seaman has been done for over a century. As one who has "lived" with him vicariously for several years, I may be privileged to imagine him as a strong man, bearded, with brown hair, blue eyes, and a serene gaze not easily ruffled. A man with a strong feeling of loyalty both to his supporters, headed by the Queen, and to his officers and men. Toward the natives he entertained liberal and benevolent feelings which, on occasion, were sorely strained. He never made any money, and his little patrimony was largely spent on the Arctic voyages which brought him nothing but fame, and little of that. He was never knighted or given any other honors, and after his death memory of him faded. But for Hakluyt, we would know little or nothing about Davis today.

Although Davis's *Seaman's Secrets* did not come out until his northern voyages were over, we may assume that the instruments of navigation he there described were being tried out in 1585–87. He says that the minimum equipment necessary for a skillful seaman consists of the compass, cross-staff, and chart, as the astrolabe and quadrant have proved to be "very uncertaine for Sea observations." Columbus and many others would have agreed heartily! He tells in detail how to use the cross-staff and his own backstaff to obtain latitude from sun or Pole Star. He improved the old traverse-board by compiling a "Traverse-Booke," and Hakluyt printed one for his third voyage. It is in the form of the standard nineteenth-century ship's log or journal; column one for courses, with the time spent on each; column two for calculated distance made good in each watch; column three for meridional observations of the sun; column four for wind direction, and a fifth for "the Discourse," what we would call "Remarks."

First Voyage, 1585

There were no Gilbertian delays to any of John Davis's voyages. He received the royal patent in February 1585 and was ready to sail in June. We are fortunate to have an account of this first voyage by a participant named John Janes, nephew "to the worshipfull M. William Sanderson," who shipped as supercargo. Here is the task organization as he gives it:

Captain and Chief Pilot, John Davis

Bark SUNNESHINE of London, 50 tuns, 23 people. John Davis, captain; William Eston, master; Richard Pope, master's mate; John Janes, "marchant." The roll includes a gunner, a boatswain, a carpenter, eleven mariners, one boy, and the inevitable four-piece orchestra. No Elizabethan voyage of discovery could do without that.

Bark MOONESHINE of Dartmouth, 35 tuns, 19 people. William Bruton, captain; John Ellis, master; "the rest mariners."

Thus the total complement was forty-two—a very modest expedition compared with Frobisher's and Gilbert's. But the sailors were picked men, as stout-hearted as their captain.

Departing Dartmouth 7 June 1585 with a moon approaching last quarter, they ran into the usual westerly winds, put into Channel harbors thrice, and only got clear of the Scillies on the 28th. Their first important event, on 19 July, was to hear "a great whirling and brustling of a tyde" and a "mighty great roaring of the Sea"; a terrifying sound in a fog so thick that neither bark could see the other. Davis, Janes, and Eston put out in a boat, and "did perceive that all the roaring which we heard, was caused oonely by rouling of this yce together." Next day "the fogge brake up" and with a full moon they raised the east coast of Greenland "which was the most deformed rocky and mountainous land that ever we saw." Snowy mountain tops stood up above the clouds, and there was a league of ice to break through before reaching shore. Greenland acquired a new name from Captain Davis: "Land of Desolation." Markham, who knew somewhat of this coast, identifies the spot as Cape Discord.* Efforts to push through the ice to the shore came to naught, and the cold so took it out of the men that the captain increased their rations. For breakfast, every mess of five would rate half a pound of hard-bread and a "kan"—a pint-size mug—"of beere." No tea, no coffee, nothing hot for Arctic voyagers in those days.

Making no further effort to explore the east coast, Davis turned south, doubled Cape Farewell without seeing it, and sailed northwesterly until 29 July when he sighted land to the northeastward. He found the latitude to be 64°15′ N; a good instance of his expertise at

* This name has disappeared from the map, but I find it in T. G. Bradford, *Illustrated Atlas of the U.S.* (1844). Apparently it is now called Cape Wallace, lat. about 60°40′.

taking and working out a sight, as Bowditch gives 64°11'. He had hit the entrance to the complex of fjords which had been the Norsemen's Western Settlement, and is now Godthaab. Davis named it Gilbert Sound.

The Englishmen's relations here with the Eskimo, who had moved in on the Northmen about a century earlier, were not altogether happy but very amusing. They announced their presence, after Davis, Eston, and Janes had showed themselves on a rocky island, by making a "lamentable noyse . . . with great outcryes and skreechings" like "the howling of wolves." The Captain's boat party converged on this island with a similar party from *Mooneshine*, which included the four-man orchestra. These, after landing, played while the captains and sailors danced. Ten Eskimo kayaks now approached, and when their paddlers landed "we allured them by friendly embracings and signes of curtesie." This approach not seeming to work, master Ellis of the smaller bark, as a self-appointed expert in race relations, alternately struck his breast and pointed at the sun, gestures which he believed would break the social ice, which they did. After depositing caps, stockings, and gloves on the ground as gifts, the Englishmen country-danced and played themselves into their boats and called it a day. What a pity that Davis did not have an artist like John White to depict this scene—fiddlers fiddling, mariners capering, and grinning Eskimo as audience.

After this overture it was easy to persuade the Eskimo to trade. The English bought five kayaks and "their clothes from their backs," for they appreciated the fine sealskin garments and boots tailored by Eskimo women and perfectly adapted to their habitat. Janes observed the dwarf willows and evergreens of Greenland, and a profusion of yellow flowers "like primroses."

On 1 August, with a fair wind, the two barks crossed the strait that would be named after their captain and made land in latitude 66°40', with no ice visible. They named it Exeter Sound, from the city that had supported Davis, and the two forelands after Sir Edward Dyer and Sir Francis Walsingham. At Totnes roadstead—named after a town up the Dart which had provided money for the voyage—and "under Mount Raleigh" four "white bears of a monstrous bignesse" were killed. Time has been kind to Davis's names, as a glance at the modern map will indicate; and his latitude is correct for Cape Walsingham.

This was the furthest north for Davis's first voyage. He amiably in-

George Clifford, Earl of Cumberland. Miniature by Nicholas Hilliard. Courtesy of Trustees of National Maritime Museum, Greenwich.

creased rations—for a mess of five men, four pounds of hard-bread daily, twelve wine quarts of beer, and six Newfoundland codfish on fast days; on flesh days, when bear meat helped out the salt beef, a gill of dried pease. But he had to cut down on their butter and cheese.

Sunneshine and *Mooneshine* made sail and departed Exeter Sound 8 August. They doubled the southernmost cape of the Peninsula on the 11th, naming it Cape of God's Mercy (God has been dropped from the name today), and entered a deep sound, hoping it would prove to be the Passage. Davis named it after George Clifford, Earl of Cumberland, a privateer owner and sailor in the war with Spain, perhaps an investor in this voyage.

They sailed some 180 miles into Cumberland Sound, and it is not

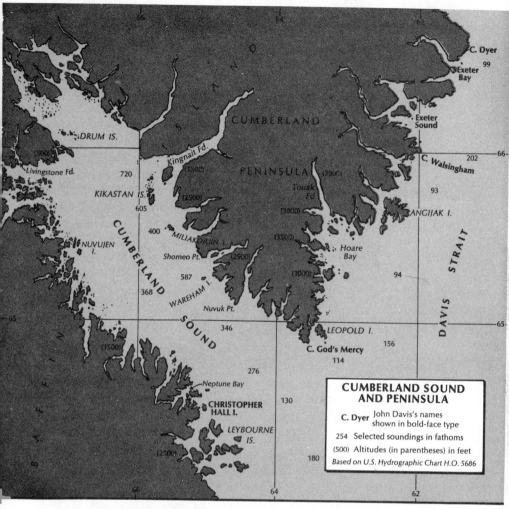

surrounding text on map:

C. Dyer
Exeter Bay
99

Exeter Sound

CUMBERLAND

C. Walsingham
202
66

93

ANGIJAK I.

DAVIS STRAIT

DRUM IS.
(500)

Livingstone Fd.
720

Kingnait Fd.
(1500)

PENINSULA
(3900)

Touak Fd

KIKASTAN IS.
605

(2500)

(3800)

C
U
M
B
E
R
L
A
N
D

400

MILIAKDJUIN I.

(3500)

NUVUJEN I.

Shomeo Pt.
(2500)

Hoare Bay

94

587

WAREHAM I.

368

Nuvuk Pt.

S
O
U
N
D

346

LEOPOLD I.
156

C. God's Mercy
114

65
65

276

(1500)

Neptune Bay

CHRISTOPHER HALL I.
130

LEYBOURNE IS.

(2500)

180

**CUMBERLAND SOUND
AND PENINSULA**

C. Dyer — John Davis's names
shown in bold-face type

254 Selected soundings in fathoms

(500) Altitudes (in parentheses) in feet

Based on U.S. Hydrographic Chart H.O. 5686

66
64
62

surprising that Davis thought this was "it." The further he sailed, the deeper the water. "Hard aboord the shoare" among islands (either the Miliakdjuin or the Kikastan group) he found no bottom at 330 fathom. No wonder, for the modern chart gives no bottom at 400 fathom off the Miliakdjuins and 485 to 605 fathom off the Kikastans. Other signs, too, convinced Davis that he was on the right course for Cathay; whales were sighted swimming from that direction, and tidal currents were swift and powerful. But, as with every other Northwesterman for three centuries, he did not press far enough to see. On arriving among islands at the head of Cumberland Sound, on 20 August, the day of full moon, the wind turned northwest. After discussion with Captain Bruton, the two masters, and the narrator Janes, Davis decided to start home. It was indeed high time, if they did not wish to be frozen in for the winter, with provisions for only six months. But Davis always regretted that he had turned back, and to Cumberland Sound he returned in 1587.

The Eskimo, doubtless remembering Frobisher's kidnapping, kept out of sight, but the Englishmen found ashore a pack of their huskies, two sleds, one of wood and the other of whalebone, and some Eskimo children's toys, including a miniature kayak.

After anchoring in a harbor on the south coast of Cumberland Sound, *Mooneshine* and *Sunneshine* cleared for England on 24 August. They picked up the "Land of Desolation" (Greenland) on 10 September, "thinking to goe on shoare, but we cold get never a good harborough," sighted England after a fast passage of two weeks, and on 30 September anchored off Dartmouth. How good those green hills of Devon must have looked! Adrian Gilbert and the whole clan warmly welcomed and encouraged Davis, who now heard what Raleigh was doing to fulfill Gilbert's plans.

Davis had enjoyed very good luck, compared with Frobisher, as it happened to be a warm summer. Even Cumberland Sound was "altogether void of any pester of ice."

Second Voyage, 1586

Captain John Davis, with the unquenchable optimism of Elizabethan mariners, now wrote to Sir Francis Walsingham about Cumberland Sound: "The northwest passage is a matter nothing doubtful, but at any tyme almost to be passed, the sea navigable, voyd of yse, the ayre tolerable and the waters very depe." The faithful merchants renewed their support, and on 7 May, with a new moon, began "The second voyage attempted by Master John Davis . . . for the discoverie of the Northwest Passage, in Anno 1586." He now had a fleet of four: ship *Mermayd* of 120 tuns, chartered by the adventurers for £100 a month, the same barks *Sunneshine* and *Mooneshine* as on the first voyage, and a ten-tun pinnace, the *North Starre,* "provided to be our scout for this discovery." A second pinnace, broken down, was carried in the ship. The total investment amounted to £1175, of which Exeter merchants contributed £475, those of Totnes £375, and London only £162 10s. Whatever the worshipful Mr. Sanderson gave is not known; but as Davis reported to him, it must have been considerable.

On 7 June, one month out, *Sunneshine* and *North Starre* broke off in pursuance of instructions to investigate the "straight over the Pole" route. We shall come back to them later.

This was a slow-sailing fleet. Not until 15 June did they raise the coast of Greenland, "mightily pestered with yce and snow, so that there was no hope of landing." The pack-ice that year extended from 30 to 150 miles off shore. Davis gives the latitude as 60° N, which is right for Cape Farewell, and even attempts to name its longitude—47° W of London. That was about three degrees off—a remarkably close longitude guess for the sixteenth century. Obviously he had been keeping accurate dead reckoning with his chip log and traverse table.

His next latitude after doubling Cape Farewell, 64° N, is exactly right for Gilbert Sound (Godthaab) and the complex of fjords behind it. The ships were not even anchored before swarms of Eskimo came out in kayaks, welcoming their musical friends of last year with embraces and gifts. Next day the Englishmen landed their knocked-down pinnace on a convenient island in the Norsemen's old bailiwick and began to assemble it. The Eskimo, forty to a hundred kayaks at a time, visited the men at their labor, bringing fish, fowl, hides, and white hares. Other Englishmen explored inland over "a plaine champion countrey" where the Norsemen had pastured their cattle. Davis with some of his men visited an Eskimo village, challenged the natives to a jumping contest, and "from leaping they went to wrestling; we found them strong and nimble, and to have skil in wrestling, for they cast some of our men that were good wrestlers."

On 4 July the pinnace was launched, with the help of forty natives shoving and hauling; and they held another wrestling match. The same day the master of *Mermayd*, on an excursion in search of firewood, uncovered what must have been the grave of Christian Norsemen, "having a crosse laid over them," since the Eskimo here were all "idolaters." "These people," concluded Davis, "are very simple in their conversation, but marvellous theevish, especially for iron." They began "to shew their vile nature" by cutting ships' cables to get the anchors. They cut away *Mooneshine*'s skiff and stole objects from the decks, to such an extent that Davis was persuaded to fire two cannon shots "which strange noice did sore amaze them, so that with speed they departed." Next day they were back, bearing propitiatory gifts but light-fingered as ever; and when prevented from boarding the ships, they threw big stones onto their decks with slings. The mariners, furious, told their Captain that that was his fault—"lenity and friendly using of them gave them stomacke to mischiefe." Better fire a broadside as a good example; but Davis "desired them to be content," i.e. tolerant; his visit was too short to convert the natives or "make them know their evils."

Following another visit on board, in which gifts were presented, the Eskimo treated *Mooneshine* to another barrage of stones, one of which hit the boatswain. Captain Davis then lost his temper, manned an armed boat, and pursued the kayaks. The natives escaped, just as they had from Frobisher's men, because no boat rowed by Europeans could ever catch a one-man kayak.

On 11 July five Eskimo came on board "to make a new truce." The Englishmen retained one as hostage for the stolen anchor, but did not wait long enough to get it back. "Within one houre that he came aboord, the winde came fayre, whereupon we weyed and set saile, and so brought the fellow with us." Davis, finding that this Eskimo "could not indure the cold" at sea, gave him a "new sute of frize after the English fashion . . . of which he was very joyfull." He lent a hand in sailing, and "became a pleasant companion among us." But he did not survive the voyage.

Sailing on 17 July, with moon in last quarter, *Mermayd* and *Mooneshine* fell in with an enormous iceberg, so big that the pinnace was sent to see if it were not land; it must have been more than one big berg as they "coasted this mighty masse of yce" for almost two weeks, their sails, shrouds, and lines becoming sheathed with ice. The men "through this extremity began to grow sicke and feeble," and respectfully urged Davis, for his own sake as well as theirs and their families, to return home. Davis compromised; *Mermayd* "not so convenient and nimble as a smaller bark, especially in such desperate hazzards," he consented to send home with about half the company, and to proceed with *Mooneshine* and the pinnace.

On 1 August, at latitude 66°33'—which is nearly accurate for the site of the present village of Inugsugtsusok—"and in longitude from the Meridian of London 70 degrees" (really 53°45' W), they "discovered the land." There they graved (cleaned the bottom of) *Mooneshine* and stowed some of *Mermayd*'s provisions in her. The Eskimo were friendly, but "a flie which is called Atuskyte . . . did sting grievously."

Leaving *Mermayd* at this spot to begin her homeward passage, Davis in *Mooneshine*, on 12 August, crossed the strait that would be named after him. Two days later he made the Cumberland Peninsula, Baffin Island, where he had been the year before. The crossing he estimated to be 210 miles, which is nearly correct, and the latitude 66° 19′, which is less than twenty miles out. Now, turning south, he passed "a very faire promontory in latitude 65°, having no land on the South." This was almost the correct latitude for Cape of God's Mercy, which Davis had named on his previous voyage. Why did he not recognize it? Davis now makes an interesting obervation which proves him to have been a careful navigator. From noon to noon, 18–19 August, "by precise ordinary care"—meaning dead reckoning, and using the chip log, "We had sailed 15 leagues South by west, yet by art and more exact observation, we found our course to be Southwest," proving the existence of a westward-running current. This means that he was taking meridional altitudes of the sun, and probably dawn and dusk sights of Polaris, with the backstaff that he had invented.

On 19 August at 6 p.m., just as those in the little bark thought they were hot on the trail to China, it began to snow. Davis hove-to all night and, when morning broke fair, turned shoreward and found a fine landlocked harbor in which to spend the night. This must have been either on Resolution Island or Hall's Island. The Captain climbed a hill to look for a possible passage, but saw only islands. How tired he must have been of seeing nothing but one archipelago after another!

Mooneshine now coasted south until 28 August when, according to Davis's calculations, they were in latitude 56° off the Labrador. They had missed the entrance to Hudson Strait, which would have led to something worth while, though considerably short of China. They called at "a very faire harbour" up which they sailed, and which we can identify from Davis's latitude as Jack Lane Bay; the inlet has been named Davis in his honor. He reported the trees and the wild fowl, "of the partridge and fezant we killed a great store with bowe and ar-rowes." Englishmen of that era were expert archers both with long bow and crossbow, and they used arrows in preference to bullets for shooting birds.

After riding out a couple of storms, Davis left this pleasant spot of the Labrador coast on 1 September, continuing south. On the 3rd at 54° 30′—which is just right for Cut Throat Tickle and Run By Guess

Island—they dropped a kedge anchor to fish, and made an apostolic haul of cod, "the largest and best fed fish that ever I sawe," wrote Davis, and "divers fishermen" with him agreed. They were at the northern entrance to Hamilton Inlet, the appearance of which gave Davis "a perfect hope of the passage," and he was eager to explore it; but a strong west wind blowing directly out of the inlet prevented.

On 4 September in a good roadstead "among great store of Isles" off Cape Porcupine and the Norsemen's Wonder Strands, Davis anchored and hauled in a "mightie store" of codfish. Wishing to save for his homeward passage the fish that they could not eat at once, he sent some men ashore, probably on the Wonder Strands at Trunmore Bay, to split and cure them on flakes. That detained them several days. On the morning of 6 September five young sailors, having rowed ashore to uncover the fish, were suddenly attacked by "the brutish people of this countrey," as Davis calls them, "who lay secretly lurking in the wood." The Captain promptly rendered gunfire support to the young men, who were fighting desperately with their backs to the sea. He slipped cables, sailed shoreward under foresail, and discharged two volleys of musketry "at the noyse whereof they fled." But two young seamen had been killed by arrows and two were badly wounded; the fifth, with an arrow through his arm, escaped by swimming.

That evening "It pleased God farther to increase our sorrowes" by blowing up "a mighty tempestuous storme" which lasted four days. The direction of the gale, north-northeast, put *Mooneshine* on a lee shore with the pleasant prospect of dragging her anchor and grounding on the Wonder Strands "among these Canibals for theyr pray." Davis cut down his top-hamper almost to bare poles, yet the windage caused the cable of his sheet-anchor to part. "In this deepe distresse the mightie mercie of God, when hope was past, gave us succor, and sent us a fayre lee." The wind suddenly backed to the westward—"so we recovered our anker again, and newe mored our shippe." They had been held "by an olde junke," * a single strand of the other cable; another proof of divine protection.

On 11 September, with a fair west-northwest wind, Davis departed the inhospitable Wonder Strands, "shaping our course for England." They arrived somewhere in the West Country at the beginning of October.

---

* The original meaning of "junk" is old rope; the naval accounts of Henry VII distinguish "old jonkes" from "hausers."

Now let us see what happened to the other half of this fruitless second voyage—bark *Sunneshine*, Richard Pope, master, with sixteen men, and pinnace *North Starre* with about ten men. They sailed with Captain Davis, took their departure from Dursey Head the same day (11 May 1586), and at latitude 60° N, by agreement, broke off to seek a passage between Greenland and Iceland up to latitude 80° N, "if land did not let us." Their plan was to prove Robert Thorne's and John Dee's scheme of sailing right over the North Pole.

No land prevented them, but ice did. They called first at Iceland, departed 16 June, and it took them three weeks to reach Greenland, which "was very high, and it looked very blew." As usual the pack-ice prevented them from landing. Ten days later they recognized a place which Captain Davis the year before had named "Land of Desolation," presumably Cape Discord. Again, plenty pack-ice and no possible landing. This indicates that master Pope gave up his polar quest before even crossing the Arctic Circle, and decided instead to nip around to Gilbert Sound (Godthaab) on the west coast, which Davis had fixed as a rendezvous. There *Sunneshine* and *North Starre* arrived on 3 August, weeks after Davis had departed. They tarried for twenty days. Although the local Eskimo at first exhibited only unfriendly and threatening attitudes (Davis having kidnapped one of them), they gradually warmed up. The English did a good trade in sealskin, bringing home 500 whole ones and 140 half-skins. "Divers times," says purser Morgan of *Sunneshine*, who wrote this narrative, "they did weave us on shore to play with them at the foot-ball, and some of our company went on shore to play with them, and our men did cast them downe as soon as they did come to strike the ball."

This first recorded international football match did not resemble anything known as football today. It must have been the English medieval village game, in which two goals were set up as much as a mile apart, and the contestants, of any number provided both sides were equal, tried to kick, butt, or throw the ball through the other side's goal. Apparently the Eskimo had a similar game but had not learned how to ward off a tackle.

On 30 August, Pope anchored in a harbor south of Gilbert's Sound. There the English had an unnecessary scuffle with the natives over a kayak which they had bought, but tried to turn in when it proved to be leaky. Bows and arrows were the weapons on both sides. Casualties were three Eskimo killed and several wounded, and one Englishman wounded. Having thus undone most of the good that Davis had done for race relations at this point, *Sunneshine* "departed from Gilberts sound for England" on the last day of August, and dropped Greenland under the horizon on 2 September.

The third day out, at night, "We lost sight of the *North Starre* our pinnesse in a very great storme," and lay a-hull for a full day hoping to sight her. But she was never heard of again. We have already observed the high mortality among pinnaces—Frobisher's and Gilbert's. The trouble with this type was its want of a complete, watertight deck, making it liable to be pooped and swamped by a heavy following sea.

Sunneshine reached Dartmouth 4 October and continued through the English Channel and up the Thames to Ratcliff, "in safety God be thanked," on 6 October.

The indefatigable John Davis, according to his report on 14 October 1586 to William Sanderson, seems to have been very pleased with himself after a voyage which had really been a failure. He is certain that the Northwest Passage "must be in one of four places, or els not at all." "This voyage may be performed without further charge, nay, with certaine profit to the adventurers." He is ready to sell his portion of Sandridge, the family estate, to "see an end of these businesses."

Never is there "an end of these businesses," even in 1970.

Third Voyage, 1587

John Davis must have been very plausible and impressive, since Adrian Gilbert, Sanderson, and other supporters now backed him for a third voyage as "Chiefe Captaine & Pilot generall, for the discoverie of a passage to the Isles of the Molucca, or the coast of China, in the yeere 1587."

His task force consisted of the old *Sunneshine* of London, 50 tuns, a Dartmouth bark named *Elizabeth* (burthen unknown), and a small "clincher" (clinker-built pinnace) named *Ellen,* or *Helene,* of London, Captain Pierson. Janes and the Captain were very doubtful of taking a clincher on so long a voyage; "neverthelesse we put our trust in God," and all three sailed from Dartmouth on 19 May, a week after full moon. The clincher made a bad start, breaking her tiller first night out. Nevertheless, says Janes, "we went forward, hoping that a hard beginning would make a good ending." And so it did.

This time they had fair northeasterly winds to clear the Channel and Scilly. One week out, *Sunneshine* sprang a leak, pumped 500 strokes a watch, but located and stopped it by shifting the ballast until the hole came out of water, while the other two vessels waited, hove-to. On the 28th *Elizabeth* for eighteen hours towed the *Ellen* "which was so much bragged of by the owners report before we came out of England, but at Sea she was like a cart drawen by oxen. Sometimes we towed her because she could not saile in a head wind." A bad handicap to the fleet's speed.

A near-mutiny broke out because some of the sailors had been promised a profitable fishing voyage and wanted to sail to the Banks right away; but "after much talke and many threatenings they were content to bring us to the land." Davis, in the column of his "Traverse-Booke" for remarks, indicates that he was constantly working out "true course"—i.e. course made good, "drawen from divers traverses." For instance, seventy-two hours' sailing 2–5 June, with wind west-south-west, he made good 135 miles "W. by S., Southerly," indicating that in mid-ocean with presumably a heavy sea, all three (the clincher some-times under tow) made good a course better than five points on the wind. Davis did not embrace this opportunity to make better northing and westing because he was bound for the west coast of Greenland and did not care to risk bumping into ice off Cape Farewell.

On 7 June wind shifted to the southeastern quadrant, and even the despisèd clincher could keep up. On the 14th, moon almost full, they sighted high land, and on the 16th, "being in the latitude of 64° through God's helpe we came to an anker among many low islands." This was already familiar Godthaab, Greenland, which Davis had named Gilbert's Sound. His latitude was correct: Bowditch gives that of Godthaab's flagstaff as 64° 10′ 36″. The Eskimo "came presently to us after the old maner, with crying *Ilyuoute*, and shewing us Seales skinnes." This slogan apparently meant "I have no knife, so let us talk."

The first job there was to assemble a second pinnace which had been brought knocked-down in the *Elizabeth*. After Davis had made the mistake of capturing "a very strong lusty young fellow" as a hostage for good behavior, the natives started stripping the planking off the new pinnace as fast as the strakes were nailed in place, "onely for the love of the iron in the boords." *Sunneshine*'s gunner fired a blank shot to make them desist, but they scampered off with their spoil to another island. Captain Davis decided that under these circumstances there was no use trying to assemble the pinnace; he had her knocked down again and stowed on board *Elizabeth* for use in fishing. William Bruton, master of *Sunneshine*, informed his captain that "the good ship which we must all hazard our lives in" was leaking 300 strokes an hour while riding at anchor. "This disquieted us all greatly." No wonder! Davis, typically, "determined rather to end his life with credite then to re-turne with infamie and disgrace," and so inspired his shipmates that they "purposed to live and die together, and committed ourselves to the ship." Since the crew of leaky *Sunneshine* as well as that of *Eliza-beth* preferred to continue their voyage fishing instead of exploring, and were likely to be mutinous and useless if denied, Davis generously released them, and on 21 June "departed from this coast, our two barks for their fishing voyage, and my self in the pinnesse for the discovery."

The main purpose of this voyage being to explore the northern part of Davis Strait, which later became Baffin Bay, the Captain set a northerly course, along the west coast of Greenland. Clincher *Ellen* crossed the Arctic Circle, and on the 24th arrived at latitude 67°40' off the modern Nordrestromfjord. That day and the next they had profit-able trucking with Eskimo who paddled thirty miles off shore to get the white men's "pinnes, needles, bracelets, nailes, knives, bels, looking glasses and other small trifles," in return for "salmon peale" (grilse), caplin, wild fowl, and seal skins. "For these last 4 dayes the weather hath beene extreame hot and very calme, the Sun being 5 degrees above the horizon at midnight," recorded Davis in his "Discourse," and he noted that the compass variation was 28° W.

On 30 June, day of full moon, after "we took the heigth and found ourselves in 72°12'," Davis continued to the site of the modern Uperna-vik, where an 850-foot cliff rises sheer from the sea. The latitude is 72°46', and this was Davis's furthest north. He named the place "Hope Sanderson" in honor of his backer; and a good hope it proved to be, as the Northwest Passage starts across Baffin Bay, in Lancaster Sound.

Sanderson's Hope disappeared from the map in the last century, but it was well known as such when the explorer Sherard Osborn arrived on Midsummer Day 1850. "We hauled-in for the land," he wrote. "Passing into a channel, some four miles in width, we found ourselves running past the remarkable and lofty cliffs of "Sanderson his Hope." . . . The Hope's lofty crest pierced through the clouds which drove athwart its breast. . . . Under its lee, the water was a sheet of foam and spray, from the fierce gusts which swept down ravine and over headland; and against the base of the rocks, flights of wild fowl marked a spot famous amongst arctic voyagers." Elisha Kent Kane followed Osborn a few years later and left us a good illustration of it.

Davis now turned west, and soon encountered the long north-south pack-ice which blocks the middle of Baffin Bay the year round, melting a little every summer and gathering more ice every winter. With a north wind blowing, he could not hope to "double it out by the North" (nor, had he tried, could he have found any end); so he coasted the mass southerly. On 6 July, seeing a gap in the ice which apparently led to clear water, Davis "put our barke with oares through," found himself in a pool surrounded by towering icebergs, and was glad to get out alive.

Not until 16 July could the clincher double the southern tip of this pack-ice. Then, after two days of fog, Davis sighted the mountains on Baffin Island, just north of Exeter Sound, where he had named a hill Mount Raleigh on the first voyage. By midnight they were "athwart the Streights," as Davis hopefully called the dead-end Cumberland Sound. Doubling Cape of God's Mercy, *Ellen* sailed up Cumberland Sound 150 to 180 miles, and on 23 July anchored "among many Isles in the bottom of the gulfe, naming the same *The Eerle of Cumberlands Isles*," and noting a 30-degree westerly variation of the compass. On the 24th Davis "set saile, departing from the place, and Shaping our Course southeast to recover the Maine Ocean againe."

Becalmed on the 25th, "the weather marvellous extreame hot," master Bruton and several mariners went ashore "to course dogs"—the first hint that Davis had with him a few couple of hounds. They had not been let ashore earlier for fear of the Eskimo huskies, with the result that they were so soft and fat from eating codfish "that they were scarce able to run." Here is the most comic episode of the voyage —musicians blowing horns, sailors trying to "sic" the hounds onto a fox or hare, all hands shouting "tally-ho!" and cracking whips, and the over-fed hounds waddling a short distance then lying down with their tongues lolling out. The Englishmen, furious at being robbed of their sport, had to call off the hunt, unsuccessful as their quest for the Northwest Passage.

On 29 July *Ellen* cleared Cumberland Sound, under a full moon,

Sanderson's Hope, almost three centuries later. From Elisha Kent Kane, *Arctic Explorations* (1856).

and on the 30th passed the mouth of an "Inlet which lay between 63 and 62 degrees of latitude, which we called *Lumlie's Inlet*." It was named after John, Baron Lumley, high steward of the University of Oxford and an important person at Queen Elizabeth's court. At that of her successor, James I, he became unpopular because he boasted too much about his ancestors; the king is said to have cut off one such harangue with, "Stop mon! thou need'st no more: now I learn that Adam's surname was Lumley!"

Lumley's Inlet must have been Frobisher Bay; the reason that Davis did not recognize it as such was that the map-makers, confused by the false Zeno chart, had driven Frobisher's discovery right through southern Greenland. Passing a headland (the southern tip of Meta Incognita or of Resolution Island) which he named Warwick's Foreland, Davis's *Ellen* fell into an "overfall" or tide-rip, "lothsomly crying like the rage of the waters under London bridge," and had the curious but alarming experience of racing an iceberg caught in the same current. It was a fair wind, and the clincher bent on every sail, but the iceberg won.

Between 31 July and 1 August she "passed by a very great gulfe, the water whirling and roaring as it were the meetings of tydes." Why

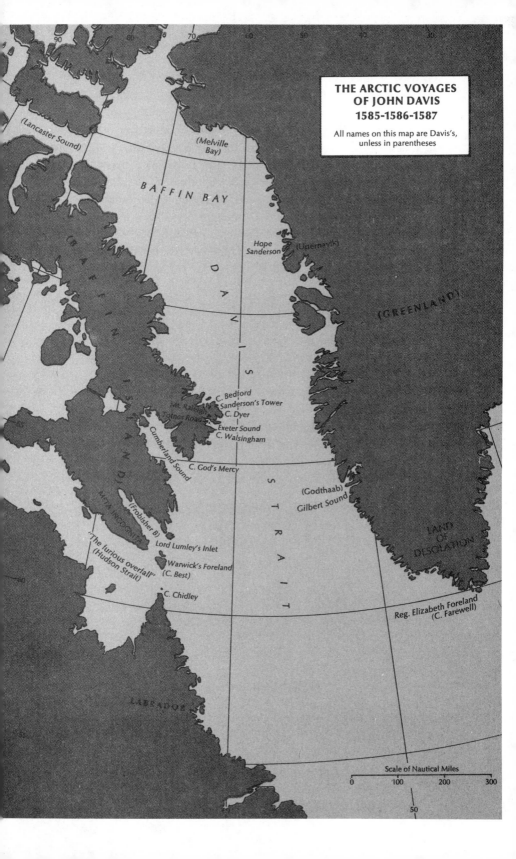

THE ARCTIC VOYAGES
OF JOHN DAVIS
1585-1586-1587

All names on this map are Davis's,
unless in parentheses

(Lancaster Sound)

(Melville
Bay)

BAFFIN BAY

(GREENLAND)

Hope
Sanderson (Upernavik)

D
A
V
I
S

BAFFIN ISLAND

C. Bedford
Mt. Raleigh Sanderson's Tower
Totnes Road C. Dyer
Exeter Sound
C. Walsingham

Cumberland Sound

C. God's Mercy

S
T
R
A
I
T

(Godthaab)
Gilbert Sound

META INCOGNITA

(Frobisher B.)

Lord Lumley's Inlet

LAND
OF
DESOLATION

"The furious overfall"
(Hudson Strait)

Warwick's Foreland
(C. Best)

C. Chidley

Reg. Elizabeth Foreland
(C. Farewell)

LABRADOR

Scale of Nautical Miles

0   100   200   300

50

did Davis not explore it? This was Hudson Strait, which would not, to be sure, have led to Cathay but to a valuable bay. Possibly "ice" is the answer, for *Ellen* had to coast "a banke of ice which was driven out at the mouth of this gulfe" before reaching the northernmost point of the Labrador. This cape, whose latitude Davis gives correctly as 60°26′ N, he named *Chidleis* after his friend, an old Devon master mariner, Captain Chudleigh. Cape Chidley it still is today.

The Captain had set a rendezvous with his barks on the Labrador coast between latitudes 54° and 53°, where they were then supposed to be fishing. He therefore ranged the Labrador as he had done the previous year, looking for the errant vessels. A "frisking gale at the west-northwest" blew up on 10 August. Next day he sighted five deer on an island that he named Darcie's after John, Baron Darcy of Chiche, father-in-law of Lord Lumley. Assuming Davis's latitude 54°32′ to have been correct, this was White Cockade or Brig Harbor Island at the northern entrance to Hamilton Inlet, where he had anchored the year before. The presence of game gave these Englishmen another chance for a hunt with their lazy hounds. The fat mutts, apparently having been put on short rations, now condescended to provide a little sport; they coursed the deer twice around the island—imagine the yapping and yelling and tooting of horns!—only to have their quarry take to the sea and escape to the next island. "One of them was as big as a good prettie Cow, and very fat, their feete as big as Ox feet," observed Janes. He did shoot a gray hare, small consolation for losing the deer.

Finding neither bark nor any "marke, token or beacon" which they might have set up, Davis sailed as far south as Château Bay, the famous fishing rendezvous on the Strait of Belle Isle. Thence, on 15 August, with a new moon "we shaped our course for England, in God's name," without even stopping to take on wood and water. Two days later they were chased by a Basque vessel on the Grand Bank, but escaped. "After much variable weather and change of windes we arrived the 15 of September in Dartmouth, anno 1587, giving thanks to God for our safe arrival." *Elizabeth* and *Sunneshine* had already arrived, their holds crammed with stockfish. This big haul convinced the dwellers on the Dart that the Newfoundland fishery was really profitable.

To Sanderson in London, Davis wrote on the 16th, "Yesterday . . . I landed all wearie therefore I pray you pardon my shortnesse. . . .

The passage is most probable, the execution easie." It was a remarkable voyage to have been made in the tiny, slow-sailing pinnace *Ellen*.

Janes's account in the 1589 edition of Hakluyt suggested to the king of Denmark that he had better assert his prior rights to Greenland (assuming his succession to King Olaf Tryggvason), or some other power would get it. Accordingly, Greenland has been under Danish sovereignty since the seventeenth century, and the Danes have dealt with the Eskimo humanely and intelligently.

No more just, courageous, and wise seaman than Davis ever sailed under the Cross of St. George. Humane, modest, a good but not stiff disciplinarian, and so intelligent a navigator as to invent new instruments and methods, he should be regarded as the greatest of not only the Devon group but of all Elizabethan mariners. It is too bad that his skills and aptitudes were wasted on an enterprise, seeking the Northwest Passage, as impossible a goal for that age as a landing on the moon would have been in 1900. Nevertheless, just as Cartier on his first voyage found the key to a major water route to penetrate the continent; so Davis, by reaching Sanderson's Hope (Upernavik) at latitude 72°46′ N, had unwittingly found the key to the Northwest Passage. Almost directly across Baffin Bay, west-northwest from Sanderson's Hope, lies the entrance to Lancaster Sound where the actual Northwest Passage begins. Less fortunate than Jacques Cartier, John Davis had many more adventures at sea before being killed by Japanese pirates in 1605 at the age of fifty-five.

Bibliography and Notes

SOURCES AND AUTHORITIES

John Davis is no favorite of the present generation of English historians, probably because he never claimed to be "first" at anything, and his life has never been the subject of intensive research as have those of the Cabots and the Gilberts. Nothing important about him has been published for ninety years. Nobody has yet combed local records in search of information about him and his ships.

The accessible sources are, every edition of Hakluyt from 1589 on, and a volume of the Hakluyt Society, *The Voyages and Works of John Davis*, well edited by Captain Albert H. Markham R.N. (London, 1880). This volume includes narratives of Davis's Far Eastern voyages, a reprint of *The Seaman's Secrets*, and a good biographical introduction.

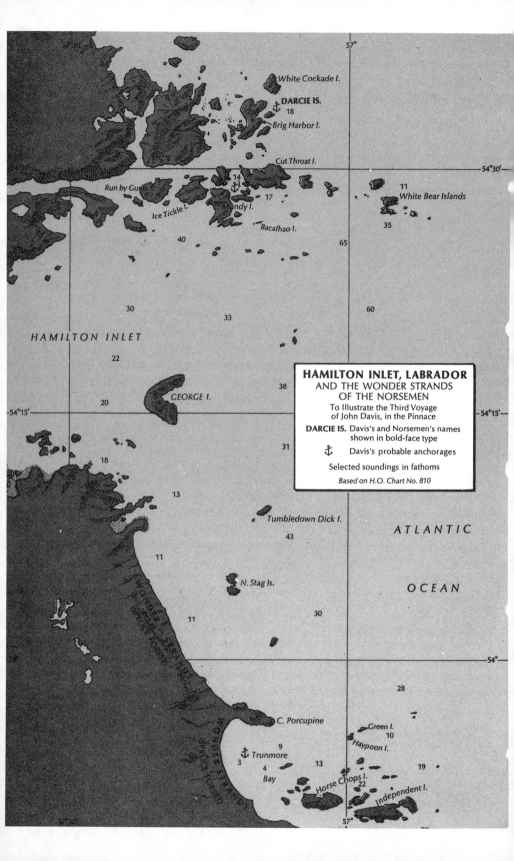

HAMILTON INLET, LABRADOR
AND THE WONDER STRANDS
OF THE NORSEMEN
To Illustrate the Third Voyage
of John Davis, in the Pinnace
DARCIE IS. Davis's and Norsemen's names
shown in bold-face type
⚓ Davis's probable anchorages
Selected soundings in fathoms
Based on H.O. Chart No. 810

Hakluyt's accounts of Davis's first and third voyages are by John Janes the "marchant"; that of the second by Davis himself, and that of the *Sunneshine* and *North Starre* cruise by Henry Morgan, "servant to Mr. Sanderson."

The only biography worth mentioning is Clements R. Markham, *A Life of John Davis* (London and New York, 1895).

Among modern mariners inspired by John Davis were Rear Admiral Richard E. Byrd USN and Robin Knox-Johnston, who in *A World of My Own* (1969), states how he was cheered by Davis's speech (quoted at the head of Chapter XVIII). Lacking a contemporary description of Davis, I like to think that he inspired his contemporary William Bourne, in his *Regiment for the Sea*, the chapter on "What maner of persons be meetest to take charge of Shippes in Navigation" which may be found in the Hakluyt Society edition, pp. 170–71.

PLACE NAMES

These are comparatively easy to identify for Davis's voyages because he took accurate latitudes, many of which are mentioned in the narratives, and his "Traverse Booke" or deck log, for the third voyage is printed in Hakluyt and in the Hakluyt Society's 1880 volume, 49–59. Nevertheless, the secondary authorities have made rather wild work of his courses, especially for the Labrador. My identification of the place where *Ellen* almost dragged ashore and two men were killed by Indians, as Trunmore Bay, is based on Davis's description and my own observation from the air. The distance from Hamilton Inlet, says Davis, is twenty-four miles, the depth four fathom, which agrees with the modern chart, and the place was "full of fayre woods." This was the unique spruce forest that grows on the narrow sandy plain bordering the Norsemen's Wonder Strands. This beach was ideal for curing fish, and nowhere else on the entire Labrador coast could Indians have issued from a forest ambush to attack men on a beach.

The *Earl of Cumberland's Isles*, where the hare hunt took place, I judge to have been Drum Island or the islands in Netilling Fjord. Although it has been stated that Davis named Cape Farewell, Greenland, I find no evidence that he did, and on the Molyneux Globe it is called Queen Elizabeth's Foreland—the name that Frobisher had given to Resolution Island off Meta Incognita. Davis had been convinced by English map-makers who stupidly accepted the Zeno map as accurate, that Frobisher's Strait ran across southern Greenland. That is why, when he saw the "Strait," he did not recognize it as Frobisher's and named it after Lord Lumley. But do not write down Davis as dumb. Even the *Atlas universel* (1841) by the eminent French geographer Alexandre E. Lapie, *premier géographe du Roi*, has (*planche* 16) a wide strait running right through Greenland, no Frobisher Bay or Strait on Baffin Island, and depicts Cumberland Sound as a strait connecting with Hudson's.

Davis's system of nomenclature was to give each of his principal backers something on the map for their money. Modestly, he named nothing after himself or his family; *fretum Davis* is first mentioned on the Molyneux Map and Globe of 1586–92.

MOLYNEUX MAP AND GLOBE

After his third Arctic voyage, Davis busied himself, with Sanderson and Emery Molyneux the map-maker, in producing the Molyneux Map and Globe to illustrate his and other discoveries. The map was not very good, since it reflected the Zeno heresy; but England was very proud of it. Shakespeare is supposed to have been thinking of this map when Maria in *Twelfth Night*, III, i, 89 says, "He does smile his face into more lines than are in the new map with the augmentation of the Indies."

Emery Molyneux of Lambeth, "Emerius Mulleneux" on the cartouche, made several globes of which two survive: the Petworth, dated 1592, in the British Museum, and one dated 1603 in the Middle Temple, London. Reproduction of the Northwest Passage part of the first is in R. A. Skelton, *Explorers' Maps* (1958), p. 123; also chap. v. The Map, which first appeared in the 1589 edition of Hakluyt's *Voyages*, is a close copy of the Globe— or vice versa. Helen M. Wallis, "The First English Globe" and "Further Light on the Molyneux Globes," *Geographical Journal*, CXVII (1951), 275–90, and CXXI (1958), 305–11. Miss Wallis interprets a legend on the Globe to mean that Molyneux sailed with Davis, but I think it means no more than that Davis helped him in its preparation. Frobisher's Strait crosses Greenland, whose west coast honestly ends with "Hope Sanderson." The east coast of Baffin Island, where Cumberland Sound, Lord Lumley's Inlet, and the "furious overfall" are entered, is depicted as part of the Labrador.

DAVIS'S NAUTICAL INVENTIONS AND LATER CAREER

The next notice we have of Davis is in 1589, when "with shippe pinnace and boat" he joined the fleet of the Earl of Cumberland off the Azores. As captain of the *Desire*, we find him in 1591 under the command of Thomas Cavendish the circumnavigator. This voyage ended with a series of disasters, including the death of Cavendish. Davis made Ireland in June 1593, with only fifteen men of his original crew of seventy-six alive. During this voyage he discovered the Falkland Islands, which England still tenaciously holds against the claims of the Argentine Republic.

John Davis now used his mathematical knowledge and maritime experience to write a rutter, *The Seaman's Secrets*. The first edition came out in 1594. This, easily the best book on navigation in the sixteenth century, imparted to all navigators, the methods, instruments, "wrinkles," etc. that Davis had worked out in his many voyages. It became the Bible to English mariners in the next century. The only known copy of the first edition is in Lambeth Palace Library; the 1607 edition is reprinted in Markham's *Voyages and Works of John Davis*. In 1595 Davis also brought out *The*

Northwest part of Molyneux Map of *c.* 1586–87. First to name Davis
Strait and to show his furthest north, Hope Sanderson. Note the Zeno
names, Friesland and Estotiland; the first Virginia colony, proving that the
map must have been drafted after 1585; and the confusion that still reigns
over the New England coast. From Nordenskjold, *Facsimile Atlas.*

World's Hydrographical Description, copies of which are in the Newberry
Library, Chicago, and the New York Public Library. These, and the
instruments, are discussed in D. W. Waters, *Art of Navigation* (1958), pp.
201–9.

Of all Davis's inventions, the backstaff was the most simple and therefore
most useful to mariners. It obviated the inconvenient glare in your eyes
when "shooting the sun," but was not too good for stars. As Davis himself

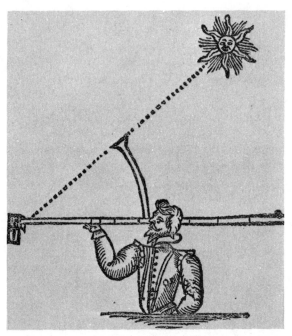

Solar altitude by Davis's backstaff. From John Davis, *Seaman's Secrets*
(Hakluyt Soc. ed. 1880).

explains in *The Seaman's Secrets*, a slit in the plate at the end of the staff
is directed at the horizon. Then you move the "transversary" until the
shadow of its upper edge, made by the sun, "doe fall directly upon the
said slitte." Then measure the height on the scale.

Davis's Quadrant, first described in 1595 but probably worked out by
Davis on his Arctic voyages, was an improvement on the backstaff. The
small arc had a lens which projected an image of the celestial body to the
sighting slot which you aimed at the horizon. The big arc, like the vernier
on a modern sextant, had a scale giving you fractions of a degree. You read
the altitude off a sliding member on the big arc which contained a peep-
hole for the observer. This instrument was so accurate as to be used long
after the invention of Hadley's quadrant; the one in our illustration was
made at Salem in 1775.

The Chip Log. This method of measuring a ship's speed is described in
William Bourne, *A Regiment for the Sea* (1574), and elaborated in the
1580 edition (page 297). It is so simple and cheap a device, one which any
good "chips" could clap together, that it is difficult to believe Davis did not
use it; but he never mentions it in his *Seaman's Secrets* or in the accounts

of his voyages. The "chip", or "log" was a plate of hardwood weighted to stand perpendicular to the surface. Attached to it by a bowline was the log line, wound on a reel. This line, beginning at 60 feet from the log, had a knot rove into it at 42-foot intervals, each being one-120th of a mile. Streaming the log properly required several persons. One sailor held up the reel; a second saw to it that the line ran free in order not to jerk the chip through the water; a third threw the chip over the taffrail, shouted "Mark!" when the first knot passed into the water; a fourth then turned up a half-minute glass (1/120th of an hour); a fifth sailor counted the knots as they went over the taffrail. The number which passed before the sand ran out of the glass indicated the number of miles per hour the ship was making. With modifications, this system lasted right through the days of sail and was used by steamers well into the last century; there is a picture of the process in Augustus Hoppin, *Crossing the Atlantic* (Boston, 1872), in a Cunarder; and midshipmen at the U. S. Naval Academy before World War I were taught how to "stream the log" on their summer cruises.

See also Notes to Chapters V and XV above.

After his return from the Cavendish voyage, Davis became flag pilot in the first fleet that the English East India Company sent to the Far East. This voyage, under Captain James Lancaster in *Sea Dragon*, lasted from 1601 to 1603.

Mr. Philip C. F. Smith shooting the sun with the Peabody Museum's Davis quadrant.

Queen Elizabeth died that year, and James I became king of England. Despite the East India Company's chartered monopoly of the Far Eastern trade, James granted to a favorite, Sir Edward Michelbourne, a license to make a voyage to "Cathaia and Japan." Davis became fleet pilot in the 240-tun ship *Tiger*—probably not Raleigh's *Tiger*, which by this time must have been scrapped. She sailed from Cowes in December 1604 and made Bantam in October 1605. On the next leg of the voyage, she fell in with a ship full of Japanese. The Englishmen treated them "with good usage" at a harbor on the eastern entrance of the Strait of Malacca. This happened on 29 December 1605. Unfortunately, the Japanese turned out to be pirates. While being entertained on board, they made a desperate attempt to capture the *Tiger* and were only driven overboard after a long and bloody fight, in which John Davis was killed.

So perished a great seaman and navigator. His unfaithful wife having died, Davis divided his property, in a will drafted just before this last voyage, into four parts: one to Judith Havard whom he was engaged to marry, and one to each of his sons Gilbert, Arthur, and Philip. Nothing seems to be known about their lives. With no leading family to promote his fame, Davis's exploits faded from view. His services to exploration and navigation have never been adequately recognized.

SUMMARY OF QUEST FOR NORTHWEST PASSAGE, 1609–1969

Stefansson rightly points out that the Eskimo were the first to get through from Asia, in their kayaks; but it probably took them centuries to get from Alaska to Greenland.

1610–11. Henry Hudson, after exploring the great river named after him up to the site of Albany, made another attempt in the bark *Discovery* of 55 tuns. Shrewdly estimating the "furious overfall" observed by Davis at the mouth of Frobisher's "Mistaken Strait," he sailed up Hudson Strait into the great bay named after him. After wintering in James Bay, mutineers captured the *Discovery* (June 1611) and marooned Hudson, his son, and six loyal members of the crew, who were never heard of again. Robert Bylot brought the ship back to England and escaped serious punishment.

1612–15. Thomas Button and Bylot, both in *Discovery*, made two voyages in search of Hudson and the Passage. They returned without finding either. William Baffin, second in command, reported Hudson Strait and Foxe Basin to be dead ends as far as the Passage was concerned, starting where Davis had left off.

1616. Second Bylot-Baffin voyage in *Discovery*. Sailed beyond Sanderson's Hope to about latitude 78° N, into Smith Sound between Ellesmere Island and Greenland. This was Furthest North until 1853. On their return, they discovered and named Lancaster Sound, true beginning of the Northwest Passage, but they thought it to be only another dead-end.

1670. Establishment of the great Hudson's Bay Company. This led to various unsuccessful attempts to get through from the Bay. None ever did—the pack-ice is too thick.

1753-54. The *Argo* of Philadelphia, Captain Charles Swaine, an expedition promoted by Benjamin Franklin and other Philadelphians. Never got very far, and several sailors when prospecting for gold were killed by Eskimo. L. W. Labaree, *Papers of Benjamin Franklin*, IV, 380-84, 448; V, 148, with many references. Ben Franklin, ever an optimistic Northwestman, fell for the phony voyage of De Fonte, alias Fuentes. See Note on Anian to Chapter XV above.

1819-22. Sir John Franklin's First Expedition. He got as far as King William Island, where his ships were frozen in. He and several members of the crew escaped overland.

1819-20. Attempt of Sir William Parry RN in bark *Hecla*, 375 tons. Sailed through Lancaster Sound to Melville Island. His way blocked by ice, he spent the winter and returned safely. Later voyages of his were even less successful.

1829-31. John Ross and his nephew Sir James Clark Ross, in 150-ton *Victory* with an auxiliary sidewheel engine, tried the Prince Regent Inlet from Lancaster Sound to the Boothia Peninsula; frozen in for the winter, the men escaped by boat and were rescued by a whaling ship.

1845-48. Sir John Franklin's expedition in H. M. S. *Erebus* and *Terror*, sailing ships with auxiliary steam engines. They were last seen by a whaler near the entrance to Lancaster Sound on 26 July 1845. They wintered at Beechey Island off southwest coast of Devon Island; next year sailed south through Franklin Strait and were frozen in on the west coast of King William Island from September 1846 to April 1848. Sir John and twenty-four men died in the meantime, and the 125 survivors, abandoning ship, started off for the mouth of the Back, or Fish, River; all perished en route. Expedition after expedition was sent to ascertain the fate of this expedition, even in hope of finding survivors among the Eskimo. Finally the truth was ascertained from Eskimo accounts, and human remains. More relics have been found from time to time; as late as 1925 Knud Rasmussen read the burial service over skeletons of Franklin's men at Starvation Cove. But these relief expeditions explored so much new land and ice in the Arctic as to pave the way for later successes, and left their names on the map.

1850-54. One of these searchers, Commander Robert McClure R.N., of H.M.S. *Enterprise*, actually got through the Passage from west to east, but partly on foot.

1903-5. Roald Amundsen bought Norwegian fishing sloop *Gjøa* (length 70 feet, beam 20 feet, registered tonnage 47), strengthened her frame, added 3-inch oak sheathing and a 13 h.p. kerosene engine, which proved a nuisance. Sailing from Oslo 16 June 1903, he took on dogs, sleds, kayaks, and provisions at Disko, Greenland, sailed through Lancaster Sound to Beechey Is-

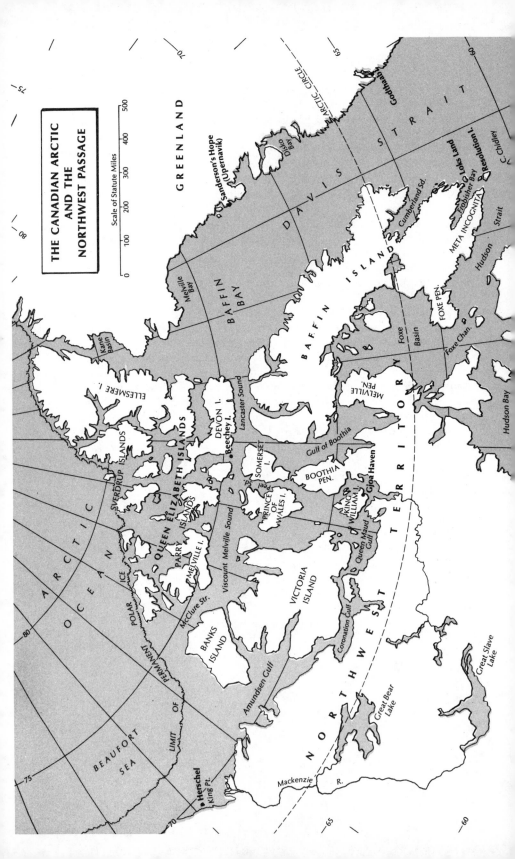

THE CANADIAN ARCTIC AND THE NORTHWEST PASSAGE

Scale of Statute Miles

0 100 200 300 400 500

GREENLAND

Sanderson's Hope
(Upernavik)

Disko Bay

D A V I S   S T R A I T

Godthaab

Loks Land

Resolution I.

C. Chidley

META INCOGNITA

Frobisher Bay

Cumberland Sd.

Hudson Strait

Melville Bay

BAFFIN BAY

Kane Basin

B A F F I N   I S L A N D

FOXE PEN.

Foxe Basin

Foxe Chan.

Hudson Bay

ELLESMERE I.

Lancaster Sound

DEVON I.

Beechey I.

MELVILLE PEN.

SVERDRUP ISLANDS

QUEEN ELIZABETH ISLANDS

SOMERSET I.

Peel Sd.

PRINCE OF WALES I.

Gulf of Boothia

BOOTHIA PEN.

Gjoa Haven

KING WILLIAM I.

N O R T H W E S T   T E R R I T O R Y

PARRY ISLANDS

MELVILLE I.

Viscount Melville Sound

Queen Maud Gulf

A R C T I C   O C E A N

ICE

POLAR

McClure Str.

BANKS ISLAND

VICTORIA ISLAND

Coronation Gulf

LIMIT OF PERMANENT

Amundsen Gulf

Great Bear Lake

Great Slave Lake

BEAUFORT SEA

Herschel I.
King Pt.

Mackenzie R.

land, turned south into Peel Sound between Somerest and Prince of Wales islands, and on 12 September 1903 anchored in a harbor of King William Island which has been named Gjøa Haven. He remained there for twenty-three months to study the North Magnetic Pole and other Arctic problems, sailing 13 August 1905 and following the north shore of the Canadian mainland. On 26 August, having traversed Amundsen Gulf (named after him), he spoke a whaling ship from San Francisco, and realized he had "made it." He arrived King Point at western end of Mackenzie Bay 1 September, wintered at Herschel Island just over the Yukon boundary from Alaska, made dog-sled trip to Fort Egbert, Eagle City, not far from Dawson, to report. He returned to his vessel February 1906, sailed in July, and on 31 August 1906 reached Cape Nome, Alaska. He proceeded to San Francisco, where *Gjøa* has become a permanent exhibit in Golden Gate Park. William A. Baker, "The Gjøa" in *American Neptune*, XII (1952), 7–21; Roald Amundsen, *The North West Passage* (2 vols., 1908).

1940–44. The first both-ways passage. Schooner *St. Roch* belonging to the Canadian Mounted Police, 100 feet long with a 150 h.p. diesel engine, skippered by Inspector Henry A. Larsen, left Vancouver 23 June 1940, reached Walker Bay east of Herschel Island 25 September, and was frozen in until 31 July 1941. From 11 September 1941 to 24 August 1942 she was frozen in at Pasley Bay, near the Magnetic Pole on Prince of Wales Island. In the summer of 1942 she managed to get through Lancaster Sound and reached Halifax, N.S., on 11 October. In July 1944, with a new 300 h.p. diesel, she started back and reached Beechey Island about 1 September. She drove through miraculously fast, taking only sixteen days from Baffin Bay via Lancaster and Melville Sounds and Prince of Wales Strait (between Banks and Victoria Islands) to reach the mouth of the Mackenzie River. Passed through Bering Strait 27 September and reached Vancouver, B.C., 16 October 1944. "The Story of the *St. Roch*" in *Swiss Air Gazette* (Zurich, 1969).

1957. U. S. Coast Guard cutters *Storis, Spar,* and *Bramble* got through with aid of Canadian icebreakers, especially *Labrador,* which had done it alone in 1954.

1958–60. Submarines U.S.S. *Nautilus, Skate,* and *Seadragon* traversed the North Pole under the ice, coming home safely on the other side.

1969. Tanker *Manhattan,* 940 ft. long, 132 ft. beam, 115,000 dwt. tons, 43,000 h.p. engine, was built at Quincy in 1961 but converted, reinforced, and provided with an icebreaking bow which increased her length to 1005 ft. Under Captain Roger A. Steward and crew of 126, she entered Lancaster Sound 5 September 1969, arrived Resolute or Cornwallis Island next day. Tried to get through McClure Strait between Melville and Banks Islands but could not buck the pack-ice, and only got free with the aid of Canadian icebreaker *John A. MacDonald,* Captain Paul Fournier, which attended her all the way. Entered Prince of Wales Strait 14 September and, debouching into Amundsen Gulf, completed Northwest Passage, via the

Beaufort Sea 15 September. She made Barrow, Alaska, on 21 September. At one point her expensive hull was holed by an iceberg, but watertight bulkheads saved her. Returning, she passed through Lancaster Sound and Baffin Bay, made Halifax 8 November 1969.

Manhattan's owner, the Standard Oil Company of New Jersey, advertised, "She did it. She conquered the Northwest Passage." Seems to me that *Gjøa* and *St. Roch* did that; and it is far from certain that the *Manhattan's* route is commercially practicable; or that exploitation of the Alaskan oilfields by this means will not pollute the hitherto virgin Arctic with spilled oil and exterminate the Eskimos' means of subsistence. See Bern Keating, "North for Oil," *National Geographic* CXXXVII (March 1970), 374–91.

Thus, in four and a half centuries, 1497–1969, the objective of the Northwest Passage search has gradually evolved from a short route to the "happy shores of Cathay" to simple geographical curiosity; and, finally, to making more money for American oil producers.

✳ XIX ✳
The First Virginia Colony

1585-1586

Of thys her Maiesties newe kingdom of Verginia: All the kingedomes and states of Chrystendom theyere commodytyes joyegned in one together, doo not yealde ether more good, or more plentyfulle whatsoever for publyck use ys needefull, or pleasinge for delyghte.

RALPH LANE TO SIR FRANCIS WALSINGHAM, 12 AUGUST 1585.

Walter Raleigh and the Amadas-Barlowe Voyage of 1584

When Sir Humfry Gilbert was "swallowed up of the sea" on 9 September 1583, his half-brother Walter Raleigh, about thirty years of age, lay basking in the rays of Gloriana. Handsome, with intense eyes of bluish gray, a gallant soldier in the French wars and in a cruel but successful one in Ireland, Walter was brilliant, versatile, and arrogant. No mean poet or historian, he had been out of a job after returning from Ireland; and there is no reason to doubt the old story in Thomas Fuller's *Worthies* that he called the Queen's attention to himself by spreading his velvet cloak over a puddle that lay in her path. For some two years now he had been Elizabeth's favorite young courtier and she had already made him a man of wealth with gifts of land, monopolies, and sinecures, and more to come. Still eager for action but unable to risk the Queen's displeasure by breaking away, he

* All the events described in this chapter and the next occurred in the present state of North Carolina, the northern boundary of which, since the charter of 1665, has been latitude 36°30′ N. But Raleigh's Virginia extended for two hundred leagues each side of his settlement, and that would have covered the entire seaboard of the Thirteen Colonies and most of Florida.

Sir Walter Raleigh at the age of thirty-six.
From a portrait by an unknown artist. In the Virginia Museum of Fine
Arts, the gift of Mrs. Preston Davie. Courtesy of the Virginia Museum
of Fine Arts.

now found a reasonable substitute by taking over Sir Humfry's ambitious scheme for an English colony in North America and pushing it to a conclusion just short of success. If Verrazzano may be called the discoverer of Virginia, Raleigh was her founder.

Since Gilbert's patent would expire by its own limitation on 11 June 1584, Raleigh sought and easily obtained (25 March 1584) a new one from the Queen. It opens with the usual stereotyped phrases on the patentee's permission "to discover search fynde out and viewe such remote heathen and barbarus landes Contries and territories not actually possessed of any Christian Prynce." Raleigh receives the same viceregal powers that Gilbert (and before him, Roberval) had briefly enjoyed, and greater than those of later lords proprietors like the Calverts. He may expel anyone not licensed by himself from a space within two hundred leagues each side of his intended colony, or any unauthorized trader "founde traffiquinge into any harbor or har- borowes Cricke or Crickes within the lymyttes aforesaid"—excepting fishermen and others driven thither "by force of tempest." The far- sighted provisions of the Gilbert patent are repeated, to the effect that all settlers licensed by the patentee "may have and enjoye all the pryvyledges of free Denizens and persons natyve of England" as if "they were borne and personally resiante within our said Realme of England." Raleigh may promulgate laws and ordinances for the gov- ernment of his planters, so long as they are compatible with the laws and polity of England, and the Church of England. But—doubtless with an eye to the peccadillos of the Gilbert family—Walter is warned that if he shall "robbe or spoyle by sea or by lande" any subject of Her Majesty or of friendly princes, he will be held to full restitution and satisfaction; which, if he give it not, he and his colony will be put "out of oure allegiaunce and protection" and become free-for-all. This did not prevent Raleigh's mariners from "spoyling" Spaniards when occasion offered, nor was it so intended.

Raleigh wisely decided first to reconnoiter his vast domain, report on the natives, climate, products, and select a site; and it is clear that he aimed at one well south of Norumbega. For this purpose he chose two gentlemen of the elaborate households that he maintained in Lon- don and Devonshire: Philip Amadas of Plymouth, only twenty years old, and Arthur Barlowe. Their fleet consisted of "two barkes, well furnished with men and victuals." We do not know their names, but they must have been small, under fifty tuns' burthen, to have entered the northern arm of Pamlico Sound. Amadas commanded the "ad- mirall," or flagship, and Barlowe the other; Simon Ferdinando, the English-naturalized Portuguese who had reconnoitered Norumbega for Gilbert, acted as flag pilot. Seven gentlemen "of the Companie" signed the official report.

The two vessels slipped out of Plymouth, unobserved by Spanish spies, on 27 April 1584 and made the Canary Islands a fortnight later. To avoid being delayed by northern gales and fogs as Gilbert had been, Raleigh ordered them to take the tradewind route inaugurated by Columbus and later followed by Verrazzano.

In June, Amadas and Barlowe arrived in the West Indies. They called somewhere—probably the aguado, or watering-place, near San Germán

Bay, Puerto Rico, which John Rut visited in 1527—for "sweete water and fresh victuall." This cured the crew from the effects of "aire very unwholesome." Departing 22 June, they sailed around Cuba to catch the Gulf Stream, "disbogging" between it and Florida, and on 2 July came onto soundings, probably off the coast of the future Georgia. There they joyfully breathed the odor of an offshore wind "as if we had been in the midst of some delicate garden." On the 4th, with moon at first quarter, they sighted the coast, probably about midway between Cape Fear and Cape Lookout. For the next nine days, with moderate winds and under a waxing moon, they followed the Carolina Banks— the long, long series of narrow islands between Cape Fear and Currituck, which Verrazzano had assumed to be a mere barrier between two oceans. Barlowe wrote a good description of the Carolina coast geography: "Wee sawe before us another mightie long Sea: for there lieth along the coast a tracte of Islands, two hundreth miles in length, adioyining to the Ocean sea, and between the Islands, two or three entrances: when you are entred betweene them (these Islands being very narrowe . . . in most places six miles broad, in some places less . . .) then there appeareth another great Sea fortie, and in some fiftie, in some twentie miles over, before you come unto the continent: and in this inclosed Sea, there are about a hundreth Islands of divers bignesses."

The Englishmen might have prepared for this region by reading Verrazzano's Letter, which Hakluyt had published in 1582; but neither their letters nor their reports make any reference to the Florentine. He had found no inlet to this inland sea, and Barlowe bears him out by stating that he found none until full moon, 13 July when, after sailing for 120 miles, Ferdinando detected one that they named after him. This entrance later closed up; Oregon Inlet, which opened in 1846 a few miles to the southward, eventually replaced it. Unwittingly, these Englishmen were on one of the most dangerous coasts in America: Capes Fear, Lookout, and Hatteras extend sandy traps for mariners (Frying Pan Shoal, Diamond Shoal, the Wimble, etc.) many miles beyond their own low, inconspicuous terrain. The United States Coast Guard estimates that along this outer shore there lies a wreck every two or three miles. These islands were more heavily wooded in Raleigh's day than in ours, since the strong winds hampered new growth once they had been deforested. They were thickly inhabited by Algonkin Indians in

Raleigh's day, but are now being subjected to "development" wherever the Federal Government has not stepped in to create a reservation.

Entering Port Ferdinando "not without some difficultie," with only twelve feet of water in the inlet at high tide, the two barks "cast anchor about three harquebushot within the havens mouth" on the southern side. The men manned their boats, landed on Hatarask Island (the native name for the long barrier island that extends south toward Cape Hatteras), and formally took possession for "the Queenes most excellent Maiestie." They found the island to be low and sandy, but so full of the small summer grape that "in all the world the like aboundance is not to be founde." They explored it and observed with delight the "goodly Cedar," pine, cypress, sassafras, tupelo, and other trees. This spot lay but ten miles south of Kitty Hawk, whose hills and vegetation so delighted Verrazzano in 1524 that he named it Arcadia, and very near to the great dunes of tawny sand which mark the modern Nags Head. The discharge of an arquebus by an Englishman raised a huge flock of cranes "with such a crye redoubled by many Ecchoes, as if an armie of men had showted all together." An exact description of the raucous cry of the sandhill crane.

On their third day at Hatarask, the Englishmen made first contact with local Indians. Three natives in a dugout canoe landed on a point near the ships' anchorage; Amadas, Barlowe, and Ferdinando rowed ashore and held parley. The principal *werowance* (the local name for chief men) "with his owne good liking" came on board and they gave him a hat and a shirt and a "taste of our wine, and our meate." The werowance then filled his canoe with freshly caught fish which he divided between the two barks, a welcome addition to their sea stores. Next day the chief's brother, Granganimeo, came on board one of the barks, and from him the Englishmen gathered that the name of the "king" or top werowance was *Wingina*, and the country's name *Windgandcon*.

Wingina was chief of the Roanoke, an Algonkin-speaking tribe who ruled the village on Roanoke Island and one on the mainland opposite. Windgandcon, according to Walter Raleigh after he had had time to study the Indian vocabularies jotted down by his colonists, meant simply, "You wear gay clothes!" It frequently happened that Europeans inquiring the name of a region (seldom named by North American

Hatarask Island, scene of first landing, 1584.

Oregon Inlet.

"One of the wyves of Wyngyno" (Wingina). Painted by John White, 1585. Her apron is a dressed deerskin. Her face, arms and legs are "pownced" (tattoed) in blue. The necklace is of copper beads. DeBry engraved the same lady for his *America*, but captioned her as "a younge gentill woeman daughter of Secota," and adds that they "cover their brests in token of maydenlike modestye." Courtesy British Museum.

Indians) were given something else—like Norumbega, for instance. Whatever it may have meant, Windgandcon (with a dozen variations) was the name used by the English for this region until it was officially changed to Virginia.

Granganimeo, representing his brother then recovering from wounds received in a recent scuffle with local enemies, was accompanied by a suite of forty or fifty men, "very handsome, and goodly people, and in their behaviour as mannerly, and civill, as any of Europe." He caused a long reed mat to be spread on the ground, sat at the far end, and beckoned the Englishmen to join him, making "signes of joy and welcome" such as striking first his own head and breast and then those of the visitors. He made a long and of course unintelligible speech, after which gifts were exchanged. A bright tin dish, which Granganimeo made into a sort of breastplate, was exchanged for twenty pelts of deer or buffalo, and a copper kettle brought fifty pelts. Next, Granganimeo brought his "very well favoured" wife and three children on board, a suite of fifty "ladies" remaining ashore. Her royal highness wore ropes of pearls, "the bignes of good peas," and acted "very bashfull"; she may have been the same wife whom John White depicted in 1585, without the pearls. Following the royal delegation, "great store of people" came on board, bringing dressed deerskins and berries that they used to make dyes. Every day the king's brother gave the Englishmen a brace or two of fat buck deer and as many rabbits and as much fish as they could eat, as well as plenty of maize, cucumbers, pumpkins, and nuts; Barlowe says that they made three crops of maize every year. "The soile is the most plentifull, sweete, fruitfull and wholesome of all the world," he adds, and grows more than fourteen varieties of hard- and soft-wood trees. It is true that the soil is good in narrow strips along the rivers and sounds, but a few miles inland one encounters heavily wooded swamps full of snakes, which have prevented the intensive exploitation to which tidewater Virginia and up-country Carolina were later subjected. The country is "flat as a pancake," but it has a peculiar beauty owing to the large proportion of water to land. Winters are never very cold, and the summers are cooled by sea breezes. White and pink dogwood blossoms herald the spring, and in the autumn the tupelo and other hardwood trees display a brilliance not greatly inferior to the foliage of Canada. Like the French there, the English never commented on the beauties of nature but concentrated on her bounties.

Hakluyt, reading Barlowe's and later reports, confidently predicted that Windgandcon would become England's Mexico; he had a vision of tidewater plantations of sugarcane, banana, pineapple, even mulberry trees to feed silkworms; and the mountains would yield gold. This dream took about a century to dispel. Upland rather than tidewater North Carolina became the prosperous section; the part explored and reported on so glowingly by Raleigh's men is now a sportsman's and fishermen's paradise, with a few beach resorts. Pamlico Sound can be very rough with a strong northwest wind, but it is also very shoal, depths of fifteen feet being uncommon. Even small craft today need to follow the channels dredged by a paternal government. Today's chart shows but six inches or a foot of water at low tide where we figure that the Englishmen first landed, and there is not more than two feet anywhere within ten miles. If Barlowe's two barks anchored inside, as his narration indicates, there must have been more depth in 1584 than in 1970.

Barlowe and seven men rowed and sailed in the ship's longboat some twenty miles up Albemarle, the sound and river next north of Pamlico. Returning, they paid a memorable visit to Wingina's village on the north end of Roanoke Island. Granganimeo's wife ran to the water's edge to welcome the Englishmen, and ordered her servants to carry them ashore, as had happened to Cartier at Hochelaga. As they were soaked with rain, she set them down by a "great fire" in the middle of the bark-covered regal dwelling, removed all their clothes, including stockings, washed and dried them, and bathed their feet in warm water. In the inner room she caused to be spread out on the sleeping-benches a feast of corn porridge, pumpkin, fish, and venison cooked in different ways, "divers fruites," and water flavored with sassafras and other herbs. "We were entertained with all love and kindness," wrote Barlowe, "and with as much bounty, after their manner, as they could possibly devise. Wee found the people most gentle, loving and faithfull, void of all guile and treason, and such as lived after the manner of the golden age. The earth bringeth foorth all things in aboundance, as in the first creation, without toile or labour." Their skin is "of colour yellowish," he wrote—just as John White depicts them—"and their haire blacke for the most; and yet we saw children that had very fine auburne, and chestnut colour haire."

Peter Martyr, following Columbus, wrote in the same strain, almost the exact words, about the peaceful Arawak of the Bahamas. Here, as there, it may have been a golden age for the invaders, but a tragic fate awaited the natives. Here, as there, the arrival of Europeans set these kindly, hospitable people on their way to extinction.

While the eight Englishmen were doing justice to their supper, some noisy braves, armed with bows and arrows, appeared in the courtyard. Their hostess, seeing her guests' uneasiness, sent menservants to take away the hunters' weapons and chase them off. When the Englishmen declined to spend the night, fearing lest hospitality be a cover for intended treachery, she sent a hot supper to their boat, with "fine mattes to cover us from the rayne," and had thirty or more of her people stand guard on shore to see that they were not molested.

That incident concludes the first English Virginia voyage. Two young natives named Manteo and Wanchese volunteered to accompany Barlowe home. On 23 August the two barks debouched from Port Ferdinando, and making a fast passage, reached England about 15 September 1584.

Windgandcon Becomes Virginia

Plenty had been going on in their absence, and more was to come. Richard Hakluyt, at Raleigh's request, wrote his *Discourse Concerning Westerne Planting*, of which we have already made a summary, to prove the value of a North American colony for England. He hoped to persuade the Queen to make this an official enterprise, and Barlowe's narrative made excellent colonial propaganda; but Elizabeth did not "buy"—she sensed what was cooking for her in Spain. She did, however, reward Raleigh with knighthood at the Epiphany of 1585, and graciously allowed him to change the name of his vast territory from the dubious Windgandcon to Virginia. Raleigh caused a seal to be cut, showing his arms (four superimposed lozenges), his crest (a roebuck), motto *Amore et Virtute*, and an inscription stating the seal to be the insignia WALTERI RALEGH MILITIS DOMINI ET GUBERNATORIS VIRGINIAE—of Walter Raleigh, knight, Lord and Governor of Virginia.

Diplomatic relations with Spain having already been broken, the Queen now began to issue letters of marque for plundering Spanish vessels wherever found, and by the close of 1585 the somewhat lukewarm war with Spain had become really hot. Sir Walter, having well learned from Sir Humfry the danger of delay, lost no time in preparing a colonizing expedition to sail in the spring of 1585. He also tried to supplement his royal patent by an act of Parliament. Several friends in the Commons promoted this bill but it failed to pass the Lords, probably because the Queen did not relish the implication that her patent was insufficient, and objected to Parliament muscling in, as it were, on royal prerogative.

The ways and means of assembling a colonizing expedition in 1585 were so odd as to be almost ludicrous. The Queen lent Raleigh *Tiger*, a ship of the Royal Navy, for his "admirall." She is the first Elizabethan discovery ship of which we have an identifiable portrait (in White's painting of the Puerto Rico camp), and she is the only one to have been immortalized by Shakespeare. In *Macbeth*, Act I, scene iii, First Witch tells how a sailor's wife insulted her, but "her husband's to Aleppo gone, master o' the Tiger," and in revenge the witch will follow him in a sieve and hex him. Shakespeare had evidently read in Hakluyt the voyage of Master Ralph Fitch to Aleppo in "a ship of London called the *Tyger*," in 1585; and as the Royal Navy was always buying merchant vessels, it is a good guess that Fitch's *Tyger* and Raleigh's *Tiger* were identical. Elizabeth also contributed £400 worth of gunpowder from the royal magazine.

To raise money, Raleigh sent forth his own *Roebuck* to take prizes, just as Roberval had done half a century earlier. One prize, the Dutch *Waterhound* of Brill, he sent in to Plymouth; she could not be condemned because her cargo consisted of French wine, but Sir Walter detained her just the same, and impressed her Dutch master, pilot, and a few sailors. They were glad to get home almost three years later, after having been forcibly sailed to Virginia and back. *Roebuck* took another Dutch ship named *Angel Gabriel*, condemned for having a Spanish cargo, and also a French ship laden with linens, whose name is not recorded. The proceeds of these prizes went into the expense account. Raleigh's own pinnace *Dorothie* joined up, and he built two new ones, Barlowe evidently having told him how necessary small craft were for exploring the Virginia sounds and rivers. Raleigh also obtained ship *Elizabeth*, owned at least in part by her captain, Thomas Cavendish, the future circumnavigator; and the *Red Lion* of Chichester, owned in part by her captain, George Raymond. As the Queen granted Raleigh power to "take up" (impress) both men and shipping, it is probable that *Red Lion* and her crew were commandeered; they certainly acted as if they had been.

Equally important were the personnel. It was out of the question for

Sir Richard Grenville. By an unknown artist; painted in 1571. Courtesy National Portrait Gallery, London.

Raleigh to go himself; the Queen promised to help with the expense only if he stayed at home and rewarded him with another sinecure office, Master of the Horse. He did not dare incur her displeasure. So, as "generall" or commander-in-chief, Sir Walter named his kinsman Sir Richard Grenville, he who later won immortal fame through his battle in the *Revenge* with a Spanish fleet. Grenville, already a prominent figure, belonged to an old Cornish–North Devon family seated at Buckland Abbey since 1541, where young Richard was born the following year. His father, also Sir Richard, became an important man in the county and a courtier under Henry VIII, and like so many other gentlemen of the time, a poet. One of the only two poems of his that are preserved might have been an inspiration to his son:

In Praise of Seafaring Men in Hopes of Good Fortune

Who seeks the way to win renown
Or flies with wings of high desire;
Who seeks to wear the laurel crown,
Or hath the mind that would aspire:
Tell him his native soil eschew,
Tell him go range and seek anew.

To pass the seas some think a toil,
Some think it strange abroad to roam,
Some think it grief to leave their soil,
Their parents, kinsfolk and their home;
Think so who list, I like it not,
I must abroad to try my lot.

After a term at the Inns of Court, Richard Jr. was elected to the House of Commons, and married Mary St. Leger, daughter of a Devonshire knight who lived near Bideford in North Devon. He fought Turks in Hungary and the Irish in Ireland whence, like so many contemporaries, he returned impoverished. Again to Parliament in 1571, when the portrait we have reproduced was painted. His full, expressive eyes are blue, his hair light brown, his glance alert and arresting. He begged the Queen to allow him to follow Magellan's route to the Pacific, but she gave that mission to Drake. Raleigh, since he could not himself go to Virginia, persuaded Grenville to take over; and (wrote Holinshed the chronicler) Sir Richard out of the "love he bore unto Sir Walter Ralegh, together with a disposition he had to attempt honourable actions worthy of honour, was willing to hazard himself in this voyage."

Unlike Frobisher and Davis, Grenville was not a professional seaman. This may be the basic reason for his quarrel with the fleet pilot, Simon Ferdinando, who had already sailed to the New World at least thrice. But Sir Richard, hot-tempered like Gilbert and Raleigh, quarreled with many others, including Ralph Lane. And (as his action in the *Revenge* proves) he learned from his Virginia voyages more ship handling than most sailors knew.

As governor of the colony Raleigh appointed Ralph Lane, a young gentleman of means who owned shares in privateers and had fought in Ireland. There he incurred the displeasure of his superiors by his greed for the confiscated land of rebels. The vice-treasurer of Ireland observed that County Kerry "was too large for Mr. Lane." Returning to England, he was appointed an equerry by the Queen. She gave him charge of twenty horsemen and forty foot, whom he was allowed to keep at the palace "in consideration of his redye undertaking the voyage to Virginia for Sir Raughley, at her Maiestie's commaundment." What qualifications he was supposed to have for governing a distant colony we know not.

Raleigh initiated for England the practice followed for over three centuries (e.g. the Wilkes Pacific Expedition of 1838–42 and the Perry Japan Expedition of 1853–54) of adding a scientific and artistic staff to the command. The scientist was Thomas Hariot. Shortly after graduating from Oxford in 1580, Hariot joined Raleigh's household on a salary in order to teach his master "the mathematical sciences." Raleigh must have observed during his brief activity at sea under Gilbert that you needed something more than a smattering of celestial navigation to guide a fleet, and Hariot was the natural choice for the expedition's scientist. Raleigh expected him to study the Indians of Virginia, to map his domain, to list natural resources, and to write a report, all of which he did; his *Briefe and True Report of the New Found Land of Virginia* (1588), translated by Theodor de Bry into Latin, French, and German, with illustrations by John White, became one of the principal sources of information about North America and its inhabitants for over a century. In preparation for his ethnological duties, Hariot took under his protection the two Indians whom Barlowe had brought from Virginia, Manteo and Wanchese; he taught them English, and himself learned at least a smattering of Algonkin. For Raleigh to have cultivated such a man and used his talents to further the colonization of Virginia is by no means the least of his titles to fame.

Another appointment that does Raleigh honor was that of artist John White, whom we have already encountered as a shipmate of Martin Frobisher. Despite his excellent work for Raleigh's Virginia, we still know next to nothing of White's origin or education. He had been trained as a surveyor and, prior to his shipping with Frobisher in 1577, had been received as a member of the Painter-Stainers' Company of London. Either William Sanderson (still Sir Walter's businessman) or Raleigh himself must have seen White's sketches of the Baffin Island Eskimo and decided to appoint him the artist-naturalist of Virginia; a very happy choice. Natural history was coming of age in England—

one remembers particularly Gerard's *Herbal*—and to all such men the new species found in America were particularly stimulating.

Simon Ferdinando, chief pilot of the expedition, had made at least three voyages to North America since entering the English service, the latest with Amadas and Barlowe, and should have been well qualified. But, as the event will show, Simon had either lost his skill or had been suborned by the Spanish secret service to wreck the expedition. For Philip II was very much interested in what Raleigh was doing—as much as his father had been in Cartier's third voyage. Spain had a good claim to North America, at least as far north as the Hudson. Gomez and Ayllón had sailed along the coast and up some of the rivers; on several Spanish maps the region now named Virginia was called *Jactán*, and Chesapeake Bay, *Bahía Santa María*. There had even been in 1570–71 a Spanish Jesuit mission somewhere on the shores of that bay, which the local Indians exterminated. Spain guessed rightly that one of the principal motives for the forthcoming English establishment was to provide a base for privateers to prey on homecoming *flotas*, just as the French had done in their short tenure of Fort Caroline, Florida. And now Spain and England were in open war. Hence we have a spate of letters to Philip II from Mendoza, his ambassador to France, who handled reports from secret agents in England; and from Spanish officials in the West Indies. None of these in the end did Spain any good, and many are wildly inaccurate—Mendoza for instance persisted in reporting that Grenville's destination was Norumbega. But all are a boon to historians avid for detail.

If Spain had defeated England in 1588–90, she would certainly have planted a chain of garrisoned forts along the North American coast, and it is doubtful whether a humbled and subjected England could have fought her way in. The ultimate fate of Virginia depended on the Spanish Armada's victory or defeat.

Grenville's 1585 Voyage, to Puerto Rico and Hispaniola

Raleigh must have been an excellent organizer to have his fleet ready to sail less than seven months after the Amadas and Barlowe reconnaissance returned. The organization of the fleet that departed Plymouth "at the pleasant prime," 9 April 1585, with moon five days full, follows:

GENERAL AND ADMIRAL OF THE EXPEDITION, SIR RICHARD GRENVILLE

TIGER, a queen's ship of 140 to 200 tuns, Sir Richard, captain; Simon Ferdinando, master and chief pilot. Complement, about 160, half of them sailors. Governor Ralph Lane sailed in her.

ROEBUCK, Raleigh's flyboat, 140 tuns, John Clarke, captain. Philip Amadas, designated Admiral of Virginia, sailed in her.

LYON or RED LION of Chichester, bark of 100 tuns, George Raymond, captain (and probably owner).

ELIZABETH, bark of 50 tuns, Thomas Cavendish, captain and high marshal (chief judicial officer) of the expedition, who probably owned her.

DOROTHIE, Raleigh's pinnace, or "small barke," tunnage unknown; captain, probably Arthur Barlowe.*

Two recently built pinnaces, names unknown, which probably sailed on their own bottoms. One was lost at sea and replaced by another built at Puerto Rico.

Total number of men, about five hundred, of which nearly half were seamen; 108 were colonists, and the rest, soldiers or specialists who were not expected to stay in the colony.

Other ships not yet ready for sea were organized as a relief expedition to depart in June, under Captain Bernard Drake.

The names of the colonists, "as well Gentlemen as others, that remained one whole yeere in Virginia," are preserved for us by Hakluyt. Most of the 108 people cannot be identified, but the list has perennial interest as the first enumeration of an English colony. There were several Irishmen, including the inevitable Kelly, and at least two others who had served under Lane in Ireland. The gentlemen included Hariot, a Stafford, an Acton, a Rowse, a Prideaux of Padstow, and Master Thomas Harvey of the London Company of Grocers, "cape merchant" (businessman or supercargo) of the expedition. There were a couple of German miners, and a Jewish mineral expert from Prague named Joachim Ganz, who appears on the list as Doughan Gannes. For the most part the colonists were men with common English names such as John Taylor, Thomas Parr, James Stevenson, and Marmaduke Constable.

---

* There is no mention of her or of Barlowe during the voyage; it is probable that she turned back early.

Three had no surnames; three others belonged to the household of Sir Francis Walsingham, a financial backer of the voyage. Since the conversion of the heathen had always been held forth as a principal object, it is strange that Grenville, unlike Frobisher, had no chaplain in his company. Few or none later joined the Virginia Company which founded Jamestown (they probably had "had it"); but one gentleman, Sir Edward Gorges, was close kindred to Sir Ferdinando Gorges who played a prominent role in the settlement of New England.

The outward passage of this colonizing expedition furnished plenty of sport, and hard work too, for all hands. Sir Richard Grenville behaved as if his main object were to capture prizes; doubtless he had to, since Raleigh had gone deeply into debt to get the fleet to sea. He took the southern route, following the belt of northerlies to the Canaries. A storm off Portugal sank *Tiger's* pinnace and scattered the fleet. *Elizabeth* rejoined the flagship at Puerto Rico, but *Lion* reached Virginia ahead of them.

Tiger continued to the Canaries, took her departure from Fuerteventura on 14 April and, following the shortest course (discovered by Columbus in 1493) to the West Indies, raised Dominica on 7 May. This was a fast but not a record passage. Three days later, she anchored for "refreshment" at an island that the English called Cotesa, or Cottea, "near the island of St. John" (Puerto Rico); probably Vieques. On 12 May *Tiger* "came to an anker in the Baye of Muskito, in the Island of St. John within a Fawlcon shot off the shore, where our Generall Sir Richard Greenvill and the most part of our companie landed, and began to fortifie, very neere to the sea side; the river ranne by one side of our forte, and the other two sides were environed with wood."

Exactly where was this fort, so accurately depicted by John White? Don Hernando de Altamorano, a Spanish gentleman taken in one of Grenville's prizes, says it was "at a port called Mosquetal," which was the original name of Guayanilla Bay. The important identifying detail is that White's pictures and *Tiger's* description show a river entering the landing beach from the north, just west of the camp; and the Rio Guayanilla does just that, entering the bay adjoining a little beach resort. The *Tiger*, says her journal, was able to anchor "a Fawlcon shot"—about 300 yards—off the shore, and the modern chart shows soundings of four fathom and one and three-quarters fathom within

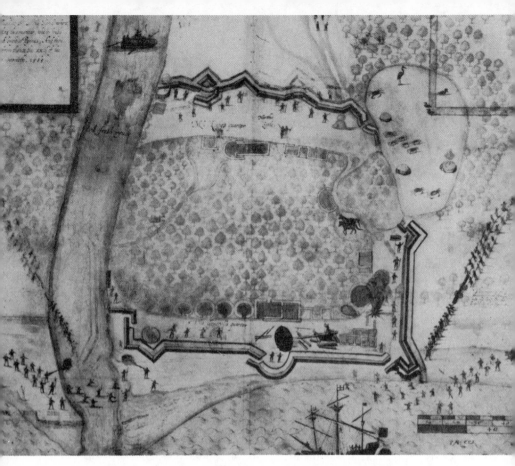

John White's painting of the fort at Guayanilla Bay, Puerto Rico. Ship
Tiger at anchor. Courtesy British Museum.

a quarter-mile of this shore near the river mouth. As almost four centuries have elapsed since Grenville's call, these soundings represent a
lot of silt deposited since 1585.

Three years before Grenville's arrival, a gang of French pirates had
entrenched themselves there and terrorized that part of Puerto Rico.
Possibly that is why Grenville chose the spot; he evidently had designated it as fleet rendezvous before leaving England, as the *Elizabeth*
turned up there on 19 May.

Grenville landed at least 120 men who, in a few days, built so strong
a fort that the Spanish authorities feared they meant to stay. But Sir
Richard only intended to build a new pinnace to replace the one lost
off Portugal, and to pick up a few head of cattle for Virginia. The
building of a pinnace must have been anticipated in England, as *Tiger*

had on board the necessary iron, sails, cordage, and wheeled truck; all that Grenville needed was timber and skill.

John White's watercolor of the fort, one of his best, shows a scene of great activity. *Tiger,* looking very taut and efficient, is moored close to the beach. The fort, a formidable affair, rests its west flank on the river. Grenville and Lane have established their shore quarters—as far apart as possible! Between "the Generalls quarter" and a sconce on the parapet, a pinnace is being built. Timber is stacked about, a fellow is boring holes in a squared-off baulk, and near by there is a fire, doubtless to forge the ironwork. Outside on the right, labeled "The manner of drawing in the timber into the fort, for the buylding of a Pynnes," a great tree balanced on two-wheeled trucks is being dragged by twelve men and followed by twice as many armed soldiers. Two horses which the English had captured are in a corral. On the west side of the river near the shore, "The Generall" is returning from his first parley with the Spaniards, accompanied by twenty-five guards armed with arquebuses, swords, and pikes. Eight men are already wading across the

Air view of Guayanilla Bay, January 1951, showing mouth of the river and site of the fort. Courtesy of Mr. Aurelio Tió.

river, and four on the other bank are prepared to receive them. Up the Guayanilla, a ship's boat is piled high with water casks. White, who loved best to depict wild life, threw in for good measure a blue heron, a ruddy duck and smaller birds, and land crabs.

The Spanish governor of Puerto Rico, and the governor of Florida then staying with him, were nonplussed. Having slight force at their disposal, whilst the English were numerous and aggressive, they dared not try to expel the intruders. A troop of horse from the San Germán garrison came to the west bank of the river displaying a flag of truce. Grenville held a parley; and the Spaniards, being assured that the English would soon depart, but if not allowed to buy provisions would "releeve" themselves "by the sword," promised to bring cattle for sale next day to a point about four miles inland. But when Grenville arrived at the rendezvous, no Spaniards showed up. Grenville, furious, "fired the woods thereabouts," returned to the fort, and, finding the pinnace all launched and rigged, destroyed his defenses and set sail. He caused to be cut on a tree trunk an inscription, which the Spaniards copied, stating that *Tiger* and *Elizabeth* were about to leave on 23 May "in good health, glory be to God. 1585."

To build a fort and a pinnace in eleven days seems an extraordinary exploit. Grenville, energetic himself, must have been able to instill energy in all his men.

In the Mona Passage between Puerto Rico and Hispaniola, *Tiger* captured a small but empty Spanish *fragata*, and a big ship laden with cloth and other merchandise. Grenville brought the larger of the two into Añasco Bay, hoping to sell her, and sent Governor Lane in the smaller one to a place near Cape Rojo (the southwestern point of Puerto Rico) to procure salt. The Spanish pilot of the *fragata* obligingly indicated where it could be had, and John White went along and sketched the scene. Lane threw up a small fort around two conical salt mounds, set his men to cutting out chunks with mattocks, and used the Spanish prisoners to load them. Before he had obtained a full cargo, a Spanish force approached. It consisted only of a lieutenant, forty horsemen, and thirty foot soldiers—the garrison of San Germán beefed up with local militia—but Lane's imagination built it up to an entire regiment led by the governor of Puerto Rico in person. Upon reporting to Grenville on board *Tiger*, Lane protested bitterly to the General for putting him and his men in jeopardy; and this precipitated a series of quarrels which tore the company apart.

By selling his large prize at Añasco Bay on the west coast, and squeezing ransoms out of her passengers, Grenville acquired money to purchase from the local haciendas several head of cattle, horses, and swine, together with plantain and sugar ratoons to transplant; but not nearly enough for his calculated needs in Virginia. So, in the latter part of May, Sir Richard set sail for another Spanish possession to "spoyle." Very glad the Englishmen were to leave Puerto Rico; they had been so "stoong" ashore by the "muskitoes." Millions more were doubtless awaiting them in Virginia, but no fresh complaints are recorded. Governor Bradford of Plymouth Colony well said that nobody should come to America "that cannot endure the biting of a mosquito."

Grenville now shaped his course, with *Tiger*, *Elizabeth*, and the new pinnace, to the north coast of Hispaniola. Crossing the much frequented Mona Passage, he took a Spanish *fragata* whose crew abandoned her "upon the sight of us," and another "with good and rich fraight" and wealthy Spanish passengers. These he ransomed on the spot and set ashore on Puerto Rico. One of them, Hernando de Altamorano, made an interesting report to the king of his experiences. He could not extract from "Verdecampo" (Grenville) and his men their ultimate destination—rather thought they intended to settle on some uninhabited island of the West Indies such as Dominica, where the Spanish had not been. The gentlemen in the *Tiger*, said Don Hernando, were served their meals on gold and silver plate. Manteo and Wanchese spoke good English and were well treated. On board were many musical instruments, including clarion trumpets, "because, they said, the Indians like music." They pressed on Don Hernando a Spanish Protestant Bible to take to San Juan in order to reveal to the inhabitants "how their priests had deceived them." This mission the Spaniard probably dared not perform for fear of the Inquisition.

Grenville now sailed down-wind along the north coast of Hispaniola, past Puerto Plata, to Isabela, Columbus's original colonial capital. Here, considering that their two countries were at war, there took place a surprisingly peaceful and pleasant get-together between Englishmen and Spaniards. On 5 June the alcalde, accompanied by "a lusty Friar, and 20 other Spaniards, with their servants and Negroes," appeared on the beach off which the English fleet lay at anchor. Grenville manned his boats "with the chiefe men of our fleete" dressed in their best, rowed ashore, exchanged salutes with the alcalde, and conferred with him. The English sailors, who had already proved themselves to be good carpenters, speedily raised two "banqueting halls," roofed with green boughs, one for the gentlemen, the other for the servants, and dished up to their hosts "a sumptuous banquet," all served on plate. It was accompanied by "the sound of trumpets" and a concert of music "with which the Spanyards were more than delighted." After dinner the alcalde brought a saddlehorse for every gentleman who cared to ride, and laid on a hunt, the quarry being three white bulls brought down from the mountains. "The pastime grew very pleasant for the space of three houres, wherein all three of the beasts were killed," one trying to escape by sea as the hunted stags do in Somersetshire. Gifts were exchanged, and next day Harvey, Grenville's cape merchant, bought all the cattle the ships' decks could hold, as well as hides, ginger, pearls, and tobacco for sale in England.

On 7 June the fleet "departed with great good will from the Spanyardes . . . of Hispaniola," Grenville attributing their hospitality to his show of strength. Possibly so; but the Spanish creoles at that out-of-the-way place were bored with life and welcomed any diversion, especially by Englishmen who, in contrast to the French corsairs who landed only to plunder, were "brave and gallant Gentlemen" and knew how to entertain. Naturally they dared not report these doings to Spain.

So far the voyage had been merry and the company united except for the spat between Grenville and Lane over the salt. On 8 June they landed at a small island of the Turks-Caicos group and took a number of seals—perhaps that is why Sir Richard wanted salt. Next day they called at Caicos to look for salt pans (with which the island still abounds), but found none, for which Simon Ferdinando was blamed. Passing outside most of the Bahamas, they anchored and landed at Cygateo (the future Eleuthera) and on the 20th fell in "with the mayne of Florida," we know not exactly where, as Florida then included Georgia and South Carolina.

Tiger almost foundered on the shoals off what Grenville took to be Cape Fear, on 25 June, first indication that pilot Simon was slipping; and the new moon was already at first quarter. It seems probable that this cape was really Lookout, not Fear, and that the harbor where they anchored next day is the present Beaufort-Morehead, North Carolina. Here they "caught in one tyde so much fishe as woulde have yielded us £20 in London; this was our first landing in Florida." Two days

Grenville arrives.
Entrance to Beaufort and Morehead City, North Carolina.

An inlet, probably the one where *Tiger* struck.

later they anchored off an inlet that they called Wococon, probably the present Whalebone Inlet. It seems odd that Ferdinando should have tried an unknown inlet at latitude 35° N (Raleigh communicated this latitude to the Dutch cartographer Ortelius), instead of continuing around Cape Hatteras to the opening named after himself and already used by Amadas and Barlowe.

In entering Pamlico Sound, Ferdinando committed the pilot's unforgivable sin. While conning *Tiger* through the inlet he ran her aground, and the rest of the fleet also hit bottom. They floated off easily, but *Tiger* pounded almost ninety times during two hours, and only good seamanship on the part of Grenville's men prevented her from becoming a complete wreck. They managed to float her, and to make her fit for sea again, but most of the provisions and supplies in her hold were utterly spoiled. Sir Richard was furious, and the officer who kept *Tiger*'s journal observed that Simon "abused our General and us, deserving a halter for his hire." Ralph Lane, after his return, when he had become Grenville's bitter enemy, denied that the grounding was Ferdinando's fault. Any sailor will doubt this verdict. The most charitable thing we can say about Simon is that he never learned his business.

On 3 July, moon two days full, Grenville sent to Wingina at Roanoke Island by boat the unwelcome news that the English were back, and a pinnace took the now bilingual Manteo to his home island of Croatoan, near Cape Hatteras. There he found that the *Red Lion*, Captain Raymond, from which they had been separated in the gale off Portugal, had called some three weeks earlier, landed thirty colonists, and sailed for Newfoundland. And Captain John Clarke's *Roebuck* must have shown up shortly, as we find her sailing for England in September.

Here ends the 1585 voyage, and the checquered history of the first Virginia colony begins.

Lane's Colony at Roanoke Island, 1585–86

The annals of this earliest English colony in America are brief and meager. While most of the company marked time, precariously anchored off the Outer Banks, Sir Richard in his barge (a Thames tilt-boat), with the new Puerto Rico-built pinnace, and a ship's longboat, led an exploring expedition of Pamlico Sound in search of a good site

The village of Secoton on the Pamlico River, 1585. Note the three plant-
ings of corn, the shrine to their god in the ripe cornfield, and the tomb
of their werowances at lower left. Original John White painting. Courtesy
British Museum.

for the colony. Pamlico is the sound that Verrazzano had mistaken for
the Pacific Ocean in 1524. Sir Richard was accompanied by Lane,
White, Hariot, Cavendish, Amadas, Manteo, "and divers other Gentlemen." The boats rowed and sailed about twenty-five miles due north,
and landed. After an inland march of a few miles, the Indian village of
Pomeiooc was encountered and a "great lake called by the Savages
Paquype." This is now Lake Mattamuskeet, and the country between it

The village of Pomeiooc, near Lake Mattamuskeet, 1585. Note the sleeping platforms in the mat-covered houses, the dog at upper left, and the long bow. Original John White drawing. Courtesy British Museum.

and the Sound is rich farm land. They then rounded Bluff Point, passed the mouths of several small bays, stood up the Pamlico River and the Pungo, one of its branches, to an Indian village called Aquascogoc. Returning to the Pamlico, on 15 July they rowed up about twenty miles farther to the village of Secoton (near the site of Bonnerton), "and were well intertayned there by the Savages." At this time, John White made his now famous sketches of Pomeiooc and Secoton. Grenville then committed an act of ruthless folly which began the ruin of friendly relations with the natives so carefully built up by Amadas and Barlowe. A silver cup had disappeared from one of his boats when they were calling at Aquascogoc. Sir Richard, assuming theft, demanded it back from the local werowance, who promised to make a search. Upon returning to Aquascogoc in his tilt-boat, and no cup being produced, Grenville "spoiled their corne" and burned the village. He would have done better, like Davis with the Eskimo, to have used a little patience, especially since his colony had to live among these people and even depend on them for food. But Sir Richard was evidently the "put the fear of God into 'em" type of explorer who would have been at home

Grenville's boat expedition.
Probable site of Secoton.

Site of Pomeiooc—Lake Mattamuskeet in distance.

among nineteenth-century gunboat diplomats. For this and doubtless other unrecorded rash and rude acts of theirs, the English planters eventually paid dear.

Back from "the discovery of Secoton," Sir Richard and his companions boarded the fleet which had been riding in safety off Whalebone Inlet and Wococon (now Portsmouth) Island, and sailed for Port Ferdinando, Hatarask Island. This ocean passage of less than sixty miles took them six days; they must have had head winds and made a long "traverse" seaward to avoid the Diamond and Wimble shoals. Upon arrival off Port Ferdinando, Wingina's brother Granganimeo came on board and invited the Englishmen to seat their colony on Roanoke Island. The invitation was joyfully accepted on the strength of Barlowe's enthusiastic description of the fertile soil and friendly natives.

On 5 August Grenville dispatched one of his prizes to England under command of John Arundel, to beg of Raleigh a prompt relief expedition, in view of the loss of *Tiger's* cargo. Three weeks later, the General himself sailed home in *Tiger*. He had performed his allotted task by landing colonists, cattle, plants, and all her freight which had not been ruined by grounding. Governor Ralph Lane, now responsible for the colony, wrote to Sir Francis Walsingham on 8 September (sending his letter in *Roebuck* which sailed for England a few days later), adverting in no mild terms to the ways in which Sir Richard "hathe demeaned him selfe" during the voyage. He had threatened to put Lane on trial for his life, owing simply to his having offered some unwanted and unpalatable advice. Lane begs Walsingham never again to place him under Grenville, for he cannot suffer Sir Richard's "intollerable pryede, and unsaciable ambycione." Grenville, undoubtedly, was a difficult person to work for, or under; but he had the guts which every colonial pioneer needs to succeed, and which Ralph Lane obviously lacked.

On her way home, *Tiger* captured a richly laden Spanish ship named *Santa Maria de San Vicente*. Sir Richard boarded her from "a little cocke boat" that his men had clapped together on board so hastily that she fell apart and sank at the Spaniard's side, like Frobisher's pinnace off Hall's Island. This indicates that the General had left behind both pinnaces, as well as the tilt-boat and other small craft, for the use of the colony. He took command of the *Santa Maria* himself, and made Plymouth on 18 October 1585. *Tiger*, having parted from her in foul weather

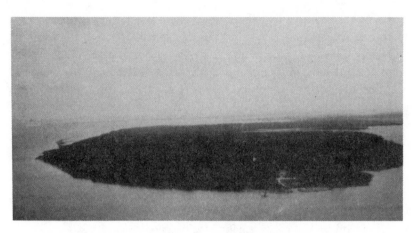

The heavily wooded Roanoke Island of 1970.

Currituck beach, 1970.

off the Azores, came into Falmouth on the 6th and then moved up to Plymouth. Raleigh and other "worshipfull friends" came to Plymouth to greet Sir Richard, who wrote proudly to Sir Francis Walsingham on the 29th, "I have god be thanked performed the action whereunto I was directed as fullye as the tyme wherein I have bene absente from hense and all possibilities wolde permitte me I have possessed and peopled the same to her Maiesties use, and planted it with suche cattell & beastes as are fitte and necessary for manuringe the Countrey and in tyme to geve reliefe with victuall, as also with such fruites and plantes as by my travaile by the waie thetherwardes I mighte procure." The sale of *Santa Maria* and her cargo, together with prizes taken in the West Indies, yielded some £50,000 which gave the adventurers a handsome dividend on their investment of £10,000.

We have very meager accounts of what went on at Roanoke Island after Grenville's departure. Winter succeeded the splendor of autumn, and the Englishmen were relieved to find it mild, and that so much verdure stayed green. They had already planted corn and seeds, and hopefully set out the ratoons and banana plants gathered in the West Indies. For defense they built a fort on the northern end of the island, designed by Hariot.

Roanoke Island, about ten miles long and two broad, heavily wooded (indicating good soil) and with a little harbor of its own (appropriately named Shallowbag Bay), was as suitable a place for a colony as any in the coastal region; but it had the fatal disadvantage of inaccessibility. Roanoke could never serve as a hideout for English privateers, because only pinnaces and small barks could sail through the inlets, as *Tiger*'s mishap proved. Lane, to his credit, soon realized that he could find no deep-water harbor hereabouts; learning of the future Hampton Roads from the Indians, he planned to go there by river and on foot, to investigate. Making a first attempt in March of 1586, Lane got no farther than a native village near the headquarters of the Chowan River; and as all Indians ran away at his approach, leaving their pets behind, the English were reduced to eating roast native dog, flavored with sassafras. On another boat trip, of which almost nothing is known, Lane discovered Currituck Sound and rounded Cape Henry into Lynnhaven Bay. He also explored the Roanoke River almost to its headwaters, looking for sources of the Indians' copper ornaments, and hoping to find gold.

There is no doubt that, following Lane's advice, Raleigh's next colony would have been pitched on the shores of Chesapeake Bay, but for an accident. In native relations Lane was inept, despite the advantage of having Manteo as interpreter. He attended the annual Indian corn-busk, the green maize festival common to all eastern tribes, in the August full moon, and reported that the assembly numbered more than seven hundred; he learned how to grow corn and even tried making syrup from the cornstalks. But, by his own showing, Lane allowed racial relations further to deteriorate.

Europeans never seemed to learn from one another's experience how to deal with American Indians intelligently, or even with Christian humanity. Columbus in Hispaniola and Jamaica, Ribaut and Laudonnière in Florida, and Cartier in Canada, were as bad as the English. Natives received the first Europeans with jubilation and overwhelming hospitality, based partly on the belief that they were "men from heaven." Both Lane and Hariot wrote that by Wingina's Algonkin tribe the English were considered supernatural, part of the evidence being that they had no women with them, yet refused the native girls. Such continence on the part of English sailors is hard to believe, especially since White's drawings show the young native women to be well formed, comely, their hair coquetishly trimmed, and provocatively attired in a single dressed deerskin. Bounteous initial hospitality always seemed to convince Europeans that they could be "freeloaders" indefinitely; that as superior beings they should be supplied with fish, corn, venison, or whatever they wanted. But, though they paid with knives, bells, and beads, "consumer demand" was soon satisfied.

Another factor in Indian life that Europeans seldom considered was the natives' habit of gorging in the fall when they had plenty of everything, and starving in the spring; they did not "gather into barns" any more than did "fowls of the air"; and before the first corn crop ripened, they were generally reduced to gathering shellfish and edible roots. Lane reported that Wingina set up fish weirs and planted corn for the English colony in April, "which put us in marveilous comfort," hoping it would see them through until summer. All they feared was "of the two moneths betwixt," during which, if the savages would not bring them edible ground roots, and if the weirs "should fayle us, as often they did, wee myght very well starve . . . like the starving horse in the stable, with growing grasse, as the proverbe is."

Why Europeans never seemed able or willing to fish for themselves is still a mystery, but a fact. In Virginia the Indians built simple fish weirs, and in the months of friendship Wingina's men built some for the English, who were incapable even of repairing them. Another source of trouble was the cattle and swine brought from Puerto Rico and Hispaniola. Unless Lane saw to it that they were surrounded by a fence "horse-high, ox-strong, and hog-tight," which is most unlikely, they must have made a beeline for the nearest Indian cornfield. That created enmity between the races in North America all through the colonial period; it was one of the principal causes of King Philip's War in New England.

Inevitably these racial dissensions, misunderstandings, and injustices led to an effort by the natives to rub out the European colony. Through Manteo (Wanchese having reverted to his native allegiance) the English learned that Wingina had summoned 700 to 800 bowmen from his subjects and his allies to do the job, on the pretense of laying on a big funeral for his lately deceased father, whom Lane credits with having so far restrained his resentful son. At a signal fire, they would surround and burn the Englishmen's flimsy wattle and bark huts, and kill each inmate as he ran out; then mop up any who were "dispersed abroade in the Islande, seeking of crabs and fish." As a preliminary, in order to soften up the English and neutralize their superior arms, Wingina gave orders to sell the intruders no food whatsoever, even for the delectable copper,* and to cut breaches in their weirs so that fish would escape. "The famine grewe so extreme among us," recorded Lane, that he sent Captain Stafford and twenty men to Croatoan Island to sponge on friendly Indians there.

After this dispersal, Lane with barely forty men knew that he was too weak to fend off an attack of tenfold his numbers armed with highly lethal bows and arrows. His own arquebuses and other hand arms, perhaps thirty to thirty-five in number, took so long to reload that an enemy could close in for the kill after his first volley. Deciding that diplomacy had failed, and with no immediate expectation of relief from England, Lane decided on a preventive war. Warned by friendly natives that Wingina's D-day was 10 June 1586, Lane planned a *cami-*

---

* One infers that Raleigh, being informed by Barlowe how highly the Algonkin valued copper, sent out a quantity of it from the Keswick copper mines as a trading medium.

sado, as the Spanish called a night attack because the assaulting party wore their shirttails loose to identify themselves. That was prematurely discovered, and called off. Next day, 1 June, in the dark of the moon, Lane and twenty-five men in his biggest boat with one canoe, landed at Wingina's mainland village of Dasemunkepeuc, found the chief sitting among his werowances, gave the agreed watchword, "Christ our victory," and opened fire. Wingina played dead, then started up and ran like a deer; but he was "shot through the buttocks by mine Irish boy" (Kelly or Glavin) with a big cavalry pistol, says Lane, then chased into the woods, and killed and beheaded by Hariot and Edward Nugent, another Irishman. The Irish may not have won every war for the English in North America, but they sure started early!

A week later, when Lane's men were fearfully guarding against counterattack, a happy message came from Captain Stafford at Croatoan. A fleet of twenty-three sail had been sighted. It was the relief!

Drake and Grenville Relief Expeditions of 1586

The first relief expedition was not the one originally planned under Bernard Drake, but an unexpected, providential visit of Sir Francis Drake. Raleigh had chartered Bernard's ship *Golden Royal*, and the *Red Lion* of Chichester (which had made a quick return to England) should have accompanied her; but on 20 June 1585, the Queen ordered both ships to join her expedition to Newfoundland. It was then that Bernard wrought such havoc among the enemy fishing fleet as we related in Chapter XIV. Going and coming, they captured five richly laden Spanish or Portuguese ships, one "laden with sugers, wynes and oliphantes teeth," and "xvi sayle of Portingalles laden with fishe in the Newe founde land." The total loot brought £60,000, and of this Raleigh got the lion's share, which the Queen had promised him in return for diverting this relief expedition from Virginia. Upon *Golden Royal*'s return to England, she was procured by Sir Richard Grenville in the spring of 1586 to accompany him, in *Red Lion*, to relieve the Roanoke colony. But the other Drake beat them to it.

Sir Francis, with a fleet of twenty-nine sail and 2300 mariners and soldiers, and Martin Frobisher as second in command in his old flagship *Aid*, had just completed a highly successful raid on the West Indies. He captured and ransomed Santo Domingo and Cartagena, then took and sacked St. Augustine in Florida with particular relish, remembering what Menéndez had done to the French Protestants. On the eighth day of June, Edward Stafford's lookouts on Croatoan joyfully beheld this veritable armada, fraught with spoils of victory, approaching their Virginia.

Sir Francis, probably at Sir Walter's request, had always intended to make this call, and he expected to leave in Virginia some Negroes whom he had captured and freed at Cartagena, and a load of the St. Augustine loot. Anchoring off Croatoan, he took on board one of Stafford's men as pilot, and by the big wherry sent a letter ahead through Pamlico Sound to make Lane "a most bountifull and honourable offer for the supplie of . . . necessities." Some of the Drake fleet managed to get through Port Ferdinando inlet to Roanoke Island, but most of them drew too much water and had to anchor "without the harbour in a wild road at sea, about two miles from shore."

Drake did not have Verrazzano's luck in open-roadstead anchoring off this coast. He was preparing to leave behind enough "shipping and victuall" to serve the colony, carrying home only such planters who were weak or sick, when on 13 June a terrific gale blew up from the northwest and continued four days. Drake, like any good mariner, sought sea room; and one of his ships, the seventy-ton bark *Francis* (which he had intended to leave with Lane) kept right on going to England. After the storm had abated, Drake returned to Roanoke and offered to give the colony another ship, but Governor Lane and his chief counselors besought him to take everybody home. And that Drake did. All 103 surviving colonists abandoned Roanoke, piled on board Drake's ships, and departed Virginia 18 June 1586.

Immediately after, around 20 June, a supply ship sent by Raleigh arrived at Roanoke, took a look around, and, finding nobody there but savages, returned home. Two weeks passed, and in mid-July Sir Richard Grenville turned up with a fleet of several ships, which had left North Devon about 2 May and had crossed direct from Madeira. He made a careful but fruitless search for the colonists, and from a captured Indian learned that they had deserted Roanoke. Sir Richard left on the island an inadequate force of eighteen men to hold the fort for England, and sailed about 25 August, looking for prizes between Newfoundland and the Azores and returning to England in December.

Drake's fleet, carrying Lane and the colonists, arrived Portsmouth 28 July.

By the time the next Raleigh colony arrived, in 1587, the men left by Grenville, led by a Coffin and a Chapman, had all disappeared. John White learned that they had been ambushed at Roanoke by double their number of natives, and smoked out of their huts before they could arm themselves properly. They fought valiantly with swords for an hour against the Indian archers, but to no avail. Four got away in their small boat to an islet opposite Hatarask, and were either pursued and killed there, or starved to death. Coffin and Chapman, mariners of Barnstaple, deserve remembrance among the unsung heroes of English colonization.

Lane and his men are not to be blamed for scuttling. After killing Wingina, they rightly anticipated an overwhelming counterattack. Grenville would not have quit, but Lane was not of the stuff of which heroes are made. He deserves particular credit for his explorations which pointed the way for the Virginia Company to the Chesapeake in 1607. His native relations were inept, but not more so than those of other pioneers; and, given the respective attitudes of Algonkin and English, it was only a matter of time before a fatal clash occurred. Europeans, even with humane intentions toward American natives, could not long live side by side with them; and the natives were mowed down by European diseases when not impoverished by the loss of their hunting range and cornfields. "Peaceful co-existence" between Europeans and natives never worked unless (as in Mexico and South America generally) on the basis of the Indian becoming the white man's slave or forced laborer. The Algonkin, Iroquois, and other natives of North America were too proud to do that; they preferred death to slavery, and although they fought bravely, and won many early encounters, they always lost in the end because incapable of preventing Europeans from being reinforced by sea.

Bibliography and Notes

GENERAL SOURCES

David B. Quinn (ed.), *The Roanoke Voyages, 1585–1590*, two volumes, issued by the Hakluyt Society in 1955, is a monument to Professor Quinn's scholarship. Every possible document from every likely source is included, the notes on ethnology, botany, and the English background are informing and voluminous; and (most unusual for an historian), Professor Quinn twice visited and examined the area described in the narratives.* The map of the area at the back of Volume II is most excellent.

Irene A. Wright, *Further English Voyages to Spanish America, 1583–1584: Documents from the Archives of the Indies* (Hakluyt Society, 1951), contains more Spanish sidelights on "Don Verdecampo" (Grenville) and "Rale" (Raleigh). Miss Wright, a specialist in Cuban history, resided in Seville for many years doing research for the Cuban government, the Library of Congress, and for any student who could convince her that he was serious—fortunately Quinn and I did! She had extraordinary flair for unearthing documents in the Archives of the Indies, and an equal skill in deciphering and translating them.

Next in importance is the monumental work edited by Paul Hulton and D. B. Quinn, *The American Drawings of John White 1577–1590* (2 vols., folio, British Museum and Chapel Hill, 1964). The second volume reproduces all White's drawings and paintings of Raleigh's Virginia, mostly in color. It is amazing that these beautiful and accurate paintings, including the best portraits of American Indians prior to Catlin, the best flora prior to John Bertram, and the best birds and beasts prior to Audubon, should have waited almost four centuries for adequate reproduction. One reason is that almost everyone assumed that De Bry's engravings were sufficient. De Bry's *America*, first published in Frankfort in 1590, and later German and French translations the same year, did make widely known the artistic work of John White and the literary work of Thomas Hariot, but the De Bry engravings are very different from the White paintings. In general, the engravings Europeanize and idealize the features of Indians, especially the women. In order to display more detail than White, De Bry changed his paintings and added to them; for example, he separates the little girl from her mother so she can hold a rattle in one hand and a doll in the other. In the picture of a native couple eating beans, De Bry adds in the foreground a squid, fish, and some ears of maize. The De Bry engravings are, however, valuable for their descriptive texts by Thomas Hariot which are not in his *Briefe and True Report;* and for that reason Hulton and Quinn have reproduced a number in the above-mentioned *American Drawings of John White.* All earlier attempts to reproduce the White drawings were failures.

The most important biographies, both excellent, are A. L. Rowse, *Sir Richard Grenville* (London, 1937) and *Raleigh and the Throckmortons* (London, 1962).

* In his company were historians Carl Bridenbaugh and John Gordon, whose report of the 1948 reconnaissance by car and motorboat he kindly lent to me. James F. Nields, Cameron W. Beck, and I covered the same area in Nields's Beechcraft in June 1970, and found no reason to disagree with Quinn's identifications.

For older books and articles, Justin Winsor, *Narrative and Critical History*, IV, 121–26, is best. But Winsor wrote too early for the works of Alexander Brown (1843–1906). A Virginian, rendered almost totally deaf by service in the Confederate Army and with no other means than the exiguous income of a country post office, Brown bravely went ahead with his research. It was he who first realized that if anything fresh were to be found on the first Virginia colony, it would be in Spanish archives. With no grant, no foundation, or indeed anything but little contributions sought by handwritten appeals to friends and members of the American Historical Association, he managed to support research at Seville and Simancas, and opened up the richest non-English source for this period of Anglo-American history, later so brilliantly and thoroughly pursued by Irene Wright. His documents are found in *The Genesis of the United States* (Boston, 1890).

For those who have no access to Hakluyt Society publications, a good substitute is Henry S. Burrage (ed.), *Early English and French Voyages, Chiefly from Hakluyt* (New York, 1906), in the Original Narratives of Early American History series edited by J. Franklin Jameson. This includes the principal narratives of the 1584, 1586, 1587, and 1590 voyages. I must here pay a "briefe and true" tribute to Dr. Jameson (1859–1937). An early graduate of the celebrated seminar at Johns Hopkins University, he devoted most of his life to historical organization: founder and first editor of *The American Historical Review*, secretary of the American Historical Association, head of the Department of Historical Research of the Carnegie Institution of Washington. As such he edited and found a publisher for this extraordinarily useful series of some twenty volumes on North American colonial history. These, a boon to young scholars, have never been superseded. Dr. Jameson was a scholar in the old-fashioned sense, at home in ancient and modern languages, impeccable in judgment, always helpful to young aspirants. For the first half of the twentieth century he worthily took the place that Justin Winsor held in the latter half of the nineteenth.

DETAILS

Outer Banks and Cape Hatteras. David Stick, *The Outer Banks of North Carolina* (1958), includes a useful table (p. 9) of the inlets, when they were open and when closed. The only one open during the Raleigh voyages, and still open in 1958, was Okrakoke, west of the island of that name. William L. Ellis, "Lonely Cape Hatteras," *National Geographic*, CXXXVI, 393–420 (September 1969), has an impressive map showing all identifiable wrecks. The Gulf Stream flows within twelve miles of Cape Hatteras, and the counter-currents, strong winds, and shifting sands are a menace to navigation even today. A Texas Tower was established off Diamond Shoals, the most dangerous, in 1966. In 1942 there were more than twenty sinkings of merchant ships by U-boats off "Torpedo Junction," as sailors called Cape Hatteras.

The Amadas-Barlowe Voyage of 1584. Quinn guesses that the flagship was the 200-tun *Raleigh,* but she could never have negotiated the inlet; and that the other was the *Dorothie,* which started on the 1585 voyage.

Raleigh's 1584 Patent is in Quinn, I, 82–89. Newfoundland, as the editor points out, was not included in Raleigh's grant. The crown may have intended to do something about a separate government for Newfoundland but did not get around to it until 1610, when James I granted a patent to John Guy to make a settlement there. Subsequently, Lord Baltimore tried one at Ferryland, found the climate too severe and moved to Maryland.

Port Ferdinando. Certain local authorities believe this inlet to have been the same as Roanoke Inlet which served the colony of North Carolina from 1660 to 1811; this was originally just south of Nags Head village, but moved south to the narrow neck where the Roanoke Sound Bridge now begins. Others, following John White's contemporary map, believe Port Ferdinando to have been a few miles further south, at about latitude 35°50', where the Outer Banks is again very narrow. At both locations, the five-fathom line, where Captain Watts's ship anchored in 1590, approaches the coast today within three-quarters of a mile. The taking possession from the southern location would have been on Cedar Point, or just south of the lighthouse, both places then being part of Hatarask (Hatteras) Island. See Stick, pp. 274–77. However, the inlets in this region change so frequently that we cannot be certain of Port Ferdinando's exact location. Lane's sketch map of the region, in Quinn, I, 214–15, shows a big gap in the Outer Banks opposite the southern end of Roanoke Island, but does not name it.

Windgandcon. The meaning is discussed by Quinn, I, 116–17, and II, 853–54. Some authorities agree with Sir Walter; others think that it means "fine evergreens," or something else.

Thomas Hariot. After Raleigh's fall in 1603, Hariot attached himself to the "wizard" Earl of Northumberland and became one of the most productive experimental scientists of the early seventeenth century. He made the earliest known map of the moon, on the basis of telescopic observations in 1609–10. Long neglected, his scientific papers that have survived are now being intensively studied at Oxford. D. B. Quinn's article on Hariot in *The Renaissance Quarterly,* 1969, and A. C. Crombie *et al.,* "Thomas Harriot 1560–1621," in *Times Literary Supplement* 23 October 1969.

John White. His life is discussed not only by Quinn, *Roanoke Voyages,* I, 42–60, but in the first volume of *The American Drawings of John White.* Certain Virginians have advanced the snob argument that the humble artist of the 1585 voyage could not possibly have been the governor of the 1587 colony. One can now safely assert that only one John White went to Virginia, although his name may be spelled in contemporary documents "Wite," "Twit," "Wright," or whatnot. Nothing is known about him subsequent to the voyage of 1590 except that he lived in Ireland.

Simon Ferdinando. Since neither Miss Wright nor anyone else has found evidence in the Spanish records that Simon was on Philip II's secret payroll, we may acquit him of treachery; but he certainly bungled. Apparently he was patronized by Walsingham, which accounts for the important positions given to him by Raleigh.

Tilt-boats. See picture of ships in the Thames in Chapter V above. The two pictures of *Tiger* off the Puerto Rico coast, and in White's Map of Virginia, indicate that Grenville erected a tilt or awning on her quarterdeck as a protection from the sun.

GRENVILLE IN PUERTO RICO

Quinn is rather foggy on Puerto Rican topography, for which I have had the help of my esteemed friend Ing. Aurelio Tió of San Juan, an expert on the historical geography of the island. Having found the name *Cottea* nowhere but in this narrative, he is convinced that the island was Vieques and the name is derived from *jicotea*, the giant tortoise which is found there. It could not have been any of the cays off the southern shore of Puerto Rico, as all are devoid of fresh water.

Tiger's calling the anchorage where the fort was built "Baye of Muskito" identifies it as Guayanilla Bay, originally called by the Spaniards *Musquetal* because of the abundance of insects. Owing to these pests and the still more annoying French corsairs who landed there to pillage at least thrice between 1569 and 1582, most of the Spanish planters, before Grenville's arrival, had removed themselves, together with their town of San Germán (already once moved since John Rut's visit) to the foothills. The several Spanish reports of English activities there leave no doubt that Grenville's fort was at the mouth of the Guayanilla River in the like-named bay, not in Tallaboa Bay as Quinn states, at I,181.

John White's painting of the fort we have reproduced from the original in the British Museum; it will be found, in colors, in *The American Drawings of John White*, II, plate 3; description in I,68. Note that the apparent bathing party on the beach at the right is a mere offset from the cavalcade on the left, caused by the painting, when folded, having been wet in consequence of a fire in 1865. Mr. Tió believes that Lane's fort and salt operations were at the mouth of the Tayaboa River where (as he proved by an air view) there are extensive salt pans today.

* XX *
The Second Virginia Colony

1587-?

Sir Walter Raleigh was one that Fortune had picked out of purpose, of whom to make an example, or to use as her Tennis-Ball, . . . for she tossed him up and out of nothing, and to and fro to greatness, and from thence down to little more than to that wherein she found him, a bare Gentleman.

SIR ROBERT NAUNTON, *Fragmenta Regalia* (1641) P. 47.

John White's Colony and Settlement

Sir Walter Raleigh, no whit discouraged by the return of Ralph Lane's people or by his reports, promptly started preparations for a comeback. His Virginia seemed to be delightful, fertile, with mild winters, promising rich rewards in sub-tropical agriculture, and prospects of copper and even gold mines in the distant mountains. The only thing wrong with the Roanoke site was inaccessibility, owing to all three inlets so far discovered being too shallow and dangerous to admit the average merchant ship or privateer. So the obvious place to seat the next colony was on Chesapeake Bay, which Lane had partly explored. That would provide a deep-water naval base for attacks on Spanish shipping, plenty of islands defensible from Indians, more arable land and less swamp than on the Carolina sounds.

Richard Hakluyt, always (as Sir Philip Sidney wrote) "a very good Trumpet" for Raleigh, and William Sanderson of Sanderson's Hope fame, "a great friend to all such noble and worthy actions," were all for another try. Hakluyt was excited over an account of Antonio de Espejo's New Mexico expedition of 1583, which had just been published, and which he republished and translated. Espejo reported silver

mines, and his longitude (as Hakluyt reported it) was so wildly inaccurate that New Mexico appeared to be at the very back door of Virginia! The war with Spain will not last forever (wrote Hakluyt),
there will be unemployment when the armed forces are disbanded, and
no fitter plan can be found to employ old soldiers than Virginia, where
"one hundred men will doe more nowe among the naked and unarmed
people" than a thousand could do in Ireland. "Yf you proceed, which
I longe much to knowe," he wrote to Sir Walter on the penultimate
day of 1586, "your best planting wilbe aboute the bay of the Chese-
pians, to which latitude Peter Martyr and franciscus lopez de Gomara
the Spaniard confesse that our Gabot and English did first discover."
Espejo's expedition "bringeth you to rich sylver mynes up in the
countre in the latitude of 37½."

Preparations for this second Virginia colony were formidable, the
voyage thither long and complicated, the outcome lamentable.

Raleigh set up a distinguished organization for his second Virginia
colony. Co-opting several friends and well wishers as assistants, and
appointing John White the artist as governor, he incorporated (in the
usual form for colonial joint stock companies) THE GOVERNOUR AND
ASSISTANTS OF THE CITTIE OF RALEIGH IN VIRGINEA. Garter King of Arms
gave the city a simple coat of arms, a cross with Raleigh's roebuck
crest in one quarter; but to John White "of London, Gentleman," he
gave a coat in eight quarterings; and to each of the assistants, their own
"Armes of Ensignes of honour," which we have here reproduced.
Probably these were emblazoned on shields, to display on the waist-
cloths of a ship; but what could have been done with them at Roanoke?
Governor White bought himself a suit of armor; everything possible
was done to dignify the City of Raleigh as a feudal community, with
an appointed aristocracy and common people to do the heavy work.

This impression of Raleigh's social plans is confirmed by the list of
planters. Unlike the men-only Ralph Lane colony, this included both
sexes and all ages. There were fourteen families which, with the un-
attached individuals, amounted to 89 men, 17 women, and 11 children.
All were middle-class English or Irish (no foreign mineral men) but
the newly armigerous assistants were expected to form an aristocracy.
One of them, Ananias Dare, had married Eleanor White the governor's
daughter; and she, although already pregnant, accompanied her husband. Dionyse Harvey, apparently a cousin to Sir James Harvey iron-

City of Raleigh   Cooper   Harvie

Ferdinando

White

Bayley

Dare   Nichols   Howe

The Virginia armorial of 1587.

monger of London, was accompanied by his wife Margery; and she too was almost ready to increase the white population of Virginia. Two or three of the men, besides the governor, had been members of Ralph Lane's colony. It is clear that this was meant to be a genuine self-perpetuating colony, not a mere trading post or garrison like Ralph Lane's. Ralph himself was conspicuously absent, but unfortunately Walsingham or Sir Walter Raleigh insisted on appointing Simon Ferdinando captain of the flagship, and he proved just such a cross to Governor White as he had been to Sir Richard Grenville. Manteo and another Indian, whom Lane had brought home, were included.

Governor White conducted a very small fleet, considering the number of passengers and the importance of his mission. His "admirall" was a 120-tun ship *Lion*—probably the *Red Lion* or *Lyon* of Chichester which had gone out in 1585. He had a flyboat, name and tunnage unknown, commanded by Edward Spicer, and a pinnace, commanded by Edward Stafford, who had been on the previous voyage. Simon Ferdinando seems to have commanded the *Lion*, and the fleet; and as White had no pretensions to seamanship Simon always played the "admirall."

The fleet departed Portsmouth 26 April 1587 and anchored same day in Cowes roads, just in time to see the new moon set. Apparently Governor White had important business there with Raleigh's kinsman Sir George Carey, captain of the Isle of Wight and governor of Carisbrooke Castle. Carey, an old hand at privateering, had recently obtained letters of marque for several ships which shortly embarked on a plundering expedition to the West Indies. Raleigh had probably planned some sort of co-operation between this fleet and White's, but they never met. Sir Richard Grenville also planned a relief squadron, whose flagship (a Spanish prize) had the curious name *Virgin God Save Her*, but never got to sea.

Final departure took place from Plymouth on 8 May 1587, moon waxing first quarter to full. Farewell forever to green and merry England, for the more than one hundred colonists stowed in makeshift cabins on board the *Lion*, the flyboat, and the pinnace. It was a late departure for starting a colony, as John White must have known; you had to get there in time to sow crops to reap that year, or you would be in a bad way by spring. But Simon Ferdinando, who took command whether or not he had the right, did not care the traditional tinker's dam for the Virginia colony. He was all for privateering; while the South Atlantic and the Caribbean were swarming with richly laden enemy ships, it would be like picking up money. And, very likely, Sir Walter, always strapped, gave him carte blanche.

Governor White's narrative of this passage to Virginia shows it to have been not quite as crazy as the Grenville and Lane voyage two years earlier. Choosing the southern tradewind route, *Lion* raised Dominica 19 June, and the flyboat, which Ferdinando (says White), "lewdly forsooke" off Portugal, turned up two days later. Passing along the superb chain of the Leeward Islands, these two and the pinnace anchored at St. Croix, probably in the future Christiansted harbor, and "all the planters were set on land" for three days, 22–25 June. Imagine what pleasure that must have given the English children; this was their first experience of tropical vegetation and gay-colored screaming parrots. But they paid dear for their fun by eating "a small fruite like greene apples," which made their mouths burn and their tongues swell. This was the poisonous manchineel, whose fruit looks like a green apple, and the eating of which causes the symptoms described. Every navigator to the West Indies, starting with Columbus, had warned against this tree, whose "very leaves drip poison," but of course the English did not know that. And so many tourists have followed suit that the local government is now trying to eradicate the manchineel.

Ferdinando assured the company that there were no man-eating Caribs on St. Croix. Wrong as usual! That was where Columbus had his first fight with the Caribs; and White, who with six others explored the interior, saw eleven of them. Fortunately these Caribs either were not hungry, or were awed by the guns of the ships, as they made no effort to convert White's "planters," as he called his colonists, into fresh meat.

Their next stop, after a brief call at Vieques, was Guayanilla Bay, Puerto Rico, already familiar to White and Ferdinando. There, unaccountably, they marooned two Irishmen, Denis Carroll and Darby Glande, who had been unwilling participants both in the 1585 voyage and in this. White tried to get salt in the bay whence Lane had been frightened off in 1585, but Ferdinando vetoed that. The governor also wanted to land in the Bay of San Germán (now Añasco) to procure live plants of orange, pineapple, plantain, and mammee apple "to set at Virginia," but Ferdinando turned that down too, insisting they could do better at Isabela, where he had made friends with a Frenchman named Alençon on his previous visit. But the bumbling Ferdinando overshot Isabela and sheered off the coast of Hispaniola for Caicos. There they made the same fruitless search for salt as in 1585, but shot plenty of wild fowl, including swan.

On 7 July 1587, with moon a week past full, they left Caicos and sailed outside the Bahamas to Virginia. The place where they hit the land, somewhere between Cape Fear and Cape Lookout, Ferdinando thought to be Croatoan; but, after anchoring off shore for two days looking for the inlet, he decided it was not. They then weighed and stood along the Carolina Banks northward, narrowly missing being cast away on Cape Lookout or Hatteras. "We were come within two cables length upon it: such was the carelessnes and ignorance of our Master," wrote White. If one-tenth of the accusations of White and Grenville against Ferdinando were true, he was one of the world's worst pilots.

Ferdinando's next decision was fatal. Their supposed planned destination was the Chesapeake; but when they called at Roanoke Island on 22 July, hoping to pick up Grenville's men and continue, Ferdinando ordered the entire contingent to land and pitch this colony on the site of Lane's. White recorded, "It booted not the Governour to contend with them." Was this owing to a weakness of character on his part, or to a secret inclination to try Roanoke again rather than push on to the unknown "Chesepiok"? Ferdinando's excuse for canceling the Chesapeake destination was "that the summer was farre spent." He was not thinking of planting corn, but eager to get at the Spanish plate fleet, which usually called at the Azores in August or early September.

All passengers, both from *Lion* and the flyboat, were landed between 23 and 25 July, and the "Cittie of Raleigh in Virginia" began its brief, unhappy existence.

The fort on Roanoke Island had been razed, but all Lane's houses were "standing unhurt." They were overgrown with gourd and pumpkin vines, and deer were "within them, feeding on those Mellons"—as the English then called every squash-like vegetable. It was obvious that Grenville's small group left there in 1586 had disappeared. The men set-to, repairing the old and building new "cottages," including one to serve as Governor White's mansion; the women washed clothes, and the children had a beautiful time running about the island, picking flowers, and catching crab.

An Indian couple near Roanoke Island, dining. Hariot explains that their dish is "sodden" (parboiled) corn, and adds: "They are verye sober in their eatinge, and trinkinge, and consequentlye verye longe lived because they doe not oppress nature. . . . I would to God we would followe their exemple." Original John White painting. Courtesy British Museum.

The blue crabmeat of this region, especially in the soft shell stage, is a great delicacy, as we know to this day; and the Englishmen's taste for it led to their first casualty, on 28 July. George Howe, one of the twelve assistants, fishing for crab two miles from the village and without arms, was murdered by a party of Indians. His body, when found by his friends, contained sixteen arrow wounds, and his head had been bashed in by a club. Whether this was revenge for the killing of Wingina, or a warning "Englishmen Go Home!," we do not know.

The event convinced Governor White that he must repair his Indian relations. Accordingly he and master Stafford and twenty other men sailed to the Island of Croatoan at Capè Hatteras, taking Manteo, whose mother and other kindred belonged to the Croatoan tribe. The natives fled from their village when they saw the Englishmen coming, but after Manteo had called to them in their own language they cast aside their bows and arrows, "embracing and entertaining us friendly" but begging the English "not to gather or spoil any of their corne, for that they had but little." The Governor assured them that he came in

Indian woman and child near Roanoke. The woman carries her right arm in a bead necklace. The band around her forehead is a sign of rank. The little girl (whose face was smudged when the painting got wet) is carrying a doll dressed in Elizabethan court costume. Hariot explains that the children "are greatlye Dilighted with puppets and babes which wear brought oute of England." Original John White painting. Courtesy British Museum.

friendship, that the English wished to "renew the old love that was betweene us . . . and to live with them as brethren, and friendes." This appeared to please the Croatoans, who invited the English to visit their "towne," feasted them, and asked for some badge or token that they might wear, in order not to be mistaken for Wingina's men when encountered far from their island. And at a conference on 1 August it was agreed that "all unfriendly dealings past on both parties should be utterly forgiven and forgotten." A date was set, a week thence, to hold a meeting of werowances with Raleigh's assistants, at Roanoke, and try to make peace with Wingina's people.

It did not work out as planned. The Indians, always casual about dates, did not turn up on the day agreed. Governor White then decided that revenge for the death of Assistant Howe should no longer be delayed. Crossing to the mainland, the English assaulted Wingina's village of Dasemunkepeuc, found it full of Indians, and killed one before the rest fled. A bad mistake, alas! These were not Wingina's people, who had deserted the place after killing Howe, anticipating an English attack; the victims of White's assault were friendly Croatoans. En route to the planned conference they had found a great store of corn, tobacco, and pumpkin at the deserted village and wished to gather it for their own use before being spoiled by deer and raccoons. Manteo "imputed their harme to their owne follie" in being late for the engagement; but the chain of friendship was broken.

It was "summer time, when livin' is easy" in those parts, as Bess sang in Gershwin's *Porgy and Bess*. Fish were easily caught by hook and line, even though the English were too clumsy to build weirs. Corn, pumpkin, and other native vegetables were ripening. Manteo doubtless taught the big boys how to shoot birds with bow and arrow, as Governor White wished to conserve his powder and ball. On 13 August Manteo was christened, and as there was no English clergyman in the City of Raleigh, Master White officiated. Also, "in reward of his faithful service," he gave Manteo a title: "Lord of Roanoke and of Dasemunkepeuc," and perhaps designed a coat of arms for him. All very feudal and proper. White, acting for Raleigh as the lord and proprietor of Virginia, appointed Manteo chief of the Roanoke tribe, and his vassal.

Five days after Manteo's promotion, on 18 August, the governor's daughter Eleanor Dare gave birth to a daughter. She was christened by her grandfather the following Sunday, and "because this childe was the first Christian borne in Virginia, she was named Virginia." She was also the first European child to be born in North America outside the Spanish dominions; at least the first since the Norseman Snorri in the eleventh century.

A few days later, Virginia was provided with a little playmate. Margery, wife of Dionyse Harvey, was delivered of a child, whether boy or girl we know not, and the governor duly christened him, or her.

All this time *Lion*, the flyboat and the pinnace, were lying at anchor off Port Ferdinando or being repaired and readied for the homeward passage. On 21 August a northeast gale made up, forcing the flagship to cut her cables and seek sea room, and it took her six days to beat back. During her absence, Governor White and his assistants discussed who should return in her to act as factor or agent for the colony in England. Obviously the City of Raleigh needed a full-time agent there to prod Sir Walter into sending relief, and to keep the English public informed and interested. Every assistant preferred to stay, none wished to go home; and after much persuasion Governor White was prevailed upon to return himself. This does not mean that he had become unpopular but that, as a friend to important persons, which none of the obscure though armigerous assistants were, he could best serve the City of Raleigh in England.

So on 27 August, after spending only a month in Virginia and probably having little time to paint more pictures, White boarded the flyboat. She was riding outside the bar with *Lion*, under Simon Ferdinando. The pinnace stayed behind to serve the plantation.

As the flyboat was weighing anchor, she underwent a grievous accident, one not infrequent in days of sail with no labor-saving devices. Twelve men were at the capstan, winding in the long, heavy cable, and had reached the point where it was badly strained, as the anchor refused to break. Then a capstan bar broke. The strain on the stretched cable was such that the capstan, with the other bars set, flew around, wounding most of the anchor detail "so sore that some of them never recovered." On a second try the same thing happened, so they were obliged to cut the cable and lose the anchor. The flyboat's crew of fifteen, weakened by this accident, managed nevertheless to keep up with *Lion*, reaching Corvo and Flores in the Azores on

17 September. There Ferdinando, in view of the flyboat's having only five men fit for duty, transferred to her some of his sailors and dispatched her to England with Governor White on board, while he cruised around Terceira looking for prizes.

Poor flyboat's troubles were not over. She encountered a northeast storm which drove her further off course than she could recover in thirteen days; and at the end of that time, with only "stinking water, dregges of beere, and lees of wine" to drink, her crew expected "nothing but by famyne to perish at sea." But God was merciful. On 16 October 1587, seven weeks out from Virginia, she raised the land and sailed right into a harbor. The poor devils, having lost their reckoning, had no idea where they were, and no boat to send ashore and inquire. In due course a boat put out from another ship and informed them that they were at Smerwick on the Dingle Peninsula, Ireland. Governor White and the flyboat's master rode across country to the town of Dingle to seek help, and transferred three sick sailors thither; but in the meantime the boatswain, boatswain's mate, and steward died. Leaving the flyboat at Smerwick to procure a new crew, White took passage in a ship called the *Monkie*, and on 5 November arrived at Marazion near St. Michael's Mount, Cornwall. Thence he proceeded overland to Southampton, arriving 8 November 1589, where he learned that *Lion* had made Portsmouth three weeks earlier. She was so disabled by sickness and death that, unable to beat into the harbor, the crew were forced to anchor outside, "and might all have perished there, if a small barke by great hap had not come to them to help them."

Thus sadly ended the 1587 voyage, whose events proved that the hazards of the sea had not abated in a century's time.

But what happened to the colony at Roanoke? That is a mystery which has never been solved.

Thomas Hariot's Account

Even before White's return the propaganda mill had been grinding. Raleigh was much annoyed by false and malicious reports about Virginia. These came partly from men who had been "worthily punished" there for misdemeanors, and partly from colonists who could not bear wilderness life and railed against the New World "because there were not to bee found any English cities, nor such faire houses, nor . . . daintie food, nor any soft beds of downe or feathers, the countrey was to them miserable." Similarly, Governor Bradford of Plymouth Colony commented unfavorably on people who are "too delicate and unfit to begin new plantations and colonies, that cannot endure the biting of a mosquito. We would wish such to keep at home till at least they be mosquito-proof."

So, Thomas Hariot's *Briefe and True Report* was rushed to completion, dated February 1588, and came out a month or two later. Hariot began with a luscious catalogue of Virginia's native commodities—silk grass (yucca), silk worms (probably tent caterpillars), alum, copperas, kaolin, and other minerals, all wrongly identified. But he also mentioned a few genuine products, some of which are still leading productions of the Carolinas after almost four centuries of non-conservation: cedar wood, then much wanted in England for furniture and wainscoting; pitch, tar, turpentine, and other pine derivatives, the ever desirable "naval stores"; furs and deer skins; grapes—from which a wine called "Virginia Dare" is still made—and sassafras which, owing to the shape of the leaf, was supposed to be a specific against syphilis. Thomas Frampton's translation, entitled *Joyfull newes out of the new founde World* (1577), of the description of American plants by the Spanish Dr. Monardes, recommended sassafras not only for venereal diseases but for bellyache, toothache, and almost every human ill. The London market went wild for sassafras; in the first decade of the next century, at least two voyages, Gosnold's and Pring's, were made to New England in search of it.

Hariot made much of prospective copper mines and of the five thousand beautiful pearls that "one of our companie" obtained by barter with the savages. Intended as a gift to Queen Elizabeth, whose court costumes were heavily pearl-embroidered, these disappeared in a storm on the passage home. Imported dyestuffs like woad could easily be grown in Virginia, and the savages were already extracting dyes from sumach, pokeweed, and other native plants. Thus, Hariot anticipated the English government's subsidizing the growing of indigo in the Carolinas in the eighteenth century. Among native foodstuffs, Hariot lists maize, the kidney bean, pumpkin and squash, saltbush, and sunflower, and he tells his readers how the Indians planted and cooked them. Nor does he neglect *uppówoc*, "the which Spaniardes generally

call Tobacco." It is a cure-all for "grosse humors" of the body, and
"of so precious estimation amongest" the natives "that they thinke their
gods are marvelously delighted therwith." And so were the English.
Since Hawkins's introduction of the weed in 1565, tobacco smoking
had become a well-established custom; Raleigh and Hariot (both heavy
smokers) now introduced the native Virginia clay pipe as a model for
English pipe-makers. "Drinking" (i.e., smoking) tobacco shortly became so popular with both sexes and all classes in England that an edict
had to be issued against smoking in church.

Hariot devotes several pages to the edible roots found in Virginia—
the groundnut, water-plantain, arrow-arum (which he wrongly identified with West Indian cassava), and wild onion. Of "fruites" he com-
mends the chestnut, black walnut, acorn, shagbark, persimmon, prickly-
pear, wild strawberry, and scuppernong, from which Virginia housewives used to make a palatable wine. There is still an immense scuppernong vine on Roanoke Island which White's colonists may have
planted.

Passing over Hariot's enumeration of "Beastes," "Foule," "Fishe,"
and building timber, all calculated to whet the appetites of prospective
settlers, we reach a chapter "Of the nature and manners of the people."
Their houses and villages are well described, as in White's paintings,
as well as their religion, polity, arts, and crafts; but their fighting pro-
pensities are glossed over with the remark that English discipline and
firearms are more than a match for them. "They shewe excellencie of
wit," he remarks, and are even intrigued by the Englishmen's instruments, including a "perspective glasse," which I take to be a primitive
sort of telescope. But he distorts the facts about Indian relations with
the colonists. He tells about Wingina joining the Englishmen's prayers
and psalm-singing, and asking them to pray for him when he fell sick
and when a drought threatened the corn crop; but he does not tell
about Wingina's turning against them, or his death. He will only admit
that "some of our companie towardes the ende of the yeare, shewed
themselves too fierce, in slaying some of the people" for trivial reasons.
Hariot does add an important fact which neither Lane nor White
mentioned, that in every native village visited by them, "the people began to die very fast" after their departure. This indicates that some
Englishman carried the germs of measles or smallpox, both of which
were fatal to the natives.

Hariot closed with the correct prediction that the English may "looke for . . . more and greater plentie" in upland Virginia, just as the Spaniards found the West Indies a mere gateway to native empires and mainland wealth. As for the "holsomness" of the climate, he recorded that, after the first three weeks, "We lived onely by drinking water and by the victuall of the countrey." Yet only four men out of the 108 died, and three of them were "feeble, weak and sickly persons before ever they came thither." He added an important item not found elsewhere, that Sir Walter had promised 500 acres of land to each planter. Nothing is said as to how the natives' consent would be gained.

While Hariot's book went through the press, Richard Hakluyt dickered with Theodor de Bry to get out multi-lingual editions of it, illustrated by his engravings of John White's drawings and maps. These began to appear in 1589 and continued for several years. Thus, England now had a more detailed and, on the whole, more truthful account of the climate, natives, and products of North America than did any other nation, even Spain, at that time. These gave a firm basis for the expectations on which the great Virginia Company of 1606 were founded.

But—could John White's colony at Roanoke Island survive?

Relief Expeditions of 1588–1590

Fifteen eighty-eight was Spanish Armada year. England needed every ship, sailor, and fighting man to defeat an invasion which would have turned her over to Spain and the Inquisition. Never, save perhaps in 1940–41, has the "happy isle" been in such jeopardy; it was no time to divert men and ships to a tiny colony overseas. The City of Raleigh had fighting men and should be able to take care of itself. Nevertheless, after White and Hariot had acquainted Raleigh with the situation at Roanoke, Sir Walter loaded a pinnace with emergency supplies and prepared to follow up with a fleet of seven or eight ships commanded by Sir Richard Grenville. All were ready before the end of March 1588, when the Privy Council ordered Grenville to "forbeare," and hold his ships in readiness to augment the royal navy. Raleigh then obtained permission to send the 30-tun bark *Brave*, Captain Arthur Facy, and the twenty-five-tun pinnace *Roe*, with John White and some fifteen civilians, to reinforce Roanoke. They left Bideford on 22

Queen Elizabeth. The "Armada Portrait," painted in 1588. The Queen's hand, it will be observed, covers most of North America. From the Woburn Abbey Collection, by kind permission of His Grace, the Duke of Bedford. Courtesy National Portrait Gallery, London.

April. But Facy, more interested in prize-taking than in relieving fellow countrymen, met his match in two "men of Warre" of La Rochelle, of sixty and one hundred tuns' burthen. In the unequal combat Facy and John White, wounded, had to surrender *Brave*. The Frenchmen —with whose country England was supposed to be at peace—looted her of supplies, munitions, and everything not nailed down, and released her in a crippled condition, forcing the bark to return home. *Roe* followed suit, and that was the end of this attempt to relieve Roanoke.

Raleigh and White now augmented the Company of the City of Raleigh by taking in new associates such as William Sanderson and

Thomas Smythe, father of the future treasurer of Virginia; but nothing got off the ground in 1588, or next year either. Nobody has been able to explain why nothing was done in 1589. A second Spanish Armada was anticipated, to be sure, but England sent expeditions to the West Indies, Brazil, and the Far East that year. Raleigh surely could have sent at least a pinnace to Virginia, had he not been so deeply concerned with other matters.

He had not lost interest in his colony. John White persuaded him to organize a big relief expedition headed by Captain John Watts, a notorious privateer commander. White, anticipating another voyage in which Roanoke would be forgotten, persuaded Sanderson to impose a bond of £5000 on Watts to sail straight to Virginia. Watts, furious over this restriction, put ashore before starting, most of the stores and all the colonists destined for Roanoke. But John White stayed with him, and this 1590 relief expedition sailed from Plymouth 20 March. It was organized as follows:

CAPTAIN JOHN WATTS, GENERAL

Ship HOPEWELL (also called HARRY & JOHN) 140–160 tuns; Abraham Cocke, captain; Robert Hutton, master; 16–24 guns and 40–84 men, according to different accounts.

Ship LITTLE JOHN, 100–120 tuns; Christopher Newport, captain; Michael Geare, master; 19 guns, "up to 100" men.

Pinnace JOHN EVANGELIST; William Lane, captain.

The second echelon, which departed later, and caught up at Cape Tiburón, Haiti:

Bark MOONLIGHT (also called MARY TERLAYNE), 80 tuns, 7 guns, 40 men; Edward Spicer, captain; John Bedford, master. The property of William Sanderson.

Pinnace CONCLUDE, 20–30 tuns; Joseph Harris, captain; Hugh Hardridge, master. Owned by Thomas Middleton of London, merchant.

John White's narrative of the 1590 voyage, which Hakluyt printed ten years later, indicates that it was even wilder than Grenville's of 1585, if relief of Roanoke were the object. On 1 April, *Little John* and the pinnace anchored in the roadstead of Santa Cruz de Tenerife. From a London ship which, in defiance of the war, was loading sugar, they purchased two shallops to replace their own, lost through being towed

John White's Map of Virginia, 1585–87, from the "Chesepiuc" (Chesapeake) to Cape Lookout. The big English ships are outside the Banks, pinnaces and canoes inside. The original is in the John White manuscripts, British Museum. Courtesy British Museum.

in rough water. Somewhere in Canary Island waters, *Little John* took as prize a Spanish "double flyboat"—whatever that may be—and sent her home under a prize crew. On 9 April both *Johns* and *Hopewell* took departure from the Grand Canary and crossed to Dominica in twenty-one days—Columbus's record, never broken for a century.

Detail of John White's map of Virginia, from Roanoke Island and Port Ferdinando (whose name, significantly, he ignores) to Cape Lookout. The arms are those of Sir Walter Raleigh. The lowest ship must be meant for the *Tiger*. Fay Foto, from the John White book.

At Dominica, unaccountably, they managed some friendly trading with the Caribs. They then sailed along the chain of the Leeward Islands, threaded the Sir Francis Drake Passage in the Virgins, coasted the north side of Puerto Rico (causing warning signal fires to be lighted), and landed "on the Northwest end" to water "in a good river called Yaguana." This was the aguada, or watering place, on the Bahía de Aguadilla, which ships had been using for a century. After taking a ten-tun *fragata* of not much value, the *Hopewell* people on 13 May landed on Mona, the island visited by John Rut in 1527. There they burned ten or twelve houses, captured a pinnace, and "chased the Spaniards over all the land; but they hid them in caves, hollow rockes and bushes, so that we could not find them." Unreasonable Spaniards!

Next call was at Saona off southeastern Hispaniola. There they hung about for several days hoping to sight ships, but none came their way. *Little John* and the captured *fragata* were left in those waters to watch for Spanish ships aiming at the Mona Passage, while the "admirall" and the *Evangelist* prowled around Cape Tiburón (now Cape Dame Marie), eastern entrance to the Windward Passage. Watts knew very well the standard course followed by the Spanish *flotas* or treasure fleets. The one from Santo Domingo sailed through Mona Passage, but the richer ones from the Spanish Main, Panama, and Vera Cruz rounded San Antonio, the western cape of Cuba, replenished at Havana, and caught the Gulf Stream in the Florida Channel.

On 2 July, when Captain Spicer and the second echelon (*Moonlight* and *Conclude*) caught up with Watts off Cape Tiburón, a *flota* of fourteen sail was sighted. The Englishmen thought they were really in the money, but the Spaniards scattered down-wind to seek security in Jamaica. Watts pursued, and next morning caught up with a big ship, *Buen Jesus* by name, and took her. He manned her with a prize crew from his own fleet, and she proved to be a valuable capture. Another prize, the sixty-tun *Trinidad* taken by *John Evangelist*, disappointed the English because a nasty Frenchman "had taken and spoiled her before we came." But the French had not taken everything, so Watts put a prize crew on board and she joined the others.

Off Cape San Antonio, another disappointment. The English sighted the principal treasure *flota* of twenty-two sail in a flat calm, and could not catch them. Here, says White, "We were much pestered with the Spaniards we had taken," for they must have had at least a hundred prisoners on board, and so set them ashore at a Cuban harbor of their own choice.

After a fruitless patrol between Havana and the Matanzas, the fleet entered the Straits of Florida. White took note of the Gulf Stream and its inshore counter-currents. August opened with "very fowle weather" —rain, thunderstorms, waterspouts—and on the 3rd they stood in toward shore and made the Carolina Banks at one of the islands south of Cape Lookout. Weather continuing "so exceeding foule," they sought sea room and did not again sight land until 9 August, when they anchored in eleven fathom at latitude 35°30′ N (so White reckoned), right off the northeast end of the island of Croatoan. Here they "caught great store of fish" and took on fresh water. Watts prudently sounded the nearest inlet from a boat and decided not to press through. Instead, he proceeded northward; on the 15th *Hopewell* and *Moonlight*—all other vessels having been detached to take prizes home or look for more off the Azores—anchored about three-quarters of a mile off Port Ferdinando, in five fathom. Smoke seen rising from (as they supposed) Roanoke Island inside, gave them good hope that the colonists were alive and flourishing.

False hope, alas. Next morning, 16 August 1590, two boats were hoisted out. With Captain Cocke of *Hopewell* and Captain Spicer of *Moonlight* in charge, and Governor White on board one boat, they rowed through the inlet. Smoke from Hatarask Island distracted them, and the business of investigating it—and finding no explanation—consumed that day. On 17 August they tried again. A northeast wind blowing in against an ebb tide was raising breakers on the inlet bar. Captain Cocke got his boat through safely, but Captain Spicer's capsized and he and six rowers were drowned.

After the boat had been righted and bailed out, they resumed this discouraging journey and soon found more to depress them. The most poignant episode in our northern voyages, since Gilbert's death, is simply described by Governor White. Arriving at the north end of Roanoke Island after dark, in the light of a forest fire, "We let fall our Grapnel neere the shore, & sounded with a trumpet a Call, & afterwardes many familiar English tunes of Songs, and called to them friendly; but we had no answere."

No living soul was there to answer.

Next morning at daybreak the men landed and walked to the place where John White had left his colony three years earlier. Fresh foot-prints in the sand indicated that natives had been there recently. On the brow of a forested sand dune they found carved on a tree C R O in "faire Romane letters." Inland they came across ruins of the fort and the houses, overgrown with grass, weeds, and pumpkin vines; and on a post by the entrance CROATOAN was carved "in fayre Capitall letters." They found cannonballs and iron bars and, by the shore, dis-interred five chests "carefully hidden of the Planters," but since "digged up again and broken." Three of these chests were White's, and he had the mortification to find his books torn from their covers, the framed maps and pictures with which he intended to adorn the governor's mansion "rotten and spoyled with rayne," and the suit of armor which he had brought to wear on ceremonial occasions, "almost eaten through with rust."

White had expected his 1587 colony to move from Roanoke Island, and on leaving himself, enjoined them to leave a carved message as to their destination, with a Maltese cross in case they did so "in distresse." But there was no such sign here, and both "Croatoan" and the un-finished "Cro" suggested that the planters had removed to the island of that name, where the chief werowance was friendly Manteo. White figured that his people had gone there voluntarily, and that Wingina's former subjects had then "spoyled" the chests and carried off every-thing they wanted.

Returning to the ships in the outer roadstead, White and the other captain agreed to sail south to Croatoan Island to investigate. But an-other storm was making up, the sheet anchor cable parted when *Hope-well* was weighing, a third anchor "came so fast home" that the "admirall" would have dragged ashore had she not drifted into a deep hole, and the men made sail promptly so she could claw off. Having but one cable and anchor left, and victuals and fresh water at a low ebb, Watts decided to let Croatoan go and drive south for a jolly prize-taking winter in the Caribbean, promising White to return in the spring and search for the lost colony. But the wind blew so strong from the west and northwest that *Hopewell* shaped her course for the Azores and *Moonlight* sailed directly to England.

On 17 September *Hopewell*, with John White on board, sighted Corvo and Flores, and anchored in Flores roadstead where five English warships and Watts's prize *Buen Jesus* already were.

After sailing with this war fleet for a couple of weeks, *Hopewell* took off for England on 27 September, and on 24 October "came in safetie, God be thanked, to an anker at Plymmouth." *Conclude* and prize *Buen Jesus* were already in London River; *Moonlight* and all other ships of Watts's fleet reached home safely. The prizes fetched several thousand pounds, but no word had been gathered of the Virginia colony except the mute evidence of ruined Roanoke.

White and Ferdinando have been blamed for locating the second colony at Roanoke, instead of taking it to Chesapeake Bay as Raleigh had planned. But there is slight possibility that it would have done any better on the Chesapeake, after communications with England had been cut. Local Indians had rubbed out the Jesuit mission in 1571, and Powhatan, the "Emperor" of these parts, would certainly have exterminated any colony planted in his dominions. The major blame should be charged to Captain Watts for fooling around the West Indies so long that he reached Roanoke in the hurricane season and dared not tarry to search for the colonists.

The Lost Colony

The planters may, of course, have already been slaughtered; but the lack of a cross on the tree where "Croatoan" was carved suggests that they departed in peace. Nobody to this day knows where they went, or what became of them.

The most likely solution is that, finding existence too dangerous or difficult on Roanoke Island, they removed to Croatoan near Cape Hatteras, where the natives were friendly. They probably found slim pickings there on the Outer Banks, and around 1650 the Croatoan tribe migrated, finally settling in the present Robeson County in the interior of North Carolina. There they were known successively as the Hatteras or Lumbee tribe, but were officially named Croatoan in the last century. These Indians have a strong tradition that the Roanoke colonists amalgamated with them; and the existence of blue-eyed and fair-haired types among them, as well as the incorporation of Elizabethan English words in their language and their using surnames from John White's lost colonists, bears this out.

Englishmen of the Jamestown Colony of 1607 were naturally curious about the fate of their predecessors. Captain John Smith in his *Generall*

History of Virginia (1624) and William Strachey in his *Historie of Travell into Virginia Britania* (1612) tell stories that they picked up. One was that four Englishmen, two boys and one maid "who escaped the slaughter at Roanoak," reached the upper Chowan River, where an Indian chief named Eyanoco took them in and employed them to beat copper; but nobody was able to find these people or get word of them. It was also rumored that the Roanoke planters joined a different tribe, which lived near Chesapeake Bay; that Powhatan made war on these people around 1588–89 and killed every one, including the English. Two men were sent from Jamestown to seek survivors in 1608–9; they brought back from Roanoke Island crosses and letters of English origin given them by Indians there, but no certain information.

Many other solutions have been offered, but all are fantastic.

Thus, the sixteenth century closed, without England or France having established a colony in North America. When the seventeenth century dawned on New Year's Day 1601, not one European was living in North America, unless some of the Roanoke planters were still alive or a few French fishermen had elected to spend the winter on the St. Lawrence. What a contrast to the wonders that the Spanish had accomplished in the West Indies, Mexico, Peru, and New Granada! So, were all the efforts by both nations, which we have described, futile? By no means. They were the necessary preliminaries to the seating of permanent colonies: Canada by Champlain at Quebec in 1608, Jamestown by the Virginia Company of London in 1607, New England by the Pilgrim Fathers in 1620. These succeeded where earlier attempts had failed, because (1) all except Plymouth had ample backing from home; (2) all kept communications open with France or England, and (3) all found native products to send home for sale—peltry from Quebec and Plymouth, tobacco from Virginia. The main lesson, which might have been learned from the Norse colonists in Greenland, is that no New World colony could survive without trade and communications. And, as Captain John Smith remarked, no colony could live on "privy men's purses," by private support alone. Raleigh is estimated to have spent at least £40,000 on Roanoke; but the Jamestown Virginia colony cost at least tenfold, contributed through long sustained national efforts. Even so, Jamestown might have succumbed but for tobacco.

Moreover, the literary and artistic products of Raleigh's experiment:

Thomas Hariot's *Briefe and True Report*, John White's paintings, and De Bry's engravings of them, provided a corpus of information upon which seventeenth-century Virginia's success was based.

In closing let us not forget the gallant ships and the brave mariners who lost their lives pursuing these voyages for a century after Cabot, or men like Raleigh who financed them: Cabot himself and both Corte Reals lost with all hands no one knows where; Gilbert, lost with all hands off the Azores; Frobisher, mortally wounded in the war with Spain; John Davis, slain by Japanese pirates; Verrazzano, killed and eaten by cannibals; Raleigh, basely executed by James I as part of his cringing policy toward Spain.

These men, and the thousands of mariners whose remains lie under the seamless shroud of the sea, deserve to be perpetually remembered as precursors of two great empires in North America.

Bibliography and Notes

SOURCES AND DETAILS

The sources for the voyages covered by this chapter are identical with those mentioned in the Notes to Chapter XIX, especially Quinn's *Roanoke Voyages*, and *The American Drawings of John White*.

The organization of the Spanish treasure *flotas* is well described in Clarence H. Haring, *Trade and Navigation Between Spain and the Indies* (1918), chap. ix.

Apropos Wingina's joining the colonists' psalm singing, North American Indians everywhere were intrigued by Englishmen's singing of psalms. Dr. J. Franklin Jameson humorously pointed out that Indians of California, greeting the first Europeans after Drake with "*Ngna, Ngna, Ngna*," proved that Drake's sailors sang psalms through their noses, as the Puritans alone were supposed to do!

Charles Manning and Merrill Moore, "Sassafras and Syphilis," *New England Quarterly*, IX (1936), 473–75.

The Virginia Armorial. The blazons are in Raleigh's Patent, Quinn (ed.), *Roanoke Voyages*, II,508–11. From them our arms have been executed by "1776 House," Boston.

THE JESUIT MISSION ON CHESAPEAKE BAY

The best account is in John Gilmary Shea, *The Catholic Church in Colonial Days*, I (1886), 147. It was organized by Menéndez de Avilés in the hope of converting the Indians living around Chesapeake Bay, and holding that region for Spain as a northern St. Augustine. The party of eight Jesuits, led

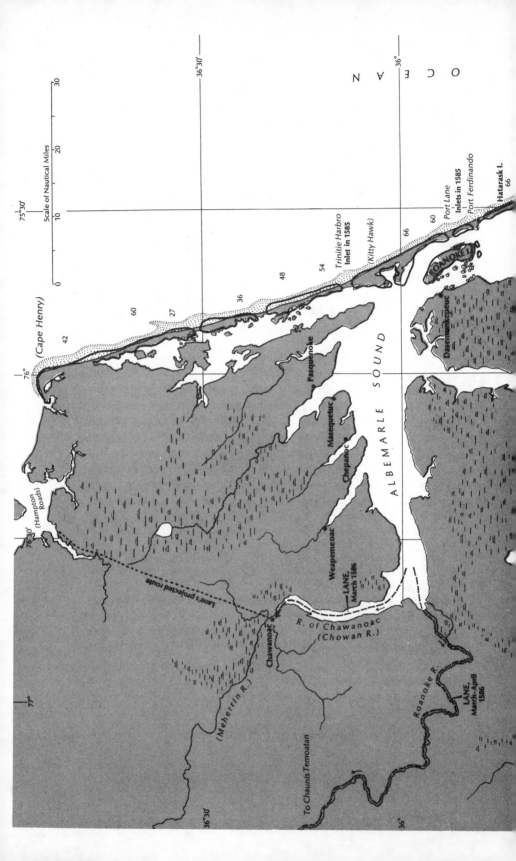

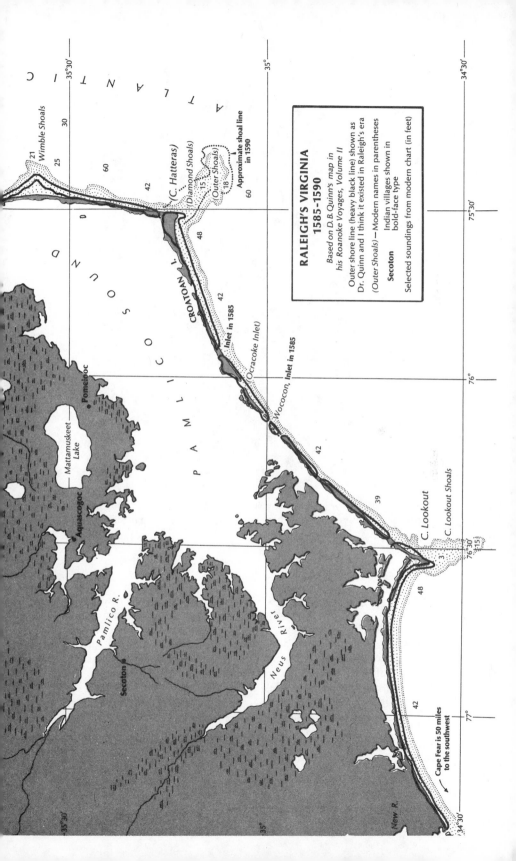

RALEIGH'S VIRGINIA
1585-1590

*Based on D.B. Quinn's map in
his Roanoke Voyages, Volume II*

Outer shore line (heavy black line) shown as
Dr. Quinn and I think it existed in Raleigh's era

(Outer Shoal(s)) — Modern names in parentheses

Secoton — Indian villages shown in
bold-face type

Selected soundings from modern chart (in feet)

Wimble Shoals

A T L A N T I C

21
30
25
60
42

(C. Hatteras)
(Diamond Shoals)
15
(Outer Shoals)
18
Approximate shoal line
in 1590
60

48

CROATAN I.

S O U N D

42

Inlet in 1585

(Ocracoke Inlet)

Wococon, Inlet in 1585

Pomeiooc

P A M L I C O

Mattamuskeet
Lake

Aquascogoc

42

39

C. Lookout

C. Lookout Shoals

3

115

48

Pamlico R.

Secoton

Neus River

42

Cape Fear is 50 miles
to the southwest

New R.

"Miss America" of 1587. Marc Gheeraerts's apotheosis of America. Note Frobisher's Eskimos among her supporters. But why the billy-goat and the wolf? From an engraving in the Rijksmuseum, Amsterdam, with their kind permission.

by their vice-provincial Father Juan Bautista Segura, sailed from Santa Elena, the Spanish post north of St. Augustine, on 5 August 1570 and arrived at their chosen destination, which the Indians called *Axacan*, 10 September. One of this party, a converted Indian renamed Luís Velasco, came from there, and invited them to the spot, the location of which is conjectural; Shea thought it was somewhere on the Rappahannock. The vessel that took them there sailed back to St. Elena on 12 September, carrying the usual urgent requests for more supplies—the ship had left the fathers with only two barrels of hardtack to get them through the winter, and the local Indians were almost starving, owing to a series of droughts. Luís defected, and on 14 February 1571, with a band of fellow Indians, attacked the mission and slaughtered every member except a converted Indian boy, Alonso.

A year or two later, Menéndez headed a punitive expedition to the site of the mission and hanged eight of the murderers at the yardarm of his ship. Shea refers to A. G. Barcia, *Ensayo Cronológico*, pp. 142–46; there is a 1951 translation by Anthony Kerrigan. Shea has an article "The Log Chapel on the Rappahannock" in *Catholic World*, March 1875. Other references are in Justin Winsor, *Narrative and Critical History*, II, 282–83.

ROANOKE ISLAND AND THE LOST COLONY

Parts of the northwestern end of Roanoke Island have eroded, submerging a lot of evidence, but the outlines of Lane's fort have been traced. In 1653 Francis Yeardley of Virginia was shown "the ruins of Sir Walter's fort" by local Indians (A. S. Salley, *Narratives of Early Carolina*, p. 26), and John Lawson (*A New Voyage to Carolina* (1709) found old coins and guns there. This part of North Carolina was settled by poor and ignorant people, including a New England Adams owner of Roanoke Island, and took slight interest in its history. After the publication of Alexander Brown's *Genesis of the United States* in 1891, interest became general. In 1926 a pageant of White's colony was given on the island. Eleven years later there was built for it a round-log structure, fearful and wonderful to behold, complete with log cabins and a log chapel. The publication of Harold R. Shurtleff, *The Log Cabin Myth* (1939), proved how wrong this was, but it took demolition by a hurricane in 1960 to have it replaced by the Waterside Theater, in 1962. There Paul Green's music drama *The Lost Colony*, first presented in 1937, is performed annually from about 20 June to the end of August.

After intermittent digging by amateur archaeologists, serious excavation of the island began in 1938 under direction of Mr. J. C. Harrington, who has described the results in *North Carolina Historical Review*, XXVI (1949), and in Quinn (ed.), *Roanoke Voyages*, II, 901–10. The fort, which has been restored, is almost an exact replica of the one that Ralph Lane built for his salt-taking operations in Puerto Rico in 1585. Inside it, traces of a two-story building about 10 by 35 feet, a well, and a powder magazine were found, together with an iron sickle, fragments of glazed earthenware, a red-clay native tobacco pipe, jettons, and other objects. These are now shown in the tourist center on Roanoke Island. Since 1941, Roanoke Island has been the Fort Raleigh National Historic Site, administered by the National Park Service of the Department of the Interior. They have issued in their Handbook Series an excellent illustrated booklet *Fort Raleigh*, by Charles W. Porter III.

The Introduction to *The American Drawings of John White* (1964), I, 59–60, has a discussion of the Lost Colony. Frederick W. Hodge, *Handbook of American Indians*, I (1907), 365, regards the theory of the Croatoan or Lumbee tribe having incorporated Raleigh's colonists, as "baseless," but admits that they show a mixture of blood; and most North Carolina historians (especially Francis L. Hawks) believe that this is the answer. So does the exhaustive study by Stephen B. Weeks, "The Lost Colony . . .

Its Fall and Survival" in American Historical Association *Papers*, V (1891), 441–80. Even the family names of forty-one Roanoke planters survive among them.

In 1937, some California tourists "discovered" near the Chowan River a hard stone on which had been crudely pecked out with a sharp instrument, a message from Eleanor Dare to her father John White, telling where to find her. This was sold to the professor of a small Southern college, who made the mistake of broadcasting a reward of $250 each for more stone-carved letters. As a result he acquired about a dozen, supposed to have been found along the Indian trail from Edenton, North Carolina, to Atlanta, Georgia. Your writer served on a committee invited to examine and authenticate them. At first glance the stone-carved letters, reputedly from Eleanor to her "dear papa", were impressive. The incised letters had the same patina as the rest of the stone; lichen had apparently grown into the letters. They tell a pathetic story of a long trek; Ananias Dare died, and Eleanor had to marry an Indian. The committee, as politely as possible, declared the stones to be fake, largely on the use of two words, "trail" and "reconnoitre" which were not in the English language for a century or more after 1590. Subsequently the *Saturday Evening Post* sent a member of its staff, Boyden Sparkes, to examine the stones, and by good detective work he found the man who faked them. His article is in the *Post* of 26 April 1941.

SHIP DESIGN AROUND 1600

Raleigh's Virginia suggested, and the 1607 colony furthered, an important development in English ship design. When ships had to carry a hundred or more passengers each, and "first class" crowded the superstructure, they became top-heavy, and their "tumbling and rowling" became almost unbearable. Sir Walter himself, about 1606, wrote "Observations and Notes, Concerning the Royal Navy and Sea-Service," which was published in his *Judicious and Select Essays* (London, 1650). He observes (p. 13) that "the high charging of ships . . . makes them labour and makes them overset." He wants "more steadinesse and less tottering Cadge worke"—"cage work" was the usual word for the lightly constructed stern and forecastles. Add one deck to the hull, he advises, making two and one-half decks in all, "sufficient to yield shelter and lodging for men and Marriners," with "only one low Cabbin for the Master" in the sterncastle. Sir Walter warns against building "cabbins" below decks, as "they are but sluttish Dens that breed sicknesse in peace, . . . and in Fight are dangerous to teare men with their splinters." Grenville's flagship *Tiger* and other vessels depicted by John White, are of the old style, with plenty of "cage work," but the modern replicas of the Virginia fleet of 1607, and of *Mayflower*, indicate that both castles had already been radically reduced. By the following century, ships in transatlantic trade were practically flush-decked.

List of Illustrations

Maps redrawn for this volume by Vaughn Gray are indicated by an asterisk (*). Photos not otherwise ascribed are by the author and his shipmates.

St. Brendan's Bay, County Kerry.	14
The Skelligs, from Skellig Michael.	15
Drying nets and carrying a curragh at Brandon Harbour, County Kerry.	17
The medieval conception of St. Brendan's Isles. Bartolomeo Pareto's Map of 1455.	21
The "Sacrificial Stone" at Mystery Village, Salem, New Hampshire.	31
Restored section of the wrecked *knarr* recovered at Roskilde Fjord, 1968.	33
Bow and triangular forward bulkhead of the smaller cargo ship excavated at Roskilde.	33
The Norsemen's "Wonder Strands" and Cape Porcupine, Labrador.	42
The Wonder Strands.	43
Iceberg stranded in cove of southern Labrador. Belle Isle in distance.	43
* Map: The Northern Tip of Newfoundland.	44–45
L'Anse aux Meadows: Air view of Epaves Bay.	46
L'Anse aux Meadows: Excavation of the Great House.	47
L'Anse aux Meadows: Salmon stream and meadow.	48
L'Anse aux Meadows: Hearth and ember box in the Great House.	48
Early Norse ironworks. Wood carving of c. A.D. 1100 in Hylestad, Norway.	50
Page from Flatey Book illustrating birth of King Olaf Trygvasson.	65
Part of page from Flatey Book with reference to "Výnlãd," Vinland.	66
* Yale's "Vinland Map" and modern map compared.	70
The Skólholt Map of c. 1600.	73
A Uniped and another monster.	79
The original Zeno Brothers' Map.	88

Earl Sinclair—"Zichmni" in Massachusetts. The "Indian Rock" at
Westford. 90
Head of chapter in Olaus Magnus. *De Gentibus Septentrionalibus* (1555),
"Concerning the Pygmies of Greenland and the Rock Hvitsark." 91
* Gago Coutinho's Map of the Azores. 98
* Sketch of Atlantic Islands based on Nautical Chart of 1424. 100
Contemporary model of a carvel-built cog, the Spaans Karveel. 113
Edward Fiennes, Earl of Lincoln, Lord High Admiral, 1550–54 and
1558–85, holding a dry-card mariner's compass. 115
Long-course Portuguese ships from the Miller I Atlas of *c.* 1525. 117
Late fifteenth-century ship heaving the lead when entering the English
Channel. 120
English shipping in the late fifteenth century. 121
Long-course Portuguese ships of *c.* 1529 from the Ribero World Map of
that date. 123
Shipping in London above the Bridge, 1600. 127
Shipboard punishments for mutiny. 133
The mariner's astrolabe, or ring. 137
Compass card with both points and degrees. 138
H.M.S. *Tegar.* 144
H.M.S. *Lyon.* 144
Ship in Dover Harbor, *c.* 1530–37. 145
Ship on the Thames below London Bridge, 1600. 146
Frontispiece of Nordenskiold's *Periplus.* 152
Taking a meridional altitude of the sun with the mariner's astrolabe. 153
* Diagram for obtaining latitude from an observed altitude for the North
Star. 154
Diagram for obtaining latitude from noon observation of the sun. 154
Nineteenth-century traverse board. 155
King Henry VII. 160
* Map: The River Avon from the Severn to the City of Bristol. 162–63
The central part of Bristol in 1673. 164
Conjectural model of Cabot's navicula *Mathew.* 168
Dursey Head and Bull Rock, Ireland. 169
Icebergs and field ice off Newfoundland, July 1885. 171
Cape Dégrat from the south. Belle Isle in the distance. 173
Capes Bauld and Dégrat from the north. 173
Quirpon Passage and Harbor (top) and Griquet Harbor (middle), where
Cabot probably first landed. 175
Cape Bonavista, Newfoundland. 176
* Map: Cabot's First Voyage, 1497. 178–79
What Cabot saw: Baccalieu Island and Grates Point; Cape St. Francis;
Cape Broyle. 182
What Cabot saw: Cape Race; Cape Pine; Cape St. Mary's. 183
* Northeast portion of the Contarini-Roselli engraved mappemonde of
1506. 188
Outline of a portion of the Ruysch Map of 1508. 189
* Map: Cabot's Idea of His First Voyage. 190
A section of Sebastian Cabot's 1544 Map compared with similar region
on Nicolas Desliens's World Map of 1541 reversed. 196

The "Cabot Rock" at Grates Cove. 204
A section of the "Munich-Portuguese" Map. 214
Sebastian Cabot in his old age. 223
* Three early maps of Newfoundland's east coast compared with modern
  map. 224
Part of "Miller I" Atlas world map. 230
The two harbors at Ingonish. 232
West coast of St. Paul Island. 232
San Germán Bay, Puerto Rico. 236
The Juan de La Cosa Mappemonde. The American part. 240
The "English coast" on the Juan de La Cosa Mappemonde. 241
New World half of the Oliveriana Map, Pésaro. 243
Three photos of Dighton Rock. 246
Jean Jolivet's two Norman ships and a galley from his map of Normandy,
  1525. 253
A 1970 view of Fécamp harbor. 256
A plan of Dieppe in 1853. 257
Dieppe and environs, 1970: Harbor and quai Henri IV. 258
Rouen in 1526. 259
* Map: Western France and the English Channel in the Sixteenth Century. 262
A view of La Rochelle. 266
The Cordouan lighthouse. 269
French nefs of 1555. 271
Posthumous portrait bust of Verrazzano. 278
Francois Ier, roi de France. 280
Giovanni da Verrazzano. Late sixteenth-century copy of an earlier
  Florentine portrait. 281
"De Guadagnis, Citizen of Florence," brother or father of Verrazzano's
  wife. 282
The Castello Verrazzano, Greve in Chianti. 283
North American part of the Girolamo da Verrazzano World Map
  of 1529. 284
A ship, probably La Dauphine. 286
The Bailly Globe, 1530, with "Sea of Verrazzano" showing the Verrazzano
  concept of North America. 291
* Map: Coast and Sounds of the Future North Carolina. 293
Verrazzano's "Pacific Ocean." The "Sea of Verrazzano" seen over the
  Carolina Outer Banks, each side of Cape Hatteras. 294
Arcadian landscape on Miller I Atlas. 296
Site of Verrazzano's Arcadia. Kill Devil Hill, Kitty Hawk. 297
Four personages of the French court, for whom Verrazzano named places
  on the American coast: François le Dauphin; Louise de Savoie,
  duchesse d'Angoulême and Queen Mother; la duchesse de Ven-
  dôme, née d'Alençon; le seigneur de Bonnivet, amiral de France. 300
* Map: New York Bay. 302
Verrazzano's Petra Viva. The Dumpling Rocks off Conanicut Island,
  Brenton Point in the background. 304
* Map: Verrazzano's point of contact with the Maine Indians. 305
* Map: Narragansett Bay. 306
* Map: Maine coast. 309

Isabeau d'Albret, vicomtesse de Rohan.   310
Monhegan Island.   311
Mount Desert Island, from Mount Desert Rock.   312
* Map: Tracings of Verrazzano's course on the Maiollo (1527) and
    Girolamo da Verrazzano (1529) maps.   321
"The Land which the Pilot Estévan Gomez Discovered," New England
    from Cape Cod to Mount Desert Island.   330
Cape Fear and Frying Pan Shoals. Probable site of Ayllón's Colony on
    Cape Fear River.   333
"Lands of Estévan Gomez and of Ayllón." The coast of North America
    from the Gulf of St. Lawrence entrance to Florida.   335
Saint-Malo, from Saint-Servan by Louis Garneray, c. 1820.   340
Sketch by M. Dan Lailler, Conservateur du Musée de Saint-Malo, of an
    early portrait of Cartier.   342
Section of the Harleian-Desceliers-Dauphin Map of 1542, with alleged
    portrait of Cartier.   343
Château Island, Château Bay, Labrador.   349
Black Bay and Red Bay, Labrador. Cartier's *Port des Buttes* and *Port
    de la Baleine*.   350
Greenly Island off Blanc Sablon.   351
The beach that gave Blanc Sablon its name.   351
The natural rock road from Blanc Sablon village to the harbor.   351
Dog Island and Le Boulet, "round as an oven," where Cartier set up
    the Cross.   353
Lobster and Rocky Bays.   353
Sketch of the scenery from Ferolle Pt. to Point Rich (Cartier's *Cap
    Double*).   356
St. Paul's Inlet.   356
Bay of Islands (Cartier's *St. Julian*), from C. Gregory to Bear Head
    (*Cap Royal*).   357
Cape St. George (Cartier's *Cap de Latte*), Newfoundland.   358
Fort La Latte, Brittany, from Cap Fréhel.   358
Fort La Latte, close-up.   358
The Magdalen Islands.   360
Bird Island (Cartier's *Ile de Margaulx*).   360
Ile de Brion.   360
Beach connecting two parts of the Magdalen Islands.   360
Southern part of the Magdalen Islands in 1969.   362
Entry Island, Magdalen Group.   362
Allezay, The Deadman.   365
Cap des Sauvages, Cape North, P.E.I.   365
View on the north shore of Prince Edward Island.   366
John Rotz's "Boke of Idrographie," 1542, folios 23–24.   367
Mouth of Miramichi Bay.   372
Cap Percé and Bonaventure Island.   372
View in Gaspé Bay.   373
Cartier's *Cap St. Louis*, East Cape, Anticosti.   376
Cap Rabast, Anticosti.   376
Limoïlou.   379

September iceberg on Cartier's route. 383
Some of Cartier's *Toutes Iles.* 383
Philippe Chabot, sieur de Brion, amiral de France. 385
La Grande Hermine sailing past Saint-Malo. 390
Cormorant Rocks and Cape Whittle. 393
Mont-Saint-Pierre, Gaspé Peninsula, Notre Dame range in distance. 393
* Map: The Gulf of St. Lawrence and Terre-Neuve. 396–97
Entrance to Bay of Seven Islands. 398
The Moisie River. 398
The Bic Islands, Cartier's *Iles St. Jean.* 400
Old Bic Harbor. 400
Mouth of the Saguenay, Tadoussac, Red Island and reefs. 402
The Saguenay, a few miles above Tadoussac. 402
Hare Island, Cartier's *Ile aux Lièvres.* 404
Baie de Saint-Paul. 404
Cartier's anchorage off *Ile d'Orléans* or *de Bacchus.* 404
North America in the Desceliers Mappemonde of 1546. 408–409
Ramusio's plan of Hochelaga. 412
* Map: Cartier's "Chemin de Canada" 1535–1542. 416
Cross on Ile aux Coudres, looking toward the north shore of the river. 422
Tip end of Cape Breton Island; Cape North, Cartier's *Cap de Saint-Paul,*
   in background. 423
Title page of Cartier's *Brief recit,* 1545. 425
La Grande Hermine. Miniature model. 427
Marguerite, reine de Navarre. 431
Charles, duc d'Orléans. 440
West Canadian part of Desceliers Planisphere, 1550. 444
East Canadian part of Desceliers Planisphere. 445
The Harrington Islands. 447
Restored Port Royal *Habitation* of 1605. 449
North American section of Nicholas Vallard Map, 1547. 452–53
Title page of *L'Heptaméron,* 1560 edition. 459
Norumbega on the Mercator World Map of 1569. 466
The entrance to St. John's Harbor, Newfoundland. 472
"Making fish" at Petty Harbor, near St. John's. 474
Dr. John Dee. 475
Queen Elizabeth the First. 495
Martin Frobisher. 499
William Borough's Map. 503
* Map: Frobisher Bay and Entrance to Hudson Strait. 509
Shooting Polaris with cross-staff. 513
Title page of George Best's *True Discourse* (1578). 514
Little Hall's Island. 520
Jackman Sound, Frobisher Bay, and part of Grinnell Glacier. 521
Part of Hall's Island (now Loks Land). 522
John White's painting of the Eskimo mother and baby captured by
   Frobisher in 1577. 524
John White's painting of the Eskimo captured by Frobisher in 1577. 525
Countess of Warwick Sound. 527

George Best's narwhal.   529
Lucas de Heere's drawing of the Eskimo's demonstration at Bristol, with
a native background.   530
A fair June day in Frobisher Bay. From foot of Grinnell Glacier looking
toward Baffin Island.   534
High summer in Frobisher Bay, 1864. Meta Incognita and Grinnell Gla-
cier in background.   536
Frobisher Bay. Meta Incognita, from Frobisher Bay. Delano Bay, on
southwest shore. *Morrissey* at anchor among the islands.   538
Sir Martin Frobisher.   541
George Best's map of the world in his *True Discourse* (1578).   546
Charles Howard of Effingham, Lord High Admiral, 1585–1618.   548
John Seller's map of Buss, from his *English Pilot* (1673).   553
Buss anchored, in Elizabethan view of Great Yarmouth Harbor.   553
Sir Humfry Gilbert.   556
Christ Church, Oxford, in Hakluyt's day.   559
Minesweeper leaving Dartmouth Harbor.   562
The River Dart at Stoke Gabriel.   562
Compton Castle.   564
Captain Thomas Lee.   567
"Sir Humfray Gylbert knight his charte," by John Dee, 1583.   581
Sandridge Barton: The farm and a view of the Dart with the great elm.   585
George Clifford, Earl of Cumberland.   590
* Map: Cumberland Sound and Peninsula.   591
Sanderson's Hope, almost three centuries later.   602
* Map: The Arctic Voyages of John Davis 1585–1586–1587.   603
* Map: Hamilton Inlet, Labrador.   606
Northwest part of Molyneux Map of *c.* 1586–87.   609
Solar altitude by Davis's back staff.   610
Shooting the sun with the Peabody Museum's Davis quadrant.   611
* Map: The Canadian Arctic and the Northwest Passage.   614
Sir Walter Raleigh at the age of thirty-six.   618
Hatarask Island, scene of first landing, 1584.   622
Oregon Inlet.   622
"One of the wyves of Wyngyno" (Wingina). Painted by John White,
1585.   623
Sir Richard Grenville.   628
John White's painting of the fort at Guayanilla Bay, Puerto Rico.   634
Air view of Guayanilla Bay, January 1951, showing mouth of the river
and site of the fort.   635
Entrance to Beaufort and Morehead City, North Carolina.   639
An inlet, probably the one where *Tiger* struck.   639
The village of Secoton on the Pamlico River, 1585.   641
The village of Pomeiooc, near Lake Mattamuskeet, 1585.   642
Grenville's boat expedition. Probable site of Secoton.   643
Site of Pomeiooc—Lake Mattamuskeet in distance.   643
The heavily wooded Roanoke Island of 1970.   645
Currituck beach, 1970.   645
The Virginia armorial of 1587.   658

An Indian couple near Roanoke Island, dining. 662
Indian woman and child near Roanoke. 663
Queen Elizabeth. The "Armada Portrait," painted in 1588. 670
John White's Map of Virginia, 1585-87, from the "Chesepiuc"
(Chesapeake) to Cape Lookout. 672
Detail of John White's map of Virginia, from Roanoke Island and Port
Ferdinando to Cape Lookout. 673
* Map: Raleigh's Virginia 1585-1590. 680-81
"Miss America" of 1587. Marc Gheeraerts's apotheosis of America. 682

Index

A

Abnaki, 185, 308-9, 312, 329, 507
Achelacy, P.Q., 410, 440-41
Adam of Bremen, 51, 64
Admiral, defined, 473, 492-3
Adventurer, defined, 493
Afonso V, 92-7, 100
Africa, voyages to, 5, 12; trade, 482-5, 497, 500
Agostinho, Col. José, 109
Aid, 117*n*, 156, 649; Frobisher's ship, 531-5, 540, 543-5, 551; inventory, 147, 517-18
Albemarle Sound, 625
Alexander VI, 60, 341, 435
Alfonce, Jean, 267, 381, 439, 443, 447-8, 481; *Cosmographie*, 347, 384, 394, 426, 445; latitudes, 512; on Norumbega, 464, 490; up Saguenay River, 451; *Voyages avantureux*, 231, 249; bibli., 457
Algonkin Indians, 307, 429, 464, 620, 651; and Raleigh colonists, 621-49 *passim*, 668
Allen, Arthur S., 200
Allen, Thomas, 544
Almagià, Roberto, 198, 318

Altamorano, Hernando, 633, 637
Amadas, Philip, 619-21, 631-2, 640-42, 653-4
Amerike, Richard, 163
Amundsen, Roald, 497, 528, 613-15
Añasco Bay, P.R., 236, 636-7, 660
Anchors, 119, 146, 540
Angel Gabriel, 627
Anglo-Azorean syndicate voyages (1501-5), 192, 213, 218-20, 225, 233, 471; bibli., 248
Ango, Jean, 260-61, 270, 275, 281, 285-6
Angoulême (New York), 301-2, 323, 490
Anguille, Cape, 359
Anian, Strait, 497-8, 545, 613; bibli., 515
Ann, Cape, 331, 369
Anne Aucher, 568-9
Anne Frances, 531, 535-6, 539, 541-2
Anne Warwick I., *see* Kodlunarn
Annunziata, 292, 295-6, 319
Anthiaume, Abbé, 274-5, 489
Anticosti I., 376-7, 394-5, 421, 479, 566
Antilia, 87, 95-104, 166, 186-7, 208, 219; bibli., 110, 320; map, 99
Anunciada, 327, 333
Arcadia, 295-9, 558, 621; bibli., 322-3
Argo, 613
Armor, 320, 426, 486, 657, 676

Arques R., 255
Ashhurst, Thomas, 218
Astrolabe, 77, 94, 136, 151-3, 287, 479, 487, 502; Davis on, 587; Gunther on, 512
Atlas, 104
Aubert, Thomas, 270
Aucher, William, 571
Audubon, J. J., 354
Avalon Peninsula, 177, 184, 186, 227; on maps, 461
Avelinda, 201
Avon River, 161-7, 186, 205, 256, 260
Ayala, Pedro, 166, 191-2
Ayllón, L. V. de, voyage and colony, 235, 287, 332-4, 631; bibli., 332-4; on map, 331, 464
Azores, 25, 83, 211, 229, 242, 661; discovered, 94-7; English ships near, 549, 577, 646, 650, 665-6, 676; focal point for discovery, 213; bibli., 109-10

B

Babcock, W. H., 84, 101, 110
Baccalaos, origin of name, 203
Baccalieu I., 181, 187, 201, 203, 227, 573
Backstaff, 587, 595, 609-10
Baffin, William, 584, 612
Baffin Bay, 600-601, 605, 615-16
Baffin I., 40-41, 69; Davis at, 601-2; Frobisher at, 314, 506-8, 520; on maps, 545, 607-8
Baptista de Lima, Manuel, 109, 242, 251
Barcelos, Diogo and Manuel, voyage, 251
Barcelos, Pedro M. de, 211-12
Barlow, Roger, 110, 150
Barlowe, Arthur, 620; praises natives, 644; voyage of 1584, 619-21, 624-6, 631, 640, 648n, 653-4; of 1585, 632
Barnaby I., 401
Bartlett, Capt. Bob, 537
Bas, Cape de, 234-5
Basque fishermen, 203, 364, 479, 604
Battle Harbor, Lab., 200, 234
Bauld, Cape, Nfld., 46, 53, 56, 172, 187, 191, 198, 202, 217, 227-8, 234; Cartier at, 347-8
Bear Head, Nfld., 356-9
Beardmore relics, 77-8
Beare, 531
Beaupré, Vicomte de, 438-41
Beck, Cameron W., 652n
Beechey I., 613-15

Belle Isle, 41, 47, 54, 227, 347, 384, 461; Breton namesake, 443
Belle Isle, Strait of, 54-6, 174, 194, 200-201, 226-8, 237, 270, 335, 342, 348, 368, 392
Bellinger, Etienne, 468, 489
Beluga, 403, 418
Beothuk, 180, 185, 203, 215-19, 228, 231, 272, 347, 355, 477-9, 492
Bernard, Jacques, 9, 112, 149, 267, 275
Best, George, 502, 505; on Frobisher voyages, 516-19, 522, 528-9, 531-6, 539-42; *True Discourse*, 487-501, 511-12, 540, 544-6, 550; map, 546
Biarni Heriulfson, 40-41, 54, 59, 62, 69, 82
Bible, the, 142-3; Cartier reads, 414; Frobisher's, 502; D. Hernando's, 637; Hakluyt quotes, 557
Bic Is., P.Q., 401
Biggar, H. P., works on early Canada, and Cartier, 242-5, 248-50, 276n, 336-7, 381, 424, 455, 491
Birds, 172; mythical, 19-23, 30; in Nfld. and Canada, 219-20, 347-8, 350, 361, 367, 392, 476, 595
Bird Rocks, P.Q., 361, 364
Bjorn, 27
Black Bay, Lab., 348
Blanc Sablon, P.Q., 200, 348-9, 354, 369, 378-80, 392, 426; whaling, 478
Blegen, Theo. C., 76-7
Block I., 303, 319, 488
Boats, 122, 574; in Canada, 371, 406, 411, 451; flyboat, 126, 659, 665-6; gundalo, 126; shallop, 126-7, 422, 438, 473, 671; tilt-boat, 126-7, 492, 642, 644, 655; see also Pinnace
Bonaventure I., N.B., 371
Bonavista, Cape, 177, 181, 184-5, 194, 199-202, 227, 230, 346
Bonne Aventure, 315
Bonne Espérance, P.Q., 352, 355, 384
Bordeaux, shipping and wine, 237, 267-8; river of, see Gironde
Borough, Stephen, 484, 487; backs Frobisher, 501; on S. Cabot, 222, 248
Borough, William, 501; map of 1576, 503 (illus.), 512, 552
Bourne, Edward G., 9; works by, 193-4, 337
Bourne, William, 139-40, 150-51, 502, 607, 610
Bradford, William, on mosquitoes, 637, 667

Bradore Bay, P.Q., 200, 350, 384
Bramble, USCGC, 615
Braithwait, Richard, 132
Brave, 669-70
Brasil I., *see* Hy-Brasil
Brazil, discovered, 210, 274, 286; trade of Dieppe, 255, 273, 314-16
Bremen, aircraft, 350, 384
Breton, Cape and I., 122, 176-7, 195-9, 363, 421; Fagundes colony, 229-31, 248; Gomez at, 328
Bretona, 332
Bridenbaugh, Carl, 652n
Brion, Philippe de Chabot, sieur de, 261, 324, 361, 384, 388, 506
Brion I., 361-3, 368, 384, 421
Bristol, 336, 470, 571; chronicles, 166, 192-3; churches, 163-5; Fernandes in, 211-12, 218; plan (illus.), 164; search for NW Passage, 211, 218-20; tides and trade, 161-6, 203-4, 561; bibli., 204-5
Brittany, 140, 253, 263-4, 279, 315, 422; Cartier in, 339, 348
Brouage, 264, 481
Brown, Alexander, *Genesis of U.S.*, 653, 683
Browne, Capt. Maurice, 572-3, 575-6
Bruton, Capt. William, 588, 591, 601
Buen Jesus, 674-7
Burcot, "Dr.," 530, 544
Burin Peninsula, 184
Burleigh, Lord, *see* Cecil, William
Burrage, H. S., *Early . . . Voyages*, 653
Buss, 552
Buss "Island," 544, 552-4; *Buss of Bridgewater*, see *Emmanuell*
Button, Thomas, 612
Bylot, Robert, 612
Byrne, James M., 205

C

Cabot, Edmund, 201
Cabot, John, 7, 97, 105, 217, 239, 267, 270, 336, 421; chart of first voyage, 178-9; coastal voyage, 177-85, 200-203, 347; conception of voyage, 186-7; departure and crossing, 167-70; first voyage, 140-42, 161-2, 170-77, 193-5; homeward passage, 185-6; landfall, 170-77, 193-200, 212; latitude data, 202; London sojourn, 187-90; navigator, 136, 153, 170, 174; objective,

159; second voyage and death, 189-92; bibli., 192-3
Cabot, Lewis and Santius, 159, 202, 248
Cabot, Sebastian, 90, 159, 188, 218, 482-4; account of discovery, 195-7; alleged NW voyage, 220-21, 558; character and portrait, 157, 221-2; map, 171, 192, 195-8, 384, 454; illus., 196; quoted, 135, 142-3; regulations, 149; tall tales, 194, 203, 225, 347; visits Cartier, 445; voyage to River Plate, 221-2, 242; death, 223-5, 487; bibli., 193, 248
Cabot Strait, 237, 363; Cartier in, 421; on maps, 461
Cabral, Goncalo, 95
Cabral, Pedro A., 210, 274
Caicos I., 638, 661
Camden, William, 139, 545
Camden, Me., gold rush, 490; hills, 467-8
Canada, 340; "*bout de l'Asie*," 187; chemin de, 395-9; name, 395, 429, 460-62; trade, 267, 477; winter in, 416 (illus.), 417; *see also* Cartier
Canary Is., 5, 24, 83, 95, 101, 253, 290; English fleets in, 619, 633
Canoes, 298, 369-70, 375, 621
Cantino, Albert, 215-16, 245; map, 69, 102, 194, 212, 217-19, 226-7, 244; illus., 224
Canto, Ernesto do, 93
Canynges, William, 163, 204
Caraci, Giuseppe, 71, 243
Caravel, 215, 327-8
Carbonariis, G. A. de, 191
Card, Antha E., 108
Carew, Capt. Henry, 531
Carib Indians, 315, 325, 660, 674
Carleil, Christopher, 483
Carolina Banks, 292, 295, 640, 654, 661, 675-7; description, 620; wrecks on, 299, 480, 620; on maps, 337; illus., 293
Caroline, Fort, 470, 631
Carroll, Denis, 660
Carta do doacão, see Letters-patent
Carthage, 5, 11, 285, 288
Cartier, Jacques, 143, 187, 273, 276, 299, 328, 336, 340, 487, 605, 647; backers, 261, 340-41, 388-9; *Brief récit*, 391-2, 405-13, 418, 421, 424, 429; commission of 1540, 187, 433-5; costume, 413, 426; crews, 389-91; finances, 389, 432, 456; fleets, 389, 437, 456; home life, 432, 444-5; identification of places, 382-6;

Cartier, Jacques (*continued*)
  objectives, 345, 391; portraits, 341-3,
  386-7, 461; *Première relation*, 346,
  354, 363, 381-2, 386; voyages, first,
  199, 346-82, second, 388-429, 462,
  third, 430-33, 437-45; will and death,
  438, 445; bibli., 381-7, 424-9, 455-8;
  chart *chemin du Canada*, 416
Cartographers, 83-4, 88, 97, 111, 219,
  233, 239, 274, 287, 313-14, 386, 640;
  and Buss, 544; and Hy-Brasil, 104-5;
  and Newfoundland, 228; and ships,
  122; Cartier influences, 458-60; Dieppe, 261, 488; English, 487-8, 607
Cary, Sir George, 659
Casco Bay, Me., 308-9, 330, 337
Catalina Harbor, Nfld., 201, 346
Cathay Company, 501, 516-17, 530-31,
  546-7, 566; bibli., 551
Catherine (1532), 265
Catherine (1598), 480
Catlin, George, 106, 652
Cattle, 593; Canada, 390, 437, 439, 446,
  456; Norsemen's, 46-7; Sable I., 480,
  575; Virginia, 634, 637-8, 644, 648
Cavendish, Thomas, 608, 627, 632, 641
Cecil, Sir William (Lord Burleigh),
  501, 514, 565
Cellère Codex, 317
Chabot, Philippe de, *see* Brion
Chaleur Bay, 368-71, 385, 421
Champernowne, Katherine, 563
Champlain, Samuel de, 264, 331, 341,
  374*n*, 387, 406, 429, 477; and Norum-
  bega, 469, 490; *habitation*, 448, 456;
  quoted on good captain, and navi-
  gator, 343-4, 443, 457; works, 248,
  381
Chancellor, Richard, 484
Chanteys, 128-9, 140, 148
Chapman, George, on Brion, 506
Charles V, 233, 240, 279, 314; and
  Cartier, 276, 435-6, 482; and Gomez,
  326-8, 331, 334; and navigation, 487,
  560
Charles VIII, 260, 264
Charlesbourg-Royal, 429, 439-43, 448
Charlevoix, Pierre de, 105, 108
Chat, Cape, P.Q., 401
Château Bay, Lab., 348, 604
Chatterton, Thomas, 166
Chaucer Bank, 96
Chaunu, Pierre, 148, 274
Chauvin, Pierre, 481
Chefdhostel, Thomas, 480-81

Chesapeake Bay, 336-7, 647, 678; Jesuit
  mission, 631, 677-83; on maps, 334,
  631; site for colony, 656-7, 661, 677;
  Verrazzano misses, 299, 316, 323
Chicora, 332
Chidley, Cape, 195, 481, 504, 604
China (Cathay), search for strait to,
  210-12, 279, 484, 498, 616; Cabot,
  170, 186, 192-4, 199, 497; Cartier, 314-
  16, 345, 355, 363, 368, 380, 399, 432;
  Davis, 591, 595, 604; Frobisher, 314-
  16, 506-8, 517, 532, 536, 545; Gomez,
  326-31; Verrazzano, 282, 287-9, 293,
  299, 314; *see also* Northwest Passage
Chip log, 136, 593, 595, 610-11
Chorruca, 332
Chowan R., 646, 678, 684
Christ Church, Oxford, 557-8
Christian I and III, 89, 92
Christy, Miller, *Silver Map of World*,
  512-14
Churchyard, Thomas, on Frobisher,
  516, 546; on Gilbert, 555, 580
Cipangu, *see* Japan
Civille, Alonce de, 442
Clarke, Capt. John, 632, 640
Clarke, Richard, 572, 576, 582
Clement VII, 341, 435
Clifford, George, Earl of Cumberland,
  590
Clothing, 35-6, 60, 131-3, 149, 517, 539
Cluverius, Philip, 489-90
Cocke, Capt. Abraham, 671, 675
Cod, Cape, 191; earlier names, 308, 331;
  on maps, 334, 377
Codfish, 254, 336, 378, 469; curing meth-
  ods, 491; names for, 203; in Nfld.
  waters, 180, 225-8, 238, 272, 359, 477,
  596; S. Cabot on, 220; *see also* Stock-
  fish
Coffin, Adm. Sir Isaac, 364
Cole, Humfrey, 487, 502, 512
Coles, K. Adlard, 124
Coligny, Gaspard de, colony, 470
Colonization attempts, 323; Canada,
  387, 424, 433, 439-41; Cape Breton,
  229-31, 248, 328; Cape Fear, 332-4,
  337; Florida, 470, 486; Norumbega,
  468, 570-71, 575, 578; Sable I., 480-
  81, 492; Virginia, 560, 651; summary,
  678
Columbus, Christopher, 3, 6-8, 29, 61,
  82, 98, 124, 132-3, 160, 170, 192, 216,
  229, 287, 308; and Antilia, 101-4, 166;
  identified as Scolvus, 94

Columbus, Ferdinand, 6, 100, 130-31, 206n
Compass, 34-5, 89, 137, 151, 479, 587; Frobisher's, 502; variation, 150, 170, 426, 505, 514, 600-601
Complaynt of Scotlande, 128-9, 148
Compton Castle, Devon, 563
Conception Bay, 227, 573
Conclude, 671, 674, 677
Conflans, Antoine de, 276, 318
Conger, Nicholas, wrestler, 523
Connolly, J. B., Out of Gloucester, 477
Convicts, as French colonists, 434, 437-9, 456, 480-81
Cook, Capt. James, 316; 1770 chart, 355; illus., 357
Cooper, Catharine M., 148, 205
Copper, 667; prized by Eastern Indians, 307-8, 395, 415, 455, 646-8
Cordeiro, António, 93
Cordouan lighthouse, 140, 181, 202, 267
Cormorant Rocks, 394, 426
Cornbread, Indian recipe, 414
Corte Real, Gaspar, 180, 212-17, 226, 231; bibli., 244
Corte Real, João Vaz, 82, 93, 108-9, 213
Corte Real, Manuel, 217
Corte Real, Miguel, 74, 213, 216-17, 245-7, 304
Corte Real, Vasco A., 213, 217
Cortés, Hernando, 277
Cortés, Martín, Arte of Navigation, 135, 150, 487
Cortesão, Armando, 10-12, 97, 101, 110-11, 244, 337
Corunna, Spain, 328, 331
Corvo I., 95-8, 665, 676
Costa, Joaquim A. de, 11, 12
Coudres, Ile aux, 403, 421
Countess of Warwick Sound, 532-4, 537-9, 542
Coutinho, Adm. C. V. Gago, 109, 244
Covell, W. King, 319
Cow Head, Nfld., 355, 378
Cox, William, 531, 572
Crignon, Pierre, 464, 489
Croatoan Indians, 663-4, 667, 677
Croatoan I., 648-50, 662, 675-7
Crone, G. R., 11, 71, 239
Crosses, erected at: Baffin I., 522; Gaspé, 375, 386; LeBoulet I., 352, 392; Mascanin Bay, 394
Cross-staff, 151, 287, 483, 487, 502, 512, 529, 587
Cumberland, Earl of, 551, 608

Cumberland Harbor, P.Q., 354
Cumberland Sound and Is., Baffin Is., 590-92, 601, 607-8; illus., 603
Currituck, N.C., 620
Cut Throat Tickle, Lab., 595

D

Darcy, John Baron, 604
Dare, Ananias, 657, 684
Dare, Eleanor, 657, 664, 684
Dare, Virginia, 54, 664-5
Dart River, 561, 584, 589, 604
Dartford, 530, 552
Dartmouth, 561-2, 568-9, 577, 588, 592, 598, 604
Dasemunkepeuc, 649, 664
Daughters of Navarre Is., 311, 323, 329, 488
Dauphin, Cape, 363-4
Dauphine, 276, 285-7, 346, 444, 501; voyages, 288-313, 316-18, 323
D'Aussilon, Paul, 449
Davies, Arthur, 242, 320
Davis, John, 136, 269, 483, 507; early life, 563, 584; Arctic voyages, first, 587-92, second, 592-8, third, 598-605; later career, 605, 608, 611-12, 679; nautical inventions, 609-11; navigator, 588-9, 595, 599; personality, 587, 605; quoted, 583; Seaman's Secrets, 587, 605, 608-10; death, 605, 612, 679; bibli., 605-7; voyages (illus.), 606
Davis, Robert, 501, 572
Davis Strait, 250, 595, 600
Day, John, Letter to Columbus, 167-9, 176-7, 184-5, 192-5, 198-200; text, 205-9
Deacon, Richard, 106
Deadman I., 364
DeBry, Theodor, 560, 630, 652, 669, 679
Dee, John, 24, 207n, 487, 497, 502, 555, 597; career, 483-4; helps Frobisher, Gilbert, and Davis, 501, 568-9, 584-5; bibli., 493; map, 84, 498, 580-81; illus., 581
Dee River (Narragansett Bay), 484, 570, 580
De Fonte, fake voyage, 515, 613
De Goís, Damião, 213, 216, 244
Dégrat, Cape, Nfld., 172-4, 177, 184-5, 195, 201-2, 227, 347, 382-4, 438
DeHeere, Lucas, artist, 529-30
Delabarre, E. B., on Dighton Rock, 245-7

Del Cano, Juan S., 277, 326
Delight, 117n, 572-8, 582
Demoiselle Is., see Harrington Is.
Demons, I. of, 457
Denmark, annexes Greenland, 605
Dennis (or Dionyse), 532-4
Denoix, Cdt. L., 387, 390, 424
Denye, 568
Denys, Jean, 270
Deschênes, E. B., 382, 386, 426
Desceliers, Pierre, 261, 465, 488; 1542 map, 337, 342, 364-6, 460-61, 343 (illus.); 1546 map, 371, 426, 461 408-9 (illus.); 1550 map, 462, 444 (illus.)
Desire, 608
Desliens, Nicolas, 261; map, 198, 460-61, 465
D'Este, Ercole, 217-19
Destombes, Marcel, 319
DeVoto, Bernard, 85, 106
"Diamonds" of Canada, 354, 432, 439, 442-3, 446, 449, 454, 531
Diaz, Bartholomeu, 105
Dieppe, 118, 140, 260-61, 270; in Middle Ages, 253; plan of, 257; situation, 253-4; trade, 255-6, 272-3; Verrazzano at, 284, 313-14
Dighton Rock, 37, 74, 245-7
Diligence, H.M.S., 371
Direction, 200
Discord, Cape, 588, 597
Discovery, 612
Dobel, Guillaume, 272
Doeg Indians, 85
Doegr, 41, 64
Dogs, 533, 601, 604
Domagaya, 389, 419, 440; and Cartier, 401-3, 406-7; in France, 375, 430
Dominica I., 632, 637, 660, 673-4
Donnaconna, 429, 462-4; and Cartier, 374-5, 391, 405-10, 415-17; in France, 430-31, 439; politician 419-20; death, 438
Dorothie, 627, 632, 654
Doublet, Jean, 272
Drake, Sir Bernard, 472, 632, 649
Drake, Sir Francis, 148, 316, 483; circumnavigation, 496-7, 533, 629; row with Frobisher, 547-9; in W.I., 406, 649-50
Drake, Capt. George, 363
Dress, 35-6, 60
Drogeo, 87

Dudley, Ambrose, 501, 518
Dulmo, Fernão, 97
Dumplings, off Newport, 303-4, 319
Dun fish, 491
Du Plessis, Pierre, 437
Dursey Head, Ireland, 169-70, 174, 194, 199, 202, 207, 533, 597
Dyer, Andrew, 519, 531
Dyer, Sir Edward, 589

E

Eames, Wilberforce, 511
Eanes, Gil, 94
Eddystone, 139-41, 267
Eden, Richard, 135, 150, 487, 550; on S. Cabot, 203n, 223-5, 248
Edward VI, 482-3
Egg I., P. Q., 399
Elephant, 568
Eleuthera I., 638
Elizabeth (Davis's), 598-600, 604
Elizabeth (Raleigh's), 627, 632-4, 637
Elizabeth I, 131, 500, 581, 586, 602, 667; accession, 485; backs Davis, 587; backs Frobisher, 504-5, 510, 516-18, 523, 528, 531-3, 547-9; character, 496; and Gilbert, 497-8, 563-6, 570-72, 576-8; and Hakluyt, 558-60; and Lane, 630; quoted, 163, 485-6; supports Raleigh, 617-18, 626-9, 649; visits Dee, 483; death, 612
Elizabethan Age, 486, 494, 507, 510, 569
Ellen (or Helene), 598-607
Ellis, John, 588-9
Ellis, Thomas, on Frobisher, 494, 539-43; True Report, 546, 550-51
Elyot, Hugh, 218-20, 233
Emanuell (of Exeter), 532
Emmanuell (of Bridgewater), 532, 537, 543-4
England, advances in navigation, 487; awakening under Elizabeth, 494; indifference to America, 430, 468-71; insecurity, 496; war with Spain, 626, 631
Englishmen, captured by Eskimos, 507-8; guaranteed rights, 567, 571-2; Roanoke settlers, 596, 650-51
English Channel, 119, 139-41, 270, 346, 533, 598
Enterprise, 613
Erebus, 613
Eric the Red, 27, 38-40, 51-5, 58-64, 184

Ericsson, Leif, 35, 38-41, 53-4, 57-62, 67, 74, 82, 347, 367; settlement, 47-52, 60, 172, 348, 489
Eskimo, 53, 68, 92, 507, 551, 613; and Davis, 589, 593-4, 599-600; and Frobisher, 143, 508-10, 523-4, 528-30, 533, 537, 542; toys and football, 592, 597
Espejo, Antonio de, 656-7
Eston, William, 588-9
Etchemin Indians, 375, 417
Exeter Sound, 589, 601
Evans, John, 86, 106

F

Fabyan, Robert, 219
Facy, Capt. Arthur, 669-70
Fagundes, João A., 122, 277; voyages, 211, 225-33, 328, 335, 366, 421, 480, 489; bibli., 248-9
Falcon, 568
Falkland Is., 608
Farewell, Cape, 29, 39, 212, 242, 503-5, 512, 552, 588, 593, 599, 607
Fear, Cape, 288-9, 313, 318; Indians, 289-92; river, 295, 320, 332-4, 337; voyages to, 620, 638, 661
Fécamp, 255, 272, 315
Fenton, Capt. Edward, 517, 522, 547-9; and Frobisher, 531-2, 539-42, 545; *Troublesome Voyage*, 510
Ferdinand II, 158, 239-40
Ferdinando, Simon, 654-5, 677; visits Norumbega, 468; voyages to Va., 619-21, 629-32, 638-40, 659-61, 665-6
Fermeuse, Nfld., 227, 573
Fernald, Merritt L., 51-2, 72
Fernandes, Francisco, 218-20
Fernandes, João, 210-15, 218-19; bibl., 242
Ferryland, Nfld., 181, 479, 654
Field, Joseph, Nfld. cruise, 201
Findlay, A. G., 104, 170, 199
Finnbogi and Helgi, 57, 62
Finus, Orontius, 436
Fischer, Joseph, on Norsemen, 63, 68
Fire-lances, 370, 386, 518
Fisheries, Acts of 1542 and 1563, 471, 491; cod, 227-8, 254-5, 270-72, 471-8, 492, 596; exports, 369; French, 265, 270-73; "wet" and "dry," 266, 270, 473-8, 491; whale and walrus, 478-80; bibli., 491-2; *see also* Grand Bank
Fitzgerald Lord Gerald, 432

Flags and shields, 119, 124; Ango's 260-61; Frobisher's, 518, 523; Virginia, 657, 679
Flamengue, 315
Fleury, Jean, 254
Flores I., 95-8, 135, 665, 676
Florida, 197, 252, 313-15, 336, 428, 445, 465, 566, 620; extent, 638; French colony, 470, 486, 631, 647; on maps, 231, 316, 320, 331, 334, 461
Fog, 167, 170-72, 177, 180, 184-5, 200-201, 355, 368, 375
Fogo I., 181, 185, 201, 227, 471
Fontoura da Costa, Capt., 109
Food, seamen's, 35, 130-31, 276
"Fool's gold," *see* Iron pyrites
Forbes, Alexander, 526, 537-9, 551
Forster, Johann R., 88
Fournier, Capt. Paul, 615
France, 334-6, 430-31; coast (illus.), 262; maritime conditions, 252-73; neglects America, 314-16, 432, 454, 470; wars, 273, 314, 500
France-Roy, 429, 448-51, 456-7
Frances (English), 532, 535
Frances (French), 568
Francis, 650
François, 481
François Iᵉʳ, 259-61, 277, 302, 384; backs Cartier, 187, 340-41, 392, 420, 433; backs Roberval, 434, 442, 462; backs Verrazzano, 279, 287, 292, 313, 323, 464; character, 279; finances, 432; Saguenay, 430-33; "sun shone for him," 435, 455-6; death, 454
François, Dauphin, 285, 340
Franklin, Benjamin, 515, 613
Franklin, Sir John, 613
Franzen, Prof. Gösta, 76
Freels, Cape, 181, 185, 194, 200-201, 227, 346-7
Fretum Trium Fratrum, 92, 483, 497
Freydis, 54-7, 62
Frisius, Gemma, 156, 483, 497
Frobisher, Dorothy (Widmerpole), 549
Frobisher, Sir Martin, 136, 143, 152, 194, 483, 592; character and early life, 497-500, 549-50; fleets and equipment, 501-4, 516-18, 531-2; general orders, 532; knighted, 547; letter to missing seamen, 524-5; navigator, 488, 504; objectives, 500-501, 517; quoted, 506, 547, 549-50; raid on W. I., 547, 649; "valiant courage," 505; voyages,

Frobisher, Sir Martin (*continued*)
first, 500-510, second, 516-31, third, 126, 531-45, 566; summary, 550; death, 549
Frobisher Bay, or Strait, 236, 503-7n, 512, 516, 519-20, 523-4, 533-43, 551, 607-8; on map, 545, 607; illus., 509; renamed Lumley, 602, 608
Fromont, Thomas, 389, 437
Fulford, Faith, 563, 584, 612
Fuller, R. Buckminster, 147
Fundy, Bay of, 161, 279, 312, 335, 392, 468-9
Funk I., 201, 312, 346-7, 392, 573
Fur trade, 369-70, 380, 418, 434, 477, 481, 492

G

Gabriel, 152; on Frobisher voyages, 501-2, 505-11, 516-17, 520, 529, 532, 535-7, 540-44, 547
Galion, *see* Pinnace
Galvão, Antonio, 100, 194
Games, 418, 428
Ganong, W. F.: *Crucial Maps*, 198, 248, 318, 336, 426; on Cartier portrait, 387; on Norumbega, 488
Ganz, Joachim, 632
Garcie, Pierre, rutter, 112, 148, 260
Gardar, 59-60
Gardner, G. Peabody, 384
Gaspé Bay and Peninsula, 368-75, 382, 417, 421, 426
Geare, Michael, 671
Gilbert, Adrian, 584-6, 592, 598
Gilbert, Sir Humfry, 85, 126, 136, 200, 547-50, 560; background and early life, 497, 563-4; backs Frobisher, 501; character, 565-6, 578; *Discourse*, 498, 555, 565; on education, ideas, 565-6, 571, 580; finances, 571; knight and M.P., 565; land grants, 488, 569-70; in Nfld., 480, 492, 574; plans for colony, 468, 490, 570-71, 575, 578; voyages: first, 568-9; second, 199, 471-3, 481, 569-78; death, 142, 577, 617; bibli., 580-82
Giovio, Giulio and Paolo, 315-17, 324
Gironde River, 207n; mouth of, 181, 198-9, 202, 265-7
Gjøa, 497, 613-15
Glande, Darby, 660
Gnupson, Bishop Eric, 58-9, 67-71
Godfrey, W. S., Jr., 74

God's Mercy, Cape, 590, 595, 601
Godthaab, Greenland, 39, 59, 589, 593, 597-9
Golden Hind, 148, 496, 533
Golden Hinde (or *Samuel*), 572-7
Golden Lion, 552
Golden Royal, 649
Gómara, Francesco L. de, 90, 220-21, 556, 657
Gomez, Estévan, 231, 287, 334, 488, 657; voyage, 320, 323, 326-31, 336, 464, 631; illus., 330
Gonçalves, Antao, 94
Gonsalves, João, 218-20
Goodwin, W. B., 30, 89, 107
Gordillo, Francisco, 332
Gordon, John, 652n
Gorges, Sir Edward, 633
Gosling, W. G., *Gilbert*, 580
Gourges, Dominque de, 470
Grace, 479
Granches, Catherine de, 341
Granches, Monts des, Nfld., 355
Grand Bank of Nfld., 177, 220, 229, 248, 491; fisheries, 227-8, 254, 263, 266, 270-74, 344-5, 390, 470, 473, 476; Gilbert and Davis on, 573, 604
Grande Françoise, 270
Grande Hermine, 138, 387, 443-4, 501-2; on Cartier's voyages, 389, 405-6, 421-3, 430, 437-8, 442; rebuilt for Expo 67, 390, 424
Granganimeo and wife, 621-6, 644
Grapes, 36, 51-4, 59, 621, 667
Grates Cove "inscription," 202-3
Guadeloupe, 315, 325
Gray, John, 531
Gray Is., Nfld., 226, 347, 573
Great auk, 228, 347, 361, 392, 492, 573
Great Britain, 161
Great Mecatina I., P.Q., 392
Great Michael, 270
Green, Oliver, on Anticosti, 377, 386
Green, Paul, *The Lost Colony*, 583
Greenland, 41, 49, 52-8, 184; Davis's "Land of Desolation," 588-90, 592-4, 597-8; Denmark annexes, 605; discovered and rediscovered, 39, 40, 198, 212, 219, 242; and Frobisher, 503-5, 519, 533, 544; Norse colony, 59-61, 678; on maps, 244, 545; bibli., 67-8
Greenly I., P.Q., 349-50, 384-5
Greenway House, 563, 568
Grenfell, Dr. Wilfred, 349
Grenville, Sir Richard, 127, 135, 146,

659, 669; appearance and personality, 629; early life, 628; fleet, 632; in Virginia, 640-43, 655; letter to Walsingham, 646; relief expedition, 649-50; returns home, 644; voyage of 1585, 631-9
Gresham, Sir Thomas, 501
Griffin, Gerald, on O'Brazil, 103
Grip, Carsten, 92
Griquet Harbor, Nfld., 174, 181, 202
Groais I., Nfld., 227, 347, 384
Gromets, 134, 276, 327, 391, 410
Grube, Master, 234, 237
Gryffyn, Owen, 501
Guadagni family, 281, 322
Guadeloupe, 315, 325
Guayanilla Bay, P.R., 633, 655
Gudrid, 53-8, 62, 245
Guillén y Tato, J. F., 239
Gulf Stream, 620, 653, 674-5
Gunnlangson, Gudleif, 27-8
Guyon, Jean, 411*n*

H

Habert, Jacques, on Verrazzano, 318, 323
Hakluyt, Richard, 273, 572-3; biography, 555-61; on Atlantic crossings, 199; on Davis, 587, 605-7; and DeBry, 560, 669; Epistle dedicatory, 556-8; on Hore, 237-8, 250; "longe voyaiges," 560; on Madoc, 85; rejects Ingram, 489; trans. of Cartier, 367, 378-9, 424, 432, 445, 455; trans. of Verrazzano, 289-90, 317; on Virginia, 625, 632, 656-7; on walrus, 479; writings and bibliography, 381, 489, 511, 551, 578-80, 626
Hakluyt, Lawyer Richard, 557, 580
Hakluyt Society, 580
Hale, Edward E., 104, 110
Hall, C. F., 514, 526-8, 551-2
Hall, Christopher, 152; on Frobisher voyages, 501, 505-7, 511-12, 517, 531-2, 536
Hall's I. and Islet, 503, 507-12, 517-19, 522-3, 535, 542-3, 595
Hamilton Inlet, 59, 596, 604, 607
Hammocks, 64, 132
Hanseatic League, 61, 114, 165, 484
Haraszti, Zoltán, 79
Hare I. and Passage, P.Q., 403, 421
Harfleur, 256, 259

Haring, C. H., Trade and Navigation, 679
Hariot, Thomas, 632, 641, 646-7; Briefe and True Report, 630, 652, 667-9, 679; kills Wingina, 649; bibli., 654
Haro, Cristóbal de, 327
Harrington, J. C., 683
Harrington Is., 394, 426, 446, 457
Harris, Capt. Joseph, 671
Harrisse, Henry, 9, 81, 93, 239, 242-4, 336, 460-61; on Ayllón, 332, 337; on the Cabots, 193-7, 248, 490
Harry Grace à Dieu, 270
Harvey, Dionyse, Margery, and child, 657-9, 665
Harvey, Capt. Edward, 532
Harvey, Sir James, 657
Harvey, Thomas, 632, 638
Harwich, Eng., 505, 510-12, 518, 533
Hastings Manuscript, 114, 119, 122, 125, 139, 141, 146, 150, 167
Hatarask I., 621, 644, 651, 654, 674
Hatteras, Cape, 288, 292, 480, 620-21, 640, 653, 661
Haugen, Prof. E. I., 64-9, 79
Havard, Judith, 612
Havre de Grace, 256, 279
Hawkins, Sir John, 428, 485-6, 668
Hawks, F. L., 684
Hawtin, Raymond, 203
Hayes, Edward, 471, 572, 582; on Gilbert, 573-80
Heavener, Okla., 78-9
Hecla, 613
Helgason, Jón, 80
Helluland, 41
Hencken, Hugh, 30-31
Hennig, Richard, Terrae Incognitae, 11, 58, 207*n*
Henri II, 255, 273, 454
Henri IV, 265, 273, 470, 480-81
Henry, Cape, 295, 323, 646
Henry VII, 130, 133, 208*n*, 222, 471, 596*n*; and Anglo-Azorean syndicate, 218-20; and the Cabots, 105, 159-60, 166, 174, 186-7, 190, 220, 279, 558; names Newfoundland, 184; patent to Fernandes, 213; subject of "Interlude," 250
Henry VIII, 129, 143, 150, 238-40, 460, 483, 628; on Cartier and Roberval, 436, 442; character, 279; Rut's voyage, 234, 237; and S. Cabot, 221; and Thorne, 233; and Verrazzano, 314, 320
Henry the Navigator, 34, 94-5, 100

Heptaméron, 302, 447, 458
Hercules, 84
Hermannsson, Halldór, 62, 67, 72, 108
Herodotus, 5, 11
Herrera, Antonio de, *Historia General*, 250
Herring, 254, 270, 273, 276, 369, 552
Hervé, Roger, 461
Hesiod, 4, 11
Hobbs, Prof. W. H., 89, 107
Hochelaga, *see* Montreal
Hoffman, B. G., *Cabot to Cartier*, 239, 248, 336, 381
Holand, H. R., 76-8, 490
Honfleur, 254-6, 260, 270, 442, 456
Honguedo, 374n, 394
Hóp, 54-6, 69
Hope of Greenway, 568
Hopewell, 140, 531, 671-7
Horace, 4, 5, 11
Hore, Richard, 233, 237-8, 250
Horsford, Eben N., 67, 469, 489-90
Howard, Lord Charles of Effingham, 547-9
Howard, Lord Edward, 234
Howe, George, murdered, 662-4
Hudson, Henry, 554, 586, 612
Hudson, Thomas, 586
Hudson River, 302, 312, 316, 336, 469, 488
Hudson Strait, 535-7, 545, 595, 604, 612
Humboldt, Alexander von, 5, 81
Huron Indians, 455, 492; and Cartier, 374-5, 386, 405-10, 423, 438-41; customs, 418; at France-Roy, 448, 450; at Hochelaga, 411-15, 428; treatment of, and fate, 420, 428-9, 439
Hutton, Robert, 671
Hvitramannaland, 27, 30-31, 57-8
Hvitsark rock, 92-3
Hy-Brasil, 102-5, 186, 208, 229, 544; Bristolians' search for, 163, 166-7, 170; bibli., 110

I

Icebergs, 23-5, 29-30, 192, 616; encountered by Frobisher and Davis, 507, 520, 534, 539, 594, 601-2; off Newfoundland, 174, 184, 200-201, 215, 234-5, 346, 392; chart (illus.), 171
Iceland, 31, 39-40, 52, 58, 62, 270; Bristol trade, 162-3 166-8; Irish settle, 25-8; on maps, 89, 92

Indians: attack Davis, 596, 607; Cabot on, 197; conversion of, 435, 633; generalities, 647-8, 651; Verrazzano's, 289-92, 296-8, 301, 322; Welsh-speaking, 84-7, 106-7; *see also names of nations*
Indies, the, 3, 105, 131, 160, 184, 190, 208n, 484, 497
Ingonish, N. S., 229-30, 248, 328
Ingram, David, on Norumbega, 467-8, 489
Ingstad, Helge, 38, 47-9, 67-9
Insulae Fortunatae, 4-5
Insurance, marine, 265
"Interlude of the Four Elements," 249-50
Inventio Fortunata, 77, 206-7n
Ireland, 54, 168-70, 202, 226, 500, 504; and Hy-Brasil, 102-5, 110; early monasteries, 13-15, 29; Gilbert, Grenville, and Lane in, 565, 629-30
Irish, 13; early American colony, 24-8, 30-31, 56-8, 74; in Virginia, 632, 649, 657
Iron pyrites, 329, 432, 439, 442, 446, 510; *see also* Marcasite
Ironworks, Norse, 49
Iroquois Five Nations, 354, 413, 417, 429, 651
Irving, Washington, 100
Isabela, Hispaniola, 105, 637-8
Islands, Bay of, Nfld., 355
Islands, mythical, 4-5, 9, 24, 69, 81-4, 96-105, 229, 242, 251, 461; Buss, 83, 544, 552-4; illus., 553; *see also* Hy-Brasil
Isle au Haut, Me., 311, 323, 330, 468, 488
Islesboro, Me., 467

J

Jackman, Charles, 139-40, 519-20, 531
Jackson, Melvin J., 194
Jacques Cartier Bay, Passage and Mountains, 352, 378, 395
Jacquette, 254, 272, 275
Jal, Auguste, 148-9, 274-6n
Jalobert, Macé, 389-91, 410-11, 437-9
James I, 473, 602, 612, 654, 679
Jameson, J. Franklin, 653, 679
Jamestown colony, 633
Janes, John, 587-91, 598, 604-7
Japan and Japanese, 100-101, 170, 191, 498, 612, 679

Jay, John, 163, 205
Jenkinson, Anthony, 484, 497, 564
Jesus, 485
João II, 95-7, 208*n*
João III, 252-4, 286, 314, 435-6
João de Lisboa, 82, 102, 111
John A. MacDonald, 615
John Evangelist, 671-4
Jones, Gwyn, writings, 63, 68-9, 72
Jones, Rev. Morgan, 85, 106
Judith, 531-4, 539
Julien, Ch.-A., works on discovery, 274-5, 318, 381, 424, 492
Junk, 519, 535, 596
Juricek, J. J., on Cabot's landfall, 194-5

K

Kalm, Peter, 52, 169
Kane, Elisha K., 601
Karlsevni, Thorfinn, 38, 53-8, 62, 245
Keniston, Hayward, 205
Kennebec River, 330, 336, 578
Kensington Rune Stone, 74-8, 490
Kent, Rockwell, 68, 200
Kildare, Cape, P.E.I., 364
King, J. E., on Saguenay, 457
Kipling, Rudyard, 477
Kirkham, John, on Frobisher, 546
Kitty Hawk, N. C., 295, 301, 323, 621
Knollys, Henry, 568-9
Kodlunarn I., 526-9, 532, 539-44, 551-2
Kohl, J. E., "Asia and America," 324, 515

L

Labrador, the, 40-41, 47, 56, 59, 194, 566; fisheries, 470; and Greenland, 212, 219; on maps, 198, 335-6, 503, 608; voyages to, 234-5, 348-52, 595, 604
Labrador, makes NW Passage, 615
Lachine Rapids, 415, 441, 451, 454
Lailler, Dan, 343, 380*n*, 387
La Latte, Fort, 359
La Morandière, Charles de, 275, 491
Lancaster, Capt. James, 228, 611
Lancaster Sound, 600, 605, 612-16
Lanctot, Gustave, on early Canada, 386, 456, 492; bibli., 323, 381
Landernan, 263
Lane, Frederic C., 112, 115, 148
Lane, Ralph, 617, 635, 668, 683; defends Ferdinando, 640; explorations, 646,

656; governor of Va., 632, 644-51; quarrels with Grenville, 629, 636-8
Lane, Capt. William, 671
L'Anse aux Meadows, Nfld., 38, 47-51, 54, 57, 60, 172; bibli., 68-9
La Pommeraye, Charles de, 411*n*
La Roche, Marquis de, 480-81
La Rochelle, 140, 264-7, 352, 442, 670; bibli., 275
La Roncière, Charles de, 9-10, 274, 318, 381, 386, 457
La Roncière, Monique, 10
La Roque, Marguerite de, 394, 426; "valiant demoiselle," 446-8, 458; bibli., 457
Larsen, Helge, 67-8
Larsen, Sofus, 92-3, 103
Las Casas, Bartolomeo, 100, 111, 206*n*, 381
LaSalle, Robert Cavelier de, 415
Latitudes: Alfonce's, 451; Cabot's, 174, 177, 181, 194, 199-202; Cartier's, 346-7, 368, 375, 426; Davis's, 588-9, 593-5, 599-600, 604; Frobisher's, 502, 512, 519, 529, 535, 551; Gilbert's, 573; sailing by, 34, 94, 170, 352, 443, 479, 504; Verrazzano's, 287-8, 307, 312, 319
Laudonnière, René de, 470, 647
Layng, T. E., 10, 239, 242, 463
Leagues and miles, 288, 303, 382, 387
Le Boulet I., P.Q., 352
LeBreton, Guillaume, 389, 410-11
Le Conquet, 263
Lee, Edward, 233-4
Leech, James, 532
Le Havre, 255, 259, 272, 315, 564
Leigh, Capt. Charles, 361, 364, 384
L'Émerillon, 433, 443-4; on Cartier's second and third voyages, 389-90, 403, 406, 421-3, 430, 437, 442; Lac St. Pierre trip, 410-11, 415
Le Pelletier family, 260
Lescarbot, Marc, 180, 476, 480, 490
Letters-patent: Anglo-Azorean syndicate's, 213, 218, 225; Ayllón's, 332, 337; Cabot's, 159-60, 167, 190-92, 208, 218, 558; Corte Reals', 214; Fagundes's, 229; Fernandes's, 211-12, 242; H. and A. Gilbert's, 566, 586-7, 618-19; Portuguese, 96-7, 160; Raleigh's, 618-19, 627, 654, 679
Le Veneur de Tilliers, Jean, 340-41
Lewis, H. F., 352, 382, 386, 394, 426
Lewis, Michael, on ordnance, 156

L'Hermine, 270
"Libel of English Policie," 157
Lièvres, Ile aux, *see* Hare I.
Lighthouses, 119, 140-41, 150, 165, 255; *see also* Cordouan
Limoïlou, 380, 432, 438, 444, 563, 584
Line of Demarcation, 212, 226
Lion (also *Red Lion*), 568, 627, 632-3, 640, 649, 659-61, 665-6
Lipinsky, L. S., on Verrazzano, 318-19
Little John, 671-4
Lloyd, Master, of Bristol, 166
Loire River, 264
Lok, Capt. John, 483, 500
Lok, Michael, 531, 550; "East India by NW," 511; and Frobisher, 501, 510, 531, 544-5; heads Cathay Co., 516; map, 320, 487
Loks Land, 507*n*
Longfellow, H. W., 37, 114, 306, 323
Longitude, 223, 287; 313, 368-9, 375, 487-8, 593-4, 657
Lookout, Cape, 288, 292, 620, 638, 661, 675
Lost Colony, the, 677-8, 683-4
Louise, 272
Louise de Savoie, 279, 303, 314, 318, 464
Lowell, J. Russell, 37
Lucas, Fred W., on Zeno brothers, 89, 107
Luís, Father, 227
Lumley, John, Baron, 602-4, 607
Lundy, 185
Lundy, Rev. J. B., 245
Lyme grass, 51-4, 367, 370-71
Lyons, France, 280-85, 314

M

MacInness, Prof. C. M., 205
Madoc, Prince, 77, 82-7; bibli., 106-7
Magdalen Is., 125, 361-4, 384, 421; fisheries, 473, 479, 492
Magellan, Ferdinand, 3, 222, 277, 285, 318, 323, 326-8
Magellan, Strait of, 326-7, 335, 503, 506-7
Magnaghi, Alberto, 324
Maine: Acadia National Park, 323; earliest map, 335; part of L'Acadie, 299; Verrazzano and Gomez visit, 308-12, 329-30; *see also* Norumbega
Maingard, Jacques, 389, 410
Maize, 374, 413-14, 647, 667
Mallart, Jean, 248, 465, 490

Malpeque Bay, P.E.I., 366
Manchineel fruit, 660
Mandan Indians, 77, 84-7, 106
Mandeville, Sir John, 56, 502
Manhattan, 615-16
Manteo, 626, 641, 659, 676; interpreter, 630, 637, 640, 647-8, 662-4
Manuel I, 211-17, 226, 229, 240-42
Maps, modern, *see* List of *Illustrations*
Maps and Globes, ancient, 81-4, 97, 210, 225, 450, 454; Avon River, Bristol to Severn, 162-3 (illus.); Bailly globe, 295, 320, illus. 291; Behaim globe, 100-101, 186; Best's, 540, illus. 546; Bianco, 69, 155; Borough, William, 512-13, 552, illus. 503; Bristol, plan of 1673, 164 (illus.); Cabot, S., 171, 192, 195-8, 384, 454, 460-61, illus. 196; Cantino, 69, 102, 194, 212, 217-19, 226-7, 244, illus. 224; *Chemin du Canada* (illus.), 416; Contarini Roselli, 186, illus. 188; Cook's charts, 355, illus. 357; Dee, 84, 498, 580-81, illus. 581; Dulcert, 102; Desceliers (1542), 337, 342, 364-6, 460-61, illus. 343; (1546), 371, 426, 461, illus. 408-9; (1550), 462, illus. 444; Desliens, 198, 384, 460-61, 465; Egerton, 279, 320; Farrer (1651), 320; Frisius, Gemma, 90, 483, 497; Gough (1360), 205; Gourmont (1548), 89; Homem, Diogo (1568), 231, 239; La Cosa, 191-5, 217-19, 244, 279, 320, bibli., 238-40, illus. 240-41; Lok, Michael, 320, 487; Maiollo, 295, 312, 319-20, 334, 490, illus. 321; Martinez (1580), 200; Mason, John (1618), 200; Mercator, 83, 384, 429, 462-7, 504, illus. 466; Miller I Atlas, 122, 226-31, 244, 319, 328, illus. 224, 230; Molyneux, 487, 552, 607-8, illus. 609; Munich-Portuguese, 212-14, illus. 214; Oliveriana, 212, 219, 242-4, 282, illus. 243; Ortelius, 239; Pareto (illus.), 21; Pizzi Nautical Chart of 1424, 84, 101-2, illus. 99; Pizzigani chart, 102; Plancius, 382; Reinel, 226-7, illus. 224; Ribero, 198, 287, 319, 323, 329-31, 334-7, 461, 464, illus. 335; Rotz, 460, 463, illus. 367; Ruysch, 187, 206*n*, illus. 189; Santa Cruz, 329-31, 337, illus. 330; Seller, 544, illus. 553; Skólholt, 72, illus. 73; Testu, 346; Ulpinus, 336-7; Vallard, 384-7, 448, 461, illus. 452-3; Verrazzano, 285, 288*n*, 289, 295-6, 311-12, 319-20, 323-4,

332-4, 464, 488-9, illus. 284, 321; Vespucci, 320; "Vinland" of Yale, 58-9, 67-72, illus. 70; White's, 655, illus. 672-3; Wolfenbüttel, 212; Zalterius, 515; Zeno, 72, 88, 462, 504, 602, 607, illus. 88

Marcasite, 508-10, 519, 530-31, 541-2, 551-2; in Puerto Rico, 236

Marguerita, 265

Marguerite, Queen of Navarre, 302, 447-8

Marie, 265

Marie Johan, 268

Mariner's Mirror, articles in, 149

Mariners' Mirrour (1588), 151

Marinus of Tyre, 8

Markham, A. H., ed. of Davis's *Voyages*, 588, 605, 608

Markham, C. R., *Life of Davis*, 607

Markland, 41, 56, 59

Marlowe, Christopher, quoted, 494-6

Marot, Clement, 434

Martyr, Peter d'Anghiera, 625, 657; *Decades*, 487, 555; on Gomez and Ayllón, 331, 337; on S. Cabot, 203, 220

Mary I, Queen, 222-3, 482, 563

Mary of Guildford, 116n, 234-7

Marye, 442

Mascanin Bay, P.Q., 394

Masefield, John, 579-80

Mathew, 119, 122, 133-4, 146, 166; name, 193; voyage, 167-87, 193-4, 199-200

Mattamuskeet Lake, N.C., 641

Mayda I., 102

Mayflower, 117n, 308, 384

McClure, Cdr. Robert, NW passage, 613

McFee, William, *Frobisher*, 511, 547, 550

Medina, José T., on Gomez, 336

Medina, Pedro, 153, 487, 502

Méndez, Diego, 235, 250

Menéndez de Avilés, 470, 650, 679, 683

Merchant Adventurers of Southampton, 571

Mermayd, 592-5

Meta Incognita, 510, 520, 531-2, 537, 543-5, 602, 607

Meteors, 542

Michael, 501-2, 505, 516-19, 532-4, 539

Michelbourne, Sir Edward, James I's license to, 612

Micmac Indians, 89, 185, 231; and Cartier, 369-71, 374, 385-6, 417; fur trade, 477, 492

Middleton, Thomas, 671

Milton, John, on Norumbega, 469

Mina, El, 485, 500

Miners, on Frobisher's third voyage, 532, 535, 540-43, 550-52

Minion, see *William*

Miramichi Bay, N.B., 368

Moisie River, 395-9

Moitessier, Bernard, 124

Mollat, Prof. Michel, 9, 112, 264, 387; bibli., 274-5, 318, 324

Moltke, Erik, 76-7n, 80

Mona I. and Passage, 235-6, 636-7, 674

Monardes, Dr., *Joyfull Newes*, 555-6, 667

Monhegan I., 311, 323, 488

Monsters, 56, 79, 420, 431; see also Unipeds

Mont Royal, 413-14, 440

Montagnais Indians, 378, 429, 477, 492

Montreal (Hochelaga), P.Q., 428-9; Cartier's trips to, 406-15, 440-41

Mont-Saint-Michel, 339-40, 368

Monts, Pointe des, P.Q., 401

Moone, 532, 535, 539, 542

Mooneshine, 588-96

Moonlight, 671, 674-7

Moore, Thomas, on Deadman I., 364

Moose, 177, 468

Morgan, Henry, 597, 607

Morrissey, 537-9

Mosquitoes, 177-80, 190, 348, 594, 637, 655, 667

Mosür wood, 51-2, 66-7

Mount Desert I., 311, 323-4, 488

Moyles, Capt., 532

Muscovy Company, 483-4, 497, 501, 565, 586

Music on shipboard, 391, 414, 568, 573, 588-601, 637-8

"Mystery Village," 11, 30

N

Nansen, Fridtjof, *In Northern Mists*, 79, 108, 110, 244, 248

Nantes, 264-5

Narwhal, 492, 528

Natashquan Pt. and Harbor, 378, 426

Nautilus, USCGC, 615

Naunton, Sir Robert, on Raleigh, 656

Navarro, Gines, 235

Navesink Highlands, 296, 301, 319

Navigation, 560; Cabot's, 136, 153, 170; Cartier's, 136, 348; celestial, 136, 174,

Navigation (*continued*)
487; Davis's, 587-9, 599; dead reckoning, 122, 593, 595; French, 140, 259; hazards, 139, 256; instruments, 139-42, 151-6, 287, 479, 483, 487, 502-4, 511-14, 605; Norse, 34; Portuguese, 94-5; traversing, 136, 147, 156; treatises on, 150; Verrazzano's, 136, 285-7, 307, 313, 488; bibli., 151-6, 608

Necho, Pharaoh, 5, 12

New England, 329-31, 334, 469, 481, 490, 561, 578

New York Bay, 301-2, 317-19; chart (illus.), 302

Newfoundland, 482; boat exchange, 423, 438; Cabot discovers, 170-84, 199-202; Cartier in, 341, 346-8, 355-9, 421-2, 443; Corte Reals in, 215; earliest names, 184; English attack of 1585, 649; fisheries, 225, 254, 272-4, 434, 471-80, 491, 604; Gilbert in, 573-5; le petit nord, 384, 477; Norsemen in, 38, 46-58, 172; on maps, 217-20, 225-8, 250, 279, 312, 320, 335-6, 460-61, illus. 44-5, 224; pre-Cabot "discovery," 166, 208n, 220, 274; recent yacht cruises, 201-2; tourist cruises 237-8, 250

Newport, Christopher, 671

Newport, R. I., 319; stone tower, 37-8, 73-5, 490; Verrazzano and Gomez at, 303-8, 331, 488

Nice, Treaty of, 432

Nicholas V, 60, 68

Nicholas of Lynn, 206n, 207n

Nicolet, Jean, 314, 324

Nields, James F., 68, 193, 652n

Niña, 114, 124, 133, 166, 390

Ninoo, O., Eskimo, 526, 551

Nisbet, John, and Hy-Brasil, 104

Noël, Etienne, 439

Noël, Jacques, 455

Nonnius, Petrus, 483

Norden, John, London, 126-7

Norman, Robert, Newe Attractive, 151

Normande, 285-6, 318

Normandy, 140, 253-63

Normanville, France, 490

Norris, Sir John, 549

Norsemen, 31-80

North, Cape (C. Breton), 198, 421

North, Cape, P.E.I., 367

North Carolina, 293-5, 617n, 625, 638, 677; coast and sounds (illus.), 293

North Pole, passage over, 233-4, 237, 558, 586, 593, 597

North Star, see Polaris

North Starre, 592-3, 597-8, 607

Northeast Passage, 132, 483-4, 497, 555, 564

Northwest Passage, 90, 93, 211, 218, 234, 482-3, 515, 555; Davis seeks, 583-4, 590-92, 598, 600-601, 605; Frobisher's quest, 498; Gilbert advocates, 497-8, 501, 564, 571; S. Cabot's "search," 220-21, 558; summary of quest, 612-16; traversed, 497, 534; see also China

Norumbega, 329, 457, 464-70, 482, 619, 631; Gilbert's intended colony, 468, 490, 570-71, 575, 578; Horsford's theory, 67, 469; name, 488-9; on maps, 198, 311-12, 464-5, 489, illus. 466; bibli., 488-91

Nova Scotia, 185, 193, 312, 316, 329, 491; names for, 231, 235, 299, 323; on maps, 331, 335

Noyes, Alfred, quoted, 493

Nunn, George E., 239, 324, 515

O

O'Brazil, see Hy-Brasil

Obregón, Mauricio, 16n, 68, 193, 205

Ohman, Olaf, 75-7

Oklahoma, Vikings in? 78-9

Olaf Tryggvason, king, 39-40, 52-4, 64, 605

Olaus Magnus, Historia, 56, 68, 79, 89, 108

Old Bic Harbor, P.Q., 401

Oleron, Isle and Laws of, 132-3

Oleson, T. J., Early Voyages, 64, 67, 75, 77n, 108, 206n; on Cabot, 193-4

Oliveriana map, 212, 219, 282, bibli. and illus., 242-4

Ordnance, 143-6, 156, 370, 518

Ore, 510, 517-19, 524-31, 536, 540-46

Oregon Inlet, N.C., 620

Orkney Is., 25, 510, 518

Orléans, Charles duc d', 364, 405

Orléans, Ile d', 405-6

Ortelius [Abraham Oertel], 483, 640

Osborn, Sherard, on Sanderson's Hope, 600-601

Ostriche, Henry, 248, 482

Ottawa R., 420, 439, 441

Oviedo y Valdes, Fernandes, 82, 105, 235-6, 250

Owls Head, Me., 330

P

Pallavicini, General, 279
Pamlico Sound, N.C., 619, 625, 640-44, 650
Parkhurst, Anthony, on fisheries, 471, 478-9
Parkman, Francis, 9, 324, 457; quoted, 341, 401, 426, 492
Parmenius, Stephen, 572-6, 580
Parmentier, Jean, 261-3, 275, 464
Parr, C. McKew, on Magellan, 337
Parry, John H., 71
Parry, Sir William, 554, 613
Paspebiac, P.Q., 369
Pasqualigo, Lorenzo, 180, 184-5, 189, 192, 244
Pasqualigo, Pietro, 216, 244
Patterson, George, 248-9
Peckham, Sir George, 106, 483, 488, 547, 570-71
Peisson, Edouard, quoted, 147
Pemaquid Pt., Me., 330
Penguin I., 228-9, 238
Penobscot Bay, 311-12, 329-30, 336-7, 464-5, 468-9, 488-90
Pensée, 254, 270, 285
Percé, I. and Cape, P.Q., 371, 386
Persia trade, 484, 498
Petite Hermine, 389, 391, 406, 410, 421
Philip II, 482, 485, 492, 511, 560, 568; annuls S. Cabot's pension, 222; interest in Raleigh colony, 631, 654; policy toward English Catholics, 570-71
Philpot, Capt. Richard, 531
Phips, Sir William, 371, 377
Phoenicians, 5, 8, 11-12, 95, 245
Pierson, Capt., 598
Pine, Cape, Nfld., 177, 181, 202
Pining and Pothorst, 82, 89, 92-4, 213, 254; bibli., 108-9
Pinnace (galion), 122, 126, 142, 332, 501, 576, 598; built in P.R., 634-5
Pirates and piracy, 34n, 82, 92-4, 161, 236, 254, 569, 572-3; French, 533, 634, 638, 655; Japanese, 612, 679; Roberval, 442
Placentia Bay, Nfld., 181, 184, 217, 226, 479
Plato, 6, 8
Pletho, 8
Pohl, F. J., 75-8, 89
Polar bears, 197, 238, 347, 447, 462, 589

Polaris, 34, 136; navigational star, 153, 170, 174, 307, 479, 502, 512, 529, 587, 595
Pollock Rip, 308
Polo, Marco, 206, 289, 515
Pomeiooc village, N.C., 641-2
Pontbriand, Claude de, 389, 411n
Pontneuf, Notre Dame de, P.Q., 410, 440
Poole, H. S., on Buss I., 554
Pope, Capt. Richard, 588, 597
Port au Port, 359
Port aux Basques, Nfld., 421
Port Daniel, P.Q., 369-70
Port Ferdinando, 621, 626, 644, 650, 654, 665
Portage (share) system, 133
Portugal, alleged policy of secrecy, 82, 101-2, 110, 208n; explorations, 225-8, 231-5; sea power, 94-7
Postel, Guillaume, 81, 105
Poulard, Madame, 339
Poullet, Jean, 411, 424
Poutrincourt, Baron de, 180, 448, 477
Prato, Albert de, 234, 386
Pratto, Cap de, 311, 386, 421
Pre-Columbian "discoveries," 81-2, 90-94, 109-11, 208n, 213
Prince Edward I., 197, 251, 328, 364-7, 384-5
"Primage" and "privilege," 327
Prowse, D. W. and G.R.F., on Cabot, 194, 200, 225, 491
Privy Council, 485, 518, 564, 569, 669
Prize money, 549, 646, 677
Ptolemy, Claudius, 7-8, 11, 104, 187, 199, 307
Puerto Rico, aguada, 619-20, 674; discovered, 105; Grenville in, 632-7, 655; Rut visits, 235-6, 620
Puntas, C., 485
Pythagoreans, 6
Pytheas, 5-6

Q

Quadrant, 94, 136, 151-3, 156, 170, 287, 487, 502, 587, 610
Quebec (Stadaconé), 341, 364, 371, 418, 429, 438-9, 448; Cartier discovers, 406, 410-11; city founded, 481; fort, 415, 418-19; Indians of, 374-5, 403, 417
Quiberon Bay, 443
Quii, 58, 68, 92, 108-9, 454

Quinn, David B., 9, 193, 208n, 248, 457, 655; editions of Gilbert and Hakluyt, 489, 510, 579-80; *Roanoke Voyages*, 651-2, 679
Quirpon I., Nfld., 54, 172-4, 201, 227; Cartier at, 347, 384, 438

R

Rabast, Cap, P.Q., 377, 394
Rabelais, François, 424, 458
Race, Cape, Nfld., 96, 102, 177, 181, 191-5, 217, 227, 231, 237, 479, 491; fog, 201-2; Gilbert's voyage, 573-6
Rafn, Carl, *Antiquitates*, 30, 37-8, 73, 245
Raleigh, 572-3, 654
Raleigh, Cary, 658
Raleigh, City of, 657, 661, 665, 669-70
Raleigh, Mount, 601
Raleigh, Sir Walter, 126, 549, 558, 562-3, 586, 655; backs Gilberts, 568-9, 571-2, 592; character, 617; colonies, 292, 428, 560, 617-79; knighthood and arms, 626; "Observations on Sea Service," 684; death, 679; bibli., 652
Ralph, Elizabeth, 205
Ramusio, G. B., 381, 429; on Hochelaga, 412-15, 428, illus. 412; on S. Cabot, 195n, 220-21, 558; on Verrazzano, 283, 313-17
Rasmussen, Knud, 613
Ravelli, Paul, 111
Rawson-MacMillan Expedition, 551-2
Ray, Jas. G., 167
Raymond, George, 627, 632, 640
Read, Conyers, *Walsingham*, 580
Recusants, 570-71
Red Bay, Lab., 201, 348-9
Red Islet Bank, P.Q., 403
Red Lion, see *Lion*
Reinel, Jorge, 231
Religion: at sea, 142-3, 171, 272; on Frobisher's voyages, 520-21, 532, 537; wars of, 265, 273, 454, 470
Renewse Harbor, Nfld., 422-3, 573
Resolution I., P.Q., 506, 512, 534, 541, 595, 602, 607
Revenge, 135, 628-9
Rhode Island, 37, 303
Rhodes, I. of, 303
Ribaut, Jean, 470, 647
Rice, Capt. Harold E., 63, 79
Rich, Pt., Nfld., 355, 378
Richelieu Rapids, 410

Rieth, Adolf, 79
Roanoke Indians, and Raleigh colonists, 621-49 *passim*
Roanoke I., 621, 640, description and cost, 646, 678; first colony, 644, 649-50; second colony, 651, 661-5, 669-71, 675-6; bibli., 651-3, 683-4
Roanoke River, 646
Roberval, de La Roque, sieur de, 347, 387, 426, 432, 566, 627; commission, 434, 480, 618; maroons niece, 394, 446-7; voyage to Canada, 267, 434-8, 442-3, 448-51, 461-2; death, 454; bibli., 455
Rocky Bay, P.Q., 352-4
Rodman, Lt. Hugh, 174
Roe, 669-70
Roebuck, 126, 627, 632, 640, 644
Rojo, Cape, P.R., 636
Roses on Brion I., 361, 384
Ross, John and Sir James, 613
Rotz, John, atlas, 460, 463, illus. 367
Rouen, culture and trade, 254-9, 314; fishery, 272-3; great families, 260
Rouge, Cap, P.Q., 439
Rowse, A. L., 510, 563, 652
Roze, cartographer, 261
Rucellai, Bonacorso, 260, 281, 287
Ruddock, Alwyn A., 150, 205-6
Ruge, Sophus, *Fretum Anians*, 515
Rummaging, 135, 542
Runic inscriptions, alleged, 37-8, 74-9
Russia, trade with, 484, 498
Rut, John, 116n, 471, 487, 550; voyage, 233-7, 386, 620, 655, 674; bibli., 250
Rutters, 136-41, 152, 261, 307; Davis's, 587, 605, 608-10; Garcie's, 112, 148, 260; Mallart's, 248, 465, 490; bibli., 150-51

S

Sable, Cape, 105, 193, 328, 491
Sable I., 229, 491, 575, 582; French colony, 480-81, 492
Sagas, the Vinland, 31, 36-41, 53-7, 63-4, 72
Saguenay, Kingdom, 56, 391, 415, 420, 430-32, 439-41, 451-4, 461-4; river, 401-3, 420, 426, 451; bibli., 457-8
Sainte-Anne, 442, 451
St. Augustine, Fla., 650
St. Augustine River, P.Q., 352-4
St. Brendan, 161-2, 265; islands, 83, 96, 101, 251; voyages, 9, 15-26, 180; bibli., 28-9

Saint-Brieuc, 437, 439
St. Charles River, P.Q., 406, 415, 418, 439, 578
St. Croix, W.I., 660
St. George, Cape, Nfld., 359
Saint-Georges, 437-9
St. John I., 229; *see* Cape Breton and Prince Edward I.
St. John's, Nfld., 181, 200-201, 235, 442-3; Gilbert at, 471, 573-5
St. Lawrence, Gulf and River, 237, 248, 265, 312, 336; Cartier in, 328, 350-75, 380, 395-9, 401; fisheries, 470, 478-80; name, 395, 429; on maps, 454, 460-63, 488
St. Lawrence Harbor, P.Q., 394
Saint-Malo, 15, 199, 260, 263, 272, 341, 437; and Cartier, 345-6, 359, 380, 432-4, 438, 455; fishermen, 363
St. Mary's, Cape, Nfld., 181, 184, 201
St. Maurice River, P.Q., 411, 415
St. Nicolas, P.Q., 394
St. Patrick, 13, 23, 24
St. Paul Bay, Nfld., 355; Cape, 421-3
St. Paul Is., 232
Saint-Pierre, *détroit*, 377-8, 394
Saint-Pierre, Lac, 411, 415
Saint-Pierre, Mont, P.Q., 393
Saint-Pierre and Miquelon, 228-9, 421-2
St. Roch, 615-16
St. Ursula and 11,000 virgins, 229
Saintonge, 253, 264, 476
Saints' names and days, 299, 337
Sakonnet Pt., R.I., 308
Salamon (*Salamander*), 532-3
Salt, 238, 264, 473, 477, 661; in Puerto Rico, 636-8, 655, 660, 683
Sampson, 116*n*, 234-5
San Antonio, 326
San Germán, P.R., 236, 250, 619, 636, 655
San Miguel, Ayllón's colony, 332-4
Sanderson, William: backs Davis, 586-7, 592, 598, 604; and Raleigh, 630, 656, 670-71
Sanderson's Hope, 600, 605, 656
Sandridge Barton, 563, 584, 598
Sanitary conditions and regulations, 134-5, 540
Sannazzaro, Jacopo, *Arcadia*, 295
Santa Catalina, 332
Santa Cruz, Alonso de, 227, 242, 328; map, 329-31, 337, illus. 330; bibli., 336
Santa Elena, S. C., 470, 682
Santa Maria, Azores, 95-6

Santa Maria, ship, 114, 194, 239, 444
Santa Maria de San Vicente, 644-5
Santo Domingo, 235, 332-4, 337, 649, 674
Sanz, Carlos, 10
Sassafras, demand for, 667, 679
Satanazes, 101, 111
Sauvages, 270, 369-70, 386, 428, 433-5
Sauvages, Cap des, P.E.I., 365-7
Schultz, Jonas, 510, 530-31, 544, 552
Scolvus (Skolp, Kolno), Johannes, 82, 90-94, 213; bibli., 108-9
Scurvy, 162, 418-19, 429-34, 441, 450
Sea Dragon (1601), 611
Seadragon, U.S. sub., 615
Seamen, 122, 128-9, 141, 151, 445, 497, 563; Cabot's, 166, 172, 185, 189-90; Cartier's, 344, 380, 389, 415; character of, 132; Davis's, 588, 593-6, 599-601, 607; duties, pay, food, etc., 132-4, 266, 276, 318, 327, 517, 531, 552; English, 481-2, 487, 496; French, 261-5, 272; Frobisher's, 535-9, 550-52; Gilbert's, 569; Raleigh's, 632, 640, 647
Secoton, 642-4
Secrecy, Portuguese, 82, 101-2, 110, 208*n*
Seguin I., 306-8, 330
Segura, Fr. Juan Bautista, 682
Seine River, 254-60
Seller, John, *English Pilot*, 544, 552-4
Sellman, Edward, 512, 544-5, 549-51
Seneca Indians, 417
Sept Isles, P.Q., 395-9
Serchthrift, 222, 484
Settle, Dionyse, 517-19, 522, 528-9, 546, 551
Seven Cities, *see* Antilia
Shakespeare, quoted, 125, 494, 608, 627
Shea, J. Gilmary, 679, 683
Shekatika Bay, P.Q., 352
Sheldon, Dr. and Mrs. P. B., 201
Shepherd, Capt. Thomas, 552
Shetland Is., 25, 505
Ships and shipping: types, 112-14, 149, 215, 268-70, 327-8, 332, 389-90, 501, 552, 568*n*; bibli., 148-9, 274-6
Ships and shipping (English), 112-48; ballast and bilge, 134-5; building, 114-16; carvel and clinker-built, 114-17, 149, 269, 272, 598-602; design, 113-14, 117-22, 125, 684; names, 116-17; rigging, 117-19, 123
Ships and shipping: French, 252-73; Irish, 16-18, 25-9, 86, 112; Norse, 34-6,

Ships and shipping (*continued*)
112-14; Portuguese, 215; *see also* Boats
Shoals, Is. of, 491
Sidney, Sir Henry, 565
Sidney, Sir Philip, 558, 570
Sinclair, Henry, 88-9, 107
Skate, U.S.S., 615
Skelton, R. A., 10, 58, 69, 195-7, 239, 338; *Explorers' Maps*, 608
Skrellings, 53-9, 68, 75, 245
Slaves, slave-trading: African, 94, 216, 332, 431, 485-6; Drake frees, 650; Indian, 105, 216, 254, 270, 309, 331-2
Smerwick, Ireland, 666
Smith, Capt. John, 134, 143, 331, 387, 677-8
Smith, P. C. F., 156
Smyth, William, 517, 532
Smythe, Thomas, 671
Snorri, 54-8, 62, 245
Soncino, Raimondo, 158, 169-70, 177, 189-90, 194
Southampton, 561, 571, 666
Southey, Robert, *Madoc*, 86-7
Spain: and Cartier, 435-7, 455-6; and England, 146, 473, 482, 487, 496, 500, 560, 569, 626, 631; fisheries, 472-3, 492; No. Amer. exploration, 326, 337; treasure ships, 254, 287, 332, 470, 485-6, 496, 549, 661, 674, 679
Spanish Armada, 389, 486, 547, 631, 669, 671
Spar, U.S.S., 615
Sparkes, Boyden, and Dare stones, 684
Spear, C., 181, 219, 227
Spicer, Edward, 659, 671, 674-5
Spices and spice trade, 105, 159, 165-6, 191, 255, 331, 431, 436, 483, 497-8
Spooning, 505-6
Squirrel, 126, 568-9, 572-6
Stadaconé, *see* Quebec
Stafford, Capt. Edward, 648-50, 659, 662
Stafford, Sir Edward, 557
Stefansson, Vilhjalmur, 612; theories of Vinland, 72-3; *Voyages of Frobisher*, 72, 511, 550-52
Stephens, Thomas, 87, 106
Steward, Capt. Roger A., 615
Stick, David, *Outer Banks*, 653-4
Stockfish, 131, 162, 207n, 276, 471, 476-9, 491, 604
Stoke Gabriel, 563, 584
Storis, U.S.S., 615
Stormy, Robert, 165
Strabo, 8

Strachey, William, *Historie of Travell*, 678
Straumey, 54
Straumfjord, 56
Sunneshine, 588-93, 597-600, 607
Swabber, 134
Swaine, Capt. Charles, 613
Swallow, 568, 572-5
Sweeps, 146
Sylvester, H. M., *Maine Coast Romance*, 489

T

Tadoussac, 401, 481
Taignoagny, 389, 420, 440; and Cartier, 401, 406-7; in France, 375, 430
Tanfield, Capt. William, 531, 541
Taylor, Bayard, on Saguenay, 426
Taylor, Eva G. R., 10, 71, 92, 107-10, 150, 250, 510; on Cabot, 195, on fake islands, 84; *Haven Finding Art*, 511; *Writings of Hakluyts*, 579
Teles, Fernão, 96, 100
Terceira, 211-13, 666
Terror, H.M.S., 613
Thanksgiving Day, the first, 520-21
Thevet, André, 479; imports tobacco, 428; *Cosmographie, Singularitez*, 457, 502; on Norumbega, 465-7, 489-90; on S. Cabot, 221; visits Cartier, 445, 457
Thiennot, Cape, P.Q., 378, 394, 426
Thomas, 531, 539-40
Thomas, John, 218
Thomas Allen, 531-3, 536, 542
Thorhall the Hunter, 54-5, 62
Thorlacius, Theodore, 71-2
Thorne, Nicholas, 220, 233
Thorne, Robert, 220, 237, 436, 558, 586, 597; circumpolar letter, 233-4, 250
Thorvald, 53-6, 62
Thorvard, 54, 57, 62
Thule, 6
Tieve, Diogo de, 95, 98, 109
Tiger (Davis's), 612
Tiger (Raleigh's), 146, 156, 612, 627, 638, 684; at P.R., 633-7, 655; grounds, 640, 644-6
Tió, Aurelio, 250, 655
Tobacco, 37, 300, 638; Arcadia, 298; Canada, 418, 428; Hawkins and, 428, 486; Virginia, 664, 667-8, 678
Torfæus, Thormodus, 36, 72
Totnes, 561, 589, 592
Tourist cruises, 237-8, 250

Towerson, William, 485
Traverse board and book, 122, 137, 153, 156, 170, 502; Davis's, 587, 593, 599, 607
Trepassey Bay, Nfld., 181
Trinidad, 674
Trinity, 205, 237
Tripp, Kenneth, 492
Triumph, 547
Trois Rivières, P.Q., 411, 415
Trudel, Marcel, 9, 248, 318, 323, 381; Atlas, 460; on Cartier, 424, 455; convicts, 456; Sable I., 481
Trunmore Bay, Lab., 596, 607
Tunnage, 124-5, 166, 501n, 659
Tutonaguy, 441, 456, 461-2
Tyrker, 40, 51, 62

U

Ulloa, Luís, 94, 109
Unemployment, colonies cure, 498, 657
Ungava Peninsula, 68, 536-7
Unipeds, 56, 62-4, 79, 420, 431
Upcot, Capt., 532, 542
Upernavik, Greenland, 600, 605
Urdaneta, Antonio, 497
Ushant, 29, 141, 150, 185, 199, 202, 260, 263

V

Valentine, 238
Vallentyne, 442
Velasco, Luís, 682-3
Velasco, Pedro de, 95, 98
Venice, 82, 87-8, 115, 158, 174, 188, 248
Ventura, 201
Verge, Enos, 491
Vergil, Polydore, 191
Verrazzano, Giovanni da, 143, 332-4, 345, 391, 464-5, 487-9; backers, 260, 281, 314; documents, 317-18; early life, 282-4; expenses, 324; Letter, 273, 285-8, 292, 299, 303, 312-13, 317-18, 558, 570, 620; navigator, 136, 285-7, 307, 313, 488; New World theory, 313; objective, 287-9; portraits, 285, 320-22; "Sea of," 292-5, 316, 320, 337; system of names, 299, 319; voyages, 231, 253, 273, 286-315, 621; death, 315, 324-5; bibli., 317-25
Verrazzano, Girolamo da, 261, 287, 315-16; map, 285, 288n-9, 295-6, 311-12, 319-20, 323-4, 332-4, 464, 488-9; illus., 284
Vespucci, Amerigo, 163, 243, 320, 324
Viana do Castelo, 228-9, 249
Vieques I., 633, 655, 660
Vigneras, L. A., 205, 337
Vikings, 24-7; defined, 31n-33n; in Oklahoma? 78-9
Vilas, C. S., 200
Villiers, Capt. Alan, 205
Vinland, 31, 34n-39, 59, 62-3, 71; Karlsevni colony, 53-7; location, bibli., 72; Thorvald expedn., 53; Thorvard colony, 57
Virgil, 6, 295
Virgin God Save Her, 659
Virginia, 469, 481, 631; armorial, 657, 679; colonists, 632-3, 640, 650, 657-60, 675-7; extent defined, 617n; first colony, 486, 517, 640-51, 657-9; Jamestown colony, 633, 677-8; name, 624-6; native commodities, 667-8; problems of survival, 648; relief expeditions to, 649-51, 671-7; second colony, 656-77; voyages to, 127, 149, 547, 619-26, 659-61, 665-6; bibli., 651-3, 679-84
Vittoria, 277, 326, 444
Voyages, doubtful or mythical, 5, 8, 11-12, 81, 87-93

W

Wahlgren, Erik, 76-8
Waist-cloths, 122-4
Walker, Hovenden, 371, 399
Walker, John, on Norumbega, 468, 490
Wallis, H. M., on Molyneux Globes, 608
Walrus, 361, 399, 418, 479, 491-2
Walsingham, Sir Francis, 531, 554, 633, 655, 659; backs Davis, 584, 589, 592; and Gilbert, 568, 571-2; Grenville's letter to, 646; and Hakluyt, 556-8; and Lane, 617, 644
Wampanoag Indians, 245-7, 415; description, 307; and Verrazzano, 304-7, 322, 488
Wampum, 414, 438-9
Wanchese, 626, 630, 637
Warburton, George, on Anticosti, 377, 386
Ward, 199
Warwick, Earl of, 564
Washburn, Wilcomb E., 71
Waterhound, captured, 627

Watts, Capt. John, 654; heads relief expedn., 671, 674-6
Weapons, 145, 456, 518, 597, 648; see also Ordnance
Webber, John W., 490
Werowances, 621, 642, 664, 676
Westford Rock, 89, 107-8
Westropp, T. J., 103, 110
Whale fisheries, 478-9
Wheaton, Henry, 36
Whidden, Roger, 111
Whitbourne, Richard, 477
White, John, 589, 654, 668, 684; accompanies Grenville, 633-6, 641-2; *American Drawings*, 652-5, 679, 683; armor, 426, 676; art work, 517, 523, 528-30, 560, 624-5, 630, 679; governor of Va., 657-66; map of Va. (illus.), 672-3; narrative, 126, 660, 671; relief expeditions, 669-77
White Cockade I., Lab., 604
White Head, P.Q., 371
Whitely, G. C., Jr., 200
Whittier, J. G., 399, 426, 490; quoted, 75, 339, 392
Whittle, Cape, P.Q., 378, 394
Wiers, Thomas, 544
Wilkins, E. H., on Arcadia, 322
Willes, Richard, *History of Trauayle*, 550, 555
William, 237-8
Williams, Roger, 74, 303-4, 307, 319, 322
Williamson, J. A., 9, 199; biog. of Hakluyt, 578; books on Cabots, 192-5, 203n, 239, 248; Fernandes-Barcelos voyage, 242
Willoughby, Sir Hugh, 132, 484
Windgandcon, becomes Virginia, 624-6; description, 624-5; meaning, 621, 654

Wine, 162, 165, 238, 264; Bordeaux, 237, 265-7
Wingina, 621, 625, 640, 644, 664, 668, 676, 679; helps English, 647-8; killed, 649, 662
Winship, G. Parker, 193, 197, 248
Winsor, Justin, 9-10, 106, 110, 195, 457; on Alfonce, 490; on Ayllón, 337; on Cartier, 458-60; on Frobisher, 511; on Hakluyt, 579; on Verrazzano controversy, 317; on Virginia, 653; quoted, 5, 67, 75
Winter, William, shipmaster, 572
Winter, Sir William, 530, 552
Wococon I., 640, 644
Wolf, H.M.S., 371
Wolfal, Master, chaplain, 539, 542
Wonder Strands, 41, 54, 64; Davis at, 596, 607; source of timber, 59
Wright, Irene A., 652-4
Wroth, Lawrence C., 283; *Voyages of . . . Verrazzano*, 317-22, 324, 336
Wyndham, Capt. Thomas, 482
Wytfliet, Cornelius, 90, 108

X-Y-Z

Yale Vinland Map, 58-9, 67-72, illus., 70
Yeardley, Francis, 683
Yorke, Capt. Gilbert, 517, 522, 531, 536
Young, G. F. W., on Dighton Rock, 247

Zeno brothers, 505; book and map, 72, 88, 504, 514; influence on maps, 602, 607-8; voyage, 82, 87-90; bibli., 107-8
Zichmni, 87-9, 107
Zocchi, Galleaggo, 285, 320-22